# MOBILE RIVERINE FORCE

America's Mobile Riverine Force Vietnam

Volume II

Nashville, Tennessee • Paducah, Kentucky

Turner Publishing Company
412 Broadway • P.O. Box 3101
Paducah, Kentucky 42002-3101
(270) 443-0121

www.turnerpublishing.com

Copyright © 2005 and Publishing Rights:
Turner Publishing Company

This book or any part thereof may not be reproduced or transmitted in any form or by any means, electronic or mechanical, including photocopying, recording, or by any information storage and retrieval system, without permission in writing from the publisher.

Library of Congress Control Number: 2005903577

ISBN 978-1-63026-966-1

Turner Publishing Company Staff:
Doug Sikes, Publishing Consultant

Printed in the United States of America.

0 9 8 7 6 5 4 3 2 1

# DEDICATION

This book is dedicated in memory of all who served in Vietnam, especially those who gave their all. It is also dedicated to those who have gone on since the war. We love and miss each one our fallen brothers daily; they will always remain in our hearts, minds, and prayers.

Over 2.6 million served
Over 58,000 gave their lives
They fought for their country
They fought for freedom
They fought with honor
In the end they fought for one another

# CONTENTS

Foreword ............................... 4

Preface .................................. 5

Mobile Riverine Force
　History ................................ 7

Personnel Killed in Action
　and Missing in Action ....... 52

Special Stories ...................... 55

Mobile Riverine Force
　Veterans ............................ 79

Roster ................................. 126

Index .................................. 150

*USS* Benewah *(APB-35). Photo courtesy of Dan Dodd, Official Navy Photographer for ComRivFlot-One MRF TF-117 68-69, Retired Chief Photographers Mate.*

# FOREWORD

This book is dedicated to all the Navy units of Task Forces 117-116-115, and to all who served in the 9th Infantry Division, be you a Navy Boat Rider, Army Infantrymen, Army or Navy Medic or Corpsman, Artilleryman, Ships Crewman, Truck Driver, Ship's Barber, or from an Army Mech Unit. I include also all supporting Navy ships and Signal Corps. I could list all the different units, ranks and rates (MOS's), but that is not necessary; you know who you are, where you served, and why you served.

Each and every one of you did an outstanding job in a war that was unpopular at home, but one fought with honor, courage, and dignity. No one can or will ever be able to take this away from us. General Fulton once told me, "Albert, I fought in three wars. And those young men who fought and served and those who died in Vietnam were the bravest young soldiers and sailors I ever had the honor and privilege to have served with".

This book should also be in remembrance of our brothers who paid the supreme sacrifice after giving so much. "They are the ones who gave all" and also in remembrance of our brothers who are still with us. Though our ranks are thinning, we still remain brothers of the Vietnam War. We have lost so many members, Army and Navy both, since the association was started in 1992 at a small reunion in Conover, NC. I remember Oscar Santiago and Budda Thomas, the first people to contact me in 1992. Both were truly heroes in my book as were the many, many more that have gone on ahead since then. I wish we had room to publish all their names. As young children growing up in NC, like most young kids, we all had our heroes: I had mine; we all had them. But now here I am in my mid 60's and guess what? I still have heroes, much as I did when I was a child; however, my list of heroes has grown very long. Each and every one of you has become my hero. You went to war and you served your country. Not many of our generation can lay claim to that. We all have this as one of many distinctions: we went and we served.

Since the small reunion in 1992, we have grown to be one of the largest, and I believe, one of the most successful Vietnam Veterans' associations around. That's because of you, the members. Without you, this could never have happened. I want to thank each and every one of you for all the support you have given the Association and me over the years; it is appreciated. Special thanks to each and every one of you, and BRAVO ZULU to all hands.

Albert B. Moore, President
Mobile Riverine Force Association

# PREFACE

I am honored and privileged to dedicate this book to the Heroes from the Army's 9th Infantry division, Navy Task Force 115, 116, 117, and all supporting units. Not only to the many friends that we left behind thirty something years ago but to the thousands that returned home to endure years of painful memories and wounds. As a rifleman, radio operator, squad leader, and platoon sergeant with Charlie Company, 4th Battalion, 47th Infantry Regiment of the 9th Infantry Division from October 1967 to October 1968 I was honored to be able to serve with the finest soldiers and sailors in the entire military. Not only did they do their job well, they did it with pride and with dignity. It hurts all of us to see the news, movies, etc. show only the negative side of the Vietnam Veteran and to never see the positive side.

In this book one will read the stories and the biographies of the real Vietnam Veteran. One will see Veterans that went on to lead productive lives, men that have been loving husbands and fathers and ones that have enriched the communities and peoples lives around them. This book is not only a tribute to the Mobile Riverine Force and 9th Infantry Division but to all Vietnam Veterans. It is my wish and hope that this book be passed from generation to generation so that the heroes we left behind, those that have since passed on, and those with us today will never be forgotten. It was an honor to serve with these men in 1967 and 1968 and it is an honor to presently serve with them as Vice President of the best Vietnam Veterans Association in America today. The Mobile Riverine Force Association.

Roy Moseman, Vice President
Mobile Riverine Force Association

# MOBILE RIVERINE FORCE HISTORY

Volume I focused on the formative years, which were primarily 1967-68. River Assault Squadrons 9 and 11 began the ironing out process of the Mobile Riverine Force – Task Force 117. Tactics and equipment were tested against an enemy who had his way in the III and IV corps regions for many years. In the spring of 1968, River Assault Squadrons 13 and 15 began crossing the Pacific to fulfill their role in the War.

Volume I leads up to the disbanding of the MRF on August 25, 1969. Volume II proceeds on by detailing the ongoing function of the Riverine Forces leading up to the final boats being transferred to the South Vietnamese Navy in December 1970. In the interim period you will see how combat-hardened sailors volunteered to be Advisors to the South Vietnamese Navy under the command of Task Force 194. Despite the outcome of the war, a legacy of honor, dedication, and heroism was left by a small band of unique young sailors and soldiers.

*Photo courtesy of Dan Dodd, Official Navy Photographer for ComRivFlot-One MRF TF-117 68-69, Retired Chief Photographers Mate.*

COMMANDER
U.S. NAVAL FORCES
VIETNAM
MONTHLY HISTORICAL SUMMARY
NOVEMBER 1969
DECLASSIFIED

## AMPHIBIOUS TASK FORCE 211

Amphibious Task Force 211, which is composed of RAIDs 70, 71, 72, 73, 74 and 75 with the combined assets of 108 riverine craft, participated in river patrols, amphibious and interdiction operations, logistics lifts and Psyops and civic action missions. The 497 river patrols and 1,447 amphibious operations that they conducted in November accounted for the major utilization of the RAIDs. The number of river patrols was comparable to the October figure. However, the number of amphibious operations dropped by more than 500 missions from the October total of 2,010 missions.

The two oldest RAIDs, 70 and 71, ATG 211.1, continued to carry out interdiction missions in Giant Slingshot operations on the Vam Co Dong and Vam Co Tay rivers from their respective bases at Tan An, CTE 194.9.4.2, and Ben Luc, CTE 194.9.0.2. Although the RAIDs 70 and 71 assets had their headquarters at Ben Luc and Tan An, their units were regularly operating out of Ben Keo (Tay Ninh), Tra Cu and Moc Hoa. (See discussion of Giant Slingshot in SEA LORDS Summary for further details of the operations of RAIDs 70 and 71.)

The ATG 211.3, composed of 52 riverine craft of RAIDs 72, 74 and 75, and the 4th and 6th Infantry Battalions, VNMC, with their supporting artillery units, aggressively pursued the enemy in the U-Minh Forest of Kien Giang Province. The RAID craft, operating from base locations at Tan Bang (VR 996 542) and Dong Hung (VR 942 621), utilized the Can Gao Canal and connecting waterways to provide their basic lift and fire support capability to the Vietnamese Marines.

The launching of the enemy winter-spring campaign in the 4th CTZ in the beginning of November was considered to have reached a high point on the night 6/7 November when 44 individual fire attacks and no ground attacks were reported in the Delta. The previous night of 5/6 November, there were 16 individual fire attacks and four ground attacks including the enemy assaults against the VNN VNMC forces positioned at Tan Bang (VR 996 542) and Dong Hung (VR 942 621). The attack at Dong Hung was the scene of the heaviest fighting that the new RAIDs had engaged in. While moored at the ATF 211 command post at Dong Hung, the RAID craft and command post came under 82 mm mortar attack at approximately 0130. The mortar attack ceased at about 0145 only to resume at 0300 with the added firepower of 60 mm mortars, B-40/41 rockets and 57 mm recoiless rifles. Under the cover of the heavy barrage of mortar, rocket and recoiless rifle fire, approximately two battalions of VC surrounded and attacked the command post. When it was imminent that the friendly positions were going to be overrun, the VNMC staff, advisors and most of the troops of the two companies of the 6th Infantry Battalion boarded the RAID boats on the west bank allowing the VC forces to destroy the tents, huts, bunkers and communications equipment that the marines were forced to leave behind. All the RAID boats traveled to the east bank. From this position, they were able to place only limited fire upon the enemy because of some VNMC that still remained on the west bank. From the CCB, the friendly forces were able to call in spooky and shadow aircraft who were able to respond to the call and remain on station until 0630 when the enemy forces broke off the ground attack.

The VC battalion had inflicted heavy casualties and damage on the VNN/VNMC forces in the isolated incident, but they paid dearly for their efforts. A total of 19 of the 21 RAID 72 and 74 boats suffered varying degrees of battle damage but no boats were sunk, and only three craft with flooded engine rooms could not move under their own power. The command post and communication center were severely damaged. The marines suffered 30 killed, 84 wounded and three missing. The two USN advisors to RAID 74, who received minor shrapnel wounds, GMG1 Garcis and BM1 Stauber, were more fortunate than the two VNN who died fighting and 36 other VNN who were wounded. The VNMC reported that 85 VC were killed in this attack and ensuing actions. The following enemy weapons were recovered: 16 AK-47s, three B-40/41 rocket launchers and one Chicom machine gun.

There were no VNN casualties or damage as a result of the mortar attack on Tan Bang on the same morning. However, later that morning, RAID 75 boats engaged in an enemy ambush while on a river patrol between Tan Bang and Dong Hung (VR 948 610). Three VC were killed and eight VNN were wounded. One ATC was slightly damaged from a B-40 rocket hit.

Seemingly undaunted in their willingness to confront the VNN/VNMC forces, the VC, estimated at battalion size, attacked the Dong Hung position on the evening of 7/8 November. Following approximately 75 rounds of 82 mm mortars, B-40 and B-41 rockets, the VC force mounted successive ground attacks from the southeast and southwest. The valiant attempts were squelched by the combined efforts of helo gunship, the RAID units and the VNMC ground forces. Twenty VC were eliminated by the friendly forces, but five marines and one VN sailor lost their lives, and eight marines and two VN sailors received wounds. Major damage was sustained in two of the RAID craft, and a third sank. As they fled, the VC were careful to pick up the weapons of their fallen comrades. Only one AK-47 was captured.

The first six weeks of the operations in the U-Minh Forest went largely unchallenged. However, faced with a continued build-up of friendly forces, the enemy had decided, at least in the opening days of November, to wage comparatively large-scale offensive operations in order to re-establish his hold on the area. The U-Minh Forest has consistently been an integral part of the enemy plans for the Delta, and the positive effects of the GVN accelerated pacification program and friendly offensive operations have definitely impaired their activities.

Because of the extensive battle damage and general material condition of the RAID 72, 74 and 75 units, 15 RAID 72 and 74 boats proceeded to the USS Askari (ARL 30) at Long Xuyen in order to carry out the required maintenance. In order to fill the craft vacancy, ten RAID 73 transited from Thoi Binh (WR 100 320) to Dong Hung on 9 and 10 November. Their arrival brought about the realignment of ATG 211.2 to include both RAIDs 73 and 75. The relief of ATG 211.3 by ATG 211.2 at Dong Hung on 10 November was affected since the majority of the RAID 72 and 74 boats had departed the area.

Amphibious operations and waterborne guardposts with Vietnamese marine units through the remainder of the month met daily resistance. On 13 November, Dong Hung came under mortar attack again with 25 82 mm mortar rounds being fired at the command post and incoming helos. One Vietnamese sailor and four marines were killed, and 18 marines, one USMC advisor and one VNN were wounded. The 6th Infantry Battalion, VNMC, was relieved by an ARVN Ranger Battalion of its security assignment at Tan Bang on 14 November. However, the marines continued offensive operations in the same general area.

In order to have the best utilization of the RAID craft, it was decided to redeploy RAID 73 to the Song Ong Doc area of operations. After lifting two companies of the 5th Infantry Battalion to Tan Bang on 25 November, the RAID 73 units proceeded to Ca Mau in anticipation of relieving USN RAD 131 units at the end of the month.

Movement of the 105 mm howitzer from Tan Bang to a new location about ten miles north northeast of Dong Hung (WR 005 780) took place on 27 November. At the same time, other equipment was moved to Dong Hung, and all the RAID craft previously located at Tan Bang were repositioned at Dong Hung. (See VNMC Summary for further details of ATG 211.2 and ATG 211.3 operations.)

As of 30 November, the Vietnamese Navy had the following number and types of craft assigned as indicated:

| | |
|---|---|
| Logistic Ships | 23 |
| Patrol Ships | 41 |
| PCFs | 33 |
| WPBs | 5 |
| 1st Coastal Zone Junks | 47 |
| 1st Coastal Zone, RAG 32 | 17 |
| 2nd Coastal Zone Junks | 57 |
| 3rd Coastal Zone Junks | 65 |
| 4th Coastal Zone Junks | 57 |
| 3rd Riverine Area RAGs | 62 |
| 4th Riverine Area RAGs | 102 |
| Amphibious Task Force 211[1] | 108 |
| Task Force 212 (RPGs)[2] | 83 |
| Central Task Force[3] | 65 |
| TOTAL | 765 |

[1.] ATF includes RAIDs 70, 71, 72, 73 and 74
[2.] TF 212 includes all PBRs assigned to RPGs 51, 52, 53 and 54
[3.] Central Task Force includes RAGs 27, 81 and 91

## VIETNAMESE MARINE CORPS

While employed exclusively in the III and IV Corps tactical areas, the Vietnamese Marine Corps and their U.S. Marine Corps Advisors aggressively sought out the enemy through the utilization of amphibious, heliborne, reconnaissance, defense and security operations. The Marine and enemy casualty statistics were almost a direct reflection of the activity of the 4th, 5th and 6th Infantry Battalions and their supporting units in the U-Minh Forest. The launching of the enemy's Winter Spring Campaign in the Delta was considered to have taken place in the period 5-8 November. On the evening of 5-6 November, the VNMC Brigade "B" headquarters, two companies of the 6th Infantry Battalion, Battery C of the Artillery Battalion and 21 RAID 72 and 74 craft at Dong Hung (VR 944 620) were subjected to a stand-off attack of approximately 500 rounds of 82 mm mortars and B-40/41 rockets. This was followed by a ground assault directed against the Brigade CP, which was successfully repulsed by the VNMC and VNN Forces. The final results were: 30 marines, two VNN and 85 VC killed; 88 marines and 38 VNN (including two USN advisors) wounded; heavy damage to the command post and to the RAID craft; 16 AK-47s, three B-40/41 launchers and one CHICOM machine gun captured.

## BRIGADE "A"

The Brigade "A" staff was in a six-hour reserve standby status to JGS until 10 November when it departed Saigon to relieve Brigade "B" located in the U-Minh Forest. The Battery "A" of the 1st Artillery Battalion joined the Brigade at Dong Tam. The relieving process was completed on 12 November at Dong Hung (VR 944 620). The Brigade "A" and Battery "A" utilized the sites vacated by Brigade "B" and Battery "C". The following day the command post came under a VC 82 mm mortar attack. Twenty-six rounds landed with pinpoint accuracy in the command post causing 25 casualties among the 4th Battalion, the artillery battery, the brigade staff and the VNN. One VNN officer was killed and the USMC artillery advisor, Captain R. Porter, received shrapnel wounds in the face. The headquarters functioned the remainder of the month as the coordinator of the marine units and air and waterborne assets that operated in the area.

## BRIGADE "B"

The Brigade "B" staff functioned as the headquarters unit for the VNMC units operating in the U-Minh Forest through 12 November. After they were relieved by Brigade "A", the Brigade "B" staff and Battery "C" traveled to Rach Soi (WS 151 007) where they remained overnight before proceeding to Saigon via Can Tho. Leaving Battery "C" at Dong Tam, the Brigade "B" Headquarters arrived at the VNMC Headquarters on 14 November and assumed the six-hour alert status to JGS that was previously filled by the Brigade "A" staff.

## 1ST INFANTRY BATTALION

The 1st Infantry Battalion was assigned a one-hour alert status as JGS reserve at Camp Nguyen Van Nho (XS 874 935) for the entire month with the exception of the period 3-9 November when it returned to its base camp at Thu Duc (XT 922 007) for one week of training and rehabilitation.

## 2ND INFANTRY BATTALION

From 1-6 November, the 2nd Infantry Battalion, stationed at Ben Luc (XS 625 756), was under the operational control of the Giant Slingshot Commander, CTG 194.9. From positions to the south and southeast of Ben Luc (XS 558 834, XS 553 809, XS 625 736), the 2nd Battalion units sent out platoon-sized patrols and night squad single guard posts. Although the battalion did not establish enemy contact during this period, they uncovered a small cache on 2 November that contained 100 handmade grenades, 143 rifle grenades and 200 rounds of carbine ammunition (at XS 547 806).

Changing operational control to the 5th ARVN Ranger Group on 6 November, the 2nd Battalion moved to a new location four miles east of Saigon (XS 754 938). There were negative results through 10 November when the battalion was assigned an operational area that stretched from six kilometers west of Saigon to the Vam Co Dong River. In order to facilitate operations in the area, the battalion headquarters and one company relocated to Fire Support Base Barbara (XW 571 856). The remaining battalion units were strategically located in the area (XS 704 845, XS 875 820, XS 587 826). The 2nd Battalion carried out air mobile operations in conjunction with the U.S. 25th Infantry Division with negative results until 24 November. After the 3rd Battalion relieved the 2nd Battalion on 24 November, the 2nd Battalion returned to the Thu Duc base camp and a six-hour alert status under JGS control.

## 3RD INFANTRY BATTALION

From 1-15 November, the 3rd Infantry Battalion underwent refresher training at the Van Kiep National Training Center (YS 400 610). With the completion of four weeks of refresher training on 15 November, the battalion was placed on six-hour alert as JGS Reserve. The following day they returned to their Thu Duc base camp. On 24 November the 3rd Battalion exchanged missions with the 2nd Battalion and came under the operational control of the 5th Ranger Group ARVN. The battalion deployed an average of eight squad and five platoon-sized guardposts per night. There was negative enemy contact for the remainder of the month.

## 4TH INFANTRY BATTALION

The 4th Infantry Battalion served in various capacities as one of the ground elements of ATF 211 in the U-Minh Forest in November. The unit met with light resistance on 5 November (VR 873 665). Five VC were killed, one VC was captured and a CKC rifle and some hand grenades were taken into custody. Contact was again established on 6 November resulting in one VC and two VNMC being killed and five marines being wounded. As a result of the enemy attack on the ATF Headquarters on the morning of 5/6 November, two companies were moved to reinforce the security of the command post at Dong Hung on the afternoon of 6 November. On 13 November when the ATF 211 Headquarters came under 82 mm mortar attack, the 4th Battalion took the brunt of the casualties. Four of their men were killed and another 14 were wounded. The same day, the 4th Battalion engaged a VC force at VR 902 605, killing two of them and capturing five grenades and one knife.

After the 4th Battalion was relieved as the ATF 211 Headquarter security force on 23 November, it was helo lifted into several areas of suspected VC activity. Three VC were captured on 25 November (VR 862 718) and one kilogram of documents was found on 26 November.

On 30 November, elements of the battalion found and destroyed a VC complex consisting of a first-aid station, an information center and an armory. Two pistols, one Russian rifle, one shotgun, 10 boxes of TNT, one PRC 25 radio, three 105 mm shells and some miscellaneous rifle parts were removed from the VC complex.

## 5TH INFANTRY BATTALION

The 5th Infantry Battalion operated as an element of ATF 211 in the Song Ong Doc District of An Xuyen Province and in the U-Minh Forest area of Kien Giang Province in November. An ambush on the evening of 6 November fourteen miles west southwest of Ca Mau (VR 926 057) ended with the death of three VC, the capture of one CKC rifle, two mines, 10 hand grenades, 500 rounds of small arms ammunition, 800 kilograms of rice and two kilograms of documents, and the destruction of one sampan. Early the following morning, a marine squad outpost (VR 977 036) was overrun by an unknown-sized enemy force after the outpost had been taken under fire with 20 rounds of 60 mm mortar, B-40 and B-41 rockets. Five marines were killed, four were wounded and five M-16s and one M-79 grenade launcher were taken from the marines. The enemy was not to be spared casualties as five of their men were killed, one was captured and 20 B-40 rockets and 12 enemy hand grenades were recovered.

Between 14 and 17 November, the 5th Battalion concentrated on operations between the western edge of the U-Minh Forest and the Gulf of Thailand. On 16 November, the marines joined forces with U.S. Air Cavalry forces to kill 41 VC and destroy 15 sampans on a small canal three and one half miles southwest of Dong Hung (VR 893 658).

Minor incidents were reported during the remainder of the month while the battalion headquarters and two companies occupied defensive positions in Dong Hung and the other companies screened an area up to five kilometers around the ATF command post at Dong Hung.

## 6TH INFANTRY BATTALION

The 6th Infantry Battalion supported ATF 211 operations in the U-Minh Forest the entire month of November. Working with U.S. Air Cavalry units on 3 November approximately ten miles southeast of Dong Hung (WR 053 473), the combined force killed 22 VC and destroyed two VC platoon-sized base camps and three sampans. Concurrent with the attack on the ATF 211 headquarters at Dong Hung on 6 November, the 6th Battalion headquarters at Tan Bang (VR 992 544) received 15 rounds of 82 mm mortars that wounded 16 marines.

After the 6th Battalion was relieved of its security mission at Tau Bang by an ARVN Ranger Battalion on 14 November, the marines initiated operations to the northwest and the west to within one kilometer of the Gulf of Thailand. Between 16 and 20 November they met with daily resistance. A strong enemy force was en-

*Photo courtesy of Dan Dodd, Official Navy Photographer for ComRivFlot-One MRF TF-117 68-69, Retired Chief Photographers Mate.*

gaged in the middle of the afternoon of 17 November and lasted until approximately 0400 the following morning (VR 850 569). Three marines were killed and another 22 were wounded in the bloody battle. A sweep of the battlefield on the morning of 18 November revealed 13 dead VC, one AK-47, three cartridge belts, twenty 60 mm mortar rounds, one B-40 launcher and 15 grenades.

Squad-size contacts on 19 November yielded five VC killed and the capturing of one VC, one submachine gun, two cartridge belts, 12 hand grenades and one kilogram of documents. Five thousand kilograms of salt and 57 sampans were also destroyed.

During the rest of the month, the 6th Battalion had almost daily contact which ended in casualties and loss of equipment to the enemy. When the VC attacked one company of marines in night defensive positions on 23-24 November, they were driven off by the organic weapons of the marines and U.S. and VN air strikes. Two marines were killed in the attack and another three were wounded. The VC lost 13 men and the use of three homemade rocket launchers, six homemade rockets, eight B-40 rockets, two belts of .50-caliber machine gun ammunition, 17 grenades and 15 TNT charges.

The discovery of a 50-bed hospital and small information center (VR 861 569 to VR 873 591) on 29 November was another indication of the heavy involvement the VC have in the U-Minh Forest. Before the marines destroyed the complex, they recovered 10 kilograms of medical supplies, one kilogram of documents, 20 1.5-volt batteries and a VC flag.

### 7th INFANTRY BATTALION

On 1 November the 7th Infantry Battalion was formed under an authorized force structure increase. The battalion has been located in the rear area of the VNMC Training Center at Thu Duc where training and further organization are being implemented. The unit strength on 1 November was 692 men including 33 officers, 80 NCOs and 579 men.

In addition to training and organization, the new battalion has been manning security outposts and escorting the movements of the two brigade headquarters and artillery Batteries A and C to and from Saigon.

### 1st AND 2nd ARTILLERY BATTALIONS

Employment of the artillery batteries is included in the Operational Control summary that follows.

### PSYCHOLOGICAL OPERATIONS AND CIVIC ACTION SUMMARY

In November, 36 VC rallied to USN and VNN forces. Although this was considerably more than the 19 who chieu hoi'd in October, it did not surpass the record high of 208 Hoi Chanh that was experienced in July. The VNN Coastal Group 14 located in the Cua Dai River Basin of I CTZ accounted for approximately one half of the ralliers. Poor living conditions and lack of interest in the fighting were relatively common reasons this particular Hoi Chanh gave for rallying to the government.

In the Danang area 8,213 Vietnamese received medical aid from MEDCAPs via the NAVSUPPACT facilities and mobile teams. The dental facilities at the NSAD station hospital and at Camp Tien Sha treated a total of 389 Vietnamese dental patients. Another 463 Vietnamese were the recipients of dental aid from the mobile teams and outlying NSA detachments. The NSA Danang rendered civic action assistance to 22 schools, three orphanages, three dispensaries and 42 separate institutions during the month. One of the special projects that is under construction is a two-story, six-room Catholic school in the nearby village of Nhuong Nghia. Most of the manpower for this project are being provided by the members of the local parish.

Elements of the Third Naval Construction Battalion accounted for 2,840 medical/dental treatments including 14 emergency evacuations and two surgical cases. The Seabee teams reported that they had completed 38 projects in November, including one school, two housing projects, three warehouses, five bridges, six public buildings, one medical facility, one …

## VNMC OPERATIONAL CONTROL SUMMARY NOVEMBER 1969

| Unit | Dates | Under The Operational Control Of | Operation Name | Mission |
|---|---|---|---|---|
| Brigade A | 1-9 | JGS | None | Reserve |
|  | 10-30 | ATF 211 (VNN/VNMC) 21st ARVN Div | Quyet Tien S.D. 21/36/211 | RIF |
| Brigade B | 1-9 | ATF 211 (VNN/VNMC) 21st ARVN Div | Quyet Tien S.D. 21/36/211 | RIF |
|  | 10-30 | JGS | None | Reserve |
| 1st Infantry Bn | 1-30 | JGS | None | Reserve |
| 2nd Infantry Bn | 1-6 | CTG 194.9 | Giant Sling Shot | RIF |
|  | 7-14 | 5th Ranger Group | None | RIF |
|  | 15-30 | JGS | None | Reserve |
| 3rd Infantry Bn | 1-15 | JGS Van Kiep NTC | None | Training |
|  | 16-24 | JGS | None | Reserve |
|  | 25-30 | 5th Ranger Group | None | RIF |
| 4th Infantry Bn | 1-30 | ATF 211 (VNN/VNMC) | Quyet Tien S.D. 21/36/211 | RIF |
| 5th Infantry Bn | 1-8 | ATG 211.2, 21st ARVN | Quyet Tien S.D. 21/38 | RIF |
|  | 9-30 | ATF 211 (VNN/VNMC) | Quyet Tien S.D. 21/36 | RIF |
| 6th Infantry Bn | 1-30 | ATF 211 (VNN/VNMC) | Quyet Tien S.D. 21/36 | RIF |
| 7th Infantry Bn | 1-30 | VNMC Division | None | Training/Organization |
| Battery A | 1-30 | ATF 211 | Quyet Tien S.D. 21/36/211 | D/S |
| Battery B | 1-8 | ATG 211.2, 21st ARVN | Quyet Tien S.D. 21/38 | D/S |
|  | 9-30 | ATF 211 (VNN/VNMC) | Quyet Tien S.D. 21/36/211 | D/S |
| Battery C | 1-30 | ATF 211 (VNN/VNMC) | Quyet Tien S.D. 21/36/211 | D/S |
| Battery D | 1-30 | JGS | None | Reserve |
| Battery E | 1-30 | CMD | None | D/S |
| Battery F | 1-30 | RSSZ | None | D/S |

## VNN/VNMC Statistical Summary

**Vietnamese Navy:**

| | Daily Average | | Searched | | Detained | |
|---|---|---|---|---|---|---|
| | Oper | Empl | Junks | People | Junks | People |
| Coastal Force | | | | | | |
| I | 49.8 | 47.7 | 14,829 | 58,777 | 22 | 121 |
| II | 42.8 | 40.4 | 44,722 | 44,722 | 5 | 52 |
| III | 46.4 | 46.1 | 8,180 | 28,180 | 41 | 135 |
| IV | 37.6 | 37.5 | 11,578 | 35,615 | 2 | 6 |
| **Subtotals:** | | 50,348 | 167,294 | 70 | | 314 |
| *Fleet Command | | | | | | |
| Patrol Ships | 26.3 | 23.3 | 1,530 | 7,071 | 0 | 0 |
| WPBs/PCFs | 29.0 | 17.4 | 3,554 | 10,940 | 0 | 17 |
| **Subtotals:** | | 5,084 | 18,011 | 0 | | 17 |
| Riverine Area | | | | | | |
| River Assault Groups | 134.3 | 127.4 | 7,100 | 39,200 | 0 | 0 |
| TF 211 | 72.5 | 71.9 | 3,390 | 8,409 | 0 | 0 |
| TF 212 | 78.5 | 65.8 | 9,601 | 31,132 | 0 | 0 |
| #Central Task Force | 44.0 | 40.0 | 0 | 0 | 0 | 0 |
| TOTALS | | 75,523 | 264,054 | 70 | | 331 |

**Vietnamese Marine Corps: (through 27 November)**

| | | | | | | |
|---|---|---|---|---|---|---|
| VC/NVA: | KIA | 249 | Captured | 33 | Suspects detained | 27 |
| VNMC: | KIA | 59 | WIA | 195 | MIA | 3 |

Hoi Chanh: 7

*Provided 28 gunfire support missions
# Includes RAG 27 and RTEG

---

**Commander
U.S. Naval Forces
Vietnam
Monthly Historical Summary
December 1969
Declassified**

... the following coordinates: from Vinh Phouc (WR 250 750) to Vinh Phong (WR 320 540) to WR 380 480 to WR 470 480 to WR 470 660 to the Cai Lon River (WR 520 710) along the river to WR 470 730 to Ap Thanh My (WR 460 770) to Cai Tu River (vicinity WR 430 770) along Cai Tu River to WR 410 750 and back to Vinh Phuoc. RAID 72 and 74 remained with the marines while RAID 75 returned to the USS Askari (ARL 30) at Long Xuyen for much needed maintenance. Utilization of the RAIDs in the Twin Rivers area included troop lifts, river patrols and WBGPs. On 23 December, RAID 25 units relieved the majority of the RAID 72 boats which returned to Long Xuyen and the USS Askari for maintenance. (See discussion of VNMC Summary for further details of ATF operations.)

RAID 73 spent the majority of the month at Dong Tam and Long Xuyen. On 27 December, they completed the trip to the ATF headquarters. The Commander TF 211 had made the decision to keep three RAIDs in the area and to rotate one RAID back to Long Xuyen for a two-week upkeep and refitting period. RAID 73's initial employment was with the Third Battalion VNMC along the Rach Nuoc Trong (vicinity WR 380 693 to WR 423 675). The RAIDs had no significant contact, and the marines were involved in scattered and light action through the end of the month.

## Vietnamese Marine Corps

The reconnaissance in force operations conducted by Amphibious Task Force 211 in the U-Minh Forest region of Kien Giang Province were officially terminated at midnight on 9 December. The cumulative result for the three-month operation which began on 8 September are as follows: VNMC – KIA 133, WIA 499, MIA 3; VC/NVA – KIA 507, VCC 54, VCS 115; HC 105. Weapons captured: 41 AK-47 rifles, 31 CKC rifles, 17 Mauser rifles, one heavy machine gun, two .50 caliber machine guns, three carbines, two French rifles, one Russian rifle, one M-16, one Chicom machine gun, one B-41 rocket launcher, two M-1s, one Chicom rifle, one U.S. shotgun, one M-60 machine gun, one M-79, five .45 caliber pistols, three K54 pistols, two M3A1 submachine guns, one .45 caliber submachine gun, one B-40 rocket launcher, one 60 mm mortar. Captured mines, explosives and ammunition: 84,600 rounds of small arms, 14 AT mines, seven anti-boat mines, 19 AP mines, 94 Claymore mines, 110 61 mm mortar rounds, 122 82 mm mortar rounds, 1,216 hand grenades, 192 rifle grenades, six mines (5 kilo), two mines (100 kilo), six 105 mm Howitzer mines, 30 57RR rounds, 53 75RR rounds, 271 B-40 rocket rounds.

During the period 8-10 December, the ATF, which at this time included the 1st, 4th and 6th Infantry Battalions, 1st Artillery Battalion and RAIDs 72 and 74, completed the move from the U-Minh Forest to the Twin Rivers area of Chuong Thien Province (WR 364 697). With the launching of Quyet Tien Su Doan 21/32, 36, 42/211 on 10 December, the ATF began watermobile operations on the Cai Lon River and connecting waterways with RAIDs 72 and 74, and airmobile operations in conjunction with U.S. Air Cavalry Troop assets that stressed Eagle Flight tactics, screening missions around the ATF 211 command post area, and company-sized lifts. Enemy contact was infrequent throughout the remainder of the month as the VC/NVA forces employed evasive tactics and resorted to extensive mining of the areas in order to combat the VNMC mission of reducing enemy infiltration.

## Brigade "A"

Brigade "A" has been absorbed into the joint staff of ATF 211. The brigade commander has been designated as the deputy commander of ATF 211. Further information of ATF 211 operations is found in the individual discussions of the infantry battalions.

## Brigade "B"

For the entire month, the Brigade "B" staff was located at the VNMC Division Headquarters in Saigon while maintaining a six-hour alert status under JGS control.

## 1st Infantry Battalion

After relieving the 5th Infantry Battalion on 6 December in the U-Minh Forest operation, the 1st Infantry Battalion, as one of the VNMC elements of ATF 211, transited to the Twin Rivers area of Chuong Province (WR 364 697) in order to begin reconnaissance in force operations on 10 December. Plagued by mining incidents and sporadic contact, the 1st Battalion concluded RIF operations to the southeast of the command post (WR 364 697) on 20 December and returned to the command post where it assumed the responsibility for the perimeter defense and the local security patrols. A surprise encounter with a small enemy unit on 26 December resulted in one VC killed, and Eagle Flight operations with a VNAF Air Cavalry Troop unit on the same day accounted for another VC killed. The 1st Battalion was relieved of the ATF 211 command post security mission on 31 December and moved to the southwest portion of the area for operations in January.

## 2nd Infantry Battalion

The 2nd Infantry Battalion was in a one-hour alert status to JGS through 13 December. The following morning, the 2nd Battalion was airlifted from Tan Son Nhut Air Base to Binh Thuy for further transfer by helo to the Twin Rivers area south of the ATF 211 command post (WR 320 680) in order to affect the relief of the 4th Battalion. Late on the afternoon of 15 December, the 2nd Battalion gained contact with an estimated enemy squad (WR 335 634). The VC/NVA soldiers broke off the fighting without leaving an indication of their casualties. Two VN marines were wounded in this action. With RAID 72 providing the transportation, units of the 2nd Battalion patrolled and carried out landing assaults throughout the remainder of the month. Company-sized and Eagle Flight operations on 21 December were successful with five VC killed and no friendly casualties.

Nine VC were captured and another five were killed by the Marines in an action on 27 December. Five VNMC suffered wounds in the same fire fight. When the contact was broken off, the VC/NVA had left behind three rifles, one B-40 launcher, 14 grenades, four claymores, two 105 mm mines and one kilogram of documents. On the last day of the year, the 2nd Battalion moved to the ATF 211 command post and began local security operations in defense of the field headquarters.

## 3rd Infantry Battalion

From 1-10 December, the 3rd Infantry Battalion conducted airmobile assault and platoon and squad-sized night operations in the area north of Ben Luc. The battalion command post and one company were in positions at Fire Support Base Barbara (XS 576 856). The remaining Marine forces were deployed throughout the area. There was no action reported through 11 December when the 3rd

*Photo courtesy of Dan Dodd, Official Navy Photographer for ComRivFlot-One MRF TF-117 68-69, Retired Chief Photographers Mate.*

Battalion was relieved by the 33rd Ranger Group. The 3rd Battalion returned to their base camp in Thu Duc (XT 922 007) and a six-hour alert status for JGS. On 14 December, they traveled to Camp Nguyen Van Nha (XS 878 929) and were designated as the CMD reserve on one-hour alert.

The 3rd Battalion came under the operational control of ATF 211 on 26 December when it relieved the 6th Infantry Battalion in the Twin Rivers area of Chuong Thien Province. With the exception of one VC who was killed on 26 December, the Marine engagements with the enemy were limited to mining incidents which have inflicted casualties on the Marines.

## 4th Infantry Battalion

Under the operational control of ATF 211, the 4th Infantry Battalion carried out reconnaissance in force operations in the U-Minh Forest until 9 December when the mission was concluded, and ATF 211 displaced to the Twin Rivers area of Chuong Thien Province. At approximately 0500 on 6 December, a VC mortar and ground assault was launched by one VC company against one VNMC company (VR 870 680). The VNMC, with the assistance of U.S. OV-10 Black Ponies, repulsed the attack and killed 19 VC and captured three AK-47s in the process. The VNMC suffered casualties of three killed and 22 wounded who were medevaced.

After the 4th Battalion had moved to a new location on 10 December (WR 355 690 and WR 358 677), they began company-sized operations. On 13 and 14 December, the 4th Battalion, having been relieved by the 2nd Battalion, was airlifted to their Vung Tau base camp via Binh Thuy (YS 276 457). From 15-26 December, the 4th Battalion refurbished their equipment and weapons while on six-hour alert status under JGS control. Moving to Camp Nguyen Van Nha (XS 878 929) in Saigon on 26 December, the 4th Battalion was placed by JGS as the CMD reserve on one-hour alert.

## 5ᵀᴴ INFANTRY BATTALION

The 5th Infantry Battalion was responsible for the security of the ATF 211 headquarters at Dong Hung (VR 944 620) from the beginning of the month until the U-Minh Forest operations concluded on 9 December. While the battalion headquarters and two companies occupied defensive positions in and near the command post, the two remaining companies screened an area up to five kilometers around Dong Hung. Operations with U.S. Air Cavalry Troops on 3 December produced seven VC killed (WR 015 695). Late on the evening of 4 December, one 5th Battalion marine was killed and another eight were wounded during a VC mortar attack on the ATF command post. The 5th Battalion departed the area on 8 December, and after a one-night stopover in Can Tho, they arrived at their base camp (XT 968 064).

After spending three days in a six-hour alert status to JGS, the 5th Battalion joined friendly forces in the RSSZ in Operation Wolfpack III, a multi-battalion operation to seek out and destroy VC sapper units in the RSSZ. The marines first established contact on 15 December when one company sighted four VC attempting to cross the Thi Vai River along the eastern boundary of the RSS7 (YS 200 730). All four of the VC were killed and one rifle, one B-40 launcher, three B-40 rockets, small arms ammunition and one cartridge belt were captured. Three enemy sampans were also destroyed.

A small unit guardpost, on the evening of 22 December, surprised a squad-sized VC element. One VC was killed and one AK-47 and one PRC 10 was confiscated in this action. Wolfpack III terminated on 24 December and the 5th Battalion returned to the Thu Duc base camp (XT 968 046) and a six-hour reserve status to JGS.

## 6ᵀᴴ INFANTRY BATTALION

The 6th Infantry Battalion, an element of ATF 211, was engaged in almost daily fighting in the final week of operations in the U-Minh Forest. On the afternoon of 4 December, a 6th Battalion unit uncovered a VC training center (VR 870 630) that was defended by an estimated VC platoon. Once the marines had silenced the enemy force, they found five dead VC, 12 hand grenades, 200 rounds of AK ammunition, and two anti-personnel mines that were not familiar. The two-house, 20-bed complex was destroyed before the Marines departed the area.

Mining incidents which have accounted for the majority of the marine casualties took three lives and wounded another 15 marines on 5 December alone. The following day, a company-sized patrol surprised a VC squad, killing three of them and confiscating their equipment which included one AK-47, one pair of field glasses, one sampan and other miscellaneous items. Later that day, the patrol received three Hoi Chanhs, possibly the remaining squad members of the earlier engagement.

The battalion traveled to the Twin Rivers area on 9 December, established the base camp (WR 364 697) and implemented perimeter security measures. There was no contact, however, the marines experienced casualties from their operation in the heavily mined area. The 6th Battalion was relieved of the ATF 211 command post security operation on 20 December. The same day, they began company-sized operations in the southeastern portion of the A.O. On 21 December, the marines made contact with a VC squad four miles south of their command post near the Rach Nga Ba Cai Tau (WR 388 623). When the skirmish ended, the marines tallied three dead VC, one AK-47, five grenades and 200 rounds of ammunition captured and seven houses destroyed.

After the 6th Battalion was relieved by the 3rd Battalion on 26 December, the battle weary troops were airlifted to the Thu Duc base camp. The 6th Battalion served the remainder of the month in a six-hour reserve status to JGS.

## 7ᵀᴴ INFANTRY BATTALION

The 7th Infantry Battalion terminated its small unit training and organization at the VNMC Training Center (XT 898 039) on 3 December. The battalion moved to the National Training Center, Van Kiep, Baila (XS 390 610), and on 8 December, the marines began seven weeks of initial unit training.

## 1ˢᵀ AND 2ᴺᴰ ARTILLERY BATTALIONS

Employment of the artillery batteries is in the operational control summary which follows.

*Photo courtesy of Dan Dodd, Official Navy Photographer for ComRivFlot-One MRF TF-117 68-69, Retired Chief Photographers Mate.*

# VNMC Operational Control Summary December 1969

| Unit | Dates | Operational Control Of | Operation Name | Mission |
|---|---|---|---|---|
| Brigade A | 1-9 | ATF 211 (VNN/VNMC) 21st ARVN Div | Quyet Tien S.D. 21/36/211 | RIF |
|  | 10-31 | ATF 211 (VNN/VNMC) 21st ARVN Div | Quyet Tien S.D. 21/36, 38, 42/211 | RIF |
| Brigade B | 1-31 | JGS | None | Reserve |
| 1st Inf Bn | 1-5 | JGS | None | Reserve |
|  | 6-9 | ATF 211 (VNN/VNMC) 21st ARVN Div | Quyet Tien S.D. 21/36/211 | RIF |
|  | 10-31 | ATF 211 (VNN/VNMC) 21st ARVN Div | Quyet Tien S.D. 21/36, 38, 42/211 | RIF |
| 2nd Inf Bn | 1-13 | JGS | None | Reserve |
|  | 14-31 | ATF 211 (VNN/VNMC) 21st ARVN Div | Quyet Tien S.D. 21/36, 38, 42/211 | RIF |
| 3rd Inf Bn | 1-10 | 5th Ranger Group/CMD | None | RIF |
|  | 11-13 | JGS | None | Reserve |
|  | 14-26 | CMD | None | Reserve |
|  | 27-31 | ATF 211 (VNN/VNMC) 21st ARVN Div | Quyet Tien S.D. 21/36, 38, 42/211 | RIF |
| 4th Inf Bn | 1-9 | ATF 211 (VNN/VNMC) 21st ARVN Div | Quyet Tien S.D. 21/36/211 | RIF |
|  | 10-14 | ATF 211 (VNN/VNMC) 21st ARVN Div | Quyet Tien S.D. 21/36, 38, 42/211 | RIF |
|  | 15-26 | JGS | None | Reserve |
|  | 27-31 | CMD | None | Reserve |
| 5th Inf Bn | 1-8 | ATF 211 (VNN/VNMC) 21st ARVN Div | Quyet Tien S.D. 21/36/211 | RIF |
|  | 9-11 | JGS | None | Reserve |
|  | 12-24 | RSSZ | Wolfpack III | RIF |
|  | 25-31 | JGS | None | Reserve |
| 6th Inf Bn | 1-9 | ATF 211 (VNN/VNMC) 21st ARVN Div | Quyet Tien S.D. 21/36/211 | RIF |
|  | 10-26 | ATF 211 (VNN/VNMC) 21st ARVN Div | Quyet Tien S.D. 21/26, 38, 42/211 | RIF |
|  | 27-31 | JGS | None | Reserve |
| 7th Inf Bn | 1-4 | JGS | None | Reserve |
|  | 5-31 | JGS (Van Kiep NTC) | None | Training |
| 2nd Arty Bn | 1-24 | JGS | None | Reserve |
| Btry D | 1-24 | JGS | None | Reserve |
| Btry E | 1-24 | CMD | None | D/S |
| Btry F | 1-24 | Rung Sat Special Zone | None | D/S |
| 2nd Arty Bn | 25-31 | JGS | None | Reserve |

*Photo courtesy of Dan Dodd, Official Navy Photographer for ComRivFlot-One MRF TF-117 68-69, Retired Chief Photographers Mate.*

From: ADMINO COMNAVFORV
To: CHINFO
Info: CINCPACFLT
Unclassified

## REPUBLIC OF VIETNAM NAVY WEEKLY HIGHLIGHTS

The following summary of VNN actions for the week of 26 Dec 69 was compiled by the VNN PAO at Vietnamese Navy Headquarters in Saigon and was released in English to the Press Corps at 271415H: Quote – Fourth Riverine's RAGs kill 25 VC in two provinces – River Assault Groups (RAGs) 21/33, 23/31 and 29 operating in the Fourth Riverine Area in Operation Quyet Thang 266/31 during the past week in Vinh Long and An Xuyen provinces killed 25 Viet Cong, took in two Hoi Chanhs and captured 12 individual weapons, 15 hand grenades and two land mines. A 10-bed aid station was also destroyed. Friendly forces took only light casualties.

RSSZ forces make large weapons haul near Nha Be – Last week, River Patrol Group (RPG) 32 and River Assault Group (RAG) 27 on Operation Chuong Duong 39/69 encountered an enemy force 21 km southeast of Nha Be in Gia Dinh Province and killed 27 Viet Cong. VNN sailors also captured six individual weapons, one PRC-10, four M-26 grenades, two land mines and an assortment of munitions. Destroyed were 29 bunkers, eight sampans, six boxes of TNT, 16 locally produced hand grenades and 12 huts. Friendly casualties were termed "very light."

CG 16 takes in, processes 21 detainees Dec 21 – Coastal Group (CG) 16 of the First Coastal Zone arrested 21 Viet Cong suspects at 1600H, Dec 21 while on patrol. Of the 21, four were found to be local-force VC, three were VC demolitions men, one was of the Viet Cong Female Cadre and 13 were suspected of being draft dodgers. The 21 were soon turned over to the national police of Quang Ngai Province for further processing. Mekong River patrols score heavily on enemy last week – Vietnamese Navy River Patrol Groups (RPGs) operating in the eastern and western river systems of the Mekong Delta last week reported killing 38 enemy and capturing another 19. Twenty-eight individual weapons were captured along with three land mines and 11 hand grenades. Enemy properties destroyed by VNN forces included 19 sampans, five bunkers, 20 fishing nets and 22 huts.

F-C PCF, "Viper" launched; F-C Junks reviewed – Two new ferno-cement prototype craft, named Ha-Tien 2 and Ha-Tien 3 were launched from the Marine railway at the Vietnamese Navy shipyard in Saigon Dec 20. Ha-Tien 2 is a mark II patrol craft, fast (PCF) or "swift boat" and Ha-Tien 3 is the new, experimental "Viper." Armed with two M-60 machine guns and an automatic grenade launcher, the "Viper" is meant for small group fire-support of river patrol boats (PBRs). Present at the ceremony were Commodore Tran Van Chon, Vietnamese Navy chief of Naval operations, Minister Yu Quoc Thuc, minister of state for reconstruction and development and Ambassador William E. Colby, deputy to COMUSMACV for cords. Following the launching, the two new craft plus the ferno-cement junk (Ha-Tien 1) and a ferno-cement fishing craft passed in review before the assemblage. The craft later carried a number of the attending military and civilian dignitaries on a demonstration ride up the Saigon River.

MEDCAPS continue throughout the republic – Vietnamese Navy Medical Civic Action Projects (MEDCAPS) during the past week aided 533 people and distributed 15,000 leaflets and posters in Ba Ngoi Village and Ninh Moa, both in Ninh Thuan Province, as well as in the Song Cau District of Qui Nhon Province and in Kam Can City in An Xuyen Province.

OFFICE OF:
Lt. J.A. Martin, USNE
006A – T-4378
Acting Force PAO
RELEASED BY:
Capt. Emmett H. Tidd, USN, Chief of Staff

*Photo courtesy of Dan Dodd, Official Navy Photographer for ComRivFlot-One MRF TF-117 68-69, Retired Chief Photographers Mate.*

Department of the Navy
U.S. Naval Forces, Vietnam
and
Naval Advisory Group, Military Assistance Command, Vietnam
FPO San Francisco 96626

NAVFORV/NAVADVGRP MACV
NOTE 05440
021:leg
1 January 1970

Confidential (Unclassified upon removal of enclosures)
NAVFORV/NAVADVGRP MACV NOTICE 05440

From: Commander U.S. Naval Forces, Vietnam/Chief, Naval Advisory Group, Military Assistance Command, Vietnam
To: Distribution List
Subj: COMNAVFORV/CHNAVADVGRP Task and Advisory Organization
Encl: (1) Task Force 115 Organization
(2) Task Force 116 Organization
(3) Task Group 194.0 Organization
(4) Task Group 194.7 Organization
(5) Miscellaneous Advisors

1. Purpose. To promulgate and forward for information enclosures (1) through (5).
2. Information. The information compiled is as of 31 December 1969 and is subject to change on short notice.
3. Cancellation. Upon receipt of the next NAVFORV/NAVADVGRP MACV Task and Advisory Organization and for record purposes on 31 March 1970.

Emmett H. Tidd
Chief of Staff

Distribution:
NAVFORV/NAVADVGRP MACV NOTE 05216 of 31 JUL 69
Case 1 – Lists I thru VIII

Copy to:
CINCPACFLT (4)
CINCLANTFLT (4)
COMPHIBPAC (4)
COMPHIBLANT (4)
COMPHIBTRAPAC (4)
COMPHIBTRALANT (4)
COMSERVPAC (4)
COMSEVENTHFLT (4)
NIOTC MARIS (2)
CTF 72 (2)
CTF 73 (2)

CNO    OP-333 (2 each)
       OP-345
       OP-04
       OP-42
       OP-43
       OP-05
       OP-06
       OP-601V
       OP-601C
       OP-602
       OP-605
       OP-92

# COMNAVFORV/CHNAVADVGRP Task and Advisory Organization
## Task Force 115

| | | |
|---|---|---|
| CTF 115 | Coastal Surveillance Force | CAPT J.J. Shanahan, USN |
| CTG 115.1 | Northern Surveillance Group (MSC/MSO/WPB/PCF/PG assigned) | CDR R.C. Kucera, USN, Commander and First Coastal Zone Advisor HQ ashore Danang |
| CTU 115.1.0 | Sea Tiger (Cua Dai River) | as assigned on scene commander |
| CTU 115.1.1 | Northern Offshore Reaction Unit One (MSO/MSC/PG/WHEC assigned) | Senior CO Offshore Patrol Area One |
| CTU 115.1.2 | Northern Offshore Reaction Unit Two (MSO/MSC/PG assigned) | Senior CO Offshore Patrol Area Two |
| CTU 115.1.3 | Northern Inshore Reaction Unit (WPB/PCF assigned) | CDR R.C. Kucera, USN, Commander and First Coastal Zone Advisor HQ ashore Danang |
| CTU 115.1.4 | Northern Barrier Reaction Unit (MSO/WHEC assigned) | Senior CO Barrier Patrol Unit |
| CTU 115.1.5 | Duffel Bag Detachment | LTJG G.L. Catlett, USNR |
| CTU 115.1.6 | Northern WPB Support Unit COGARDIV 12 (WPB assigned) | LCDR T.C. Volkle, USCG Commander Coast Guard Division 12 |
| CTU 115.1.7 | Northern PCF Support Unit | LCDR D.R. Breckenridge, USN Commander Coastal Division 12 |
| CTU 115.2 | Central Surveillance Group (MSO/MSC/WPB/PCF/PG/WHEC assigned) | CDR H.C. Boschen, USN, Commander and Second Coastal Zone Advisor HQ ashore Nha Trang |
| CTU 115.2.1 | North Central Surveillance Unit | LCDR Duong Van Qui, VNN Commander and Qui Nhon CSC Officer HQ ashore Qui Nhon |

| | | |
|---|---|---|
| CTU 115.2.2 | South Central Surveillance Unit | CDR H.C. Boschen, USN, Commander and Second Coastal Zone Advisor HQ ashore Nha Trang |
| CTE 115.2.2.1 | Socen Offshore Reaction Element Four (MSO/MSC/WPB/PCF assigned) | Senior CO Offshore Patrol Area Four |
| CTE 115.2.2.2 | Socen Offshore Reaction Element Five (MSO/MSC/PG/WHEC assigned) | Senior CO Offshore Patrol Area Five |
| CTE 115.2.2.3 | Socen Inshore Reaction Element (WPB/PCF assigned) | CDR H.C. Boschen, USN, Commander and Second Coastal Zone Advisor HQ ashore Nha Trang |
| CTE 115.2.2.7 | Socen PCF Support Element COSDIV 14 (PCF assigned) | LT D.J. Sullivan, USN Commander Coastal Division 14 |
| CTG 115.3 | Southern Surveillance Group (MSO/MSC/WPB/PCF/WHEC/LST assigned) | CDR P.A. Yost, USCG, Commander and Third Coastal Zone Advisor HQ ashore Vung Tau |
| CTU 115.3.1 | Southern Offshore Reaction Unit Six (MSO/MSC/PG/WHEC assigned) | Senior CO Offshore Patrol Area Six |
| CTU 115.3.2 | Southern Offshore Reaction Unit Seven (MSO/MSC/PG/WHEC assigned) | Senior CO Offshore Patrol Area Seven |
| CTU 115.3.3 | Southern Inshore Reaction Unit (WPB/PCF assigned) | CDR P.A Yost, USCG, Commander and Third Coastal Zone Advisor HQ ashore Vung Tau |
| CTU 115.3.4 | Market Time Raider Unit | as assigned |
| CTU 115.3.5 | Market Time Raider Unit | as assigned |
| CTU 115.3.6 | Southern WPB Support Unit COGARDIV 13 (WPB assigned) | LCDR D.P. Gatto, USCG Commander Coast Guard Division 13 |
| CTU 115.3.7 | Southern PCF Support Unit COSDIV 13 (PCF assigned) | LCDR J.W. Streuli, USN Commander Coastal Division 13 |
| CTU 115.3.9 | Southern Operation Support Unit | Senior CO/OIC as assigned |
| CTG 115.4 | Gulf of Thailand Surveillance Group | CDR Kiem, VNN |
| CTG 115.5 | | Unassigned |
| CTG 115.6 | Gulf of Thailand Offshore Patrol Unit (WHEC assigned) | CO WHEC assigned Area Eight/Nine |
| CTG 115.7 | Sea Float Commander/ Gulf of Thailand Sea Lords Commander | CDR J.C. Patrick, USN, Commander Mobile Advanced Tactical Support Base |
| CTU 115.7.0 | Sea Float/Sea Lords Logistic | as assigned Support Unit (LST) |
| CTU 115.7.1 | Sea Float/Sea Lords Operations/Planning Unit | as assigned |
| CTE 115.7.1.1 | Sea Float/Sea Lords Waterborne Units (PCFs assigned) | Senior OIC PCFs assigned |
| CTU 115.7.2 | Sea Float Base Defense Unit | as assigned |
| CTE 115.7.2.1 | Sea Float EOD/UDT Det | as assigned |
| CTU 115.7.3 | Sea Float NGFS Unit | CO PG assigned |
| CTU 115.7.4 | Sea Float Ground Security Unit (WHEN assigned) | U.S. advisors as assigned |
| CTU 115.7.5 | Sea Float VNN POLWAR Unit | as assigned |
| CTU 115.7.6 | Sea Float SEAL Detachment Special Operations Group One | LT M.F. Crane, USN OIC Seal Delta Platoon |
| CTE 115.7.6.1 | Special Operations Group Two | LTJG C.S. Prouty, USN OIC Seal Mike Platoon |
| CTE 115.7.6.2 | Special Operations Support Unit | LTJG J.G. Engstrom, USN, OIC Mobile Support Team Two Det ECHO |
| CTU 115.7.7 | Sea Float/Gulf of Thailand Sea Lords Support Unit (An Thoi) | LCDR C.L. Miller, USN Commander Coastal Division 11 |
| CTU 115.7.8 | Sea Float Air Reaction Unit (Seawolves) | as assigned |
| CTU 115.7.9 | Sea Float/Gulf of Thailand Sea Lords Air Recon Unit (LOU/SLICK assigned) | as assigned |
| CTG 115.8 | Operational Readiness Group | CAPT J.J. Shanahan, USN, Commander |
| CTU 115.8.1 | WPB Operational Readiness Unit | CAPT D.E. Perkins, USCG Commander and COMCOGARDRON One |
| CTU 115.8.2 | PCF Operational Readiness Unit | CDR L.R. Jefferis, USN, Commander and COMCOSRON One |

| | | |
|---|---|---|
| CTU 115.8.3 | Harbor Defense Readiness Unit | CDR G.H. Overstreet, USN<br>Commander and OIC<br>IUWG 1 WESTPAC Det |
| CTU 115.8.4 | PG Operational Readiness Unit | LCDR J.R. Swain, USN<br>COMCOSDIV 32 |
| CTG 115.9 | Harbor Defense Group | CDR G.H. Overstreet, USN<br>Commander and OIC<br>IUWG 1 WESTPAC Det |
| CTU 115.9.1 | Harbor Defense Unit<br>Vung Tau | LCDR R.G. Montgomery, USN<br>OIC Harbor Defense |
| CTU 115.9.2 | Harbor Defense Unit<br>Cam Ranh Bay | LCDR W.G. Dyer, USN<br>OIC Harbor Defense |
| CTU 115.9.3 | Harbor Defense Unit<br>Qui Nhon | LCDR H.L. Barnes, USN<br>OIC Harbor Defense |
| CTU 115.9.4 | Harbor Defense Unit<br>Nha Trang | LCDR W.G. Murphy, USN<br>OIC Harbor Defense |

## COMNAVFORV/CHNAVADVGRP Task and Advisory Organization
### Task Force 116

| | | |
|---|---|---|
| CTF 116 | River Patrol Force/<br>River Patrol Flotilla Five | CAPT J.E. Faulk, USN, Deputy<br>First Sea Lords COMRIVPATFOR/<br>COMRIVPATFLOT FIVE |
| CTG 116.4 | VAL-4 (Binh Thuy) | CDR M.S. Schuman, USN, CO, VAL-4 |
| CTU 116.4.8 | VAL-4, Det ALFA<br>(Binh Thuy) | LCDR R. Ballard, USN<br>OIC, VAL-4, Det ALFA |
| CTU 116.4.9 | VAL-4, Det BRAVO<br>(Vung Tau) | LCDR J. Butterfield, USN<br>OIC, VAL-4, Det BRAVO |
| CTU 116.6.7 | Special Operations Support Unit<br>(Binh Thuy) | LT T.A. Mason, USNR<br>OIC Mobile Support Team Two |
| CTE 116.6.7.1 | Special Operations Support Element A<br>(Nha Be) | ENS R.S. Scott, USNR, OIC Mobile<br>Support Team Two, Det ALFA |
| CTE 116.6.7.2 | Special Operations Support Element B<br>(Ben Luc) | LTJG C. Bortell, USNR, OIC Mobile<br>Support Team Two, Det BRAVO |
| CTE 116.6.7.3 | Special Operations Support Element C<br>(Song Ong Doc) | LTJG J. Todd, USNR, OIC Mobile<br>Support Team Two, Det CHARLIE |
| CTE 116.6.7.4 | Special Operations Support Element D<br>(Nha Be) | LTJG S.B. Hazard, USNR, OIC Mobile<br>Support Team Two, Det DELTA |
| CTU 116.6.8 | Beachjumper Unit One<br>Team 13 (Binh Thuy) | LTJG G. Gottemueller, USNR<br>OIC, BJU 1, Team 13 |
| CTU 116.6.9 | EOD Team (Binh Thuy) | WO-2 J.R. Lundberg, USN<br>OIC EOD Team 38 |
| CTG 116.8 | Helo Support Group (Binh Thuy) | CAPT R. Bechwith, USN, CO, HAL-3 |
| CTG 116.9 | Rung Sat Special Zone<br>River Patrol Group (Nha Be) | CDR C.J. Wages Jr., USN<br>COMRSSZRIVPATGRP |
| CTU 116.9.1 | RSSZ River Patrol Unit<br>(Nha Be) | LT T.P McGinley, USN<br>COMRIVDIV 531 |
| CTU 116.9.2 | RSSZ MCM Unit ALFA<br>(Nha Be) | LT R.H. Champion, USN<br>COMINEDIV 112 |
| CTU 116.9.5 | Special Operations Unit A<br>(Nha Be) | LTJG A.Y. Bryson, USN, OIC Seal<br>Team Det ALFA, 10th Platoon |
| CTU 116.9.6 | Special Operations Unit D<br>(Nha Be) | LT W. Gardner, USN, OIC Seal<br>Team Det ALFA, 9th Platoon |
| CTU 116.9.8 | RSSZ Helo Unit A<br>(Nha Be) | CDR W.E. Serig, USN<br>OIC HAL-3, Det Two |

## COMNAVFORV/CHNAVADVGRP Task and Advisory Organization
### Task Group 194.0

| | | |
|---|---|---|
| CTG 194.0 | First Sea Lords Commander<br>(Can Tho) | RADM W.R. Flanagan, USN<br>Commander First Sea Lords/NAVLE<br>DMAC/Deputy COMNAVFORV |
| CTG 194.1 | Crusades Commander | CAPT J.R. Faulk, USN<br>COMRIVPATFOR/<br>COMRIVPATFLOT FIVE |

| | | |
|---|---|---|
| CTU 194.1.0 | Deputy Crusades Commander (Saigon) | CDR D.J. Walter, USN |
| CTU 194.1.2 | Breezy Cove Crusades Commander | as assigned |
| | | (Song Ong Doc) |
| CTU 194.1.3 | RSSZ Crusades Commander | LTJG J.M. Hogan, USNR |
| | (Nha Be) | OIC CTF 116 Monitor Team Two |
| CTU 194.1.4 | Barrier Reef West | as assigned |
| CTU 194.1.5 | TF 115 Crusades Commander | CAPT J.J. Shanahan, USN |
| | | COMCOSURVFOR |
| CTE 194.1.5.1 | Cua Dai Crusades Commander | as assigned |
| CTE 194.1.5.2 | Sea Float Crusades Commander | as assigned |
| CTE 194.1.5.3 | Qui Nhon Crusades Commander | as assigned |
| CTU 194.1.6 | Vinh Te Crusades Commander | LT R.F. Krebs, USN |
| | (Ba Xoai) | OIC TF 116 Monitor Team One |
| CTU 194.1.7 | TG 194.7 Crusades Commander | RIVSTRIKEGRP Monitor Team |
| | (Dong Tam) | as assigned |
| CTU 194.1.8 | Barrier Reef East Crusades Commander | as assigned |
| | | (Thuyen Nhon) |
| CTU 194.1.9 | Giant Slingshot Crusades Commander | LT J.C. Young, USNR |
| | (Tra Cu) | OIC 116 Monitor Team Three |
| CTG 194.2 | Breezy Cove Group Commander | LCDR L.H. Thames, USN |
| | | COMRIVRON 53 |
| CTU 194.2.1 | Patrol Unit (PBR) | LT N.W. Berry, USN |
| | | COMRIVDIV 572 |
| CTU 194.2.3 | Patrol Unit (RAC) | OIC RAD 131 and 152 |
| CTU 194.2.4 | LST Support Unit | CO USS Garrett County |
| CTU 194.2.5 | Helo Support Unit | OIC, HAL-3, Det 6 |
| CTU 194.2.6 | Special Warfare Unit | LTJG R.Woolard, USNR, OIC Seal |
| | | Team Det ALFA, 3rd Platoon |
| CTE 194.2.6.1 | Mobile Support Team Two | as assigned |
| | | Detachment CHARLIE |
| CTG 194.3 | Search Turn Group Commander | as assigned |
| CTU 194.3.1 | Patrol Unit | LT W.H. Graham, USN |
| | | COMRIVDIV 513 |
| CTU 194.3.2 | Patrol Unit | LT G.N. Eischen, USN |
| | | COMRIVDIV 553 |
| CTU 194.3.3 | Interdiction OPS Helo Support Unit | LCDR D.W. Strey, USN |
| | | OIC HAL-3, Det 8 |
| CTU 194.3.4 | LST Support Unit | CO USS Harnett County |
| CTU 194.3.5 | Patrol Unit | LT E.E. NcNeely, USN |
| | | COMRIVDIV 554 |
| CTU 194.3.6 | OIC SEAL PLTN K Det G | as assigned |
| CTE 194.3.6.1 | A Squad | as assigned |
| CTE 194.3.6.2 | B Squad | as assigned |
| CTG 194.4 | Barrier Interdiction Group Commander | CDR T.F. Mullane, USN |
| CTU 194.4.0 | Deputy Interdiction Group Commander/ | LCDR Lam, VNN |
| | | Commander Tran Hung Dao I/CTG 212.4 |
| CTU 194.4.1 | Commander Western Sector Tran Hung Dao | LCDR Que, VNN |
| | | (Ha Tien) |
| CTE 194.4.1.1 | CG 41/42/43/44 (Ha Tien) | LT Lo, VNN |
| CTE 194.4.1.2 | PCF Element (Ha Tien) | Senior OIC |
| CTE 194.4.1.3 | RIVDIV 532 | LT J.B. Bishop, USN |
| CTU 194.4.2 | Commander Central Sector Tran Hung Dao I | LT D.A. Spaugy, USN |
| CTE 194.4.2.1 | RIVDIV 535 | LT R.R. Lepak, USN |
| CTE 194.4.2.2 | RIVDIV 512 | LT D.A. Spaugy, USN |
| CTE 194.4.2.3 | RIVDIV 515 | LT T.F. O'Connor, USN |
| CTE 194.4.2.4 | RIVDIV 551 | LT A.R. Smelley, USN |
| CTE 194.4.2.5 | RIVDIV 573 | LT G.J. Ellis, USN |
| CTE 194.4.2.6 | RIVDIV 571 | LT J.W. Luksich, USN |
| CTU 194.4.3 | Commander Eastern Sector Tran Hung Dao I | LT Thinh, VNN |
| CTE 194.4.3.1 | RAD 132 Det A | Senior Boat Capt |
| CTE 194.4.3.2 | Kenner Ski Barge Element | LTJG An, VNN |
| CTE 194.4.3.3 | RIVPATGRP 54 | LT Thinh, VNN |
| CTU 194.4.4 | Commander Ha Tien Support Unit | LCDR J.F. Neese, USN |
| CTU 194.4.5 | Commander Barrier Reef | LT M.B. Connolly, USN |
| CTE 194.4.5.1 | Commander Barrier Reef West | LT J.E. Roper, USN |

| | | |
|---|---|---|
| CTE 194.4.5.2 | Commander Barrier Reef Central | LT G.H. Sturvist, USN |
| CTE 194.4.5.3 | Commander Barrier Reef East | LT W.L. Messemer, USN |
| CTE 194.4.5.4 | RIVDIV 514 | LT J.E. Roper, USN |
| CTE 194.4.5.5 | RAD 132 | LT M.B. Connolly, USN |
| CTE 194.4.5.6 | RAD 152 | LT W.L. Messemer, USN |
| CTE 194.4.5.7 | RIVDIV 592 | LT J.R. Poe, USN |
| CTU 194.4.6 | Commander Helo Support Group | LCDR E.F. Yaeger, USN |
| CTE 194.4.6.1 | HAL-3, Det 3 | LCDR B.W. Borquist, USN |
| CTE 194.4.6.2 | HAL-3, Det 5 | LCDR E.F. Yaeger, USN |
| CTE 194.4.6.3 | HAL-3, Det 9 | LCDR R.J. Touhey, USN |
| CTU 194.4.7 | Commander Border Interdiction Patrol | LT R.J. Aurin, USN |
| CTE 194.4.7.1 | MSR Border Interdiction Element | LT R.J. Aurin, USN |
| CTE 194.4.7.2 | PCF Border Element | Senior OIC |
| CTE 194.4.7.3 | Minesweeper Element | LT R.J. Aurin, USN, COMINEDIV 113 |
| CTE 194.4.7.4 | PCF River Element | Senior OIC |
| CTG 194.5 | Sea Lords Coastal Incursion Commander | CAPT J.J. Shanahan, USN COMCOSURVFOR |
| CTG 194.6 | Upper Saigon Interdiction Group Commander | as assigned (Phu Cuong) |
| CTU 194.6.1 | Upper Saigon River Patrol Unit | COMRIVDIV 593 |
| CTU 194.6.2 | Upper Saigon River Patrol Unit | as assigned |
| CTG 194.9 | Interdiction Force Commander/Deputy | CDR A.C. Sigmond, USN Interdiction Force Commander Trung Hung Dao II (Ben Luc) |
| CTU 194.9.0 | Ben Luc Interdiction Unit | as assigned |
| CTE 194.9.0.1 | PBR Element | COMRIVPATGRP 53 |
| CTE 194.9.0.2 | RAC Element | RAID 71 |
| CTU 194.9.1 | Tra Cu Interdiction Unit | as assigned |
| CTE 194.9.1.1 | PBR Element (Tra Cu) | COMRIVDIV 552 |
| CTE 194.9.1.2 | RAC Element (Tra Cu) | RAD 151/RAID 71 |
| CTU 194.9.2 | Go Dau Ha Interdiction Unit | COMRIVDIV 573 |
| CTE 194.9.2.1 | PBR Element (Go Dau Ha) | COMRIVDIV 594 |
| CTE 194.9.2.2 | RAC Element (Go Dau Ha) | RAD 151 |
| CTU 194.9.3 | Ben Heo Interdiction Unit | COMRIVDIV 552 |
| CTE 194.9.3.1 | PBR Element (Ben Heo) | COMRIVDIV 594 |
| CTE 194.9.3.2 | RAC Element (Ben Heo) | RAD 151 |
| CTU 194.9.4 | Tan An Interdiction Unit | COMRIVRON 513 |
| CTE 194.9.4.1 | PBR Element (Tan An) | COMRIVPATGRP 53 |
| CTE 194.9.4.2 | RAC Element (Tan An) | RAID 70 |
| CTU 194.9.5 | Tuyen Nhon Interdiction Unit | COMRIVDIV 153 |
| CTE 194.9.5.2 | RAC Element (Nha Be) | COMRIVDIV 153 |
| CTU 194.9.7 | Moc Hoa Interdiction Unit | as assigned |
| CTE 194.9.7.1 | PBR Element (Moc Hoa) | COMRIVDIV 511 |
| CTE 194.9.7.2 | RAC Element (Moc Hoa) | vacant |
| CTU 194.9.8 | Can Giouc Interdiction Unit | as assigned |
| CTE 194.9.8.1 | PBR Element | vacant |
| CTE 194.9.8.2 | COMRIVDIV 151 | as assigned |
| CTU 194.9.9 | Support Unit (Ben Luc) | as assigned |
| CTE 194.9.9.1 | OIC Seal Team Det GOLF | as assigned BRAVO Platoon (Ben Luc) |
| CTE 194.9.9.2 | EOD Element | OIC EOD Team 44 |
| CTE 194.9.9.3 | UDT Element | vacant |
| CTE 194.9.9.4 | Mobile Support Team Element | OIC Mobile Support Team Two Det BRAVO |
| CTE 194.9.9.5 | ACV Element (Ben Luc) | as assigned |
| CTE 194.9.9.6 | Southern Air Support Element (Ben Luc) | OIC HAL-3, Det 4 |
| CTE 194.9.9.7 | Northern Air Support Element (Tay Ninh) | OIC HAL-3, Det 7 |

## COMNAVFORV/CHNAVADVGRP Task and Advisory Organization
### Task Group 194.7

| | | |
|---|---|---|
| CTG 194.7 | Riverine Strike Group Commander | COMRIVSTRIKEGRP CAPT C.H. Blair, USN |
| CTU 194.7.3 | Riverine Assault Squadron One Three Commander | COMRIVRON 13 LT M.B. Connolly, USN |

| | | | |
|---|---|---|---|
| CTE 194.7.3.1 | Riverine Assault Division One Three One Commander | COMRIVDIV 131 | LT W.M. Kahn, USN |
| CTU 194.7.4 | Riverine Assault Squadron One Five Commander | COMRIVRON 15 | LT G.H. Sturvist, USN |

## COMNAVFORV/CHNAVADVGRP TASK AND ADVISORY ORGANIZATION
### ADVISORS

| | | |
|---|---|---|
| Senior Naval Advisor | Saigon | CAPT C.F. Rauch Jr., USN (ARVN 40895) |
| Deputy Senior Naval Advisor | Saigon | CAPT E.I. Finke, USN (T-3329) |
| Assistant Senior Naval Advisor | Saigon | CDR R.G. Hamm, USN (ARVN 40895) |
| Senior Marine Advisor | Saigon | COL W.M. Vanzuyen, USMC (T-4113) |
| Assistant Senior Marine Advisor | Saigon | LCOL T.D. Parsons, USMC (T-4113) |
| First Coastal Zone Advisor | Danang | CDR R.C. Kucera, USN (Foothill 928) |
| Second Coastal Zone Advisor | Nha Trang | CDR H.C. Boschen, USN (Nha Trang 3905) |
| Third Coastal Zone Advisor | Vung Tau | CDR P.A. Yost, UR, USN (SVN3-6537) |
| Fourth Coastal Zone Advisor | An Thoi | CDR B. Clark, USN |
| Third Riverine Area Advisor | Saigon | LCDR J.P. Boyd, USN (ARVN 40524) |
| Fourth Riverine Area Advisor | Can Tho | CDR R.A. Clark, USN |
| RSSZ Advisor | Nha Be | CDR C.J. Wages, USN |
| Fleet Command Advisor | Saigon | CDR G.W. Ducharme, USN (ARVN 40956) |
| Senior Shipyard Advisor | Saigon | CDR R. Matzner, USN (ARVN 40468) |
| CTF Clearwater | Cua Viet | CAPT J.E. Edmundson, USN |

### PATROL UNITS LOCATED IN I CORPS AND UNDER THE OPERATIONAL CONTROL OF CTF CLEARWATER

| | |
|---|---|
| CDR Hue River Security Group | LT J.B. Bishop, USN, COMRIVDIV 521 |
| CDR Dong Ha River Security Group | LT S.H. Jones, USN, COMRIVDIV 543 |

*Rocket damage. (Courtesy of Ralph Bakle.)*

### JANUARY 1970

### OPERATION SEA LORDS SUMMARY

During the month of January, combined Sea Lords forces operating in the Giant Slingshot, Border Interdiction, Search Turn, Ready Deck, and Breezy Cove campaigns accounted for a total of 384 enemy killed (by body count) and 17 captured. These totals are not too dissimilar when compared with December's 378 enemy killed and 47 captured, and they reflect similar overall activity levels for both months, which ranged from low to moderate. Friendly casualties for this period increased moderately from 12 killed and 84 wounded in December to this month's 22 killed and 122 wounded. In January, Vietnamization continued as Operation Ready Deck was removed from the Sea Lords Campaign and redesignated as a 3rd Riverine Area VNN operation with both VNN and USN units assigned. A breakdown of complete USN and VNN Sea Lords statistics for January and statistical totals computed since the start of operations are located at the end of this section following the discussion of the various campaigns.

### GIANT SLINGSHOT

During January, there were an average of 63 U.S. Navy craft and 55 VNN craft assigned to the Giant Slingshot Campaign, and, in addition to performing escort duty, troop lifts, and blocking and support missions, these craft set a daily average of 22 WBGPs along the Vam Co Dong and Vam Co Tay Rivers. During the month, enemy activity remained at the low to moderate level with enemy casualties increasing from December's 142 killed to January's 182 killed. However, this increase did not come about without cost to friendly units. Friendly casualties also increased from nine killed and 37 wounded last month to this month's 18 killed and 72 wounded.

In addition to other duties, CTG 194.9 assumed the opcon, 5 January, of all elements assigned to Operation Deep Channel II, one of the largest combat demolition jobs in the history of the Navy. The purpose of this operation is to connect the Kinh Gay and Kinh Lagrange Extension, using military explosives. This will in turn provide a patrolling route for river patrol craft in a formerly inaccessible area and established a cordon to enemy infiltration from the tip of the "Parrot's Beak" southwest along the Kinh Bo Bo - a known enemy infiltration route. The new six mile channel when completed will have the added benefit of providing the civilian population in the area with a short cut between Tuyen Nhon and Tra Cu, thus making it easier for them to transport products to the market in Saigon, Tay Ninh City, and elsewhere. By the end of January, Detachment Delta of Underwater Demolition Team Twelve (UDT-12) and a detachment of Vietnamese Navy Frogmen, all under LTJG Walter R. Harvey, were well on their way to completion of the channel blasting. In addition, other units were involved as seen on the Task Organization Chart below.

The following narrative includes examples of the more significant incidents occurring in the Giant Slingshot AO in January.

On the first day of the month, two VNN PBRs of RPG 53 were in WBGP on the Vam Co Dang River, three miles west northwest of Ben Luc (XS 573 777), when they observed a sampan moving north along the west bank. The Vietnamese units, with U.S. Navy advisor EM1 Hererra aboard, waited until the sampan closed within 20 yards, then opened fire killing all four occupants. The sampan was then searched and found to contain an AK-47, two ammo cans containing political progress reports, and medical and supply lists. Black Ponies placed a strike on the west bank, but there was no further contact.

On the night of 2 January, two Seawolves flown by Commander Hamman and Lieutenant Catone were diverted to assist TU 194.9.7 craft in contact with VC six miles northwest of Moc Hoa on the Vam Co Tay River (XT 965 965). The two aircraft received and suppressed light small arms and automatic weapons fire as they placed multiple rocket and machine gun strikes on the target. A later sweep by 194.9.7 units revealed that the airstrikes had killed six VC, mid subsequent intelligence reports from agents in the area indicated that an additional five VC had been killed and 12 wounded.

Beginning at 1400H on 8 January and continuing into the morning of 10 January, RF troops made contact with an estimated VC/NVA battalion located in a rubber plantation five miles north of Go Dau Ha (XT 360 332). U.S. Navy units from Go Dau Ha provided blocking forces and waterborne guardposts in the Vam Co Dong River while Seawolves and Black Ponies conducted air strikes in support of the operations. At the same time, RAC at Go Dau Ha were standing by to lift additional troops into the area should a need for them arise. As it turned out, there was no need since the enemy was resoundly defeated and lost 89 VC/NVA killed while inflicting only light casualties on friendly forces - two RF killed, one RF wounded, and two U.S. Army wounded.

In the meantime, on the afternoon of 9 January, Navy Seawolves scrambled to support ARVN and U.S. troops in heavy contact 11 miles southeast of Ben Keo (XT 370 350). The two Seawolves, flown by Lieutenant Catone and LTJG Pinegar, arrived on the scene and coordinated with a U.S. Army FAC as they placed multiple rocket and machine gun attacks on two sides of the friendly position. After returning to Tay Ninh to rearm and refuel, the LHFT arrived back in the contact area as armored vehicles, which had been moved in to suppress the enemy offensive, began taking heavy RPG fire. The aircraft placed strikes in support of retreating friendly forces until their ammunition was expended, and their fuel state required them to return to their home base. By this time, TACAIR was en route. The Navy helos were credited with 10 probable kills, and, despite receiving heavy A/W fire on all passes, suffered no casualties with the exception of two small holes in one of the aircraft.

In the same general area, also on 9 January, four RIVDIV 594 PBRs were en route to night WBGP positions when they came under heavy B-40 and A/W fire from the south bank of the Vam Co Dong River three miles south of Ben Keo (XT 223 433). A total of nine B-40s were fired, and one of the PBRs took two hits resulting in a three foot hole in the port bow and shattered coaming on the portside forward.

To avoid sinking, the PBR beached on the north bank west of the contact area and twenty minutes later was taken in tow to Ben Keo by an ATC with a Monitor providing cover. An artillery sweep of the contact area was followed by Army LHFT and Navy Black Pony airstrikes. However, enemy casualties were unknown. Friendly casualties were one USN killed and four USN wounded who were medevaced less than 16 minutes after the start of the action.

SEALs of SEAL Team, Det Golf, were inserted by LSSC three miles northeast of Ben Luc (XS 586 770) on the evening of 13

| Task Designator | Title | Commander | Execution |
| --- | --- | --- | --- |
| A. TG 194.9 | Giant Slingshot | COMMANDER, Giant Slingshot | Provide overall coordination |
| B. TG 115.9 | Coastal Surveillance Group | COMMANDER, TG 115.1 | Provide UDT personnel |
| C. TG 115.7 | Solid Anchor | COMMANDER, TG 115.7 | Provide UDT personnel |
| D. TU 194.9.1 | TRA CU Interdiction Unit | COMRIVDIV 552 | Provide support as requested by CTE 194.9.9.3 |
| E. TU 194.9.5 | Tuyen Nhon Interdiction Unit | COMRAD 153 | Coordinate employment of USA infantry platoons |
| F. TE 76.0.6.2 | UDT Twelve | COMMANDER, UDT Twelve | Provide one officer/10 enlisted to CTE 194.9.9.3 |
| G. TE 194.9.9.3 | Kinh Gay SPECOPSGRU | OINC, Kinh Gay SPECOPSGRU | Assume opcon UDT personnel. Direct extending and clearing operations. Coordinate between USA and USN |
| H. TE 194.9.5.3 | USA INF PLT as assigned | CO, USA INF PLT as assigned. | Provide direct support to CTU 194.9.5 |
| I. | Naval Support Activity, Saigon | COMNAVSUPPACT SGN | Provide logistics support |

January. The nine SEALs, two of which were LDNNs, under LTJG Duggan, patrolled north about 600 meters to an east-west commo-liaison trail discovering five bunkers along the route. Turning east on the trail, the SEALs had patrolled another 500 meters when they heard numerous voices from a large hooch nearby (XS 590 775). One of the LDNNs stated that the voices were directing preparations for a VC meeting, which he estimated 20 VC were attending. While maneuvering toward the hooch, the SEALs observed nine VC armed with AK-47s moving east. The SEALs set up on the hooch, called for Seawolves, then initiated fire after which they withdrew 50 meters to direct the Seawolf airstrikes. During the subsequent strikes, the Seawolves received light A/W fire, and, as the SEALs moved south for extraction, they also received fire. The results of the action were 15 VC probably killed (five by air) and no friendly casualties.

One platoon of MSF troops and four PBRs of TU 194.9.7 were operating together an 16 January and were in night WBGP when they sighted approximately five VC on the south bank of the Vam Co Tay River, four miles northwest, of Moc Hoa (WS 951 974). The PBRs, under Patrol Officers SMC Chambless and BMC Blackwell, made firing runs and received two B-40 rockets and small arms fire in return from an undetermined size force. Seawolves were diverted to the scene and placed two strikes in the contact area followed by an MSF troop sweep which netted two VC bodies, two AK-47s,and one B-41 rocket. The boats reset the WBGP, and when it became light, another troop sweep was made recovering a B-40 round and 25 back packs filled with personal gear and khaki colored uniforms. Later in the morning, an informant, relating information obtained from villagers in the area, reported that 11 VC had been killed and 12 wounded in the action. There were no friendly casualties.

The enemy had better success an the 21st day of January in an action against the ATSB at Go Dau Ha on the Vam Co Dong River. At 0111H, an explosion occurred between the galley ammi of the ATSB and an ATC (T-36) which completely demolished the galley and caused the ATC to sink within three minutes. General Quarters was set immediately on the ATSB, and fields to the north were straffed with machine gun and mortar fire. In addition, boats dropped concussion grenades into the water in the vicinity. A VC was seen evading to the west along a canal by the north perimeter. Seawolves were scrambled and upon arrival, observed several VC evading to the west, 800 meters south of the base. They were taken under fire by the Seawolves, and artillery was called in and fired blocking rounds to the north and southwest.

Of the six U.S. Navy crewmen onboard the ATC four escaped. Two men, below decks at the time of the explosion, were killed. Of the four that escaped, three were slightly wounded. Enemy casualties are unknown.

The same day, after having been alerted to enemy movement by portable sensors, CTU 194.9.7 PBRs set up in night WWP five miles northwest of Moc Hoa (WS 948 978). Sighting approximately 30 VC on the river bank, the four PBRs, under Patrol Officers SMC Chambless and BMC Lewis, took the enemy under fire and received grenade and heavy automatic weapons fire in return. Seawolves and a U.S. Army LHFT conducted numerous strikes in the contact area. Also, a Shadow aircraft arrived an the scene but was unable to fire because of clearance problems. The afloat units discovered four VC bodies in the river after the strikes. There were no friendly casualties.

## BORDER INTERDICTION

At the end of January, there were 278 river craft and six helos assigned to the Border Interdiction Campaign. During the month, these units continued to hamper the VCs slowly disintegrating logistics chain despite the seasonally decreasing water level which was detrimental to waterborne interdiction efforts. The number of enemy contacts sightings in the Border Interdiction AO indicates that the enemy is still trying to move through the Tran Hung Dao and Barrier Reef interdiction barriers, and this month that effort cost him 41 confirmed killed, and 67 more probably killed. On the other hand, friendly Border Interdiction forces suffered no kills during December and at month's end had only 33 wounded.

The degree of effectiveness of Navy forces in the Border Interdiction Campaign was reflected in a statement by a VC who had surrendered to friendly forces. He revealed that a 300 man unit with needed weapons and supplies had been prevented from crossing into the "Seven mountains" area for several weeks by Navy forces. Major General Wetherill, CG DMAC, had passed to the units concerned, a message which contained a well done for their unsurpassed "Courage, determination, and aggressive action." The following incident narrative includes examples of such action.

At 0205H on 3 January, a VC/NVA element of unknown size launched a coordinated attack on the Vinh Gia Special Forces Camp and waterborne units in guardpost positions nearby. The camp, located 30 miles southwest of Chau Doc, in the central sector of the Vinh Te Canal, received four recoilless rifle rounds and AK-47 fire; 10 minutes later, a RIVDIV 512 PBR in WBGP five miles west of the camp (VS 733 612) began receiving automatic weapons fire. Seawolf support was requested at this time, and even though HAL 3, DET 3 helos were theoretically "pinned down" at Vinh Gia due to the incoming enemy fire, LCDR Thomas and LTJG Watts made emergency takeoffs in order to provide support for the PBR, including Medevac. While the Medevac was being conducted, a RIVDIV 515 PBR came under B-40 and heavy automatic weapons fire one mile east of Vinh Gia (VS 815 612). An Army LHFT in the area observed the attack and diverted to assist, arriving prior to HAL 3, DET 5, Seawolves scrambled from YRBM-16. Airstrikes were placed in the ambush area, and a Medevac was conducted. Another RIVDIV 515 PBR, also at VS 815 612, reported that an 82mm mortar round had landed on the boat and fortunately failed to detonate. The crew was evacuated to the cover boat and a security perimeter was set. Later, EOD personnel were lifted to the scene to dispose of the dud mortar round, and they arrived shortly after 40 MSF troops who were lifted in by PBRs and inserted near the westernmost contact area (VS 730 613) for a sweep. Results of the action were three VC killed and seven USN and three VNN wounded. In addition, an AK-47, 100 rounds of AK-47 ammunition, numerous hand grenades, and miscellaneous personal and medical gear were recovered.

That night, just to the east of the previous incident, a fierce battle erupted. Initially, the attack was launched by an estimated 100 VC/NVA against a RIVDIV 535 PBR, under Patrol Officer BMC Marriner, in WBGP 24 miles southwest of Chau Doc (VS 840 612). During the action, heavy automatic weapons fire was received from the north bank and random small arms fire was received from the south bank by the PBR. At one point, the enemy approached the boat closely enough to throw a hand grenade at it. Fighting was so intense that the PBR had to be rearmed. By this time, two Seawolf Det's, three flights of Black Ponies, and Army Hunter-Killer Team, and TACAIR were supporting the action, which was characterized by a series of individual engagements in which the enemy would initiate fire on the PBR, followed by airstrikes suppressing the enemy fire, only to have the enemy open fire again a short time later. The next morning MSF troops were inserted, and they found one NVA body and evidence of five more enemy probably killed. In addition, mortar positions, one 105mm booby trapped projectile, and a small amount of ammunition were found. Remarkably, there were no friendly casualties.

On the same night, still further to the east, a RAD 132 ATC reported receiving A/W fire and B-40 rockets from the north bank of the Vinh Te Canal, five miles southwest of Chau Doc (WS 058 803). The ATC (T-2), with GMG2 Jones aboard as Patrol Officer, returned and suppressed the fire. Another ATC (T-19), with GMG1 Johnson as Patrol Officer, also came under fire one half mile to the southwest (WS 053 798) while en route to assist T-2. Seawolves of HAL 3, DET 9, placed two strikes in the vicinity of WS 049 798 where six people were sighted on the north bank. There was no further contact or any friendly casualties. PF troops were, inserted into the area after the action and captured a VC who was suffering from a serious face wound. Rapid interrogation of the prisoner while awaiting Medevac revealed that he was part of a 14 man team assigned to attack boats on the Vinh Te Canal. The PF troops also recovered a small amount of ammunition including two B-40 rockets wired for command detonation.

Not all the significant action occurred in the Vinh Te Canal Section of the Border Interdiction AO. In the Barrier Reef AO, on the night of 10 January, an RF guard post on the Grand Canal seven miles west of Ap Bac (XS 047 744) was attacked by an unknown sized enemy force. RIVDIV 551 PBRs, under Patrol Officer PR1 Davidson, picked up 20 troops at a Vietnamese outpost located two miles to the east and inserted them at the contact site. The PBRs provided fire support for one and a half hours until extraction. The following morning a troop sweep revealed three VC bodies, 1,000 rounds of AK-47 ammunition, six rifle grenades, and same miscellaneous supplies and documents (boobytrapped). Friendly casualties in the engagement were two RF troops killed and one wounded.

Moving back to the Vinh Te Canal, on the night of 17-18 January, an enemy crossing attempt by approximately 100 VC was thwarted by RPG 54 PBRs, MINDIV 113 MSRs, RAD 132 RACs, and Hal 3, Det's 3 and 5, Seawolves. The first crossing attempt of the night was foiled at 2230H when, in response to NOD and radar sightings, Seawolves and Black Ponies placed rocket and machine gun strikes in the contact area, 12 miles southwest of Chau Doc (VS 972 752). Fifty minutes later, four VNN PBRs of RPG 54 in WBGP a half mile to the northeast (VS 979 755 and VS 989 760) spotted an estimated 100 VC approaching their position. When the enemy was within 20 meters, the PBRs opened fire and called in Seawolves, who again placed machine gun and rocket strikes. Both the Seawolves and the PBRs received return fire. Later, daylight sweeps of both areas produced five VC bodies and numerous blood trails leading toward Cambodia. Aircraft, as a result, were credited with 25 probable kills. In addition, a small amount of enemy ammunition was captured in the actions that yielded no friendly casualties. In a smaller engagement at VS 990 763 that occurred later still, KSB personnel accounted for four additional VC killed (two probable) as the VC were observed crawling toward a nearby PBR.

Several nights later, on the Grand Canal (Barrier Reef), a Monitor (M-3) of RAD 132, while in WBGP 14 miles west of Ap Bac (WS 920 769), received seven B-40 rockets and heavy automatic weapons fire from both banks. The Monitor returned fire even though she had sustained six rocket hits. An ASPB and a Zippo nearby broke their guard post position to assist, and arriving on the scene suppressed the hostile fire. The Monitor, escorted by the ASPB, cleared to the west to Medevac four wounded USN, while the Zippo remained behind destroying enemy positions. Seawolves, in addition to Medevac services, placed strikes on the enemy positions.

A troop sweep the following morning revealed eight civilian hooches destroyed, five civilians killed, and seven civilians wounded (all medevaced). Enemy casualties are unknown.

On the night of 25-26 January, RIVDIV 573 PBRs in WBGP eight miles northeast of Vinh Gia, on the Vinh Te Canal, sighted two VC 150 meters north of their guard post. CIDG troops, attached as boat security, pursued the VC north until contact was lost. Seawolves were overhead at 2046H, 20 minutes after the initial sighting, and illuminated the area. While placing airstrikes, the Seawolves, flown by LTJG Watts and LTJG Leach, received return fire. At 2228H, PBRs initiated fire on at least 12 VC observed south of the boats, this time Black Ponies were on hand and raked the area with fire until they were relieved by Seawolves. At 2305H, PBRs of RIVDIV 571, in the contact area, observed two VC running from the scene and took them under fire with unknown results. Seawolves, providing support, were seen taking automatic weapons fire from the eastern end of Nui Gia Mountain. At 0330H, 20 MSF troops swept the area while under Black Pony cover with the following results: eight VC killed (one by air); six AK-47s; numerous hand grenades, and two pistols captured; and numerous documents confiscated. There were no friendly casualties.

## SEARCH TURN

With an end of month asset strength of two Seawolves and 36-water craft, which included 29 PBRs, three Boston Whalers, two MSDs one CCB, and one LSSC, Search Turn units (TG 194.3) continued their interdiction operations in January with patrols in the Gulf of Thailand and the Three Sisters area and with waterborne guardposts on the Ba The and Rach Gia-Ha Tien Canals and along the Kien An coast, an area indicated in intelligence reports as the site of a major enemy resupply effort.

January also saw Search Turn personnel aid the victims of a VC terrorist attack in Rach Gia. At 1955H on 7 January, CTG 194.3 NOC was notified that a terrorist had thrown a grenade into the Chau Van Theatre in downtown Rach Gia. Five civilians were killed and 25 were hospitalized, eight of which required emergency surgery. The VN TOC initiated a request for blood and a medevac to be sent from Can Tho. U.S. personnel in Rach Gia and at the Naval Base at Rach Soi responded with immediate, blood donations.

On the 15th of the month, the USS Hunterdon County (LST 838) arrived on station in the vicinity of Rach Gia to relieve the USS Harnett County (LST 821) and assumed task designator CTU 194.3.4.

Hostile fire incidents in the Search Turn A.O. dropped again in January with only 14 recorded as compared to 19 in December. Enemy losses, however, rose during the month from 12 kills and 18 probables in December to 24 kills and 20 probables.

PBRs of RIVDIV 553, under Boat Captains BM1 Kovi and GMG2 Goodwin, were on a routine gulf patrol in the Three Sisters area (VS 872 156) in the early evening of 21 January when a sampan with four occupants was observed close to the beach in a 24 hour curfew area. Upon illumination, the occupants jumped from the sampan and were then taken under fire. Two VC were killed, and two were seen running for the beach. Twelve to 15 more were observed to come out of the tree line in an apparent attempt to retrieve the bodies and the sampan. They were taken under fire by the PBRs; there was no return fire. At this time, nine bodies were clearly sighted in the contact area. Seawolves then put in a strike and provided cover while an attempt to recover the sampan was made. This try, however, was thwarted by shallow water and enemy LAW fire from the tree line on the beach. Black Ponies also arrived on station and put a strike into the contact area, and PBRs, while firing into the area, observed one large secondary explosion. With the assistance of Sector artillery illumination, the contact area was kept under surveillance throughout the night. Another attempt to retrieve the sampan during the early morning using a borrowed Army Boston Whaler with Seawolves overhead was prevented by shallow water and deep mud. The sampan was then destroyed. Enemy losses also included nine VC killed. There were no friendly casualties.

While en route WBGP on the following evening, PBRs of TU 194.3.2 observed five VC crossing a field south of the Rach Gia

Ha Tien Canal and took them under fire at 500 meters; there was no return fire. Thirteen minutes later, artillery, illumination was requested, and the first round went out 35 minutes later. Five minutes after, the units investigated the contact area and found one VC body and one heavy drag trail. Air assistance was not requested because of the scene's proximity to a populated area. The enemy suffered one VC killed and one VC probably killed while friendly casualties were held down to one USN slightly wounded.

During the early morning hours of 24 January, units of RIVDIV 553, while in WBGP under Patrol Officer LTJG Nickerson, received sensor activation and observed four VC approaching their position 14 miles northwest of Rach Gia (VS 957 238). These four were taken under fire, but no return fire was received. Seawolves were requested on Scramble III. They arrived on station and put in a strike 15 minutes later. There was no further activity, and the units re-established their guardpost position. About four hours later, the units again received sensor activation and observed VC moving in the contact area. Once again, the enemy were taken under fire with no return fire being received. Illumination was requested, and a sweep by the units produced one heavy blood trail. The enemy suffered one VC probably killed. There were no friendly casualties.

## RIVERINE STRIKE GROUP

During January, as last month, all RAC formerly assigned to CTG 194.7 (Riverine Strike Group) remained out-chopped to other operational commanders with the exception of those craft undergoing overhaul.

## BREEZY COVE

The level of activity in the Breezy Cove AO decreased slightly during January. Enemy KIAs dropped from 40 killed last month to this month's 30 killed, and there was a corresponding decrease in friendly casualties which dropped from 12 wounded to four wounded. The total number of ENNIFs, FRIFFs, and unilateral firings did increase slightly, however, from 56 to 59.

At the end of January, 26 craft and two Seawolves were assigned for operations as follows:

CTU 194.2.4 USS Garrett County (LST 786)
CTU 194.2.1 10 PBRs, 2 Boston Whalers
CTU 194.2.3 5 ASPBs 5 ATCs, 1 Monitor
CTU 194.2.5 2 UH-1Bs
CTU 194.2.6 1 HSSC, 1 LSSC, 1 Boston Whaler

On 7 January, the USCGC Dallas (WHEC-716) provided Breezy Cove with its first naval gunfire support in reaction to a PBR contact. Additional support by Dallas is included in the following narrative which contains the more significant incidents occurring in the Breezy Cove AO during January.

Four SEALs and two LDNNs, under Platoon Leader LTJG Mihalic, were inserted by sampan three miles northeast of Song Ong Doc (WR 007 052) on the afternoon of 2 January. Shortly after setting up a guardpost, male voices were heard to the west. A Seawolf was scrambled, and when it was overhead, the SEALs moved into some huts west of the guardpost and captured three VC.

On the afternoon of 6 January, Pham Van Trang rallied to a PBR patrol under the Chieu Hoi program. Upon his initial interrogation by NILO Song Cing Doe, the Hoi Chanh revealed the location of 100 VC five miles northeast of Song Ong Doc (NR 052 046 to WR 063 052). That night an airstrike was placed on the target with unknown results; the pilots reported receiving ground fire. On 9 January, a NILO Ca Mau agent reported that 32 VC had been killed as a result of the airstrike.

On 8 January, Pham Van Trang was shot and killed by a petty officer of the Vietnamese Navy.

After he had turned himself in, the Hoi Chanh was quartered ashore under 24 hour surveillance. During this time, he passed intelligence information to NILO Song Ong Doc, helped plan a SEAL operation, and made a psyops tape urging his friends to rally to the side of the government. SEALs and LDNNs, however, considered the Hoi Chanh's suggested operation as a possible trap. The suspicion clouding Trang's true feelings were further heightened when he requested a weapon from the NILOs interpreter. Thus, arrangements were made to turn the Hoi Chanh over to local authorities as quickly as possible.

On the 8th of the month, at 0830H, Trang was placed in the custody of a sentry, on the ASPB to be turned over to local authorities about an hour and a half later. At 08335H, PO2 Vu Ba Hung of the Vietnamese Navy took Thang to Vam Song Ong Doc for a requested cup of coffee. While in a restaurant, the rallier insisted upon seeing a sister in town and persuaded Hung to let him go and see his sister alone. Petty Officer Hung had noticed that Trang was acting strangely, so he followed him from a distance. When Thang realized that he was being followed, he told Hung that he had changed his mind and would return to the ASPB by himself. Hung, however, again followed Thang closely.

At approximately 0900H, the Hoi Chanh looked back and saw the trailing Hung. The petty officer then observed Thang reach into his shirt where he detected a large bulge. Hung draw a .45 cal pistol and shot the Hoi Chanh twice. This shooting was witnessed by CPO Lee Anh Hoang also of the Vietnamese Navy who was on his way to the village market at the time. Hung and Hoang examined the body of Thang and found a fragmentation grenade clipped to his waistline.

The village doctor, Dang Van Kim, pronounced the false rallier dead, and village officials accepted custody of the remains.

The village chief commended Hung's sharp observation and quick reaction which saved the lives of both civilians and allied sailors.

Petty Officer Hung has been recommended for the U.S. Navy Commendation Medal with Combat "V" for meritorious service while serving in a joint Vietnamese and United States Navy Task Group.

In another action involving aircraft, two Seawolves sighted three evading sampans 11 miles north of Song Ong Doc (VR 827 184) on the afternoon of 14 January. As the helos arrived in the vicinity of the sampans, they received automatic weapons fire from both banks of the canal. The aircraft returned fire on the enemy positions, and, after successive strikes, the A/W fire still continued. At this point, CTG 194.2 requested and received clearance for naval gunfire support from the PSA An Xuyen. The USCGC Dallas arrived in the area and commenced fire until Seawolves and Black Ponies arrived back in the area to place additional airstrikes. After the airstrikes (which still received return fire), the USCGC Dallas opened fire again, pausing briefly for TACAIR strikes. When all fire finally ceased, enemy casualties were 13 VC killed and six more probably killed. There were no friendly casualties.

### FEBRUARY 1970

## OPERATION SEA LORDS SUMMARY

During the month of February, combined Sea Lords forces operating in the Giant Slingshot, Border Interdiction, Search Turn and Breezy Cove campaigns, accounted for a total of 337 enemy killed (by body count) and 27 captured.

Friendly casualties for this period were 20 killed and 86 wounded. A breakdown of complete USN and VNN Sea Lords statistics for February and statistical totals computed since the start of operations are located at the end of this section following the discussions of the various campaigns.

## Giant Slingshot

During February there was an average of 55 U.S. Navy craft and 24 VNN craft assigned to the Giant Slingshot Campaign, and in addition to performing escort duty, troop lifts, blocking, and support missions, these craft set a daily average of 24 WBGPs along the Vam Co Dong and Vam Co Tay Rivers. The above figures for the number of units assigned to the Giant Slingshot Campaign are much reduced from those figures of the preceding month. Several units were shifted to other operations that were taking place or were anticipated to take place in the operations areas farther westward than the area encompassed by the Giant Slingshot area of operations (AO). Intelligence had indicated that VC/NVA forces could be expected to execute a major push from the area of the Cambodian border farther to the west during the early days of February. The major offensive was to coincide with the period of celebration of TET in South Vietnam. Other units had been shifted in conjunction with the phased turnover of boats to the Vietnamese Navy under the ACTOV Program.

Even with the reduced number of units available, units of Giant Slingshot still were able to maintain a daily average of 24 WBGPs along the Vam Co Cong and Vam Co Tay Rivers. However, several of these WBGPs, were conducted using only one boat in position.

The level of general activity remained nearly the same as reported in January, with the number of sightings of suspected VC only slightly reduced. The number of enemy killed in action by all units conducting operations in this area dropped from 182 killed in January to only 55 killed during the month of February. Friendly casualties for the month of February were five killed in action and 35 wounded in action.

During the month of February, Operation Deep Channel II was successfully completed. On 8 February 1970, the final demolition charge was exploded resulting in the connection of the Kinh Lagrange (canal) and the Kinh Gay (canal), thus providing a direct navigable waterway between the cities of Tuyen Nhon and Tra Cu for both the Vietnamese civilians living in the area and for the USN VNN forces manning the waterways of the Giant Slingshot AO.

The demolition experts continued work after the official opening of the new canal until 24 February in order to widen the canal to an average width of 25 feet and an average depth of five feet. Areas were also blasted clear for turnaround points for the patrol boats which would use the canal. The final size of the canal, as determined by the demolition experts, is 28,675 feet in length by 25 feet in width and by five feet in minimum depth.

Some problems have already been encountered in the operation of boats on this new canal. One problem that was probably expected by all is that the banks are eroding rapidly, mostly from the loosening effect of the explosives used. Another problem, an unexpected one, is that the tides in the canal appear to be independent from either side. This tidal problem tends to build up debris in the canal and also creates unexpected periods of low water. By closely observing the tidal conditions, the boats have been able to transit the canal at medium to high tide carrying several combat troops without running aground. COMRIVDIV 551 conducted several experimental transits of the canal under varying tidal conditions. On one of these transits, at a reduced tidal condition, his boat ran aground. COMRIVDIV 551 reported it to be a "lonely feeling to sit high and dry on a PBR with no place to go."

Highlights of operational activity within the Giant Slingshot AO during the month of February are included in the following narrative descriptions.

On the night of 6 February, the base at Tra Cu (XS 477 983) Hau Nghia Province came under enemy mortar attack. At 0157H two mortar rounds exploded just outside the base defense wire to the west. General Quarters was sounded and the personnel proceeded to their assigned bunkers. There was a lull in firing by the enemy. PBR boat personnel then proceeded to scramble the boats. The enemy mortar battery commenced fire again and the next three rounds impacted in the vicinity of the pier resulting in numerous friendly casualties. Enemy fire ceased after firing six rounds at the base. The last mortar round exploded between the observation tower and the sick bay, with the observation tower and the adjacent water tank receiving shrapnel. Air and artillery assistance were called, but the enemy had now ceased all activity and Civilian Irregular Defense personnel were operating in the area. Helicopters evacuated all casualties.

As a result of the mortar attack, friendly casualties were: one USN KIA, six WIA, and six VNN WIA. The U.S. Navy personnel were EN3 Niemi, USN KIA; LTJG Rees, USN WIA (serious); SM1 Pierce, USN WIA (serious); EN3 Parshal, USN WIA (serious), EN3 Wurtzburger, USN WIA (serious); GMG3 Hollister, USN WIA (serious); EN3 Warnick, USN WIA (serious).

A later inspection of the base revealed that the observation tower, water tower, and generator shack received shrapnel with no apparent damage. One fuel hose was severed by shrapnel and several boats had shrapnel holes above the waterlines.

On 7 February, in Tay Tinh Province, approximately 10 kilometers from Tay Tinh City (XT 160 425) a daylight patrol under patrol officer BMC Dennis, with BM2 Sanders as Boat Captain embarked in ATC-32 and with GMG3 Ray as Boat Captain and embarked in monitor M-5, discovered three nippa palm rafts. The rafts were approximately three feet square with each raft having a four foot bamboo mast. Attached to the mast of each raft was a bundle of propaganda leaflets written in both English and Vietnamese and addressed to U.S. military personnel. The rafts appeared to have been placed in this location for interception by a U.S. Navy river patrol craft.

In the early morning of 9 February, in Long An Province (XS 789 646) approximately four kilometers west of Can Giouc City and approximately 15 kilometers southwest of Saigon, Boat Captain BM1 Groce embarked in his Zippo boat (Z-5) and Boat Captain BM2 Knott embarked in his ATC (T-35) joined forces with a Regional Forces/Popular Forces (RF/PF) unit to attack a VC/NVA base camp. Intelligence had indicated that this base camp was operated by 25-40 NVA and was used as a munitions factory. At 0400F, the RF/PF deployed to form blocking units. At 0445H Z5 entered a canal adjacent to the above listed position and commenced burning. Fifteen secondary explosions were observed. The RF/PF reported making contact with VC/NVA running to the south. Seawolves were called in and placed a strike on the area of the base camp. After the air strike, RF/PFs closed in and inspected the area. Twelve bunkers were observed. Nine bunkers had already been destroyed by the Seawolves' air strike. A RF/PF demolition team destroyed the remaining three bunkers and also destroyed two booby traps.

The significance of this action is that this was the first time that a ground assault on this area was possible. The ground forces attributed that the burning conducted by Zippo-5, which cleared the area of the majority of the booby-traps, had been the major factor in the success of the ground sweep.

The U.S. Navy personnel assigned to conduct operations in the Giant Slingshot AO have learned that the enemy is tenacious when he wants to be and respect him for his tenacity. The following is an example of the enemy accomplishing his mission despite all the obstacles placed in his way.

In Hau Nghia Province at Go Dau Ha City (XT 383 250) the bridge across the Vam Co Dong River was mined on 13 February at 0220H. A first hand witness, the skipper of OSB-2, who was on watch on his boat, described that he had seen an electrical flash and heard a muffled explosion, which he evaluated to mean that the explosive charge was set deep. He observed that one concrete pillar rose slightly before toppling into the river.

One span of the bridge was destroyed by the explosion but navigation of the river was not hampered by the destruction of the bridge span due to the depth of the channel under the bridge.

In carrying out his mission, the enemy sapper had successfully evaded all attempts by friendly forces to protect the bridge. On examination, the forces assigned to protect the bridge were all actively carrying out their assignments. There were Popular Force (PF) guards at each end of the bridge and a roving guard on the bridge. Floodlights were illuminating each pillar of the bridge as well as each end of the bridge. An ATC had conducted a chain sweep at irregular intervals. Concussion grenades had been randomly thrown from an ATC and from the CSB-2. There was a swimmer net around each pillar of the bridge constructed of 55 gallon drums, expanded metal, and angle iron. However, the swimmer net around the pillar which was destroyed was rusty and deteriorated.

In the evening of 23 February, in Hau Nghia Province, 12 kilometers from Tra Cu City (XT 426 093) Patrol Officers RMC Gage and BMC Wicklund with Boat Captains EN1 Girard in PBR 866, BM1 Cain in PBR 868, BM1 Studds in PBR 870, and GMG2 Farley in PBR 706 were proceeding at idle speed to a WBGP waiting for an artillery mission to be concluded when the boats were attacked by an enemy unit using a 75mm recoilless rifle. The first round fired by the enemy passed over the boats and exploded on the west bank of the river. One of the covering boats immediately opened fire on the east bank. As the attack continued, the lead boat, PBR 868, was hit by two, 75mm recoilless rifle rounds, one round hitting in the chief's quarters which damaged the radios and one round exploding on the coxswain's flat which killed Patrol Officer Gage instantly and maimed Boat Captain Donald M. Cain.

The units continued to receive recoilless rifle and automatic weapons fire but this time from both banks. The wounded Boat Captain managed to turn his boat around and clear the kill zone. The Vietnamese gunner expended all of his 50 caliber ammunition, then manned an M-60 machine gun and took over the helm so that the rest of the crew could administer aid to the wounded Boat Captain.

The boats all cleared the kill zone but remained in the area. A medevac helicopter (Dustoff) and artillery assistance was requested. At 1937H, an Air Force Forward Air Controller arrived on station and air elements worked over the area until 2120H, expending four, 500 pound bombs, four Napalm bombs, in addition to smaller caliber ammunition. Enemy casualties are unknown.

On 25 February, in Tay Ninh Province, 9.5 kilometers from Tay Ninh City (XT 181 13) Patrol Officer SM1 Whitesell with Boat Captains EN2 Haynes in PBR 8118 and GMG2 Grosz in PBR 8120 were en route to night WBGP when at 2037H they came under intense enemy rocket and automatic weapons fire. One B-40 rocket exploded against the fiberglass shield on the starboard side of boat 8118 injuring five of the embarked personnel. The units returned fire on the enemy position and cleared the area. Artillery, air, and medevac assistance was requested. Artillery took the enemy ambush area under fire from 2044H to 2051H. Black Ponies arrived on station at 2052H and commenced strikes which lasted until 2107H. Artillery and additional air strikes were conducted until 2334H. Personnel wounded in this ambush and medevaced were: EN2 Leo H. Haynes, USN WIA (serious); ENEN Michael C. Perex, USN WIA (serious); SM1 John R. Whitesell, USN WIA (minor); SN Dale R. Williams, USN WIA (minor); and GMG3 Stanley H. Gaines, USN WIA (minor).

## April 1970

### Giant Slingshot

During April, political events occurring in Cambodia had an influence on the Giant Slingshot Area of Operations (AO). During the latter half of the month, refugees from Cambodia began crossing the border in large numbers into Tay Ninh Province in the Giant Slingshot AO.

There was a larger than usual amount of activity in the Giant Slingshot AO this month, but most of the activity had nothing to do with actual enemy activity. The activity was in preparation for the scheduled turnover of assets to the Vietnamese Navy. On 5 May 1970, the Vietnamese Navy is scheduled to assume Operational control of the Giant Slingshot AO. After 5 May, U.S. Navy personnel will assist the Vietnamese Navy only in an advisory capacity.

During the month of April, there were 76 engagements with enemy forces. U.S. Navy forces accounted for seven enemy killed while suffering ten USN wounded.

During the month of April, there were 76 engagements with enemy forces. U.S. Navy forces accounted for seven enemy killed while suffering 10 USN wounded.

### Significant Engagements During The Month Of April

On 1 April, two U.S. Army LCMs were mined at the Advanced Tactical Support Base (ATSR) Tuyen Nhon. The mine had apparently been placed by sappers between the LCMs and approximately 15 feet forward of the sterns. PBRs immediately attempted to assist the LCMs to dewater, but the damage was too extensive. Both boats sank at their moorings. Divers investigating found that one boat had a seven foot by two foot hole in the side and bottom, and the other boat had a three foot by two foot hole in the side and bottom. EOD personnel estimated that a 50 pound charge of C-4 would be required to produce such extensive damage.

On 7 April, PBRs 62 and 135 were proceeding to a Waterborne Guardpost (WBGP) in Kien Tuong Province when they came under B-40 and heavy automatic weapons (A/W) fire from a position at WS 902 945. PBR 62 received a hit on the 60mm mortar mount which wounded all five personnel an board and set the PBR on fire. Both boats were able to return fire and cleared the area. Three additional PBRs were diverted from WBGP to assist. A USA LHFT put in a strike on the enemy, than hovered over the stern of PBR 62 and evacuated two critically wounded USN personnel. The personnel remaining on the boat put out the fire. Additional personnel were later evacuated from the boat, and the boat was taken in tow back to the base at Moc Hoa. Black Ponies and Seawolves provided support.

On 7 April, PBRs assisted U.S. Army personnel in locating a large cache in Hau Nghia Province at XT 461 055, approximately three kilometers from Tra Cu City. The cache was reported as: 134 B-40 rockets with boosters. 50 Chicom grenades, 16 Chicom anti-tank mines, two 107mm rockets, 12 60mm mortar rounds with fuses and boosters, and 24 82mm mortar rounds with boosters. All of the captured material was in usable condition. An EOD team later disposed of most of the captured material.

On 9 April, two boats were entering WBGP in Long An Province, about five kilometers from Ben Luc with U.S. Army personnel embarked.

U.S. Army personnel began insertion into ambush positions. When the point man was approximately 20 meters from the boats and approximately one-half of the troops had debarked, an explosive device was detonated Which was directed toward the boats. Seven personnel were wounded including two USN. A VNN crewmember observed one man approximately 150 meters inland fleeing the area. It is believed that the mine was command detonated.

On 13 April, the first of several MEDCAPs for refugees from Cambodia was conducted at a camp near Go Dau Ha in Tay Ninh Province.

On 16 April, two unidentified personnel were observed in the vicinity of the ATSB Moc Hoa. Later, four males were spotted in the water under a canal bridge directly across from the ATSB. Clearance to fire in the area of the swimmers was requested but was denied due to friendly personnel operating in an adjacent area. Swimmers were then observed to work their way downstream. The lead swimmer was on his back towing a package. A PBR was scrambled to attempt to intercept and apprehend the swimmers. The swimmers gained the bank and disappeared into tall grass. The bank was taken under fire. The attack was thwarted, but the sapper team escaped.

On 19 April, the ATSB at Ben Keo came under rocket attack. The crews of one PBR and a Monitor were in a position to observe the incoming rockets. Ten rockets were observed. All rockets cleared the base by a good distance. An LHFT later conducted a strike on an area from which the rockets were believed to have been fired.

On 30 April, a Boston Whaler was in WBGP at XS 578 786, approximately seven kilometers from Ben Luc in Long An Province. A supporting Army unit was proceeding to an ambush position approximately 50 meters inland. The Army unit encountered two enemy personnel who apparently mistook them for friendlies as they beckoned and called for the Army personnel to follow them. Army personnel took the enemy under fire and saw both men fall.

## Tran Hung Dao V/Operation Ready Deck

On 1 April, additional units of RPG 52 arrived in the operating area. The arrival of these units brought the total of assigned boats to 48. On 10 April, the 10 PBRs of RIVDIV 593 departed the operating area en route to the vicinity of Chau Doc on the Bassac River for assignment to the Operation Barrier Reef forces.

With the departure of RIVDIV 593, all operating forces an the Saigon River are now units of the Vietnamese Navy. U.S. Navy advisors are, however, still on the scene and taking an active part in all operations.

On 20 April, Operation Ready Deck, which had been designated TG 194.6, was redesignated TG 215.1 and assumed a Vietnamese Navy Task Force designator. RAG 24, RPG 52, and RAG 30 are now designated TU 215.1.11 TU 215.1.2, and TU 215.1.3, respectively.

During the month, USN and VNN forces were involved in 27 firefights. As a result of these encounters, 23 VC were killed. Friendly casualties were three U.S. Navy personnel wounded and four Vietnamese Navy personnel wounded.

## Significant Activity During the Month of April

On 3 April, two U.S. Navy PBRs of RIVDIV 593 were in Waterborne Guardpost (WBGP) at XT 598 336, approximately 28 kilometers northwest of Phu Cuong on the Upper Saigon River in Binh Duong Province. At 2328H, one VC approached the boats. No additional VC were sighted, so the boats held their fire until the VC reached a range of only 15 feet. The VC was taken under fire at this close range and killed.

In a very similar situation on 6 April, within approximately 600 yards of the position of the firefight on 3 April, two Vietnamese Navy PBRs, with EM1 Moceri embarked as an advisor, had two VC approach their boats. The VC were taken under fire at a range of only 30 feet. In this instance, however, it is not known if the VC were actually killed.

On 6 April, two U.S. Navy PBRs had assumed WBGP at XT 666 295, approximately 30 kilometers northwest of Phu Cuong. At 2239H, one VC swimmer attempted to board one of the PBRs. He was immediately killed.

On 7 April, two VNN PBRs were in WBGP at XT 722 223, approximately 12 kilometers northwest of Phu Cuong. At 2009H, a VC threw a grenade which landed on one of the boats. A quick acting VNN crewmember kicked the grenade over the side. The detonation of the grenade caused some minor hull damage, but there were no personnel casualties.

On 17 April, two VNN PBRs were in WBGP at XT 652 315, approximately 30 kilometers northwest of Phu Cuong. At 2135H, the PBRs were attacked and received a total of five grenades thrown from the east bank of the river. One VN was slightly wounded, and material damage to the boats was light. The bank area was taken under fire, and two VC were probably killed.

In approximately the same position on the night of 21 April, two VNN PBRs observed one VC about 50 meters distant. The units broke WBGP and took the man under fire. In return, the boats received heavy A/W fire from a nearby treeline. A helo fire team was requested and later placed strikes in 'the area. Two U.S. Navy advisors and one Vietnamese crewmember were slightly wounded in this encounter.

## Border Interdictions

Border Interdiction operations as reported in this section will include only those operations conducted by units assigned to the Barrier Reef Area of Operations (AO). Operations conducted in the Tran Hung Dao I AO are contained in the Naval Advisory Group Summary.

During the month of April, the forces assigned to the Barrier Reef AO engaged the enemy on 28 occasions. U.S. Navy units accounted for 11 enemy killed while the Vietnamese Navy units accounted for three enemy killed. Friendly losses for the month totaled three U.S. Navy personnel killed and four wounded.

The number of boats assigned to the Barrier Reef AO for the month averaged 100. The average number of boats available for daily assignments was 78, while the average number of Waterborne Guardposts (WBGP) established by the available boats was 66. On the last day of the month, RPG 56 units departed the Barrier Reef AO for the adjacent Giant Slingshot AO, reducing the number of units assigned to the Barrier Reef AO to 80.

## Significant Engagements During the Month of April

On 2 April, a Strike Assault Boat (STAB) of STABRON 20 was in WBGP near the north bank of the Grand Canal at WS 947 765, approximately 20 kilometers west of Ap Bac. The boat was hidden in a dense treeline port side to the north bank with rain falling and sheet lightning illuminating the area. At 020010H, the boat crew heard movement on the opposite bank, breaking twigs, and voices talking. The boat captain was requesting Sector clearance to take the movement under fire when the enemy initiated the attack. All the other boat crew members were manning their weapons ready for unrestricted combat. The enemy launched a veritable barrage of B-40 rockets and heavy automatic weapons (A/W) fire. The boat received three B-40 rocket hits almost sim1taneously which killed three crewmembers instantaneously and wounded one other member of the crew. The boat lost all communications, but due to the communications conducted prior to the enemy attack, Seawolves were en route and arrived on the scene in less than ten minutes. After the enemy attack, the boat broke WBGP using the one engine still in commission. One crewmember returned fire on the enemy positions with an M-60 while another crewman controlled the boat proceeding to join ATC-1 at a WBGP at WS 951 764. The one wounded crewmember was transferred to the ATC and medevaced by helo.

An inspection of the STAB after the above action indicated that the boat had been hit by two B-40 rockets. One rocket penetrated the forward starboard side near the waterline and detonated adjacent to the forward fuel bladder such that fragments penetrated the fuel bladder which self-sealed. The second B-40 detonated on the starboard side amidships dishing in the hull, ceramic armor and penetrating the ballistic blanket with fragments apparently crossing the cockpit and penetrating the port ballistic blanket and the port hull.

The inspection report further specified that "another possible recoilless round detonated stbd hull penetrating ballistic blanket and after portion of stbd cockpit severing and causing extensive damage to control cables from instrument panel to stbd engine rendering stbd engine inoperative."

The inspection report concluded that from the B-40 rocket which detonated adjacent to the fuel bladder, it is evident that the combination of the ceramic armor and foam helped absorb the detonation, and the, foam-filled fuel bladder prevented a gasoline explosion by self-sealing. In the amidships area, the combined ceramic armor and the ballistic blanket reduced the penetration fan of fragments, but did not stop them entirely.

This was the first STAB damaged so extensively in an engagement with the enemy.

On 5 April, ATC-28 was in WBGP at XS 000 754, approximately 17 kilometers west of Ap Bac. At 2253H, T-28 came under heavy B-40 and A/W attack from the vicinity of a lighted hooch on the south bank. T-28 sustained nine B-40 rocket hits and numerous A/W hits injuring all the personnel on board; two VNN were killed; four VNN were wounded; and three USN were also wounded. The rockets had been fired in three volleys of three rockets each.

T-28 broke WBGP and proceeded east. T-33, in WBGP one kilometer to the east, and T-29, in WBGP one kilometer to the west, broke their respective WBGPs and proceeded to the contact area. At 2258H, T-28 reported the status of the wounded and requested a medevac helo. By 0056H, medevac was completed.

Black Ponies and Seawolves reported overhead but could not obtain clearances for conducting air strikes due to the number of friendlies reported to be in the area and the close proximity of several hooches occupied by local Vietnamese.

At 151257H April, PCF 59, on the Mekong River border patrol, observed what appeared to be a major firefight on the Cambodian side of the border. Approximately 150 people were seen fleeing from the market area of the village at WT 204 060 and two large junks were afire near the village. PCF 59 remained clear of the area but continued to keep the area under surveillance. At 1400H, PCF 59 observed four craft at WT 208 088. Two of the craft were 80 foot junks, cue craft appeared to be an LCM-6, and the other craft appeared similar to an ATC. The boats under observation received heavy fire from both banks. The two wooden junks caught fire and later sank. The other two craft sailed out of sight to the north. A short time later, two T-28 type aircraft appeared and put in repeated rocket and machine gun strikes in the vicinity of WT 200 065. The aircraft had no identifying markings.

At 161220H April, PCF 97, on the Mekong River border patrol, chased and apprehended a water taxi sampan at WT 206 048. The water taxi had one U.S. civilian male wearing camouflage greens and three Vietnamese males on board. The U.S. male readily identified himself as an NBC correspondent. He stated that he was in the area to verify a report of 400 to 600 Vietnamese bodies floating down the Mekong River as a result of a massacre of Vietnamese by Cambodians. Since the correspondent had no military escort or apparent permission to be in the border control region, PCF 97 was instructed to deny access to the border control region to the newsman and the others in the water taxi and to escort the taxi south and out of the area. The newsman stated that he would return to Chau Doc and await further developments.

While the taxi occupants were being questioned, a Piper Cub type single engine aircraft passed close overhead. The plane had unknown markings. The newsman stated that the occupants of the plane were probably CBS correspondents on a similar assignment to his own. The water taxi departed the area at 161315H.

At 161925H April, a PBR of RPG 56 was proceeding at top speed down the Grand Canal en route to WBGP. Suddenly, the boat lost steering control. Before the boats speed could be reduced, the boat hit the canal bank and turned over at WS 530 809, approximately 11 kilometers east of the Mekong River, and sank with only the bow remaining above water. All crewmembers and advisors escaped unhurt with the exception that one VNN crewmember was missing. ATC 22 proceeded to the scene to assist. An unsuccessful attempt was made to right the boat. Divers conducted a search for the missing crewmember in the forward and midships section of the boat with no success. It was concluded that the missing crewmember must possibly be trapped between the stern and the canal bottom.

On the following day, the body of the Vietnamese sailor was located. On 18 April, ATC 22 and the USS SATYR salvage crew completed salvaging the PBR. Hull damage to the PBR was considered slight.

At 171108H April, PCF 97, on the Mekong River border patrol, once again apprehended a water taxi with the same NBC correspondent and passengers as apprehended on 16 April. The correspondent was on the same mission and still lacked military escort or apparent permission to be in the border patrol area. He was once again escorted clear of the area.

On 21 April, a PBR of RPG 56 was returning from night WBGP in the early morning at high speed through the Grand Canal. At 0710H, the PBR careened off the bank of the canal and capsized at WS 515 811, approximately 10 kilometers from the Mekong River. A short time later, salvage assistance arrived an the scene. Salvage operations were completed by 1600H. The PBR suffered heavy damage and required extensive work by a repair facility.

## OPERATION BREEZY COVE

Operation Breezy Cove, designed to pacify the Ca Mau peninsula in conjunction with Operation Sea Float, experienced the same drop in activity in April as other naval operations. The nine enemy killed was the lowest total in five months while the number of craft assigned to Operation Sea Lords' smallest component remained at about 23. No Americans were killed in April and 14 were wounded.

COMUSMACV conducted an Operations Security Survey of CTG 194.2 during April in an effort to minimize the enemy's prior knowledge of Breezy Cove operations. The inspection team's findings are applicable to all allied units participating in shallow water counterinsurgency programs. While Breezy Cove's security was evaluated favorably, the six following weaknesses were found:

1) A large AO precludes the necessary density of craft to thoroughly patrol waterways.
2) Noise of approaching boats forewarns the enemy.
3) Guerrilla mobility permits enemy to initiate the majority of firefights.
4) Size of PBRs and limited camouflage capabilities contribute to easy detection of WBGPs.
5) Pattern of never setting a WBGP in the same place allows enemy "safe" use of the area where one was previously set.
6) Some communication equipment is not secure.

## Significant Combat Activity During April

The Breezy Cove patrol craft themselves reported only scattered action throughout the month. Combined air and land retaliatory strikes accounted for the majority of enemy casualties.

On April 9, CTG 194.2 scrambled Seawolves in answer to an attack on a water taxi at WR 005 044. Forward air controllers called in ARVN artillery strikes to hold the estimated 25 enemy troops until the helicopters arrived. Black Ponies joined the attack, hitting Viet Cong who were running through an opening for a hooch line. PBRs landed 30 ARVN troops at Old Song Ong Doc and stood by for support. The entire action lasted over three hours. A thorough sweep of the area revealed seven VC killed (BC), five probably killed, three wounded, and two captured. Allied forces suffered no losses.

On April 11, PBRs 141 and 767, patrolling 14 kilometers east of New Song Ong Doc, observed two rockets fired at them from the north bank. They returned fire while clearing the area and called in air support from Seawolves. Breezy Cove transport units landed troops summoned from Old Song Ong Doc. They captured two rocket launchers and one B-50 rocket 100 meters from the bank and found two blood trails. There were no friendly casualties.

An unexplained explosion sank PBR 101 150 meters south of Song Ong Doc on April 19. The boat was withdrawing from the beach after landing SFAL team members when an underwater blast destroyed the starboard pump, sinking the craft in four feet of water. The boat captain surmised that a dud round had been sucked into the pump. Salvage operations raised the craft.

On April 23, guerrillas rocketed two Armored Transport Craft (ATCs 10 and 12) carrying civilian workers back to Old Song Ong Doc. One B-50 rocket exploded in the port side bar armor of ATC 10. The units returned fire but cleared the area because of the civilian passengers. Seawolves struck the area and received no return fire. One American sailor and one Vietnamese civilian incurred slight wounds.

One unfortunate incident marred Breezy Cove's record during the month. On April 11, during a routine patrol by units of RivDiv 572, a young Vietnamese trainee on PBR 767 accidentally discharged a 40mm mortar round on the roof of a civilian home in Vam Song Ong Doc. Three civilian occupants were slightly wounded and were treated and released by an ATSB corpsman. Property damage was minimal.

## Proposed Improvements For Operation Breezy Cove

By the end of April, LCDR L.H. Thames, Commander of Operation Breezy Cove, foresaw the need for re-evaluating the Navy's assets and tactics in the Song Ong Doc District. Pacification efforts in the district had been progressing favorably as 7,500 refugees had come to the area in the last six months, but certain USN and VNN weaknesses threatened to reverse the trend. As in most areas of Vietnam, the Navy, expecting the enemy to move at night, had emphasized nocturnal patrols and WBGPs. Recent intelligence now indicated that the Viet Cong were now conducting the majority of their infiltration, propaganda, and tax extortion in the daylight hours. In addition, increased demands for transportation by ARVN troops in the district rendered the present number of Breezy Cove units inadequate. CTU 194.2 consequently made the following recommendation to First Sea Lord. 1) Employ only 30 per cent of assets in nightly WBGPs, freeing the remainder for daytime patrolling; 2) Increase the number of River Assault Craft by seven; 3) Permanently locate River Assault Division 13 at Old Song Ong Doc to provide greater operational flexibility and control.

## June 1970

## Operation Tran Hung Dao XI

United States Navy assets and advisors continued to take part in Operation Tran Hung Dao XI during the month of June. A heavy portion of the burden of the operation was borne by the Vietnamese Navy and at the end of the month, with the withdrawal of all U.S. forces from Cambodia, the operation became entirely Vietnamese.

At the beginning of the month the task organization of the operation was as follows:

| | |
|---|---|
| TG 194.0 | Tran Hung Dao XI |
| TU 194.0.1 | Amphibious Assault Unit: RAIDs 71-75, LSIL 329, 5 VNN PCFs, 10 USN ATCs of RAS 13/15. |
| TU 194.0.3 | Air Support Unit One: HAL-3 |
| TU 194.0.4 | Air Support Unit Two: VAL-4 |
| TU 194.0.6 | River Security Unit: 11 PBRs of RIVDIV 593, 5 PCFs of TU 194.5.1, 3 STABs of STABRON 20. |
| TU 194.0.7 | Flag Support Unit: USS BENEWAH, ASKARI SATYR, USS HUNTERDON COUNTY, YRBM-16, YRBM-21. |
| TU 194.0.8 | LSM(H)400, LSSLs 225 and 226, 10 VNN PCFs, 9 VNN PBRs. |

At 0200H on 1 June, US ATC 50, while on routine night patrol about nine kilometers south of the Neak Luong Ferry (coordinates WT 265 335), was taken under fire by small arms and B-40 rockets. ATC 50 and ATC 47 returned the fire and cleared the area. One USN was wounded as a result of the action.

On 4 June ASKARI departed the area of operations, towing the ferries which had been salvaged in May to Dong Tam. She chopped to NSA Saigon upon her arrival at Dong Tam.

At 0700H on 6 June, Seawolves of HAL-3 Det 9 on patrol received heavy automatic weapons fire from a point about 15 kilometers north of the border (coordinates WT 270 250). They returned the fire and called in Black Ponies for assistance. They made two hot turnarounds off the USS Hunterdon County (LST-838) and continued to place strikes until the Black Ponies arrived. The Seawolves made one last strike after the Black Ponies had finished making their air strikes. Initial results were reported as three structures destroyed and two damaged. At 1830H on the same day Seawolves again took fire from the same area. Black Ponies were again called in, but they were unable to suppress the fire. The next day, June 7, the 520th Tactical Air Squadron placed heavy air strikes in the area.

At 1000H on 8 June, the Hunterdon County moved from its position in Cambodia to a point just south of the border. One US ATC was left in Cambodia for communication purposes.

On 14 June a major reorganization took place due to the dwindling U.S. role in the operation. River Division 593 was chopped to CTG 194.8 (THD I) and the STABs were chopped to CTG 194.4 (Barrier Reef). The USN PCFs returned to the operational control of CTF 115 but CTG 194.5 was tasked to provide five PCFs as a contingency for Cambodian operations until 25 June.

About 1200H on 16 June, four VNN sailors from the monitor HQ 6518 of RAG 26 went ashore against orders about 10 kilometers south of Neak Luong (WT 268 308) to visit a coffee house. While drinking coffee, one of the other customers, apparently a VC, started a brawl. Two of the sailors managed to escape, one wounded in the head, but the other two were captured and presumed dead. There were no U.S. advisors present during this incident.

SEALs carried out operations during the month in the Tran Hung Dao XI area of operations. On the night of 16 June LDNN

Group A, consisting of nine VNN SEALs and two U.S. advisors, acting on NILO intelligence, was inserted by STABs at a point about 10 kilometers north of the border. They set up an ambush at a small road (WT 243 251). At 2320H two men on bicycles sped past the alert and watchful SEALs too quickly to be taken under fire. The SEALs then extracted. The next night, 17 June, the SEALs returned with a ploy to outdo the wily bicycle riders. A wire was rigged across the road. At 2110H a man came along the road on a bicycle and ran into the wire. He was captured but released when it was found that he had no documents or weapons. The SEALs, their ambush site compromised, then extracted.

At 1330H on 20 June a VNN sailor against orders took a sampan into the beach about 20 kilometers north of the border (WT 298 380). He was taken under fire which he returned until he was subdued by an unknown number of VC. Three other VNN sailors heard the fire and went to his assistance. They were taken under fire by about 30 VC and two were wounded, losing an M-16 rifle and an M-79 grenade launcher. The sailors returned to HQ 1201 of RAID 70. The RAID commander led a 16-man landing party which searched up to 800 meters inland. They came under B-40 and small arms fire before withdrawing. Then the RAID units launched a two hour assault, destroying a village and numerous bunkers.

At 1325H on 21 June, VNN ATC HQ 1233 received a sniper round which killed one VNN sailor. At 1520H units of RAIDs 74 and 75 and RAGs 23/31 proceeded to the area and took 20 VC in houses and bunkers under fire. Seawolves scrambled and placed multiple rocket and machine gun strikes at the direction of USN advisors aboard RAID 74/75 boats. Nine houses and one sampan were destroyed and one VC was killed by air.

At the end of the month the withdrawal of all U.S. personnel and assets from Cambodian territory was carried out. At 1055H on 29 June, USN PCF 74, while on its way out of Cambodia, received B-40 rocket and sniper fire about 12 kilometers south of Neak Luong (WT 290 365). The PCF did not return the fire but cleared the area. One USN sailor was slightly wounded. All USN/USMC personnel had withdrawn from Cambodia by 291427H June.

The evacuation of refugees from Phnom Penh by ships of the Vietnamese Fleet Command, which had been interrupted briefly around the beginning of the month, continued during the month. By 30 June the total number of refugees brought out of Cambodia was 37,720.

## OPERATION SEA LORDS SUMMARY

During June Rear Admiral H.S. Matthews, Deputy COMNAVFORV and First Sea Lords (CTG 194.0) continued to concern himself primarily with the Cambodian operation as naval action in Vietnam itself continued along the same sporadic course of the past several months. The only organizational change of note in TU 194.0 was the disestablishment of River Assault Squadron 13 and River Assault Divisions 131 and 132 on 19 June. The remaining assets and personnel from these units were assigned to River Assault Squadron 15.

First Sea Lords expressed concern for the growing number of sniper attacks in June. In addition, he pointed to evidence that the Viet Cong and North Vietnamese were reorganizing and infiltrating with the civilians into villages along the Mekong and her tributaries in an effort to regain dominance in that area. RADM Matthews warned against a tendency for U.S. boat crews, relaxed after the initial lull in Cambodian operations, to anchor too close to shore without proper lookouts, to wander ashore in unauthorized groups, and to swim within sniper range. The battle against boredom is one of the greatest struggles in which a river sailor must engage. The long hours, emotional strain, and oppressive heat normally work with the communists in weakening the Americans' guard.

With the withdrawal of all U.S. forces from Cambodia on 30 June, COMNAVFORV reiterated the necessity of practicing navigational exactitude to prevent the diplomatic embarrassment of a patrol boat inadvertently straying across the border. He pointed out that in the past boredom and routine have contributed to carelessness and inefficiency of patrols along the border regions,

## BREEZY COVE

Throughout June Operation Breezy Cove continued to be the most active operation in the entire Sea Lords area. There were 15 friendly-initiated firefights, 11 enemy-initiated actions, and 30 unilateral firings by allied forces. USN/VNN forces killed 63 of the enemy and captured eight, while suffering only six wounded themselves.

Seawolves accounted for the largest number of enemy killed in a single June action in the Breezy Cove AO. Before dawn on 11 June, Seawolves 62 and 63 scrambled to assist ARVN and U.S. troops in contact with a battalion-size enemy element 12 kilometers north of Thoi Binh (WR 09 44). They placed two air strikes in the area during a 90-minute period and received sporadic AK-47 fire. The allied ground elements counted the bodies of 15 dead Viet Cong.

Unit commanders in Vietnams two southernmost AOs, Breezy Cove and Sea Float, experienced difficulty in making necessary repairs on their heavily committed river craft. The services provided by the USS Krishna (ARL-38), although of excellent quality, have been only barely adequate because of the large number of boats needing repair. It often took a week or more before the ARL could accept a boat for repair, and repair time averaged one to ten days. The small craft in these AOs are expected to receive even less maintenance as the number of River Assault Craft (RAC) will be increased from 21 to 45 in the coming weeks.

Breezy Cove units experienced the first sapper swimmer attack on USN river assets since the operation began in September 1969. Early on the morning of 11 June, boats of RIVDIV 554 had just shifted their WBGP toward the mouth of a canal six miles east of Song Ong Doc (VQ 890 975) when a crew member spotted a man swimming south along the canal, approximately 10 meters from one of the PBRs. The swimmer was going against the current and carrying a rectangular object. The swimmer dove under the water and reappeared 10 feet from the boat. The units attacked the man with concussion grenades, apparently killing him. They sank the small rectangular floating object rather than risk bringing it aboard. Intelligence analysts believed this assailant to be a member of the sapper element of the 95th North Vietnamese Regiment known to be operating in the area. Day rocket attacks on the PBRs had generally been ineffective, and an increase in night sapper activity against the vulnerable WBGPs was expected.

The United States' most effective counter-guerrilla forces, the Navy SEALs, were quite successful during June operations at Breezy Cove.

At 1445H on the afternoon of 9 June, a nine member SEAL platoon of Detachment ALPHA inserted by air at VQ 902 928 along the Song Dong Dung with a Viet Cong Hoi Chanh as guide. They fired at two males running into a treeline and then discovered a VC rice cache pointed out by the Hoi Chanh. The 3600 kilos of rice were in huge bins and could not be salvaged, so the SEALs destroyed them. The SEALs entered the hooch of the VC village chief 50 meters away, captured a one kilo pile of documents, and then retreated to the proposed pickup area. While waiting for the helicopter, the SEALs saw a woman pointing them out to a man with a K-54 pistol. The man spotted the Vietnamese guide and fired at him, wounding him in the forearm. The patrol took the area under fire and called in air strikes. Another Vietnamese was wounded by VC automatic weapons fire when he ran into the open to recover the K-54 pistol. When enemy fire was suppressed, the SEALs and the two wounded Vietnamese were extracted by an Army Slick.

On 17 June, LT Boink led a squad of SEALs from Detachment ALPHA to VQ 902 900. They were operating along with Vietnamese counterparts and inserted in sampans. The SEALs established a guardpost along a trail and at 1020H encountered two men. The men began to run, and the SEALs killed one and captured the other. These men were later identified as the VC province chairman of finance and economy and his assistant. An estimated eight Viet Cong then attacked the SEALs who called in Seawolves to cover their escape. One Vietnamese agent was wounded as they boarded the sampan and a Seawolf hovered to evacuate him in the midst of the firefight. The Seawolves continued air strikes until the SEALs successfully extracted.

LT Boink's platoon successfully captured three other members of the Ca Mau Viet Cong infra-structure on the morning of 22 June. Acting on Hoi Chanh intelligence, the SEALs departed Ca Mau by MSSC and landed 13 kilometers NE of Ca Mau (WR 289 223) on the Quan Lo River 0245H. Two men crawled into a nearby hooch pointed out by the Hoi Chanh and encountered two male and one female VC. The female struggled briefly with one SEAL, and one of the men tried to stab LT Boink with a bayonet. The SEALs quickly withdrew with their prisoners and returned to Ca Mau. The captives were identified as the village propaganda chairman, a bodyguard of the Ca Mau City committee chairman, and a member of the VC female proselytizing cadre.

## BARRIER REEF

The Area of Operations of Barrier Reef was one of the most active for the Brown Water Navy during June. In eight firefights, allied forces accounted for 27 enemy KIA and one captured. No Americans or Vietnamese were killed in the month's operations, but 11 allies (8 USN, 3 VNN) were wounded.

The only major personnel change in CTG 194.4 came on 15 June when LCDR Richard E. Barbour relieved LCDR Paul T. Souval as COMRIVRON 55.

The Vietnamese peasant who occasionally cooperates with allied forces is by far the best source of information on Viet Cong activities. Guerrillas who travel by night in small groups are often visible only to the indigenous population and must depend on them for supplies and geographical information. On 31 May a local farmer at Thanh Loi (WS 7977785) informed ARVN forces that five Viet Cong planned to cross the canal adjoining his land within two days. Units of STABRON 20 and an Army Hunter Killer Team set a WBGP at the designated point on the evening of 1 June. At 2200H STAB 7015 and 708 sighted two persons fording the canal and opened fire with M-60 machine guns and M-79 grenade launchers. After the assailants lost sight of their prey, four persons (3 USN, 1 VNN) from STAB 7015 landed to investigate while STAB 708 provided illumination. The landing party discovered two men hiding in a ditch, one of whom tossed a grenade at the group, wounding the Vietnamese. The landing party and STAB 708 saturated the area with bullets while STAB 7015 evacuated the wounded man to ATSB Phuoc Xuyen. Seawolves from Detachment SEVEN, aided by an Army Cobra Team, placed air strikes along the bank of the canal. The allies reported that two VC were killed in the action.

A USN investigation of the area the following morning resulted in the capture of one of these "dead" Viet Cong. During interrogation by the national police at Phuoc Xuyen, the 31-year-old suspect admitted to being a communist from Hanoi who had lived in the village for six years. He had two other VC working for him and reported to a Viet Cong captain on the hull numbers and types of boats on the canal each night. The VC captain had been the other man who was wounded in the previous night's conflict. The Phuoc Xuyen police reported the rather incredible fact that the man's wife and child were unaware that he was a VC.

The Viet Cong apparently carefully monitor all U.S. traffic along the canals - at least in the Barrier Reef AO. The national police from Hoa discovered two VC located in hooches on the south bank of the Grand Canal near WS 801 785 whose job was to relay information by radio to their cohorts waiting for a safe moment to cross the canal. The Barrier Reef commander instituted a twofold scheme to thwart VC canal crossings. Strike assault boats began random day patrols, and troops covered by assault boats were occasionally inserted in between areas covered by nightly WBGPs.

Viet Cong intimidation continued at a high pace along the border areas despite these efforts. A mid-June intelligence report indicated that the guerrillas had ordered inhabitants in the Phuoc Xuyen vicinity to do away with their dogs as they often barked and compromised Viet Cong positions. An old man living at VS 903 771 on the Grand Canal reported that VC had ordered him not to stray more than 50 meters from his hooch as the entire area was booby trapped. The national police also reported that the VC has forced the local population to inform on the location of U.S. craft and in one case had murdered a VN male for giving GVN officers information about communist troop movements. In times of war,

the civilian population has always suffered from the destruction surrounding them. In Vietnam this suffering often results from methodical terrorism against a people caught in the middle.

The treacherous currents of South Vietnam's small rivers and streams claimed the lives of several U.S. Naval personnel in June, one of whom was EN3 Warnick, an advisor with RPG 59 under CTG 194.4. PBR 708 was at a WBGP 16 kilometers SE of Moc Hoa (XS 119 791) on 7 June when it sighted two Viet Cong on the east bank of the Kin Moi Hai. It broke its guardpost to make a firing run on the area. Petty Officer Warnick, who had been lying on the canopy of the PBR, fell into the canal and was never seen again. PBRs 742, 773, and 774 joined in the search, and Black Pony/helicopters provided illumination. The PBRs dragged the canal bottom without success and Regional Force personnel conducted an abortive search of the surrounding area.

Seven U.S. Navy personnel were wounded on the evening of 20 June when a satchel charge was tossed into ATC 50 while it was in a WBGP near WS 935 766. Air support was not immediately available so a nearby STAB made a firing run along the canal bank. All the wounds were fortunately of a slight nature and were quickly cared for by an embarked Navy corpsman.

PBR 145 of RIVDIV 532 in a WBGP 16 kilometers south of Moc Hoa on 25 June sighted a moving light on the north bank at WS 995 755. The PBR fired a short burst at the light and moved to a new guardpost. Thirty minutes later, the boat stopped a lighted sampan moving west along the canal with a young girl aboard who was in serious condition from a bullet wound in the hip, probably as a result of fire from the PBR. The boat crew took the girl to Military Advisory Team 61 for treatment, from where she was medevaced to Tan An. The girl was subsequently identified as a Viet Cong whose job was to signal the position of U.S. river boats to VC units in the area.

## RIVERINE STRIKE GROUP

Midway through June, the commander of Riverine Strike Group (CTG 194.7) sent the following message to COMNAVFORV: "Riverine Strike Group will disestablish without ceremony 30 June 1970. All remaining river assault craft were reassigned on that date to COMRIVRON 15 under the administrative and operational control of COMRIVPATFLOT Five.

For the past seven months CTG 194.7 had been a skeleton force. During. November 1969, as U.S. Naval forces began a buildup of interdiction forces along the Cambodian border, most Riverine Strike Group units were out chopped to other Sea Lords components. Since that time CTG 194.7 had controlled only those boats which were returned for alterations and repairs.

U.S. NAVAL FORCES
VIETNAM
MONTHLY HISTORICAL SUMMARY
JULY 1970
DECLASSIFIED

## BREEZY COVE

CTG 116.2 forces at Song Ong Doc continued to experience a high level of hostile activity during July. One VNN sailor was killed and another wounded as Breezy Cove units participated in 17 firefights (11 initiated by friendly forces and six initiated by the enemy). There were no USN casualties in July.

A collision on the Song Ong Doc River accounted for the death of one Vietnamese sailor on 2 July. Monitor 1 and Zippo 3 were proceeding east as PBRs 44 and 101 were traveling west in a heavy rainstorm. The boat crews did not see each other until they were less than 10 meters apart, and their efforts to avoid collision were futile. Zippo 3 struck PBR 44 on the port side, knocking one VNN crewman, Chinh Vo Van, into the river at VR 890 003. The boat crews cut their engines when they heard cries for help, but the sailor was never seen after he fell into the seven-knot current wearing rain gear and a flak jacket. The four craft illuminated and searched the riverbanks but found no signs of the missing man, reportedly a non-swimmer.

The USS Garrett County (LST 821) left the Breezy Cove AO after spending three and one-half years in Vietnam when the USS Jennings County (LST 846) relieved her of her support functions on 8 July. The Garrett County now proceeds to Guam, after a brief visit to Bangkok, for decommissioning. She will eventually be turned over to the Vietnamese Navy.

The ATSB at Song Ong Doc went to general quarters at 2134H on the evening of 9 July when it was learned that several Viet Cong had infiltrated the city of Song Ong Doc. A VNN landing party was organized to investigate. Within an hour the Vietnamese force returned to report that two VC had entered the village, distributed propaganda leaflets, and departed immediately. The base secured from GQ without firing a shot.

The Viet Cong introduced a new weapon to the allies in the Song Ong Doc area when they attacked a PBR with an RPG 7 rocket. VNN PBRs 38 and 39 of River Patrol Group 62 were attacked with five rockets and small arms fire while on patrol 14 miles east of Song Ong Doc (VR 920 012). One VN sailor was wounded seriously by a rocket which exploded close aboard the lead boat and a bullet which struck him in the cheek. The PBRs suppressed the enemy fire and rushed the wounded man to Song Ong Doc for evacuation. A portion of the rocket fragments which hit the PBR were recovered and evaluated as portions of an RPG 7, a highly accurate, short-range communist rocket which had heretofore not been encountered in the Breezy Cove AO. In addition, a bullet fragment in the boat was believed to have come from an American M-16 and not an AK-47. A troop sweep into the area failed to recover a launcher, but intelligence indicated that a platoon-size enemy force had spent two days in bunkers near the ambush site waiting for a riverboat to pass. The Song Ong Doc NILO, LTJG J.W. Tapscott, reported that the enemy combination of small arms fire and rocket attacks was highly effective against river craft, especially if the VC continued to use the RPG 7.

PBRs 62 and 78 of RPG 62 initiated a major firefight from their WBGP one and a half miles east of Vam Song Ong Doc (VR 835 994) on the evening of 21 July. When the PBRs commenced firing at a movement along the north bank, they received heavy small arms return fire. Monitor 1 and Zippo 3 came to the area to assist, and saturated the contact area with flames and 105 mm shells. The VNN PBRs then illuminated the area and searched along the banks with negative results. About 15 minutes later (at 2205H), there was a Duffle Bag sensor activation two kilometers northwest of the original contact area, and a NGFS ship fired 25 rounds of 5-inch shells into the area, believed to be the hiding area of the ambush team. A Popular Force platoon made a ground sweep and reported 10 Viet Cong killed (probable) on the basis of numerous blood trails.

Six SEALS of Detachment ALPHA, 6th Platoon made a rather unique discovery 16 kilometers southwest of Ca Mau (WR 017 080) on the afternoon of 24 July. LT Boink's squad entered a hootch suspected of being a Viet Cong supply point, but found nothing. About 150 meters eastward, however, they found a heavily camouflaged mound which hid a very large and operationally sound French tractor with a wheel diameter of 4.3 feet. The SEALS marked the vehicle with smoke so that aircraft could destroy it after extraction. Two men then successfully escaped a nearby hootch, despite SEAL efforts to stop them. The hootch itself was a VC workshop complete with tools and metal from a wrecked

*Photo courtesy of Dan Dodd, Official Navy Photographer for ComRivFlot-One MRF TF-117 68-69, Retired Chief Photographers Mate.*

aircraft being used to make rocket motors and parts. The SEALS marked this site also and extracted by air. Intelligence sources indicated that this area was along the communist supply route from the U-Minh Forest sanctuaries to the Song Ong Doc River, and the VC probably used the tractor for nocturnal transportation of heavy equipment. Seawolves 63 and 68 and an Army Forward Air Control plane quickly deprived the VC of their vehicle and hobby shop.

## RUNG SAT SPECIAL ZONE

Combined operations were continued in the Rung Sat Special Zone (RSSZ) during the month of July. Five such operations were conducted and were named Chuong Duong 27-70 through Chuong Duong 31-70.

Provincial Reconnaissance Units (PRUs) were also active during the month within the confines of the RSSZ. A typical PRU operation was conducted on 11 July in the Thanh Duc District of Long An Province, approximately seven kilometers south of Nha Be Navy Base. Thirty PRUs, with advisors, inserted by LCM and conducted a sweep. Results of the sweep were two VC killed and three captured. They also captured a small amount of documents, three AK-47 rifles, one K-54 pistol, one 61 mm mortar and 4,000 rounds of 7.62 machine gun ammunition. The PRUs destroyed five bunkers, a small amount of rice and a small amount of clothing.

The Chuong Duong operations were all very similar in concept with Chuong Duong 29-70 forces encountering the majority of enemy contacts. Forces participating in the operation were USA Slicks; a USA LHFT; USN Black Ponies; USN ASPBs; USN PBRs; RSSZ RF Companies 121, 362, 601, 908 and 999 with advisors; VNN LCMs; VNN RPGs; RAG 27 units; USAF Forward Air Controllers; the RSSZ EOD Team and the RSSZ Psyops Team. The operation was conducted in Nhon Trach District in Bien Hoa Province, approximately 12 kilometers east of the Nha Be Navy Base and in Quang Xuyen District, approximately 22 kilometers south of the Nha Be Navy Base. The operation was characterized by multiple troop insertions, sweeps and extractions. Extensive use was made of psyops material and broadcasting facilities during the operation. Psyops personnel conducted both live and taped broadcasts from helicopters and dropped a total of 280,500 leaflets. The leaflet drops included Safe Conduct, Return to GVN, Rally to GVN, Chieu Hoi, Hoi Chanh and Weapons Reward leaflets.

Results of the Chuong Duong 29-70 operation were one RF trooper slightly wounded, 15 VC killed and four probably killed. Friendly forces captured one U.S. .45-caliber submachine gun with four magazines, two CKC rifles, one M-1 carbine, one AK-47, assorted small arms and automatic weapons ammunition, one transistor radio, approximately six pounds of documents, assorted clothing and cooking utensils, food and VN $1,500. The forces destroyed seven sampans, 22 bunkers, 11 structures, three cooking hootches and one 105 mm round.

The only other Chuong Duong operation which had significant contact with enemy forces was Chuong Duong 31-70. The most significant feature of one such contact with the enemy during this operation was that the enemy forces attempted to use tear gas (CS) against the friendly forces.

PRU and Chuong Duong operations during the month accounted for 34 enemy killed and 11 probably killed. Eleven VC were captured. Two crew-served weapons and 34 individual weapons were captured. Friendly casualties during the month were one RF trooper killed and 13 wounded.

Accounts of actions involving assets of individual River Patrol Groups may be found in those sections of the summary which discuss specific operations.

## RAIDS

On the morning of 10 July, 11 units of RAID 75, under the command of CTG 211.3, departed Cambodia and proceeded to Ca Mau (WR 17 15) via Can Tho. The boats arrived in Ca Mau at noon on 12 July, and USN advisors boarded them there. The units again got underway at first light 13 July and sailed to Thoi Binh (WR 10 33) on the Song Trem Trem to work with RAG 25/29 supporting the ARVN 21st Division, 33rd Regiment.

RAID units saw no action worth reporting, and they spent the duration of the month doing troop insertions and conducting WBGP along the Song Trem Trem, both north and south of Thoi Binh, and along the adjoining canals. Ca Mau is the homebase for the operation. All other RAIDS are still operating with TF 210 in Cambodia.

## RIVER ASSAULT GROUPS

During July, the River Assault Groups (RAGs) of the Vietnamese Navy continued to carry out normal river interdiction and troop lift operations. A list of the RAGs and their areas of operation is appended.

Units of various RAGs were engaged in a number of small actions during the month. At 1615H on 5 July, units of RAG 25/29 on patrol about 15 miles southeast of Ca Mau (WR 398 021) received approximately two rounds of B-40 rocket fire and six rounds of small arms fire which they returned with 40 mm, 81 mm, 20 mm and machine gun fire. The units then began to patrol the Ganh Hao River and at 2230H discovered a quarter-inch cable stretched across the river at WR 386 023. The cable prevented them from continuing the patrol so all units returned to base. At 0023H on 7 July two FOMs and one Monitor apparently interrupted a major crossing of the Ganh Hao River about 17.5 miles southeast of Ca Mau (WR 418 008). Many voices were heard from both banks and three rounds of small arms fire were received from a sampan on the north bank. A second heavily loaded sampan was sighted on the south bank. Both banks and sampans were covered with fire and all units returned to base.

At 1500H on 19 July an LCM of RAG 25/29 had just extracted the 974 RF Company about 15 miles north of Ca Mau (WR 142 370) when it took one B-40 round through the overhead weathershield. Twelve RF soldiers and one VNN sailor were wounded. The angle of fire indicated that the B-40 had been fired from a tree.

At 0310H on 24 July, an FOM of RAG 25/29 on patrol 23 miles northeast of Ca Mau (WR 503 205) struck a sharp submerged object and sank immediately in 15 feet of water. The crew was unable to remove their weapons and ammunition before the craft sank.

At 0930H on 20 July while transiting the Song Tac Canal seven kilometers northwest of Cat Lai, Commander 6012 of RAG 30 came under B-40 rocket and AK-47 fire from the east bank. Three rockets hit the boat and it suffered minor damage. The fire was returned with unknown results.

---

U.S. NAVAL FORCES
VIETNAM
MONTHLY HISTORICAL SUMMARY
AUGUST 1970
DECLASSIFIED

## BREEZY COVE

United States Naval forces of Operation Breezy Cove (TG 116.2) scored several important victories during August in the Song Ong Doc area where enemy activity continued at a high pace. The month's highlight came with the liberation of 28 Vietnamese prisoners of war in the first successful Navy-led assault on a communist prison camp. While there were only three enemy-initiated firefights during August, intelligence sources indicated extensive enemy operations southward from the U-Minh Forest sanctuaries. In addition to fighting guerrillas, TG 116.2 personnel had to contend with threatening rains and seas at mid-month.

The greatest tragedy of the month was the death of LTJG K.W. Tapscott, Operation Breezy Cove's Naval Intelligence Liaison Officer, killed in action seven kilometers east of Song Ong Doc on 6 August as he was on a routine patrol with units of RPG 62. PBRs 20, 31 and 36 came under intense rocket and automatic weapons fire from the north bank at VQ 854 999. After the lead boat on which the NILO was riding sustained a rocket hit on the port bow, the three craft made a second firing run through the contact area, again receiving a heavy barrage. One B-40 rocket struck LTJG Tapscott in the chest and shoulder, mortally wounding him. The second boat received three rocket hits which wounded four Vietnamese sailors. Within 20 minutes of the initial attack, Seawolves arrived overhead to place rocket and minigun strikes along the canal bank. Monitor 1 was summoned from the Song Ong Doc Advanced Tactical Support Bast (ATSB) and arrived on station to lob 35 105 mm shells into the enemy's ambush site. The entire exchange lasted over an hour, and the ensuing ground sweep by VNN sailors revealed a hat riddled with bullet holes near a pool of blood. LTJG Tapscott, who had been Song Ong Doc NILO since May 1970, was recommended for the Bronze Star for meritorious service.

PBRs 33 and 38 intercepted three Viet Cong sampans 13 kilometers east of Song Ong Doc (VR 926 009) on the afternoon of 8 August. While transiting from Binh Thuy to Song Ong Doc, the two RPG 62 craft noticed the Vietnamese sampans taking evasive action. When they gave chase, the sampans beached and Viet Cong on both sides of the canal opened fire on the allies with automatic weapons. Two other PBRs of RPG 62 arrived to make firing runs through the contact area and

## RIVER PATROL GROUPS

| Unit | # of PBRs | Homeport | Operation |
|---|---|---|---|
| RPG 51 | 4 | Cat Lai | RSSZ |
| RPG 52 | 20 | Phu Cuong | Ready Deck/THD V |
| RPG 53A | 10 | Ben Keo | Giant Slingshot/THD II |
| RPG 53B | 10 | Ben Luc | Giant Slingshot/THD II |
| RPG 54A | 10 | My Tho | THD VIII |
| RPG 54B | 10 | Tan An | Giant Slingshot/THD II |
| RPG 55 | 20 | Chau Doc | THD I |
| RPG 56 | 8 | An Long | Barrier Reef/THD IX |
| - | 3 | - | THD XI |
| RPG 57 | 20 | Nha Be | RSSZ |
| RPG 58 | 20 | Rach Soi | Search Turn/THD VI |
| RPG 59 | 20 | Tuyen Nhon | Barrier Reef/THD IX |
| RPG 60 | 10/10 | Tan My/Hoi An | Sea Tiger/THD VII |
| RPG 61 | 20 | Ha Tien | THD I |
| RPG 62 | 20 | Song Ong Doc | Breezy Cove/THD X |

Seawolves 66 and 67 scrambled to place air strikes. After the firing subsided, a VNN boat crew and a Popular Force company from Song Ong Doc made a ground sweep and captured the three sampans, three kilos of rice, and Viet Cong documents, including three personal letters, training documents and pay records.

The ATSB at Song Ong Doc was apparently threatened by sappers during the morning of 12 August. At 0930H, a large junk stopped briefly about 500 meters west of the pontoon complex and then proceeded toward the sea. Within 15 minutes, the fantail watch on the ATSB reported bubbles coming from under the western pontoon. An American officer who observed these bubbles believed that they were similar to those coming from the discharge of a scuba regulator at the respiratory rate of a working diver. The base went to General Quarters as boats of RIVDIV 152 came alongside and the sailors began throwing concussion grenades into the water around the ammi complex. The bubbles ceased after the explosion of the first grenade, but within 10 minutes a knocking sound was heard under the eastermost pontoon. The sound traveled the length of the pontoon, apparently with the current, but nothing was seen emerging from the opposite end. Divers were flown in from Solid Anchor and searched among the ammi hulls and mooring cables with negative results. The base secured from battle stations at 1311H.

Monsoon rains and heavy seas proved to be a greater threat to the Song Ong Doc base during August than the enemy itself. A storm on 16 August with winds of 30 knots gusting to 40 knots created two-foot waves around the ATSB ammis. The initial period of adverse weather carried away the bridge between the ammi complex and the shore, the communication lines to the Seawolves and Duffle Bag installations, and the AN/GRC-10 antenna. The weather slackened during the night but the seas rose again the following day, putting tremendous strain on the cables mooring the ammis. No further damages resulted although the torrential rains threatened the foundations of the Seawolf helicopter pad. Although it took several days to repair the damage, CTG 116.2's support capabilities were not seriously hampered.

*Photo courtesy of Dan Dodd, Official Navy Photographer for ComRivFlot-One MRF TF-117 68-69, Retired Chief Photographers Mate.*

ATCs 7 and 50 were on routine patrol on 22 August at the southern end of the "VC Canal" (VQ 890 962) when ATC 7 struck a mine at the mouth of "VC Lake." The explosion did not entirely disable the craft, and the RIVDIV 152 units limped back to Song Ong Doc for assessment of damages. The blast had damaged both screws and the rudder post, but the hull appeared to be in sound condition.

U.S. Naval SEALs accounted for the most daring and prestigious victory of the August Breezy Cove operations when they led the rescue of 28 prisoners of war on 22 August. This feat, the first successful rescue attempt of Operation Brightlight, was dependent upon the combined forces of the Army, Navy, Australian Air Force and Vietnamese Regional Forces.

Acting on intelligence provided by an escaped POW, Australian B-57s began placing 750-pound bomb strikes on the morning of 22 August along a canal near the camp, located 39 kilometers southeast of Ca Mau (WQ 440 928) to establish a blocking force on one side. At 0910H, SEALs of Detachment ALPHA, 6th Platoon, led by LT Boink, and the 974th Regional Force Company inserted by air approximately six kilometers north of the camp (WQ 445 931) along a narrow beach line. Upon insertion, the SEALs shot an armed VC who attempted to enter a nearby bunker. Army gunships began placing heavy rocket and minigun fire into the jungle north and west of the POW camp to establish a further blocking force. When the escapee led the SEALs and RFs into the POW camp, the allies noticed many fresh footprints heading south. Army gunships, Seawolves and the USS Southerland (DD 743) were directed to saturate the area 500 meters south of the camp in an effort to cut off escape and hopefully force the communist guards to release their captives. The ground forces continued their southerly pursuit for over two hours, following a trail of abandoned clothing and gear. At 1245H, they linked up with 28 POWs whose guards had just fled the area. An Army Slick recovered the ex-prisoners and took them to Ca Mau. Seven of them, including the former company commander of the 1109th Viet Cong Company, were former VC who had been captured while attempting to Chieu Hoi.

Two separate patrol groups of RPG 62 were attacked with B-40 rockets and small arms fire six kilometers east of Song Ong

| RIVER ASSAULT AND INTERDICTION DIVISIONS | | | | | | |
|---|---|---|---|---|---|---|
| Division | AO | ATC | ASPB | MON | CCB | Zippo |
| RAID 70* | An Long | 7 | 9 | | | |
| RAID 71 | An Long | 9 | 3 | 2 | 1 | |
| RAID 72 | An Long | 8 | 5 | 2 | 1 | |
| RAID 73 | An Long | 8 | 5 | 1 | 1 | |
| RAID 74 | Rach Soi | 8 | 4 | 2 | 1 | |
| RAID 75 | Dong Tam | 8 | 4 | 1 | | 1 |

*RAIDs 70-73 are currently operating under CTF 210 in Cambodia.

| RIVER INTERDICTION DIVISIONS | | | | | | |
|---|---|---|---|---|---|---|
| Division | AO | ATC | ASPB | MON | CCB | Zippo |
| RID 40 | Go Dau Ha | 6 | 6 | | 1 | 1 |
| RID 41 | Tan Chau | 8 | 6 | 1 | | |
| RID 42 | Chau Doc | 3 | 9 | | 1 | 1 |
| RID 43 | Tan An | 3 | 8 | 1 | 1 | 1 |
| RID 44 | Tra Cu | 4 | 9 | 1 | 1 | |
| RID 45 | Sea Float | 7 | 5 | 1 | 1 | |

Doc (VR 865 001) at 0735H on 30 August. The lead boat of one patrol was struck by a rocket which did not detonate, but the cover boat sustained two rocket hits which wounded both the forward and after .50-caliber gunners, the boat captain, the M-60 gunner and the American advisor. The forward .50-caliber gunner was carried aft for treatment, whereupon he got up and manned the M-60, only to be mortally wounded by an AK-47 round. Monitor 1 and Zippo 3, assisted by Seawolves and a third PBR patrol, entered the contact area and quickly suppressed the enemy fire. The USCG C Ponchartrain (WHEC 70) fired to the north of the area to cut off the enemy's escape route as Seawolves evacuated the wounded personnel. Fireman Nguyen Viet Tam, the gunner killed in action, was recommended for the American Bronze Star for heroic action.

Navy Seawolves accounted for the largest single combat success of the month when they killed 25 of the enemy on 30 August 10 kilometers east of Song Ong Doc (VR 904 040). The helicopters of Detachment SIX placed heavy air strikes against an estimated company-sized Viet Cong force in contact with a unit of the 33rd ARVN Regiment, and when they departed to refuel and rearm, were replaced by Seawolves of Detachment THREE from Ca Mau. These Seawolves received heavy small arms fire and called for additional assistance from the OV-10s. All enemy fire was suppressed by 0015H on 31 August, two hours after the fighting began. An intercepted communist transmission revealed that the aircraft had killed 25 of the enemy.

## Search Turn

Navy SEALS were the most active members of TG 116.3 during August as they worked throughout the month to halt daytime Viet Cong travel and detain VC suspects in the Kien Luong Province. River units of Operation Search Turn were involved in 12 firefights, more than any other SEA LORDS group with the exception of Operation Sea Float. The boats and crews of River Patrol Group 58 were complimented by Deputy COMNAVFORV, RADM H.S. Matthews for their exceptional condition and high degree of readiness.

Acting on a Kit Carson Scout (KCS) and informer intelligence, SEALS of Detachment GOLF, KILO Platoon, and a KCS squad attempted to capture two district-level Viet Cong political leaders in the early morning of 12 August. LTJG Stubblefield's SEALs and Vietnamese counterparts left Rach Soi shortly before midnight on 11 August, heading for a hamlet 11 kilometers south of Rach Gia on the Cai Lon River. While approaching the insertion point, the MSSC was ambushed with B-40 rockets and automatic weapons from both sides of the canal while passing through a row of fish stakes at WR 108 955. Though the enemy silhouetted the allies with parachute flares, they were unable to inflict any casualties. Seawolves 85 and 86 scrambled to place air strikes on the enemy positions, and when these were completed, the SEALs made another firing run through the area, suppressing the enemy fire which they received and destroying several sampans along the canal bank. The body-snatching mission was aborted.

A Duffle Bag monitoring team stumbled onto what was apparently a Viet Cong monitoring/communications base on the morning of 16 August. Members of Duffle Bag Team NINE were working three kilometers northeast of Rach Soi at WS 152 065 when they discovered a recently abandoned enemy encampment. The most important equipment found was a commercial transistor short wave radio modified to receive FM transmissions, an unsophisticated but effective example of guerrilla ingenuity. Unfortunately, a Regional Force soldier who was accompanying the sensor team inadvertently changed the monitored frequency before it could be recorded. No other crypto gear or intercepted messages were discovered. A meal for approximately 30 men was still on the fire, indicating the enemy had fled as the Duffle Bag team approached. The camp, surrounded by booby traps, consisted of two large hootches and five bunkers, all fully camouflaged to preclude aerial detection. Seawolves and OV-10s were called in to destroy the complex, but as the monitoring team withdrew toward their PBRs, a small group of the enemy attacked with small arms fire. The aircraft covered the ground forces' extraction and then destroyed the small base. There were no personnel casualties, but Seawolf 83 incurred minor damage from the ground fire. All of the sensors planted in that area were active that evening, indicating extensive enemy movement in a northerly direction from the camp site.

## Rung Sat Special Zone Shipping Incidents

Almost two months had passed without an attack being aimed at merchant ships transiting the Long Tau Shipping Channel, when on 20 August, the USNS Herkimer, while transiting north, was the recipient of four B-41 rockets fired from the south bank in the vicinity of YS 065 632, approximately 20 kilometers southeast of the Nha Be Navy Base. Only one rocket hit the ship which resulted in negligible damage and no casualties. Friendly forces arrived at the scene at 1355H, within 10 minutes of the initial attack, but were unable to locate the enemy forces.

On 25 August, the SS Raphael Semmes, transiting north, was taken under fire with two B-40 rockets at 0704H from the southwest bank from the vicinity of YS 125 633, 25 kilometers southeast of the Nha Be Navy Base. The Raphael Semmes suffered two hits and no casualties. The rockets did only superficial damage to the forward deck area near a cargo hatch. Seawolves, on a routine patrol, were on the scene in three minutes and placed strikes on the suspected enemy position. A troop sweep located two B-41 rockets and fresh footprints but no enemy troops. The rockets were destroyed in place.

DEPARTMENT OF THE NAVY
U.S. NAVAL FORCES, VIETNAM
FPO SAN FRANCISCO 96626
FFS-16/023:RSD
5750
SER: 6518
8 NOVEMBER 1970

Confidential/Declassified

From: Commander U.S. Naval Forces, Vietnam
To: Distribution List
Subj: U.S. Naval Forces, Vietnam Monthly Historical Summary for September 1970

1. The U.S. Naval Forces, Vietnam Monthly Historical Summary is forwarded for information and retention.

W.O. McDaniel
Chief of Staff

Distribution:
CINCPACFLT (4)
COMUSMACV (Hist. Branch, SJS)
COMUSMACV (Doctrine Branch J-343)
COMUSMACV (COC, JOD)
COMUSMACV (J3-12)
CNO (OP-09B9) (3)
CNO (OP-09B91E)
CNO (OP-03, 04, 05, 06) (1 ea)
CNO (OP-34)
CNO (OP-92)
CNO (Ops. Eval. Group)
OPNAV (OP-601V)
CINCLANTFLT
COMFIRSTFLT
COMSECONDFLT
COMSIXTHFLT
COMSEVENTHFLT
CHNAVMAT (Code 04)
COMSEVENTHFLT (Hist. Team)
PRES NAVWARCOL

## FOREWORD

Enemy activity within the Republic of Vietnam remained low to light in all Military Regions during most of the month of September.

Of particular interest was the increase in mining incidents which affected all Military Regions. Mining on the Cua Viet River reached an all-time high when on 27 September, seven mines were discovered within a 15-hour period.

Commander
U.S. Naval Forces
Vietnam
Monthly Historical Summary
September 1970

Force Historians .............................. LCDR D.G. Roller
LCDR E.F. Sienicki
Field Historians .............................. LTJG Stephen W. Frantz
LTJG Richard C. Schisler
LTJG George G. Lynn
LTJG Michael W. Taylor

Historical Journalists ..................... JO1 Joe LeClerc
JO2 Don H. Stephenson
JOSN Robert S. Drew

## CURRENT OPERATIONS
(AS OF 30 SEPTEMBER 1970)

| VNN Designation | USN Designation (Nickname) |
|---|---|
| TRAN HUNG DAO I (TG 214.2) | No USN nickname; originally part of Border Interdiction |
| TRAN HUNG DAO II (TG 214.1) | GIANT SLINGSHOT |
| TRAN HUNG DAO IV | SOLID ANCHOR (TG 116.1) |
| TRAN HUNG DAO V (TG 216.1) | READY DECK |
| *TRAN HUNG DAO VI | SEARCH TURN (TG 116.3) |
| TRAN HUNG DAO VII (TG 221.1) | SEA TIGER |
| TRAN HUNG DAO VIII (TG 217.1) | No USN nickname |
| TRAN HUNG DAO IX (TG 212.3) | BARRIER REEF |
| **TRAN HUNG DAO X | BREEZY COVE (TG 116.2) |
| TRAN HUNG DAO XIV (TG 217.2) | No USN nickname |
| TRAN HUNG DAO XV (TF 213) | MARKET TIME Inner Barrier |
| TRAN HUNG DAO XVI (TF 210) | Cambodian Operations |

*TRAN HUNG DAO VI will operate as TG 212.5 when activated.
**TRAN HUNG DAO X will operate as TG 212.6 when activated.

## OPERATION SOLID ANCHOR (THD IV)

Operation Sea Float passed into the annals of Naval history on 1 September when CTG 116.1 moved ashore to the Solid Anchor site. All remaining personnel were transferred ashore by 3 September. Unfortunately, this move ashore did not solve the many problems which plague the CTG 116.1 forces. Instead, it brought about another serious problem, that of base defense.

This problem of base defense was the subject of a great deal of study by the U.S. Navy command throughout the month. Aside from a shortage of both USN and VNN personnel to man the base, and the shortage of defensive material and weaponry (a number of U.S. and VN sailors were sent to Solid Anchor without weapons – a situation which was later corrected), the disadvantages of the Solid Anchor site itself were brought to light. In a message sent to COMNAVFORV on 20 September CTG 116.1 stated that: "The physical Solid Anchor site is considered unsatisfactory from a defensive point of view. The frontage is long and the depth is narrow. The appendage of a helo pad and airstrip, the lack of adequate ammo and POL storage and the neat symmetry of the quarters and warehouses all provide advantages to the attacker."[1]

This shaky defense posture was not enhanced by the disestablishment of the Kit Carson Scouts which also occurred during the month. The loss of the KCS and their camp on Solid Anchor's eastern flank "creates an exposed relatively open flank to the enemy, which Solid Anchor is incapable of filling at this time."[2]

The assets of Solid Anchor did, however, receive a most welcome addition when the 6th Vietnamese Marine Battalion, along with an artillery battery, were ordered into the Solid Anchor area of operations on 2 September. The last of these troops arrived on 5 September. Their presence provides the Solid Anchor command with the large strike force which it had been sadly lacking since the departure of the Mobile Strike Force troops in May of this year.

*Photo courtesy of Dan Dodd, Official Navy Photographer for ComRivFlot-One MRF TF-117 68-69, Retired Chief Photographers Mate.*

Another continuing concern of CTG 116.1 has been the deplorable material condition of the RID 45 craft assigned to Solid Anchor. This condition reached its nadir on 25 September when of the 11 RID 45 craft assigned, nine were non-operational due to material deficiencies and the other two were sunk. (The sinking of these two craft will be discussed later). In an attempt to bolster the River Assault Craft forces, RID 41 was ordered to replace RID 45 at Solid Anchor. This shift had not yet occurred at month's end.

A group of dignitaries visited Seabee (Third Naval Construction Battalion) construction sites during September.

Colonel S.F. Lapping, deputy chief of Psyops Division, COMUSMACV, gained some firsthand knowledge of U.S. Navy psyops efforts during his visit on 30 September.

Commander M.B. Brisbois relieved Commander T.A. Kellerher at CTG 116.1 on 1 October.

Operational activity in the Solid Anchor area of operations remained at a high level throughout the month. There were a total of 13 ambushes of Solid Anchor units by the enemy in September. These attacks resulted in damage to three PCFs, two ATCs, an LSM and a civilian tug, and the wounding of three USN and nine VNN personnel. The enemy also successfully attacked two RID 45 units nested off the Solid Anchor site on 25 September with water mines. ASPB 5167 and ATC 1269 were sunk while ASPBs 5165 and 5166, and ATC 1267 were damaged. Six VNN personnel were wounded while another eight were missing and presumed drowned. One U.S. Navyman was injured during rescue attempts.

In a tragic incident on 27 September, two U.S. Navy Seawolves sighted smoke from campfires and requested firing clearance from the Solid Anchor NOC. The NOC granted clearance and the Seawolves commenced their strike. They immediately ceased fire when they observed a yellow smoke grenade, indicating a friendly unit. Unfortunately, seven Vietnamese Marines, part of a company-sized unit making a sweep, were wounded before the cease fire. Only the quick reaction of the Seawolves in halting the strike when they observed the yellow smoke averted what might have been a more serious incident.

SEALs from Zulu Platoon of SEAL Team ONE, Det GOLF hit the jackpot on a mission conducted 13 kilometers east of Solid Anchor (vicinity WQ 128 720) on 23 September. The SEALS found a bunker and hootch complex containing a VC or VNA rocket and rocket launcher factory and weapons repair facility. The SEALs, along with a UDT demolition element, destroyed hundreds of rockets, numerous rocket launchers and mines, approximately 350 disassembled SK3 rifles, plus a wide range of weapons manufacturing machinery and other assorted weapons. They also captured 45 pounds of documents. In all, the SEALs and UDT personnel destroyed 80-90 percent of the munitions and severely damaged the machinery before extracting. A follow-up patrol the next day destroyed more of the munitions and machinery. The SEALS on this patrol noted that the bodies of three VC killed the previous day had been removed from the area, indicating that the VC had returned after the SEAL attack.

SEALS from GOLF Platoon under LT Dyer, along with Kit Carson Scouts, did not meet with the same success as their comrades when they attempted to raid a VC training camp 22 kilometers northeast of Solid Anchor (vicinity WQ 208 740) on 26 September. Instead of the eight armed VC their intelligence source had indicated would be present, they ran into a heavily armed force of approximately 20 men. This force hit the SEALs with M-79 grenades and heavy automatic weapons fire which wounded three SEALs and three KCSs before the SEALs were able to call in Seawolves which provided cover for a medevac and a successful extraction by MSSC and LSSC. Ten of the enemy were killed during the encounter (five body count, five probable).

1. CTG 116.1 msg DTG 200940Z Sep 70
2. CTG 116.1 msg DTG 18160Z Sep 70

## OPERATION BREEZY COVE

While Operation Breezy Cove SEALs and river assets experienced a moderate measure of hostile action in September, an encounter between Navy Seawolves and a massive enemy ground force was the most significant action reported by CTG 116.2. There were a total of 12 firefights during the month, and the allies reported finding the bodies of 12 enemy troops.

Navy SEALs of Detachment GOLF made several contacts with the Viet Cong after inserting in the area south of the Bay Hap River on the morning of 13 September. The SEALs first battled a five-man enemy unit armed with automatic weapons at VQ 953 743, and shortly thereafter encountered 40 communist troops at VQ 964 736, seven of whom were wearing light blue uniforms. The SEALs reported killing six of the enemy (body count) and six (probable). They recovered assorted weapons and communist documents.

Seawolves from Song Ong Doc were involved in one of the Navy's greatest operational losses in September. On 15 September three American helicopters (two USN, one USA) were shot down in the vicinity of "VC Lake" (VQ 94 95). The incident began in mid-afternoon when Seawolves inserted elements of a Regional Forces company six kilometers south of the city of Song Ong Doc (VQ 93 97). Shortly thereafter, the ground troops made contact with a large enemy force and urgently requested medical evacuation for six seriously wounded troops. Dustoff 86 attempted extraction, but heavy ground fire drove it away, and it was forced to wait for helicopter gunship support. While waiting, it withdrew southward to Solid Anchor, approximately 30 kilometers away, to medevac two life or death cases. Seawolves 12 and 32 of Detachment Three were scrambled from Ca Mau, and Seawolves 62 and 65 left Solid Anchor to provide cover for the second extraction attempt. As they overflew the contact area at 1700H, all four aircraft were hit almost immediately. Seawolf 62 was saturated with large caliber machine gun fire and crashed into a rice paddy dike at VQ 930 960 with two of its crew killed and two wounded. Moments later Seawolf 12 was hit, and the pilot radioed that the ship was going down. To avoid a ground assault by the enemy, the pilot elected to guide the disabled aircraft into the shallow "VC Lake." Seawolf 65 sustained hits in the pilot's pedal linkage and was forced to withdraw and limp toward Ca Mau. Seawolf 32, flown by LTJG Xucuhko, was simultaneously hit in the fuel cell, and though losing fuel at a critical rate, hovered over her Detachment Six sister ship to provide cover for Dustoff 86 which sought to extract the crew of Seawolf 12. In the process, Seawolf 32 sustained at least eight additional hits but was able to remain airborne. This task completed, the rescue helicopter braved withering fire to save the two wounded survivors of Seawolf 62. Seawolf 32 then escorted Dustoff 86 out of the fire zone and headed toward Song Ong Doc, requesting that boats be sent up the Song Ong Doc in case the crippled helicopters could not make it to the ATSB. CTG 116.2 responded immediately, sending boats eastward from Song Ong Doc and calling additional boats from their assigned patrols in case assistance was needed. Meanwhile, Dustoff 86 flew to the 3rd Surgical Hospital in Binh Thuy with the two wounded men. Throughout the episode, Army Cobra helicopters in the area were unable to provide assistance as they were involved in other actions.

At 1732H, three Navy Slicks arrived at the crash site to recover the bodies of the two Seawolf 62 crewmen but could not land because they had no gunship cover. They were able to land an hour and a half later when an Army Cobra arrived to provide fire protection. The enemy's anti-aircraft gunners had apparently stayed in place for they then shot down the Cobra whose crew was quickly extracted by a Dustoff helicopter. One of the SEA LORDS Slicks then landed to extract one of the bodies from Seawolf 62. Navy OV-10 aircraft waiting overhead were denied firing clearance because of the presence of friendly troops in the area.

By 2255H it was reported that Seawolf 62 was engulfed in flames, and it appeared that the enemy forces had moved on the helicopter after dark, removed the remaining body, stripped away the guns and set the aircraft on fire. The following morning, the body was found a short distance from the helicopter. OV-10s then destroyed the downed Seawolf 12 in VC Lake and an ARVN demolition team blew up Seawolf 62. An Army Chinook helicopter lifted out the Cobra.

The total friendly casualties for this engagement were two USN killed and two USN wounded. LTJG William A. Pedersen and ADJ3 Jose Pablo Ramos were killed when Seawolf 62 crashed. The other two crewmen of that aircraft, LTJG William L. Ford and AMS3 James P. Plona, were both wounded.

The helicopter crewmen involved in this massive battle agreed that the incident showed signs of a skillfully planned ambush rather than of spontaneous anti-aircraft fire. Several men, probably guerrillas acting as decoys, were spotted in close proximity to Seawolf 12 after it crashed and seemed to be attempting to draw the other aircraft in for a landing by waving white or red flags or handkerchiefs. The NILO at Ca Mau indicated that there were no friendly units within two kilometers from the crash site. Whenever the Seawolves would make a pass, the hidden enemy gunner units would not disclose their positions by firing until the helicopters' ordnance would no longer bear on them. According to the pilots involved, the enemy force numbered approximately 500 to 1,000 men who, because of their deadly accuracy with large caliber automatic weapons, appeared to be extremely well trained.

This battle was the first significant contact to be reported in the "VC Lake" vicinity in some time. According to ARVN intelligence sources, the headquarters of the 95th North Vietnamese Army Regiment has been located in this area, but the unit was beginning to move into the U-Minh Forest as the local Viet Cong were unable to support them. This attack, according to intelligence analysis, might indicate a reverse of that trend.

The only major administrative change for the month occurred when CDR C.R. Christensen, USN, relieved LCDR K.J. Rhea, USN, as CTG 116.2 and SOPA ATSB Song Ong Doc on 22 September. CDR Christensen was formerly assistant senior advisor to CTG 212.

## OPERATION SEARCH TURN

COMNAVFORV ordered an increase in the number of day time patrols and inspections of river traffic in the Search Turn (TG 116.3) Operation area during September. Intelligence reports had indicated possible enemy movement of war materials from the U-Minh Forest to Cambodia. Possibilities for communist mobility was great as the heavy monsoon flooding in the area allowed the Viet Cong and North Vietnamese to travel in sampans over normally dry land. Allied river craft, engaging in a total of nine firefights, battled several large enemy units in the last week of September and reported killing eight (body count) by the end of the month.

PBRs of River Patrol Group 58 battled with an estimated company-size communist force on the night of 23 September. The crews of PBRs 51, 54 and 55 observed heavy movement 100 meters inland from their WBGP position on the Kinh Tu Canal, eight kilometers northeast of Rach Gia (WS 141 119). At 2009H, the allies began firing into the area with all weapons and finally received automatic weapons fire in return. Navy Seawolves expended all their ordnance on the target site, and soldiers from a nearby ARVN outpost at WS 136 112 began firing at the enemy but could still not suppress the return fire. Two Search Turn OV-10s patrolling nearby arrived to place their entire load on the estimated 50-100 man guerrilla force which then temporarily ceased firing. At 2110H, the ARVN outpost itself was attacked as the defenders observed numerous lights moving toward them. The PBRs and Detachment Eight Seawolves rushed to the area to assist, and after a brief exchange of fire, the lights were extinguished, and firing on the outpost ceased. As the river craft returned to the original contact area, crew members observed troop movement along the bank and interpreted it as enemy forces sweeping for battle casualties. The PBRs and Seawolves again fired into the area, and this time received no return fire. As the ground movement ceased, the sailors heard sampans moving west along Ta Keo Creek and adjoining canals, but the proximity of their allied boats precluded the use of artillery. OV-10s placed air strikes, and Seawolves illuminated the area with flares, but no enemy were sighted. There were no more incidents during the night.

The following day several local inhabitants told an allied interpreter that the Viet Cong had suffered six killed and 10 seriously wounded in these engagements. The communists had aroused animosity among the indigenous population by forcing them to treat the wounded and bury the dead. The Viet Cong apparently extorted a considerable amount of money to conduct the burial ceremony.

SEALs of Detachment GOLF, KILO Platoon captured a Viet Cong tax collector on 25 September in a village 21 kilometers south of Rach Gia (VR 966 880). Reacting on intelligence provided by a Kit Carson Scout, the SEALs inserted in the small village at 1515H, and were searching hootches when they heard movement and voices in the adjacent woods. One man, armed with a rifle, escaped as the allies approached, but another Viet Cong, identified as a tax collector, was captured. The allies began to receive small arms fire from a position 50 meters away, but a Seawolf was called in to suppress fire. The ground troops extracted without casualties and returned to Rach Soi.

A column of eight boats of RPD 58 was ambushed six kilometers southeast of Rach Gia (WS 130 025) on the evening of 26 September while enroute to a WBGP. PBR 7649, the third boat in the column, received two B-40 rockets on the starboard side and was forced to break away from the column with five wounded VNN sailors. The remaining boats, assisted by Seawolves and additional RPD 58 PBRs, took the contact area under fire, and crew members claimed killing five of the enemy. They also reported seeing over 30 NVA fleeing the area. PBR 7649 attempted to return to the Rach Soi base at top speed, but was forced to beach after covering only about three kilometers. The river craft sank to the extent that only one inch of freeboard existed, but within 30 minutes the boat had been pumped out enough to allow towing back to Rach Soi.

Intelligence investigation revealed that the ambush team, probably the same group which had attacked PBRs 51, 54 and 55 three days earlier, had forced the civilian population to move out of the area earlier in the day. The nearby Regional Force personnel were aware of these developments but made no effort to warn the PBRs, according to VNN officers and USN advisors.

## RUNG SAT SPECIAL ZONE

Combined operations were continued in the Rung Sat Zone (RSSZ) during the month of September. Six such operations were conducted and were named Chuong Duong 38-70 through Chuong Duong 43-70. The Chuong Duong operations were all very similar in concept, with the usual insertions by Slick helicopter, cover by USN and USA LHFTs, sweeps by RF companies and PRUs, and extractions by ASPBs or Slicks.

The most significant Chuong Duong operation was 38-70. At 030628H two ASPBs at XS 969 581 were fired upon with two B-41 rockets and other small arms fire from the west bank near Quang Xuyen, 12 kilometers south of the Nha Be Navy Base. One ASPB received one B-41 rocket on the port side resulting in four USN personnel wounded. The ASPB although damaged continued in company and commenced a firing run to the north where additional fire support was requested from USN LHFT on an enemy position located at XS 968 580. Results of Chuong Duong 38-70 were six U.S. wounded, nine VN wounded and two VN killed. Four bunkers were destroyed and assorted turtle mines, M-79 duds and booby-trap grenades were captured.

In a special operation (110600H-151800H) near Long An and Can Giuoc (XS 807 745), 15 kilometers southwest of the Nha Be Navy Base, two PF platoons supported by a Zippo boat and Douche boat (water Monitor) and Seawolves conducting a sweep northward through the area came into contact with enemy forces. At 151000H, the Zippo boat and Douche boat came under B-40 rocket and heavy automatic weapons fire at XS 807 745. Three B-40 hits were received by the Zippo, wounding two USN personnel and two PF personnel Plus moderate damage to the boat. One B-40 round glanced off the Douche boat bow causing light damage. USN helicopters and fire teams were scrambled to the area and placed suppressing fire on the enemy position.

Various other insertions, sweeps and extractions were made during this period. In addition, the Zippo boat made burn runs for a total of 20 minutes of flame time. Douche boats destroyed two bunkers and accumulated 30 minutes of water time. Results of the Long An (PF waterborne) operations were two PFs missing, three PFs wounded, two USN wounded, four enemy killed and three captured. Materials captured were: two B-40 rocket launchers, two B-40 rocket rounds, three AK-47 rifles with magazines, 40 rounds of 7.62 ammunition and a small quantity of food.

PRU and Chuong Duong operations during the month accounted for 14 enemy killed and 10 probably killed. Three enemy and 15 individual weapons were captured. Friendly casualties during the month were six killed and 22 wounded, of which eight were USN.

## RSSZ SHIPPING INCIDENTS

Harassment on the Long Tau Shipping Channel continued when at 011330H, the U.S. civilian tug Santiam, with a barge in tow transiting north, came under fire from three B-40 rockets shot from the south bank at YS 066 623. There was no damage or casualty to the Santiam.

A USN Light Helicopter Fire Team (LHFT), a USAF Forward Air Controller and RF Company 908 responded to the incident. The RF company swept the area with negative results.

*Photo courtesy of Dan Dodd, Official Navy Photographer for ComRivFlot-One MRF TF-117 68-69, Retired Chief Photographers Mate.*

U.S. NAVAL FORCES
VIETNAM
MONTHLY HISTORICAL SUMMARY
NOVEMBER 1970
DECLASSIFIED

Department of the Navy
U.S. Naval Forces, Vietnam
FPO San Francisco 96626

FF5-16/023:rsd
5750
Ser: 0139
9 February 1971

From: Commander U.S. Naval Forces, Vietnam
To: Distribution List
Subj: U.S. Naval Forces, Vietnam Monthly Historical Summary for November 1970

1. The U.S. Naval Forces, Vietnam Monthly Historical Summary is forwarded for information and retention.

Richard S. Moore
Chief of Staff

Distribution:
CINCPACFLT (4)
COMUSMACV (Hist. Branch, SJS)
COMUSMACV (Doctrine Branch J-343)
COMUSMACV (COC, JOD)
COMUSMACV (J3-12)
CNO (OP-09B9) (3)
CNO (OP-09B91E)
CNO (OP-03, 04, 05, 06) (1 ea)
CNO (OP-34)
CNO (OP-92)
CNO (Ops. Eval. Group)
OPNAV (OP-601V)
CINCLANTFLT
COMFIRSTFLT
COMSECONDFLT
COMSIXTHFLT
COMSEVENTHFLT
CHNAVMAT (Code 04)
COMSEVENTHFLT (Hist. Team)
PRES NAVWARCOL
COMPHIBLANT
COMCBPAC
COMCBLANT
COMINEPAC
Commandant, Armed Forces Staff College
Commandant, U.S. Army War College, (Attn: Library U-393), Carlisle Barracks, Pa. 17013
COMNAVFACENGCOM
SUPT USNA
CHINFO
CO NAVPHIBSCOL LCREEK
CO NAVPHIBSCOL Coronado
PHIBTRADET MARIS
NSRDC PANFLA
NIOTC MARIS
Project Manager, Naval Inshore Warfare Project, Washington, D.C. 20360
CG Aerospace Studies Institute (Code ASAD), Maxwell AFB Ala. 36112
CHNAVSEC C&GS Col., Ft. Leavenworth, Kansas 66027
CHNAVSEC Air University (Attn: AUL (SE) – 69-10), Maxwell AFB
USA Special Warfare School (Attn: USN/MC Liaison Officer) Ft. Bragg, N.C. 28307
USMC Rep., U.S. Army Infantry School, Ft. Benning, Ga. 31905
DIA (DIAAP-4A2/Pentagon)
Office of the Senior Marine Advisor, Naval Advisory Group, Box 9 FPO San Francisco 96626
Commander Naval Ship R&D Center, Washington, D.C. 20007
Commander Mine Squadron ELEVEN
Commander Naval Special Warfare Group, Atlantic, NAVPHIBASE, LCREEK, Norfolk, Va. 23521
Commander, NAVSPECWARGRUV, NSAS, Box 25

NAVFORV & NAVADVGRP MACV NOTE C5216 of 1 Oct 1970
List II.A. (SNA)
List II.B. (SMA)
List III (Less E)
List IV (Less D&E)
List V (A)
List VI (A1&2, D1 E&H14)

COMMANDER
U.S. NAVAL FORCES
VIETNAM
MONTHLY HISTORICAL SUMMARY
NOVEMBER 1970

Force Historian .................................LCDR Edward E. Sienicki

Field Historians .................................LTJG Stephen W. Frantz
LTJG Richard C. Schisler
LTJG George G. Lynn
LTJG Michael W. Taylor

Historical Journalists ..........................JO1 Joe LeClerc
JO2 Don H. Stephenson
JO3 Robert S. Drew

## FOREWORD

The level of enemy-initiated activity remained low throughout the country during the month. In the First Military Region friendly and enemy forces alike were still recovering from October's inclement weather.

November will nevertheless remain an important month in the annals of the Navy's Vietnamese effort. For the first time since the 1968 Tet Offensive, a North Vietnamese trawler was challenged and sunk. After an extended period of covert tracking, U.S. Naval and Coast Guard ships finally sank the trawler after she had entered the 12-mile limit on 22 November at 0006H.

Another significant coup occurred on 22 November when a group of SEALs accompanied by PF troops, assaulted an enemy POW camp near Nam Can in the Cau Mau Peninsula and freed 19 South Vietnamese prisoners.

U.S. Navy and Coast Guard in-country strength continued to decline in November. As of 26 November, there were 17,389 Naval and Coast Guard personnel in South Vietnam, a reduction of about 500 men over the course of the month.

## Current Operations
### (As of 31 November 1970)

| VNN Designation | USN Designation |
| --- | --- |
| TRAN HUNG DAO I (TG 214.2) | None |
| TRAN HUNG DAO II (TG 214.1) | GIANT SLINGSHOT |
| TRAN HUNG DAO IV | SOLID ANCHOR (TG 116.1) |
| TRAN HUNG DAO V (TG 216.1) | READY DECK |
| TRAN HUNG DAO VI (TG 212.5) | SEARCH TURN |
| TRAN HUNG DAO VII (TG 221.1-CHI LANG I) | SEA TIGER |
| TRAN HUNG DAO VIII | None |
| TRAN HUNG DAO IX (TG 212.3) | BARRIER REEF |
| *TRAN HUNG DAO X | BREEZY COVE (TG 116.2) |
| TRAN HUNG DAO XIV (TG 217.2) | None |
| TRAN HUNG DAO XV (TF 213) | MARKET TIME Inner Barrier |
| TRAN HUNG DAO XVII (TF 210 as of 1 DEC '70) | None |

*Not yet turned over

## Operation Solid Anchor

Solid Anchor units scored a smashing victory against the enemy on 22 November. While newspapers around the world were telling of the unsuccessful attempt to liberate U.S. POWs in the Son Tay prison camp in North Vietnam, 10 SEALs of WHISKEY Platoon of SEAL Team One, Detachment GOLF led by LT Couch, along with 19 PF troops, were doing some liberating of their own. In an area 15 kilometers east-southeast of New Nam Can (VQ 880632), the SEALs and PFs freed 19 South Vietnamese POWs after carrying on a running firefight with 18 VC guards. The aggressiveness of the SEALs and PFs was clearly exhibited in this team operation. Two VC were also captured along with numerous documents in the raid. Worthy of note is the fact that this was the first in-country operation for WHISKEY Platoon and its supporting unit, MST Det Charlie.

Rocket ambushes and mining attempts continued to plague the waterborne units assigned to Solid Anchor, but the frequency of the attacks dropped off sharply in November. There were three rocket ambushes which resulted in minor damage to LSSL-230 and PCF 3919 and two mining incidents which caused moderate damage to A-5164 and minor damage to A-5165 and T-1272. Nine VNN personnel and one U.S. Navy advisor were wounded in these attacks, but fortunately their wounds were minor.

Heavy weather in the South China Sea accounted for the only major losses to Solid Anchor units during the month. Six VNN PCFs transiting from Solid Anchor to Cat Lo on 2 November were buffeted by extremely high seas caused by a tropical storm Nora. PCF 3907 swamped and sank (XR 645160) and 10 hours later PCF 3904 met the same fate. Both crews were rescued without loss of life and the remaining swifts arrived at a safe haven off Coastal Group 36 at Long Phu.

A search and rescue mission for these PCFs, and also for a VNN PGM, a VNN WPB and three USN PCFs, was coordinated by CTF 115. With the exception of two Solid Anchor PCFs, all units reached safety.

In a command shift on 1 November, CAPT E.I. Finke, USN, formerly the senior Naval advisor to the Vietnamese Navy, assumed the position of CTG 116.1. CAPT Vuong Huu Thieu, VNN, became his deputy task group commander and chief staff officer.

The 6th VNMC Battalion departed the Solid Anchor area of operations on 4 November. This battalion was responsible for 61 enemy KIA and 10 captured as well as the capture of a large number of weapons and supplies in the two months it spent at Solid Anchor AO. The 6th VNMC Battalion was relieved by the 7th VNMC Battalion which acquitted itself well in November. The Marines killed 13 of the enemy and captured three more. They also took part in a two-day operation in conjunction with VNN river craft, a first in the Solid Anchor VNMC operations.

The nomenclature of the two hamlets adjoining the Solid Anchor complex underwent another change in November. Although the hamlets have been referred to as Ham Rong I and II by Navy sources in the past, their names within the GVN structure are listed as Ham Rong (Ham Rong I) and Thi Tran (Ham Rong II). The GVN nomenclature will henceforth be used.

Although their nomenclature was changed, the problems of the hamlets remained basically the same in November – adequate defense against the enemy. The PF outpost under construction at Thi Tran was hit by two B-40 rockets on 4 November (no damage) and an RF outpost on the Kinh Ngang Canal eight kilometers from Solid Anchor (WQ 019743) received 20 rounds of 81 mm mortar fire on 30 November, killing one RF and wounding 10 others.

The distribution of the 59 M-1 carbines received by CTG 116.1 in October to PSDF personnel in Ham Rong and Thi Tran was delayed until a PSDF recruiting drive in these hamlets is completed. CTG 116.1 is retaining the carbines until the Nam Can District senior advisor requires them for the new PSDF troops.

VADM J.H. King Jr, COMNAVFORV; RADM Tran Van Chon, CNO, VNN; and BGEN Nguyen Huu Hanh, Dep CG IV Corps, were on hand for the dedication ceremonies of the Solid Anchor air strip on 26 November.

## Breezy Cove

At the beginning of November, CTG 116.2 was faced with reconstructing his totally destroyed Advanced Tactical Support Base at the mouth of the Song Ong Doc River. A large-scale enemy attack on 22 October had driven away the allies and razed the floating base, but within a week, COMNAVFORV issued orders to rebuild it at its original location. During the reconstruction period, the Breezy Cove Naval Operations Center was located on the USS Garrett County (AGP-786) anchored off shore. The PBRs and River Assault Craft returned to the ATSB for staging.

During the first week of November, these initial plans were modified by COMNAVFORV. The new projected plan provided for relocation of the main Breezy Cove base to Ca Mau with an advanced staging base situated at Song Ong Doc, 15 kilometers from the river's mouth. Deputy COMNAVFORV delineated the following advantages of this relocation.

1. The capability to cover Song Ong Doc from Ca Mau to the Gulf of Thailand. Advanced staging from Old Song Ong Doc would provide continued allied presence in the western portion of the AO and hence preclude adverse psychological effects on the civilian inhabitants of the Song Ong Doc District.
2. The tactical versatility of concentrating forces in either the eastern or western portion of the AO, depending on the threat.
3. Enhanced base defense posture at both bases.
4. Improved communication capability from the Gulf of Thailand through Old Song Ong Doc to the new base at Ca Mau.
5. Closer and improved liaison with the district chief of Old Song Ong Doc and the Ca Mau Province chief for combined operations.

6. Improved overland logistics capability from LSB Binh Thuy to Ca Mau.

The advanced base at Old Song Ong Doc was to be a simple, floating complex, similar to the original one at the river's mouth. Two ammis were towed under escort from Solid Anchor as were the undamaged ammis from the original ATSB.

The entire relocation was completed by 25 November and the Breezy Cove logistics and gunfire support ships were released from duty. The construction of the new operations center at Ca Mau involved a much longer process, not scheduled for completion until March 1971. In the meantime, the province chief offered the Navy temporary use of the PRU camp located three kilometers northwest of Ca Mau on the Song Tac Thu. Because of this shift, the turnover of Operation Breezy Cove to the Vietnamese Navy, originally scheduled for 1 December, was postponed. While there were a few scattered incidents, the enemy did not attack in force during this period of instability. The new NILO at Song Ong Doc reported that Communist concentration in the area remained high and seemed to be increasing. Navy OV-10 aircraft and Seawolves operating in the area reported extensive troop movement, and bunker construction near the old ATSB. At mid-month, a reliable local Vietnamese informer stated that the Viet Cong planned to attack the Song Ong Doc base on 25 November with an even larger force than before. The man claimed that one group of the enemy was going to attack from fishing junks returning from sea while a second element would move through the village to prevent the shore-based allies from reaching their boats. This assault never materialized. The only direct enemy activity involving the defenders of the ATSB was sniper fire on 19 November which wounded BM3 Eugene J. Jones, who was standing a perimeter watch.

Because of the heavy enemy threat in the Song Ong Doc District, the CNO of the Vietnamese Navy ordered River Interdiction Division 43, heretofore attached to Tran Hung Dao II to the mouth of the Song Ong Doc River to protect base reconstruction efforts. It was estimated that these boats would reinforce TG 116.2 for a period of six weeks. On 20 November, RID 43 relieved River Assault Squadron 15, which proceeded to Dong Tam for stand down and eventual turnover to the VNN.

Base security around the destroyed ATSB remained a problem pending relocation because of the paucity of ground troops. CTG 116.2 depending almost entirely on Dufflebag sensors, requested that a company of Vietnamese Marines be sent to Song Ong Doc, but was denied. On 17 November, however, a battalion of the 32nd ARVN Regiment arrived to protect the area. The unit's four 105 mm howitzers supplied vital striking power for the immediate vicinity.

The only major action involving Breezy Cove river boats in November occurred on the 20th of the month when two PBRs received B-40 rockets, five kilometers east of the Song Ong Doc ATSB (VR 846002). The lead boat escaped without mishap, but the cover boat caught fire and exploded before sinking. The crew, including two wounded VNN sailors and a slightly injured USN advisor, ADR1 C.R. Benson, were quickly rescued by Zippo-3. Two days later Explosive Ordnance Disposal divers recovered all serviceable weapons and blew up the sunken PBR.

While the riverine units of Operation Breezy Cove enjoyed a rather peaceful month, U.S. Navy SEALs were highly active in their efforts to neutralize members of the Viet Cong infrastructure in the Song Ong Doc area. On the evening of 5 November, seven SEALs of Detachment ALFA, 9th Platoon, led by a Kit Carson Scout and a local informer, captured two VC four kilometers south of Ca Mau (WR 182108). Upon returning to their base camp, the SEALs persuaded their captives to divulge the whereabouts of their village cadre leader. Within three hours, the commando squad had captured him as well.

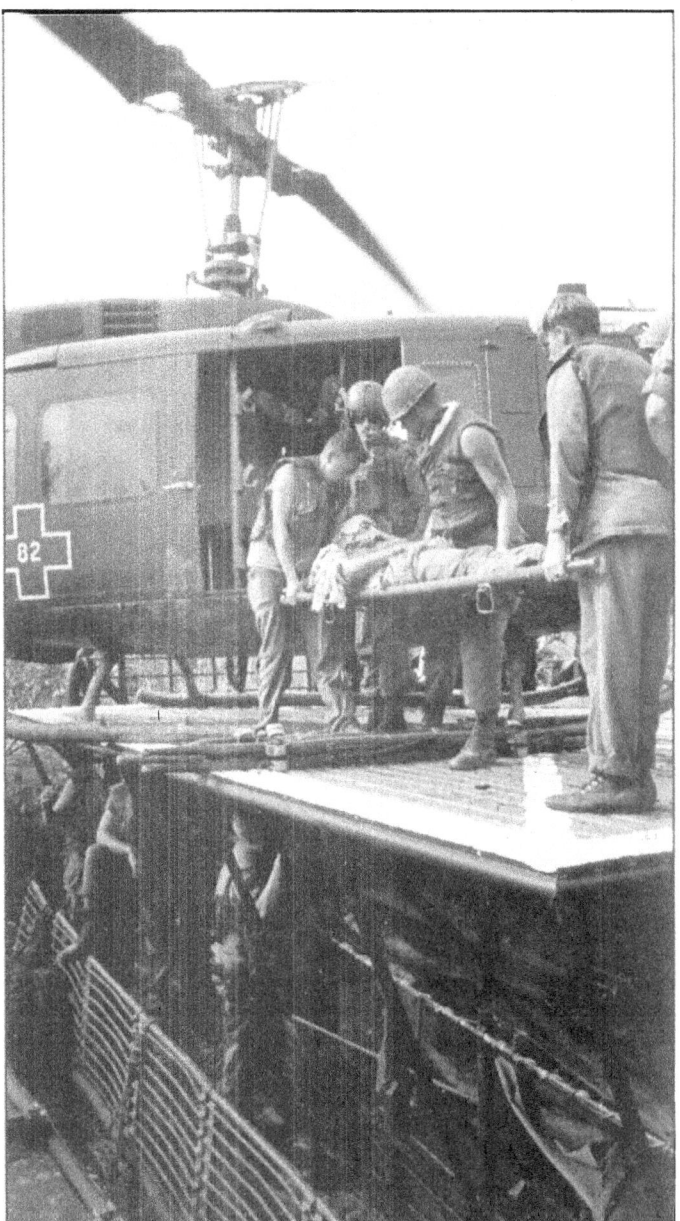

*Photo courtesy of Dan Dodd, Official Navy Photographer for ComRivFlot One MRF TF-117 68-69, Retired Chief Photographers Mate.*

LT Moran's 9th Platoon captured three more VC just two days later. A pair of Hoi Chanhs led the SEALs to a small village 15 kilometers southeast of Ca Mau (WR 238040) on the night of 7 November. They immediately entered the suspects' hootch and captured three men, two of which were hamlet level guerrillas and the other a village level VC. When the SEALs began to withdraw, they received continuous sniper fire and as they were scrambling into the extraction helicopter, EM1 John S. Fallow was wounded slightly in the leg.

Another USN sailor became the victim of the swift currents of the Delta waterways in November. EN3 Bruce C. Hunt, a crewmember of ATC-2 of RIVDIV 152 drowned near the ATSB Song Ong Doc on the third day of the month. It was believed that he fell from the nest of RACs while carrying a seabag and was swept under one of the ATCs. Hunt had been proceeding to the helicopter pad for a flight to Binh Thuy, and his disappearance was not suspected until his body was discovered the following day.

Evidence of skillful joining of allied communications in the Ca Mau Peninsula presented itself again during November. On the afternoon of 6 November, the USS Hunterdon County (LST-823) launched an LCVP to investigate two contacts six kilometers off shore from the north of the Song Ong Doc River (VQ 743974). Both craft were sampans, one occupied by two men with fishing gear and the other by six men, resting at anchor. When the LCVP boat captain tried to contact the Hunterdon County for instructions, his broadcast was blocked by loud Vietnamese music. The jammed frequency was the standard one used by the USS Garrett County, the USCG C Yakutat and the USS Hunterdon County for communication with their LCVP craft. According to the Song Ong Doc NILO, the timing of the jamming indicated that the jamming station was either aboard one of these two sampans or in contact with their crews. Neither of the sampans was boarded or inspected, according to the commanding officer of the Hunterdon County, because they did not appear to be a threat and because of lack of boarding and search experience on the part of the crew.

A SEA LORDS helicopter was ditched in the Gulf of Thailand on 26 November when it ran out of gas attempting to reach the USS Garrett County (AG-786) off the coast near Song Ong Doc. The crew was rescued and for the next three days, high winds and seas prevented salvage divers from reaching the sunken helo, and when they were able to dive, they could not find it.

On the day after the helicopter loss, LCM-6, after battering against a YFU alongside the Garrett County, in heavy seas, sank in 24 feet of water. On 28 November, a PBR broke loose from its moorings at the Garrett County and sank in heavy seas before it could be recovered. In both cases, the suddenness of high winds was cited as the reason for failure to take sufficient preventative action. COMNAVFORV, however, concerned with this triple loss in three days, ordered an investigation of the Garrett County's boat and helicopter control procedures and adequacy and timeliness of weather forecasts.

## OPERATION BLUE SHARK

The highly successful Operation Blue Shark closed out its assignment on 15 November. Blue Shark, which was mounted following the disestablishment of the Market Time Raider Program in May of this year, went out as it had come in – in style. The success of the operation is attested to by a message from COMNAVFORV to CTG 116.5 (Commander, Blue Shark) which stated that:

"Along the coastline from the southern border of the Rung Sat Special Zone to Vinh Chau District, and up the Bassac and Hau Giang Rivers you kept the enemy off balance and on the defensive with your board and search operations, inshore surveillance, river patrols, SEAL insertions and attacks on enemy base camps and supply points. Yours was a difficult operating area, with heavy foliage, shallow and often uncharted waterways and shifting sand bars, but you covered it well."[1]

In one of the last Blue Shark missions, PCFs 45, 87, 93 and 692 lifted a KCS/SEAL team to the Thanh Phu Secret Zone (vicinity XR 802952) on 12 November. As the Swifts entered the northern mouth of the Eo Lon Canal 26 miles south-southeast of Ben Tre, they received two B-40 rockets and small arms fire. The enemy fire was suppressed, and the SEALs and KCSs inserted to conduct a pincer sweep. Black Ponies provided covering strikes during the sweep. Two VC were killed and an enemy arms cache consisting of over two tons of arms and equipment was discovered during the ...

## RUNG SAT SPECIAL ZONE

For the forces of the RSSZ, it was again a month of furious activity that required an enormous amount of patience and diligence. On 1 November at 0120H, personnel on a Boston Whaler assigned to pier security for the logistical base at Nha Be spotted floating vegetation and debris approximately 100 meters east of the deep water piers. The crew made a routine inspection of the debris and decided to disperse it with a concussion grenade. The result was a minor secondary explosion. No damage occurred and the incident was regarded as a possible enemy mining attempt.

On 3 November at 1920H, a reconnaissance squad from RF Company 999 was inserted by Slick 15 miles east of Nha Be (YS 191 760) and patrolled an assigned perimeter. One sampan with three persons aboard was sighted and taken under fire, probably killing three VC. The sampan was destroyed and 20 kilos of food captured. Seawolves were called and placed air strikes in the vicinity with unknown results.

Between 0900H and 1800H on 5 November, RSSZ PRUs conducted a special operation supported by Slicks, Seawolves and Black Ponies. The PRUs were inserted by Slick aircraft into an area 11 miles northeast of Nha Be and began a sweep of the area. Two contacts were made with an unknown size VC force during the operation. Results of the operation were no friendly casualties, 11 VC killed and two captured. Items captured included five B-40 rocket rounds, 1,000 AK-47 rounds, four claymore mines and a large number of documents. Three hundred kilos of rice, two sampans, two anti-vehicle mines, 10 kilos of TNT and five fortifications were destroyed.

From 1330H to 1815H on 6 November, RSSZ PRUs conducted a special operation in an area 11 miles northeast of Nha Be (YS 070 950). The operation was supported by Slicks and Seawolves. Immediately after insertion, the PRUs engaged a large enemy force and with effective air strikes and overhead cover suppressed the enemy fire. Seven VC were killed and two VC were captured. Four small arms weapons, five anti-vehicle mines and many documents were captured while three bunkers were destroyed. There were no friendly casualties.

Operation Chuong Duong 50-70 commenced at 0800H on 7 November approximately 27 kilometers northeast of the Nha Be Navy Base in the vicinity of YS 158 198. Two VNN PBRs received fire from the west bank in the vicinity of YS 182 800, but could not return the fire due to the close proximity of friendly troops. RF Company 121 made contact with an unknown number of VC which lasted intermittently until 1300H. RSSZ Pysops Team and BJU-1 Team 13 conducted 20 minutes of taped loudspeaker broadcast with the Chieu Hoi theme. The results of Chuong Duong 50-70 were one friendly casualty, nine VC killed and one VC captured. A large amount of documents, medical supplies, one AK-47, two wrist watches, two transistor radios and three kilos of fish were captured.

Based upon intelligence in Nhon Trach (YS 15 75), 22 kilometers east of the Nha Be Navy Base, PF Platoon 018 and the Quang Xuyen Intelligence Squad were inserted by Slicks on 10 November to search for a possible weapons cache. At 1120H, the contingent discovered the enemy cache in the vicinity of YS 153 756 which included 14 CKC rifles, five 9 mm grease guns, one light machine gun DPM Chicom type 53, and one Mauser rifle. In addition, they destroyed 1,200 K-54 rounds, 750 AK-47 rounds and 20 60 mm mortar rounds.

Chuong Duong 51-70 commenced on 13 November at 0855H in the vicinity of YS 075 535, 36 kilometers southeast of the Nha Be Navy Base. The district operation was secured due to no contact with the enemy. The result of the operation was six bunkers destroyed.

Chuong Duong 52-70 District Operation commenced on 17 November at 0730H in the vicinity of YS 95 68 – YS 99 68, 14 kilometers south of the Nha Be Navy Base. On 18 November at 1530H, the operation was secured due to no contact with the enemy.

Chuong Duong 53-70 Headquarters Operation commenced on 19 November at 1600H in the vicinity of YS 14-80 – YS 21 77, 23 kilometers east of the Nha Be Navy Base. The results of the operation were one RF wounded, two bunkers and one sampan destroyed.

In one of the more tragic operations that started on 20 November at 0930H in the vicinity of YS 075 922, 16 kilometers northeast of the Nha Be Navy Base, a PRU tripped a booby trap, wounding seven personnel, four seriously, who were immediately medevaced by Slick to the 24th Evacuation Hospital in Long Binh. A sweep of the area brought them in contact with an unknown size VC force. USN LHFT placed air strikes on the enemy which resulted in four VC killed and one captured. Items captured were five individual weapons, four B-41 rockets, two claymore mines, two grenades and four kilos of documents. Three base camps and four camouflaged hideouts were destroyed.

Chuong Duong 54-70 Headquarters Operation commenced on 25 November at 0800H in the vicinity of YS 175 801, 21 kilometers east of the Nha Be Navy Base. In one of the most relentless pursuits of the enemy by RSSZ units, results were finally established which reflected the tenacious struggle. On 28 November at 1400H, Chuong Duong 54-70 was concluded with one RF wounded, 50 VC killed, one VC wounded and two captured. Five individual weapons, three watches, two radios, three batteries, assorted electronics equipment and codes and five kilos of documents were captured. Ninety kilos of food and clothing, 30 kilos of rice, eight base camps, 11 bunkers, three sampans, 14 sleeping platforms and 15 kilos of eating utensils were destroyed.

For the month of November, RSSZ units accounted for 87 VC killed, four probably killed, nine VC and 31 weapons captured, while suffering only one friendly killed and 13 wounded.

River Assault Division 153 departed Nha Be on 9 November and marked the end of the U.S. patrol and assault boat operations in the RSSZ. CTG 116.9 stated:

"In the 17 months that your unit was employed in the Rung Sat as part of TG 116.9, your performance served as an outstanding example of exemplary courage in combat for others to follow. During this period, your units participated in more than 75 major combined air mobile-water mobile operations in addition to the multitude of other tactical assignments to which you were tasked. The alpha boats commonly known as the dreadnoughts of the Rung Sat were vital to the success of the elimination of over 500 Viet Cong."

## LONG TAU SHIPPING CHANNEL

With the abatement of hostile activity on the Long Tau Shipping Channel, COMNAVFORV saw fit to recognize this accomplishment with the following statement to the senior advisor, Rung Sat Special Zone:

"I note with pleasure that the passing of September and October completed two consecutive months during which there were no attacks on shipping transiting the Long Tau Channel. An accomplishment of this nature is tangible evidence of the continuous pressure you have maintained on the enemy through extensive offensive operations, increased security, your overall professionalism and the outstanding spirit of teamwork which exists in the RSSZ. Every effort should be taken to exploit this success by maintaining continuous pressure and relentless pursuit against the enemy."[1]

But the lull that persisted in the past two months was suddenly broken when on 1 November at 1415H, the SS President Coolidge, transiting north on the Long Tau Channel, came under fire from the east bank, three miles southeast of the Nha Be Navy Base. An estimated three B-41 rockets were fired at the ship, but there were no hits. Seawolves were denied clearance to place strikes on the suspected enemy positions because of close proximity of an RF outpost. An aftermath investigation revealed that some debris from the air burst settled on the fantail of the vessel.

U.S. NAVAL FORCES
VIETNAM
MONTHLY HISTORICAL SUMMARY
DECEMBER 1970
DECLASSIFIED

Department of the Navy
U.S. Naval Forces, Vietnam
FPO San Francisco 96626

FFS-16/021C:dhs
5750
Ser: 0173
15 February 1971

From: Commander U.S. Naval Forces, Vietnam
To: Distribution List
Subj: U.S. Naval Forces, Vietnam Monthly Historical Summary for December 1970

1. The U.S. Naval Forces, Vietnam Monthly Historical Summary is forwarded for information and retention.

Richard S. Moore
Chief of Staff

Distribution:
CINCPACFLT (4)
COMUSMACV (Hist. Branch, SJS)
COMUSMACV (Doctrine Branch J-343)
COMUSMACV (COC, JOD)
COMUSMACV (J3-12)
CNO (OP-09B9) (3)
CNO (OP-09B91E)
CNO (OP-03, 04, 05, 06) (1 ea)
CNO (OP-34)
CNO (OP-92)
CNO (Ops. Eval. Group)
OPNAV (OP-601V)
CINCLANTFLT
COMFIRSTFLT
COMSECONDFLT
COMSIXTHFLT
COMSEVENTHFLT
CHNAVMAT (Code 04)
COMSEVENTHFLT (Hist. Team)
PRES NAVWARCOL
COMPHIBLANT
COMCBPAC
Commandant, Armed Forces Staff College
Commandant, U.S. Army War College, (Attn: Library U-393), Carlisle Barracks, Pa. 17013
COMNAVFACENGCOM
SUPT USNA
CHINFO
CO NAVPHIBSCOL LCREEK
CO NAVPHIBSCOL Coronado
PHIBTRADET MARIS
NSRDC PANFLA
NIOTC MARIS
Project Manager, Naval Inshore Warfare Project, Washington, D.C. 20360
CG Aerospace Studies Institute (Code ASAD), Maxwell AFB Ala. 36112
CHNAVSEC C&GS Col., Ft. Leavenworth, Kansas 66027

CHNAVSEC Air University (Attn: AUL (SE) 69-10), Maxwell AFB
USA Special Warfare School (Attn: USN/MC Liaison Officer) Ft. Bragg, N.C. 28307
USMC Rep., U.S. Army Infantry School, Ft. Benning, Ga. 31905
DIA (DIAAP-4A2/Pentagon)
Office of the Senior Marine Advisor, Naval Advisory Group, Box 9 FPO San Francisco 96626
Commander Naval Ship R&D Center, Washington, D.C. 20007
Commander Mine Squadron ELEVEN
Commander Naval Special Warfare Group, Atlantic, NAVPHIBASE, LCREEK, Norfolk, Va. 23521
Commander, NAVSPECWARGRUV, NSAS, Box 25
COMNAVORDSYSCOM (ORD-08)

NAVFORV & NAVADVGRP MACV NOTE C5216 of 1 Oct 1970
List II.A. (SNA)
List II.B. (SMA)
List III (Coastal Group Commands and Activities)
List IV.B. (MINEDIVs)
List IV.F. (Aircraft Squadrons)
List V. A1. (NSF Danang)
List V. A2. (NSAD Nha Be)

## COMMANDER
## U.S. NAVAL FORCES
## VIETNAM
## MONTHLY HISTORICAL SUMMARY
## DECEMBER 1970

Force Historian ..................... LCDR Edward E. Sienicki

Field Historians ................... LTJG Stephen W. Frantz
LTJG George G. Lynn
LTJG Michael W. Taylor

Historical Journalists ........... JO2 Don H. Stephenson
JO3 Robert S. Drew

## FOREWORD

As 1970 unceremoniously drew to a close for the 16,757 U.S. Navymen in South Vietnam, and desultory toasts were downed in myriad hootches and barracks throughout the country, another landmark in Naval history was reached as the last assets of the "Brown Water Navy" and coastal patrol forces were officially transferred to the VNN. In relinquishing operational control of its small combatants, the USN is gradually reverting to the strictly advisory role it played prior to the large build-up of U.S. Armed Forces in South Vietnam in 1965.

The Vietnamese Navy launched another major campaign on 1 December with the inception of TRAN HUNG DAO XVII, the first combined all-out assault on the VC-controlled U-Minh Forest in the history of the war. The operation includes assets from RAIDs 70 and 71, RID 40, RAG 25/29 and RPD 61, all engaged in providing logistics support, troop lifts and blocking forces for components of the ARVN 21st Division.

The Saigon headquarters of U.S. Naval Forces, Vietnam, was exposed to the first threat of violence in many months as activity in the capital city increased during December, partly as the result of student activity and partly from VC terrorism. On 15 December at 2050, two Vietnamese civilians placed a plastic bottle filled with gasoline into the gas tank filler neck of a USN vehicle parked outside the NAVFORV Compound, but no explosion was caused and only minor damage done to the vehicle. At 2255 the same night, about 10 students gathered on Doan Thi Diem Street adjacent to NAVFORV Headquarters with the expressed intention of burning a USN Jeep. Members of the Vietnamese Security Force arrived and dispersed them before any damage could be done. In their wake, the students left a leaflet stating that their activity was to revenge the death of a fellow student killed in Qui Nhon by U.S. Forces.

The Military Sealift Command, Vietnam, reported a possible Saigon Harbor attack the morning of 19 December, when at 0210 two 122 mm rockets impacted in the city at XS 863 919 and XS 876 916, killing six Vietnamese civilians and wounding eight. Nine MSC vessels were moored in the harbor at that time, four of them USNS ships.

On a more cheerful note, VADM Jerome H. King, commander, Naval Forces Vietnam, relayed to U.S. Navymen in the First Coastal Zone a letter of gratitude from President Thieu to General Creighton Abrams, COMUSMACV, thanking and praising U.S. Forces who were instrumental in providing flood relief for the people in the area during the disastrous storms of October. General Abrams added his own commendation to that of the president, stating "this act of humanitarianism contributed significantly to the overall Vietnamization program."[1]

## SOLID ANCHOR

During the month of December, Operation Solid Anchor was plagued with a series of logistics, personnel and material problems which would have tried the patience of any responsible commander. In addition to the types of problems cited above, the enemy scored several successes during the course of five ambushes of boats, two mining incidents and one mortar attack on the northern edge of the perimeter of the Solid Anchor base itself. In operations during the month, one VNN sailor and one Philippine civilian were killed, three USN and 12 VNN sailors plus four Philippine civilians were wounded. Friendly forces killed a total of 29 of the enemy and captured 61. The enemy sank one ATC and damaged one monitor, one ASPB, one PCF and two civilian tugs. There were 11 friendly initiated firefights, while the enemy initiated 12.

Colonel F.W. Tief, USMC, the senior Marine advisor, was sent to Solid Anchor as a relief for Capt E.I. Finke, as commander of TG 116.1 on 9 December.

Among the problems to which the commander of Solid Anchor was forced to address himself were contamination of the fuel in the JP-5 ammi, resupply of JP-5, a lack of emergency electrical power backup for the base, the need of a significant portion of the

## CURRENT OPERATIONS

| VNN Designation | USN Designation |
|---|---|
| TRAN HUNG DAO I (TG 214.2) | None |
| TRAN HUNG DAO II (TG 214.1) | GIANT SLINGSHOT |
| TRAN HUNG DAO IV | SOLID ANCHOR (TG 116.1) |
| TRAN HUNG DAO V (TG 216.1) | READY DECK |
| TRAN HUNG DAO VI (TG 212.5) | SEARCH TURN |
| TRAN HUNG DAO VII (TG 221.1) | SEA TIGER |
| TRAN HUNG DAO VIII (TG 217.1) | None |
| TRAN HUNG DAO IX (TG 212.3) | BARRIER REEF |
| TRAN HUNG DAO X (TG 212.6) | BREEZY COVE |
| TRAN HUNG DAO XIV (TG 217.2) | None |
| TRAN HUNG DAO XV (TF 213) | MARKET TIME Inner Barrier |
| TRAN HUNG DAO XVII (TF 210) | None |

*Photo courtesy of Dan Dodd, Official Navy Photographer for ComRivFlot-One MRF TF-117 68-69, Retired Chief Photographers Mate.*

assigned river assault craft for repairs which strained or were beyond the Solid Anchor repair capability and the arrival of relief PCFs in a material status which precluded operations.

On 12 December, CTG 116.1 in a message to COMNAVSUPPACT Saigon noted that 18 out of a total of 25, or 72 percent, of his assigned assault craft were in need of repairs which required outside assistance, such as engine overhauls, bar armour repair, hull welding, and strut and rudder repair. In that day's situation summary, he reported that only nine of his assigned 25 RAC were available for patrol. The command faced the same staggering casualty problems in regard to its PCFs. On 20 December, CTG 116.1 reported that out of 10 assigned PCFs, only one was fully operational, five were only partially able to carry out their mission and four were in a completely non-operational status. This problem had been exacerbated about a week earlier by the arrival at Solid Anchor of two relief PCFs with one operational engine apiece. CTG 116.1 brought to Senior Advisor COMCOSFLOT Five's attention the fact that PCFs with one engine were ineffective on combat patrols in the Solid Anchor area of operations. COMNAVFORV ordered SA CTF 213 to take immediate remedial steps to correct the asset situation.

On the personnel front, acute problems developed also. In order to reduce the theft of personal items, a big morale factor, and the pilferage of military goods, CTG 116.1 requested the assignment of six men to form an internal security force. COMNAVFORV turned the request down, reminding CTF 116 that although Solid Anchor had an allowance of 59 NSAS personnel, over 160 were actually assigned and stating that he felt the assignment of additional personnel would only aggravate a problem which was going to have to be solved in any case as a result of the forthcoming reduced space ceiling which would become effective 1 May 1971.

On 9 December, the VNN EOD Team refused to do any more work and stated their intentions to the VNN operational commander. They then packed their bags and departed Solid Anchor for Saigon, leaving the two-man U.S. advisory team to handle all EOD work. On 22 December, EOD personnel reported there was a three-man VNN EOD team at Solid Anchor again, but reported that one assigned member who, when informed that VNN EOD personnel were tasked with accompanying the 7th Battalion VNMC on an operation, departed the area and missed the operation.

The month concluded with a cholera epidemic, which broke out in Ham Rong Village on 30 December. Ten cases appeared, three of which resulted in death. The hamlets were immediately declared out-of-bounds to all base personnel. The Solid Anchor medical team and MAT 67 immediately went to work, and by 1 January, the spread of the disease was reported under control. Four people were reported dead and 13 were medevaced, with a total of 31 people still sick.

Meanwhile there was a high level of activity as operations against the enemy continued. The month's most serious incident occurred on 2 December. Boats of RID 41, proceeding south down the Rach Ong Dinh with 200 VNMC embarked, were ambushed 11 miles southeast of Solid Anchor (WQ 015 635) at 0807H. Two B-40 rockets hit the port side of an ASPB causing moderate damage and wounding the VNN forward gunner. The force then came under automatic weapons fire. The boats suppressed the fire, and VNN personnel went ashore to investigate the ambush site. They found it heavily booby-trapped and collected eight claymore mines, three B-40/41 rockets and four B-50 launch bombs. The captured ordnance was placed topside on the bow of a monitor, and the boats continued south to the point where the VNMC were to be inserted, some 300 meters south of the ambush site. While attempting to beach during the insertion, the monitor carrying the ordnance struck a mine, and its bow from the waterline upward was blown off. LT S.V. Ethridge, BM 1 H.E. Sampsell, and one other USN advisor were wounded and eight VNN personnel were wounded. Recognizing the imminent danger posed by the more than 100 rounds of 105 mm ammunition in the monitor's magazine adjacent to the bow section, WO-1 Benjamin W. Rand, EOD team leader, led a group of advisors and VNN EOD personnel aboard the sinking craft and removed the most dangerous portion of the ammunition. Warrant Officer Rand was recommended for the Silver Star, three men were recommended for the Bronze Star and seven men, including two VNN EOD personnel, were recommended for the Navy Commendation Medal for their actions during the incident. The sinking monitor was towed back to Solid Anchor by two ATCs. A VNN crew member of the monitor was found to be missing upon arrival at the base, and his body was later found in the canal.

At 0830H on 3 December while en route north patrolling on the Kinh Cai Nhap, two ATCs of RID 45 were mined about seven miles northwest of Solid Anchor. One boat was undamaged, but the other suffered major shock damage and sank immediately. Two VNN sailors were wounded, one seriously. An ASPB was sent to provide assistance and Seawolves provided air cover for the helicopter which medevaced the wounded. En route to the boats, the medevac helicopter came under automatic weapons fire which was suppressed by the Seawolves. The ASPB, proceeding to the mined craft's assistance, observed a water mine explosion close aboard to port but suffered no damage or casualties.

Photo courtesy of James Kelley.

At 1745H on 11 December, two PCFs, escorting the civilian tugs Stanford and Skipjack west on the Song Bo De, came under automatic weapons and B-40 rocket fire 10 miles west of Nam Can (WQ 243 681). Two rockets hit Skipjack, one in the pilot house and one in the stack, causing moderate damage. The PCFs suppressed the fire and Seawolves placed strikes in the area. There were no friendly casualties. Again at 0940H on 19 December, the civilian tug Stanford and escorting PCFs were ambushed on the Song Cua Lon while proceeding toward Solid Anchor about 8.5 miles east of the base (WQ 111 692). Three rockets struck the tug, killing one civilian and wounding four, and one struck an escorting PCF wounding one VNN sailor. Advisor RM 3 M.J. Murphy suffered minor cuts caused by flying glass. All units proceeded to Solid Anchor under their own power.

At 1405H on 20 December, boats of RID 44 transiting the Rach Cai Nhap toward Solid Anchor came under B-40 rocket attack eight miles northeast of the base. There were no direct hits and Seawolves arriving only a minute later placed strikes in the area (WQ 082 740).

At 0840H on 27 December, an ATC on routine patrol discovered and broke a wire which they believed led to a command detonated mine in the Rach Cai Nhap about 6.5 miles northeast of Solid Anchor (WQ 078 765). EOD personnel were called to the scene, found a mine, recovered and disarmed it. The mine consisted of 60 pounds of plastic explosives in a wooden box with five electric and two non-electric blasting caps.

Beginning at 0405H on 27 December, 20 to 30 rounds of 82 mm mortar fire landed on the northern edge of the perimeter of the Solid Anchor base causing no casualties or damage. The fire was immediately returned with mortars, automatic weapons and small arms. Crater analysis indicated that the enemy mortar position had been to the northeast at extreme range. A thorough sweep of the area was conducted with no results.

At 1835 on 28 December, Seawolves on routine patrol about eight miles southeast of Nam Can received a heavy volume of automatic weapons fire (WQ 073 566). One helicopter flying at about 1,000 feet took two hits, but fortunately continued to operate. After placing a strike, the Seawolves returned to their base. Examination of the holes in the aircraft indicated that they were made by rounds from a .51-caliber machine gun.

SEALs of Whiskey and Zulu Platoons of Detachment Golf, SEAL Team One carried out a vigorous schedule of operations during the month. On 20 December, seven SEALs from Zulu Platoon paddled in sampans to the mouth of the Trai Cheo Canal (VQ 978 766), six miles northwest of Solid Anchor, and spied a VC proceeding upstream. They followed him and 11 more VC in six sampans appeared. The SEALs challenged the group of VC, and all initially obeyed the instructions. When two of the captives suddenly attempted to seize hidden weapons and evade, the SEALs took them under fire. Eight of the VC were killed in the ensuring melee, and two more were probably killed as they fled. The SEALs took no casualties.

Vietnamese Marines of the 7th Battalion and Battery B VNMC continued to carry out reconnaissance in force operations in the Solid Anchor area of operations during December. They killed 10 and captured two of the enemy while suffering four killed and seven wounded themselves. They captured four rifles, one pistol, 65 grenades and miscellaneous medical supplies. In addition, 16 craft and 45 bunkers were destroyed.

## BREEZY COVE

Allied units of Operation Breezy Cove (CTG 116.2), seeking to stabilize operations following base relocations to Ca Mau and Old Song Ong Doc, experienced a hectic month during December. The still uncompleted base at Ca Mau was attacked, and river units engaged in 11 firefights. While there were several intelligence reports of large troop concentrations in the Song Ong Doc and Cai Nuoc districts, the allies did not engage in any large confrontations. Yet when the operation was finally turned over to the Vietnamese Navy at month's end, the new VNN commander inherited responsibility for one of the most hostile areas in Military Region IV.

Two boats of RID 43, returning up the Song Ong Doc River after resupplying from the USS Garrett County (APG 786) on 10 December, were ambushed by B-40 rockets, recoilless rifles and automatic weapons fire at VR 869 002. An Armored Troop Carrier received rocket rounds through the pilot house and canopy while an ASPB sustained two hits at the waterline. Two American advisors, EN 3 N.H. Demski and BMC J.D. Howe, and five Vietnamese sailors were wounded. Seawolves from Ca Mau placed air strikes on suspected guerrilla positions but reported no enemy casualties.

VNN PBRs of River Patrol Division 62 moving east along the Song Ong Doc River were attacked by B-40 rockets and automatic weapons fire during the early evening of 17 December. The boats, aided by Seawolves, suppressed enemy fire and withdrew without casualties. The attack was potentially effective, however, as it came from both banks of the river rather than from one isolated position. This new tactic, according to NFV analysts, suggests either new and more effective leadership or the presence of well-trained North Vietnamese reinforcements.

Throughout December, salvage operations were conducted to recover the Seawolf helicopter, HSSC 5634, and the PBR lost in late November near the USS Garrett County (APG 786) off the coast of Song Ong Doc. The salvage ship, USS Reclaimer (ARS 42), finally located the HSSC on 15 December after five days of searching and, following a week of on-station patching, delivered the refloated craft to the repair ship USS Krishna (ARL 38). The following day, the Reclaimer raised the sunken helicopter and, after stripping off the weapons and classified equipment, jettisoned the wreckage in deep water. By the end of the month, the missing PBR still had not been recovered.

CTG 116.2 suffered his greatest loss since the razing of the Song Ong Doc ATSB when his new headquarters at Ca Mau was bombarded with mortar fire on the night of 26 December. One U.S. sailor, EN 2 E.V. Rochez, and an Army advisor were killed while 13 American and eight Vietnamese sailors were wounded. A generator and guard tower were destroyed, and a PBR and two LCM craft sustained minor damage. Two Ca Mau Seawolves scrambled to place air strikes on the suspected enemy positions. A ground sweep the following morning recovered several communist small arms and two sampans with blood in them.

Following the attack, the Song Ong Doc NILO reported that a local sympathizer had reported that the Viet Cong would attempt to destroy patrol craft at the Ca Mau base by dropping mines from sampans near the piers. Because of the increased threat to the base, two Regional Force companies and two Popular Force platoons began deploying nightly south of the river near the PRU camp. In addition, PRUs began setting regular night ambushes to the north while PSDF troops operated in hamlets east and west of the compound.

Lieutenant Moran's SEALs of Detachment Alpha, 9th Platoon, enjoyed another successful month in their efforts to eradicate the Viet Cong infrastructure in An Xuyen Province. In the early morning hours of 4 December, a four-man squad ambushed and killed four Viet Cong 12 kilometers southwest of Hai Yen (VQ 797 722). After the initial contact, the group relocated 50 meters away. They ambushed a sampan at dawn, killing one of the VC and two hours later, killed still another guerrilla and captured his comrade. One of the dead Viet Cong was identified as a deputy province level finance section chief.

Two days later, the SEALs attempted to aid one of their Kit Carson Scouts whose mother and brother had been abducted by the Viet Cong. A squad led by three scouts inserted near the man's hootch 11 kilometers south of Ca Mau (WR 205 040) and rescued the man's son who had successfully hidden himself when the VC came. The party was unable to locate the two kidnap victims but captured one guerrilla cadre member during the search.

The SEALs were more fortunate on the evening of 7 December when they captured a communist hamlet assistant military chief and a supply section chief in a village 15 kilometers southeast of Ca Mau (WR 233 038). After entering the targeted hootch, pointed out by a local informer, and capturing the two men, the five-man squad remained secluded in the structure throughout the night. Shortly after daybreak, a 15-man unit of Viet Cong, apparently aware of allied presence in the area, began sweeping through the nearby area, firing their AK-47 rifles. The out-numbered SEALs called in a Seawolf strike on the enemy, and escaped during the air attack.

SEALs of the 9th Platoon attempted to rescue Vietnamese prisoners of war being held in a camp 12 kilometers southeast of Hai Yen (VQ 932 768) on 27 December. Reacting to ARVN intelligence and led by local guides and a Kit Carson Scout, the five-man squad attacked the small camp defended by a dozen guards. All the prisoners had recently been removed, but the SEALs killed four of the guards with assistance from Seawolves and captured communist weapons, documents and medical supplies.

Operation Breezy Cove officially became TRAN HUNG DAO X (CTG 212.6) on 29 December when Lieutenant Commander Nhan, VNN, relieved Commander Christensen, USN, as operational commander. The Ca Mau ceremony was attended by Vice Admiral King and Rear Admiral Chon, the Vietnamese CNO. The U.S. Navy will continue to provide air and logistical support, and the new CTG 116.2, Lieutenant Commander W.D. Dannheim, will act as both senior advisor and officer in charge of the operation's two support bases.

## Task Fleet 21

The Christmas Season failed to provide a respite for the combined allied forces of Task Fleet 21. The operations and units still controlled by the U.S. Navy, including Breezy Cove, Solid Anchor and the Seawolf helicopters and OV-10 aircraft, continued to encounter the most extensive enemy resistance in the vast Mekong Delta and Ca Mau Peninsula. Combined ARVN and VNN forces of TRAN HUNG DAO XVII, an operation launched at the heart of the Viet Cong stronghold of the U-Minh Forest in early December, sustained the greatest casualties among Vietnamese forces.

December also witnessed the further Vietnamization of riverine warfare in the Delta as command of Operation Breezy Cove and of the Tan Chau, Kien An, Chau Doc and Ha Tien operating bases was transferred to the Vietnamese Navy. Symbolic of the waning role of the American naval forces was the disestablishment of River Patrol Flotilla V after the official turnover of the last PBR of the Brown Water Navy at the end of December.

CTF 116, who has exercised administrative control over all river patrol boats for the past two years, assumed the title of commander, Delta Naval Forces. Captain R.E. Spruit, the senior advisor to CTF 212, was assigned this position as additional duty.

COMNAVFORV expressed concern over two vital aspects of naval operations in the Delta during December: base and boat security against sampans, and helicopter control. The former problem developed from the accidental deaths of several non-hostile Vietnamese civilians who had unintentionally entered defensive water areas. COMNAVFORV ordered extensive notification of the location of defensive areas and the posting of warning signs to keep civilians and sampans clear of these secured zones. Warning shots, fired in the air, were to be used only as a last resort in clearing a prohibited area.

The mysterious crash of a Seawolf helicopter in the jungle north of Ca Mau led to a revamping of the Navy's aerial control procedures. On the morning of 19 December, a helicopter of Detachment 3 departed the repair facility at Binh Thuy and headed for its home base at Ca Mau. The last contact with a control center was at 1025H. At approximately 1100H, the air craft crashed in an unsecured area, 26 kilometers short of its destination (WR 321 437), and all four crewmen perished. For the next two days, the helicopter lay undiscovered, and no aviation commands, including HAL-3, reported that any aircraft were missing. Finally, on the afternoon of 21 December, a 7-year-old Vietnamese girl inadvertently stumbled upon the wreckage and reported it to the local authorities. The next morning, an Army Reconnaissance Team located the helicopter. The bodies of the crewmen, LTJG R.H. Buzzell, LTJG A.O. Ortiz, AEC J. Ratliff and ADJ 2 R.E. Worth, were found in shallow graves near the wreckage. Evidence of enemy presence in the area was extensive as the helicopter, which had crashed upside down, had been riddled with bullets and stripped of all vital parts and weapons.

COMNAVFORV ordered a thorough investigation of the circumstances surrounding this bizarre and unreported crash. In addition, an extensive revision of aircraft control procedures was instituted to ensure that all Navy planes would be accounted for at all times.

# U.S. Naval Forces CTF – 117 – Mobile Riverine Force
# PERSONNEL KILLED IN ACTION/MISSING IN ACTION
## Southeast Asia Theater of the Vietnam War 1960-1975
### "May our Brothers Rest in Peace"

**CTF-117 River Assault Flotilla One**

**River Assault Squadron 9 – River Assault Division 91**

09/27/67 – Wiselee Smith, BM3, San Francisco, CA – ATC-91-10 (Kien Hoa)
09/27/67 – David Du Wayne Knowles, SN, Eatonville, WA – ATC-91-10 (Kien Hoa)
09/27/67 – Marc S. James, SN, Bronx, NY – ATC-91-3 (Kien Hoa)
02/01/68 – William M. Comer Jr., BM2, Larned, KS – BC – ASPB-91-2 (Dinh Tuong)
07/23/68 – John F. Bobb, BM1, Erlanger, KY – BC – ASPB-91-4 (Kien Hoa)
07/23/68 – David A. Pearson, FN, Town Tonawanda, NY – ASPB-91-4 (Kien Hoa)
11/10/68 – Sammy J. Cross, GMG3, Hominy, OK – M-91-2 (Kien Hoa)
12/23/68 – Wallace Going, BM2, Watson, OK – ASPB-91-5 (Kien Hoa)
01/10/69 – Daniel L. Westlie, EN3, Augusta, WI – ATC-91-1 (Kien Hoa)

**River Assault Squadron 9 – River Assault Division 92**

04/12/67 – Michael J. Smith, SA, Kansas City, KS (Kien Hoa)
12/21/67 – Frank H. Buck, FN, Wenonah, NJ – ATC-92-10 (Dinh Tuong)
02/06/68 – Samuel M. Boyce, RM3, Dardanelle, AR – ASPB-92-2 (Vinh Long)
03/02/68 – Michael A. Evenson, RM3, Lakota, ND – ASPB-92-7 (Phong Dinh)
03/18/68 – David H. Wyrick, LT, Alliance, OH – 1100 – CO – M-92-1 (Dinh Tuong)
04/04/68 – Samuel C. Chavous Jr., BMC, Cross City, FL – BC – M-92-2 (Kien Hoa)
04/04/68 – Douglas G. Morton, FN, Phoenix, AZ – M-92-2 (Kien Hoa)
04/04/68 – John D. Woodard, BM3, Clyde, NC – M-92-2 (Kien Hoa)
08/02/68 – Charles H. Dellinger, SN, Gibsonia, PA – ATC-92-8 (Phong Dinh)
05/12/69 – David J. Boron, SN, Cleveland, OH (Go Cong)

**River Assault Squadron 11 – River Assault Division 111**

09/15/67 – William H. Little, EN2, Weymouth, MA – M-111-3 (Dinh Tuong)
09/15/67 – Richard A. Cheek, SN, Oregon, IL – M-111-2 (Dinh Tuong)
09/15/67 – William T. Diamond Jr., SN, Ottawa, IL – ATC-111-6 (Dinh Tuong)
12/04/67 – Adrian E. Howell, FN, Lucedale, MS – ATC-111-8 (Dinh Tuong)
12/04/67 – Robert J. Moras, FN, Escanaba, MI – ATC-111-8 (Dinh Tuong)
12/21/67 – Frederic P. Webb, RMSN, Redmond, OR – ASPB-111-4 (Dinh Tuong)
02/07/68 – Maynard L. Smith, EN3, Troy, KS – ATC-111-? (Vinh Long)
02/27/68 – James L. Lien, BM2, Lead, SD – BC – ASPB-111-4 (Military Region-4)
02/27/68 – Jeider J. Warren, BM1, Castor, LA – ASPB-111-4 (Military Region-4)

03/09/68 – Eugene E. Swift, BM3, Hyattsville, MD – ATC-111-5 (Bien Hoa)
05/04/68 – Charles L. Perry, BM3, Columbus, OH (Dinh Tuong)
05/09/68 – Roy A. Cox, BM3, Ft. Worth, TX – ATC-111-7 (Dinh Tuong)
05/10/68 – Kenneth A. Carroll, BM2, Ohley, WV (Go Cong)
05/26/68 – Ronald W. Durbin, BM2 – Cumberland, MD – BC – ASPB-111-1 (Kien Hoa)
05/26/68 – Jerry L. Williams, RM3, Picher, OK – ASPB-111-1 (Kien Hoa)
07/23/68 – Charles S. Roy, EN2, Rock Springs, WY CCB-111-1 (Dinh Tuong)
08/21/68 – R.D. Sullivan, BM1, Centerville, TN – ATC-111-10 (Dinh Tuong)
11/01/68 – Harry J. Kenney, EN3, Cincinnati, OH – USS Westchester County LST-1167 (Go Cong) **MIA**
11/11/68 – Eddie M. Adams, FN, Hadley, MA – ASPB-111-1 (Dinh Tuong)
11/11/68 – Theodore Harrison Jr., SN, Chicago, IL – ASPB-111-1 (Dinh Tuong)
03/09/69 – Jackie R. Morgan, BM2, Oklahoma City, OK – BC – ATC-111-9 (Tay Ninh)
03/31/69 – Donald L. Bruckart, GMG3, Redlands, CA – ATC-111-2 (Kien Tuong)

**River Assault Squadron 11 – River Assault Division 112**

07/11/67 – Howard W. Bannister, BMC, Delbarton, WV – M-112-1 (Long An)
03/01/68 – Leslie E. Murray, BM1, Chehalis, WA – ASPB-112-8 (Phong Dinh)
03/14/68 – Edward J. Hagl, BM1, McAllister, MT – BC – ATC-112-7 (Quang Tri)
03/14/68 – Frankie R. Johnson, EN3, Toppenish, WA – ATC-112-7 (Quang Tri)
03/14/68 – Ernest W. Wiglesworth Jr., BM3, Greensboro, NC – ATC-112-7 (Quang Tri)
03/14/68 – Eugene Nelson, FN, Lug Off, SC – ATC-112-7 (Quang Tri)
03/14/68 – Robert W. Cawley, SN, Butte, MT – ATC-112-7 (Quang Tri)
03/14/68 – Joseph S. Perysian, SN, Butte, MT – ATC-112-7 (Quang Tri)
05/24/68 – Frederick V. Arens Jr., FN, Boston, MA – ASPB-112-1 (Go Cong)
8/18/68 – Stephen C. Brunton, BM3, Ukiah, CA – ASPB-112-2 (Dinh Tuong)
08/18/68 – Billy D. Roy, BM3, Oklahoma City, OK – ASPB-112-1 (Dinh Tuong)
08/18/68 – Edward R. Darville III, GMG3, Hialeah, FL – ASPB-112-2 (Dinh Tuong)
08/18/68 – Patrick J. Griffin, RM3, Topeka, KS – ASPB-112-1 (Dinh Tuong)
12/16/68 – Charles L. Kneece, BM3, Chillicothe, OH – ASPB-112-1 (Kien Hoa)
01/31/69 – Ronald Chapman, ENFN, Columbia, MS (Gia Dinh)
02/16/69 – Nelson Ramirez, SN, Bronx, NY – ASPB-112-5 (Hua Nghia)
02/23/69 – Nicholas I. Pyle, SN, Columbus, OH – CCB-111-1 (Hua Nghia)

### River Assault Squadron 13 – River Assault Division 131
08/02/68 – William R. Taylor, BM2, Honolulu, HI – ATC-131-9 (Chuong Thien)
11/12/68 – James A. Myers Jr., GMG2, New Harmony, IN – ASPB-131-2 (Kien Giang)
03/15/69 – Harvey Lee Basco, BM2, Alexandria, LA – ATC-131-8 (Go Cong)
06/07/69 – Curtis L. Hendrickson, SN, Winger, MN – ATC-131-10 (Long An)
02/26/70 – Norman K. Byassee, En2, Litchfield, Park, AZ – UH1B Helicopter (An Giang)

### River Assault Squadron 13 – River Assault Division 132
02/06/69 – Mark Siedentopf, SN, Fremont, CA – ATC-132-1 (Kien Hoa)
02/22/69 – Victor G. McCall, EN2, Brevard, NC – ATC-132-6 (Kien Hoa)
04/29/69 – Richard L. Keller, EN3, Lomita, CA – ASPB-132-3 (Chuong Thien)
04/29/69 – Terry N. Thompson, FN, Gulfport, MS – ASPB-132-3 (Chuong Thien)
05/24/69 – Ronnie G. Klomstad, SN, Rochester, MN – ATC-132-10 (Bien Hoa)
08/28/69 – Richard E. Martinez, BM1, Renton, WA – ATC-132-15 (Dinh Tuong)
09/05/69 – Terry D. Mason, RMSN, Toppenish, WA – ATC-132-22 (Tay Ninh)
11/17/69 – James F. Rost Jr., LTJG, Malverne, NY – 1105 – ATC-132-6 (Vinh Long)
12/30/69 – Doyle H. Parson, BMC, Weeping Water, NE – Z-132-1 (Bac Lien)

### River Assault Squadron 15 – Staff
06/23/70 – Harold L. Linville, HM2, Reno, NV – Helo SeaFloat

### River Assault Squadron 15 – River Assault Division 151
01/14/69 – Jose B. Campos, BTFN, Seguin, TX – ATC-151-5 (Chuong Thien)
01/14/69 – David A. Land, SN, Wichita, KS – ATC-151-5 (Chuong Thien)
04/21/69 – Thomas W. Gaudet, EN3, Salem, NH – ATC-151-3 (Chuong Thien)
06/01/69 – Iris H. Harrington, EN3, Iowa, LA – ATC-151-1 (Long An)
01/21/70 – Ronald S. Athanasiou, BM3, Jacksonville, TX – ATC-151-36 (Hua Nghai)
01/21/70 – James C. Baumer, ENFN, Huron, OH – ATC-151-36 (Hua Nghai)

### River Assault Squadron 15 – River Assault Division 152
12/27/68 – Barry M. Barber, SN, Las Vegas, NV – ATC-152-10 (Kien Giang)
02/28/69 – William A. Hanna, BM2, Ft. Smith, AR – ATC-152-3 (Vinh Long)

### River Division 595/River Assault Division 153
12/11/69 – Larry R. Dameron, BM3, Burlington, NC – ASPB-153-6849 (Tay Ninh)
12/11/69 – Joseph F. Benak, FN, Jupiter, FL – ASPB-153-6849 (Tay Ninh)
08/23/70 – James R. Hunt, QMC, Columbus, IN – PO – ASPB-153-? (Go Cong)
11/04/70 – Bruce C. Hunt, EN3, South Pasadena, CA – ATC-153-2 (An Xuyen)

### USS Askari (ARL-30)
12/03/67 – John R. Ruoho, MR1, Florence, WI (Off Shore)
07/21/70 – Scott F. Wemette, DCFN, Malone, NY (An Giang)

### USS Benewah (APB-35)
05/24/67 – Sandy M. Rivers, SN, Philadelphia, PA (Phuoc Tuy)
11/28/69 – Michael L. Ferguson, RD1, Rockwood, TN (Kien Phong)
11/11/70 – John E. Hollis, SN, Apple Spring, TX (Kien Phong)

### USS Colleton (APB-36)
05/03/69 – Edward N. Barr, SN, Brevig Mission, AK (Kien Hoa)

### USS Krishna (ARL-38)
07/01/69 – Richard Garza Jr., SFP3, San Jose, CA (Kien Giang)

### USS Tom Green County (LST-1159)
11/29/66 – Stephen C. Sharp, FN, Houston, TX (Quang Nam)
01/21/69 – Ray L. Sharp, CS2, Ridgeway, MI (Bien Hoa)
01/21/69 – Raymond J. Krekelberg, CSSN, St. Paul, MN (Bien Hoa)

### USS Mercer (APB-39)
11/22/68 – Thomas E. Sheppard, CSC, Lake Worth, FL (An Giang)

### USS Nye County (LST-1067)
11/24/66 – James R. Willeford, SA, Hartford, IL (Thua Thien)

### USS Outagamie County (LST-1073)
08/27/67 – James E. Young, FA, Houston, TX (Quang Tri)

### USS Westchester County (LST-1167)
05/10/65 – Dudley W. Mayo, SN, Bellflower, CA (South China Sea)
11/01/68 – Rodney W. Peters, RMC, Grants Pass, OR (Go Cong)
11/01/68 – Anthony R. Torcivia, CS1, Easton, PA (Go Cong)
11/01/68 – Richard C. Cartwright, SK1, Jamestown, OH (Go Cong)
11/01/68 – Aristotoles D.R. Ibanez, SK1, Cavite City, Philippines (Go Cong)
11/01/68 – David G. Fell, PN1, Van Wert, OH (Go Cong)
11/01/68 – Jerry S. Leonard, YN1, Greensboro, NC (Go Cong)
11/01/68 – Chester D. Dale, QM2, Capitan, NM (Go Cong)
11/01/68 – Thomas G. Funke, ETN2, Coeur D Alene, ID (Go Cong)
11/01/68 – Thomas H. Smith, QM2, Markesan, WI (Go Cong)
11/01/68 – Floyd W. Houghtaling III, QM3, Canajoharic, NY (Go Cong)
11/01/68 – Keith W. Duffy, RD3, Yonkers, NY (Go Cong)
11/01/68 – Gerald E.B. Hamm, RM3, Camden, AR (Go Cong)
11/01/68 – Joseph A. Miller Jr., RM3, Lebanon, PA (Go Cong)
11/01/68 – Reinhard J. Schnurrer Jr., RM3, St. Paul, MN (Go Cong)
11/01/68 – Cary F. Rundle, YN3, Aldan, PA (Go Cong)
11/01/68 – Timothy C. Dunning, SMSN, Santa Ana, CA (Go Cong)
11/01/68 – Jackie C. Carter, SA, San Jose, CA (Go Cong)

### CTF – 194 Commander Naval Forces Vietnam

### CTG – 194.9 Commander River Patrol Forces (Staff)
01/08/70 – James C. Mitchell Jr., EM1, Torrance, CA (Kien Giang) UH1B Helicopter

### CTU 194.9.7 Riverine Strike Group
09/25/69 – Lonnie R. Parker, FN, Bessemer, AL (Gia Dinh) USS Benewah (APB-35) Nha Be River

# SPECIAL STORIES

*Photo courtesy of Dan Dodd, Official Navy Photographer for ComRivFlot-One MRF TF-117 68-69, Retired Chief Photographers Mate.*

# Military Police Operations in the Mobile Riverine Force's Area of Operations 1967-1968

*by Louis J.M. "Joe" Carson*

Vietnam redefined the mission of the military police in the combat zone. Before Vietnam in a typical combat zone, the military police were charged with the security behind the MLR (main line of resistance) commonly known as "the front."

But as we are all well aware there were no front lines in Vietnam and consequently military police resources were usually stretched to the max. The 9th Infantry Division had one organic military police company as did all Army infantry divisions. The 9th Military Police Company was made up of four platoons with a headquarters section, motor pool section with an assortment of trucks and gun jeeps mounted with M-60 machine guns. The divisions TO&E stated: at the discretion of division commanding general, the MP company can be used as infantry. Because of the nature of the war in Vietnam, the line between many non-combat MOSs and actually being involved in combat operations became somewhat blurred. At the jungle warfare school at Bearcat one of the infantry S.F.C.s conducting one of the classes asked a group of troopers what were their MOSs. Only one young trooper answered 11 Bravo. The S.F.C. vented his anger by saying, "No, no, no. This is Vietnam and this is the 9th Infantry Division. You were all trained as basic infantrymen. You all will be expected to defend the camps your assigned to, the convoys you ride in and your buddies and yourself anytime you're outside the camps."

During its early deployment, the 9th MP Company retained its headquarters and two platoons at Bearcat, one platoon was detached to Tan An and the remaining platoon, 2nd Platoon, was detached to the 2nd Brigade as part of the Mobile Riverine Force's area of operations and its supply lines. Many people are not aware that the American Army did not have POW camps in Vietnam. If a Viet Cong or NVA soldier was captured, he was processed through our detainee compound either at Dong Tam or on the detainee barge that accompanied the MRF of operations. If the detainee was brought in because he was suspected of being a VC or NVA he could only be detained three days before being released. During this time, the military intelligence team questioned him to try to determine his status. Anyone brought in as a regular VC or NVA

*Two scout dogs at the MP detainee compound at Dong Tam. The scout dog handlers would sometimes bring their dogs over to the compound to get the scent of the VC detainees.*

soldier was passed on to the ARVN 7th Division Headquarters after the MI team questioned them.

The International Red Cross inspected the detainee compound at Dong Tam to be sure the detainees were being properly treated and were receiving their native meal at least once a day, of rice and fish, to supplement the c-rations we gave them. We all knew in our hearts that our POWs in North Vietnam were not being treated this way and they weren't getting steak and potatoes once a day (our native meal). In most military police units discipline, law and order is usually its primary function. Fortunately at Dong Tam everyone was too busy to get into much trouble. Plus the nightly mortar and rocket attacks kept overnight mischief to a minimum.

One unique facet of the military police duties at Dong Tam and other camps was security escort for the combat engineers' early morning mine and booby-trap sweep detail. The MPs would supply an M-60 gun jeep with three MPs, and the combat engineers would supply two to four men with mine detectors to sweep the road for three to four klics from Dong Tam, where we were supposed to meet the ARVNs sweeping the road in the opposite direction. The first morning after arriving at Dong Tam, I was placed on the mine sweep detail. As the sun slowly crept over the horizon, we started down the road from the main entrance to Dong Tam toward My Tho, one MP driver and one MP on the M-60 and myself walking with the combat engineers to cover their backs from snipers so they could devote their undivided attention to ferreting out the ingenious ways the VC tried to conceal their mines and booby traps. On this morning, a staff sergeant working one of the mine detectors told everyone to stop, he had something. He told everyone to go back behind the gun jeep that was trailing us by 50 meters. I told him I was supposed to watch his back and I couldn't do it from 50 meters down the road. All he said was, "It's your funeral," and turned around and started probing the area he suspected. After what seemed like an eternity of probing he finally found an old c-ration can. When he turned around, I think he was surprised to still see me standing there. With a visible sign of relief on his face, he said, "I guess if we are the combat engineers that makes you guys the combat cops."

Convoy escort and security was another function that fell to the military police with usually one or two gun jeeps escorting the convoys between the camps.

As Dong Tam grew from a small fire support base to a full brigade size camp, so did the military police's role. To help build and support the camp many local Vietnamese were hired, which meant they all had to be searched every morning going into Dong

*Sgt. Joe Carson behind M-60, CPL Newan standing in driver's seat, SPC Hunsberger walking between truck and gun jeep. Two MP gun jeeps getting ready to escort ammo convoy from Dong Tam to fire support base.*

*Group of detainees brought in by helicopter (departing in the background) to the MP detainee compound. The U.S. Army did not hold POWs during the Vietnam War. We could only detainee a Vietnamese for three days in which time military intelligence had to classify them as innocent civilians and they were released or classify them as POWs after which we transported them to My Tho and turned them over to the ARVNs. If they had been captured during a fight, classification wasn't a problem. But if they were only suspects, didn't have an identity card, etc., then the M.I. detachment classified them.*

Tam and every evening when they left. Combined operations with the Vietnamese National Police and ARVN MPs throughout the MRF's AO became common. Usually operations consisted of four or more MPs and a dozen or so of Vietnamese National Police or ARVN MPs being taken by an LCI to a village where a thorough search was done. These operations many times resulted in the discovery of munitions, contraband, VC suspects and documents for military intelligence. As more troops were deployed to Dong Tam, I was appointed provost marshall investigator for the MRF's AO. The provost marshall investigator's job was to investigate any violations of the uniform code of military justice and on more serious offenses take care of the preliminary investigation until a CID officer could arrive from Bearcat. The use of drugs in Vietnam by the American Army is still the subject of great debate. I can say unequivocally that during my time with the 9th MP Company, both as an NCO and a provost marshall investigator, this was not the case.

There were a few cases we investigated during this time and most of these were cases where men in the offenders' own unit turned them in, obviously not wanting to be out on an operation with someone impaired. An army is only a reflection of the society it represents and, as drug use became more prevalent in our civilian society at home, I would have to suspect so did its use in Vietnam during the later stages of the war. The American society I left in 1965, when I enlisted in the Army, was not the same American society I returned to in 1968.

## OPERATION STABLE DOOR, CTF 115.9
*by Rudd Cunningham*

There are many aspects in the history of a Naval Unit. Taken alone most are as dry and dull as a popcorn fart during 'water hours.' Combined they give a reader the flavor of what occurred.

### 1966

Inshore Undersea Warfare Group ONE, Western Pacific Detachment (IUWG-1, WESTPACDET) was established on 15 November and designated Operation STABLE DOOR(CTG 115.9). Operational control was under Commander Coastal Surveillance Force (Combined Task Force (CTF) 115), Vietnam, Operation MARKET TIME.

The STABLE DOOR assigned mission to: "Conduct harbor patrols and surveillance operations as directed in order to protect friendly shipping and military vessels within the assigned harbors from attack by enemy sneak craft, swimmers, sabotage, and other threats."

The first Commanding Officer was LCDR L. S. MARSH, USN. Initial strength was 27 officers and 437 enlisted.

MIUWS ELEVEN and THIRTEEN deployed from Group ONE, Long Beach, California to Cam Ranh Bay and Vung Tau respectively.

MIUWS TWENTY-TWO and TWENTY-THREE deployed from Group TWO, Little Creek, Virginia to Nha Trang and Qui Nhon respectively.

*HECP personnel with U.S. detainee. "Don't these people own uniforms?"*

Basic units consisted of Mobile Inshore Undersea Warfare Surveillance Units (MIUWS) and Harbor Patrol Elements.

Harbor Patrol Elements utilized Landing Craft, Personnel Light(LCPL). The 36' boats were outfitted with fore and aft M2 .50 calibre machine guns, RADAR, portable searchlights, high frequency and very high frequency transceivers. Quarter-pound concussion grenades, 1 pound TNT blocks, Mark 40 depth charges, hand-held flares, and 12 gauge fleshette rounds were the primary anti-swimmer devices.

On 21 November the first group of Southeast Asia Semi-permanent Harbor Patrol(SEASHARP) personnel deployed from Little Creek, Virginia.

First to turn over was Qui Nhon. The Harbor Patrol Unit and Harbor Entrance Control Point(HECP) were integrated into one group and designated Unit THREE. Explosive Ordnance Team(EOD) 20 was assigned with the tasks:

1) daily anchor chain and hull inspections.

2) render safe any explosive devices as requested by higher authority.

3) salvage operations when requested by other commands on a not-to-interfere with primary mission basis.

December 9th SEASHARP and EOD Team 22 relieved MIUWS 11, and Cam Ranh Bay became Unit TWO.

### 1967

In January, 16 foot Boston Whalers(Skimmers) augmented the PLs. The high speed and shallow draft of the civilian craft made them ideal for inner harbor patrol, amphibious infiltration and exfiltration, and as a quick reaction force. In addition to personal small arms and antiswimmer devices, skimmers were armed with the M60 .30 calibre machine gun.

SEASHARP and EOD Team 23 replaced MIUWS 22 as Unit FOUR at Nha Trang on 22 January.

MIUWS 13 turned over operations to Unit ONE at Vung Tau On 13 February 1967. Two weeks later the Royal Australian Navy Clearance Diving Team THREE was assigned.

In May Picket Boats were added to patrol elements. The 45 foot , twin engine, wooded craft had longer endurance, greater seakeeping ability, and improved habitability. Armed amidship with a twin 50 mount they were well suited for patrolling outer harbors.

During August, in conjunction with COMNAVFORV, COMINEDIV 93, and MINERON 11, a plan was developed to position Mine Sweeper Boats (MSB) at Cam Ranh Bay. OpCon under Unit TWO they would conduct routine, periodic sweeps of Stable Door harbors.

### 1968

Unit Five was established in February. Years earlier a battle known as the "Vung Ro incident" established the need for Operation MARKET TIME. The unit was hard pressed by enemy forces.

For his part the enemy improved the quality of his efforts. Highly trained NVA swimmer/sapper teams infiltrated the Republic of Vietnam to employ extremely sophisticated methodology.

Understanding the increasing nature of the threat, units commenced rear action defense tactics. Expanded patrol areas, waterborne ambushes, and shoreline reconnaissance were initiated to deny access to the enemy. STABLE DOOR sailors worked closely with U.S. Army Special Forces and Republic of Korea units to maximize the pressure on the enemy.

The effectiveness of these special ops was evidenced by the violence of the enemy's increased retaliations.

On June 6, a mortar and rocket barrage covered the approach of elements of the 30th VC Main Force Battalion. The two prong infantry assault succeeded. Unit FIVE was overrun. The unit continued its' mission despite the attacks on it. During one such attack in November an estimated 40 mortar rounds hit the tiny unit.

In the Christmas attack, sappers infiltrated the Qui Nhon MARKET TIME base. Bypassing the Swifties, chiefs, and officers quarters, the fight was initiated by attacking the harbor patrol barracks.

### 1969

In January the U.S. Army assumed harbor defense responsibilities for Vung Ro.

WestPacDet's vigilance and commitment to carry the war to the enemy's hidden strongholds countered attacks through out STABLE DOOR.

The need for specialized training in land warfare to minimize casualties became apparent. Early in the year Unit THREE personnel became the first naval graduates of the MACV, 5th Special Forces Group RECONDO school in Nha Trang.

Volunteers soon filled the training programs begun at the units. By early spring the naval LRRPs were hampering the enemy's ability to move freely. The position of Sniper was incorporated into the recon team. This adaptation added the obvious offensive strike capability and increased its' overall defensive posture.

One unique evolution, HECP personnel regularly flew backseat with the U.S. Army 203rd Reconnaissance(Hawkeye) Squadron.

The First Swimmer Defense Doctrine was produced in June . Its' detailed Standard Operating Procedures led to the publication of <u>COUNTERING THE SWIMMER/SAPPER</u>.

### 1970

23 Jan as part of President Nixon's plan to pull out of the conflict, STABLE DOOR was ordered to commence Accelerated Turnover to Vietnamese(ACTOV). A proposed Task, Organization, and Equipment for Vietnamese Navy Harbor Defense was approved by COMNAVFORV and the Vietnamese Chief of Naval Operations. "Load list" for patrol craft and on-site training programs were drawn up.

This was in addition to operational commitments. For his part, the enemy intensified his efforts to attack shipping in STABLE DOOR ports/harbors.

15 June Unit THREE turned over.
1 July Unit FOUR turned over.
1 September Unit ONE turned over the harbor Patrol element.
25 November, remaining elements of STABLE DOOR turned over. Albeit brief, Inshore Undersea Warfare Group ONE, Western Pacific Detachment performed in the highest traditions of Naval service.

### CAMPAIGNS

During its' activation Inshore Undersea Warfare Group ONE, Western Pacific Detachment took part in eleven of the war's seventeen campaigns. They were:

Vietnamese Counteroffensive Phase II
Vietnamese Counteroffensive Phase III
Tet Counteroffensive
Vietnamese Counteroffensive Phase IV
Vietnamese Counteroffensive Phase V
Vietnamese Counteroffensive Phase VI
Tet 69/Counteroffensive
Vietnam Summer-Fall 1969
Vietnam Winter-Spring 1970
Sanctuary Counteroffensive
Vietnamese Counteroffensive Phase VII

### Tribute to LTC William W. Poole Jr.

Lieutenant Commander William W. Poole Jr. (SS), USN, commanding officer of Unit THREE was typical of WestPacDet's unit commanders.

Enlisting in 1940, he served as gunnersmate and mineman aboard diesel-electric boats out of Manila, Perth, Mare Island and Pearl Harbor. He was an "old salt" before most of his command was born.

Commissioned in 1961 as a limited duty officer (ordnance), he was a tough weather-beaten image of a Naval officer. The welfare and safety of his men were paramount to him.

The old man never drank. One night I asked him about it. He said, "I like to have a drink. But I don't want even one beer in me when I have to make a decision that can cost someone his life." His leadership taught: you can delegate authority, but you can never relinquish responsibility.

### MAY THEY REST IN PEACE...
Undersea Warfare Group ONE (I.U.W.G.-1),
Western Pacific Detachment
"There is a port of no return ..."
Seaman Daniel Eugene Moore Jr., USN, 22 February 1967
Boatswainmate Third Terry Lee Davis, USN, 24 February 1967
Seaman Michael Joseph Dinapoli, USN, 23 December 1967
Signalman Second Donald Francis McDowell, USN, 26 December 1967
Radarman Second Anthony Barton Brown, USN, 6 June 1968
Radioman Second Thomas James Meenan, USN, 6 June 1968
Electronics Repairman Second Norman Laforest McKenny, USN, 6 June 1968
Lieutenant (junior grade) William T. Morris III, USN, 6 June 1968
Quartermaster Second Howard Frank Burnes, USN, 11 August 1968
Signalman Second Robert Louis Bouchet, USN, 11 August 1968
Gunnersmate Third Herman A. Miller II, USN, 11 August 1968
Quartermaster Third Delbert Leo Singler Jr., USN, 3 March 1969
Sonar Technician First Freddie Leslie Tapper, USN, 27 September 1970

"Sailor, rest your oar ..."

## THE LAST AMERICAN PIRATE
*by Herschel Hughes, Jr.*

Today, Captiva Island, just off southwest Florida, is the site of carefree getaway vacations, but its name reveals its darker, much romanticized connection with ferocious pirates of the Caribbean and Gulf of Mexico. This island is where history and legend has it that pirates, like Jose Gaspar, repaired their war-torn ships and imprisoned beautiful female captives.

Until now, no one has even suspected that right in the middle of the Vietnam War, between tense combat operations, one final act of piracy by an American sailor was perpetrated, one more beautiful female captive was taken – not just taken, but invited to dance for the ship's crew! This is the story of that sailor, the story of the last American pirate.

One winter afternoon of 1968-69, this sailor was tasked to take his captain's gig ashore to the division headquarters at Dong Tam, to check on some work being done ashore for the ship. Upon arriving at the dock there stood a most remarkable and unexpected sight – a tall, young and beautiful western woman. In stark and poetic contrast, a burley, unshaved midget accompanied her. Well, a beautiful, buxom, western woman and a midget were the two most unlikely objects to find on a Dong Tam dock. They were entertainers, she a singer/dancer and he her drummer, both from Australia, sent down to the USS *Benewah* by the special services officer to put on a show.

Now, this was the "pre-TQL" Navy. For those folks who stayed in the Navy into the '90s and have taken Total Quality Leadership courses, you have been informed that we are all on the same team. The crews from our sister ships are patriotic Americans, too. As good "TQL-ers," we don't compete with other ships' crews for scarce resources anymore! But this was before that, when we did compete, vigorously, with other ships for scarce resources, and beautiful, buxom western women were extremely scarce in the

*LCPLs prowled the waters in and around five ports in Vietnam. The turbo-charged diesel was capable of 25 knots.*

MRF. In addition, the *Benewah* was our commodore's flagship, which is like being "teacher's pet" because we already thought they were the favored ship.

Alas, this young sailor was NOT from the *Benewah*, but WAS from a ship that looked like the *Benewah*; in fact, only one number painted black on the dark green bows distinguished them at all. Within a flash, this otherwise honorable "officer and gentleman" made his decision to carry out an act of piracy. He told the buxom lass and her short friend he would gladly take them to his ship, the "Benewah," and with a nod to his coxswain gave the order, "Take us back to our ship, coxswain!" At that point, the lass and the midget were technically captives.

The entertainers were happily bound for the "Benewah," while this young pirate was anxiously laying the groundwork for the next phase of the plan. Washington in all his glory did not cross the Delaware with more sense of mission than this young officer brought his newly found treasure across the Mekong River to where the ships lay anchored. As the gig arrived alongside the pontoon that served as the ship's loading dock, little difficulty was found getting dock space as shipmates, and the embarked boat crews, became aware of his cargo. After firmly assuring the bug-eyed quarterdeck watch that "No official measurements of anything were needed for the ship's log," the young pirate escorted the lady and her drummer to the wardroom. He quickly moved to put his plan into place. The trickiest part would be handling the captain. It was this young officer's job to know the ship's operations well in advance, and a special service show of this "magnitude" would certainly have been well planned and the skipper briefed.

Swallowing his pride, the rookie pirate lied to his deeply respected CO for the first and only time. Confessing he had somehow missed the ball on this one, he informed his captain that special services had, for some reason, sent us a show.

"Does the skipper want me to sent her away?" the sailor asked.
"Where is she?" responded the CO.
"She's in the wardroom, sir."
"Perhaps I should go meet her?"
"I think it would be worth your time, sir."

The plan was in the bag the second the skipper laid eyes on her. This fine captain had never been known to move about his ship with any clumsiness whatsoever, but as he made visual contact with this young lady's most prominent features, he tripped over the threshold of his own wardroom door. Following introductions, the skipper ordered work to stop and a "Tango" boat with a flight deck be requested to tie up amidships to function as the stage. The sailors and soldiers could "man the rail" on all decks on the starboard side for the show.

Perhaps the show would have had a little more "atmosphere" in a darkened nightclub, but the young lady and her drummer put on a whale of a show that afternoon. Most of the crew had not seen a western woman for six months, some close to 10 or 12. This lady from Australia was a sight for sore eyes. It was a reminder that home still existed where, hopefully, we would return soon. After the show, the "hostages" were thanked and taken back to the post at Dong Tam.

Somewhere in Australia is a retired singer/dancer and her drummer who have fond memories of their performance on the "Benewah." Now you know they never made it to the Benewah, because they were victims of the last American pirate. To the crew of the *Benewah* and their embarked troops, this old retired pirate will try to make it up to you at some future reunion. But to his faithful shipmates, you know I did this for you, God bless you all. And if those old *Benewah* sailors, who never took any TQL courses, catch up with me and do me in, shipmates, just scatter my ashes…well…how about on Captiva Island!

## A DAY REMEMBERED
*by Raymond W. "Padre" Johnson*

Rach Gia River, June 19, 1967
previously published in *River Currents*, A Publication of the
Mobile Riverine Force Association
Volume 1, Number 5, Summer 1994

Chaplain Raymond W. "Padre" Johnson will always remember June 19, 1967 as his longest day.

Ray "Padre" Johnson was the first U.S. Navy chaplain for the men of River Assault Flotilla One – Task Force 117. Due to his earlier medical background, he was assigned to accompany each field mission in a field medical capacity and as chaplain. He also recalls the frequent "eyeball to eyeball" range of Mekong Delta Riverine warfare.

During Chaplain Johnson's tour of duty in Vietnam, he wrote many letters to his family and friends. They weren't your ordinary letters. The letters provided "a uniquely believable and candid insight into the situation in Vietnam."

Although the letters were quite personal (not intended for publication), Chaplain Johnson's insight gave a very moving account of the war. He was consequently persuaded to release them for publication combined with an extensive narrative into the sights and sounds of this far-away field of combat. A selection was made from the magnitude of letters and in 1968 they were published by the Fleming H. Revell Company of Westwood, NJ, under the title: "Postmark: Mekong Delta."

Johnson recalls a time when he was on a medevac boat working its way through the narrow, twisting tributaries of the Rach Gia River. "Company A of the 4th Battalion, 47th Infantry, 2nd Brigade of the 9th Infantry Division, was on our right, about to leave the semi-shelter of a sporadic tree line for a few hundred yards of open rice paddies."

The intelligence reports which were circulated depicted the area as having a small force of guerrillas in the immediate vicinity, nothing of any threatening size. The reports weren't accurate.

Our unsuspecting soldiers weren't aware of the 1,000 hardcore Viet Cong that moved into ambush positions in the area during the previous night. Johnson describes what happened to A Company. "Suddenly, the VC opened up from an L-shaped tree line with machine guns and recoilless rifles – unbelievably accurate fire." They were trapped, caught in the open being cut down like sickled weeds. The fighting was "… just too unreal to grasp. I had had firsthand experience with the fury of action, but nothing like this!"

The intense firefight wasn't an isolated incident. It turned into a battle involving hundreds of men. Navy monitors of the Mobile Riverine Force moved into positions against the heavily fortified bunkers and Air Force dive bombers used tactics to support the troops on the ground.

The air was filled with artillery smoke. Somehow a wounded radioman attempted to make his way towards the medical aid boat. He was hit again. Chaplain Johnson will never forget the look on his face as he reached for help. It was simply a matter of instinctive reflex. "I left the boat and somehow was able to carry him back toward the semi-protection of our aid facility. While I was giving him medical assistance, he informed me that all of the platoon leaders and medics were either dead or seriously wounded. The battle was unmerciful. No one dared to venture out or even move." The wounded soldiers were in desperate need, many were bleeding to death. Three major areas of serious casualties were identified by the wounded soldier. Chaplain Johnson realized that someone was going to have to reach the wounded. With a silent prayer in his soul for the dead and wounded Army and Navy casualties reported, he asked for volunteers to assist.

Under heavy cover fire from their gunboat, two members of the boat crew, another man named Johnson and Dosell, volunteered to help Chaplain Johnson to evacuate the wounded. They zigzagged their way toward the mass of wounded and dead.

During their first attempt, the three brave men managed to crawl through the heavy gunfire and explosions to the protection of a dike. At that point, Chaplain Johnson realized that he had been hit in the legs and flak vest, ripping away the sleeve on his left arm. After he compressed the bleeding of his left thigh, he made a judgement that his wounds were not serious enough to prevent him from continuing his original purpose.

Before attempting to reach more of the wounded, Chaplain Johnson tried to orient himself in mapping out a strategy. He felt a huge thud. "It felt like the wallop of a baseball bat" against his chest and resulted in two cracked ribs. He was covered so heavily with mud that he failed to notice the entrance of the missile through the zipper lining of his flak vest. The missile was stopped by his New Testament, which for the first time, he stuffed into his pocket prior to battle. When he recovered, he directed his stretcher-bearers toward a group of wounded soldiers that were huddled behind a mound of mud.

The volunteers had to run 75 yards through open terrain. Chaplain Johnson and others watching remember the mud kicking in front of him and along his left side as the VC failed to connect.

Chaplain Johnson attended the wounded and then decided to carry the two most seriously wounded by stretcher back to the medevac boat.

Johnson and one of the soldiers who was not wounded carried one stretcher while Chaplain Johnson and Dosell carried the other. The stretcher-bearers were faced with a 200-plus-yard dash-and-carry. "It seemed like an eternity" as they made their way back through the mud. "I shall never forget the wounded men's eyes and 'Thank God!' and their expressions of thanks when we reached the medevac boat."

To help them return, the boats of the Mobile Riverine Force unleashed a wall of heavy gunfire support which aided immensely in reducing Charlie's accuracy, securing their safety. On their way to the medevac boat, Chaplain Johnson noticed another soldier trying to move and who also needed immediate help. The chaplain shouted, "Play dead," and assured the soldier he would return. After the chaplain's third return to the wounded, he collapsed, checked his wounds and vomited.

It didn't take long to fill up the medevac boat with wounded soldiers and sailors. The dismal sight continued. While the wounded awaited evacuation, four helicopters were shot down, one exploded during its valiant attempt to evacuate the wounded.

More rescue parties were encouraged to form and engaged in a "… daring and miraculously successful attempt to clear the field of the seriously wounded …" because of Chaplain Johnson's medical intervention and successful rescue attempts (quoted from Chaplain Johnson's Silver Star Citation).

It was obvious that more aid was needed. Chaplain Johnson went back in the battlefield with his medical aid kit, helmet and punctured flak vest. He continued to help others by providing medical support and words of encouragement and assurance into the night. He refused to be evacuated because of the short supply of medical assistance.

While reading Chaplain Johnson's account of that day in June, 1967, it wasn't hard to understand his expressed emotions. It seemed like he was near his destiny. "Twice men were hit while I was rendering them assistance…right beside me. That close!" stated Chaplain Johnson.

Commanding Officer Ray Riesco, who was taking continuous bunker fire to his own boat, said that each time he watched the chaplain move back into the field, he felt that the chaplain would not return. Yet, each time he did return – and stayed to help at the boat before once again returning to the field. It seemed impossible! He must have had two angels protecting and guiding him.

This operation was dubbed Concordia I. It was detailed in both Time and Newsweek magazines and in the award-winning book, "Brown Water Black Beret," by Thomas J. Cutler, LCDR, USN, and the Naval Institute Press, 1988.

The battle lasted through the night; it continued for two more days. Many lives were lost. Cutler wrote, "The final casualty counts

listed 46 Americans killed and approximately 150 wounded. The Viet Cong left 255 dead on the battlefield … as a result of the engagement, the Viet Cong were rendered ineffective in Long An Province for more than a year."

In recognition of his outstanding service in Vietnam, Chaplain Johnson received two Purple Hearts, two Silver Stars, the Legion of Merit with Valor and the Vietnamese Cross of Gallantry. In January 1969, he was honored as one of the Ten Outstanding Young Men of America by the U.S. Jaycees. This honor was given in recognition of his service to the men of River Assault Flotilla One, the Vietnamese people and the writing of his book, "Postmark: Mekong Delta." In previous years, this honor was given to such notables as John F. Kennedy, Leonard Bernstein, Orson Welles and Henry Kissinger.

During my recent conversation with Chaplain Johnson, I agree that he was given an extension in life beyond Vietnam, in order that he could complete his recent 15-year research project and exploration with the people of 159 nations. The entire journey is recorded in his new book, "Journeys with the Global Family." This book provides an insight into his personal philosophy, life, historical insights and excellent photo-reproductions of over 500 portraits of the people he lived with during this 15-year period. The 500 portraits are recorded on 25 regional paintings that premiered at the United Nations, in December 1992, and are currently on tour throughout America and in selected overseas cities. The exhibition is entitled, "Faces of the Global Human Family." It will eventually return to the United Nations as part of their permanent collection.

*About Ray "Padre" Johnson:* International author, art critic and United Nations historian, Dr. Noel Brown, writes in his biographical presentation of Padre Johnson that "Padre has truly lived the adventure of the renaissance man in our time." He further writes, "To understand the natural spirit of freedom and breathing quality in Padre's unique forms of art creativity and written insights, you have to appreciate the influence that his unusual range of life events and job descriptions had in shaping the quality of his present artistic and written accomplishments."

Some of these influences include drawing portraits at the age of 10 with unusual likeness, living the life of an authentic working cowboy with a number of major Wyoming and Montana ranching outfits, laboring as a blue-collar worker in heavy construction and industry, competing as a very successful college athlete, working as an emergency room medical technician, serving as an ordained Lutheran Church in America pastor, holding state and national leadership positions in government and human services and being the recipient of advanced degrees in theology and cultural anthropology as well as many achievement awards in recognition of his art, humanitarian and written accomplishments.

## ATTACK OF ADVANCED TACTICAL SUPPORT BASE SONG ONG DOC ON NIGHT OF OCT. 20, 1970
*by Ron Mitchell*

We (Tango-3) were on patrol a few clicks up river when we saw a good-size explosion followed by a huge one (the float that held all the fuel drums). This was followed right away by a lot of radio traffic and at that point we turned back toward the base as fast (6 knots?) as our boat would go.

By the time we arrived the two boats that didn't go out that night had loaded up as many of the support personnel as they could carry, dropped their lines and headed out to mid-river to return fire, which was coming from both banks and also from the village of Song Ong Doc.

*Advanced Tactical Support Base Song Ong Doc under attack on Oct. 20, 1970.*

*In spite of Advanced Tactical Support Base Song Ong Doc being destroyed, the American flag did not burn.*

*Advanced Tactical Support Base Song Ong Doc the day after it was attacked on Oct. 20, 1970, note the American flag still flying.*

Seawolves and OV-10s along with a few Cobras were in the air raining rockets and minigun fire on both sides of the river. Our boat captain elected to pull alongside the float as we saw probably a dozen or more guys, some wounded, waiting for their turn to get off. As I remember we took off the last load of wounded and those that were tending them.

There was an LST off the coast and that's where we took them. A Tango boat isn't the best way to quickly evacuate wounded on a stretcher but we were the last chance these guys had and we got the job done.

The intention was to stay alongside the LST that night but the sea was too rough and would have taken our decks off if we stayed much longer, so back to the ATSB we went and kept a real sharp eye until daylight when some ARVNs were inserted.

United States Navy
for service as set forth in the following
CITATION:

"For professional achievement while serving with friendly foreign forces engaged in armed conflict against the North Vietnamese and Viet Cong communist aggressors in the Republic of Vietnam from May 1970 to April 1971. While serving as a gunner in River Assault Squadron One Five, Seaman Mitchell participated in 60 combat patrols and engaged the enemy on two occasions. During those patrols, he boarded and searched numerous junks and sampans, interdicted cross-river traffic, enforced curfew, inserted and extracted friendly forces in hostile territory and provided fire support for besieged units and outposts. His technical knowledge and long, arduous hours including a particularly strenuous period during Operation Breezy Cove were directly responsible for the constant state of readiness of his river assault craft. On 20 October 1970, Seaman Mitchell was on routine night patrol when his craft went to the assistance of Advanced Tactical Support Base Song Ong Doc which was under mortar, rocket and heavy automatic weapons fire. He assisted in the evacuation of base personnel and rendered medical treatment to wounded persons in his craft. Later serving on the Staff of Commander Coastal Surveillance Force, he handled supplies and maintained vehicles belonging to that command. Seaman Mitchell's exemplary professionalism, devotion to duty and courage under fire were in keeping with the highest traditions of the United States Naval Service."

The Combat Distinguishing Device is authorized.
For the Secretary of the Navy

## Reunited After 35 Years
*by Robert Daniel Pawlicki*

March 1967. As they stepped aboard Tango 111-11, it would be the first time that Robert Daniel "Polak" Pawlicki and Herman Michael "Mike" Hall would meet.

From March through December, both teens were in charge of the boat's .50-caliber machine guns: Mike was on the starboard while Polak was on the port. They protected the boat and its crewmen. They became friends, sharing many tragedies and also some good times. On December 22, as they came in from patrol, they were informed to pack their bags. They were finally going home.

Celebrating Christmas with their families, they realized they knew little about each other, only that Polak was from Detroit and Mike was from somewhere in Louisiana. As the years passed, both men often thought about each other but were unable to make contact.

On September 11, 2001, lives in America were changed forever, and our country reunited. For the two teens of Tango 111-11, fate would bring about their reunion as well.

*Bob Pawlicki, third from left, and Mike Hall, fourth from left; Tango 111-11; 1967.*

*Bob Pawlicki, left, and Mike Hall, right, reunited after 35 years; 2002.*

Mike had been working for the U.S. Border Patrol most of his life following the military. In October, as security across the nation increased, he was sent to Port Huron to patrol the Bluewater Bridge that connects Michigan and Canada. He returned again in January for the entire month. During Mike's assignment, he thought about his friend from Detroit, but not knowing the correct spelling of his name, was unable to locate him.

When Mike returned home in February, he got online and clicked on a link that brought up the MRFA site. He was unaware that the Mobile Riverine Force Association even existed. As he reviewed the site, he came across a board member who was on Tango 111-11. It was Robert Pawlicki. Staring him right in the face was his address and phone number. He resides in Port Huron with his family. Mike contacted Bob and a friendship that began 35 years ago was excitedly renewed. They met in August when Mike returned to Port Huron on assignment. It was an emotional reunion between two teens who once covered each other's back on the river…between two men who can now share their experiences and a lifetime friendship as well.

## Snoopy's Nose
*by Robert Daniel Pawlicki*

On Sept. 15, 1967 (my birthday), I was manning a .50-caliber machine gun on one of several Attack Troop Carriers of the Task Force 117.2 as part of Operation Snoopy's Nose. We were to insert several Marine troops deep in the Rach Ba Rai River in the Mekong Delta. As the boats moved toward the landing area, the lead boat began taking heavy fire from machine guns and RPGs from both

*Army going out on patrol, 1967*

*Observation chopper coming in for a landing.*

*Medevac taking out wounded, 1967.*

sides of the river. I began firing at muzzle flashes on shore thinking that we were all going to die.

I saw VC running towards the river and I concentrated my fire on them. I could hear explosions, metal tearing and shrapnel whizzing by. We were getting pounded from both sides of the river and smoke filled the area making it impossible to see. Boats were running into one another and into the shore. The order was given to regroup down river.

There were already a lot of casualties and we were going to go back again. Over the radio came a plea for help as this boat was returning from the ambush. We could hear the explosions and the man on the radio was fleeing for his life and screaming that everyone was dead. When this boat stopped we were ordered to come alongside the craft. I jumped on board the other boat and what I saw terrified me. The port .50-caliber was hit with a rocket blowing a hole through both sides of the mount and spraying shrapnel all over the gun mounts.

I literally had to scrape the remains of Bill Diamond's upper torso off the walls of the mount. The water that was being pumped out was red with blood and body parts. I saw brain matter and guts splattered all over the boat. I saw an eye rolling back and forth in the red water.

The boat gun was replaced and the crew that were still alive were medevaced out and replacements were put in place. I lost two more friends during this first round. Pete Bonachi lost a leg when a rocket went through his gun mount and then got shot while being moved to the medevac. "Little" was killed when a rocket exploded and hit him in the head.

We headed back up the river and were met with a barrage of rocket fire. I was firing into the vegetation with my .50-caliber. I used the belt-fed M-79 grenade launcher, firing into the shore and trees. I had to duck quickly so that I would not get hit by shrapnel from my own grenade. There were VC running all over. At an arranged site we turned into shore to drop off the troops we were carrying. I was on hyper alert knowing that something was going to happen.

We kept our guns trained on the opposite bank to cover the landing. We backed off and headed up river to set up a perimeter.

The boat was rocked by an explosion on the starboard side. I opened up with the .50-caliber catching movement of VC off the port side. The flurry lasted a short time and I was scared to look at the other gun mounts, thinking they might have been killed. Luckily they were all right and we continued toward our patrol area.

## HAPPY NEW YEAR VIETNAM
*by Gary A. "Doc" Voelker*

My name is Gary Voelker, but in 1968 I was known as "Doc," a combat medic assigned to Red Platoon, B Company 3/47th Infantry, 9th Infantry Division, South Vietnam.

It was December 30, 1968, the day before New Year's Eve, although no one in my platoon could have told you. Holidays did not mean much in Vietnam. All that really mattered was staying alive for another day.

I was awakened by the Ell Tee, who was our platoon leader. It was Red Platoon's turn to patrol the perimeter of Tiger's Lair, our company base camp. Tiger's Lair was built by our company after we left the ships, about 30 miles south of Saigon. I rolled back over to get some extra shuteye. Although breakfast was being served, the food was not worth the lost sleep so I opted for the extra few minutes rest. I did not know then that I would need it more than ever that day.

The Ell Tee hollered "Saddle up!" and within a few minutes we were a platoon ready to fight. I carried an M-16 rifle, a .45-caliber pistol, C-rations and, of course, my aid bag. The men in my platoon carried much more weight than I did, especially the M-60 machine gunner who not only carried his weapon, the heaviest in our arsenal, but many pounds of ammo as well.

The point man started out first. It was still dark but it would be light soon. The rest of the platoon filed in behind him with the "headquarters" men (RTO, medic and platoon leader) falling in about the middle.

We made our way out of the compound, down a paved road (one of the few found in the Delta), through the ARVN compound that was next to us, through a nearby village and onto Dead Man's Trail.

Dead Man's trail got its name because the body of a dead VC was left on the trail about a fourth of a mile from the village. It began to decay quickly in the heat, and finally a woman from the village buried him. But the name Dead Man's Trail stuck.

That first quarter-mile of the trail was "safe" since the village people frequented it, but after that it was very dangerous. It was full of booby traps. If you stayed on the trail long enough an ambush was certain to happen.

Once we reached the quarter-mile mark we veered off, as we always did, to walk through the canals. It was slow and difficult going. Most of the time, the G.I. in front of you had to give you a hand up to get you out of the last canal and into the next. It was exhausting.

After a while we would come to a series of rice patties. The walking was better but much more dangerous. Once out in the middle of a patty, we were like ducks in a shooting gallery.

When we were in the jungle, the walking was much easier. The jungle gave us cover and occasionally we could use a trail if we had a good point man that could spot booby traps and on this day we did.

That day we were lucky. We did not see any VC, although they may have seen us. Our main objective in these patrols was to let the VC know that if they got too close to our base camp that they would pay the price for it. And since battalion headquarters was just across the road from us it became necessary to show our strength often.

We headed back to base camp. Back through the jungle, the rice patties, the canals and finally to Dead Man's Trail. A sigh of relief would go over the platoon when we reached Dead Man's Trail because it meant that we made it through the day without anyone getting killed or wounded. Nightfall was coming and we were grateful to get back.

The day's patrol was about five klicks. Not a bad walk through a park you might say, but this was no park. Five klicks through this terrain, in this heat, left a man completely exhausted.

It was then that I saw our company commander Lt. Dennis Tomcik heading toward us. Tomcik was the consummate officer. He became company commander as an Ell Tee while most company commanders were captains. Behind him was a point man, two other G.I.s, Lt. Tony Pino (a forward observer), an RTO and Larry Cook (White Platoon M-60 machine gunner).

Tomcik stopped to talk to our platoon leader then started down Dead Man's Trail. When he got to me he grabbed me by the shirt and said, "Yeah, we need a medic. Fall in behind the RTO." Which I did without question. We began to march down Dead Man's Trail. I became a little nervous as I knew there were only six men in front of me and usually there would be up to 15-20 men in front of me and as many behind.

As usual we veered off into the canals and after a long day being completely exhausted I was back at it again. While helping M-60 machine gunner Cook out of a canal I asked him how many men were behind him, he replied "None." "None!" I gasped. "Are you crazy? There are only six men in front of me. Do you mean there are only eight of us out here…in the boonies!?" "Yep," said Cook. "We all volunteered for this night patrol. We are looking for a company of VC that the Ell Tee said are out here."

Volunteered! I did not volunteer, I was selected. That's twice I was "selected" and lived to regret it. The first was when I got the letter from President Nixon informing me that for the next two years I would be working for the government.

Cook went on to explain that we were not supposed to make contact with the VC but only find them, call in artillery on them and then get out of there. That is why the forward observer was with us. The 3/39th Artillery Unit was located about a mile from our base camp. They were good, and Lt. Pino was the best we ever had.

After a while, we stopped in a canal. Tomcik suspected that a company of VC had set up camp near a hooch in the area. He took the point man and went on ahead and gave us instructions to wait in the canal for his return. We immediately set up a defensive position and waited for Tomcik to return.

After a while, we heard rifle fire nearby. Our first instinct was to head for the gun fire and help our company commander. But his instructions were to wait, so we did. After a short while, Tomcik and the point man came running down Dead Man's Trail screaming for us to open fire. The VC were in close pursuit and bullets were flying everywhere.

We immediately returned fire with everything we had on the VC. I fired all my ammo from my M-16 and .45-caliber pistol. Cook looked like Rambo as he fired the M-60. The barrel on his gun got so hot that it quit firing. There was no time to call for back up. We were out of ammo, out of time and out of luck.

Just then Lt. Pino told us to get down as an artillery round struck the canal just 10 feet in front of us. During the firefight, he had gotten on the horn and had his artillery unit zeroed in on our position. He ordered a "hot" round at the exact moment we needed a diversion to confuse the VC so we could get up on the trail. The live round was incredibly accurate when you consider that the artillery guns were firing from nearly four miles away.

Tomcik then ordered us to get out of there and run for it. Run we did – disregarding the booby traps, right down Dead Man's Trail. We had to run and run fast to survive. Tomcik and the point man had run into the VC and were spotted. Tomcik shot two of them right away and the rest began shooting back.

*"Doc" Voelker at entrance to Tiger's Lair, 1968.*

Running down the trail looked like a John Wayne movie. Dirt was being kicked all around us where bullets hit the ground and the tree leaves and branches were falling as we ran from the AK-47 rounds hitting them. I had never been so scared in my entire life. Not so much that I would be hit, but that one of the men would be hit and I would have to stop and take care of him and be overrun by the VC.

I had someone ask me once if I was ever worried about a bullet with my name on it. Actually I wasn't. But I **was** very worried about all those that said "to whom it may concern" on them.

After a few seconds, I heard another 105 artillery round fly close to my head and land behind me. Cook was last in the formation and that meant he was closest to the enemy and I was next. Lt. Pino was screaming into the RTO mike "Drop 10, drop 5, drop 20!!" He was telling the artillery gunners to adjust each round so it would follow us down the trail between us and the VC. Now if the VC did not get us or Pino misjudged our speed, or we slowed down, we would be killed by our own artillery. It looked like we were all going to die, either at the hands of the VC or our own artillery.

Then the worst happened. Cook fell down. He was totally exhausted. He had carried that M-60 and all that ammo at full run for several minutes and he was completely done in. He had also been shot in the leg a few months earlier. I went back to help him up although I was exhausted after my own five klick patrol earlier in the day.

As we got closer to camp I saw some of our troops heading toward us down Dead Man's Trail at a full run. The entire company was there. They had been listening to the radio at battalion headquarters and when the battalion commander said, "Saddle up!" they were all ready to go. My platoon, who had been out all day with me, tired, dirty and hungry, were the first men I saw. They came to save their "Doc."

After seeing what appeared to me a legion of angels coming to my rescue, I fell to the ground totally exhausted. The trail had been completely destroyed with artillery fire. No one, civilian or military, ever used it again.

The hero of the day was Lt. Anthony Pino, the best artillery forward observer ever. Without his skill in sending that artillery down the throats of the VC I know none of us would be alive today.

So that is how I brought in the new year in 1969. The fireworks were incredible but I would not want to see them again. Ever!

*Photo courtesy of Robert Crago.*

# MACV Naval Advisory Group RAID 72 (ATF-211)
*H. Bruce "Mac" McIver*

On March 31, 1969 Radioman Seaman Bruce McIver was wounded by a Viet Cong rocket propelled grenade that struck his T-131-7 boat during an intense ambush on the Giao Hoa Canal south of Ben Tre in Kien Hoa Province. After putting out a gasoline fire started by the flying shrapnel, Seaman McIver rushed over to attend to the serious wounds of a hospital corpsman who was along on the operation. Realizing that the corpsman's life was threatened, McIver performed an emergency tracheotomy. After loading the corpsman on a medevac helicopter, Seaman McIver returned to help suppress the Viet Cong ambush.

BM1 John Thibadeau, Boat Captain of T-131-7, began the process of putting Mr. McIver in for the Silver Star Medal for his heroics. Somewhere along the line the recommendation was lost or not followed up on.

Bruce and John found one another in 2003 after many years of searching. Soon after John contacted the Secretary of the Navy regarding the Silver Star award. The paperwork was re-initiated and Bruce received his much deserved Silver Star Medal 34 years after his heroic efforts.

For years Bruce did not know the name of the corpsman or if he lived. While perusing the Naval Archives in April of 2003 he located a document listing the wounded from the March 31, 1969 ambush. The corpsman's name was Zeph Lane. There was a "next of kin" address so Bruce tried calling the number when he arrived back to his motel room. Much to his surprise, Zeph's mother answered the phone. She reported good and bad news. The good news was that Zeph had not only survived, but he had become a doctor and a pilot. In the early to middle 1980's he returned to the site where he was seriously wounded and helped build a medical clinic. The bad news was that his private plane crashed shortly afterwards killing he and a relative.

Through the process Bruce has received some much needed "closure." He is now in contact with Zeph's widow and children. New life is coming out of the sufferings and heroics that took place so many years ago during the Vietnam War.

# Military Assistance Command Vietnam (MACV) Naval Advisory Group (NAG) – ATF-211

In the summer of 1969, President Nixon and his advisors had started to actively turn the war over to the Vietnamese in a program called "Vietnamization." The U.S. Navy began assuming a large role in this process because massive numbers of U.S. river assault craft, PBR's, etc., were ceremoniously turned over to the Republic of Vietnam. For a number of reasons, this created a need for U.S. Naval and U.S. Marine advisors to coordinate the war effort and to provide technical and liaison support. Having promised our Vietnamese allies that we would support their effort against the Viet Cong and North Vietnamese Communist aggressors, President Nixon wanted a smooth transition.

There was urgent need for men possessing real combat experience to fill the advisor slots, as well as to improve the training of the U.S. officers and petty officers slated to become combat advisors. The new advisors were then in training in the Vietnamese language and culture and in the combat skills required by their future role as combat advisors.

### RAIDs 70 through 75

The concept of the RAIDs was integration of a completely self-contained Task Force capable of taking the fight to the enemy. The RAID units consisted of river assault craft manned totally by Vietnamese. The RVN Marines or "Thuy Quan Luc Chien Viet Nam," formed a proud and capable fighting unit. In addition, we had artillery and air support specifically designated to be available mainly for our operations, including OV-10A "Bronco" aircraft of the VAL 4 "Black Pony" squadron, COBRA gunships, HA(L)-3 "Seawolf" helicopter gunships, Douglas AC-47 "Spooky" gunships, and close air support from Navy carrier air groups, as well as USAF bases in Thailand.

By the fall of 1969 we had five (5) RAID Units Operating from Tay Ninh in Operation Giant Slingshot and south to the heart of the U Minh Forest in Kien Giang and Chuong Thien Provinces. As advisors we, in many instances, operated alone with the Vietnamese marine and navy units. Our duties were to coordinate everything between the Vietnamese commanders in the field and the U.S. units and commanders in the vicinity.

As American advisors ("Covan My" in Vietnamese), it was imperative that we maintain good relations as well as good communication. When in the field, I lived as the Vietnamese did. They caught our meals from the canals by stringing a net across the canal downstream and dropping a few concussion grenades upstream...instant meal! Plenty of rice, soy sauce and nuoc mam (made from the drippings of fish fermented in a vat—not my favorite!). By having our meals with them, respecting their culture, we fostered in them a new and valuable respect for us as we lived and fought together, and we certainly gained the same respect for them.

Our toughest engagement occurred at Dong Hung, a former village where we had established a small fire support base. It was deep in the U Minh Forest, a notorious VC and NVA sanctuary. As November 1969 rolled in enemy activity increased, we started receiving nightly mortar and rocket attacks followed by ground probes. Our response to these attacks clearly demonstrated the fighting spirit of the new Task Force team members: (from official records now declassified)

"At approximately 0130H, the ATF-211 CP and RAID craft at Dong Hung came under intense attack from 82MM Mortar, 60MM Mortar, B40, B41 Rockets and 57 MM Recoilless Rifle. AT Approximately 0300H two battalions of main force VC surrounded the CP and artillery positions manned by two companies of VNMC from the 6th Battalion; RAID 72 AND RAID 74, VNN and U.S. advisors. Under cover of a heavy barrage of mortar, rocket and recoilless rifle fire, the two battalions of VC and NVA attacked and overran the CP, destroying tents, huts, bunkers and communication equipment; forcing withdrawal of VNMC staff, advisors, and most of the troops from the west bank of the canal. VNMC embarked in raid craft on the west bank and all boats crossed to the east bank of the canal."

Some Vietnamese Marine Corps troops remained on the west bank in hand to hand combat. The fight raged on for over five hours until approximately 0630 when the enemy withdrew. Of the 21 RAID boats, 19 had taken multiple rocket, recoilless rifle, and mortar hits. Casualties: VNN and VNMC: 44 KIA, 151 WIA; enemy body count within the CP was 75 KIA.

Although we were attacked in force and heavily outnumbered, the Vietnamese displayed bravery and gallantry in combat against a superior numbered enemy force that had not been witnessed prior to this action. Navy Lieutenant Al Bell, our RAID 72 Senior Advisor, maintained communication with our Vietnamese counterparts throughout the night.* The NVA and VC, monitoring our communications, had waited to attack until our FAC Observer aircraft had signed off for the night to return to base. This resulted in a loss of communications that prevented us from getting any outside support until a nearby medevac helo was able to relay requests for assistance. This resulted in air support from Black Ponies, Spooky A/C gunships, and Cobra gunships assisting. Until their arrival after what seemed like hours of fighting, we had depended totally on the gunfire from the RAID river assault craft and the VNMC and VNN units that had moved to the east bank of the canal.

The Vietnamese sailors and marines with whom I served in the RAID units had what it took to carry the fight to the enemy, as well as to repel enemy attacks such as described above. I was proud and humbled to be among their company. As my Vietnamese counterpart told me, "Mac, I'll die in this war." That stunned me, so I asked why he felt that way. His response changed my perspective. Nguyen looked me straight in the eyes and said, "You here one, maybe two year then you go home." He continued, "I am home, I'll die in this war."

The Vietnamese Marines and Sailors deeply appreciated the U.S. support and would continue to depend upon our assistance. However, they knew they must take over the war because the U.S. was pulling out. By March 1973, the U.S. had pulled out all combat troops. With that withdrawal, President Nixon promised continued financial and other necessary support. In 1975 all U.S. support ceased; Saigon fell to the Communists April 30th, 1975. This in no way diminished the heroic efforts of the Vietnamese Navy and Marine Corps along with their U.S. advisors. I am proud and honored to have served with ATF-211 RAID 72 Naval Advisory Group. The RAIDs made a difference and with continued U.S. support, I think the outcome of the Vietnam War would have been different. I do know that when I returned to the U.S., we were winning the war. In the Mekong Delta and III Corps this success was largely a result of the actions of RAID units that had been established in the fall of 1969.

The U.S. advisors I served with were, LT C. A. "Al" Bell (Senior USN Advisor), Major Mike Cerreta (Senior USMC Advisor) Bill Arbogast (current member of MRFA), Dave Bell (Bill, Dave and I went through NIOTC together), Tom Vriesenga, and others who were in the field as combat advisors, we were proud to be known as "Covans."

*Sgt. Dennis Causso and scout "Hai."*

*A 3d Brigade, 9th Infantry Division Ranger shoves through the Plain of Reeds as an Air Cushion Vehicle waits the call for support.*

*Dusty Rhodes with a B-50 rocket, 1967. (Courtesy of Foddrill.)*

*3d Brigade, 9th Infantry Division Rangers look for boobytraps and bunkers as they search a traditional enemy hiding area in Long An Province.*

*Bill Otterlei and Robert Schade at Rach Kien, 1967.*

*Tet Unit 2/47th near Bien Hoa. (Courtesy P.C. Steffy.)*

Bakle, Ross, unidentified, and Harris at Song Ong Doc. (Courtesy of Ralph Bakle.)

Rocket damage, October 23, 1969. (Courtesy of Ralph Bakle.)

Eddie Scott, USO entertainer (right), with Ralph Bakle at Song Ong Doc, 1970. (Courtesy of Ralph Bakle.)

Admiral Zumwalt with LT Commander Connolly at Vin Ghiu, October 1969. (Courtesy of Ralph Bakle.)

T-15 RivDiv 132 after night ops. (Courtesy of Ralph Bakle.)

*ATSB at Song Ong Doc following rocket-mortar attack, November 1970. (Courtesy of Ralph Bakle.)*

*Alpha 8 Crew: BM2 Harris, BTSN Boyer, RM3 Bakle, GMG3 Ross; Dong Tam, first night from Vallejo. (Courtesy of Ralph Bakle.)*

*(Courtesy of Ralph Bakle.)*

*Water skier at Song Ong Doc ATSB, 1970. (Courtesy of Ralph Bakle.)*

*Bill Boyer checking out RPG damage. (Courtesy of Ralph Bakle.)*

*Tango 23 on Vinh Te canal, September-November 1969. (Courtesy of Ralph Bakle.)*

*Vinh Te Ops on a narrow, deadly canal. (Courtesy of Ralph Bakle.)*

*GMG3 Charlie Ross, April 8, 1972. (Courtesy of Ralph Bakle.)*

*RAD 132 boats going up the Vinh Te Canal, 1969. (Courtesy of Ralph Bakle.)*

*Local barber at Song Ong Doc. (Courtesy of Ralph Bakle.)*

*Vietnam, 1968. (Courtesy of Lilyard N. Lucas.)*

*Villagers on the Vinh Te Canal. (Courtesy of Ralph Bakle.)*

*T-151-5 is a sunken Armored Troop Carrier. (Courtesy of Richard Lorman.)*

*Courtesy of P.C. Steffy.*

*Courtesy of P.C. Steffy.*

*Major weapons cache. (Courtesy of P.C. Steffy.)*

*Bob Hope Show, 1967. (Courtesy of P.C. Steffy.)*

Members of Co. B, 2nd Bn., 47th Inf., 9th Inf. Div., fire on North Vietnamese Army positions while in close contact south of the "Y" bridge.

VC bunker along a trail. (Courtesy of Don Isble.)

Headquarters at Tan-Tru, January 1969. (Courtesy of J.D. Dodson.)

Christmas, 1967, at Dong Tam. (Courtesy of Foddrill.)

An Assault Support Patrol Boat (ASPB) attached to River Assault Flotilla One. (Courtesy of G. C. Skaggs.)

*U.S. Navy Armored Troop Carrier 112-3. (Courtesy of S.C. Skaggs.)*

*Left to right: (top) Hunford, Hockaday, Mangan and Stumpf; (bottom) Johnson, Brannen, Oulette and Pribnow. Echo Co. 3/60, August, 1968. (Courtesy of R.J. Stumpf.)*

*Rick Chapman, 81mm mortar monitor.*

*Tango boats tied up to the USS Benewah. (Courtesy of Michael Marquez.)*

*LST-1167 Westchester County, November 1, 1968, with two holes from mines, 27 injured, 25 killed.*

*Courtesy of Richard Lorman.*

*An Army HU-1D "Huey" helicopter lands aboard a Navy Armored Troop Carrier of River Assault Flotilla One in the Mekong Delta of Vietnam. (Courtesy of G.C. Skaggs.)*

# MOBILE RIVERINE FORCE VETERANS

**MARSHALL G. "SHANE" ADAMS** born May 23, 1948, LaHarpe, IL. Graduated LaHarpe High School 1966 and enlisted in the Army in January 1968. Attended basic training at Ft. Leonard Wood, MO, advance infantry training at Ft. McClellan, AL. (Tiger Land) and jump school at Ft. Benning, GA. Arrived RVN in August 1968 and was assigned to 3rd / 47th, 9th Inf Div at Dong Tam. Unit was moved to the U.S. Westchester County and participated with MRF operations. Provided perimeter defense for FBS David (The Mudhole). Transferred to 9th Division Finance and was part of the first 25,000 troops sent home in July of 1969 as part of President Nixon's Vietnamization Program. Honored in ceremonies in Saigon and Seattle, WA. Awards include CIB, Paratrooper Badge, Army Commendation with Oakleaf Cluster and unit citations for Gallantry and Civil Actions.

Upon returning stateside, married Carlene Walker, high school sweetheart and was stationed at Ft. Riley, KS with 1st Infantry Division. Separated from active duty as an E5 in 1971 and attended Kansas State University, earning a BS in Accounting in 1973 and an MBA in 1974.

After college, joined the Phoenix, AZ office of a large national accounting firm and have since served as controller and financial officer for several privately held companies. Founded Adams Accounting and Consulting Services and wife, Carlene is a National Account Manger with Waste Management. We currently live in Dallas, TX.

**MICHAEL L. "MOON" AITCHISON** was born April 28, 1950 in Woseca, MN. He graduated from Annandale High School in 1968 and attended the University of Minnesota from 1972 until 1973.

Aitchison joined the US Navy in September 1968. He served with LSD-27 Whetstone, LST-1179 Harnett County, APB-35 Benewok, NAG- Cat Lo, Cho Moi. He achieved the rank of CS3. Most memorable experiences include frequencies of air conditioner failures on ships, showering in the rain at Cat Lo and MedCops in Cambodia where the locals had never been around Westerners before.

Aitchison is single but committed to Denise Liebl. He had one son, Adam. Civilian employment includes working as a corrections officer for Wright County Jail.

**DANIEL "DAN" ANDERS** Sergeant Major, born March 18, 1946 Siloam Springs, AR, graduated high school Elbing, KS 1964 and earned a BA Liberal Arts at Wichita State University, Wichita, KS in 1981. Joined US Army National Guard 1966. Basic training at Ft. Jackson, SC 1966; AIT, Ft. McClellan, AL 1967; KSNG NCO Academy Wichita, KS 1968; US Army Reserve: Fire Suppression Operation Course, Chanute AFB, IL 1978; MOLC Camp Parks, CA 1982; Senior NCO Course 1984; Sergeant Major Academy, Ft. Bliss, TX 1991.

Duty assignments 1966-1969. Co. A, 1st BN, 137th Infantry, 69th Inf. Bde. KSNG Winfield, KS activated May 1968 to Ft. Carson, CO; Co. B, 3rd BN, 60th Inf., 9th Inf. Division RVN; HHC Band and DISCOM 9th Inf. Division RVN., Co. A 9th Sig. Bn., 9th Inf. Div, Schoffield Barracks, HI; HQ 89th Div (TNG) and HQ 89th USARCOM Wichita, KS through 1985. From 1985-1990 served as an IRR soldier with annual training assignments at numerous locations. Assigned as an IMA to US Army Corps of Engineers Missouri River Div. Omaha, NE in 1990. Activated January 2002 in support of Operation Enduring Freedom, served a one year tour with the Far East District USACE, Seoul, South Korean and one year a the USACE Pacific Ocean Div. Emergency Operations Center, Ft. Shafter, HI.

Decorations: Combat Infantryman's Badge, Army Service Ribbon, Army Overseas Service Ribbon, Republic of Vietnam Campaign medal with 60 device, Vietnam Service Medal with two bronze devices, Armed Forces Reserve Medal with silver hourglass and M device, NCO Professional Development Ribbon with four device, Good Conduct Medal, Army Reserve Components Achievement Medal with silver OLC, National Defense Service Medal with two bronze devices, Army Achievement Medal with two OLC's, Army Commendation Medal with OLC, Air Medal, Legion of Merit. Unit awards: RVN Cross of Gallantry and RVN Civil Action.

After 37 1/2 years of Reserve and Active Duty with the US Army, SGM Anders will transfer to the Retired Reserve mid-February 2004.

Dan and Louise were married on Jan. 20, 1968. They have two children, Christopher and Shelly, and have six grandchildren. Civilian employment is with ClubMed at Mt. Crested Butte, CO.

**DONALD E. ANDERSON**, E-5/SP-5, born Sept. 15, 1944, San Antonio, TX, graduated from Thomas Jefferson High School, 1962. Joined US Army March 1967; Ft. Polk-Basic, Ft. Leonard Wood-AIT. Arrived RVN July 1967, assigned Co. D, 3rd Plton, 15th Combat Eng. Bn. Supported Mobile Riverine Force as a demolition specialist/rifleman. On the *Benawah*. Missions in Rung Sat Special Zone, Snoopy's Nose area and other areas up and down the Mekong River and tributaries. Puled air sorties also. Supported units of the 60th and 47th Inf. Including Mech. Bn's. Spent my first day with the MRF at a Beach Party in Vung Tau.

My most memorable mission was on Sept. 15, 1967. I don't know the name of the canal or stream we were on, but I will never what happened. The lead Monitor was hit by a RPG/B40. As the column tried to backup a rear Monitor was also hit and all hell broke loose. An RPG hit the canopy frame of my boat, throwing shrapnel everywhere, killing some and wounding most. The other engineer, Willie J. Shell was sitting under the explosion, he wasn't hit, but he couldn't hear for hours. I was leaning against the ramp, I wasn't hit but the sergeant sitting next to me was killed, he had three days left. He was on the mission because the LT sitting next to him was green. After the dead and wounded were taken off there were only eight of us left including the Navy crew.

That was my birthday, I turned 23 years "old"!

I had pen pal, Cindy Holmes, while I was there and when I returned to the states we were engaged at Christmas 1968, married June 1969 and are still happily married with two daughters, Carin and Melisa. I took an early out to return to the University of Houston. I am an Engineer with a local government agency.

I wrote a book about my experiences entitled *Intermission*. Copies are at the Vietnam Archives at Texas Tech University and the Vietnam Memorial in Angel Fire, NM.

**TED "ARBO" ARBOGAST** was born Dec. 17, 1935 in New Frankfort, MO. He graduated from Slater High School in Slater, MO.

Arbogast joined the US Navy on Jan. 17, 1954. He served with *USS Woodson* DE359, *USS Bristol* DD857, *USS Howard* D Crow DE252, *USS Enhance* MSO 437, *USS America* COA66. Military locations and stations include VA, ComServ POC, Pearl Harbor, leading Gunners mate on CCBI Riv Ron 11.

Awards and medals include Purple Heart, Vietnam Service Medal with bronze star, Republic of Vietnam Campaign Medal with device, Bronze star with Combat V, four good Conduct Awards, Navy Achievement metal with Combat V, Navy Commendation, Combat Action Ribbon, Presidential Unit Citation, Navy Expeditionary Medal (Cuba), National Defense Service Medal. Most memorable experience was a fire fight in Snoopy Nose and an ambush at night coming out of plain of reeds as well as many other ambushes and fire fights. He retired Aug. 10, 1973.

Married to Diana, they have four children, Raymond, Dawn, Virginia and Veronica. They also have five grandchildren, Ashton, Joshua, Amanda, Andrew and Nicholas. Arbogast also worked as a mechanic, carpenter and construction in his own business. He is still employed.

**WILLIAM J. "ARBO" ARBOGAST** was born May 18, 1948 in Minneapolis, MN. After graduating from high school, he joined the US Navy on Oct. 10, 1966.

Arbogast served on the *USS Dale* DLG 19, Sere School Widbey Island, WA. Military locations and stations included NIOTC Mare Island, CA; River Assault Division 131; River Squadron 13; Mine Division 113; Naval Advisory

Group; Raid 72. He served six campaigns in Vietnam. Awards and medals include Bronze Star with combat V device; Presidential Unit Citation with one star; Vietnam Service Ribbon with six campaigns stars; Naval Unit Commendation with two stars; Meritorious Unit Commendation; Combat Action Ribbon; National Defense; Vietnam Campaign Ribbon with 60's device; Vietnam Cross of Gallantry with palm; Vietnam Civil Action with palm. He achieved the rank of E4 3rd Class Boatswain mate. Memorable experiences include Crossroads, Ben Tre, Snoopy's Nose, Vinh Te Canal, U Minh Forest.

Arbogast is married to Cindy and they have two daughters, Julie and Rachel. Civilian employment includes forklift mechanic with Super Valu Stores, Inc. for 30 years. He retired May 1, 2000.

**RONALD LEE BAKERT** was born March 29, 1948 in Independence, MO. He graduated from Northwest High School in Hugesville, MO. He joined the US Navy in May 1967.

Units served with and ships served on include *USS St. Francis River* LSMR 525, *USS Colonial* LSD 18, Naval Support Activity Dong Tam- Mobile Riverine Force- APL 26, *USS Midway* CVA 41. Military locations and stations were Basic Training Great Lakes, IL; School Fleet Training Center San Diego, CA; Survival, evasion, resistance and escape training Coronado, CA and Camp Pendelton, CA; Dong Tam, Vietnam; Nha Be, Vietnam. He served in Operation Deckhouse V- Operation Game Warden and Market Time. Bakert was awarded Vietnam Service Medal, Vietnam Campaign Medal, Republic of Vietnam Armed Forces Meritorious Unit Citation of the Gallantry Cross with Palm, Navy Unit Commendation- *USS St. Francis River*, Presidential Unit Citation (Navy) Mobile Riverine Force- Task Force 117, Good Conduct and National Defense. He achieved the rank of Engineman 3-Class Petty Officer before being discharged on Feb. 9, 1971.

Bakert says, "Although I remember, the sounds of Choppers in the air, the sight of Tracer Fire at night, B-40 Rockets incoming, sighting of V.C. swimmers in the water, dropping grenades into the river all night, working long hours with no sleep, repairing our Diesel Engines, while still in the water, using Maps as head gaskets. Heat and monsoon rains. Wounded receiving Medical attention before being transported on to a Hospital. Beer calls, receiving a Telegram letting me know that my first child had arrived (a baby girl). Reading a letter, telling me that Mike a schoolmate, had been killed, in Long An. Oh yes, getting awakened in the middle of the night, dropping a grenade down a launcher, and forgetting to cover my ears, SAY WHAT? But an experience that effects my life today is watching the Vietnamese children eat our garbage. The first time I took our garbage to dump in the river, Vietnamese Sampans came to get our garbage to feed their pigs, etc. The Vietnamese children began to pick up half-eaten cookies, apples, oranges, etc. and eat them. After that I would fill my pockets with fruit, cookies, etc. and give the children, so they would not have to dig from the garbage. As my children grew up, I always made them eat all food from their plates, as I do my grandchildren today. Then I remind them of the Vietnamese children in Vietnam. I often wonder what their lives are like today. I thank the Lord for my life, my family, and my country, the land of freedom and bountiful supply."

Bakert is married to Phyllis Ann and they have four children, Connie, Christine, Malinda and Robert. They also have nine grandchildren, Jonathan, Joshua, Jason, Justin, Zackary, Matthew, Brittany, Angela and Jasmine. Bakert has worked for the State of Missouri in the Department of Mental Health as a Plant Maintenance Engineer, where he retired June 2000.

**RALPH J. "BAKE" BAKLE** RM3 was born May 30, 1944 at Fort Wayne, IN. He graduated Central Catholic High School and then attended Indiana University at Ft. Wayne. Joined Navy April 1968. Attended basic training at Great Lakes NTC. Basic electricity and radioman A&C school at NTC San Diego. Two months aboard *USS Eldorado* and then NIOTC at Mare Island. Married pen pal Peggy 11 days after meeting in person in 1970. They have four children, Debbie,

Mark, Cathy and Kimberly with three grandchildren Eli, Jackson and Kessler. His original crew that trained together at Mare Island was assigned to RIVDIV 132 aspb-8. What an experience four green pea river rats thrown on a boat together-talk about McHales Navy! First operations were on the Vinh Te Canal September through December. Oct. 23, 1969 as second boat in the column heading for WBGP us and the tango boat in front of us took some rockets. He was on the fantail and the first round a HEAT round went about a foot under him and into the engine compartment, they were running with one engine to begin with and now they were dead in the water. A second round hit their starboard bow area and they took several VN militia casualties. Set out the next couple of weeks at the repair tender. After Vinh Te operations they were sent to the south of Cau Mau area a little ATSB at Song Ong Doc. Again they were hit with rockets on April 8, 1970 with the gunner and himself getting a little shrapnel. Later they got hit with 10 155mm from a Coast Guard Cutter while anchored at the ATSB. Left Song Ong Doc and Alpha 8 to go home on 30 days leave for extending his tour. Got married Aug. 10, 1970 and came back to Song Ong Doc to be radioman and 20mm top gunner. Loved humping 105 shells and drinking beer. Their boat *Moniter 152-1* was involved in the last American firefight in Vietnam. That ATSB was rocketed in November and they left shortly for Dong Tam to turn the American boats over to the Vietnamese. Sent to Comcenter in Nha Be until March of 1971 and then to Charleston, SC to the destroyer tender *USS Yellowstone*. He has worked in the retail auto industry for the past 30 years.

**JOHN ED "RED JOHN" BALLARD** was born Oct. 14, 1947 in Graves County, KY. After graduating from high school, Ballard was drafted in the US Army on Nov. 14, 1967. He served with Co A 3rd BN 47th INF. He served in Vietnam. Achieved the rank of SGT E-5 and was discharged on July 10, 1969.

Ballard is single and worked at the Goodyear Tire Plant before retiring on Dec. 31, 2002.

**PLUMER MITCHELL "MITCH" BARDEN JR.** Master Sergeant, born Aug. 20, 1931, Lawrenceville, GA, entered the US Army Jan. 24, 1952 and took basic training and AIT training at Camp Roberts, CA.

After basic he served tours of duty in Hawaii with the 25th Inf Div, 1955-1958 and again in Korea 1961-1962.

He served two tours in Vietnam, first as a Platoon Sergeant with "B" Co. 3/60 Inf. 9th Inf. Div. August 1970-August 1971 with HHC 1/11th Inf. 5th Mechanized Div. as Operations and Intelligence Sergeant.

Married Mary Helen Holland in 1958 and had a son, Anthony "Tony" Wayne. Married Laura Ellin Jameson on Jan. 24, 1969. She is now deceased; they had two daughters, Kimberly Michelle Barden Goss and Monica Alison Barden and one granddaughter, Megan Michelle Goss and four grandsons, Justin, Daniel, Nicholas and Bradley.

He retired as a Master Sergeant on Jan. 30, 1972 with 20 years of service. Awards include the Good Conduct Medal (5), National Defense Service Medal with OLC, Vietnam Cross of Gallantry with palm, UN Service Medal, Bronze Star with OLC, Air Medal, Purple Heart, Vietnam Campaign Medal an the Combat Inf. Badge (2nd Award).

He was employed with Coats and Clark Inc. until retirement on March 1, 1992.

## WILLIAM W. "BILL" BASKIN

was born April 2, 1945 in Chickasha, OK. He graduated from Chickasha High School and one year at Oklahoma University. He joined the Navy October of 1966 and attended training at NTC San Diego. Served as a Company Commander's Aid and then transferred to NAAS, Fallon, NV, working a target (practice bombing) and obtaining GMG3. Attended training at Mare Island, Valle

Jo, CA; survival school at Whidbey Island, Washington and in country January 1970. Served River Assault Division 152 on Monitor 7, until turning the boat over to the Vietnamese. Served on RIVDIV 45 at Operation Sea Float, Tran Hung DAO III; a lot of action at that location. Received National Defense Service Medal, Vietnam Campaign Medal, Vietnam Service Medal, Combat Action Medal (Ribbon), and Silver Star Medal. After discharged from Long Beach Naval Station Jan. 20, 1971, returned to Reno, NV. Now retired from the Sheriff's Office and residing with wife of 34 years.

## THOMAS FINA "TOM" BENNIS

was born July 12, 1945 at Allentown, Lehigh County, PA. He graduated from Allentown Central Catholic High School in 1963 and attended Moravian College, BA (CJR) 1980.

Bennis joined the US Navy on Oct. 16, 1962. He served on the *USS Manley DD-940, USS Sea Owl SS-405, Comrivflot one*. He served at NTC Great Lakes, RM "A" School Bainbridge, MD, USNRTC Allentown, PA, NIOTC ValleJo, CA, MRF Dong Tam, RVN. He retired Dec. 12, 1968.

Bennis is married to Gwendolyn McCowan and they have the following children, Jeanne-Marie, Rebecca, Thomas F. Jr., Maria, Gerald, Joseph, Joshua, Amanda and Julie. They also have the following grandchildren, Patricia, William, Cara, Lindsay, Ashley, Tyler, Darren, Joshua and James. Bennis was Captain at the Allentown, PA Police Department. He retired Feb. 9, 1996.

## BRUCE D. BISELY

was born June 14, 1948 in Algoma. After receiving his high school diploma, he joined the US Navy Reserve on March 13, 1967.

Bisely served with the River Assault Flottila One- ASPB III-7. He attended boot camp at Great Lakes Naval Training Center; River Assault Training at More Island, Vallejo, CA; and Survival, Evasion, Resistance and Escape (SERE) Training at San Diego, CA. Battles and Campaigns include Coronado 4 and Coronado 5, Battle for Vinh Long-Snoopy's Nose-Rung Sat Special Zone. June 1967 he served one month on Swift Boat-Coastal Division 13- Cat Lo S. Vietnam. July and August he served two months on Monitor III-2 (Gunners Mate) waiting for Alpha Boats to arrive. September 1967 to June 1968 he served nine months on ASPB III-7 (20 MM Gunner) Stationed out of Dong Tam. After Vietnam he served three months on *USS Walworth County-LST*- Little Creek, VA. Awards and Medals he received include National Defense Service Medal-Vietnam Service, Vietnam Campaign Medal, Republic on Vietnam, Cross of Gallantry-Combat Action, Navy Unit Citation-Presidential Unit Citation-Navy Achievement with Combat V. He achieved the rank of GMG3 (Gunners Mate Gunner). He was discharged on Oct. 3, 1968.

Bisely's civilian employment has included working for WS Packaging-Label Company- Rewind Department- Rewind Operator.

## THOMAS R. BLAKLEY

was born Oct. 30, 1946 at Brookside, Harlan County, KY. He graduated from high school in 1964.

In January 1966 he joined the US Navy. He served on the *USS Braine DD630*; transferred to Coastal Squadron One/ Division 13 (CatLo)/ CTF115 1968; transferred *USS Shield* August 1969 (trained Reserves); transferred *USS Marysville PCER* November 1969, released January 1970. Battles and Campaigns include Operation Sealords, Swiftraider, Sea Tiger and numerous other special operations. Awards and medals he received include PHM, Nam w/V, CAR, PUCR, NUCR, MUCR, NDSM, VSM w/ 4BS, VCM w/1960, Vietnam MUC Gallantry Cross w/ palm, Vietnam Civil action w/ palm and GCM. He achieved the rank of Engineman Second Class and was discharged in January 1970. He most memorable experience was being wounded in action on March 29, 1968, serving on PCF 98 under LTJG Wade Sanders and the friendship of his crew members.

Blakley is married to Donna. His civilian employment includes DNC Machinist/ CNC certified and he is currently working GE Aircraft Engine Group in Cincinnati, OH.

## NICK BLAZEK

was born Nov. 28, 1928 in Milwaukee, WI. After high school he attended two years of college at the University of Vienna, Austria.

On Nov. 19, 1944 he joined the US Army. He served with the 88th INF DIV WWII-HQS. USFA-970th CIC-1st CAV DIV-25th INF DIV-4th ARMD Div-XIV USA CORRS-HQS. 2nd BDE 9th INF. DIV. Some locations and locations include Italy WWII, Austria, Germany, Korea, Ft. Hood, TX, Fort Snelling, MN, Fort Riley, KS and Vietnam. Battles and campaigns include Mount Casino Italy WWII; Hungnam, Korea; Kumwha Valley, Korea and Vietnam engagements. Blazek was received the Silver Star, Bronze Star, Commendation Medals, Purple Heart (3), CIB (3rd Award) and 16 other medals and awards. He achieved the rank of Command Sergeant Major (E-9).

His most memorable experience was being assigned as the first Command Sergeant Major, 2nd BDE and given the opportunity to be the right hand Baver and member of the staff for the finest officer and gentleman he had every served for, Lt. Gen. William B. Fulton (then Colonel). Those moments and memories are very precious to him and will never be forgotten.

Blazek has been married since 1958 to Germaine. They have five children, Michael, Scott, Troy, Trent and Tania; also one grandson, Gabriel. His civilian employment includes working for Farmers Insurance Group and Strohs Brewery. He retired on Aug. 30, 1967.

## DAVID W. BOHMER

SPC4 (Acting E5); born May 16, 1946; Brooten, MN; graduated from Brooten High School 1964; drafted into Army May 1968; Basic at Ft. Campbell, KY; AIT at Ft. Lewis, WA; 2nd Platoon, Co. A, 3rd of 60th, 2nd Brigade, 9th Inf. Div, Vietnam September 1968 to July 1969; Brigade S3 Clerk for several months; Acting DI for Basic Training Company in Fort Ord, CA from September 1969 until discharged March 1970. Graduated with a BS in Business Finance 1970; became a flight instructor/charter pilot; post-graduate work in Denmark; owned and operated an independent insurance agency/ real estate sales from 1975-2000; president/ partner in Bonanza Valley State Bank, Brooten, MN 2000- present. Dave was married in 1976 and has three grown children. No grandchildren. Divorced in 1987 and still single.

Memories of Vietnam are mostly negative. He was stationed on the troop ship *Ben Tre* as part of the Mobile Riverine Force and inserted by helicopter or boat into areas designated by headquarters. Troops were usually brought back to the ship after three days because of health problems associated with constant exposure to water and mud. He was in the permanent point squad for the first five months and involved, primarily, in platoon-sized operations. He declined the offer of becoming company clerk in order to stay with his friends. The platoon was sent on long-range ambush operations and seemed to serve as "bait" to draw enemy fire: Reinforcements would occasionally be sent in if the platoon sustained enough casualties. The last months of his tour were especially bad- it seemed that officer's and NCO's did not want to be in the field and the platoon was commanded by a "shake and bake: E6. Extensive casualties were sustained from booby traps and snipers. It seemed that shortly after the platoon accumulated more than 25 men, it would be sent into a hazardous area and come back with as few as seven men. Casualties were high during his entire period of service.

Dave left his infantry company because of severe immersion foot in February 1969 and became Brigade S3 Clerk. Brigade Headquarters was moved to the city of Ben Tre shortly after. He volunteered to return to his unit when the headquarters "downsize" in the spring. Only one of his original platoon members remained. Dave was assigned to a basic training company in Ford Ord, CA upon his return to duty in the USA. He served there as an Assistant Drill Instructor until his early release in March 1970 to return to college.

His best memories are of his original Vietnam platoon including Lieutenant Dennis Bassett, Baldo Morales and "Doc" Gonzales. At the end of Dave's tour, Carlos Penya was the only other man left in the platoon who arrived in the summer/fall of 1968. Dave's worst memory is pulling his dead mentor's body away from a machine gun complex shortly after joining the platoon. He received a Bronze Star for Valor for actions that day. After that, emotional distance was kept from replacements to avoid the pain of seeing them wounded or killed; it didn't work.

## GLEN "FRENCHY" BOYETTE

was born Sept. 2, 1948 in Los Angles, CA. He joined the US Navy in September 1966. He served on the USS Klondike AR22, USS Renville APA227, USS Skagit AKA105, USS Nereus AS17. He received the following awards and medals, Nat Def Pres UC, Navy Unit Com- Presidential Unit, Republic of Vietnam- Vietnam Service, and Republic of Vietnam Gallantry Cross. Boyette was discharged in May 1972.

Boyette is married to Mary Boyette and they have a daughter, Sara. He has enjoyed retirement since Jan. 2, 2004.

## RAYMOND "RAY" BRADBURY

was born June 20, 1945 in Seattle, WA. He graduated from Rainer Beach High School.

In February 1963 Bradbury joined the US Navy. He served on the USS Whitehurst DE634, USS Topeka CLGE, USS Nueces APB40, USS Norton Sound AVM1, USS Paul Revere AOD248, USS Newport New CA148. He was stationed out of San Diego, Norfolk and Long Beach. He received awards and medals including Combat Action, Nat. Def. Pres. Unit Citation, Vietnam Campaign, Republic of Vietnam Meritorious Unit Citation with Gallantry Cross, Hon. Disch. Bradbury's most memorable experience was moving up and down the rivers to different areas where the boats were operating; leaving Vietnam from Dong Tam to Saigon and home via Subic Bay, Yukosuka- Honolulu.

Bradbury is married to Magda and they have three children, Stefin, Becky and Sarah. They also have five grandchildren, Elsie, Trentin, Nathanial, Nathan and Cassie. He has worked as Transit Driver in Tacoma, WA.

## CECIL V. "C. B." BRELAND

from the Bogalusa, LA newspaper: "My boats was one of 15 river assault craft proceeding in a column to a vital water crossroads 10 miles Southeast of the city of My Tho, deep in the Mekong Delta of Vietnam," remarked a Navyman from Mt. Hermon, LA.

Chief Boatswain Mate Cecil V. Breland, son of Mr. and Mrs. J. C. Breland of Mt. Hermon, was recalling recent action in which his river assault craft came under heavy Viet Cong attack.

"We moved into the landing area and reconned the beach with 20mm, .50 and .30 caliber machine gun fire," he continued. "Our reconning was to divert Charlie's attention from the Army infantrymen offloading from my boat and other troop-laden assault craft of the column. Seconds after we finished reconning the beach, the lead boat in the column was hit by a boat in the column was hit by a Viet Cong B-40 rocket in the vicinity of their .50 caliber machine gun mount. Moments later, the entire column came under enemy B-40 rocket, automatic weapons and small arms attack from both banks of the river."

Breland was the boat captain of Armored Troop Carrier (ATC) 92-3, which operates with the unique Army-Navy Mobile Riverine Force (MRF) in Vietnam's Mekong Delta.

As a member of this unique striking force, he is attached to River Assault Flotilla One, a unit of the Amphibious Force, Pacific Fleet.

Breland and other combat sailors of the Flotilla man heavily armored gunboats, most of which are conversions of World War II conventional landing craft. Providing close logistic and fire support for Army infantrymen, these small boats navigate the treacherous inland waterways in search of Viet Cong guerrillas.

On that day, MRF forces came under one of their heaviest enemy attacks in a day-long battle on the narrow Ba Lai River 10 miles Southeast of My Tho.

Fighting broke out at 8:45 a.m. when a column of troop-laden assault craft from River Division 92 were hit from heavily fortified enemy bunkers just as they were moving in to beach and offload Army troops. Ten Army and Navy men were killed in the vicious day-long fighting.

"I proceeded past the ambush site and then turned in to off-load my troops. My boat was still receiving automatic and small arms fire, but it wasn't as heavy as before. I beached my infantrymen and then backed out into mid-stream. An armored troop carrier behind me was proceeding into the beaching area when his bow ramp was blown off from an enemy B-40 rocket. He was unable to navigate his craft, so I attempted to tow him. I then noticed that he still had Army personnel aboard so I took them on my boat and went in to offload them. As soon as we hit the beach, we were hit with B-40 rockets and machine gun fire in the welldeck, injuring six Army personnel. After the troops were offloaded, I proceeded back to a medical aid boat to evacuate the wounded," he concluded.

Breland's armored troop carrier is designed primarily to transport Army soldiers into combat areas.

Each ATC is capable of carrying a platoon of 40 fully equipped infantrymen into virtually any canal, river or stream that interlaces the land. Bar trigger shield and a special hard steel plate protect the ATC's against enemy recall unless rife and small arms returned. Many of the ATCs have been re-configured with a helicopter deck to accommodate flight operations for medical evacuations, resupply and personnel transfers.

Prior to entering the Navy in June 1950, Breland attended Mt. Hermon High School in Mt. Hermon.

River Assault Flotilla One, commanded by Capt. Robert S. Salzer, USN, is homeported in San Diego, CA.

Breland was born June 25, 1933 at Washington Parish, LA. After high school, Breland joined the US Navy on June 25, 1950.

Breland served on the USS Lenawee-Latimer-ARNEB-Oglithorpe-Ashtabula-Kennebec. Military stations and locations include Tugs at Roos Rds. Puerto Rico and Midway Island 406-87-Nav. Sta. L. Beach. He achieved the rank of BMC E-7 before being discharged on Feb. 1, 1971.

Breland is married to Dorothy and he has four stepchildren, Tommie, David, Jackie and Linda. They have three grandchildren, Derek, Joshua and Dustin; one great grandchild, Avery Ann. In civilian employment he worked as a paint inspector and coordinator for Dow Chemical. He retired in June 1995.

**LAWRENCE E. "GRAMPS" BRENNAN** was born on Nov. 17, 1946 at Clinton, IA. He graduated from St. Mary's High School in Clinton. He earned AA degree at Clinton Community College in 1979.

Brennan joined the US Navy in October 1966. He served with the USS Samuel Gompers AD-57 1967, 1968; ASPB A-112-5 Vietnam 1969 and on the USS Hunley AS-31 1970, 1971. Locations and stations include West Pac Cruise on USS Samuel Gompers, engineman on A-112-5 Vietnam, Weapons Station and Sub base Charleston, SC on USS Hanley. He received many awards and medals including Republic of Vietnam MUC Gallantry Cross, Purple Heart, National Defense, Navy Achievement with Combat V, Vietnam Service, Vietnam Campaign, Combat Action Ribbon and Navy Unit Commendation. He achieved the rank of EN3 (E-4). He was discharged in February 1971. At the age of 22 years, he was the oldest on the boat crew; this was how he got the nickname "Gramps." His most memorable experiences include 50 gunner Nelson Ramirez killed Feb. 16, 1969 on A-112-5 and Nick "Gomer" Pyle killed on Feb. 23, 1969 at Go Dau Ha. During their second firefight of the day CMDR Carl Petersen was killed April 2, 1969. Also, another officer (name unknown) and Brennan were wounded when rockets hit them.

Brennan is married to Candace Ann and they have three children, Larry, Mike and David. They also have two beautiful granddaughters, Chloe and Lauren. Brennan worked for 33 1/2 years at the Du Pont Factory in Clinton, IA. He retired on Dec. 31, 1999.

**STAN BRODA** was born Dec. 2, 1946 in Chelsea, MA. He attended high school at Engiweman A. School. He joined the US Navy on Sept. 7, 1965.

Units and ships that Broda served on include Dennis J. Buckley DD808, River Assault Flotilla One Boat T-91-13 (Charlie Chaser). Locations and stations include San Diego Home Port DD-808 September 1965 and Dong Tam Mobile Riverine Force. He was awarded the Purple Heart, Navy Commendation Medal with Combat V for Heroic Achievement and Navy Achievement Medal with Combat V. Broda achieved the rank of E5.

Broda has one son, Joe. He also has two grandchildren, Joseph and Madison Broda. He retired in December 2002.

**LARENCE H. BROWN** was born on April 15, 1934 in Washington, D.C. He enlisted in the USN on Sept. 17, 1951; received boot training at NTC San Diego, CA and served onboard USS Prairie during the Korean Conflict, 1951-1954, in optical ship and NAS Great Lakes, IL, January-April 1955. Re-enlisted and served onboard USS Everglades, in optical shop, July 1955-December 1959, making several Mediterranean and Caribbean cruises; Naval Training Command, Great Lakes, IL. Class C Periscope School, July–August 1956; Submarine Base, New London, CT, optical/periscope shop, January 1960-October 1963.

Commissioned ensign in November 1963 and attended Officer Orientation School. Newport, RI; Officer Engineering School, San Diego, CA; served onboard USS Maunakea and USS Regulus; COMFOUR Staff, Philadelphia; Naval Inshore Operations Training Center, Mare Island; Gamewardens, RVN, Riv. Divs. 552 and 513, Vam Co Dong, and Vam Co Tay Rivers, Tra Cu, Ben Luc and Ha Tien near Cambodian border; USS Arco, XO, Guam, M.I.; Naval Training Publications Detachment, Navy Yard, Washington, D.C.; NS Annapolis, MD; USS Carol Sea. Transferred to Fleet Reserve in 1975 with 24 years of active service. Retired in 1975 with rank of lieutenant commander. Awarded Navy Commendation Medal with Combat V for meritorious combat service in the Mekong Delta.

Married Gloria J. of Annapolis, MD on July 14, 1988. Fully retired and does volunteer work in the county public school system. He is a member of FRA Branch 24. Also has BS degree in mechanical engineering and MS in marine engineering.

**GARY D. BRUCH** GMG2, was born Nov. 13, 1946 in Kingman, KS. Graduated from Lake County High School, Leadville, CO in 1965. Joined US Navy June 7, 1966; attended basic training San Diego, then on the Gunner's Mate A School at Great Lakes, IL September 1966 to February 1967. Served aboard the USS Neches (AO47), an oiler, from February 1967 to February 1968 with two tours off the coast of Vietnam

refueling ships in Yankee and Market Station. Attended River Assault Craft training at Vallejo, CA February 1969 to May 1969. Served with RivDiv 595 RivRon 5 May 7 to August 30, 1969 aboard Alpha 6856 as 20 mm gunner and RivDiv 153 RivRon Aug. 30, 1969 to May 5, 1970 aboard Alpha 6856 as 20 mm gunner and as boat captain from February to May 1970. Participated in Operation Giant Slingshot. Home base was at Nha Be operating in Rung Sat Special Zone. Also division outpost in Tuyen Nhon operating in Plain of Reeds and performed some operations out of Tan An and Moc Hoa. Separated from active on duty May 12, 1970. Married Nancy Crabb June 12, 1971 in Portland, OR. Two daughters, Kerry (Nov. 29, 1972) and Tammy (Dec. 19, 1974). Worked for US Forest Service for 25 years as Civil Engineering Tech-designing and building forest roads. Retired end of December 1999. Enjoys traveling, working in yard and flower garden, elk hunting, restoring 1958 Chevy truck, and playing with the five grandkids.

**GARY C. BRUNO**, RM-3, was born Aug. 2, 1949 in Denver, CO, graduated from George Washington High School, 1967. Joined the US Navy Oct. 17, 1967; attended basic training at San Diego, CA; served with task force 117 aboard the USS Benewah, APB-35 from Feb. 1, 1970 through March 1, 1971. Participated in the Cambodia invasion of June 1970. Other military stations were: Electronics School, Sane Diego, CA Jan. 3, 1968 to Feb. 15, 1968; Radio School, San Diego, CA Feb. 16, 1968 to June 15, 1968; Naval Communication Station, Stockton, CA June 16, 1968 to Jan. 31, 1970.

While onboard the USS Benewah, I served as radioman in the communication room. Most watches consisted on 12 on/ 12 off shifts. I was in charge of processing all incoming and outgoing communications including medical evacuations. During the invasion of Cambodia, communication demands were 10 fold due to the assault and the fact that the USS Benewah was the flagship for the invasion. Though my position aboard the USS Benewah was that of a support role I did spend a considerable time onboard the assigned assault craft as advisor and support personnel during missions of humanitarian relief.

In late November of 1970, the USS Benewah was ordered to leave the Mekong Delta and proceed to Subic Bay, Philippines. The orders included an R&R stop in Singapore, which was most needed for the ship's crew. Looking back on my experience on the USS Benewah, I would have to include the fact that I was part of the last crew to sail on the ship. For when we arrived in Subic Bay, we were officially relieved of duty and sent our separate ways, only to learn later that our ship was officially decommissioned and scrapped, scuttled and finally sank as part of a coral reef program off the coast of the Philippines. The USS Benewah served her country from WWII through the entire Vietnam Conflict. At one time she was the most highly armed vessel to experience warfare in Vietnam. I am deeply proud to be a part of her lengthy history. Separated from active duty, March 5, 1971 Treasure Island, CA and discharged Oct. 17, 1973 with the rank of RM3 (E-4).

Currently married to the former Mary Lynelle Lynch with two daughters from a previous marriage, Regina Lynn; born Feb. 2, 1972 and Rebecca Marie; born May 11, 1974. I have spent the majority of civilian time being self-employed in the field of manufacturing, marketing and research of flexible packaging in Aurora, CO.

**KENNETH V. BRYANT** was born July 21, 1944 in Point Clear, AL. He received a BS degree, sociology/minor: foreign language (German) and psychology; 4-year scholarship (Piano) at Tuskegee University in Tuskegee, AL. He graduated in 1967.

Bryant joined the US Army on April 16, 1968. He took basic training at Ft. Benning, CA; AIT at Ft. McClellan, AL and RVN with 9th Inf. Div./ 3rd Platoon, Co. B, 2nd Battalion, 39th Infantry (1st Recondo Battalion). He was awarded Combat Infantry Badge, three Bronze Stars (one with "V"), Purple Heart, Air Medal, two Army Commendation Medals (one with "V"), Good Conduct Medal, RVN Cross of Gallantry Medal with Palm, National Defense Ribbon, Vietnam Service Ribbon and Vietnam Campaign Ribbon. Bryant achieved the rank of SGT E5 and was discharged on April 15, 1970. Military location and stations include RVN: grenadier for five months with 3rd Platoon, Company B, Company Commander's radio operator (RTO) and Battalion legal clerk, HHC, 2Bn, 39th Infantry. With USA returned to US July 1969, Range Inspector at Ft. Hood, TX until discharged in April 1970.

Bryant's most memorable experiences were numerous. Some of them include being wounded on Oct. 21, 1968. Another was the loss of his friend, bunkmate and fellow grenadier David P. Nash: While on a night ambush patrol on Dec. 29, 1968, the patrol was ambushed by a VC element. During the action that followed David made the supreme sacrifice for his fellow comrades. He was awarded the Congressional Medal of Honor (posthumously) in April 1970. The third most memorable experience was the Battle of Sa Dec. Jan. 6, 1969: On the night of Jan. 6, he witnessed another extraordinary act of battlefield courage in the person of SSG Don Jenkins, Company A, 2nd Bn. 39th Infantry. Jenkins became the second of only two 2/39th Infantry soldiers to be awarded the Medal of Honor during the Battalion's tour of duty in Vietnam. He was present at both engagements, and that's an experience he'll never forget.

Bryant's civilian employment includes being an Employment Representative, Personnel Department, University of Michigan, Ann Arbor, MI for two years; Radio announcer for WKRG-FM and WABB AM-FM for two years at Mobile, AR (1972-1974); Manager, Jobs for Veterans, National Alliance of Businessmen (NAB), at Washington, D.C. (1974-1977). The most rewards of all his jobs were to create and develop job opportunities for Vietnam-Era Veterans in the Metro Washington, D.C. area. Also planned and conducted the Veterans Employment Seminar Program (VESP) which brought unemployed veteran and employees together in a workshop format. VESP was also conducted on a monthly basis at the Pentagon as part of the Army Education Office HQs retirement/separation program. NAB also conducted an annual "Hire a Veteran Day" telethon campaign on Veteran's Day each year to solicit jobs for local Vietnam Vets. Other employment: HS Basketball/Football coach (1967); Social Services/ Public Information (10 years); and pianist (performance).

Bryant is married to Carolyn and they have two children, Patrick and Helen; stepdaughter, Rita; and four stepchildren by marriage: Diane, Walter, Melissa and William.

**GERALD WAYNE "JERRY" BURLEIGH** was born Dec. 3, 1947 in Lake Charles, LA lives in Orange, TX, was attached to the Mobile Riverine Force RivRon 132 River Assault Div. 132, Tango 132-13 later changed to T-27, while serving in South Vietnam Delta from May 1969-May 1970. As EN3 primary duties were MK-19 gunner and engineer.

I graduated from Orangefield High School in 1966. Joined the USNR in Beaumont, TX 1967 and went active in January of 1969. Received special boat training from March to May at Mare Island in Vallejo, CA, SEAR at Whidbey Island, WA; and gunner training at Camp Roberts, CA.

Most memorable experience was the firefight on his last night on the boat, he helped patch up and load his wounded buddy, Harry Kahn, on a helicopter; and then later locating him back in Indiana.

Throughout his service he received the PHM, NA with combat V, RVN Service Medal w/ BSs, RVN Campaign Medal w/1960 Device, RVNM Unit Citation w/ Color Palm, MUC Ribbon, National Defense Medal; Combat Action Ribbon, Presidential Unit Citation and Good Conduct Medal.

Married to Shelia D. Doyle on June 21, 1968, and has two sons, Michael Shane, Eric Lee and one daughter, Terry Renee. Worked a Bayer Rubber Plant for 32 years and retired in January 2003.

Hobbies are wildlife photography hunting and fishing, traveling around the United States, and working with Veterans and Family Traveling Tribute Museum.

**JOSEPH V.R. CAMARA** BM2, was born July 12, 1943 Santa Barbara Sao Miguel Acores, Portugal, immigrated to United States Dec. 1, 1954 and resided in Fall River, MA. In April 1961 became a US citizen by way of naturalization. Earned a GED while in the military.

Joined the USN in December 1964; attended basic training in Great Lakes, IL; first duty station was in Newport, RI. In 1965 he received orders to report to Norfolk, VA for precom school, later being assigned to the newly built *USS Truxton*. As a member of its first crew he became a plank owner. (When the ship was decommissioned it was scrapped and pieces of the keel were polished and engraved and given to the plank owners that attended its first reunion.) When the ship was commissioned in June 1967 it was taken around South America to its homeport in Long Beach, CA. Upon arriving at Long Beach he volunteered for shore duty in South Vietnam with the Mobile Riverine Forces. Attended training for assault boats at Mare Island, Vallejo, CA, and survival, training at Whidbey Island, WA. Nov. 26, 1967 assigned to Division 111 Tango 111-8 as its coxswain. Dec. 4, 1968 on his first operation the column was ambushed from both sides of the canal with his boat receiving a direct hit on the coxswain flat killing the radioman, a gunner, and five Army soldiers on deck, as well as wounding all on board including Camara and the boat captain (as his citation reads) that badly wounded he maneuvered his boat out of the danger zone, saving the rest on board and landing the boat on its designated beach. Other citations also read that he operated in over 25 combat operations in which he was highly decorated including two Purple Hearts.

In 1966 married Barbara and was later blessed with two daughters, and now has two granddaughters. In 1969 became a letter carrier with the US Postal Service. Later on becoming a supervisor and retiring in 1992 with 30 years of service.

His most memorable experience was the satisfaction of serving this great country in a time with it needed him the most. He wanted to give back a little to thank America for adopting him.

**RONNIE ERNEST "GUNNER" CAMPBELL** was born Feb. 5, 1946 in Marion, VA. He graduated from high school. On Sept. 26, 1965 he joined the US Navy. Ships that Campbell served include *USS Ingersoll*, *USS TE Chandler*, *USS Belmont*, *USS Accokee*, RivRon 9 and units include River Division 91, T-91-8. He was stationed at San Diego, Japan, Vietnam and Norfolk. He did three tours in Vietnam. Campbell was presented with the following awards and medals: Republic of Vietnam Campaign medal w/ 1960 Device; Republic of Vietnam Meritorious Unit Citation (Gallantry Cross medal Color w/ Palm); Presidential Unit Commendation Ribbon; Navy Unit Commendation Ribbon; Purple Heart; CAR; Vietnam Service Medal w/ one Silver Star; Vietnam Campaign Medal; National Defense Service Medal and Navy Achievement Medal w/ Combat "V". He achieved the rank of GMG2 and was discharged on Oct. 31, 1969.

Campbell is married to Beverley Laprado Campbell and they have a son, Ronald Wayne Campbell. They also have a grandson, Trevor Wayne Campbell. He worked maintenance at Roanoke City Schools until he retired in August 1999.

**DOYLE LEE CANNON** was born July 28, 1947 in Lamar County, AL. He graduated in 1966 from Marion County High School in Guin, AL.

Cannon joined the US Navy on Dec. 14, 1966. He served with T-91-3, RivRon No. 9, River Assault Flotilla One. Military location and stations include basic training at Great Lakes, IL; served on *USS Floyd* San Diego, CA; Vietnam. He served at Rung Sat Special and Mekong Delta. Cannon received Citation for serving against Viet Cong and Rung Sat Special Zone and the Mekong Delta, Navy Achievement Medal and Vietnam Service Medal. Cannon achieved the rank of 3rd Class Petty Officer, BM3, Seaman, .50 Caliber gunner. He was discharged in October 1970.

Cannon is divorced and has one child, Darryl Cannon and two grandchildren, Adreanna and Brianna Cannon. After leaving the military, he has worked as a truck driver.

**LEE R. CARMEAN** was born Dec. 9, 1943 in Mishawaka, IN. After high school, he attended college and earned 24 college credits. On March 10, 1965 he joined the US Navy. Carmean served on the *USS White River LSMR536* and *Montrose APA212*. He received many awards and medals including NUCR, NDSM, VSM (02) and VCM (P). Carmean achieved the rank of E-5 and was discharged on March 14, 1969.

Carmean has four children, Shanann, Shawna, Kim and Holly. Civilian employment includes being a welder. He retired on S. S. Disability.

**JAMES J. "JA-CEE" CARROLL** was born March 20, 1947 in Boston, MA. He graduated high school in Boston, MA and attended Newbury Junior College in Boston, MA for two years. He was draft into the US Army on Feb. 21, 1967. Units he served with include 1097th Trans. Co. (Med. Boats), 9th Infantry Boat (Lucky 13 Can-Do) Vietnam. He took basic training at Ft. Campbell, KY; A.I.T. at Ft. Knox, KY (Armor) Tanks, Perm. Party 198 Trans. Co. Ft. Knox, KY. Battles and campaigns were Can-Tho, My-Tho, Ben-Tre and Ben-Luc. Carroll was awarded Army Commendation Medal, Good Conduct Medal, National Defense Service Medal, Vietnam Service Medal, Republic of Vietnam Campaign Ribbon w/ Device (1960), four Bronze Service Stars and Marksman- Rifle. He achieved the rank of SP/5 E-5 and was discharged on Feb. 13, 1969.

Carroll says that his most memorable experience was a canal at Ben-Tre. The night was coal black and the time was 01:50 hours. Rubin Rodriguez and Carroll replaced two members of the artillery unit of their shift on guard duty. After Carroll scanned the perimeter with the starlight scope to confirm no enemy activity, Rubin did the same. They both agreed that the area was quiet. Well, just at that moment the barge that housed the artillery men and the 105-Howitzers exploded. (Picture enclosed) A couple of Huey's arrived and cleared the area of hostile activity. Carroll suspects an after action report was conducted. The only names of casualties he can remember are nicknames, Tiny (from Texas) and Slim (origin unknown).

Carroll is married to Jean McAlpin and they have two daughters. Denise is married to Ted and they have a son, Ryan. Lisa graduated from Massasoit College with an Associates Degree. Carroll worked as Superintendent of Postal Operation. He retired on Sept. 18, 1996.

**LOUIS J. M. "JOE" CARSON** was born Feb. 10, 1945, Cleveland, OH. Father was MIA WWII. Graduated Lancaster High School in 1963. After graduation worked as draftsman while attending Ohio University and raced motorcycles. Enlisted in the US Army June 1965.

Took basic training at Ft. Gordon, GA, then attended Military Police School back at Ft. Gordon, GA. Stationed with the 67th Military Police Co, Paris, France. The 1st Sgt. Read a directive saying the army was critically short of Military Police MOS's in Vietnam and asked for volunteers. Even though Paris was a great duty station many of us volunteered. Arrived in RVN in July 1967 and assigned to 9th MP Co. Went through the Jungle Warfare School at Bearcat including the night ambush patrol. Upon reporting to the 9th MP Company at Bearcat I was sent to the 2nd platoon at Dong Tam the next day. Worked various details including mine sweep, security, patrol, convoy escort and Provost Marshall investigator. I think everyone stationed at Dong Tam remembers the nightly mortar attacks; our hooch was hit on three different occasions. Was infused April 1968, to the 716th MP BN's 527th MP Co in Saigon. I was assigned as patrol supervisor for first precinct downtown. Later during mini TET was assigned as NCOIC of Ambassador Bunkers security detail. I rotated home and was Honorably discharged June 1968. I went back to my drafting job, attending Ohio University and racing motorcycles. I started a part time racing motorcycle shop in 1969. Opened shop full time in 1971, bought out Honda Dealer in 1972. I married my wife Laurene "Renie" in 1975. Bought out the Harley-Davidson dealer in 1980. Recently moved both franchises to a new location. Past President and 20-year member of Mt. Pleasant Kiwanis, Board member of Fairfield County Salvation Army, appointed by Governor of Ohio to Ohio Bureau of Motor Vehicle Dealers review board to represent the motorcycle industry. Still love my wife and riding motorcycles.

**LEAL R. CASON** RM2, was born March 11, 1948. Enlisted in the Navy in 1966. My father John Cason former MM2, in the Navy during WWII and Korea, encouraged my enlistment. Went to boot camp at Great Lakes, IL. Went to basic electricity and electronics school at Great Lakes, IL. Attended Radioman "A" school in Bainbridge, MD. Was stationed on the *USS Mercer APB-39* (plank owner) in Vietnam 1968-

1969. Other duty stations were the *USS Mullany DD528*, after Vietnam the *USS Talladega APA208* (decommissioned the Talladega), *USS Alamo LSD33* until the end of enlistment. After my enlistment attended Alan Hancock College in California for an AA in Business then the University of Laverne in California for my BA in Business Management. After the Navy I went to work for the US Bureau of Prisons for 14 years then transferred to the US Mint in Denver, CO and am currently retired. I have one daughter, Tamara Cason, currently working in the medical field, one son Trent Cason AT1 currently in the Navy flying as part of a Tacamo crew (looks like he is going to be a lifer), my daughter-in-law Sacha, and granddaughter Joni from my daughter, and three grandsons, Eddie, Sidney and Christian from my son and daughter-in-law. Memorable experience was first reporting to the *USS Mercer*. When I got to the dock all I saw was basically a shell. It was late at night and there was one lone welder on the deck welding. When I went on board I asked him where the Quarter Deck was so that I could report in. He said "What Quarter Deck? This thing isn't even built." I had to walk back to the Main Gate and found out sure enough, it wasn't. A couple of weeks later a few of us were in the warehouse across from the ship being watched by the Chief Bosun Mate and I noticed that they were painting the ship green. I told the Chief that that was the weirdest undercoat I had ever seen. He said, "Son, where we are going, you are going to be glad she is painted green." That is when I found out where we were going. To make a long story short, they kept pushing up our departure date and the next thing we know, we are putting together the inside of the ship as we are going across the Pacific.

**WILLIAM CATRON** was born in 1932 in Wayne County, KY. He earned BS, MA at Western Kentucky University 1975-1976. He joined the US Navy in 1951.

Catron served with the Riv Div 513 (PBR's) 1967-1968. Military locations included the Mekong Delta in Vietnam. Catron was at the TET Offensive in 1968. He was awarded Navy Combat Action Ribbon and a Presidential Unit Citation. Achieved the rank of ENCS (SS) E-8. He retired in 1973. Catron says that his most memorable experience was to serve as "Patrol Officer" with Riv Sec. 513. He was on patrol when the "TET" attack actually started. For the next five days, they only came in to re-arm and re-fuel then right back out. He retired from the Navy in 1973. Used the GI Bill for college for a second career in education. Taught middle school and adult education.

Catron has been married to Shirley since 1954. They have four children, Becky, Doug, Mark and Katrina. They also have seven grandchildren and two great-grandchildren. Catron not only was a teacher, but also vice-principal. He retired from the Navy in 1973 and retired from teaching in 1996.

**RICK J. CHAPMAN** GMG3, born Dec. 18, 1947 in Chicago, IL. Graduated Chicago Vocational High School. After the service, received a BSME degree on the GI Bill, and now owns two businesses. They are a home maintenance company and a pawnshop.

His military life started in January 1967, as a reservist USNR and training at Great Lakes, IL and the *USS Parle (DE708)*. He was activated for River Assault training at Mare Island, Vallejo, CA and survival, evasion, resistance and escape training at Whidby Island, WA during the summer of 1968 and reported to Dong Tam Vietnam on Oct. 19, 1968. He was assigned to RivRon 11 Zippo 111-7 (Flame-thrower Boat). His first night on the boat was Halloween Oct. 31. Tied up to the pontoon of the *USS Westchester County (LST 1167)* at 3 a.m., two 500-pound mines were attached to the side by enemy swimmers that got through killing 25 and injuring 27. It was the largest single loss of the Vietnam War. Parts of the Mailshack came down on their boat. On Feb. 27, 1969 they came under heavy enemy attack which wounded four on his boat and was medivac to Dong Tam. He was awarded the Bronze Star and Purple Heart. Later he was reassigned to Tango 111-6, which turned over to the Vietnamese-Navy. Then transferred to *Monitor 132*, left Vietnam on Aug. 25, 1969 with memories that will never be forgotten.

**JOHN P. "CHRZ" CHRZANOWSKI** was born July 12, 1948 in Jersey City, NJ. He earned BS in business administration with Magna Cum Laude Honors through the G.I. Bill (Jersey City, NJ State University).

Joined the Army-Infantry June 5, 1968. Served with 9th Infantry Div. M.R.F. A Co. 4/47th, Benewah; B Co. 6/31st, Nueces and Can Gouic Base Camp. Basic training at Ft. Dix, NJ; AIT at Ft. Polk, LA; NCO Academy at Ft. Benning, GA; RVN IV Corps A.O (South of Saigon). Water Borne, Airmobile, Vehicle Insertions and Drop-offs in Free- Fire-Zones for Patrolling and Ambush Functions. He was awarded various infantry-action type medals; however, no Purple Heart. He achieved the rank of SGT E-5 11B40 Senior Rifleman with no Secondary MOS. Discharged March 17, 1970 in Ft. Dix, NJ. His most memorable experience was in country award of the CIB. He will also never forget the sounds of the expanded rounds' casings bouncing onto the Helo Deck during the Memorial Services, 21-Gun-Salute, an all too frequent event.

Married to Dorris, he has two daughters by previous marriage, Gina and Diane. They have three grandsons, Andrew John, John William and Jason William. Civilian employment includes Municipal D.P.W. Supt. 10 years and Marine Engineer for 18 years.

**GREGORY M. "GREG" COFFMAN** was born on Dec. 13, 1942 in Connersville, PA. He graduated from Torrance High School in 1961. Joined the US Navy in December 1966.

Units and ships that Coffman served on include: RTC Boot Camp, 1966, San Diego, CA; NTC 1966 San Diego, CA; Midway Island 1967-1968; NIOTC and T-131-5 RVN 1967-1968 TF 117; LST-902; River Div 151 Run TF 116; ARG-4; ACB-1 DAB Coronado, CA; AD-15; North Island; RTC San Diego, CA; BB-62; and AMPHIB GP3.

Coffman was awarded several medals and awards that include: Bronze Star Medal w/ Combat "V;" Good Conduct Medal (5) Award; National Defense Medal; Combat Action Ribbon; Navy Unit Commendation Ribbon (2) Award; Presidential Unit Citation (2) Award; RVN Campaign Medal; Vietnamese Medal of Honor First Class; Vietnamese Gallantry Cross with Palm; Vietnam Service Medal; Deployment Ribbon (8) Award; Surface Warfare Insignia; Purple Heart; Navy Meritorious Unit Commendation (2) Award; Navy "E" Ribbon; Expert Rifle; Expert Pistol; and Patrol Boat Pin.

Coffman was discharged on Aug. 1, 1986 and had achieved the rank of GMG-1. He is married to Rose Coffman. His civilian employment includes apartment management. He is a lifetime member of VFW, DAV, MOPH, NCOA and Gamewarden of Vietnam.

**MARTIN W. "BILL" COOK** was born July 4, 1945 in South Bend, IN. He completed three years at Indiana University. He joined the US Army (Infantry) on Oct. 29, 1965.

Units that he served with 2nd BE 3rd BN 60th INF 9th INF Div. *USS Colleton USS Benewah*. He served at Mekong Delta and Dong Tam Base Camp. He also served with ABOUG Unit from October 1967 to October 1968. Cook was awarded Combat Infantry Badge, Bronze Star w/ V and Air Medal. He achieved the rank of 1 LT and was discharged on Dec. 20, 1968. His most memorable experience was surviving an ambush as Recon Platoon Leader West of Dong Tam.

Married to Debra, they have five children, Betsy, Cheryl, Bill, Adam and Shannon. They also have five grandchildren, Jenny, Hunter, Thalia, Kurt and Aubrey. Civilian employment includes retired Police Officer (Patrolman-Division Chief). He retired on Feb. 18, 2000.

**DICK "BUFF" COWDEN** was born May 21, 1947 in Washington, D.C. He attended City University in Seattle, WA. Joined the US Navy on Nov. 4, 1967. He achieved the rank of Storekeeper Senior Chief (E-8) and was discharged on Oct. 31, 1992.

Career duty stations were November 1967 Naval Training Center, San Diego, CA; Naval School of Music, Little Creek, VA; Navy Band #193, Norfolk, VA; Navy Storekeeper "A" School, Newport, RI; Counterinsurgency/ Survival Training, Little Creek, VA; Naval Support Activity, Danang, Republic of Vietnam 1969; Naval Support Detachment Tan-My/Hue, Republic of Vietnam, 1969; Naval Support Activity, Danang, Republic of Vietnam, 1969; YRBM-21, Mekong Delta, Republic of Vietnam, 1970; *USS Sperry AS-12*, San Diego, CA; Naval Reserve Center, Daytona Beach, FL; *USS William R. Rush DD-714*, Bronx, NY; Chief of Naval Reserve, New Orleans, LA; Naval Reserve Center, Vallejo, CA; Naval Reserve Readiness Command, Region 19, San Diego, CA; Inshore Undersea Warfare Group 1, San Diego, CA; Craft of Opportunity, Mine Squadron 11, Seattle, WA; Naval Reserve Readiness Command, Region 22, Seattle, WA; 11/92 Retirement Ceremonies at Naval Reserve Center, Seattle, WA; and 11/97 Transferred to Naval Fleet Reserve.

Cowden is married to Cheryl and they have two children, Grady and Mitchell. His civilian employment includes working for Bayer and the Boeing Company. He retired in November 2001.

## ROBERT DAVID "CLUTCH CRAGO" CRAGO

(he ruined a few clutches driving jeeps and trucks, which got him the nickname) was born Aug. 7, 1947 in Denver, CO. He earned a Bachelor Science Degree Electronic/Electrical Engineering Columbia Pacific University 1984, Master's Degree Science Business Administration Columbia Pacific University 1987.

Crago joined the US Navy on Aug. 26, 1967. Units served with were Naval Electronic Warfare, River Assault Group, Boat Service Units, Naval Support Activity Da Nang, Vietnam, Task Force 116, Mobile Base One Tan My/ Cua Viet, and Dong Ha, Duties: Electronic Technician (Communications, RADAR, Electronic Warfare), 1060 1070, USS *Manley* DD 940, Destroyer Re-Commission Unit, with Duties as: Electronic Operations and Maintenance Petty Officer, 1970-1971. *USS Mount Whitney LCC-20* Flag Ship Amphibious Atlantic Fleet, Duties: Secure Communications Petty Officer, Section Supervisor, 1971-1973.

Military locations and stations were Great Lakes, IL Training Command; Portsmouth, VA Training Command; Coronado Training Command, San Diego, CA; Da Nang Naval Support Vietnam (Cua Viet & Dong Ha); Philadelphia, PA Naval Command; and Norfolk Naval Command, Norfolk, VA.

Battles and Campaigns: "Project Duffel Bag", Doc Mieu Base and Dong Ha (eight miles from the DMZ), Operations and Maintenance of McNamara's Wall (DMZ) Electronic Warfare Sensor Grid. "I Corps Tactical Zone" Operations and Maintenance of boat Pathfinder, RADAR, UHF ground to air, and ship to shore communications systems- Supporting Sea Lords, and Game Warden operations in I Corps Tactical Zone, plus the Special Operations Unit into the northern territories along the water portion of the Ho Chi Minh Trail. Post 1968 Tet Offensive "Task Force Clearwater" in defense of the Khe Sanh Marine Base and the recapture of the city Hue in support of the III Amphibious Marines. The recapture of the Cua Viet, Perfume and Hue Rivers. "Operation Chu Hoi (Open Arms Program)" Civil Action Corps. An effort to win over the hearts and minds of the Vietnamese people, orphanage volunteer work, bringing food and medical supplies to remote regions of the northern territories. "Yom Kipper Egypt/ Israel War" 1972 NATO Observation Corps. Joint service action of the coast of Egypt during the conflict served on the *USS Mount Whitney LCC-20*. Duties were as a cryptographic communications section supervisor for US Navy/ Marine Amphibious Forces Atlantic/ Mediterranean.

Awards and Medals: Good Conduct Medal, National Defense Service Medal, Vietnam Service Medal, Vietnam Campaign Medal, Combat Action Ribbon, RVN Cross of Gallantry Medal with Bronze Star, Navy Unit Commendation with Combat "V" Medal, Vietnam Civil Action Service Medal and Honor Man Award, Graduated 1st in his class in Cryptographic Communications School, 1968.

Rank achieved was 2nd Class Petty Officer, Electronic Technician RADAR (ETR2). Discharged on Dec. 23, 1973.

Married to Sandra Crago. Civilian employment was Sr. Communications Project Engineer and Telecommunications Project Manager for over 25 years. At the time of this writing, he is one year away from retirement.

Memorable experience: The US Navy training was the best he ever received in his life. The orphanage volunteer work they did was the most fulfilling thing he did in Vietnam, maybe in his life. As an advisor to the South Vietnamese Navy they enjoyed a sense of doing the right thing for them. The Seabees worked miracles for them when they needed them. The friends he made in Vietnam were the best people he ever knew. The ones that did not come back alive, he misses the most. The greatest honor he has ever felt was being a part of the support personnel to the bravest people in the world. In 2002, he revisited Vietnam, as a businessman and found the people in the north and south open and friendly to Americans.

Crago graduated from West Jefferson High School, 1965. He joined the US Navy in August of 1967 in the Advanced Electronics Program, six-year enlistment. Much of training in the Advanced ET area was communications, RADAR, plus basic electrical/electronics. The basic and advanced electronics training was completed at Great Lakes Training Command. He attended two voice cryptographic communication schools, he graduated 1st in his class and was given the "US Navy Honor Man" award, 1968. The training was completed at Portsmouth, VA. The cryptographic equipment repair schools emphasized the need to keep the codes a secret, and away from the enemy. He was given a temporary Top Secret clearance to handle the equipment, and the codes changers.

His training in anti-insurgency (guerilla warfare) and boat operations was at Coronado, and Camp Pendleton (US Marine Weapons Training).

He was not considered a boat crewman. His job was the make sure that all the electrical and electronic systems on the various Navy vessels inland operated correctly. They rotated from Da Nang up the rivers to Cua Viet, and Dong Ha, bringing back gear and supporting the sensor grid at the DMZ. The type of duty allowed him support to many different groups in country, SEAL Team (1), Mobile Riverine Forces, PBR gunboats (20) River Division 54, River Section 543, LCVP personnel and material carrying vessels, and helicopters. Ground to air and ship to shore communications was vital to the success of a boat's mission. When aboard the boats he manned the M-60 machine gun rear mounted or an M-79 grenade launcher when called upon. They did encounter heavy action along the rivers in the I Corps. Tactical Zone, after Tet 1968.

Much of the work accomplished by the ET/ EW personnel in Vietnam was behind the normal operations due to the sensitive nature of the secure communications and various types of electronic warfare methods deployed during the war.

The boat RADAR units had to be in good shape for night operations. The small pathfinder RADAR manufactured by Bendix, and Raytheon were made to withstand the hardships of water combat.

The UHF communications systems on the boats were of a major importance along with the voice cryptographic units attached to them. The communications systems assured the boat Captain he could call in air support and maintain contact with his cover boat.

The electronic grid of sensors along the DMZ was an impressive system backed by claymore mines to prevent the NVA from over running the five marine firebases just south of the DMZ along Highway 9. They city of Quang Tri and Hue would have been over run, as well. The special operations personnel had the job of going into the grid to replace and move sensors and mines. A switchboard was utilized to monitor the grid. If a unit of NVA would enter into the area, an operator could ignite the mines. The KIS of NVA was very high.

The DMZ was the 17th parallel with the Ben Hai River near the middle of the zone. The area just south of the DMZ was scene of some of the bloodiest battles of the conflict such as Quang Tri, The Rockpile, Khe Sanh, Lang Vei (US Army Special Forces Camp, on the Laos border), and Hamburger Hill (west of the Dakrong River, Ashau Valley, Hill 881). The gunboats and supply vessels tried to support this region, but it was difficult due to the terrain and NVZ/ VC forces in the region. The US Navy bases of Cua Viet and Dong Ha were overrun by the NVA during TET of 1968. Both bases were recaptured and a split effort of the fuel and ammunition was implemented to prevent further destruction. During that time various LSTs were used as maintenance ships with gunboat flotillas. The *USS Caroline County LST-525* and *USS Harnett County LST-821* were two in the I Corps Tactical Zone.

They tried to improve the back tracking RADAR to spot B-40 rockets and artillery positions across the DMZ, but they proved to be rather poor.

On the other side of the DMZ to the east were the Vinh Moc Tunnels. This was the staging area for the "Water Sappers" who tried to attack floating vessels in and around the area, both by river and sea.

The NVA and VC called the area west along the boarders of Laos and Cambodia from North Vietnam crossing the DMZ "Heaven's Gates." This is the area in which many B-52 strikes hit the VC and NVA soldiers bringing supplies down the Ho Chi Minh Trail.

Rivers of major operations in this region were the Cua Viet River, Quang Tri River, Cam Lo River, Perfume River and Dakrong River.

In Da Nang the support camp for our ET work was accomplished at Camp Tien Sha Annex/ Small Craft Repair Facility, located at the foot of Monkey Mountain. The primary communications operations center was located at the Triangle Relay Center. This facility was handed over to the South Vietnamese at the end of 1970.

Chaplin Corps were a part of the Chu Hoi Program- Civil Action engaging people of South Vietnam to show them we were friendly, by helping the locals with education, food and medical support. One program that Crago volunteered to be a part of was the orphan children volunteer program west of Da Nang. He would go to the local orphanages with supplies, and meet with the children. In addition, they brought rice and medical supplies to the villages along the river routes north. The motive was to have the village people tell them about VC movements in the area. This part of the Vietnam tour was the most satisfying. The units were awarded the Civil Action Service Medal. This medal made them feel very proud to be a part of the whole program.

In 1970, the US decided to turn over the operations of the I Corps. Tactical Zone to the South Vietnamese Navy. The Units were turned in advisors with a Vietnamese counter part to train. When Crago left Vietnam, no US Navy person replaced him; a South Vietnamese ETR-2 took over his responsibilities. Nguyen Van Phong and Crago became close friends. Crago was very sorry when he left. In Phong's face Crago could see the future for the people of South Vietnam. It was going to be very difficult for them to win with conflict without the US military behind them.

**SAMUEL C. CRAWFORD**, born Oct. 26, 1949 and enlisted in the US Navy in 1968 after graduating from Baltimore City College.

His first assignment out of boot camp was to the Mobile Riverine Task Force 117, onboard the *USS Satyr ARL-23*. Sam has written a novel series capturing his most memorable Vietnam experiences titled *BrownWater- Getting There is Half the Fun, BrownWater II- Now the Adventure Begins,* and *BrownWater III- Time to Go Home*.

After a number of tours in Vietnam with the MRF, Sam served a tour of duty with VQ4 (Fleet Air Reconnaissance Squadron Four) and VP30 (Patrol Squadron Thirty) at the Naval Air Test Station, Patuxent River, MD.

Honorably discharged and is a current member of the MRF. Awards and decorations include, National Defense Service Medal, Vietnam Campaign Medal w/ 60 device, Vietnam Service Medal w/ four Bronze Stars, Navy Unit Commendation Ribbon while serving with River Assault Flotilla One, Meritorious Unit Commendation, Combat Action Ribbon, Presidential Unit Citation for Extraordinary Heroism, and the Good Conduct Medal.

Married Patricia in February 1976 and they live in Middletown, DE with their daughter, Stephanie. Sam is presently employed as a Computer Programmer for an international consultant firm in Philadelphia, PA.

**DAVID CZECH** was born on May 15, 1949 in St. Cloud, MN. He joined the US Army in November 1967. Units that Czech served with was Co. B 3rd Platoon, and 4th Platoon 4/47 9th Infantry Div. He served in Dong Tam and also onboard the *USS Benewah*. He was awarded CIB and Air Medal. Achieved the rank of Spec 4. He was discharged in September 1971.

Finished his Army tour in Germany, ETS 1971. Got married in Minnesota in 1972 and moved to Alaska. He lived his high school dream in Alaska by homesteading, hunting and fishing. He worked on the oil pipeline in the mid-1970s and also construction related jobs around the state. He has a wonderful wife and four fine children, two of who are in the military now, one an oil refinery worker and his only daughter, Sarah who is an EMT. Czech was born again in 1976 and attends Bible Baptist Church in Fairbanks. Czech says, "I'm 'saved' to serve. God Bless the USA."

Most memorable experience was serving with the bravest, greatest and most dedicated men that he has ever known. The day in August 1968 when B Company did an Eagle Flight and Sgt. Joseph Salazzar single-handed charged a machine-gun bunker and saved perhaps many lives. (May his tribe increase). The day Bravo 4-Oscar "Jim Dalton" and Bruce Thuler 4th Platoon gave the ultimate sacrifice (KIA). You are not forgotten. Never will Czech see a finer bunch of men then those of you that he served with. His is looking forward to seeing a whole lot of you when he gets home!

**ORVILLE LEE "LEE" DALEY** was born on Feb. 10, 1936 in Shawnee, OK. He joined the US Navy on Feb. 23, 1955.

Units, locations and stations where Daley attended include the following: Naval R Training, San Diego, CA 1955; NRS(T) Lualualei, HI 1955 to 1956; *USS Bon Homme Richard CVA31*; *USS Norton Sound, AV1*; USN MC B-4 Davisville, RI- Guantanamo, Cuba; Argentina Newfoundland- Rota Spain; Naval Air Station Dallas, TX; *USS Askari ARL 30* (Vietnam) with the MRF; *TF 117* in the Mekong Delta 1967-1968; *USS Cocord AF5* San Diego, CA (Plank Owner); Naval Station Norfolk, VA; Naval R Training Center Orlando, FL.

Daley received many awards including the following: Navy Good Conduct Medal with two stars; Armed Forces Exped Medal; National Defense Serv. Medal; Navy Expeditionary Medal; Vietnam Campaign Medal; US Vietnam Service Medal with two stars; Combat Action Ribbon; Navy Presidential Unit Citation; Republic of Vietnam Unit Gallantry Citation; Republic of Vietnam Civil Action Unit Citation; Vietnam Presidential Unit Citation and US Presidential Unit Citation.

Retired with the rank of CS1 E6 on Sept. 17, 1974. He made a lot of sailor shipmates happy with all the good baking that he did.

Daley is married to Joan and they have three children, Susan, Patty and Robin. They also have four grandchildren, Kristene, Courtney, Blayze and Chantz. His civilian employment includes being a warehouse manager. He has been enjoying retirement since March 7, 1998.

**DAVID A. DESIDERIO** served with the US Navy (1961-1964), the US Naval Reserve (1964-1967) and the US Coast Guard (1967-1987).

Ships that Desiderio served on were *USS Arnold J. Isbell (DD869)* 1962-1964, *USCGC Taney (WHEC37)* 1967-1969, *USCGC Pontchartrain (WHEC 70)* 1969-1971, *USCGC Midgett (WHEC 726)* 1973-1975 and *USCGC Morgenthau (WHEC 722)* 1985-1987. He was stationed at USNTC (Recruit Training) July 1961 to September 1961; US Fleet ASW School, San

Diego, CA (Sonar "A" School) September 1961 to May 1962; Coast Guard Training Center, Yorktown, VA (OCS) January 1969 to July 1969; US Fleet ASW School, San Diego (Staff) 1971-1973; Coast Guard Vessel Traffic System, San Francisco 1975 to 1978 and 1982 to 1985; and Coast Guard Training Center, Alameda (Staff) 1978 to 1982.

Campaigns that he was involved with were Vietnam Advisory (*USS Arnold J. Isbell*, 1963 and 1964), Vietnam Winter-Spring 1970 (*CGC Pontchartrain*, 1970), Sanctuary Counteroffensive (*CGC Pontchartrain,* 1970), Counteroffensive, Phase VII (*CGC Pontchartrain,* 1970). Awards authorized are National Defense Service Medal, Armed Forces Expeditionary Medal (waived in favor of the VSM), Vietnam Service Medal, Vietnam Campaign Medal, RVN Meritorious Unit Commendation Gallantry, RVN Civil Actions Unit Citation, Navy Meritorious Unit Commendation, Coast Guard Meritorious Unit Commendation (2), Coast Guard Expert Rifleman Medal, Coast Guard Sea Service Ribbon, Coast Guard Commandant's Letter of Commendation Ribbon, Coast Guard Achievement Medal and Permanent Cutterman's Designator Pin.

Desiderio retired on March 31, 1987 as a Commander. His most unforgettable experience was having been given the opportunity to serve in support of our brothers in Vietnam, and the satisfaction of having done so honorably.

## FRANK M. DETTMERS SR.
was born June 28, 1934 at Trinidad, CO and graduated from high school.

On March 22, 1952 Dettmers joined the US Navy and served with the following units or ships: *AKA-20 USS Viego, CVA 15, USS Randolph, DDE871, USS Damao, APA 228 USS Rockbridge,* Amphibase, Little Creek, Can Ceu Des Pac (COF Coxswain, *USS Caoberve CAG-2),* Seaman Guard, Com Fiar SD (Admiral's Bridge). He was stationed with RivRon 13, Alfa 28, CCB-1, ATC-6, ATC-54 Vietnam, FIT Training Group, San Diego, CA; VF126 MIRanis; SOSP Downtown San Diego; Night Ops Supervisors. He was in campaigns in Korea, Vietnam, the Cuban Blockade.

During his career he received the following awards and medals: Six Good Conduct, Combat Action, National Defence, Korea, Armed Forces Expenditionary, Vietnam, President Unit Commendation, Vietnamese Cross of Gallantry.

By date of discharge on Jan. 5, 1976, he had achieved the rank of CPO Boatswains Mate.

His memorable experiences included the CCB-131-1 sunk by enemy mine in humid forest, Oct. 23, 1969 at 1612 p.m. Four injured, three VAC. Estimated 500 pounds mine. In 9160 on board *USS Danato DDE 871* crossed equator while chasing a modern day pirate on the Santa Maria. He was given asylum in Recife Brazil.

Dettmers was married to Marlene J. Dettmers (deceased) and they hand the following children: Debra Lynn, Diana Jean, Frank M. Jr. and Eugene Frank. Grandchildren are Tiffany, Scott Young Jr., Derrick Young, Frank III, Alexander and Wyatt.

In civilian life, Dettmers worked 19 years on turbines, assembler. He retired Jan. 31, 2004.

## WILLIAM E. "DUTCH" DEUTCHER
was born in Cleveland, OH on Oct. 29, 1942. He attended college for three years. Joined the US Army in May 1966.

Units served with and ships served on were 1st Platoon "A" Co./3/60th Infantry/9th Infantry Division, *USS Benewah.* Military locations and stations were Fort Benning, GA; Fort Riley, KS; RVN; Bearcat; Mekong Delta and Dong Tam. The names of battles and campaigns weren't important to Dutch. As a medic, he made sure that his aid-bag was fully equipped and then he would privately pry to St. Jude and ask him to give Dutch the courage to perform his duties to his men and leaders, no matter what the circumstances. Thank you, St. Jude.

Awards and medals are Combat Medic Badge, Army Commendation Medal and Special Promotion, RVN National Defense Ribbon, etc., etc. He was discharged in February 1968 with the rank of E-5.

Most memorable experience was the unforgettable honor of serving with some of the finest and bravest young men he has ever met. After 29 years and 51 weeks, finally locating and meeting up with Sgt. Wayne C. Merriman. The day that Wayne stepped on that land mine still haunts Dutch. Dutch knew Wayne had lost both legs, but he didn't know what Wayne's future held in store. Dutch is happy to report that Wayne has a beautiful family and is as good as he can be. After 30 plus years, Dutch was also reunited with his squad leader, Col. Rodney Morris (ret) and Chaplain James D. Johnson, Lt. Col. (ret). Both reunions took place in San Diego, CA. He also met up with a few of the guys at the 2002 MFRA reunion. He is looking forward to this year's reunion and more to come. God Bless each and every one of you and God Bless America.

Dutch is separated and has two children, Michele and Gregory. He also has two grandchildren, Keely and Mlya. His civilian employment includes working for Cleveland Building Trades/ Pipefitter Local #120. He retired in August 2001.

## STEPHEN T. "STEVE, DEX" DEXTER
was born Oct. 23, 1943 in Salem, MA. He attended Marblehead Public Schools, the University of Pennsylvania (BA) and Old Dominion University (MS Ed.).

Dexter joined the US Navy on May 27, 1965. MRF units served with was Supply Officer, APL 30 (NSA Saigon det). Military locations and stations *USS Granville S. Hall (YAG 40);* NSC Newport; *USS Dixon (AS 37);* Fleet Assistance Group, San Diego; Navy TAFT; Bandar Abbas; Aviation Supply Office, Philadelphia; *USS Independence (CV 62);* NAS Sigonella; *USS Ranger (CV 61);* Staff, COMNAVAIRLANT, Norfolk; and NSC Norfolk. Awards and medals are MSM (2), JSCM, NCM, NAM, CAR, PUC, NUC (2), MUC (3) plus various service and campaign medals and ribbons. Achieved the rank of Captain, Supply Corps, US Navy and was discharged on Sept. 1, 1991.

Memorable experiences was the MRF was his first large-scale military task force and he was and still is amazed at how well things seemed to work, particularly the spirit of cooperation between Army and Navy. The mining of the *USS Westchester County* and the sinking of the *YLLC-4* made those of us afloat feel just a little less secure and more in tune with the lives of those who fought on the rivers and rice paddies. Those and his single day of action, in the field near Ben Tre with C Co 3/60th made for a very exciting year in which he made a bunch of close friends and with many of whom he corresponds with to this day.

Dexter has been married since 1980 to Deborah "Debbie" and they have three children, Erin, Matthew and Audrey. They don't have grandchildren yet, but give them time. Civilian employment includes being a middle and high school teacher from 1991 to 1998; since then an analyst/consultant at US Joint Forces Command, Norfolk developing concepts and conducting experiments in logistics for future joint war fighting.

## C. DAVE DIVELBISS
was born June 12, 1935 in Kirksville, MO. His education includes BA in Economics and BA in Education both from Central Washington University in Ellensburg, WA and Master's in Business Administration from George Washington University in Washington, D.C. He joined the US Navy in 1952.

Units he served with and ships served on were *USS Mauna Kea, USS Mt. Katmai,* ComRiv Flot One, Nato Saclant, Comsublant, DLA and DLA-IO. Military locations and stations were Port Chicago, CA; Defense Depot Tracy, CA; Amphib. Base North Island, CA; Saclanteen La Spezia, Italy; Naval Station Norfolk, VA and DLA Washington, D.C. Divelbiss served in Vietnam from 1967 until 1968. Awards and medals are Joint Service Commendation, Navy Commendation, Vietnam Medals, Presidential Unit

Citation and Navy Unit Citation. Achieved the rank of Commander and was discharged on June 30, 1978. His most memorable experience was being a plank owner of *River Assault Flotilla One* and serving with unit in Vietnam.

Divelbiss has been married to Fran since 1958 and they have three children. David owns his own brokerage firm in food service and resides in California; Kathy is a nurse and resides in Washington; Carla is a real estate agent and also resides in Washington. Divelbiss has four grandchildren Kristin, Jason, Ryan and Alycia. His civilian employment includes being a teacher, Mayor of Roslyn, WA and Councilman.

**DANIEL DODD** was born June 25, 1931 in Kingston, PA. He joined the US Navy on Sept. 8, 1950. Dodd achieved the rank of PHC and was discharged on March 16, 1970.

**MICHAEL R. "MIKE" DOE** was born Feb. 16, 1944 in Holdridge, NE. He obtained his GED in 1961, went to college for one year, and attended many Navy Training Classes. He joined the US Navy on Feb. 24, 1961.

Units served with include *USS Iwojima (LPH2)* and *USS Tanner (AGS-15)*. Military locations and stations include being a boat captain of armored troop carrier T-91-9 (River Assault Squadron Nine). He was also a part of TET (168). Awards and medals include Navy Commendation Medal (September 1967-September 1968), Good Conduct Medal (November 1968), National Defense Service, Republic of Vietnam Campaign Medal (1968) and Vietnam Service Medal (1968 and 1969). He achieved the rank of BM1 and retired in August 1969. Doe says that his most memorable experience was everything about TET! He remembers the closeness of the boat crews in Vietnam and especially the great Bar-B-Que's. "We all needed the break so much!"

Doe has been married for 35 years to Glenna and they have three children, William, Lisa and Michael Jr. They have seven grandchildren: Alex, Jake, Sauanna, Ryan, Elizabeth, Amanda and Adam. Civilian employment includes being a Journeyman Industry Maintenance Mechanic, Gates Rubber Company in Denver, owner Doe Trucking Company in Denver, Poker Room Manager at Station Casinos in Las Vegas. He's not retired, yet!

**JAMES M. "JIM" DORLAND** was born Sept. 23, 1946 in Anaconda, MT. He earned his BS in 1976 at Portland State University. He joined the US Navy on Dec. 29, 1964.

Dorland served on *USS Enterprise CVAN-65, USS Constellation CVA-64, USS Colleton APB-36* and *USS Hunterdon County LST-838*. He had Recruit Training at San Diego, ET "A" School at Treasure Island, San Francisco, and Crypto Repair School at Vallejo. He has been awarded the Purple Heart, Presidential Unit Citation (2), Navy Unit Commendation (4), Combat Action, Gallantry Cross w/ Palm, RVN Campaign w/ 1960 Devise, Vietnam Service Medal, Vietnam Campaign Medal and National Defense. He achieved the rank of ETN-2 and was discharged on Dec. 14, 1968. His most memorable experience was being a part of TET.

Dorland is married to Teddy Loreine and they have three children Jennifer (R.I.P.), Jake and Mike. They have one grandchild, Evan. Dorland has been employed as Manager at Pacific Northwest Bell. He retired in June 1998.

**WILLIAM J. DUGGAN**, BM3, graduated from St. Patrick's High School in Ryan, IA in 1965. Left for Memphis, TN and started work on the Illinois Central Railroad until July 1966 when he enlisted in the Navy. Completed Boot Camp in San Diego, CA and was assigned to the *USS Coontz*. Made one West Pac Tour doing Search and Rescue, and upon returning Stateside, volunteered for the MRF. After training in Mare Island, CA he was assigned as boat coxswain on the *Monitor 131-2*. This boat was subsequently turned over to the South Vietnamese Navy where he was reassigned to A Mine Sweeping detachment in Nha Be for the completion of his one-year tour. Upon returning Stateside he was given orders to IUWG-1 in Long Beach, CA and was sent to TAD to Sasebo Japan for the duration of his enlistment.

After he was discharged from the Navy, he returned to Memphis, TN and back to work with the Illinois Central Railroad where he worked through the management ladder with work locations in Memphis, TN; Mobile, AL; Meridian, MS; Marshall, MO; Mattoon, IL; and Champaign, IL, his last position with the Illinois Central Railroad being Superintendent of Engineering for the North half of the railroad system. In June of 1989, he resigned from the Illinois Central Railroad to accept the position of Vice President Engineering at Iowa City, IA with the Iowa Interstate Railroad, a position held until May 1996, when he was promoted to Vice President Operations of the company. On April 15, 1999 he resigned from the Iowa Interstate Railroad to accept the position of Vice President Operations of Railroad Development Corp. of Pittsburgh, PA; a railroad investment and operating Management Company. RDC Corp. currently has properties in Argentina, Peru, Malawi Africa, Mozambique Africa, Estonia and Guatemala, Central America, where Bill also serves as President of the Railroad, and the Iowa Interstate Railroad headquartered in Iowa City, IA USA.

Bill has four children and three stepchildren, and is married to Cindy Duggan and they enjoy 15 grandchildren to date. They make their home in Champaign, IL, USA where they intend to one day make their retirement headquarters. Bill also looks forward to a year when schedules permit to attend an annual reunion of the MRF.

**MICHAEL R. "MIKE" DYER** was born Nov. 11, 1946 in Ajo, AZ. After high school, Dyer went on to earn his BA and MA. He joined the US Army on Sept. 15, 1966.

Military locations and stations include Ft. Bliss, Ft. Polk, A/5$^{th}$ 60 9$^{th}$ ID, Ft. Hood and Ft. Huachura. He served with A/5$^{th}$/ 60. Served in Vietnam, Colorado, and the Army-Navy Joint in Delta-Plain of Reeds area. Achieved the rank of E6 before retiring in June 1969. Dyer has been awarded the Purple Heart two Oak Leaf Clusters, CIB and others. His most memorable experiences were the friends, being in hot wet mud and the leaches.

Dyer is married to Rosemarie and the have three children, Tammy, Heather and Joshua. They also have one grandchild, Wesley. Civilian employment includes being a teacher, coach and athletic director.

**RONALD W. EDWARDS** was born Oct. 29, 1946 in Lumberton, NC. He graduated from West Columbus High School and attended three years at Cape Fear Technical College. Joined the US Army on April 12, 1967.

Edwards served with the 3/60 Inf., 9$^{th}$ Inf. Div. in Vietnam. He was stationed at Fort Bragg, NC for Basic Training, Fort Jackson, SC for AIT and also in Vietnam. Edwards served with the MRF from Jan. 9, 1968 until Dec. 20, 1968. He became Squad Leader in 2$^{nd}$ Platoon Charlie Company. He has been awarded Air Medal, two Bronze Star (one with Valor), Purple Heart, Combat Infantry Badge, three South Vietnamese Badges and Good Conduct Medal. Edwards achieved the rank of E6- Platoon Sgt. He was discharged in February 1969.

Edwards' most memorable experience is printed as follows; "Our Company had gone out to secure an Alpha boat that was partially sunken in the river by a rocket propelled grenade. We landed on a muddy beach where a hard-fought battle had taken place two days prior. While crawling up to try to set up security, I saw a hill that looked to be dry. My RTO and I crawled up on it. I looked down and saw a piece of wire between my legs and without thinking I pulled on it. As I did, the lid for a bunker came open and immediately sprung back shut. My RTO and I decided to attach a rope to the lid and pull it off. When we did, four sets of hands came out in surrender. We put the injured Vietnamese on a helicopter and flew them to Intelligence. In the bunker we found quite a bit of money, two AK's, two pistols and some Chicom grenades.

"The next morning the report came down-we had captured a Private, a Sergeant, a Lieutenant and a Battalion Commander from the 538 North Vietnamese Battalion. From this we found several weapon caches and sampan routes that the Vietnamese were using to get their weapons to the Delta. This turned out to be the largest Intelligence that the 9$^{th}$ Division had ever gotten from the VC at that time. Although I received no medal for this experience, it still remains my most memorable."

Edwards is married to Karen and they have a son and daughter-in-law, Michael and Heather Edwards. They also have two grandchildren, Justin and Olivia. Civilian employment includes working for General Electric for two years- Welder/Machinist and Precision Cams-family business. He retired in 1988.

**JOSEPH B. EHRENHARDT** was born June 21, 1948 in Brooklyn, NY. After high school, he went on to earn his BS in Criminal Justice. He joined the US Army Security Agency on Sept. 27, 1966.

Units that Ehrenhardt served with were the 335th RRC/ *USS Benewah*. Military locations and stations were Basic Training and Adv Ind Training at Fort Dix, Radio TIUP Fort Gordon, 335 RRC VN, CO B 319th USASA Germany. Ehrenhardt served in VN Counter Offen PH III, VN Counter Offen IV, and TET Counter Offen. He was awarded ASR, GCM, ACM, VCM, NDSM, VCM, Merit Unit CIT and REPVCG/w Palm. Achieved the rank of Sgt. before being discharged on Sept. 14, 1970. His most memorable experience was making friends over a few beers, Diego Ramirez Jr., and then losing the friend in a ambush the next day; Never Forget.

Ehrenhardt has been married for 32 years to Yvonne and they have three children, Joseph, Nicole and Sabrina. They also have a grandchild, Sabrina. Civilian employment includes being retired from NYPD and he is currently PA Park Ranger Supervisor.

**EDWARD ELIAS** was born Aug. 24, 1946 in Ramallah, Israel. After high school, he attended some college. Elias joined the US Army in 1965.

Elias served with the 9th Infantry 3rd/34th Artillery, 3/47 Infantry and on the *USS Benewah*. He was stationed at Fort Benning, GA; Fort Still, OK; Fort Bliss, TX and Vietnam. Elias was apart of the assault on My Tho, Can Tho, Dong Tam and TET Offensive. He was awarded the Purple Heart (2), Silver Star, Bronze Star, Soldier's Medals, Vietnamese Service Medal and Vietnamese Campaign Medal. Before being discharged in 1968, Elias achieved the rank of Sergeant E5. His most memorable experience was teaming up with the Navy in the Mekong River. They Navy provided barges while the Army provided artillery firepower down the river. This was the first time the Army and Navy put up artillery units on barges to float down the river. They had heavy causalities and called for air strikes and gun ships.

Elias has been married for over 33 years to Rima, and they have four children, Tina, Tammy, Robert and Nancy. They also have four grandchildren, Kristin, Jordan, Grant and Sophia. Elias has been a business owner and real estate investor. He retired in January 2003.

**JOHN A. "SLICK" ERICKSON III** was born July 5, 1947 in St. Paul, MN. After high school, he joined the US Navy in July 1966.

Units served with and ships served on include *TF117*, RivDiv-112, A-112-1 30 days, Swift Boats-Danang. He attended Radio School in San Diego, CA; More Island Vallejo, CA; Dong Tam, Danang, Vietnam; and on the *USS Thomas J. Gary* at Keywest, FL. Erickson achieved the rank of E-4 before being discharged in September 1970. Erickson says that his most memorable experience was Snoopy's Nose on Dec. 5, 1967.

Erickson is married to Aliese Marie and they have one daughter, Melissa. They also have a granddaughter, Mia. Civilian employment includes being a truck driver, salesman, owner Ace Worldwide Mug in Rochester, MN.

**LARRY C. "SQUATTY BODY" ETHRIDGE** entered the Navy OCS on Valentine's Day, 1969, after graduating from Duke. Assigned as Gunnery Officer on the *USS Askari ARL-30*, numerical relief for college classmate, George Fields. Arrived on Askari the same day man landed on the moon, also transited to

Japan for repairs and participated in the Cambodian Incursion. Hitchhiked through Europe, then returned to attend Law School and the University of Louisville. Graduated in 1975 and (in one of the best moves of his life) married Edith Kirkbride Gilbert on May 29, 1977. Daughter, Elizabeth (24) is a graduated of the University of Georgia and an entrepreneur, and son Grant (21) attends the University of Louisville. Recruited by Albert Moore while in a hospital bed and has served as the MRFA's since 1994. Values the MRFA because so many people who served in the Delta now have a means for getting together to share life experiences at the Reunions.

**CHARLES E. "BUTCH, DOC" FISHE** was born Aug. 5, 1950 in Americus, GA. He graduated from Staley High School in Americus, GA and attended two years at Troy State College in Troy, AL. On Feb. 17, 1969 he joined the US Army.

Units Fishe' served with were B, 6th BN 31st INF 9ID, 123 MED Co (CLR), 2nd GEN HOPS 4th MED Bn, 197 INF Bede, 34th MEN Bn, 130th STA Hosp and 320th Sta Hosp, MEDDAC Ft. BNG. Military locations and stations include Vietnam; Ft. Lewis, WA; Ft. Carson, CO; Ft. BNG, GA; Germany Stewart Army Base, NY; Ft. ORD, CA; Ft. Polk, LA; and Ft. Sam Houston, TX. He served in TET 1969 and Counter Offensive 1969. Fishe' has been awarded MSM, Air Medal, ARCOM 2 OLC, ARCOM w/ V Device, Achievement Medal 1/OLC, Purple Heart 2nd AWD, and Combat Medic Badge. He achieved the rank of SFC/E-7 and was discharged on June 30, 1992. His most memorable experience was on the first day when he was called "Doc" and also the day he was awarded the Combat Medic Badge.

Fishe' is married to Fraby (Staten) Fishe' and they have three children, Charles E. Fishe' II, Vitus E. D. Fishe and Ufrabyu L. Fishe'. They also have five grandchildren, Christoper, Kenshala, Alexes, Zyon and Kyshon Fishe'. Civilian employment includes being a nurse where he is still employed.

**WILLIAM C. "BILL" FODDRILL** was born Oct. 3, 1946 in Des Moines, IA. He graduated from Des Moines Technical High School in 1964.

Began employment at John Deere Des Moines. Worked May 2, 1966 in Product Engineering Department. He retired from John Deere in August 1999 as an Engineering Designer. His wife's name is Sharon (Shari) and they have two sons, Brian and John, and a daughter, Shelly.

Foddrill joined the USNR Oct. 20, 1965 and began active duty on Jan. 24, 1967 as SN (E3). He received orders for ASPB small craft duty in Vietnam and trained in a group of 40 men (eight 5-man boat crews) at Coronado, Camp Pendelton, Warner Springs, and Mare Island in Vallejo, CA.

The ASPB's for River Division 112 were not yet in Country when they arrived July 8, 1967 so they were temporarily assigned to PCF (Swift) Boat Duty. Half of them were sent to Danang, and half to Chu Lai.

Foddrill's boat crew, A112-8, went to Chu Lai until August 4 when they were then sent to the PCF Base at Cua Viet on the DMZ (NVA Artillery Range).

All crews were ordered back to Dong Tam (Mekong Delta) Sept. 21, 1967 for temporary assignments on ATC and Monitor Boats. Foddrill served as 50 cal. Gunner on 112-7 and Coxswain on T112-2. His boat (A112-8) arrived at Vung Tau in the fall of 1967, and they were sent to outfit it. They finally had their own boat! They participated in numerous s/d operations and the TET Offensive of 1968.

Foddrill left Vietnam July 24, 1968 and was sent to Treasure Island, CA for separation on Aug. 7, 1968. His discharge date was Oct. 19, 1971.

The boat crew members for A112-8 were: Leslie E. Murray, BM1 (Boat Captain); Samuel T. Brasswell, EN2 (Engineman); Whitney O. Smith, BT3 (50 cal. Gunner); Robert E. Spanos, RMSN (Radioman); and William C. Foddrill, SN (20 mm Gunner).

Leslie E. Murray was killed near Can Tho when their boat was hit with a rocket at 2:30 a.m. while they were guarding another alpha boat which was hit and sank to the river bottom the day before.

**PATRICK M. "DOC" FOGARTY** was born July 16, 1947 at Mt. Clemens, MI. He received his high school diploma, attended a four-year lineman program, and also was a civilian paramedic. On Oct. 6, 1966 he joined the US Army.

Units that Fogarty served with include 2nd Plt E Co 4th/47th 9th INF Div (Mobile Riverine Force) and onboard *USS Benewah* and *USS Colleton*. Locations and stations were Basic Training at Fort Knox, KY; Medical Training at Fort Sam Houston, TX; Fort Stewart, GA; and Hunter Army Airfield. He also served in the TET Offensive. Fogarty has been awarded Combat Medical Badge, Air Medal (3), Army Commendation w/V Bronze Star, Good Conduct and RVN. He achieved the rank of SP5 and was discharged in November 1968. Fogarty says that his most memorable experience was being with guys who had same thoughts "Survival"- acting as he did in combat. Taking care of wounded G.I.'s and knowing that maybe he could make a difference in their survival w/ extreme wounds. All of the firefights were memorable as well as the River Assault Boats.

Fogarty is married to Barbara and they have two grown children, Patrick and Heath. Fogarty also has three stepchildren, Kimberly, Ray and Elizabeth. He also has six grandchildren, Jonathan, Alexis, Jake, Nicolas, Robert and Nathan. His civilian employment includes being a Journeyman in Hi-Voltage, Lineman, Detroit Edison Co. Fogarty says that he is still climbing poles!

**JACK FOGEL** was born Sept. 21, 1943 in Berkeley, CA. His education includes AAS Mech. Engineering 1988, AAS Computer Engineering 2001, 5"/54 Gun School Great Lakes, IL, Instructor Training Norfolk, VA. He joined the US Navy in October 1960.

Units served with and ships served on were the *USS Piedmont (AD17)*, *USS Los Angeles (CA-135)*, *USS Edson (DD-946)*, *USS Gallant (MSO-489)*, *USS Norton Sound (AVM-1)*, SERE training at Warner Springs, CA, NSA NhaBE VNM, *USS Braine (DD-631)*, NAVINSHORSTRACEN Mare Island, CA, SERE training at Whidby Island, WA, Survival training Subic Bay Philipines, Served as Boat Captain in RivRon 13 and RivRon 15 on the following boats: *Tango 22, Zippo-1, Tango-50, Tango-51*, served in Vietnam from December 1967 to October 1972, Fleet Training Center San Diego as a Weapons Instructor, SSC Naval Training Center Great Lakes Gun School (5"/54 MK42), *USS Rathburne (DE-1057)*, *USS Brewton (DE-1086* later changed to *FF-1086*, FLETCOMBATRACENLANT as a Weapons Instructor (Coordinated team on developing 5"/54 training in Dan Neck, VA), last tour was at Chief of Naval Technical Training as a Training Program Coordinator for four Weapons schools in the US.

Fogel achieved the rank of GMCS (E-8) and retired in April 1986 with 26 years of service. He has been awarded Bronze Star w/ V, Purple Heart (3), Navy Commendation (3) w/ V, Navy Achievement, Combat Action Ribbon, Presidential Unit Citation, Navy Unit Citation (2), Meritorious Unit Citation, Battle Efficiency Ribbon (3), Navy Good Conduct (4), Navy Expeditionary Medal, National Defense, Armed Forces Expeditionary (2), VSM (10), Navy Humanitarian Medal, Sea Service Ribbon (4), Vietnam Cross of Gallantry, Vietnam Civil Action 1st Class Medal, Vietnam Campaign Medal, Navy Rifle Expert Medal and the Navy Pistol Expert Medal.

Fogel says of his most memorable experience, "I was Second Class Gunnersmate and made First Class while I was in Vietnam. Through the many firefights, TET Offensive there were good and bad times. The numerous exposures I have had facing life and death decisions and dealing with those decisions added to my growth in life. The shipmates that I served with and lost due to war and peace, I pray for daily. In my summation the Mobile Riverine Force and Supporting Activities along with the other Armed Forces Unit I worked with in various operations will not ever get the recognition for their achievements as they should."

Fogel has been married for 23 years to his bride, Julia E. Fogel. They have two children, Joyce Galloway (Computer Engineering degree) and John Darrohn (Civil Engineering Degree). They also have two grandchildren, Kristin and Taylor. Civilian employment has included State Technical Institute of Memphis (Instructor), Transact International (Project Manager), Williams-Sonoma (Maintenance Planner) and FEDEX Ground (Line Haul Maintenance Manger).

**KEN FORD** was born July 23, 1944 in Chicago, IL. He attended Lane Technical High School in Chicago, DeVry Technical in Chicago, Assec Elect Technical in Acc, NC and received a diploma in carpentry.

Ford joined the US Navy on Sept. 15, 1965. He served with Assault Craft Unit Two, *USS Spiegel Grove (LSD-32)*, Mobile Riverine Group Bravo, and RivFlot One. He has served at Little Creek, VA; Norfolk, VA; Great Lakes Training Center; One Med Cruise, 3 Carib Cruise, Counter Insurgency School Coronado; Jungle School Panama; SERE Training; Warner Springs, CA and Vietnam. Ford was at Giant Slingshot and Silver Mace II and was in many campaigns. He was awarded the usual Gedunk Medals, including NDSM, VNSM, VN Campaign, Navy Achievement w/ combat "v", Combat Action Ribbon Cross of Gallantry, Civil Action 1st Class, Presidential Unit and Navy Unit Citation. He achieved the rank of Radioman Third Class (E-4) and was discharged in May 1971. His most memorable experience was getting on the Freedom Bird and going back to the world.

Ford is single. His civilian employment has included Electronic Service Technician. He retired in November 1991 due to combat related disability.

**TOMMY "TOM" GARLAND** was born May 1, 1941 in Cabot, AR. He graduated from high school, attended two years of technical school and received his Associates Degree. He joined the US Navy on May 6, 1958.

Units and ships that Garland served on include NAS Memphis, TN; *USS Graham, LST-117; USS Mt. McKinley AGC-7; USS Barney DDG-6; USS Biddle DLG-34;* NAS Corpus Christi, TX; River Assault Boat Training Center, Mare Island, November 1968 to January 1969; Com. RivRon Nine January 1969 to March 1969; Com. RivRat Flot Five March 1969 to August 1969; Com RivRon Fifteen August 1969 to January 1970 and various other ships until retirement. Battles and campaigns include serving in many campaigns along the Mekong Delta and along the Horseshoe near Cambodia.

Garland has been awarded various campaign medals including Presidential Unit, Good Conduct (4), Purple Heart and a Bronze Star w/ V. He achieved the rank of BMC E-7 and was discharged on March 26, 1979, after more than

21 years of service. Garland says of his most memorable experience was setting ambush as "Boat Captain" of ASPB 115-41 and later as Patrol Officer of ASPB's in Riv. Div. 115. Another one was while serving on the US Navy Stream Team training crews in transferring cargo, ammo and food.

Garland has been married since 1960 to Lorena "Tinnie" and they have four children; a son, Jerry, and daughters, Theresa, Melissa and Rebecca. They also have seven grandchildren, Alexander, Haley, Lucus, Malory, Macy, Mason and Austin. Civilian employment includes from 1983-2001 instructor (Collision Repair) Foothills Tech. Inst. (18 years) from which he retired. Presently he is owner of Tom's Rod Shop.

**JOHN L. GIBBS** was born Feb. 14, 1945 at Wichita, KS. After graduating from Wichita High School East he attended Wichita State University. He joined the US Navy Reserve in April 1968.

Gibbs served in Naval Support Activity in Saigon. He was a courier driver, worked in administration department, NHA BE Navel Base and RVN. Gibbs has been awarded NDSM, Combat Action Ribbon and VSM. He achieved the rank of E-4 and was discharged in April 1974.

Gibbs recounts his most memorable experience. "I was a courier for the Naval Support Activity. Twice daily I would haul Guardmail from NHA BE Naval Detachment to various Navy installation in Saigon.

"One day, I was told to pick up a Chief Mozingo at Tan Son Nhut. I found out that he was the most decorated enlisted man in the "Brown Water Navy." I spent the day driving him to several places in the Saigon area and finally dropping him off at Admiral Zumwalts Villa. He shook my hand then told me the VC had a million-dollar piaster bounty on him. He also told me he would rather be in a dozen firefights than do what I did for the "Man's Navy." For the rest of my tour I had a new-found pride for what I did."

Gibbs is married to Joan and he has a daughter, Nancy. They have two grandchildren, Klisten and Michelle. Gibbs has worked as a golf course superintendent and the City of Wichita.

**PHILLIP GOMEZ** was born Sept. 10, 1947 in Las Vegas, NM raised in Texas. Attended Poteet High School. Joined the Navy in 1965. Basic training San Diego, CA. First naval assignment was the Ernest G. Small DDR 838. Provided gunfire support from N. Vietnam to the tip of S. Vietnam. Volunteered for Swift boats after 18 months but wound up in the MRF. Started MRF training and SERE training at Coronado Island, CA. Finished at Mare Island, Vallejo, CA. Arrived with his class in Vietnam

just in time for TET 1968. Was assigned to River Assault Flotilla 1, RivRon 9, RivDiv 92, and to ASPB 92-4. This experience would bring great moments of camaraderie as well as explosive moments of shear terror. Our first major battle came on April 4, 1968. We took 3 RPG's that wounded half the crew. One memorable night, when we were assigned to the artillery barges, while out on the parameter with the Army. One of the guys was going to earn his jumping wings. He was jumping from the rim of the foxhole when all of a sudden I smelled terrible body odor; I was telling the guys to keep it down because we were very close to a bunch of VC. The next day one of our columns was ambushed not far from where we were that night. I still remember that night and the smell to this day. There are still many stories to tell of my experiences while with the MRF as well as the times I spent in the hospitals from Vietnam, Japan and finally to Corpus Christi, TX. After two Purple Hearts, and several other medals I am honored to have been part and to have served with great men who were and are the Mobile Riverine Force.

**PEDRO GONZALEZ** was born Sept. 29, 1946 in Weslaco, TX. Enlisted on Feb. 12, 1965. Attended boot camp at San Diego, CA. Assigned to NAVCOMSTAPHIL. Went TAD to VP-50 where he first got introduced to Vietnam in November 1965.

Cruised the Gulf of Tonkin twice onboard the *USS R. K. Turner DDG-20*. Assigned to the Riverine Force in 1968 and served with RIVRON 13, RIVRON 15 Staff, Tango 8, RIVDIV 152 on Mike 1, last sited RVN December 1970. Other duty assignments: IUWG 1, MIUW 13, BCT Whidbey Island, WA, NAVCRUITCOM San Francisco, CA, *USS Waddel DDG-24*, *USS Paul F. Foster DD-964*. Joined the Submarine Force and made five patrols on the *USS Ulysses S. Grant SSBN-631* Blue Crew. Retired at COMNAVSUBLANT 1986 as RM1 (SS). Awards include: RVN Service Medal, Vietnam Campaign Ribbon, Vietnam Gallantry Cross w/ Palm, Combat Action Ribbon, RVN Civil Action Citation, Navy Commendation w/ Combat V, Presidential Unit Commendation, Navy Unit Commendation, Meritorious Unit Commendation, Navy Achievement Medal, Armed Forces Expeditionary Medal, NDSM, Sea Service Deployment Ribbon 5th Award. Enlisted Submarine Insignia, SSBN Deterrent Patrol Insignia w/ 4 Gold Stars.

He has a son, Tony, a daughter Vicky and two stepsons Robert and Randy.

**EDWARD F. "GREY GHOST" GORMAN** was born Nov. 24, 1933 in Brooklyn, NY. He joined the US Army in April of 1951. Gorman served with "B" Company, 3rd 60th 9th Inf. Div., *Benewah, Colleton, Washtenaw* LST-11-66. He served in Dong Tam, 2nd Tour, MAT Team, Highlands with Advisor Team in Phu Bon Prou. He was awarded CIB, Air Medal, VSM, VCM, ACM w/ V, and Bronze Star Medal. He was discharged in July 1971 with the rank of PSG E-7.

Gorman is married to Alphine and they have five children, Kathy, Arlene, Connie, Betty and Karen. They also have nine grandchildren and nine great-grandchildren.

**RON GORMAN** was born May 21, 1943 in Inglewood, CA. He earned his Associate Degree in General Studies. On July 17, 1967 he joined the US Navy.

Gorman served with RIVRON 9, R91-10, *USS Tallahatchie County AVB-2*, Atlantic Fleet Combat Camera Group-AFCCG and COMNAVAIRPAC. He was stationed at RVN; Naples, Italy Naval Air Station; Norfolk, VA; NAS North Island in San Diego, CA. Medals and awards that Gorman received include Good Conduct (2), Presidential and Navy Unit Citation, Vietnam Service, Combat Action Ribbon, National Defense and Aircrew Wings. He says his most memorable experience was the birth of his two sons while He was in the Navy. He had a gallbladder attack on detail to Sauda Bay Crete and hospitalized in a Greek Naval Hospital. When he made Photographers Mate and received Aircrew Wings. The friends he made. Some of them he communicates with today. Being able to travel to many exciting places. Being able to serve his country for nine memorable years. Gorman retired in May 1976 with the rank of Photographers Mate 2nd Class.

Gorman is married to Wanda and they have three children, June, Ronnie Jr. and Rodney. They also have two grandchildren, Missy and Marnita.

Gorman has been employed as USPS Tractor-Trailer Driver. He retired on April 7, 2003.

**DANIEL A. "DANNY" GRAVES** is a 1966 graduate of Nashville, Arkansas High School; he enlisted in the US Navy in 1968. He was assigned to ComRivRon One Eleven on ASPB-111-1 from March 169 to July 1969. He was transferred to RAS 151, serving on T-151-36, serving mostly in the Parrot Beak's Region. His primary duties were radioman, navigator and 20MM gunner. He served aboard T-151-36 until tragically it was mined and sunk during TET 1970, killing two shipmates and injuring four others.

He was a transmitter site supervisor in Western Australia, and was separated in 1972. He earned a law degree from the University of Arkansas in 1983 and has been a private attorney, deputy prosecutor, and municipal judge. He is a member of Mensa.

Judge Graves has two wonderful daughters, Blair and Bret Graves and lives in Nashville, AR where he practices law, hunts ducks and struggles on the golf course.

**LEO GREENFIELD**, born Dec. 25, 1923 in Middletown, New York, enlisted in the Aviation Cadet program in 1942 while he was attending the University of Miami in Coral Gables, Florida. He graduated in Class 44E and was commissioned as a Second Lieutenant at Craig Field, Slema, AL.

After training in P-40's and P-47's, he was assigned in 1944 to the 493rd, "Fix-Up" squadron of the 48th Fighter Group, 9th Air Force. He flew 38 missions through V.E. Day and was primarily engaged in destroying supply routes, ammunition dumps, close support of tanks and artillery as well as escort missions for medium range bombers and protective coverage on the "Ramagan Bridge"; and penetration and disbursement of counter-attacking forces at the "Bridge." On his tenth mission, his aircraft was shot up by 20 mm ground fire during a dive bombing attack on selected ground targets near Cologne, Germany. He stayed with his burning aircraft, crossed back into friendly territory, and bailed out near Maastricht, Holland. After two weeks of hospitalization, he returned to duty with his squadron.

After V.E. Day, he was selected for training in the P-47N, for long range escort of B-29's in the Pacific Theater, however, with VJ Day he was returned home and discharged into the reserves. He is the holder of the Air Medal with four clusters, Purple Heart, the Presidential Unit Citation and the Belgian Fourragere. He was released from active duty in 1946.

In 1948, he graduated from the University of Miami Law School with a degree of Juris Doctor and in 1950 obtained his Bachelor of Business Administration from the University of Miami. While practicing law in Miami, he simultaneously was an Instructor of Law at the Law School of the University of Miami.

He continues to practice in Miami, Florida where he heads up a successful law firm with offices at 1680 N.E. 135th Street, North Miami, Florida. He is primarily engaged in trail and real estate practice and is known in the State for his expertise in usury law.

He is a 32nd Degree Mason, a Shriner, and a member of the Florida Bar as well as other various affiliations. He is a lifetime member of the P-47 Thunderbolt Pilots' Association.

In 1959 he married the former Barbara Anne Merritt of Miami. They have two daughters, Jacqui who is eighteen and Heidi who is fifteen and reside in North Miami Beach, Florida.

**PAUL DEAN GREW** joined the Navy on Feb. 25, 1968 and reported to active duty on June 4, 1968 at San Diego, CA for Basic Training.

After Basic Training, he went to Submarine Base Pearl Harbor for temporary duty August 1968 until January 1969. Then in January he reported to the Naval Inshore Operations Training Center for River Assault Craft Training and Advanced Gunnery Training at Mare Island Vallejo, Ca.

Grew then went to Faltupac Detachment Whidbey Island, Washington for instruction in Survival, Evasion, Resistance, Escape Training February 1969.

Received the National Defense Service Medal, Vietnam Service Medal (One Bronze Star), Vietnam Campaign Medal, Combat Action Ribbon, Presidential Unit Citation, Navy Commendation Medal with Combat "V" for valor and a Citation from the Secretary of the Navy. He was discharged from the Navy on March 16, 1970 from Naval Station, Norfolk, VA.

His most memorable experience was after returning home he received a letter from the commanding officer Naval Reserve Training Center McKaigs Hill in Cumberland, MD 21501 stating that Grew had received the Navy Commendation Medal with Combat V for Valor and a Citation from the Secretary of the Navy and they wanted to have a ceremony to present to him.

Grew is married to Dottie. His civilian employment has included SCI Highlands State Correction Institution, Correction Carpenter Trades Instructor at Somerset, PA.

**THOMAS R. "GRIFF" GRIFFIN** was born Dec. 1, 1946 in Topsfield, MA. He graduated from Masconomet Regional High School in 1964. Drafted into the Army on Jan. 6, 1966 while working at Pratt and Whitney Aircraft in East Hartford, CN. Took Basic Training and AIT at Fort Hood, TX. Primary MOS was 82C20 Artillery Survey, Secondary MOS 13 A 10 RTO. Assigned to HQ. Battery 2nd Bn. 4th Arty. 9th Inf. Div. in July of 1966. Traveled to Vietnam on the Troop Ship *USS Gen. John Pope* with the 2nd Brigade. Arrived Vung Tau on Jan. 30, 1967. Convoyed to Bear Cat, stayed for three weeks. Led 2nd Bet. 4th Arty. convoy to Tan An as Col. King's Driver. The 2nd Bn 4th Arty. was among the first major units into the Mekong Delta to conduct sustained operations. The 2nd Bn 4th Arty. fired support for all three brigades of the best division in Vietnam, the 9th Inf. Div., and led the 9th Div. Arty. in casualties. The 9th Inf. Div. conducted 42 operations in 11 different provinces from December of 1966 to December of 1967. The 9th Inf. Div., "The Old Reliables" was the only Division in Vietnam to win the Vietnamese Cross of Gallantry twice.

Memorable experiences include six-hour nightshifts atop the 90 foot radio tower at 3rd Bde HQ at Tan An. Also, helped to deliver 128,000 rounds of 105 Howitzer ammo to Tan Tru, Rach Kien and Bien Phuc and helped to build a playground for the children of Tan An. Participated in Vietnam counter offensive Phase II and Phase III, Operations Enterprise and Coronado.

Awards include: National Defense Service Medal, Vietnam Service Medal, Vietnam Campaign Medal, Vietnam Cross of Gallantry Medal with palm, Civil Action Honor Medal, Sharpshooter M-14, Driver's Badge, Free World Forces Tab.

Married to Brenda for 33 years. Two children, Brian and Beth. Retired Hoisting and Operating Engineers, Local 4, Boston, MA. Life member DAV and VVA. Also, a member of the American Legion. 100 percent PTSD Permanent and Total 1992.

**HORACE GLENN "HG" GRIMES** was born May 15, 1947 in Swainsboro, GA, the only child of H.D. and Sybil Grimes. He graduated from Swainsboro High School in 1965 and joined the US Navy June 6, 1966. He received basic training at Great Lakes, IL. He received his river warfare and SERE training in California (Class 18-R) and served in Vietnam from May 1968 to May 1969 with RivRon 11, RivDiv 111 as coxswain and machine gunner aboard A-111-5, A-111-7 and T-111-2. Other assignments were the *USS Berkeley (DDG 15)* and *USS Yosemite (AS 19)*. He was field promoted to BM2, while serving in Vietnam, and was released from active duty Feb. 13, 1970.

His decorations include the Navy Achievement Medal w/ "V", Combat Action Ribbon, Presidential Unit Citation, Navy Unit Commendation, Vietnam Service Medal w/ 4 Bronze Stars, Vietnam Campaign Medal w/ Date Bar, National Defense Medal and RVN Meritorious Unit Citation w/ Palm.

Married to Mary F. Grimes, they have two children, Tammie and Glenn Jr., and three grandchildren, Lexie, Taylor and Thomas. Mary is an OR Nurse, Tammie is a data processing technician and Glenn Jr. works with the US Postal Service. He is medically retired from Southern Nuclear Operating Company where he worked as a nuclear security supervisor at Plant A.W. Vogtle. He is a member of the Mobile Riverine Force Association, Alee Shrine Temple, Scottish Rite, Anderson Lodge NO. 243 F&AM and the Vietnam Vets Motorcycle Club USA, Chapter E, Georgia.

**FRANK J. "GUBBBER" GUBALA** was born Nov. 15, 1947 in Buffalo, NY. He received an Associated Degree in Electronics, Bachelor of Science in Data Communication, Advance PC Applications and Computer Art.

Gubala joined the US Army on Aug. 20, 1967. He served with A Co, 3rd Battalion, 47th Infantry Regiment, 3rd Platoon, 9th Infantry Division February 1968 until July 1968; A Co 7th Battalion, 6th Infantry Regiment, 2nd Armor Division "Hell on Wheels" from January 1969 until May 1969. He served in Dong Tam, onboard the *USS Benewah* and at Ft. Hood, TX. He was awarded two Purple Hearts and a Combat Infantryman Badge. He achieved the rank of SP4. Gubala says of his most memorable experience, "I lived to talk about Nam and the Great Men I had the Honor to served with. I have since started a web site '9th Infantry Division Delta Dawgs.' With the names of over 10,000 men from the 9th Inf Div. Several hundred men have found the Buddies on it."

Gubala is married to Joyce and they have two children, Julie (who helped him put Nam behind him) and Jeff (who is a Marine). His civilian employment includes working at Burroughs Corp 12 years Computer Engineer and Owner of In-Focus Photography for 15 years.

**ROGER D. "HOOGIE" HAGER** was born June 3, 1947 in Scott's Bluff, NB. Graduated Central High in Cheyenne, WY. Drafted on Oct. 25, 1966. Served at Bear Cat, Vietnam with B. Co 2 Bn 47th Inf. 9th Inf Div April 8, 1967 until April 8, 1968 as RTD then F.O for 81 mm mortars, 3d Platoon. July 22, 1967 received Purple Heart, spent one month in hospital. Soon after he and squad seized patrol discovered a NVA Flag, partially hidden, what became the largest weapons cache found at the time.

During TET 1968, he witnessed Ammo Explosion at Long Bien. Feb. 2, 1968 received Arcom W-V for carrying his CO from a Vietnamese Cemetery back to safety near Long Thanh. Captain Keats didn't survive his injuries. He participated in Battle of Widows Village, Saigon, Bien Hoa. Spent six months at Ft. Benning then got out.

He re-enlisted June 1, 1970 and returned to Vietnam to B Co, 2d BN, 8th Cav, 1st CAV Div on Dec. 3, 1970. On Feb. 7, 1971, his platoon was ambushed. As one of 15 casualties, he was Medivac to Fitzsimmons. After one year in recovery, Hager was reclassified to 71L-Admin. Retired from TRADOC, in Ft. Leavenworth, KS on March 1, 1990. He has "Seen the world" and would like to thank the lifetime friends, Rickie Goff, Joe Adams, also inspirational to his career, Lt. Barens, Ltc. Murphy, Gen. Maddox, Col. Nash, Col. Appler and Gen. Robinson. Retired from Jackson County, MO in November 2001.

He is at home with wife, Linda. He has four children, Kim, Desiranne, Ammanda and Matthew also serving in the Army. He has four grandson, Kyle, Jacob Singleton, Ethan and Jack Fenner. Enjoys traveling, hunting, fishing and whatever else he pleases to do.

**MICHAEL DOUGLAS HANMER** was born Jan. 23, 1947 in Stambaugh, MI. He attended Iron River High School, MI Tech University (Forestry) 1972, Bay de Noc Community College, Vincennes University and received various Military education.

Hanmer joined the US Navy in 1967, MI ARNG in 1974 and the US Army 1985. He joined the US Navy on Nov. 11, 1967. He served with MRF 13, Alphas, Tangos- MRF 15 Alphas and Riv Div 132. Locations include Dong Tam, Vung Tau, SaDec, Tram Chin Canal, Binh Thuy, Chau Doc. He received basic training at San Diego, CA and NAS at Corpus Christi, TX. Hanmer was involved with Campaigns X1-XLL Summer and fall. He was awarded NDSM w/ star, VSM w/ four Bronze Stars, Navy Com Ribbon w/ V, Meritorious Unit Comm Ribbon, RVN Meritorious Unit Citation, Gallantry Cross Medal w/ Palm, CAB, Army Good Conduct, Master Recruiter Badge, Career Counselor Badge and AR Comp Achievement. In the Navy he achieved the rank of E4, in MIARNG E6 and in the US Army E7. He retired on June 30, 1998.

Hanmer is married to Susan K. Hanmer and they have two children, Rochelle and Michael. His civilian employment has included Policeman/ Fireman (retired 1985) and construction.

**WILBERT "BIG GARLOU" HANNAH** was born Nov. 20, 1946 in Jacksonville, FL. After receiving his GED, he attended two years of college and other trade schools. He joined the USNR on Feb. 2, 1965.

Units and ships that Hannah served with include the *USS WhiteRiver LSMR 536* (Rockets), Inshore Fire Support Div 93, NAVCOM Pacific 7th Fleet, California. Locations were Great Lakes, IL; Long Beach, CA; San Diego, CA; Pearl Harbor, HI; Yokosika, Japan; Subie Bay, Philippines; Vietnam, Danang. Battles include Operation "Mobile," Operation "Oakland," Operation "Deckhouse III," and Operation "Franklin," and endless other fire missions in 1st and 2nd Corps Zones. He was awarded National Defense Service Medal, Navy Unit Commendation Ribbon, Vietnam Service Medal with two Bronze Stars, Republic of Vietnam Campaign, and Republic of Vietnam MUC Gallantry Cross. He achieved the rank of E-3 before being discharged on Feb. 18, 1967.

Hannah says of his impression, "I remember how unprepared I was when hearing the reports and results of our first live action mission. The destruction and devastation pounded upon the enemy targets by our 5", 40 MMs, and eight twin tube rock-launchers were always total and complete. Delivered paid in full by a well trained E expert crew. The realization of it all was that it was not a TV movie. I love and miss my shipmate's. God Bless them all."

Hannah was married first to Flora and they had a son, Wilbert Hannah Jr. He is married currently to Viola Hannah and they have a son, Carl Jamaine, and also two stepsons, Cordell and Earl (deceased). His grandchildren include Jason, Jamaine, James Earl Jr., Cordell Jr. and Sophia Amariah. Civilian employment is working at St. Matthew's Baptist Church in Jersey City, NJ.

**JOHN S. "WHITEY" HANTTULA** was born Feb. 26, 1948 in Carlsbad, NM. He received A/A at NMSU 1979 Graphic Arts, B/A at UNM 1981 Photography-Printmaking. He joined the US Navy on April 27, 1966.

Units that Hanttula served with were Mine Force-Minesweep Boats 1967, MRFA M-112-2 January 1968 to February 1969. He served in Saigon River; Dong Tam; Cua Viet to Dong Ha; Mekong Delta area of operations. He was forward gunner- M-112-2, CUA-Viet-Dong Ha Combat Tour, Mekong Delta Combat Tour and Saigon River. He was awarded PHM (2), NAM w/ Combat "V," Navy-Marine Comd. w/ Combat "V," PUCR, VSM, VCM, VCG and Life Member DAV. When Hanttula was discharged in April 1972 he was a Seaman Gunnersmate. His most memorable experience was the numerous combat battle situations and the dependable crew and gunners of M-112-2. Most devastating was Aug. 18 and Aug. 19, 1968; they took 13 rockets hits, as point boat in Snoopy's Nose, many crew wounded and Medivac.

Hanttula has been married for 30 years to Beckie. His civilian employment has included photographer at Technical Imaging, and specialist at National Pack Service SSO.

**MICHAEL A. HARRIS**, (RM2), Born August 3, 1948 in Seattle, Washington. I grew up in and enlisted from Coos Bay, Oregon and attended Boot Camp, Basic Electricity and Electronics, Radioman "A" School and Intermediate Speed Morse Code School in San Diego, California. After volunteering for riverboat duty I was transferred to Mare Island for boat training. My portion of River Assault Division 152 arrived in Vietnam on July 22, 1968. We were billeted aboard the USS Bexar off the coast of Vung Tau until our new Program V boats began arriving on merchant ships from the states. I was assigned to T-152-1. Tangos 1, 2, 3 and 5 arrived first. We rode the ship to Saigon and offloaded them. Then we outfitted them in Cat Lo and Nha Be.

After outfitting was completed the (4) RAD 152 Tangos were "chopped" to River Assault Squadron 13 for operations. Our first time out we were in a serious ambush. The canal was so narrow that VC tossed grenades on a couple of boats. It was our "Baptism of Fire". In a couple of months RAD 152 was fully operational just in time to take part in Operation SEALORDS. RAS 15 combined with RAS 13 in a serious campaign to root out the NVA and VC in the U Minh Forest Region. We were hit hard, but we also took it to the enemy and came out victorious. At the time we did not know that our division would spend a lot of time operating in Base 480 with the Vietnamese Marines in Chuong Thien and Kien Giang Provinces.

On the way north in November 1968 my boat and T-152-10 were "chopped" to TF-116 for operations out of the small Vietnamese Naval Base at Rach Soi, which was 5 klicks south of Rach Gia. We spent about 10 weeks there. On December 27, 1968 Tango 10 took 4 rockets killing Barry Barber and wounding several other crewmembers. Not long after that the brass moved us back in with the main unit.

On June 13, 1969 a group of 8-9 river assault craft from RAD 152 were viciously attacked south of Ben Tre. We suffered 4 Army dead and many Army and Navy wounded. On June 15th we were ambushed again. This time the ramp cable on my boat broke leaving us disabled on the riverbank. M-152-1 pulled alongside and fired (3) 105 rounds into the jungle ahead of us. They almost knocked me down as I was rigging the chain hoist to raise the ramp manually. Eventually (3) craft took rocket hits.

Lt. Tom Kelley was critically wounded, but he continued to direct fire until the enemy ambush was thwarted and we moved to safer ground. Later Tom Kelley would receive the Medal of Honor for his bravery that day.

After many years as a General Building Contractor I started a "Point Man Ministries Outpost" in my hometown in 1989. Then my wife and I moved to the HQ office in Seattle and worked fulltime in ministry. Eventually we became Christian Missionaries to S.E. Asia with our target country being Laos. I was able to travel back into Vietnam on (5) occasions in the 1990's.

Now that I'm retired I truly enjoy helping out with the Mobile Riverine Force Association.

**DANIEL P. "BULLDOG, SHORT ROUND" HAYES** was born May 26, 1928 in Pittsburgh, PA. He enlisted in the Army in July 1946 and served in 1st Cav. Div 1946 to 1947 in Japan. He remained in the Reserves and after obtaining a Bachelors Degree from Duquesne University, he was commissioned a second time in Artillery in 1951. Recalled to active duty May 1952 and served as Fire Director Off. "A" Battery, 623 FA Bn (Korea) Exec. Off. "C" Btry 623 and FA Bn and Battery Commander "C" Btry 623 FA Bn (1952-1953).

Involved in Battles for "Old Baldy" "Pork Chop Hill." Supported 1st Marine Div. 2nd Inf. Div. and 7th Inf. Div. during the 1952-1953 time period. Served in many command and staff assignments in CONVS and Europe, plus attended Artillery Officers Basic Course, Artillery Officers Advanced Course and Air Force War College Courses during the 1953-1967 time period.

Served in many command and staff assignments in CONUS and Europe, plus attended Artillery Officers Basic Course, Artillery Officers Advanced Course and Air Force War College Courses during the 1953-1967 time period.

"Draden Down" (i.e. returned to CONUS earlier than expected) in 1965 became I.G. for Fort Bragg Replacement Training Center while awaiting orders for Vietnam.

Arrived in Vietnam in May 1967- assigned to 9th Inf. Div. at Bear Cat.

Assigned as Bn CO 3rd BN 34th Artillery in June 1967- engaged in the "Coronado" series of Missions. Led Bn in fights in Rung Sat, Go Cong Provence (near French Fort (Cai Lc and Cai Be and up the canals in and around Dong Tam and Cai Be. Was awarded S.S. for action in December 1967. Relieved as Bn CO in late January 1968- assigned to I Force V Artillery as Operations Officer. Just in time for TET Offensive. Wound up in 8th Field Hospital for a 20 day stay- then returned to duty for balance of Vietnam Tour awarded Legion of Merit for efforts as S-3.

Returned to the States- served as Training Officer 6th Army in San Francisco and later as G-5 Plane Assistant at STRIKE Command at MacDill AFB in Tampa, FL- several trips to Middle East between 1969 and 1972.

Retired July 31, 1972. Civilian life has been rewarding. Taught American History and Economics for over 17 years, and obtained a Masters Degree in Educational Administration. He took up painting (oils and watercolors) as a hobby 30 years ago. Became a snake, spider and scorpions hand for a children's museum. He fully retired at age 74.

**HOMER GARRISON "H. G." HELMS** was born Feb. 4, 1938 in Gastionia, NC. He joined the US Navy in 1956. He received his training at Great Lakes, IL.

Units served with and ships served on were the *USS Neches*, *USS Newport News*, Nato Cruise 1971 and US Atlantic Fleet. He served at Norfolk, VA; Second Fleet; Comsecondfit October 1970 to September 1975; *USS Chemong* 1962-1963. From 1969 to 1970 Helms was boat Captain on Assault Support Patrol Boat 152-3; 15 enemy firefights. Helms received a Vietnam Service Medal, Navy Unit Commendation, Combat Action Ribbon and Navy Achievement Medal with Combat "V." He achieved the rank of BM1 and was discharged in September 1975.

Homer past away on Nov. 15, 2002. He never talked about his experiences in Vietnam but he was very proud of his service to the United States of America. He has three honorably discharges.

Helms' widow is Vearl D. Helms. They have three children, Mark, Homer Jr. and Deanna. They also have four grandchildren, John, Madison, Melissa and Taylor. He worked at Wix-Dana as Leadsman over the shop. He retired on Feb. 4, 2000.

**ROBERT J. HELMS** was born Dec. 11, 1946 in Chicago, IL. He joined the US Army in July 1968. He served with 4/47 A Co and 6/30 B Co. and *USS Colleton*. He served in Dong Tam, Ben Tre and Tan Ninh. Helms has been awarded the Purple Heart, Bronze Star, Air Medal, CIB, AR Com, Vietnam Campaign and Good Conduct. He achieved the rank of E-5. Helms trained at Ft. Polk, LA; arrived in Vietnam in November 1968 until January 1970. He hated Monsoon season in the fields, and still doesn't like wet feet.

Helms is married to Renee and they have two children, Robert and Tasha. He has been employed at General Motors. In September 1993, Helms retired.

**STEPHEN A. HENLEY** was born May 23, 1941 in Cincinnati, OH; graduated from Indiana University Dental School and reported for duty with the US Navy at Norfolk, VA.

After attending C. I. School at Little Creek, he then went to Philadelphia as a member of the recommissioning crew of the USS Benewah. He was its dental officer when it was stationed on the Mekong River. He participated in over a dozen Army Dentcap Operations. At the end of 1967, he was transferred to Lemoore, NAS, CA, and left active duty in 1968 to begin his dental practice in Rensselaer, IN.

In 1982 he sold the practice and began working in dental missions in Grenada, Haiti, China, Indonesia, Kenya, Micronesia, Zaire, Cambodia, Thailand and Vietnam. He continued to be active in the Reserves achieving the rank of Commander, and was discharged in 1994; awarded the Navy Commendation Medal.

**JAMES O. HENRY** was born April 12, 1948 in Forest Grove, OR. After high school, he joined the US Army on Jan. 3, 1968. He served with 9th Infantry Division 3rd/ 47th USS Apple APL-26 and USS Colleton. Henry took his Basic Training at Fort Lewis, WA; AIT at Fort Jackson, SC and Instructor OCS at Fort Belvoir, VA. He has been awarded Army Commendation (3), Bronze Star w/ V-Device, Purple Heart (2), Air Medal and CIB. He achieved the rank Sgt E-5 and was discharged on Dec. 17, 1969.

Henry says that his most memorable experience was getting together with three friends (John Thompson, George Adams and Ken Schmidt) that he went to high school with; they got together in Saigon for several days. Also, while in Dong Tam, running into his next door neighbor, 1st Lt. Phill Wolever who was the XO of the 9th MP's in Dong Tam.

Henry is married to Kahna. He has the following children, Nick, Larry and Tim Henry, Kelli and Aaron Lee. He also has two grandchildren, Jake and Kamryn. He has also been a heavy equipment operator and a bartender.

**BRUCE C. HIATT** was born June 17, 1937 in St. George, UT. He earned his Master of Science in Mechanical Engineering. He joined the US Navy on July 14, 1955.

Ships and units that Hiatt served with include USS Wedderburn (DD685), USS Piedment (AS15), USS Interdiotor, USS Canon (PG90), and USS Chevalier (DD). He took Basic Training NTC San Diego, CA; Fleet Training Group San Diego, CA; NROTC Unit University of New Mexico; ASWGROUP 5; China Source and Vietnam Service. Awards and medals that Hiatt received Navy Commendation w/ Combat V, Good Conduct (3), Combat Action, Presidential Unit Commendation and Navy Unit Commendation. He achieved the rank of QMC and was discharged on July 1, 1975.

Hiatt says that his most memorable experiences were serving with MRF as the pilot 1968-1969; touring the world onboard his tours of duty; his service on the USS Benewah (APB-35) was one of his most memorable. He had many firefights, and recon trips on ASPB's to find safe passage and make surveys.

Hiatt is married to Sharon. They have the following children: Rochelle, Gina, Benton, Deborah, Jerry, and Robert. Grandchildren are Samantha, Stacy, June, Jane, Ethan, Forest, Aaron, Zachary, Chandler, Hillary and Aubrey. Civilian employment has included Mechanical Engineer. He retired on July 1, 2002.

**BRUCE ROBERT HIERSTEIN** was born Aug. 15, 1949 in Burlington, IA; graduated from Norview High School in Norfolk, VA in June 1967; Master of Urban Studies Degree in Public Administration, December 1979 from Old Dominion University, Norfolk, VA.

Enlisted in US Army July 1, 1968; attended basic training, Fort Benning, GA; Co. E, 2nd Bn., 1st Training Bde.; AIT Fort McClellan, AL, Co. B, 2nd Training Bn., AIT Bde.; Vietnam, 3rd Plt., Co. B., 4/47th Inf. Regt., 9th Inf. Div., with the MRF 1968-1969; Schofield Barracks, HI, Co. C, 3rd Bn., 14th Inf. Regt., 25th Inf. Div.

Discharged June 1970 with the rank of Sergeant. Awarded the Combat Infantry Badge, Bronze Star w/ V, Air Medal, Army Commendation Medal, Purple Heart, Vietnam Service Medal and Vietnam Campaign Medal.

Married since 1972 with a son and daughter. He has been with the Norfolk Police Department for 28 years and is now an assistant chief.

**DANNY L. HIGGINS** was born March 8, 1944 in Mitchell, SD. He obtained his high school diploma and he is an Accredited Financial Counselor (AFC).

Joined the US Navy on June 27, 1962. Served on the USS Brisckinredge TAP 176; USS Abnaki ARF-96; RivRon T-91-8; USS Hull DD-945; USS Jourett DLG-29; USS Sample FF-1048; USS Kirk FF-1087; and USS LaSalle AGF-3. Military locations include RTC San Diego; FAAWTC Point Loma; ISMF Pearl Harbor; NIATC, Vallejo, Mare Island; NUWFS Washington; Puget Sound Naval Shipped. He was awarded Bronze Star w/ Combat V, Purple Heart, Navy Commendation with Combat V plus three stars, Combat Action and Navy Achievement with four stars. He achieved the rank

of E-9 Master-Chief Boatswains Mate. He was discharged Aug. 1, 1992. Higgins says that his most memorable experience was all 30 years of serving with the best professionals in the world, Go Navy! Also, time served with RivRon 9; the year served on the LaSalle in the Persian Gulf and the rescue of 23 Merchant Seaman from their sinking freighter.

Higgins has been since Aug. 4, 1968 to Elaine. They have two children, Juliet and Danielle. Other work for Higgins includes working for the Department of Defense. He is still employed.

**JIM "DOC" HILSHEIMER** was born Aug. 12, 1947 in Chicago, IL. After high school, he attended Ohio State University. He joined the US Navy in January 1966. He served with Naval HSP Portsmouth, VA; Operating Tech School; Surgical Team Z; Dong Tam; USS Mercer APB-39 and USS Benewah APB35. Awarded CG, ND, VF, VC, PUC and NUC. Achieved the rank of E4 HM3, or Tech. He was discharged in October 1970. He says of his most memorable experiences was seeing Bob Hope in Dong Tam; also, the kids- he has so many pictures of the kids; the big green boats (that always made then crazy) in the middle of the river surrounded by Tangos; the darkroom aboard the Mercer; Med Caps; Stokel, Tom Cooley, Chuck Banworth, Watley, Dale Swensen and Murph.

Hilsheimer is twice divorced and has three children, Dan, Eric and Annie. He has a grandson, Jimmy. Civilian employment includes sales in medical until 1985 and then sales, computers, graphic designer, photographer, and video prod. He retired in May 1999.

**CHARLES ANTONE HILTON** born April 6, 1948 in Worcester, MA. Graduated form Provincetown High School, June 1966. Drafted April 2, 1968, attended Basic Training at Ft. Dix, NJ and A.I.T. at Ft. Polk, LA (Tigerland). From Sept. 2, 1968 to July 20, 1968. He served with A Co. 2/47th Mechanized Inf. 9th Inf Div., Binh Phouc, Vietnam. Was RTO to Platoon Sergeant for first six months and squad leader for final three months of tour. Awards received are the Combat Infantryman Badge, Bronze Star with V, Army Commendation Medal with V, Purple Heart, Vietnam Service and Campaign Medals.

Memorable experience-generally a mechanized outfit, but on this day they were air mobile into the Plain of Reeds. We caught hell as soon as we hit the ground, by a company size element of NVA well dug in a woodline. That was their first and only drop of the day.

He spent his last eight months at Fort Carson, CO, with the 5th Mech. Inf. Div.

He received an Associates degree in Hotel/Restaurant Management and Accounting at Cape Cod Community College. Currently employed by the US Postal Service for the last 16 years. Married to Deborah Annis 20 years, 1980 to 2000, but recently divorced. He has one daughter, Sarah Elizabeth. She is currently attending Eastern Nazarene College in Quincy, MA and is studying religion.

Hilton is currently living in Dennisport, MA (Cape Cod).

**ALAN "HODGY" HODGKINSON** was born Nov. 27, 1947 in San Francisco. He earned his Master's Degree in Creative Writing. On Jan. 3, 1968 he joined the US Army. Hodgkinson served with A Company and HHC 3/60th 9th Division. He served as U Mihn Forest West, Rung Sat East, Mo Cai South and the Plain of Reeds North. Awards and Medals include Bronze Star, Air Medal (3), Army Commendation with "V" device. He achieved the rank of Sergeant and was discharged in August 1969. Memorable experience was the day he arrived in Vietnam, the next day, and the next day and all the way to the last day in the country.

Hodgkinson is married to Akata. He has been employed as a writer and retired in 1997.

**HERSCHEL HUGHES JR.** graduated from the US Naval Academy in 1966. After serving two years aboard *USS Ault (DD-698)*, which included a Westpac deployment and attacks on coastal SAM sites in North Vietnam, he was assigned to the *USS Colleton (APB-36)* as Operations Officer. Herschel also served as *Colleton's* OOD for most river transits. Learning the navigational intricacies of the Mekong River and out as one of the memorable challenges of the MRF tour.

Following his return from Vietnam, he was assigned to RTC, Orlando, where he became involved in ADM Zumwalt's motivational initiatives in the behavioral sciences. This triggered a life long interest in psychology and a commitment to use that interest on behalf of Navy men and women.

LT Hughes completed his Master's in psychology at NC State University while teaching NROTC at UNC-Chapel Hill. Subsequently recommissioned in the Medical Service Corp as a clinical psychologist, he served a tour at NTC, San Diego. Remaining in the Naval Reserve, he then studied Navy training systems as a civilian psychologist in Orlando, for six years, and returned to clinical work as the Director of Family Assistance, Family Service Center, NTC, Orlando, in 1984. In 1988 Herschel left full-time government service and with his psychologist wife and partner, Anne, began a successful counseling practice in Orlando, which is described at www.qualitycounseling.com.

CDR Hughes' 19-year Naval Reserve career culminated in two tours as CO of a USMCR field hospital followed by his retirement in 1996 after serving 34 years of combined active and reserve duty. He then completed his doctorate from the University of Central Florida.

Their blended family of four boys, Kip, Ken, Kasey and Matt, and one girl, Heather, are grown and most have started families of their own, yielding three grandsons thus far. One daughter-in-law, Mai, is a Vietnamese-American, a constant reminder of how wonderful blessings can come out of tumultuous events. Herschel and Anne enjoy traveling to visit family, watching western movies, sailing their catamaran, and hosting family get-togethers around their pool.

**DAVID R. HUNT** was born Nov. 11, 1947 in Door County, WI. He was drafted into the US Army in August 1967. He had basic training at Fort Campbell, KY; AIT at Fort Eustis, VA; and River Assault Craft Training at Mare Island, CA. He served 458th PBR at Cat Lo (1968 to 1969) and 612th LCU at Fort Eustis, VA (1967-1968). He achieved the rank of E-4 before being discharged in 1969.

Hunt has been married since January 1974 to Rita. They have two children, Megan and David II. Civilian employment has included Chief Engineer- Inland Steel, Great Lakes Ore Carrier (1967-1994); Marine Surveyor- American Bureau of Shipping (1996- ); Owner- Door County Mustard (1996- ); and Owner- Overboard Nautical Gifts (2003- ).

**WILLIAM H. "BILL" JEFFERS** was born April 26, 1946 in Aladena, CA. He graduated from high school. On May 10, 1966 Jeffers joined the US Navy. He served on the *USS White River* and SMR 536 Boat Support Unit One, MST 2, B, PT Boat. He  served on the South to North Shore of Vietnam, Coronado, CA, Benhuc Vietnam and Pear Harbor, HI. Jeffers received the Combat Action Ribbon. He achieved the rank of GMG3 and was discharged on May 10, 1970.

Jeffers says that his most memorable experience was meeting the lifetime friends on the White River LSMR; night operations; taking the SEAL Unit on their missions; spending three months in Hawaii and running around the Islands on a PT Boat.

Jeffers is single. His civilian employment has included Keokux National Cemetery WL8-5. He retired on June 1, 2003.

**PAUL H. "JEFF" JEFFERSON** was born April 9, 1944 in Cambridge, MD. After graduating from high school, he attended two years of college.

Jefferson joined the US Navy and served two tours. The first tour was April 4, 1962 to April 8, 1965; and the second was Dec. 30, 1968 to Nov. 20, 1972. Units served with and ships served on include *USS Hunley AS-31*, *USS Proteus AS-19*, RivRon- 13, RivDiv 132, T-26. Military locations and stations include NAAS Chase Fzold, Beeville, TX; Charleston, SC; Mare Island Naval Shipyard, Vallejo, CA; Dong Tam/ My Tho, Vietnam. Battles and campaigns include Operation Giant Slingshot MRF TF-117 Dong Tam/ My Tho area Riverine Strike Force TG 1947 w Sealords and Operation Barrier Reef. Awards and medals that Jefferson was awarded were Purple Heart (2), Navy Commendation w/ Combat "V," Good Conduct Medal and Vietnam Service Medal. He achieved the rank of E-5.

His most memorable experience was three months of training and one year of "in country" service with a great boat crew. Not a bad life when the rockets and bullets weren't flying. "Lucky to make it back."

Jefferson is single; his significant other is Debbie. His civilian employment includes being a crane operator and crane operator supervisor. He retired on March 31, 1998.

**RICHARD JENKINS** was born Dec. 29, 1945 in Portland, OR. He graduated South Eugene High School in 1964 and Portland State University in 1972 with a BS degree in Business Administration.

Jenkins was drafted into the US Army in August 1968. He served in Co. B, 2 Bn, 60th Inf, 9th Inf Division January 1969 to March 1970 in Vietnam, most as a squad leader with 2nd Platoon, finished extended tour with Battalion HHC. Military locations include Tan Tru and Thu Thua. He was involved in numerous large-scale battles, mostly around the Plain of Reeds. He was awarded Silver Star, three Bronze Stars w/ "V," two Army Commendation Medals one with "V," two Air Medals, Purple Heart, Combat Inf. Badge, Good Conduct Medal and Unit Citations. He achieved the rank of SGT E-5 and was discharged in March 1970.

Jenkins says his most memorable experiences were the choppers, LZ's, ambushes, mud, booby traps, brave men, and the "Great Silver Bird" lifting off; those are his memories.

Jenkins is married to Sue. His civilian employment includes being a Record Studio Manager in the early 1980's, Owner- Wood Stove MFG in the 1980's and 1990's, and owner of Video Stores in the 1990's. He is semi-retired now.

**RAYMOND W. "PADRE" "DOC" JOHNSON** Padre's most recent achievement as an internationally celebrated artist and author involved the completion of his 14-year project/journey with the people of 159 nations. His "Faces of the World" art exhibition and his book *Journeys with the Global Family*, which features his philosophy of life and reproductions of his award winning western, wildlife, and global portrait renditions, were both featured at a very successful United Nations, New York, premiere opening. This was the first one-person exhibit in the history of the UN.

An international art critic and Patron of the Arts has written, "To understand the natural spirit of freedom and aliveness in Padre's unique forms of art creativity, you have to appreciate the influence that his unusual range of life events and job descriptions had in shaping the quality of his present artistic accomplishments." Some of these include drawing portraits with exceptional likeness at the age of ten, the life of an authentic working cowboy, blue collar worker in industry and heavy construction, successful college athlete, emergency room medical technician, Lutheran minister, author, holder of key leadership positions in government and human services and the recipient of many prestigious achievement awards in recognition of his humanitarian and written accomplishments.

During his service in the Vietnam War, he was wounded twice while leading successful medical rescue missions with the River Assault Flotilla One unit. For his rescue efforts he was highly decorated and also honored as "One of the Ten Outstanding Young Americans" by the United States Jaycees. IN previous years, this honor was given to such notables as John F. Kennedy and Henry Kissinger.

Currently, Padre continues to receive many invitations to speak and exhibit at international conferences, colleges, universities and schools of all grade levels overseas and throughout the United States.

**DALE S. "DOC" JONES** was born April 11, 1947 in Albany, OR. He received a degree in Criminal Justice. Jones joined the US Army on March 14, 1968. He served with B. Co. C Co. 4/47th Inf. and 9th Inf. Div. He served in Ft. Lewis, WA; Ft. Sam Houston, TX; Dong Tam, Vietnam; and Ft. Rucker, DC. Jones was awarded Vietnam Service, Vietnam Campaign, DRCUM, Air Medal, Bronze Star OLC V Device, Combat Medical Badge, Purple Heart and Soldiers Medal. He achieved the rank of SP/5 E-5 and was discharged on March 14, 1970.

Jones says that his most memorable experience was to provide medical care to Americans finest; being part of a brotherhood that civilians can not or will not ever understand.

Jones is divorced and has one child, Kyle and two grandchildren, Korry and Kaylee. He has been employed as a Criminal Investigator. Jones retired on Jan. 1, 2001.

**JOHN D. JONES JR.** was born Oct. 2, 1945 in Kings Creek, KY. He earned his Bachelor of Science in Law Enforcement from Eastern Kentucky University. He joined the US Navy in February 1966.

Ships and units that Jones served with were the *USS Observer*, Mobile Riverine Force (T-91-9) Tango Boat-Brownwater Navy. Military locations and stations include Philadelphia Naval Base; Vallejo, CA for Combat Training; Mekong Delta Vietnam; and Charleston, SC Naval Base. He also served in TET Offensive in Vietnam.

Jones was awarded the Bronze Star Medal, Meritorious Unit Commendation Ribbon, National Defense Service Medal, Navy Achievement Medal with Combat "V," Navy Expert Rifle Medal, Navy Unit Commendation Ribbon with one Bronze Star, Presidential Unit Citation Ribbon, Purple Heart Medal, Vietnam Service Medal with four Bronze Stars, Republic of Vietnam Campaign Medal, and Republic Vietnam MUC Gallantry Cross. He achieved the rank of E-3 Engineman Third Class and was discharged on Nov. 5, 1969.

Jones says of his most memorable experience was the survival of B40 Rocket entering his 50 caliber gunmount on Dec. 4, 1967 and also, realizing the limits of the human body during the eight weeks of the TET Offensive (no sleep, little food and being on the run from village to village).

Jones has been married since Dec. 27, 1969 to Janet Lee Hall Jones. They have two children, Callie Anne and Cara Rae. Civilian employment for Jones has included Service Manager of Appalachian Leasing Service.

**HARRY A. KAHN** was born July 9, 1947, Indianapolis, IN. Graduated from Shortridge High School in 1965 and from Indiana State University of Evansville in 1985 with a BS degree. He enlisted in the Navy on March 24, 1967 and served with RVAW 110 at North Island and then went to DP "A" School at Treasure Island. From there he somehow ended up in COMRIVRON 13 for the remainder of his service. He was retired on Aug. 17, 1970 from the Navy. He served on TANGO 26 and 27. While on Tango Boats, he completed 212 combat patrols and was involved in 13 firefights. He received the Bronze Star Medal with combat V, two Purple Hearts, Navy Commendation, Presidential Unit Citation, Combat Action Ribbon, Vietnam Service Medal with Bronze Star, Vietnam Compaign Medal and the National Defense Service Medal.

Kahn worked for the Department of Veterans Affairs for the next 25 years, retiring as a Field Examiner. He has one son, Adam, who just graduated from high school.

The hardest part of this was the memorable experiences; transporting the bodies of children killed while playing with an unexploded bomb back to their village, or the time a certain LTJG took a group of boats to a new base camp and made a wrong turn, got lost and ran out of gas. It could easily be the night their boat captain stopped the My Tho ferry at Dong Tam and thought that all the civilians on board were VC. However, Kahn says that his most memorable experience was the last night he spent on the river. He had the last watch that night and the next day he was off the boat as his tour was up and he had his discharge papers for an early out. They were ambushed shortly after he assumed his watch. They were hit with RPG and AK fire. He was wounded in the leg and upper thigh. After a short firefight, Gerald Burleigh put a tourniquet on Kahn's leg, splinted it and rushed him off the boat to a waiting Medivac Helo. He then finished his service by touring various military hospitals. He spent 365 days in Vietnam and has a story for every day, because each day he spent in 'Nam was a memorable day.

**ALLEN T. KAWABATA** was born March 31, 1947 in Wailkuku, Maui, HI. He graduated from Abraham Lincoln High School in San Jose, earned his Associate of Art degree in Drafting and Design from D.S. Lancaster College in Clifton Forge, VA.

Kawabata joined the US Navy on Dec. 27, 1965. In 1966 he served on board the *USS George Clymer*, 1967 with MRF RIVDIV 111 Tango 111-10. He had boot camp in San Diego, CA; 1968-1969 he served at Little Creek Amphibious Base, Virginia Beach, VA. He was awarded Navy Achievement Medal with Combat "V" and Vietnam Campaign Medal with Device. Achieved the rank of GMG3 and was discharged on Oct. 16, 1969. His most memorable experience was the shellback initiation for crossing the Equator.

Kawabata is married to Patricia. They have three children, Monica, Christina and Jennifer; and one grandchild, Kyle. Civilian employment has included Engineering Designer with General Electric for 29 years. He retired on May 30, 2002.

**JERRY J. KAWECKI** graduated from Central Catholic High School in Portland, OR in 1965. He attended Portland State University for two years, then decided to work for a while after two years of college with intentions to go to Oregon State University on the GI Bill after Army service. He was drafted into the US Army in March 1968, did basic training and AIT at Fort Lewis, WA and was sent to the 3/47th Inf., 9th Inf. Div. in Vietnam.

He received Expert M-16 Rifle and Expert M-60 Machine Gun Badges, Combat Infantry Badge, Vietnam Service Medal, Vietnam Campaign Medal and the Purple Heart. He was wounded by machine gun in the chest and lung and by B-40 rocket in the right leg on Nov. 22, 1968 and was medevaced to Japan, to California to Madigan Hospital at Fort Lewis, WA for about a four-month stay. After that he was sent to Fort Hood, TX to finish his two years.

His most memorable experience was his last firefight when he was shot through the chest and lung. He thought he was going to die and his mother was going to get a letter that he had died in Vietnam. But he made it back and couldn't wait to kiss the ground when he got off the plane.

He returned to Oregon and finished up three more years of college at Oregon State University on the GI Bill with a BS degree in pharmacy. He graduated from Oregon State University in 1973 as a pharmacist and married his wonderful wife of 22 years, Pattie Phillips Kawecki, on June 25, 1977. He is currently a community pharmacist in Gresham, OR. His hobbies include golfing, skiing, traveling and guns.

**JAMES V. "LUCKY 13" KELLEY** was born Nov. 5, 1942 in Wetompica, AL. He received his high school diploma. He joined the US Army in December 1959.

Units that Kelley served with include CO A 4th 47th 9th Inf. from 1966 to 1968. Military locations include Ft. Benning, GA for two years; Ft. Hood, TX seven months; Schien Fort, Germany two and one-half years; two years with 9th Inf. at Ft. Riley; Ft. Campbell, KY and Ft. Benning; and one year with the 9th Inf. Div in Vietnam. Kelley was awarded the CIB, the "is been there, done that medals." He achieved the rank of MSG E-8 after serving eight years in the Army and 14 years in Alabama National Guard. He was discharged in 1994.

His most poignant memory occurred on June 17 and 19, 1967, when his company was wiped out losing 53 dead and 47 wounded.

Kelley has been married for 40 years to Barbara. They have two children, Kristy and Kenneth; and four grandchildren, Laurel, Lexie, Andrew and James. Kelley has enjoyed 30 years of employment at the CSXT Railroad as Conductor. He retired in 2002 from the railroad.

**RON KIRKWOOD** was born Sept. 19, 1942 in Abbington, PA. After he graduated from high school, he earned his BA degree. He joined the US Navy in 1964.

Kirkwood served with RIVRON 15, Zippo 5 (FlameThrower Boat). He served in South Vietnam in the Delta area. He was awarded Marksmanship Ribbon, Combat Action Ribbon, Presidential Citation, National Defense Medal, Service Medal and the Bronze Star. He achieved the rank of E-2 and was discharged in 1970. Kirkwood says that his most memorable experience was to served on Zippo 5 (FlameThrower) in South Vietnam in 1969.

Kirkwood is divorced and has two children, Lark and Brent. He is the owner of a photo processing business.

**GEORGE A. "GHOST RIDER" KITCHEN** was born Oct. 29, 1939 in Houston, TX. He graduated from Needville High School in 1958. He attended Texas A&M in 1962 and received degree in Education/ Biology

Kitchen joined the US Navy in May 1962. He served on the *USS Hull (DD945)*; TACRON

12; Recomm crew of PBR Mother Ships; OPS OFF *USS Hunterdon CTY (LST838)*; MRF Staff then O in C of RIV DIV 92. After Vietnam Kitchen was OPS OFF of *USS Yancey (LKA93)*; Asst. Intel. Off for COMNAVMAR on Guam. Got out of the Navy in July 1972 and joined the Texas National Guard in 1978. Entered as E-4 and retired as 1st Sgt of a Tank Co in May 1990. He served June 19, 1967 at Snoopy's Nose; Rocket Alley (Ben Tre River), TET, Vinh Long and Parrot's Beak. He was awarded Bronze Star, Army Commendation, Cross of Gallantry w/ Silver Star, Combat Action, Presidential Unit Citation and Gov. of Tex. (individual award). Kitchen says that his most memorable experience was being chosen as the person to represent the whole corps of cadets at Texas A&M, for the Vietnam era, during the 125th Anniversary of the college in 2001 as an honor of a lifetime.

Kitchen is married to Diane, a library teacher. They have two children, Allen and Christine, and have two grandchildren, Sandra and Lisa. Before retiring in November 1999, Kitchen was employed at Phillips Pet. Co. operating Eng. He is now an avid deer hunter in Texas.

**EDWARD O. "RUSTY" KOHLER** was born Feb. 9, 1946 in San Antonio, TX. He attended Sydney Lanier High School in Austin, TX where he graduated in 1964; and earned BAAS Southwest Texas State University, San Marcos, TX and graduated in 1979.

Kohler joined the US Army in June 1967. He served with 9th Inf. Div., 9th M.P. CO., Mobile Riverine Force (Delta) on a LCM-80 (MP Boat). Kohler served at BearCat, Dong Tam, Tan An, and on River Boats (Floating Fire Support Bases). He was at TET (1968), but mainly along Mekong on the boats, Ben Tre and many others. He was awarded Vietnam Campaign, National Defense Service Ribbon, Good Conduct and Army Commendation Medal. Achieved the rank of Sgt. E-5 Military Police. He was discharged in June 1973. Kohler says of his memorable experiences were building bunkers and barracks in Dong Tam; working Highways 4, 1 and 2, Main Gate and Patrol Duty in Dong Tam; and lastly, working on the River Boats in the Delta for last six months, with rest and refuel stops on *USS Benewah*. This was a floating (mobile) fire support base. He was the Sgt. in charge of the MP-Prisoner Boat. They towed gun barges.

Kohler has been married for over 30 years to Kay. They have two children, Michelle Rene and David Lee, and two grandchildren, Garrett Lee and Emmalee Rose. Civilian employment has included being a Senior Patrolman, City of Austin, TX Police Department. He is currently Deputy Sheriff with the Bastrop County Sheriff's Office, Bastrop, TX. He retired in December 1996 from Austin Police Department after 25 years of service.

**LEE KOLSTAD** was born Oct. 30, 1946 in New York, NY. He earned BBA at Bernard Baruch College. He joined the US Army on Jan. 30, 1966.

Kolstad served with Company D, 15th Eng. Battalion. He had basic training at Fort Jackson, AIT at Fort Leonard Wood, OCS at Fort Belvoir, and served in Vietnam and at Fort Campbell. He was awarded Good Conduct, Bronze Star, National Defense, Vietnam Service and Vietnam Campaign. Achieved the rank of 1st Lt. He retired on June 1, 1969. Most memorable experience was the TET Offensive put the words Vietnam experience in perspective for me. A desperate enemy that we "let off the hook." The "professionalism" of the combat soldier and sailor no matter what rank, gave us all hope for the future.

Kolstad is married to Janet. They have two children, Jason and Elizabeth and have one grandchild, Danielle. He worked for Xerox Corporation. He retired Feb. 28, 2003.

**DENNIS KOTILA** was born Nov. 14, 1949 in Hancock, MI. After high school, he attended two years of college.

Joined the US Navy in December 1968. Units served with include Task Force 117, Tango Boat, T-131-2, Mobile Riverine Force. Military locations include Mekong Delta, River Assault Div. 131  served on Alpha, Mike and Tango Boats. Operated all over Mekong Delta with Task Force 117. Awarded Purple Heart, Combat Action Ribbon, Navy Achievement Medal with Combat Device and Vietnam Service Ribbon. Achieved the rank of E-4 and was discharged on Feb. 3, 1970. One of his most vivid memorable experiences was the four firefights he was in the first day on a RiverBoat (Mike Boat). He participated in Operation Giant Slingshot for months and was in many firefights. Also, transporting snipers at night to pick off the enemy.

Kotila is married to Judith and they have two children, Matt and Brenda. Civilian employment includes 798 Pipeliner. He retired October 1991.

**SAM KUBALA** was born May 17, 1945 in Corpus Christi, TX. He graduated from high school. Joined the US Navy in 1962.

Units that Kubala served with include *USS Hopewill DD681*, *USS Springfield C167*, Com RIVRON 9, RIVDIV 91 ASPB1. He served in San Diego, CA, France and Vietnam. Battles and campaigns include Snoopy's Nose, Long Am, Go Cong Provinces and Rung Sat. He was awarded Vietnam Service Medal, Vietnam Campaign, National Defense and Purple Heart. He achieved the rank of EN 2 and was discharged in February 1968. Kubala says of his memorable experience that he remembers coming through a Vietnamese village about 3:00 a.m. They had their sampans tied up to a wire across the river to a post. There was just enough room between the post and riverbank for them to get through. Their sweep gear caught on the post and when Kubala looked back, they were pulling fleet of sampans behind them.

Kubala is married to June and they have two children, Jonathan and Jennifer. Civilian employment includes working for Lonestar Gas Company. He retired on June 1, 2003.

**THOMAS "DOC" LAFLAM** was born June 5, 1948. After graduating from high school, he earned AS Associate of Science. On Oct. 5, 1966 he joined the US Navy.

Units served with include MCB 1, MCB133, RPD 531 and 592, 5 25 MIG, and 5th Special Forces. He served at Phu Bai, Go Dau Ha, Nam Can and various other locations. Battles and campaigns that he took part of were Operation Giant Slingshot and Operation Sea Float. Achieved the rank of HM3 and was discharged in March 1970. Most memorable experience was operating the dispensary in Go Dau Ha and doing Med Caps every day for the five months he was there. Then working for the 5th Special Forces and MAC until March 1970.

Married to Katherine, who is a RN at the VAMC in White River Junction, VT. They have three children, William, Timothy and Jonathan; and one grandchild, Nathan. Civilian employment has included being a carpenter and cabinetmaker.

**LARRY C. "WHISTLER" LAMB** was born Aug. 26, 1948 in Tracy, MN. He graduated from high school. Joined the US Army on May 23, 1968.

Units served with include C-3/47-9th Inf. 68-69-RVN, MRF-*USS Benawah*- 69 1st Inf. Div. Ft. Riley 1970. Military locations and stations include basic Ft. Campbell, KY-AIT-Ft. Lewis, WA-USARV-Ft. Riley, KS-USAR Winthrop, MN. Battles and campaigns include VN Counter Offensive Phase V, 9th Campaign VN-named. Awards and medals include BS w/v-NDSM-Air Medal (2)-ACM/A-USM-VSM-VCMw/60DVC-CIB-ARCAM (3)-AFRM. Achieved the rank of SFC. Discharged from active duty May 22, 1970 and from USAR in 1995. Memorable experiences MRV-1969, Combat Sniper-69 and Desert Storm-1991.

Lamb is married to Patricia and they have three children, Krista, Kerry and Katharine. They also have a grandchild, Marcus. Civilian employment held Masonry Const-33 years/Sales and drawing at local lumber and building center.

**JOHN J. LANE** was born Sept. 26, 1947 in Chicago, IL. He attended Cooley Voc High School in Chicago. He joined the US Navy on April 12, 1965.

Units served with were TF117 River Assault Division 92 Boat T-92-8 *USS Saratoga CVA60 Howard W Gilmore AS-16*. Military locations and stations were Basic Training Great Lakes, Mare Island, Vallejo, CA. Served in nine campaigns and three major battles. Awards and medals were VSM w/ two Bronze Stars, RVCM, NDSM, CAR, Purple Heart, Navy Achievement Medal w/ Combat V. Achieved the rank of Engineman second class E-5. Discharged on Sept. 5, 1968. Memorable experience was he remembers Sept. 15, 1967 ambush on the Rach Ba Rai just as they made a hairpin bend in the river past Snoopy's Nose. Their boat was hit several times with rocket-propelled grenade launcher. Most of them were wounded but thank God they all came back alive.

Lane is married to Marge. They have four children, Jimmy, Tina, Theresa and Tracey. They also have six grandchildren, Heather, Sara, Jeremy, Kelly, Ryan and Shawn. Civilian employment has included Auto Mechanic and Master Mechanic. Lane retired in May 2003.

**PHILLIP W. LANGSTON** was born March 24, 1944 in Seminole, OK. He earned his BS at Oklahoma State University and MS degree at the University of Cincinnati. Joined the US Navy in June 1967.

Units served with include Navy Schools Command-New Port, RI; *USS Betelgeuse AK (FBM) 260*, RivRon 15-RivDiv 152 Chief Staff Officer. Military locations and stations include New Port, RI; Charleston, SC; Amphibious School Coronado, Mare Island and Sere Training Whidby Island, NHABE, Dong Tam, Tuyen NHON. He served in Operation Barrier Reef and Cambodian Campaign. Awards and medals received Navy Commendation w/ Combat V and Combat Action Ribbon. Achieved the rank of LT. Discharged in September 1970. Memorable experience was interdiction patrol on Vam Co Tay, south of Parrots Beak, two weeks at ferry crossing in Cambodia supporting Marine operations, and when he left Vietnam, at Midnight, they fired a flare so the plane could taxi and take off. It seemed the appropriate last thing to see as he left Vietnam.

Langston is married to Linda and they have two children, Harper Leigh and Phillip Ryan. Civilian employment has included health care administrator and Oklahoma State Department of Health.

**DANNY LARA** was born on Jan. 14, 1947 in Thrall, TX. He earned his Masters degree, LMSW, social worker. He joined the US Army on Dec. 12, 1967.

Units served with include 3/60 Mobile Riverine Force, 9th Infantry Division in the Delta, on *USS Benewah*, Dong Tam base, Training at Bear Cat, US Basic, AIT at Fort Polk, LA (Tigerland). Awards and medals he was awarded include Vietnam Service Medal with four Bronze Stars, Vietnam Campaign Medal with Device 60, CIB, Air Medal with Oak Leaf Cluster, Good Conduct Medal, National Defense Medal, Purple

Heart, and Commendation Medal with V Device and Oak Leaf Cluster. Achieved the rank of Specialist Four and was discharged Nov. 28, 1969. Lara says that his most memorable experience was having been on a six man team that circled behind and overtook a bunker nest holding a company; also, knowing that you were part of the best machine gun team in the company thanks to Bell and Sonny.

Lara is married to Velma "Cissy" and they have a daughter, Rebecca. They also have a grandson, Jeremy. Civilian employment has included Department of Veterans Affairs Outpatient Clinic, Mental Health Social Worker and PTSO Counseling Specialist.

**ARTHUR "LASH" LARUE** was born April 21, 1949, Quincy, MA graduated from Havelock High School, Havelock, NC, in 1967. Joined the USN Dec. 20, 1967; attended Basic Training a Great Lakes, IL; Served aboard *USS Vulcan* December 1967 to August 1969. From January 1970 to June 1970 he served with Riv. Div. 131 and 152 aboard Zippo-3 as 50 cal./20 mm gunner.

From June 1970-January 1971 served as advisor to RID-45 aboard Alpha-67 at Seafloat and later at Dong Tam. Memorable experiences include a sapper attack on RID-45 boats as Solid Anchor in which his alpha boat was destroyed and three of his crew killed. Separated from active duty, Jan. 20, 1971. Received BS in Marine Biology form UNC-W in 1975. Served in USMC from August 1975 to April 1978 as Assault Amphibian Platoon Commander. Served in USN from August 1979 to July 1991 when he was discharged with the rank of Lt. Ships and commands served during this time include *USS Corry, USS Coronado, USS Dale, SCU-2, USS Hermitage* and *USS Charleston*. Attended Jacksonville University September 1991 to June 1993 and received Masters in Teaching. He resides in Orange Park, FL and has been teaching middle school science for 10 years in Green Cove Springs, FL. He is married to Judy Kanarek, a former USN nurse, and they have one son, Stephen. When he is not helping coach his son's sports teams he likes to scuba dive.

**THOMAS A. LAVENDER** was born Aug. 2, 1946 in St. Gordon, GA. He graduated high school from Wilkinson Co. High School. He joined the US Navy in July 1965.

Units and ships that Lavender served on or with include *USS Rexburg EPCER855*, Trained for Vietnam a Vallejo, CA and Whidbey Island, WA. Locations and stations served include RivRon 13, Boat number M-132-1 1968 to 1969, *USS Floyd B. Parks DD884* 1972 and 1973 and the *USS Tripoli LPH-10* 1973 and 1974. He's not sure what all battles he was involved with however, both ships were directly involved when the south began its retreat to the south during the US pull out. Some long days and nights in the Gunmounts. Lavender was awarded Navy Ach. with Combat V, Vietnam Service Commendation, Presidential and others. Achieved the rank of BM-2. Lavender's most memorable experience was on the monitor seems like they were in constant contact with VC; Snoopy's Nose rings a bell and operations along the Cambodian boarder, especially Christmas 1968; many night ambushed with special forces; they took several rocket hits and auto weapon fire which is always memorable!

Lavender is married to Linda, who he credits with saving his life 15 years ago. He has three children, Clay, Jenelle and Danielle. Civilian employment has included Kaolin Mines, store manger, prison, truck driver, career student and construction.

**NATHAN OTTO LOESCH**, a native of Iowa, was educated at Concordia College, Milwaukee, Valparaiso University in Indiana, and graduated from Concordia Seminary, St. Louis in 1955. He is the son of the sainted Pastor and Mrs. Luther H. Loesch, formerly of Pensacola, FL. Pastor Loesch's maternal grandfather, Pastor Ott Von Gemmingen, three uncles, and four cousins have served as Lutheran pastors. He spent his vicarage (intern years) in two congregations, Bergland and Topaz in the Upper Peninsula of Michigan.

After Seminary graduation, he served Immanuel Church, Bonners, Ferry, Idaho and at the same time was founding pastor of Christ the King Church in Coeur d'Alene, ID. In 1961 he became pastor of Good Shepherd Church, Portland, where he served until the end of 1966.

Commissioned as a Lieutenant (Junior Grade) in the Chaplain Corps of the United States Navy in 1962, Pastor Loesch accepted a call from the Church's Armed Forces Commission to report for active duty on Dec. 31, 1966. His tours of duty included Naval Chaplain's School, Long Beach, CA. From Dec. 22, 1967 to Dec. 23, 1968, Chaplain Loesch served in Vietnam with River Assault Flotilla ONE. His military decorations include two Bronze Stars with combat "v," two Navy Commendation Medals with combat "v," the Combat Action Ribbon, Presidential Unit Citation, Navy unit Commendation, National Defense Service Medal, Vietnamese Campaign Medal with five battle stars, Vietnamese Cross of Gallantry with silver star, the Vietnamese Service Medal and the Navy Reserve Medal.

Chaplain Loesch was released from active duty in January 1970 and "retired" in 1989 after 23 years of federal service with the rank of Commander. In 1990 Pastor Loesch received St. Martin of Tours medal from the Lutheran Church-Missouri Synod.

During his years of parish ministry, he served as pastoral advisor of the Evergreen and Oregon Districts of the Walther League, director of public relations for the Northwest District, member of the summer faculty at Holden Village in Washington, Northwest District representative of Wheat Ridge, six years as a member of the Board of Directors of the Pacific Southwest District, nine years as second vice president of the Pacific Southwest District, and a senior pastor of Bethany Lutheran Church in Long Beach, CA since Jan. 11, 1970. During his years at Bethany, the congregation completed two major building programs, in 1973 and 1997.

Pastor Loesch and his wife Meg have two children, Rachel Klitzing of Irvine and Jonathan Loesch of Rancho Cucamonga. Rachel and Jonathan and their spouses, Mark and Tonya, respectively, are full-time church workers. The Loesch's have five grandchildren, Anna and Nathan Klitzing and Bethany, Luke and Hannah Loesch.

Loesch says of Vietnam experience, the things you don't like about it is: C-Rations for chow day after day, 30 muggy days in a row, coming back from R&R, a fly doing the backstroke in your kool aid, when your shot record gets lost, a lousy movie, an all male U.S.O. Show, war.."Somebody out there hates me!," toe poppers (landmines), muddy Mekong River and Vietnam. The things that you really like are: a "care" package from home, beautiful children of Vietnam, when you're next in line, a firefight between two confused VC platoons, a U.S.O. Show with 30 beautiful girls, "Good Morning, Vietnam!," a letter from home, the Navy Hymn: "Eternal Father, Strong to Save," a Vietnam sunset, closer than brothers-guys you serve with, anything that's not in the other list and Vietnam.

**LARRY DEAN "CALIFORNIA" OR "CRAZY LARRY" LONG** was born June 17, 1949 at Hamilton, MT. He is a vocational certified horseshoer and obtained AA degree from American River College. Joined the US Army in June 1966. He did not enlist for draft.

Units served with include 3rd Marin Division, B Co 2nd BN 60th Inf 9th Inf Div, 5th Division RVNPOR School, and 3rd Platoon 3rd squad. Military locations and stations include Fort Ord, Fort Gordon, Germany, Vietnam and

Fort Riley, KS. Long served in Ben Tre, TET and French Fort. He was awarded the Combat Infantry Badge, Bronze Star with V and the Purple Heart with Oak Leaf Clusters. Achieved the rank of Sgt. E5 (Squad Leader) and was discharged in June 1969.

Long says that his most memorable experience was walking point four months, TET, (June 13, 1968) hitting anti-tank mine while driving 3/4 ton truck "Suicide Alley" out of Dong Tam and losing Bobby Hamilton on Jan. 8, 1968 at French Fort- they came to Vietnam together.

Long has been married since Sept. 14, 1968 to Joan Hacker Long. They have two children, Cristen and Matthew. They also have three grandchildren, Melissa, Alexis and Jacob. Civilian employment has included truck driver for two major companies. He retired in June 2001 due to medical conditions.

**RICHARD E. LORMAN** born June 24, 1946, Boston, MA, graduated high school (by the skin of his teeth). Joined the USN Sept. 12, 1966, and was stationed at Great Lakes, IL, furniture mover, naval housing, one year; Engineman School, Mare Island; boat training included SERE at Whidbey Island, WA, assigned ATC-152-6 (Z-152-1), then Chelsea Naval Hospital, Boston, MA.

Memorable experiences were of their most valuable crew member, Louie Bokusky, cooking up casseroles from C-rations and fixings he scoffed from any ship or base they came close to, they were delicious; SERE training, having been separated from the group quite a while for resisting quite properly and being walked (with a black hood over his head) to God-only-knows-where, only to have it yanked off and being so joyful at being reunited with the rest of the boys, standing in a corral/compound, that he grabbed the cheeks of, and kissed, the highest ranking officer on the lips, he was right in front of him and he probably was as surprised as Lorman was; seeing six inches above the knee of a Red Cross girl as she stepped down to a lower pontoon at Dong Tam-from 200 yards (and being excited); listening to "Chicken Man" and a lovely voiced Vietnamese girl disc jockey and especially to "the weekly polka hour" on armed services radio; his relatively short, but memorable, stint on Z-151-1, around May 1969, why is it that "Zippo" crews were so, well, different and nuts?!

He never married and has no children. He is a "greedy land lord" and "half-ass carpenter." Retired from the USN May 22, 1970, and is permanently disabled due to wounds received June 13, 1969, Ben Tre River.

**LILYARD N. LUCAS** was born March 21, 1926 in Woodbury, NY. He joined the USN in September 1944.

Units that he served with include boat patrol 15 Manila, APA 108, LSD 15, AGC17/AGC17, DE418, APS7, DD702 and Tug Master Phila. Pa. He served at Bainbridge, MD; Pungo NAAS, VA; Willow Grove NAS, PA; RivRon 13 and Z132-2 June 1968 to June 1969. Lucas achieved the rank of BMC and retired in January 1973.

Lucas is married to Martha K. Lucas. Civilian employment has included Rigger 1st Phila Naval ShipYard Pa. He retired April 1988.

**STEPHEN E. "STEVE" LUTH** was born July 20, 1948 in Orange, CA. He attended three years of high school and earned his GED in 1966. Joined the US Navy on Oct. 21, 1965.

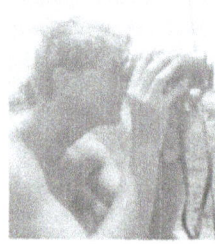 

Luth served on the *USS Monticello LSD-35* January 1966 to February 1968, Riv Ron 15 April 13, 1968 to June 1969 and Monitor 151-2 and Zippo 131-2. He was stationed at San Diego, CA (boot camp); Mare Island; Nha Be; Dong Tam and Ben Tre. He was a part of Operation Sealords Jan. 12, 1969 and Operation Homestead. He was also in many firefights. Awards and medals Luth earned include Combat Action Ribbon, Navy Commendation Ribbon with Combat V, Purple Heart and Navy Achievement. Achieved the rank of BM3 and was discharged on June 13, 1969.

Luth says that his most memorable experience was on the *USS Westchester Country* which was mined on the My Tho River, Monitor 151-2 lead boat in formation; he was driving when a boat behind then was mined and sunk on Song Cai Tu, they were hit with one rocket on May 1, 1969, five wounded four Medivacs, he got a Purple Heart.

Luth is married to Esther and they have two children, Joe and Rowena. Civilian employment has included general store and grill owner. He retired USPO June 1988.

**LARRY J. LYONS** was born on June 22, 1946 in San Antonio, TX. He earned his Associates of Arts degree. Joined the US Navy in July 1963. Units and ships that Lyons served with include *USS Oriskany (CVA-34)*, River Boat C-112-1, *USS Providence (CLG-6)*, *USS Oklahoma City (CLG-5)*, Seal Team 1, Underwater Demolition Team-13, Underwater Demolition Team-12, *USS Mount Vernon (LSD-39)*, and *USS Okinawa (LPH-3)*. Lyons achieved the rank of MA1 and medically retired in June 1984.

Lyons says he has many memorable experiences including surviving the 122 mm rocket the hit the air terminal in Saigon on Feb. 19, 1968 while awaiting a flight out to Conus; completing and graduating from UDT/Seal Team Training on July 25, 1969; Basic Airborne Training in August 1969; and returning to Vietnam as a Navy SEAL in 1970-1971.

Lyons is married to Karen and they have seven children and seven grandchildren. He became an ordained minister with Independent Assemblies of God, a mission chaplain with the Chaplaincy Full Gospel Churches. He started a church in St. Petersburg, Russia in 1994.

**BRIAN J. MAHONEY** was born May 2, 1946 in Detroit, MI. He graduated from high school. Joined the US Navy in October 1965. Served with FOCC PAC and aboard *USS Sphinx ARL24*. Military locations and stations include CINC PAC Fleet Hawaii and FOCC PAC Kunia. Achieved the rank of RM2 and was discharged on Nov. 1, 1969.

Mahoney says that his most memorable experience was while going from the *Sphinx* to the *Benewah*, almost being swamped by a tug coming up to pull the APL up River, he was half way out when his supervisor S. Cobb grabbed his vest and pulled him back in to the boat, thank God!

Mahoney is married to Audrey Jeanne and they have two children, Jennifer and Holly. They also have three grandchildren, Jessica, Jillian and Deanna. His civilian employment has included supervisor-merchants terminal-Corp, frozen food warehouse.

**ROBERT W. "DOC" "BOB" MALONE** was born July 14, 1936 in Crenshaw, MS. He graduated from Batesville High School in Batesville, earned AS at Olympic Community College in Bremerton, WA and BS at Southern Illinois University at Carbondale, IL.

Malone joined the USMC on March 19, 1955 and the US Navy on Jan. 23, 1957. Units and ships he served on include Nav Hops Corps School in San Diego, CA; NH Charleston, SC Nav Hosp; Portsmouth, VA, 2nd Marine Air Wing, Cherry PT, NC, Nav Hosp SCH, San Diego, CA,

NH San Diego, CA; RivDiv 112, RivRon 11, Task Force 117, *USS Ticonderoga CVS14*, ADCOP, Bremerton, WA, NA, Great Lakes, IL, Station Hosp. Whidbey Island, WA, Nav Sta Seattle, WA. He served in various campaigns and battles from March 1967 to March 4968. Malone was awarded the Silver Star, Bronze Star "V," Naval Commendation, Combat Action Medal, Presidential Unit Citation, Navy Unit Citation, Good Conduct with stars, National Defense, Vietnam Campaign with star, and Vietnam Service with device. Achieved the rank of Master Chief Hospital Corpsman. He was discharged on Sept. 1, 1981.

Malone says that his most memorable experience was being Master Chief Corpsman for three space recovery mission –Apollo 16, Apollo 17, SkyLab "1"; graduating college, project director for 35 cities director of operation, Chicago Market Michael Reese and Humana HMO, Shelton School District, NJROTC Instructor Shelton, WA.

Malone is married to Theresa and they have three children, Debra, Jacque and Robert Jr. (MST USMC). They also have six grandchildren, Joseph, Katrina, David Jr., Weston, Kay Lee and Richard. Civilian employment has included American Hospital Supply (Facility Mgr.), Michael Reese HMO and Humana as director of operations. He retired from Humana on July 11, 1997.

**FRANK S. MAJ JR.** was born June 5, 1946 in Detroit, MI. After he graduated from high school, he earned his BS degree in Business Administration.

Maj joined the US Army in December 1967. He served with "A" Company 2$^{nd}$ 47$^{th}$ Inf. 1$^{st}$ and 3$^{rd}$ Platoon. He was stationed at Ft. Knox, Ft. Dix, Ft. Benning, Ft. Lewis, Vietnam-Bearcat, and Ben Phuoc. Awarded the Purple Heart, Army Commendation and CIB. Achieved the rank of Staff Sergeant and was discharged in September 1969.

Maj is married to Tonya and they have two children, Frank and Eric. Civilian employment has included working at General Motors Lansing Car Assembly.

**MICHAEL A. MARQUEZ** was born June 6, 1948; Sacramento, CA graduated from Norte Del Rio High School, Sacramento, CA, in 1966. Joined the US Army Aug. 18, 1967; attended basic training at Ft. Bliss, TX; AIT at Ft. Polk, LA; and NCO School at Ft. Benning, GA. Stations were Mekong Delta; Vietnam; and Ft. Hood, TX. Served with Co. A, 3$^{rd}$ Bn., 60$^{th}$ Inf., 9$^{th}$ Inf., Div., MRF, in Vietnam July 1968 to July 1969; and the 2$^{nd}$ Arm. Div. at Ft. Hood, TX, August 1969 to August 1970.

Memorable experiences include a very hot LZ on Oct. 23, 1968, his longest day and night of his tour; and being a member of the MRF.

Discharged Aug. 17, 1970, with the rank of E-5. Received the Combat Infantry Badge, Bronze Star w/ OLC, Purple Heart, Army Commendation w/ Device w/ 4 OLCs, Air Medal w/ 2 OLCs, Good Conduct Medal, National Defense Medal, Vietnam Service Medal w/ 4 BS, Vietnamese Cross of Gallantry w/ Palm, Civil Actions Medal w/ OLC and RVN Campaign Medal.

He is divorced and has three children and two grandchildren. Works as a clerk for the US Postal Service. He enjoys fishing, hiking, camping, hunting and model railroads.

**JOHN P. "JACK" MARSHALL** was born July 16, 1943 in Pittsburgh, PA. He attended Ohio State and earned his BS degree and also attended St. Francis University and earned Master of Science in Health Service Administration.

Marshall joined the US Navy in September 1961. Served on the *USS Assurance, MSO521*; Mine Division 113, MSM5, NHA BE; *USS Donner, LSD20*. He was stationed at Panama City, FL, NHA BE Ben Luc, Vietnam; Cua Viet, Vietnam; and Chau Duc, Vietnam. Battles and campaigns involved with were Giant Slingshot, Game Warden and Market Time. Awarded Bronze Star and Combat "V." Achieved the rank of Lieutenant and was discharged in December 1970.

Marshall had many memorable experience and a few of those were being aboard *USS Benewah* when neighboring LST was blown open by V.C. mine; seals captured a 500 pound mine which exploded at their NHA BE Base, killing nine sailors; and inadvertently sailing too far up the Mekong into Cambodia.

Marshall is married to Carol and they have two children, Jack and Mike. They also have four grandchildren, Sean, Sara, Enzo and Erin. Civilian employment has included working as administrator, Latrobe Mental Health Center, and as director of Jefferson Regional Medical Center.

**RAY J. MARSHALL** was born on June 9, 1933 in Oklahoma City, OK. After high school, Marshall joined the US Navy on Feb. 28, 1951. Units served with and ships served on include *USS O'Bannon (DDE-450), USS Cascade (AD-16), USS Hailey DD-556, USS R. K. Huntington DD-781, USS Litchfield County LST-901, USS Henrico APA-45, USS Coontz DLG-9*, and *USS Providence CLG-6*. Military locations and stations were Naval Reserve Center Oklahoma City, OK; Recruit Training Command Great Lakes, IL; Radio School Imperial Beach, CA; Commissary Store Jacksonville, FL; River Squadron San Diego, CA; and Naval Amphibious Base Coronado San Diego, CA. Battles and campaigns were Korea and Vietnam. Awards and medals he received were National Defense (Bronze Star); Vietnam Service Medal (two Bronze Stars); Vietnam Campaign; Good Conduct Medal (three Bronze Stars); and Gallantry Cross.

Marshall says of his most memorable experience, "Usually the first and last day of the tour in Vietnam was deadly. More of our people died at this time than any other on our River crews. The first day of my last week in country Charlie hit our ammo dump. I was at Dong Tam, home base for RiverRon 13, awaiting a new set of orders to go home on leave. It had taken Charlie a whole year to hit the ammo dump, but hit he did. Falling debris hit the man behind me (a new arrival), before we reached the bunker (Navy side) that was about 1800. About 2000, we were told the Navy side was not safe. We started running to the Army side (about 1/2 mile away). About 2200 we were told this was unsafe also, so we started running to the Air Force side (about 1/2 mile away), stayed there until morning. That morning we found unexploded shells still laying about as crews were cleaning up the mess. The Navy side was hit the hardest. Our huts were damaged along with the building where our service records were located. I went to Vietnam in 1968 and left in 1969."

Marshall is married to Joyce E. Marshall and they have two children, Kelly and Amy. They also have four grandchildren, Ashlea, J.T., Nickolas and Lani. Civilian employment has included working as Forman at Harter Concrete and also at Designer Cast Stone. He retired on Oct. 16, 1973.

**OSCAR T. "TIM" MATHISON** was born Feb. 23, 1947 in St. Paul, MN. He joined the US Army on May 15, 1966. He served with A Co. 4$^{th}$ / 47$^{th}$ / 9$^{th}$. Mathison served in BearCat and Dong Tam. He was awarded the Combat Infantry Badge. Achieved the rank of Sgt. E5 and retired on May 15, 1968. His most memorable experience was the most difficult day of his life. It was the battle on June 19, 1967 Rach Gia River in Long An Province.

Mathison has been married since 1971 to Debi and they have two children, Lane and Tony. They also have three grandchildren, Kelsea, Cassy and Sara. Civilian employment has included V.P. Construction at Lehhar Corp.

**JOE "J. T." MATTIE** was born May 16, 1947 in Youngstown, OH. He attended Struthers High School and attended two years at Grossmont College. Joined the US Navy in September 1965.

Mattie served with the following units and aboard the following ships: the *USS Jason AR8, USS*

*Prairie AD*, Danang East Security, UDT21, MRF, Danang Naval Advisor Group and Shore Patrol. Military locations and stations he served with were Danang RVN 1966-1967; Key West, FL Dive School 1967-1967; Airborne School, Georgia 1967-1967; UDT21 (E-3) 1967-1968; MRF 1968-1969; and Danang RVN 1969-1970. Battles and campaigns include Aug. 18, 1968 battle with Battalion size NVA soldier, June 1968 U-MINH Forrest Operation. Mattie was awarded Purple Heart w/ two stars, NAVCOM w/ V, Meritorious Unit Cit w/ V, Combat Action, Presd. Unit Cit., Nav Unit Cit. w/ three stars, Good Conduct, National Def. Viet w/ three stars, and USN Pistol/ Rifle Medal. Achieved the rank of E5 and was discharged in March 1973.

Mattie says of his most memorable experience, "Aug. 17, 1968, Petty Officer (Radioman) Griffin told me that he was going to die. I told him that he would not. He even traded position with forward gunner. He was the first to die. During the battle on Aug. 18, 1968, after running out of ammo, I began to bandage the wounded, and giving morphine shots to the wounded. Just recently I had received a phone call from one of the wounded I worked on. He had not only survived, but done very well with his life."

Mattie is married to Debra Taylor and they have three children, Joseph, Anthony and Matthew. They have two grandchildren, Ryan and Michelle. Civilian employment has included working as a Detective at San Diego County Sheriff Department (Retired). He retired on March 21, 2002. He also had joined US Army Reserve, 1st SPC Forces, 12th Group "C" Company from 1976-1978.

**JOHN "MAC" MCLAUGHLIN** was born Dec. 29, 1947 in Chicago, IL. After high school, he earned a two-year degree in electronics technology. He joined the USNR on Jan. 11, 1967. Units served with and ships served on include RivRon 9 M-92-2, RivRon 13 T-131-4, M-92-2, October 1968 until turnover T-131-4 Turnover until August 1969. Battles and campaigns served in were Giant Slingshot, Sea Lords, etc. Rank achieved was EN3 and was separated in October 1969.

McLaughlin is married to Carole and they have three children, Todd, Claudia and John. Civilian employment has included Electrical Power Plant Operator.

**HUGH N. MCNEAL, DM3, Tango 1f1 4** Coxswain-four months-Boat Captain-nine months. Born Jan. 13, 1947 in Idabel, OK, Gray High School, 1965. Boot Camp San Diego August 1966 to November 1966. December 1966 to December 1967 1st Beachmasters Unit 1, Amphibious Base Coronado; January 1968 to March 1968 2nd Mare Island Warfare Training; May 1968 to June 1969 3rd MRF; and July 1969 to June 1970 4th Seabees-Amphib Base Coronado.

After USN, received BS degree in Mgmt/ Accounting from Southeastern State College in 1974. In 1976, I married the best thing that's ever happened to me, Pamela Andrews. We have two fantastic daughters, Natalie, an honors grad from OU College of Law and Lindsey, an honors student in OU's College of Pharmacy.

I worked for Wal-Mart from 1975-1985, when we returned to SE Oklahoma. Pamela and I are involved in our Purebred Charolais Ranch and I work for INW in Durant, OK.

Memorable experiences: That first real firefight. We had about 80 on T-151-4 (according to Tony). One of the most memorable was in U Minh Forest in a heavy firefight and we had to pull alongside a Tango dead in the water and I had to tie us up with more lead in the air than you can imagine. We towed the boat to safety, while taking and giving fire. Without a doubt, my mother's prayers pulled us through that day, and every day.

I feel everyone should that know from our arrival until our departure, we left much safer and secure area for the locals to live.

It's been 34 years, not much memory of names and places, battles for medals won. My father was a proud and decorated WWII Vet. I served willingly and am a proud Vietnam Vet.

He regrets that there are hardly any pictures, none of us had a camera! Also, not getting our crew together one more time: Tony Day, Steve Bowers, Joe Cheboygan, Richard Diggs and Matt White, all kids who became men really fast. We were really good at what we did. T-151-4 was always ready to go at any time, we would patch her up and take on more ammo and head out again. I do remember we won the Divisions 1st Excellence Flag.

Saddest times for me were the first time I sent Steve and Richard out on a Medivac Chopper. I knew it wasn't life threatening, but I didn't know how bad they were. We all took a little shrapnel, but they looked pretty bad. They were back very shortly, ready to go again!

**WAYNE R. MEEKS** was born Oct. 28, 1946 in Barksdale Field, LA. He earned Associate of Science degree in Photo-Offset.

Meeks joined the US Navy on Nov. 17, 1966. Units served with and ships served on include Air Test and Development Squadron 5 and RivRon 1f (106mm Monitor 6). Military locations and stations were Naval Air Facility, China Lake, CA (1967-1969) and Vietnam (1969-1970). Battles and campaigns were Vietnam Summer-Fall 1969 (June 9, 1969 to Oct. 31, 1969), Vietnam Winter-Spring 1970 (Nov. 1, 1969 to April 30, 1970) and the Sanctuary Counteroffensive (May 1, 1970 to June 30, 1970). Awards and medals include Combat Action Ribbon, Meritorious Unit Commendation, Southwest Asia Service Medal, Vietnam Service Medal, Republic of Vietnam Gallantry Cross Unit Citation, Republic of Vietnam Civil Actions Unit Citation and Republic of Vietnam Campaign Medal. Achieved the rank of E3 and was discharged July 9, 1970. Memorable experience was his daughter, Donna, who was born on Nov. 17, 1969. It's a day he'll never forget, for it was the same day they were engaged in a firefight with the NVA on the Cambodian border.

Meeks has been married since March 29, 1969 to Charlotte and they have two children, Donna and Wendy. They also have two grandchildren, Jessica and Andrew. Civilian employment has been November 1970 to November 1974 employed at Continental Data Graphics as a Off-Set Pressman, moved to China Lake, CA in November 1974 as a Bindery Worker to start his career in Federal Service, March 1975 RIF to Supply Department as a Warehouseman, March 1983 RIF to Engineering Division in the Public Works Department as a Data Engineering Tech, then moved to the Information Technology Branch, Nov. 1, 2002 as a Reference Tech.

**JAMES E. MEEHAN JR.** I was born in Whitestone, (Queens) New York, and July 27, 1944 in a nice little brick house, I have two sisters Pat and Kathy. We were all two years apart I am the youngest, I completed high school at Brentwood High Long Island, NY.

I joined the Navy the May before my 20th birthday on May 19, 1964. Went to Boot Camp at Great Lakes, IL, from there I went to Sub School New London, CN. Took a look around and was out of there. From there I went to the *USS Essex CVS-9*. While there I went home and married my high school sweetheart Geraldine "Gerry" Jaeger. Her father was a Pearl Harbor survivor on the *USS Blue Ridge*. After a year and a half I was sent orders to go to Vietnam (5-66) 6-28-66. My first son was born July 5, 1966 James E. Meehan III. I was in California after a five-day train ride, because the airplanes were on strike. There I attended IUWG-1 training, followed by training at Camp Pendleton, CA for survival and weapons training. Then we were flown out of California at night at Barbers Point, HI, and then we changed planes again and this time we were on a Market time B-25 2-engine prop job. We stopped on a very little island for fuel. When we took off from the Philippines we had engine trouble and had to turn back and wait for a new starter for the port engine. After three days we took off for Vietnam in Cam Thone Bay, then took another plane to Nha Trang. There I spent a year on the rock. Some days were good and some weren't. We got through them though. The rest of my career was on the USS *Twining* DD-540, then US *Hopper* DE-1026. Acting Chief engineer of Water Transportation Ford Island HI Hawaiian Armed Servers Police (HASP) then to

New Commission *USS Fort Fisher LSD-40*. In 1974, I gave up the seas for the harbors around New York and became a Chief Engineer of Motor Vessels working on Tug Boats in New York Harbor Union Local 333.

I have had three more children, Michael J., Kenneth S. and a girl, Colleen K. My wife has passed on, and I am looking forward to retiring in 2 1/2 years. I am now the president of IUWG1VETS, and on the board of MRFA. I belong to the VFW, and the American Legion. That is about it. God Bless Us All.

## WILLIAM PAUL "METZ" METZLER

was born Jan. 25, 1947 in Philadelphia, PA. In 1964 he graduated from high school at Bonner High School in Drexel Hill, PA. Drafted in mid-1966 and had Basic Training and AIT in Fort Rucker, AL.

Early in 1967 at Fort Benning, 5th/ 31st Infantry in support unit for the Infantry OCS. Arrived Bihn Phuoc early June of 1967 and was assigned 2nd Platoon Bravo Company, 5th / 60th Mech. Named 2nd Platoon RTO. Became Bravo Company RTO August 1967.

Metz was wounded Nov. 16, 1967 in the airmobile operation leading up to the events at Firebase Cudgel and was a survivor of the battle at Firebase Jaeger on Feb. 25, 1968. He was awarded Purple Heart- Bronze Star. He achieved the rank of Sgt. E-5 and was discharged in June 1968.

Stateside moved to San Francisco, graduated from the University of California and worked in the Dental field. In 2003 he and his long time wife and best friend, Barbara Bedell, retired and have moved to Rio Vista, CA.

Made return trips to Vietnam in 1996 and in 1997. Metz is currently the Secretary of the 5th Battalion, 60th Infantry Association.

## JOHN L. "SKIP" MILLER

was born Aug. 2, 1943 in Indianapolis, IN. He graduated from Purdue University. Miller joined the US Navy Reserve on Feb. 16, 1965.

Units served with and ships the he served on were M.R.F.A.-A-111-5 and aboard the *USS Tidewater (AD35)*. Military locations include Radio "A" School Bainbridge, MD; NIOTC Mare Island, CA; MRFA-Dong Tam, RVN and SERE Training. He was also a part of Coronado I-IX. Awards and medals were Navy Unit Commendation, Presidential Unit Citation,  Good Conduct, National Defense, Vietnam Service (three stars), Gallantry Unit Citation RVN, and Combat Action. Achieved the rank of RM3 and was discharged on Feb. 16, 1971.

Miller says of his memorable experience, "TET Offensive in 1968, having watched a friend drown and couldn't help from where I was. Having to recover a fellow radioman's body the day after a night offensive. Watching boys arrive "in country" and watch men leave. Watching a friend who had dark hair leave country with white hair. Finally, leaving country myself."

Miller is married to Suzanne and they have two children, Mark and Matthew. They also have a granddaughter, Emma. Civilian employment has included Senior Systems Analyst for Farm Bureau Insurance Company.

## RICHARD H. "RICH" MILLER

was born Dec. 7, 1946 in Glendale, CA. He attended Pasadena High School, earned AA at Pasadena City College, BS at University of California, Irvine, and MS at University of Utah.

Miller joined the US Army on March 6, 1966. He served with 2nd Platoon, B Company, 4/ 39 Battalion, 9th Infantry Div. He served at Bear Cat, Binh Son Rubber Plantation, FSB Sword FSB Dagger, Nha Be, Pink Palace, FSB Cambert, FSB Moore, FSB Mohawk, Cat Lai, Cai Lay, Xuam Loc, Tan Tru, and My Phouc Tay. Miller was at TET 1968 at Widow's Village and "Valentine's Day" at Xom Dong Phu. He was awarded Soldier's Medal, Air Medal, Army Commendation w/ Oak Leaf, Purple Heart, National Defense, Good Conduct, CIB, and Presidential Unit Citation. Achieved the rank of 1st Lieutenant and was discharged on March 30, 1969.

Miller's most memorable experiences were the death of Lt. Thomas York Osborne on Feb. 14, 1968; the guys of "my" platoon; and Lee Kunkle's advice and wit ("We need more gooks who can shoot like that!") while he was holding a cut-off radio handset after being sprayed with automatic weapons fire.

Miller is married to Sarah and they have two children, Michael and Eleanor. Civilian employment has included being a Violin Maker for 15 years. He retired in December 1997.

## RON MITCHELL

was born Oct. 1, 1946 in Ravenna, OH. He graduated from Garden Grove High School, attended Orango Coast J.C. and Long Beach State.

Mitchell joined the US Navy Reserve in 1969. He served with RAS 15 Tango 3 and was stationed at SVN. He was a part of Breezy Cove and Barrier Reef. Mitchell was discharged in 1971. His most memorable experience was when they landed at Saigon and the Stew said, "Welcome to Saigon, Republic of South Vietnam." Another memorable time was Operation Breezy Cove.

Mitchell is widowed and has two children, Zachery and Kristin. His civilian employment has included being a driver for Albertson's Grocery.

## JOSEPH R. MOON

was born Sept. 15, 1938 in Greenville, SC. He is a high school graduate. Joined the US Navy on Sept. 15, 1955. Ships served on were *USS Iona BB61*, *USS Canberra CAG7*, *USS Newport News*, *USS New DD818*, *USS Maderia City*. Military locations and stations include NAS Pensacola; NSA Danang; RVN; Z 151-1; Assault Squad 15 RVN; Advisory Group RVN. He was awarded Navy Commendation (v) 2, Purple Heart (1) and RVN eight Stars. He achieved the rank of BM1 E-6 and was discharged on Jan. 31, 1975.

Moon says of his memorable experience, "While on Operation Sea Lord on the Cai Lon River RVN. We had left two Tango boats, blocking for RVN Paratroopers, unknown to us, Charlie had crossed the river and was on both banks. Charlie ambushed the Tango. When we heard it on the radio we turned around and went to the North Bank where much fire was coming from. As we approached the shore we opened up with our flame, 20 mm and .50 cal. In about what seemed like a lifetime (about 15 minutes) we had suppressed the fire.

Moon is married to Sylvia and they have three children, Martin, Erica and Brian. Civilian employment has included working in sales at Wilford Propane.

## DENNIS P. "MOE" MOORE

was born Nov. 11, 1946 in Boston, MA. He earned his Master of Science in Taxation (MST) MBA, BS. Joined the US Navy. Units served with was River Squadron 13 and aboard *USS Glover (AGDE-1)*. Military locations and stations were Dong Tam, Vietnam, *USS Glover* homeport: Newport, RI. Battles and campaigns include Operation Slingshot; Vinh Te Canal, Grand Canal. Awards and medal were Bronze Star and Navy Commendation with "V" Presidential and Navy Unit Citation.

Moore is married to Gulzhan Abildinova whom he met in Kazakhstan. They have no children. He is employed by Worcester State College in Worcester, MA. He also consults overseas (former Soviet Union states).

Moore says about his memorable experiences, "I kept a daily diary, but have never read it. One day. Arrived April 12, 1969 flew to some Army base. Got separated after arrival. Following morning, firefight at base. I hid behind a woodpile and watched. Arrived at Dong Tam. Very hot and humid. Dong Tam had been severely damaged during mortar attack three weeks previous.

"First firefight was May and Boat Captain (Siebren) was relieved for something. We were very inexperienced. B-40 hit a few feet from me while firing 50. Nearly sank.

"June 6 (around Go Da Ha) another firefight. Village across from sugar canes. A recoilless or B-40 bounced off well deck without exploding. I believe Bud Roley was firing. Bud had been relieved of firing the Mark-19 (which always jammed). Following day he was showing the Boat Captain and someone else his problems and it accidentally went off, hitting the bank across river. Shrapnel wounded Kurt Dahl. I replaced Bud at the Mark-19. I hated that gun. This was Operation Slingshot up by Tay Ninh. While swimming in canal, some Army guy got bitten by a snake. He was swimming next to me. He died. Hated it when snakes got on board.

"Vinh Te Canal in Chau Doc region was heaviest firefighting. One time we went out with only three crewmen. I was on ASPB-10 now (after having been on Tango-24, I believe). One day Monitor from RivDiv 15 came up to help out. They just got in country. Cocky as hell. They had a boa constrictor on it. The Monitor was hit for three consecutive nights losing most of its crew. It limped out back to Big Blue (Mekong River). Well, we were hurting. Many boats had many crewmembers out either KIA or WIA, so volunteers came to help. I believe, XO from USS Mercer and 3 ET Chiefs, plus some GMs. I believe XO was wonder, one chief KIA, and the other two WIA. No more volunteers.

"We had to take the fuel barge out. We loved this (needed an Alfa boat to tow it) because we were going back to Benewah; movies and hot food. Stopped to swim while towing it back. Threw some grenades in the water to get rid of the snakes and then played "King of the Mountain" or "King of the top-20-MM turret." Across the way were 30 to 50 black-clad Vietnamese. We thought they were friendly's. We waved. They waved back. We did this for an hour or so and then left; waving again. Come to find out (according to intelligence) they were VC or NVA. That was something.

"Anyway back at the Benewah, I had to stay on board the A-10 while the rest of the crew went to eat. Some medic came down to the boat and asked what happened to Bill Harris's dog. It died on the way back and we threw it overboard. We were confined because they thought the dog had rabies. When the crew got back from chow, we topped off the barge, and got underway (a no-no) for night and steamed back to the Vinh Te (about seven hours or so). I remember I was driving with some Lieutenant (who was subsequently killed, a close friend of Mr. Connolly, the best officer I ever served under) and steamed thru a hooch. I was blinded by a "hurricane" lamp.

"In the Grand Canal, I was the Bravo Charlie of A-10 now. Got into a firefight January 6 or 12. Anyway, we were almost run down by a Zippo that was squirting. I screamed at Zito to steer to port. The Zippo sideswiped us and pushed us onto the bank where we damaged a screw (not uncommon). Heavy fighting and many casualties. Tracers; red and green all over, yet we never took a hit. An old 40-MM monitor was on fire and all her crew either dead or wounded. A few days later, there was an inquiring about civilian casualties. I was very nervous. The next day, looking at that burned out village from the Zippo, helos, enemy, who knows; I wondered where my life was going. I can't believe we got thru that firefight.

"In March, after 11 months on the boats, I was transferred my last three weeks to Danang. I realized I would never see any of River Division 13 again."

**RUSSELL "GUNNER" MOORE**, GMGC, born July 4, 1948, Philadelphia, MS, completed the 12th grade. Joined the USN July 21, 1965, and was stationed in Dong Tam. Served with A-91-1, A-92-5 and Raid 73. Participated in Operation Giant Slingshot and served as advisor for SVN Navy.

Memorable experiences include being in-country.

Retired Nov. 30, 1985, with the rank of GMGC. Received the Navy Commendation, three Purple Hearts and the Silver Star Medal.

Married Alice July 17, 1971. He retired Nov. 30, 1985.

**RONALD D. "RON" MORGAN** was born March 15, 1947 in Hillsboro, WI. He graduated from Hustisford High School in Hustisford, WI. Joined the US Navy on June 7, 1965. Served on the USS Tortuga LSD-26, USS Constellation CVA64, RUAH-5, River Assault Squadron 111. He was stationed at San Diego, CA; Albany, GA; and Sanford, FL. Morgan was awarded National Defense Service Medal, Vietnam Service Medal w/ one Silver and one Bronze Star; Navy Unit Commendation Ribbon, Republic Vietnam Meritorious Unit Citation and Republic Vietnam Campaign Medal with 1960 device. Achieved the rank of E-4 and was discharged on June 6, 1969.

Morgan is married to Susan and they have two children, Ronald and Amy. They also have two grandchildren, Holly and Abby.

**FRANK S. MORRIS** was born Feb. 17, 1948 in Detroit, MI. He took his GED, attended two years at Community College as machine tool operator at Kirtland Community College, Rocommon, MI.

Joined the US Navy in April 1965 in Detroit, MI. Units served with and ships served on were USS Ability (MSO519); US Naval Station in Charleston, SC; Mare Island Vallejo, CA; FFT, CO River Squadron Nine OVTUS-PAC; River Division 92 T-92-7; USS Kearsarge (CVS-33); SSC N.T.C. Great Lakes, IL; Engineman (C) School; Naval Station Key West, FL shore duty; USNS Harkness Oceanographic unit five; USS Gilmore (AS-16); and USS Hunley (AS-31). Awards and medals were National Defense Service Medal (first award); Vietnam Service Medal (one silver star in Lieu of five Bronze Stars); Vietnam Campaign Medal with Device; Republic of Vietnam Meritorious Unit Citation (Gallantry Cross Medal Color with Palm); First Good Conduct Award for period ending Jan. 28, 1974; Navy Unit Commendation (2); Presidential Unit Citation; Navy Meritorious Unit Commendation and Combat Action Ribbon. Rank achieved was Engineman Sec. class and was discharged on Oct. 31, 1975.

**DAVID T. MURRAY** was born Nov. 21, 1946 in Orange, NJ. He joined the US Navy on March 8, 1966.

Murray served on the USS Buchana DDG 14 San Diego, CA June 1966 to September 1968, as Gunners Mate; two cruises to South Vietnam for support Mare Island, Vallejo, CA PBR School September 1968 to December 1968 and Survival and Escape Training at Whidby Island, WA; Coronado, CA Language School December to January 1969; My Tho South Vietnam, River Di-

vision 533 January 1969 to August 1969; PBRs Twin .50 Cal Gunner Nha Be South Vietnam River Division 153 ASPBs Top 20 MM Gunner, until promoted to GMG2 then Boat Captain of ASPB 6848 for remainder of tour.

Murray was awarded the Bronze Star w/ Combat V. He achieved the rank of GMG2 and was discharged on Jan. 23, 1970.

Murray says this of his experiences, "I was very lucky only to see action a few times. In early December 1969 we set up a night ambush a few miles from Cambodia on the Van Cotry River. The north side of the river for a mile or so was a grassy plain. We cut our engines and beached. About half way through the night, a new kid (only one-week in country) was in the top 20MM on the lead boat. He was using a starlight scope and he reported to his boat captain he was observing five or six guys coming across the field, two with B40 rocket launchers. His boat captain and patrol officer didn't believe him. It was his first patrol and when they looked they saw nothing. About 5:00 a.m. we broke ambush. The lead boat pulled away. I lagged behind; one of my engines wouldn't start up at first. Just as I got my engine started, the lead boat was hit by B-40 rockets and small arms. First, they took two hits from the B-40s one in the coxswains flat wounding the patrol officer, the other on the engine crew area on the stern. It glanced off but wounded the engineman. We pulled into the fire zone and took a B-40 rocket in front of the helm in a cooler we had recently built. It absorbed the blast. My two 20MM Gunners opened up raking this river bank with fire. We pulled up and towed this other boat out of the fire zone. We called in a medavac to meet us at a CIDG base and got the patrol officer out by helo. The engineman only had a leg wound. We took him to the base corpsman. The corpsman pulled a poncho strap out of his thigh. Later that morning we went back to check out the place they had ambushed us. We found half a dozen spider holes on the bank. One had a VC in it with his finger still on the trigger of a loaded B-40 rocket launcher. He had been killed by a tiny fragment from the 20MM. We lucked out twice that night."

Murray is married to Gloria and they have four children, David, Sean, Christopher and Michelle. They also have a granddaughter, Meghan. Civilian employment has included working at Dave's Wheelchair, Inc. as president.

**HERVY L. MYERS** was born Oct. 3, 1947 in Alvin, TX. He received his GED. Joined the US Army on Jan. 8, 1968. Served with Bravo and HHC 4/39. Military locations and stations include basic training at Ft. Polk, AIT at Tigerland, Ft. Polk-Bearcat/Dong Tam-Knebe-Cailay-Ft. Benning, 3rd Training Brigade. Battle and campaigns include Snoopy's Nose (July 1968), Nha Be (August 1968) and Coco Canal (March 1969).

Myers was awarded three Bronze Stars, Army Commendation for Valor, Air Medal, CIB and Vietnamese Citations. Achieved the rank of Sgt. E-5 and was discharged on Jan. 8, 1970. His most memorable experience was serving four and a half months with David Hackworth. Lost good friend, Robert Petraco on Aug. 25, 1968. July 1968 Vietcong ambushed their Tango at Snoopy's Nose.

Myers is married to Judith and they have a son, Joseph Michael. Civilian employment has included working for Chevron/ Phillips Chemical as Operations Supervisor.

**RICHARD E. "DOC or ROCKY" NELSON** was born Aug. 8, 1930 in Minneapolis, MN. After high school, he played professional baseball from 1946-1962. In June 1949 he joined the USNR, serving until joining the US Navy in 1962. As a reservist he received training in the Hospital Corp, physical training, and FMF schools. He served on several small craft in RivRon in RVN from May 1969 to May 1970. He retired with 22 years of service at the MCRD Parris Is., SC on January 17, 1971.

His medals include 16 Battle Stars, Civil Action Honor Medal, Presidential Unit Citation, Combat Purple Heart, Navy Commendation Medal, RVN Cross of Gallantry, Army Navy Medal for Combat, and 4 Good Conduct medals.

Nelson vividly recalls his first operation behind My Tho and its 38 casualties as well as a Vietnamese scout holding a whole Tango crew at bay with a grenade at the pontoon of *USS Benewah* until LCDR Bartlett and he talked him out of it.

After his Navy service and college he worked as a construction company safety director until retiring in 1992. He lost his 1st wife and 3 children in a car crash in 1965 and another son in 1969. Today he winters in Florida and summers in Georgia where he is active as a baseball scout and tours with music groups along with his companion Stella DeMarr Nelson. To his MRFA comrades he proclaims, "Vaya con dios hombres!!"

**AARON "GARY" NEWMAN** MAC (USN Retired) was born Feb. 28, 1942, Centerline, MI, attended numerous schools throughout the United States and received a GED High School equivalency from New York State. Enlisted in the US Navy on March 15, 1959 at Kodiak, Alaska; attended basic training at Naval Training Center, San Diego, CA; served onboard the *USS Ammen (DD-527)* at San Diego, *USS Henry W. Tucker (DD-875)* at Long Beach, CA; *USS Orleck (DD-886)* at Yokuska, Japan; *USS Maddox (DD-731)* at Long Beach, CA; US Naval Magazine, Subic Bacy, Philippines TAD to Armed Forces Police Department, Olongapo, PI; Commander River Squadron Eleven, Mekong Delta, Vietnam onboard CCB-112-1; Armed Forces Police Department, at Brooklyn Naval Station, NY; *USS Zellars (DD-777)* and *USS John R. Pierce (DD-753)* at Brooklyn Navy Yard, Brooklyn, NY; *USS Howard W. Gilmore (AS-16)* at La Maddelena, Sardinia; Security Department, Naval Air Stations, Jacksonville, FL. Retired from active duty on March 15, 1978 with the rank of Master at Arms Chief Petty Officer. Awards and commendations include: Combat Action Ribbon, Presidential Unit Commendation, Navy Unit Commendation, Meritorious Unit Commendation, Good Conduct Medal (Fourth award), National Defense Service Medal, Vietnamese Service Medal, Expert Rifle and Navy Achievement Medal with Combat "V." Also received a Meritorious promotion to TM1 while serving in Vietnam.

Married to Mary Anne, formerly from Brooklyn, NY and have two children: Suzanne Renne and Daniel Vincent. After leaving the US Navy in March 1978 served as a Deputy Sheriff, Clay County, Florida until Aug. 3, 1983 at which time was hired as Chief of Police, Security Department, Naval Air Station, Jacksonville, FL. Served as Chief of Police with 270 military and civilian police officers assigned until promoted to Deputy Director of Security in May 2002.

Most memorable moments include having been in Alaska and Hawaii before they became States; having completed basic training and completed a six month cruise before my 18th birthday; having been onboard the *USS Maddox* on Aug. 3 and 4, 1964 during what has become known as the "Tonkin Gulf Incident"; being re-enlisted by Commander "Dusty" Rhodes while out on patrol; being on the first selection of a new Navy Rate-Master at Arms; seeing both of my children graduate from college.

**JOSEPH D. "JOE" NICHOLS III**, Major, Infantry, USA, Retired. Born July 11, 1942, Pittsburgh, PA, graduated Peabody High School, 1960. Joined the US Army Sept. 23, 1960; attended basic training at Fort Knox, KY and AIT Fort Knox, KY. Served with the 52nd ADA Bde from January 1961 to August 1962. Served in Korea from September 1962 through October 1963- 4th Signal Battalion. Graduated from Infantry Officer Candidate School May 1964, graduated from Airborne School Fort Benning, GA June 1964, graduated from Army Intelligence School, Fort Holabird, MD September 1964. Served with the 1st Bn 31st Infantry, 7th Infantry Division, Tong Du Chon, Korea September 1964 to May 1966. Served with the 9th Infantry Division, Fort Riley, HHC 3rd Bn 39th Infantry June 1966-December 1966. Movement to Vietnam on the MSTS General Rose. Served in country with the 3rd Bn 39th Infantry until March 15 1967. Assumed command of Company C, 3rd Bn, 60th Infantry, 9th Infantry Division on March 15, 1967 from Captain Charles E. Lytle and relinquished command on Oct. 25, 1967. During his tour of duty he participated in Operation Colby, Operation Junction City, Operation Enterprise, Battle of Doi Mia Creek, Battle of Ap Bac, Operation Coronado I, Operation Coronado II and Battle of Rach Ba Rai River September 1967. He received the Combat Infantryman Badge, Silver Star, Bronze Star, Purple Heart, ARCOM w/ Device and 2 OLC, Meritorious Service Medal with 3 OLC, Cross of Gallantry with Gold Star, Air Medal, AFRM, NDSM, Army Occupation Medal (Berlin), Vietnam Campaign Medal w/2 Battle Stars, Vietnam Service Medal, Army Good Conduct Medal, Aircraft Crewman Badge, Senior Parachutist Badge, two Overseas Bars, Presidential Unit Citation, Valorous Unit Citation, Meritorious Unit Citation, Korean Presidential Unit Citation, Philippine Presidential Unit Citation, RVN Unit Cross of Gallantry w/ Palm and Civic Action Honor Medal 1st Class Unit Citation.

Subsequent to Vietnam he attended the Armored Officers Advance Course, Fort Knox, KY, Special Forces Officers Course, Fort Bragg, NC. Served with Co C 1st Special Forces Group (Airborne), Okinawa 1970-1973. Graduated with honors from University of Nebraska-Omaha BS Criminal Justice-Law Enforcement 1974, Served with 3rd Bn 6th Infantry, Berlin Brigade. Promoted to Major in May 1974. Served as a Ground Liaison Officer with the 601st Tactical Control Wing, Sembach Air Force Base, Germany 1976-1977. Graduated from Ball State University with honors received Masters of Arts-Public Service July 1977. Attended Advanced Criminal Investigation Course and Physical Security Officers Course Fort McClellan, AL July to September 1977. Served as Provost Marshall Operations Officer 728th Military Police Battalion, Camp Walker, Taegu, Korea October 1977 to October 1979. Served with the 519th Military Police Battalion and Criminal Investigational Division Fort Meade, MD November 1979 to October 1980. Retired from the United States Army October 1980. He has owned and operation Nichols Welding Service Inc. since October 1980. He is very active in Veterans Organizations and Community Service. Major Nichols is extremely proud to have been the Company Commander of Charging Charlie, C-3-60 Infantry and immensely enjoys the annual Company reunions. He says that 35 years later visiting The Wall with the men of Charlie Company to pay homage to the men of Charlie Company who paid the price is priceless.

**CLAYTON N. "OGGIE" OGDEN** was born in Salida, CO on Aug. 27, 1949. After high school, he attended trade school (gunsmith). Joined the US Navy on Nov. 12, 1968. Units served with and ships served on were RAS-15 (Tango 53), NIOTC RSG 4-70, *USS Saytr ARL-23*, *USS Comstock LSD-19*. Military locations and stations were Tram Chim, Vietnam (French Grand Canal), Dong Tam (a little bit of everywhere in Mekong Delta), Served all four corps on *USS Comstock* (Wes Pac). Ogden served in several battles and campaigns and received the usual medals. He achieved the rank of GMG3 and was discharged in September 1972. Ogden says that in Vietnam, every day and night, is a memorable experience that lives forever. Time in USN was some of the best. T-53 call sign, Snake King Moble, Bogus. (Anyone remember Cider Press Yankee, Brassrail, Pepperstump.)

Ogden is divorced and has three children, Clay, Anna and Christina. He also has three grandchildren, Chance, Blake and Isiah. Civilian employment has included Chaffee County, CO Road Supervisor. He is looking forward to retirement.

**RONALD K. OLNEY** born Nov. 26, 1948, in Camp LeJuene, NC, graduated from Toppenish, WA High School in 1966 and attended community college until entering the active duty in the US Navy on May 23, 1968. Ron was shipped to Subbase Pearl Harbor where he ran the Military Amateur Radio System (MARS) facility until checking into NIOTC at Mare Island, CA.

He arrived in-country as RM3 with RIVRON 13, assigned to T-132-1, spending the first three months in combat action as the boat crew's Radioman, Navigator and below deck's gunner in the Mekong Delta. He was later assigned to manage the Strike Force's tactical and operational communications, while also constructing and operating MARS station in Dong Tam. He was discharged from active duty on May 23, 1970, returning to his wife and son and re-entering college.

Awards include: Combat Action Ribbon, National Defense Service Medal, Navy Unit Commendation Ribbon w/ Combat V, Vietnam Service Medal w/ three Bronze Stars, RVN Campaign Medal, Navy Achievement Medal w/ Combat V, and the RVN Military Unit Citation/ Gallantry Cross.

Ron earned a degree in Computer Programming and Systems Analysis and majored in Electrical Engineering. After 11 years in commercial radio and television broadcasting, he became a telecommunications consulting engineer establishing his own company. Designing over 100 telephone systems, 100 cellular radio, microwave and fiber optic networks, he consulted as a Senior Engineer, managing the East Coast sector of the US, at Stanford Research International for the Next Generation Weather Radar System and was instrumental in the design and implementation of the Terminal Doppler Weather Radar (TDWR) System. He served as one of four Senior Engineers in the planning design and implementation of both radar networks.

He has one son, Ronald Kris, and one daughter, Heather Lynne. Olney was forced into retirement from a service-connected disability in 1998 and now resides on the Olympic Peninsula in Washington State.

**JOHN J. "BUGSIE" ORTEGA** was born on May 25, 1948 in Rock Spring, WY. He attended two years Business College, Pike Peak Community College after graduating from Palmea High School in 1967.

Ortega joined the US Navy in October 1967. He served with Squadron 11, Div 112-2 (Tango). He participated in numerous combat missions, which struck deep into the enemy infested waters of the Mekong Delta. He was awarded the Navy Achievement Medal w/ Combat. Achieved the rank of E3. Ortega says of his experience, "I had a great time with all of my friends on my boat. I will never forget them. They were a great bunch of sailors. All of the other sailors on the Div were great guys."

Ortega is divorced and has two children, Carol and John Jr. He also has two grandchildren, Eddie and Elijah. Civilian employment has included working as librarian tech. He retired in April 2002.

**WILLIAM H. "BILL" OTTERLEI** SP4 born Aug. 16, 1946 San Diego, CA and received his BS degree in Business in 1972 from San Jose State University.

Bill was drafted into the Army May 16, 1966 and was stationed at Fort Ord for Basic Training and AIT at Fort Polk. He served with Co A 3/39 9th Inf. in 1967.

Was at places called Plain of Reeds, French Fort, Cross Roads and Rach Kien. Once while on search and destroy mission in 1967 he came across a cache of VC supplies. There were two flags among the items (North Vietnam and Russian Flags).

Discharged (60 % disabled) with the rank of SP4 on May 16, 1968. His awards include two Purple Hearts and the Combat Infantry Badge.

Single, he has two children, Janell who is a schoolteacher, and Kristen who is attending college. Bill owns his own construction business, William H. Otterlei Construction.

**JAMES E. "JIM" PARIS** was born Aug. 2, 1946 in Champaign, IL. He earned his GED and then his Associates Degree in Business Administration.

Paris joined the US Army on Dec. 29, 1964. He served with F-Troop 2/2 Alc (Germany); A Company, 1st Bn 41 Inf 2 Arm. Div (Ft. Hood); C Company 4th Bn 47 Inf 9 Inf Div. He was stationed at 2nd Cav, Bambeilg, GR; Ft. Hood, TX; Tropic Test Center, Panama; Dong Tam, Vietnam; US Army Hospital Okinawa. He was awarded Vietnam Service Ribbon; Combat Medal; Purple Heart; CIB; and National Defense Ribbon. Achieved the rank of Sgt. and was discharged Aug. 9, 1969.

Paris says about his experiences, "I joined the Army in December 1964, in Chicago, IL, my time in the Army spanned four years, seven months and 12 days. Served in Fort Knox, KY (basic); Fort Polk (AIT); West Germany with the 2/2 A/C on the East/West German border; Fort Hood, TX; Panama Canal Zone and C Company, 4/47 Bat., 9th Inf. Div.

"I arrived in Vietnam on April 6, 1969, Easter Sunday with SSG Elmer Pittman. SSG Pittman was wounded less than a week later on our first patrol in country. I saw him only once more before he was shipped out.

"Two days later I joined C Company. There I was placed in charge of a squad. Spec4 Alfonso Hernandez and PFC Dale Fahrni are the only ones I remember. The reason I remember them is that we were all wounded on the same day, May 7, 1969. Unfortunately Dale died from his wounds two days later. I do not know what happened to Hernandez but would like to.

"Myself, I was sent to Okinawa and spent the next five and half months there prior to being sent home and discharged from the military. I would like to locate both Sgt. Pittman and Spec4 Hernandez."

Since leaving the military, Paris has worked for Kraft Foods, and retired on Aug. 1, 2003 after 34 years. He lives in Mansfield, IL with his wife of 37 years, Helga. They have two daughters Claudia and Lora Lee and one granddaughter Sydney E.H.L. Paris.

**DAVID PAUST** was born Jan. 11, 1936 in Madison, WI. He graduated from high school. He joined the US Navy on July 12, 1954.

Ships that Paust served on were *USS Monogohela AO-42* November 1954 to May 1955; *USS Corregidor TCVU-58* May 1955 to August 1958; *USS Saratoga CVA-60* October 1958 to August 1962; *USS McNair DD-679* August 1962 to April 1963; *USS St. Paul CA-73* May 1963 to February 1965; *USS Mispillion AO-105* February 1965 to August 1965; *USS Firedrage AE-14* August 1965 to August 1966; *USS James E. Kyes DD-787* April 1970 to February 1972; *USS Kiska AE-35* November 1972 to August 1974; *USS Tolovana AO-64* August 1974 to April 1975 and *USS Kilauea AE-26* May 1975 to May 1976.

Paust was stationed at RTC Great Lakes IL from July 1954 to October 1954; US NAVORDFAC, St Mawgan, England October 1966 to October 1968; NAVINSHOPTRACEN Mare Island, CA December 1968 to March 1969; COMRIVRON 11, VN, RivDiv 112, March 1969 to June 1969; COMRIVRON 13, RivDiv 131, June 1969 to March 1970; and Traron 21, Kingsville NAS, Texas, April 1972 to October 1972.

He was awarded Bronze Star, Purple Heart and CAR. He achieved the rank of BMC and was discharged March 17, 1976.

Paust says that his most memorable time was with RivDiv 131 on M-1 (105 Monitor) firing at electronic sensors 5-6 miles away.

Paust is married to Grace.

**ROBERT DANIEL "POLAK" PAWLICKI** was born Sept. 15, 1947 in Detroit, MI. He graduated from high school. Joined the US Navy on Sept. 15, 1965 on his 18th birthday. Units served with include *USS Tortuga* ('66), River Assault Squadron Task Force 117, Tango 111-11 ('67) Plank Owner. Stationed in Mekong Delta 1966 and 1968, Davisville, Rhode Island and Seabee Base 1968. Pawlicki participated in Operation Game Warden 1966 and River Assault Squadron numerous battles 1967. Awarded Navy Commendation Ribbon, Vietnam Service Medal w/ four Bronze Stars, Combat Action Ribbon, National Defense Service Medal, Navy Achievement w/ Combat V, Republic of Vietnam Campaign Medal and Republic of Vietnam MUC Gallantry Cross. He achieved the rank of BM3 and was discharged on Sept. 13, 1968.

Pawlicki is married to Linda and they have two children, David and Stacy. They also have two grandchildren, Hannah and Zander. His civilian employment has included working as a Journeyman Toolmaker- Retirement will be Michigan Upper Peninsula. He is also an active board member of UAW Region One Veterans Counsel and board member of MRFA.

**WILLIAM A. "BILL" PERKINS** was born Jan. 29, 1948 in New Orleans, LA. After he graduated from high school, he attended two years of college.

Perkins joined the US Navy in September 1965. He served onboard the *USS Currituck AV7*, with RivRon 11, Task Force T-111-2 Starboard .50 cal. Gunner. He served in Vietnam and Mekong Delta. Perkins was involved in Coronado V in September 1967. He was awarded the Naval Achievement Combat V, Purple Heart, Vietnam Campaign Medal w/ device, Presidential Unit Citation and Vietnam Service Medal w/ three Bronze Stars. Achieved the rank of E3 and was discharged September 1968.

Perkins says of his memorable experience, "A typical night in the Mekong Delta, hot, humid and scary. Place and date I do not remember because I choose not to remember. We were running standard river patrols near a fire support base, at the time we were only receiving small arms fire. ARVN outpost was approximately 300 meters up river and was suddenly overrun by Charlie. We proceeded to that location to assist in recapturing the outpost. At that time we began receiving automatic weapons fire and rockets. The sky was lit up with tracers coming from the outpost and our boat. While looking through my .50 cal mount I saw the flash of a rocket being launched in my direction. I opened fire at the point of where the rocket was launched, using that as a target. The darkness of the night prevented us from seeing anything on shore, other than the flashed from gunfire and rockets. This firefight seemed to go on for hours. Suddenly all became quiet for a few moments. That's when the horror began. As we sat dead in the water, in the darkness of the night, the sounds of horror began to come over the radio. The alpha boat, which had been running river patrol in the sector up river from us, was being attacked. The voice coming over the radio was pleading and crying for God's mercy and help. His boat captain and cox'n were dead; the gunner was critically wounded as he was. The sounds of screaming and the tone of his voice will never be forgotten. We attempted to proceed to their location to assist, but we began to receive weapons fire, which stopped us from getting to their location. It wasn't until the following morning that we learned the tragedy of the alpha boat. All of its crew had been killed and the alpha boat sunk.

"This is only one of many recalls I have, but to this day I want to forget, but can't."

Perkins has been married for 34 years to Judy and they have two children, Keith and Corey. They also have two grandchildren, Ethan and Aiden. His civilian employment has included working at Chillco, A.C. Tech.

**ANTHONY "TONY" PERRY** was born Oct. 27, 1947 in Coatesville, PA. He joined the US Army on April 24, 1968. Served with

USAMMAC (GS) Det #2 served on FMS 811. Military locations and stations include Vung Tau, Cam Ranh Bay and Dong Tam. He was awarded NDSM, SPS M-14, VSM, VCM, GCMDL, VCM w/ Device and two O/S bars. Achieved the rank of Spec 5 and was discharged on April 23, 1974.

Perry is married to Victoria and they have one child, Shawn Justice. They also have three grandchildren, Tabitha, Emily and Brooke. Civilian employment has included LNP Div of GE Plastics.

## THOMAS W. "TOMBO" PESCE

was born on Sept. 12, 1949 in Brooklyn, NY. He graduated from high school in June 1967. Joined the US Navy on Jan. 15, 1968.

Pesce served onboard *USS Mercer APB39* –TF117, US Submarine Base Groton Conn. Military location and stations include BASSAC River Mekong Delta, Dong Tam, Vinh Long, My Tho, MyTho Nah Be, Ben Tre. Pesce was awarded all awards from the *USS Mercer APB39*, and he is a plankowner from March 1968 to May 1969. Achieved the rank of CS3 and was discharged on Jan. 14, 1971. His most memorable experience was picking up anchor and traveling with TF117 to a suspected POW Island.

Pesce is married to Joan and they have two children, Thomas and Michael. They also have a grandchild, Alyssa. Pesce has been self-employed and owned two businesses. He retired in September 1996.

## KEITH PHILLIPS

was born March 18, 1948 in Kinston, NC. He graduated from high school, then earned AA in Police Science. Joined the US Navy on Sept. 14, 1967. Served with River Assault Squadron 13, volunteered for RiverBoat Duty. Awarded Purple Heart, PUC, Navy Unit Commendation w/ Combat V, National Defense, Combat Action Ribbon and Expert Pistol. Achieved the rank of RM3 and was discharged in March 1971.

Phillips says of his most memorable experience, "It was the first firefight, Kein Giang Province near Cambodia. It was pitch dark and a jungle canopy was beginning to enclose our three boats, two PBR's and our Alpha boat. The lead boat was hit by several rockets and we all opened up. I got off a couple of hundred rounds when my 20MM locked up. I stood up in my gun mount and began firing an M-79 grenade launcher. The three boats suffered 11 wounded and two killed out of 16 sailors."

Phillips is married to Susan and they have three children, Stephen, Carrie and Jeffrey. He is a retired Virginia State Police Officer. Retired on Sept. 1, 1997.

## PATRICK T. "P. T." PHILLIPS

was born Sept. 29, 1946 in White Mills, KY. He graduated from Pleasure Ridge Park High School in Louisville, KY. He joined the US Navy on May 8, 1966. Served onboard *USS Monmouth Country LST 1032* from Aug. 15, 1966 to Oct. 15, 1967 and with the Mobile Riverine Force ASPB112-3 from Jan. 20, 1968 to Oct. 15, 1968. Phillips served at Dong Tam. He participated in the Battle of Ben Tre, 1968 TET Offensive, Plain of Reeds, Snoopy's Nose, Sz Dec Aug 18, U Minh Forest, My Tho, Seal inserts. Achieved the rank of E4 Diesel Engineman and was discharged on Dec. 12, 1968.

Phillips is married to Carolyn. They have three children, Christopher, Julie, Joshua, and three grandchildren, Dylan, Shane and Austin. Civilian employment has included working for Fort Motor, Kentucky Truck Plant, Co. He retired on Jan. 1, 2001 with 32-plus years.

## FREDDIE PICOU

was born Oct. 22, 1945 in Washington, LA. He graduated from high school, attended SOWELA Tech-Inst. electronic Instrumentation / Commercial Pilot/CFI. He joined the US Army on June 8, 1963 and the US Navy in October 1966.

Picou's history of assignments include: June 8, 1963 Army Recruit Training Center; June 1963 to May 1966 2nd Airborne Infantry Fort Bragg, NC; May 1966 to October 1966 509th Airborne Infantry Div. Meinz, Germany; October 1966 to January 1967 Navy Recruit Training Center San Diego, CA; January 1967 to March 1967 Navy FLETTRACEN San Diego, CA; March 1967 to April 1967 Naval Shipyard Puget Sound, WA; April 1967 to December 1967 *USS Sterret DLG-31* Long Beach, CA; February 1968 to February 1969 Navy River Assault Craft I Republic of Vietnam; February 1969 to October 1972 Naval Reserve Center Lafayette, LA; October 1972 to November 1974 NRSURFDIV –25 (M) NRC Lake Charles, LA; November 1972 to October 1976 NR Ship Activation Maintenance Repair Unit Det 6210 NRC Orange, TX; January 1978 to July 1986 NR Assault Craft Unit 1 NRC Orange, TX; and July 1986 to March 2001 Executive Officer NR PHIB CB-1 Det 211 NRC Orange, TX. Picou participated in the Navy River Assault Craft 1 - Republic of Vietnam.

Picou has been awarded Navy Marksman Pistol Ribbon, Navy Expert Rifle Medal with Silver E, Republic of Vietnam Campaign Medal with Device, Armed Forces Reserve Medal w/ two hour glasses, Vietnam Service Medal, National Defense Service Medal Second Award, Naval Reserve Good Conduct Third Award, Navy Good Conduct Award, Meritorious Unit Commendation (MUC), and Navy Achievement Medal with V for Valor (Combat Duty in Vietnam).

Picou has held the following ranks: Army Recruit E-1; Army Private E-2; Army Private First Class, E-3; Navy Boatswain Mate Seaman, E-3; Navy Boatswain Mate, Petty Officer Second Class, E-5; Navy Boatswain Mate, Petty Officer First Class, E-6; Navy Boatswain Mate, Chief Petty Officer, E-7; Navy Chief Warrant Officer, CWO2; Navy Chief Warrant Officer, CWO3; Navy Chief Warrant Officer, CWO4; Navy Lieutenant Junior Grade, LTJG, O-2; and Navy Lieutenant, O-3. He retired after 34 years of service.

His memorable experience was completing Army Parachute training, achieving rank of CPO, CWO4 and LtO3, Completing Commercial Pilot/ Flight Instructor (light aircraft) training.

Picou is married Linda Ann. His civilian employment has included Chemical Plant Operator and Commercial Pilot. He retired on April 24, 2001.

## NATHAN "NATE" PLOTKIN

was born Feb. 1, 1928 in Detroit, MI. He earned his AB, MA and MS degrees. Joined the US Army, Sgt. Sept. 18, 1946 to Jan. 15, 1948; also, June 15, 1952 to Oct. 31, 1972.

Plotkin served in many units including Hg. 2nd Bde, 9th Inf. Div. He served everywhere and in Vietnam from January to December 1967. Achieved the rank of O-5 LTC and retired on Oct. 31, 1972.

His most memorable experience was serving with the 2nd Bde, 9th Inf Div, MRF as Sig O of Brigade. Outstanding leaders and outstanding men who gave their best and beyond.

Plotkin is married to Anne.

## WILLIAM R. "BILL" POSEY

was born Jan. 14, 1935 in Chattanooga, TN. He graduated from high school. Joined the US Navy on Nov. 13, 1953.

Units and ships that Posey served with include *USS Tulare AKA 112*, *USS Mobile LKA 114*, *USS Arneb AKA 56*, Small Craft, YTM414, YFU-59 Danang RVN, YTB-

785, Mekong-Delta RVN YTM-369, Subicay, Philippines. Locations include US Naval Training Center, San Diego, CA; US Nel San Diego; US Naval Depot Wiykelie Hawaii; US Naval Base, Yokusuka, Japan. He was awarded Navy Commendation, Good Conduct four Stars, Antarctica Expedition, Presidential Unit Citation, Vietnam Services Ribbon, and medals, various other commendations for achievements.

He says of his most memorable experience, "I was craftmaster of YTB785 RVN, during TET 1968. We were leaving Nha Be RVN, on a normal trip up river. We came under a rocket attack leaving the channel at that base to head up river. He had no KIA's, but two were slightly wounded. We continued our mission without further incidents. That really got the crews attention. Who fired to rocket was never seen."

Posey is married to Bobbie Faye and they have four children, Vicki, Becky, Lanny and Shirley. They also have eight grandchildren and three great grandchildren. Civilian employment has included Military Sealift, Truck Driver, TVA and various other jobs. He retired on July 1, 1974.

**PETER B. RANKIN** was born Nov. 4, 1941 in Phila, PA. He earned his BA at the University of North Carolina at Chapel Hill. Joined the US Navy Reserve in January 1966.

Units and ships served on were USS Bexar (APA-237), River Division 111, and Coronado Amphibious Base-Instructor. Military locations and stations include San Diego, CA; RVN, Mekong Delta; and Amphibious Base at Coronado, CA. He participated in the battles and campaigns that RivDiv 111 was engaged in from December 1967 to December 1968 including TET. Awards and medal he was awarded include Silver Star, two Bronze Star, Navy Commendation Medal, Purple Heart, Vietnamese Cross of Gallantry with Silver Star and various unit citations. Achieved the rank of Lt. and was discharged in May 1969. His best memories are of serving with the men of River Division 111 for one year.

Rankin is married to Ellen and they have two children, Peter and James. Civilian employment includes Owner of Southport Harbor Assoc.

**JOHN SCOTT RATH** was born Nov. 15, 1945 in Defiance, OH. He earned BBA at Ohio University. Joined the US Army in 1967. He served with 3rd Platoon/ Bravo Company/ 3rd 60th. Stationed at Vietnam from 1968 to 1969. Awarded Purple Heart, Air Medal and CIB. Achieved the rank of Sergeant (E-5) and was discharged in 1969.

Rath says that most memorable experiences usually had bad results. "June 1, 1968- we lost many lives in our platoon in an ambush trying to support another element in contact.

"Nov. 1, 1968- the USS Westchester County was mined by Vietcong sappers with extensive damage to the ship and many lives lost. Bravo Company 3rd/ 60th was the Army Company on board and had six KIA.

"Another memorable experience happened on a night L.P./ ambush- our four-man group got word to saddle-up and return to the rest of the company. The boats were coming to pick us up- GREAT NEWS! Crawling back from retrieving our claymore mine, "Wildman" Watkins stuck the cut end of the det-cord in my face so I could see it. No Claymore- just the cut det-cord. My hair stood straight up, my helmet with it. We feared something bad was going to happen, but we all made it out OK, making this a good memorable experience."

Rath is married to Doris and they have one daughter, Erin. His civilian employment includes working as a Salesman for National Door and Trim.

**DONALD W. REEDER** was born May 22, 1942 at Ventura, CA. He earned his BS degree. Joined the US Navy in June 1965. Served onboard USS Northampton CCI and USS Sphinx ARL24. Locations and stations were NOB Norfolk, VA and Vietnam. Achieved the rank of LTJG. His most memorable experiences include the friendships, traveling the rivers watching the Vietnamese survive and live on the river.

Reeder is married to Bonnie and they have two children, Audra and Keith. They also have three grandchildren. Civilian employment has included working as a citrus and avocado farmer.

**ROBERT K. "BIRDDOG" REIDEL** was born May 5, 1947 in Libertyville, IL. He graduated from high school. Joined the US Army on June 27, 1967. Units served with and ships served on include 9th Inf 3/60 Co C 4 Plt 2nd Armored Div. Military locations and stations were Ft. Leonardwood, MO; Ft. Polk, LA; Dong Tam, Vietnam; and Ft. Hood, TX. He participated in the TET Offensive. Awards and medals include Purple Heart, Bronze Star, CIB and Air Medal. Achieved the rank of Sgt. E-5 and was discharged on June 29, 1969. His most memorable experience were all the great people that he served with in Vietnam.

Reidel is widowed. He has four children, Rachele, Emily, Cari and Jake. Civilian employment includes being a Police Officer for 31 years at Lake Forest, IL, as Commander. He retired April 29, 2000.

**WILLIAM L. "BILL" REYNOLDS** was born Aug. 5, 1946 –Crazy Water Hotel downtown Mineral Wells, TX. Grew up in the San Fernando Valley (north of Los Angeles, CA)- graduated 1964, Cleveland High School, Reseda. Worked at General Motors in Van Nuys while attending Pierce College before drafted May 17, 1966.

I joined Lt. Jack Benedick's outstanding 2nd Platoon, Charlie Company, 4th/ 47th Battalion when the 9th I.D. reactived at Fort Riley, KS in May 1966. As a proud original member, I'm extremely fortunate to have served with the 2nd Platoon until January 1968. My prized possessions are Combat Infantryman Badge and Purple Heart. Of all the firefights and skirmishes, our May 15, June 19 and July 11 battles are most memorable. The battle of June 19 near AP Bac Village left an indelible imprint in my life- the tragic loss of our heroic medic, Bill Geier, and approximately 50 4th/ 47th troopers can never be forgotten. My last three months in the Army, I assisted training Basic Trainees at Fort Leonard Wood, MO. Discharged May 16, 1968.

Married Meg Ann O'Brien Nov. 1, 1969- we have two children and three grandchildren. I retired in 2001 after 28 years of service in Facilities Engineering at Lockheed Martin Corporation. Activities are helping family members and friends with home projects, playing guitar and managing a Web Site, www.9thinfantrydivision.com, which is dedicated to preserving the memory of 4th/47th soldiers, especially those who gave the ultimate sacrifice in Vietnam.

**EUDON ALVIN "RHY" RHYMER** was born April 30, 1943 in Nashville, TN. He earned his AA degree, BA degree and MFA degree.

Joined the US Navy on July 29, 1960. DESRON 9- Report for Duty May 23, 1967. USS COLLET DD730- Report for Duty May 23, 1966- Departed Feb. 21, 1967; June 15, 1966 to Sept. 5, 1968, Navy Unit Citation-Bronze Star; Nov. 4, 1966 to Nov. 5, 1966 Republic of Vietnam Gallantry Cross; Aug. 2, 1966 to Sept. 6, 1966 Vietnam Service Medal; Oct. 2, 1966 to Nov. 14, 1966 Vietnam Service Medal; and Jan. 3, 1966 to Feb. 7, 1967 Vietnam Service Medal.

USS DEHAVEN DD 727- Report for Duty March 17, 1967- Departed Oct. 23, 1967; Aug. 25, 1967 Combat Action Ribbon; Sept. 3, 1967 to Sept. 7, 1967 Combat Action Ribbon; Sept. 13, 1967 Combat Action Ribbon; June 15, 1966 to Aug. 20, 1968 Navy Unit Citation; Oct. 4, 1966 Republic of Vietnam Gallantry Cross; April 10, 1967 to May 17, 1967 Vietnam Service Medal; and Aug. 11, 1967 to Sept. 2, 1967 Vietnam Service Medal.

TF 117- Report for Duty Feb. 2, 1968- Departed Dec. 31, 1968; Jan. 29, 1968 to March 4, 1968 Presidential Unit Citation.

MRF 117- Report for Duty Feb. 2, 1968- Departed Dec. 31, 1968; May 31, 1968 Combat Action Ribbon; Jan. 29, 1968 to March 4, 1968 Presidential Unit Citation; March 5, 1968 to Jan. 24, 1969 Navy Unit Citation; Jan. 29, 1968 to March 4, 1968 Republic of Vietnam Gallantry Cross; March 28, 1968 to Oct. 14, 1968 Republic of Vietnam Gallantry Cross; Dec. 19, 1968 to June 22, 1969 Republic of Vietnam Gallantry Cross; Jan. 18, 1968 to Feb. 5, 1968 Vietnam Service Medal; Feb. 6, 1968 to Feb. 21, 1968 Vietnam Service Medal; March 1, 1968 to March 21, 1968 Vietnam Service Medal; March 28, 1968 to Oct. 15, 1968 Vietnam Service Medal; and Dec. 19, 1968 to June 22, 1969 Vietnam Service Medal.

Various other medals include Vietnam Campaign Medal, National Defense Medal and Navy Meritorious Unit Citation.

Rhymer had this to say of his memorable experiences, "The people I met and friends still in contact with- Hey "DT" Dennis Thompson-

Buffalo- "Gravel" William Bill Dargavel- Utah. All of the people that I will never forget and good days as well as the bad days. I will never forget. Well, maybe someday."

Rhymer is single and has a daughter, Eilene Anita.

## GENE "LT RICHY" RICHARDSON

was born Aug. 28, 1944 in Tallahassee, FL. He attended high school in Texas, Lamar University and earned his BS degree and earned his Master in Liberal Arts from SMU.

Joined the US Army in February 1966. Has basic/AIT, 5th Mech. Ft. Carson, OCS Ft. Benning, GA, 41st Inf. Ft. Hood, 9th Inf. Div 2nd 60th Inf. Platoon Leader XO Co C, Platoon Leader Co B, Company Commander Co E (67-68). He participated in the TET Offensive. Awards and medals he received were CIB, Silver Star, Purple Heart, Soldiers Medal, Bronze Star w/ V OLC, Air Medal, Vietnamese Cross of Gallantry, Good Conduct Medal-Vietnam Service, and Presidential Unit Citations (2).

Richardson's most memorable experience was the events leading the award of the Silver Star. It is recounted as follows: "For gallantry in action involving close combat against an armed hostile force in the Republic of Vietnam: First Lieutenant Richardson distinguished himself by exceptionally valorous actions on April 29, 1968, while serving as a Platoon Leader with Company B, 2nd Battalion, 6th Infantry, on a reconnaissance in force mission near My Tho. As his company started on a sweep of a woodline, they came under intense fire from a numerically superior Viet Cong force and the point element became pinned down in an isolated position. Realizing that the men would need immediate help, Lieutenant Richardson courageously maneuvered his machine gun team to within 25 meters of an enemy bunker and, after killing the occupants, moved further forward and directed airship strikes against the enemy. While his company moved to a more strategic location, Lieutenant Richardson, armed with an M-79, destroyed two more bunkers and kept the enemy force occupied, thus avoiding further casualties. First Lieutenant Richardson's extraordinary heroism in close combat against a Viet Cong force is in keeping with the highest traditions of the military service and reflects great credit upon himself, the 9th Infantry Division and the United States Army."

Richardson is married to Shannon and they have three children, Danielle, Justice and Ashton. Civilian employment has included working as Director of Criminal Investigations, US Agency for International Development. He retied in 1994, but is still working as Wildland Firefighter, at a ski resort and a railroad museum.

## EDWARD EVERETT RIDDLE

born Oct. 30, 1948, Vallejo, CA, graduated high school and received a one-year college certificate. Joined the US Navy Oct. 16, 1966. Stations were *USS Osford (AGRT-1)* and RivRon 9. Served with River Assault Sqdn. 9, Div. 91, T-91-9. Participated in Operation Giant Slingshot, Yankee Station.

Discharged Oct. 16, 1972, with the rank of BM3. Received the Navy Commendation w/ V, Navy Achievement w/ V and Purple Heart. His most memorable experience was the night of March 25-26, 1969. Sappers blew up the ammo dump at Dong Tam. He was sleeping approximately 400 yards from it. It was mass confusion.

He has been married to Ana Maria Fernandez since Dec. 19, 2002. He has a son, John Lewis Meyer (Edward Thomas Riddle). He is disabled- 70% PTSD, 30% Unemployability/40% Prostate Cancer. His civilian employment has included working as a mailing machine operator for the State of California.

## SAMMIE J. "BOATS" RINGER

was born on Nov. 19, 1946 in Hudson, NY. He gradauted from high school and attended two years of college. Joined the US Navy on Jan. 22, 1966. Served on the *USS John W. Thomason DD760*, and with the Mobile Riverine Force. Also with R-112-1, T-151-1 and in Vietnam-Dong Tam. He was awarded Navy Commendation with Combat V for Valor (twice). Achieved the rank of BM-3 and was discharged in January 1970.

His most memorable experience was on April 16, 1969 while in the Ben Tre area, took a B-40 rocket hit on R-112-1. The boat was on fire, with 1200 gallons of gasoline burning in the bow. They all managed to jump in the river with Charlie firing at them from the opposite bank. A Mike Boat #92 coxswained by Robert Sutton stayed in the line of fire between them and the enemy until they could be picked up by another boat. This happened at 9:35 a.m. They were extracted after 5:00 p.m. in the afternoon. It made for one long day!

Ringer is married to Joann and they have two children, Tammy and Terry. They also have two grandchildren, Nickolas and Madison. He has been enjoying retired since Sept. 14, 1999.

## HAYWOOD C. ROGERS

was born Aug. 3, 1947 in Hobgood Halifax County. He attended 12 years of school and went to Scotland Neck High School. He joined the National Guard-Navy-Army on Aug. 3, 1964.

Rogers served with Mine Div 112, MSB 18, Vietnam-Nha Be, *USS Catskill*, MCS-1 in the States. He was stationed at San Diego; Long Beach Navy; National Guard and Army-Fort Jackson, Germany. He participated in Vietnam Nha Be, Sara Saubia Abrain and Desert Storm. He was awarded National Defense, Good Conduct, Vietnam Campaign (both Ribbon), Sharp Shooter Rifle, and Navy Commendation Medal. He achieved the rank of E6 and was discharged on May 15, 1991.

Rogers says that his most memorable experience was when they were going down to Long Tau River. A rocket came over the boat, missed by about a foot, and they opened fire. The PBR's that ran gunboats got shot at; they got put in crossfire with each other. They ran aground about four hours before they could get off the sand bar. This was in February 1969.

Rogers is married to Regina Ann and they have two children, Haywood and Sharon. They also have a grandchild, Emily. Civilian employment has included working for Professional Diagnostic Service.

## JOSEPH K. ROSNER,

co-founder and the original editor of *River Currents*, the MRFA quarterly newsletter. Doug Brown of Brown Printing was the other co-founder. The name, *River Current*, was Jose Rosner's idea.

He is a plank owner of the MRFA. He was born in Oak Park, IL on July 27, 1949. Entered the US Navy on Aug. 28, 1967 and separated on May 19, 1971. Character of service, honorable.

Decorations, medals, badges, commendations, citations and campaign ribbons awarded or authorized: Vietnam Service Medal w/ Silver Star, RVN Campaign Medal w / 1960 Device, RVN Meritorious Unit Citation (Gallantry Cross Medal Color with Palm), RVN Meritorious Unit Citations (Civil Action Medal, first Class Color with Palm), Meritorious Unit Commendation Ribbon, Combat Action Ribbon and National Defense Service Medal.

Graduated from Northern Illinois University in 1977. Married Bonnie Cafferty on May 13, 1989 and they have two children, Matthew Joseph and Jaclyn Nicole. Joe has another daughter, Emily Kristine. Joe works for the US Small Business Administration.

## DELOS RANSON RYANT JR.

My military time started in the Naval Reserve in Oshkosh, WI. I joined the Reserved on my 17th birthday (Feb. 20, 1962). I think they actually swore my in about three hours before midnight, so technically I was still 16!

In 1965 I graduated from Oshkosh High School on June 10. Got married to Susan on August 7; then went on active duty for two years of December 20. I reported aboard the *USS Pulaski County LST 1088* on Jan. 8, 1966 in Norfolk, VA. We left for Vietnam on January 27, going through the Panama Canal and on to Hawaii. We arrived in Saigon on about April 10; delivering an LCU there to use in offloading ships.

From then until December 28 when I got transferred to the *USS Talladega APA 208* out of Long Beach; we made 12 more trips to various places in Vietnam. Made most to Chu Lai; but also went to Vung Tau, DaNang and Phan Rang.

On one of our "shuttle trips" to Japan, we ran into Typhoon Judy (I think that was her name). We took some damage from her, as we had a little crack in our main deck, and lost one of the blades to one of our two screws. Took a lot longer to get to Japan with only one screw! We had to go into dry dock for about three or four weeks in Sasebo, Japan.

My last trip aboard her was in December 1966. We went to Korea to pick up a load of Crown Beer for the Korean troops in Vietnam. We delivered it to DaNang, and I was transferred on December 28. The Air Force flew me back to the States. I went on about 30 days leave. Went home to Wisconsin and got my wife, and we headed for Long Beach, CA where I reported aboard the *USS Talladega APA 208*.

We left for WestPac in July 1967. Only made one trip into Vietnam with the Talladega. We returned home to Long Beach on Dec. 1, 1967, where I went on leave for six days until I got my Honorable Discharged on Dec. 7, 1967. During that six days; went down to San Diego to meet the *USS Constellation* come in, as my brother Mike Ryant was aboard; and returning home from WestPac on December 5. He got discharged himself a few days later. It was a very happy time for the Ryant family. My parents, and three other brothers, and sister had moved out to California in July 1967, so now we were all together in the same area; and my brother and I were ready to start the rest of our lives with the War finally behind us. Although a part of us will always be there. We were proud to have done our little part for our country, and the people of Vietnam.

As far as medals and such, I think I should have a couple more, and am in the process of checking it out, but DD214 says National Defense Service, Vietnam Service with two Bronze Stars. I think there were a couple of medals given out from the Vietnam government for "in-country" service members, of who I was one; having been "in-country" 14 times in all.

Still am married to Susan. Have been married for 38 years and still going! We have one daughter who was born May 30, 1977. He name is DeeAnna Lee Ryant. She and Roberto Nocelo have given us three wonderful grandchildren. Their names are Summer who is 8, Jessamyn who is 4, and Enrique who just turned 3.

I have worked as a Computer Specialist for the Department of Defense, US Army, since 1972. Started my career at Fort McCoy, WI, then to Fort Belvoir in 1979; Fort Leavenworth in 1981; back to McCoy in 1984; then to Fort Richardson, Alaska in 1986, where I have been ever since. I plan to retire in 2004 with almost 34 years total time. Guess that is about all to my story.

**MICHAEL SALABA** was born Aug, 25, 1843. He served as E-4 in the US Navy during 1968 and 1969.

Michael was on the boat *A-112-4* when it was hit in February 1969.

**TOM "SANDI" SANBORN** was born May 5, 1947 at Stockton, CA. He attended Foothill High School in Sacramento, CA, graduating in June 1966 and received his B. A. degree from California State University Chico, at Chico, CA.

Sanborn joined the US Army on Oct. 18, 1967 and served with A Company, First Platoon, 4th Battalion, 47 Infantry Regiment, and 9th Infantry Division Vietnam. He was stationed at Bear Cat Base Camp and Dong Tam Base Camp.

His most memorable campaigns were on August 12, 18 and 24 with Alpha Company and Charlie Company of 4/47 Infantry, where they were engaged in ambushes against the enemy forces. Sanborn received the Combat Infantry Badge, Air Medal, Army Commendation with Oak Leaf Cluster, Good Conduct Medal, and four Presidential Unit Citations. He achieved the rank of Sergeant E-5 before being discharged on June 12, 1969.

According to Sanborn, his memorable experiences included "serving with a lot of young, outstanding individuals who endured many difficult and frightening moments during a long 12 months of uncertainty. God bless all members of the Mobile Riverine Force for your service in Vietnam, and your contributions to the MRFA."

Sanborn has one child, Kris Sanborn. He is now a California State Peace Officer – Supervisor and will retire in December 2006.

**ROBERT L. "SANDY" SANDERS** was born Oct. 19, 1946 at Beech Grove and received his A. A.

In 1963 Sanders joined the US Navy and served on the *USS Sarsfield* (DD-837), *USS Benewah (35); USS Ticonderoga* (CVS-14), *USS Hassay AMP* (AO-145). "Sandy" was at F Mag at San Diego, CA, transferred to Long Beach, CA and then transferred to Alameda.

Before being discharged on Feb. 2, 1976, he had achieved the rank of BM 1. He was proud to serve aboard the *USS Benewah* in Vietnam. He was also on the second ship, the *USS Ticonderoga* (CVS-14) for the APOLLO 16 and 17 pickup.

Sanders and his wife, Deborah J. Sanders have two children, Robert L. Jr. and Cindy J and one grandchild, Joshua Michael Greeson. Sanders is on Social Security and VA disability.

**RONALD "RONNIE" B. SANTORO** was born March 12, 1947 at Portland, OR. He graduated in 1965 from Hillsboro High School and attended Portland State University for one year.

Ron joined the Navy in May 1966. He attended Basic at NTC San Diego. From there he went to Great Lakes Engineman School until December 1966. In January 1967 he flew to the Philippine Islands to catch the destroyer ship *USS O'Brien*. He spent over two years aboard the *O'Brien* on two West Pac tours to Vietnam and a Taiwan Patrol. In late January 1969 he went to Vallejo, CA for training on river boats. In May 1969 he picked up an ATC number T-151-3. In June 1969 the Navy asked for volunteers for Sniper Training with the 9th Infantry in Dong Tam. A few volunteers from the Navy River boats were trained in country as Navy Snipers. He was sent to several Duty Stations as a sniper to include Dong Tam Coastal DIV 15 Qui Nhon, IUWG-1, West Pac Div Qui Nhon with Recondo team, SEA COBRAs, COMCOSURVFOR (CTF-115) Operation Sea Float and Cam Ranh Bay. He achieved the range of EN3 (Engineman) before being discharged in May 1970.

One of his most memorable experiences was with the Sea Cobras – a Recondo team from IUWG-ONE, Wes Pac Det, Unit 3. They went on several ops in the inner harbor islands of Qui Nhon. Ron Smith and Ron Santoro were snipers. They were with 10 to 12 others on night operations. One evening, Ron spotted a sampan in his starlight scope. He asked to fire, but was told to wait to see what they were going to do. As the sampan made shore all hell broke loose. They were in a firefight with NVA regulars and VC. They were overwhelmed and being surrounded. The only way out was by water on their Boston Whalers. So they fought their way back to the boats; and got the hell out of there, while calling in heavy artillery. By the grace of God, they suffered no casualties.

On July 7, 1983 he was married to Cindy Santoro and they have three children, Angela Santoro, Adam Santoro and Christopher Simmons. Their grandchild is Laura Higashi. Ron retired June 6, 2003 after working with Freightliner Truck Manufacturing LLC for 31 1/2 years, purchasing agent, raw materials.

**JOHN M. SCHLEICHER** graduated from New Britain High School, New Britain, CT in 1965 and attended the University of Connecticut for one semester. He joined the USN Aug. 1, 1966; attended basic training at Great Lakes, IL and electricians mate "A" school, graduating February 1967. Served aboard the *USS Persistent (MSO 491)* from March 1967 to December 1968. The ship completed a West Pac cruise from August 1967 to May 1968, having taken part in three Market Time Patrols. January and February 1969 was with IUWG-1 training at Long Beach and Survival, Evasion, Resistance, and Escape training at Coronado, CA. Stationed at the Harbor Entrance Control Post, IUWG-1 Unit Two (Cam Ranh Bay) from March 1969 to May 1969. Volunteered for SeaFloat (ATSB-Nam city) duty in May and was the electrician for the unit. Sea Float was fitted out in Nha Be, loaded on three LSD's and then off loaded at the mouth of the Bo De river. It was towed up that river into the Cua Lon river and anchored. Served aboard SEA Float until Sept. 10, 1969. Returned to IUWG-1 Unit Two HECP and finished duty tour. Separated from active duty March 1970 with the rank of EM2 (E5). Received the NDSM, VCM, VSM(5), NUC(2), MUC.

Married Donna Sanderson in 1971. They have a son Karl, daughter-in-law Ruby and two grandsons, Keenan and Jackson. John is a self-employed electrician living in Cape Code, MA.

**RICHARD L. SCHMUTTE** was born in Indianapolis, IN on Jan. 1, 1948. He graduated from Cathedral High School 1966 and enlisted in the Naval Reserves in May 1966.

He took basic training at Great Lakes, IL; began active duty May 1967. He received training at Coronado, San Clemente, Mare Island, CA and Whidby Island, WA before going to Vietnam, where he served as a 40 gunner on M-91-2 from September 1967 through September 1968. He was released from active duty when he got back to the States. He states of his experience, "Short but rather eventful tour in our US Navy."

After discharge, he attended Indiana University for 2 1/2 years. He worked various jobs, some of which were as an inspector for Allisons, pipe fitter for the local gas company, opened a record shop, had a small trucking company, heavy equipment operator mechanic, and finally settled down and is currently working as a machinist at Amtrak in Beech Grove, IN and owns a small farm on the north side of Indianapolis.

**JOSEPH "JOCCO" SCZYREK** was born Aug. 23, 1947 at Los Angeles, CA. He enlisted in the US Navy upon graduation from Nutley, (New Jersey) High School in 1965. After completion of recruit training at Great Lakes, IL, he was assigned to the *USS Holmes County, LST 836* where he served as an Engineman in the main propulsion Room. The *Holmes County* provided amphibious support to US Forces by transporting supplies, armament and ground forces between our base in Subic Bay, Philippines and various locations in the Mekong Delta including Da Nang, Chu Lai, Cam Ranh Bay, and Saigon. He left the *Holmes County* in May of 1966 to enter MM "A" School. After completing "A" School, he was later assigned to the *USS Douglas H. Fox DD779* in 1967 as a Machinist Mate Third Class. He later achieved the rank of Machinist Mate Second Class and served as P.O.C. of the After Engine Room. The *Fox* also served in Vietnam between March and July of 1969. During that time, the *Fox* provided support to both air and ground forces by serving as a plane guard during takeoff and landing of carrier based sorties and close range shore bombardment operations with the *Battleship USS New Jersey.*

After discharge from the Navy in 1971, he attended Saint Peters' College in Jersey City, NJ and graduated with a B.S. in Business Management in 1975.

Joe met his wife, Sarah, as a blind date in 1969 while on leave, and they were married in 1971. Today they are happily married for 33 years and both enjoy successful careers. Sarah is a Public School Guidance Counselor and Joe is a Senior Vice-President with a financial services organization.

**EDWARD CONNIE SHOEMAKER** was born July 20, 1943 at Nowata, OK and received his B.A. degree from Oklahoma State University.

In April 1967, Shoemaker joined the US Navy. He served on the *USS Gallant – MSO 489* from 1967 to 1968 and on the *USS Nueces APB 40* from 1968 to 1969. Before being discharged in December 1969, he achieved the rank of Personnelman 3$^{rd}$ Class (E-4). During his service he received the Good Conduct Medal, Combat Action Ribbon, National Defense, Republic of Vietnam Campaign Medal and Vietnam Service Medal.

Homeward Delay: The night before our transit from the Bassac River to the blue waters of the Pacific, the *Nueces* had anchored for the night. Our company of 160 men had combed this murky river for 13 months. During routine Special Sea and Anchor Detail, the crew had discovered an attachment to the anchor chain. The Explosive Ordnance Demolition (EOD) was called in to assess the problem. They examined the lines below water level and discovered a 300-pound *command detonated mine*. It had not exploded because the wires had been cut, either by one of our security boats or by one of the many Vietnamese riverboats crossing nightly. The EOD team decided to cut the holding lines to salvage the mine. After the four hour delay, our crew only wanted to get to the Pacific and get our butts out of that river and head for home. Cries of approval sounded as the holding lines were cut. As irony has it with any undertaking in Vietnam, one of the team members did not have a secure hold on the line and the mine sunk to the bottom of the Bassac River. Luckily it was not our problem. We continued to hoist anchor, secure the ship, and left with the EOD crew still trying to recover the mine and bitching as to whose fault it was. God were we happy to get underway.

Shoemaker is married to Doris Darlene (Dewberry) Shoemaker. His civilian employment has been Director of Research Management, Oklahoma Historical Society.

**CHARLES "CHARLIE" R. SINGLETON** was born Aug. 31, 1943 at La Port, IN.

In February 1964, Singleton joined the US Navy. He served on the *USS Peoria*, Riverine A112-3/112-7 Debuque, *USS Enterprise VF 143, USS Downes, USS America.* He was located at SIMA 32$^{nd}$ St, NTC San Diego, Danang Vietnam, Port OPTS San Diego Tug master. He was also involved in the Giant Sling Shot.

During his service, he received the Combat Action, four Navy Achievements, Vietnam

Service, Good Conduct and Sea Service. By the time of discharge in June 1990, he had achieved the rank of Chief Boatswain mate. His memorable experiences included meeting all the different people and making new friends.

Charles and wife, Noel, have been married 31 years and have three children; Noella, Tammy and Heather. They have five grandchildren: Alethea; Joseph; Abrianna; Anthony and Alyssa. Charles has worked for Civil Service, Doct Master 32nd St.

**DAVID M. SMITH** was born May 18, 1945 at Norfolk, VA. He received his B.A. from Old Dominion University (1968) and M. S. at Virginia Commonwealth University (1980).

On Aug. 29, 1968 Smith joined the Army. He served with the 25th Infantry Division – My Tho, the 9th Infantry Div. (Co B 2/60), Tan An and the 9th Division October 1969 to May 1970. He had achieved the rank of Sergeant E-5 by the time he was discharged on June 1, 1970. During his service, he received the Bronze Star, Purple Heart, three Army Commendation Medals, three Air Medals, and the Combat Infantryman Badge.

David and wife Patricia have two sons and one daughter; Matthew, Andrew and Elizabeth. After leaving the military, he spent 24 years with the Virginia State Police, retiring in 1995. He is currently a Transportation Specialist with US Department of Transportation in Washington, D.C.

**THOMAS E. SMITH**, Sergeant E-5, was born in April 1947 in Philadelphia. He graduated from Father Judge High School in 1965. Drafted in September 1966, attended basic at Fort Gordon, GA and advanced training in Fort Knox, KY and Fort Lee, VA. Friendships made during these times would often resurface in Vietnam and years after. He was in the first group assigned to the Mobile Riverine Force by the 9 S and T Battalion. This determined group of young soldiers set up the procedures, methods and layout of the first LST supply ship. During the next 15 months, under Tom's leadership, this expanded to include Graves Registration, ammo re-supply, and direct supply support to the brave Army and Navy Combat units. Tom was lucky to be assigned with many talented people and they were often recognized for various medal and unit awards. During his service, Sergeant Smith was awarded the Bronze Star Medal, and five Army Commendations medals, various Vietnam Combat Ribbons and the Good Conduct Medal.

Separated from Active Duty in June of 1968, Tom returned to his many friends and family. Tom received his College Degree from LaSalle University in 1975 and continued to applying the many management lessons learned in Vietnam in the Paint Retail and Distribution Field. In 1988 Tom purchased a Florida-based Paint Distribution business, and started Smith's International Traders for Pain sales throughout the Caribbean. This career includes many Industry related Board and Leadership positions along with South Florida based Community organizations.

During all this, Tom has had a great partner in his wife, Lorraine. They will be married 30 years in 2004. Their children, Sabrina and Alex, continue to be a great joy and mystery to their parents, while continuing their college studies in Florida.

**JON BRADLEY "MONSTERCHEF" SODER** was born Sept. 19, 1947 at Brainerd, MN. He graduated from high school in 1965 and received his A.A.S. Supervisory Management in 1998.

In May 1966, Soder joined the U.S. Navy. The units he served with were NTC – San Diego; NWC – China Lake, CA; *USS Hunterdon County LST* 838 – TF116 Vietnam; *USS Coral Sea CVA 43* – Vietnam; Naval Air Station Cubi Point, Philippines; Naval Air Station, Beeville, TX; *USS Flint AE 32*; Reserve Naval Mobile Construction Battalion DET 1225; *USS Connole FF 1056*; Mobile Inshore Undersea Warfare Unit 111. Soder was stationed in California, Vietnam, Philippines, Japan, Okinawa, Texas, Hong Kong, Hawaii, Rhode Island, Florida, Washington, Guam, Midway, Puerto Rico, Cambodia, Tennessee, Virginia, Minnesota, Mississippi and Alaska.

Soder was in the Tet Offensive, Operation Gamewarden, *USS Hunterdon County* ambushed August 1968 (don't remember all of the campaign names for TF116 during in country stay from 1967 – 1969). During his career he received the following awards and medals: Navy Achievement Medal, Combat Action Ribbon, President Unit Citation, Joint Meritorious Unit Award; two Navy Unit Commendations, two Good Conduct Medals, three Naval Reserve Meritorious Service Medals, National Defense Service Medal, Armed Forces Expeditionary Medal, seven Vietnam Service Medals, Armed Force Reserve Medal, Republic of Vietnam Gallantry Cross Unit Citation, and Republic of Vietnam Campaign Medal.

Duty aboard the *USS Hunterdon County LST 838* – River Patrol TF 116, Mekong Delta, Vietnam was the most exciting part of his Navy career. This Tank Landing Ship converted for use as home-base for 12 PBR boats and two helicopters and their crews. This ship and others like it were part of Operation Game Warden. Operation Game Warden was a mission that took place on the rivers of the Mekong Delta in South Vietnam for the purpose of denying the Viet Cong the use of these waterways. Although this was the most dangerous duty of my career, it was also the most personally rewarding. The crew of the *Hunterdon County* was small and worked well as a team. We worked hard and played hard. Most of my 18-month tour consisted of baker duty on graveyard shift. My bread-making and a specialty for caramel and pecan rolls got quite a reputation on the rivers. Sometimes PBRs and other small boats from other units would stop by the *Hunterdon County* to get some of our bread and rolls. I also met my wife Esmenia during a period that the *Hunterdon County* was in the Philippines for repairs. It took more than a year of bureaucratic red tape to finally get approval for us to get married. We have been married 35 years now. I have lots of river patrol photos/stories on my website at www.monsterchef.net.

Soder and wife Esmenia, have a daughter, Sharon Barker. Soder retired from the Navy in May 1993, and is still working as a manger for Computer Information Technology for the state of Minnesota. He has also been a restaurant manager, interstate truck driver, truck cop, and computer information manager.

**RONALD F. SPIVAK**, Sergeant E-5, was born April 15, 1948 and graduated from Westinghouse Memorial High School. Entered the United States Army on Oct. 4, 1967; Basic Training at Fort Jackson, SC and Advanced Individual Training (AIT) at Fort Polk, LA. Served in Vietnam with Company C, 3/39 Infantry, 9th Infantry Division from March 7, 1968 to May 8, 1969; participated in Tet '68 Counter-Offensive, Phase IV, V, and VI Counter-Offensive, and Tet '69 County-Offensive.

Sgt. Spivak was discharged May 8, 1969. His military awards and decorations include: Combat Infantry Badge (CIB); Air Medal, Army Commendation Medal with "V" device and oak leaf cluster; Vietnam Service Medal; Vietnam Campaign Mode; National Defense Service Medal and Vietnam Unit Citation.

Mr. Spivak is divorced with two children, Kristin Lee and Joseph. Mr. Spivak is a life member of the American Legion, Veterans of Foreign Wars (VFW), Disabled American Veterans (DAV) and the Amvets.

**DOUGLAS A. STEARNS** was born July 8, 1949 at Bangor, ME. He has attained his AS, BA, MA (History) and MA (Political Science)

Stearns joined the US Army on June 26, 1967. He served with E and D Company, 4th BN/47th Infantry, *USS Benewah*, B Company BN 8th Cav. 1st Cav. Div., MACV Adv. Tm 23. He was stationed at DongTam, Fort Belvior, VA; Fort Benning, GA; Baumholder, Germany, Fort Dix, NJ; Fort McClellan, AL and 3rd ROTC Region.

Stearns took part in the Tet County Offensive, VN Counter Offensive Ph IV, VN Counter Offensive Ph V, VN Counter Offensive Ph VI, VN Winter-Spring 1970, Sanctuary Counter Offensive and VN Counter Offensive Ph VII. During his career he received the National Defense Service Medal; three Army Commendation Medals; Good Conduct Medal (7th award); Vietnam Service Medal; Vietnam Campaign Medal; Vietnam Cross of Gallantry; Purple Heart; Meritorious Service Medal (one OLL); Combat Infantryman's Badge; Bronze Star Medal; Air Medal (one OLC); Army Service Medal; Drill Sergeants Identification Badge; NCO Professional Development Ribbon; Civic Action Honors Medal and Valorous Unit Award. He achieved the rank of First Sergeant by the time he was discharged on April 30, 1989.

His memorable experiences included the Fire Fight March 7 and 8, 1968; ambush at the Crossroads (Wagon Wheel) and Ben Tre Canal, Fire Fight on Aug. 18 and 30, 1968; his friendship with Gary Morgan (KIA) and Barry Baron (WIA) and West Bank Security.

Stearns and wife, An Po Stearns, have one child, Latisha. Stearns civilian employment is as a Central Alabama Community College History/Political Science Instructor.

**JOHN F. "JACK" STONE** was born Feb. 26, 1940 in Boston, MA and is a high school graduate.

Jack joined the US Navy on Nov. 17, 1959 and served on seven ships including *USS Harnett CTY LST-821* from Aug. 2, 1968 to April 14, 1970. He was stationed at Three Shore Station, Moffet Field, CA, San Diego, CA and FMAG Norfolk, VA.

During his career took part in the ORP Giant Sling Shot on the Vam Co Dong at Ben Luc, Bassac River, Gulf of Siam and Rach Gia. He received the Combat Action Ribbon, PUC, NUC (two), Good Conduct (five), Navy Exp. Medal, National Defense, Armed Forces Exp. V.S.M. V.C. of G.

His memorable experiences included being part of ORP. Giant Sling Shot, when they trans the Vam Co Dong River to the Bridge at Ben Luc. They were landlocked for five months. They supported all the units in the area. They had their action with two rocket attacks. On the lighter side, Stone says they had beer call nightly. "If you ever stopped for a beer or soda, I probably was your bartender." By the time of Retirement on May 22, 1979, Stone had achieved the rank of MR1 (E-6).

Stone and wife, Lydia C., have three children; Mary, Debbie and Michael. They have five grandchildren: Ben, Aaron, Pete, Shawn and Thimary. Stone's civilian employment included C and K Company, Inc. and ADP Eng., Inc.

**DAN EARL STOVER,** SP-4, born into a military family on March 26, 1948, a good Friday. His fate was sealed. Born at Oakland Naval Hospital, Oakland, CA. Raised on tropical islands and military bases. He knew he'd travel to foreign lands one day. Dropping out of high school (Sunnyvale High) form South Bay area at age of 18, he enlisted on April 27, 1966 and took basic at Fort Ord, CA.

Basic was a brand new world (a real eye opener), discipline was sift and hard, dealt with severely. One man got sentenced to 14 years hard labor for not picking up a rifle. Sent to Leavenworth, KS, a military prison. I never seen so many men, huddled in one area to be molded into green Death machine. Marching songs all the while being sung. Ain't no use looking back Jodie got your car and girl at home. Better lean your hand to hand because you're going to Vietnam! When basic ended, he also took his AIT at Fort Ord, CA. Became 36 A-10 communication expert wireman. By September 1966, he was ordered to Fort Lewis, WAV, there the military had assembled five battalions of construction engineers, 63rd, 73rd, 93rd and two others.

The 4th Infantry Division had just left the area for Vietnam: the area had remnants of them everywhere. The feeling was of ghost with no body around, a emptiness loomed over the whole area as to say you next?

After lot of training the military made a decision in December of 1966 only one battalion was going, the 93rd. I was ordered to that unit. After doing jungle training in the snow in December, I thought how dumb. By May 1967 we knew for sure that we were heading for the war zone of Vietnam. Reason being the 34th Engineer Group Left in March 1967 which became the 20th Engineer B and E Station in Vung Tau Vietnam.

Also in May I received my GED. June 1, 1967 movement order came. Leaving behind the world as we knew it! Early in the morning a lonely Army band played the Army Hymn. No goodbye, just the band played on. Leaving by ship from the Port of Tacoma, WA on military troop transport ship, named *USS Upshar*, spending 21 days going across the Pacific Ocean.

Tensions were running high, thus when battalion arrived in the Philippines at Subic Bay, the battalion raised hell, 47 drunk and disorderly court martials were given out.

Arriving in Vietnam, landed at Vung Tau thus flew to Long Bien Airfield by C-123 and C130, then were transported by truck to an area outside Bear Cat 9th Infantry Division. In Vietnam I got attached to many different units in Vietnam, one was Co. A 9th Inf. Division S and T Supply and Transportation. Also attached of 4/47 Co A Infantry Division One Mission. Other units: 69th Engr's MAC-V 52 Advisory Team, stationed in Cantho, Dong Tam, Soc Trang, all areas of Mekong Delta.

Jan. 13, 1968 was a shocker. This was the day I knew the meaning of the world is not safe. Even in a military compound. I had orders to go on R and R that night. However Saigon came under attack for next 30 days, I watched in horror what war could do. As carnage of people within reach of me, bullets whizzed by; I returned to base, watched name tags lifted from beds, knowing friends had been killed; six in all.

Returning back to world, no homecoming, full of skin rashes, returning one by one, getting a change of clothing at Oakland Army Terminal in chow hall! There was a huge American flag with a sign in the middle of it, have a steak on us (military) for a job well done. I felt like a sin eater for all America and its blood it was spilling.

After 30 days leave, I was sent and stationed at Fort Sill, OK. They decided to train me in MP training as a stockade jailer, then a riot guard. In December 1968 this landed me at National Democratic Convention in Chicago, holding people off at gun point, told to bayonet people, told hold off the peace creeps, hippy scum, and to stab them at will, if ordered.

After service, Stover worked various jobs, then joined GI movement, worked in Outreach Programs in VA Hospitals. Retired in 1997 due to health and war-related injuries. Now teacher in martial arts, a motorcycle enthusiast, collector of Sci-Fi and old LP records. Happily married with eight children and five grandchildren.

Awarded the Defense Ribbon Vietnam Ribbon, Vietnam Service, Vietnamese Cross of Gallantry with Palm. Served from 1966 to 1969 and 1974 to 1975. Honorable discharge June 1, 1975.

**JOHN T. "JACK" STRICKLAND** was born April 30, 1944 at Pasadena, CA. He received his BS in Marketing at University of Colorado, 1970.

Jack entered the US Army in September 1966 and took Infantry Basic Training at Fort Bliss, TX; AIT at Fort Ord, CA; Infantry OCS at Fort Benning, GA. September 1967, commissioned 2nd LT, 5th Mechanized Division, Fort Carson, CO; Jungle Survival School Panama. September 1968, 3/60th Mobile Riverine Force, Dong Tam, Vietnam, D Company's 3th Platoon Leader. Became Battalion Intelligence and Psychological Warfare Officer. July 1969, first combat division to return to the USA where he separated from the Army.

Memorable operations were Thanksgiving 1968, Platoon Sergeant Richard Hunford, Tiger Scout Nyugen Phouc and Strickland killed two VC snipers at a very close range. December 1968, while Bob Hope gave a USO show in Dong Tam, they encountered heavy contact. The noise made Hope comment" "General, do they know we are trying to put on a show here?" The crowd went wild. I had the privilege to serve with Captain Paul E. Blackwell (retired as LTG). He kept most of us alive.

Medals received were Army Commendation Medal with V, Bronze Star 3 Oak Leaf Clusters with V's, Air Medal, Combat Infantry Badge, Vietnamese Cross of Gallantry.

Civilian employment: Mobil Oil, three years; Heublein Wines four years; Anheuser-Busch eight years; commercial real estate 10 years. 1997 retired, work part-time in a ski shop and as a golf course marshal.

**GARY D. STUDLEY** was born Jan. 12, 1949 at St. Paul, NE and graduated high school.

On July 16, 1968 he joined the Army and served with C, Co. 4th, 47th 9th Inf. Div. Studley took basic training at Fort Lewis, WA, AIT at Fort McClellan, AL and was at Scofield Barracks, HI.

During his service he received the Combat Infantryman Badge, Bronze Star Medal, National Defense Service Medal, Vietnam Campaign Medal, Army Commendation Medal, Vietnam Air Service Medal and Air Medal. Studley had achieved the rank of SP 4 by his date of discharge on April 16, 1970.

His most memorable experience was the first MRFA and 9th Inf. reunion that he went to, meeting old friends.

Gary and wife, Reynetta, have two children, Dallas and Darrin.

**KENNETH SUNDBERG** was born June 29, 1943 at Geneva, OH and graduated from high school.

On Oct. 10, 1966 he entered the Army and served with 5th of the 60th, 9th Inf. Div., H.H.Q., 598 Light Maintenance Bat., 67 Light Inf. Div. He was stationed at Fort Benning, then to Fort Dix, then to Fort Benning, to Bien Phoug and then back to Fort Benning.

During service he received all the Vietnam medals and a Bronze Star with V device for heroism. By discharge on July 8, 1969 he had achieved the rank of Spec 4.

He states, "Now that I look back, I loved the time I spent in the Army. The year I spent in Vietnam made me strong enough to cope with life. I was in business delivering milk for 28 years through hell and high snow. I am very proud of what I did and what the 9th Inf. did. I will never forget my friends that died; Mike Sheahan, Bobby Conley, Joe Peake, and many others. If I do forget them, then they died in vain. God bless them and God bless America."

Sundberg and wife Barbara have three children, Christopher, Tiffanee and Tracee and grandchildren Josh, Jeremy, Jacquie, Angeline, Tabipha and Garrett. Kenneth has been a milkman in civilian life.

**EDDIE W. "LUCKY" TENPENNY** was born Sept. 10, 1947 at Woodbury, TN and graduated from high school.

On Aug. 9, 1965 he joined the US Navy and served with the *USS Ticonderoga CVA-14*. He was stationed at San Diego, CA. "Lucky" received the Navy Unit Commendation with one Bronze Star, Armed Forces Expeditionary Medal (Korea), Republic of Vietnam Meritorious Unit Citation, Gallantry Cross with Palm, National Defense Service Medal, and Vietnam Service Medal with Bronze Stars (four stars). By Sept. 7, 1968 he had achieved the rank of E4.

His memorable experiences included: "I remember having to go to Korea when the *USS Pueblo* was captured. I volunteered to serve with the Mobile Riverine Force on Jan. 6, 1967. I never made it to the River Patrol but served my country in Vietnam with Task Force 77."

Tenpenny's wife is Killeen, and he retired from the US Army July 9, 2003.

**MAURICE J. THIBAUDEAU** was born Jan. 18, 1948 at Manchester, NH and graduated from high school.

On Sept. 29, 1966 he joined the US Navy and served on the *USS Chicago (CG-11)* and with the River Assault Div. 132. He was stationed at North Island, San Diego, CA and Dung Tam Republic of South Vietnam.

He took part in the Silver Lance II, Giant Sling Shot, Sea Lords, Barrier Reef Grand Canal and received the National Def. Medal, Combat Action Ribbon, Vietnam Service Medal, Rep. of Viet Campaign Medal, Meritorious Unit Combat Ribbon, Navy Commendation Medal. By date of discharge on May 25, 1972 he had achieved the rank of BM 2.

His most memorable experience occurred when he first arrived at Dong Tam. They were billeted into a newly built barracks that had been just constructed. They were assigned to a bunk before being given their duty stations. Then during the night or very early morning, he was awakened along with the rest of the group by some incoming rounds and explosions. Then after a few minutes, they were told to evacuate. The shelling was so tremendous that while entering the shelter the concussion was so great that it actually pushed him into the shelter. What was being aimed at and actually hit was the ammo dump on the Navy side.

After regaining his composure, he left along with the other guys and headed for the Army side of Dong Tam which was not being shelled. The next morning he, along with the rest of the sailors, returned and witnessed the damage that had been done. The barrack that he had been assigned to had nothing but the foundation and broken up wood framing remaining. "The VC gave me an eye opening welcome that was not forgotten."

Thibaudeau and wife, Carol Ann, had two children, Michael and Jeffrey. Maurice retired in September 2001 after working for Verizon as lineman, station assigner, garageman, Admin. Asst., and local testman.

**HARLEY G. TIMMERMAN** was born March 17, 1947 and joined the US Navy on July 3, 1967.

He served with the RivRon 13, Tango Boat 132-10 from June 1968 to June 1969 and YRBM20, July 1969 to July 1970. He achieved the rank of Engineman/Gunner MK 19 Top Turret.

His memorable moments include meeting the freighter that brought the boat over, going up to Saigon and unloading it. It was the last voyage for the civilian freighter and was to be scrapped. The crew "cleaned house" and gave us tools, equipment and anything else that wasn't bolted down. Operation Giant Slingshot up by the Parrot's Beak and the trip to the Cau Mau Peninsula.

Timmerman and wife, Sue, live with a fine dog named Delta.

**ARTHUR "ART" ROBERT TRAENDLEY** was born March 5, 1947 at Englewood, NJ and graduated from high school.

On July 21, 1966 he joined the US Navy. He served on the *USS Wexford CTY (LST-1168)* and was also stationed at San Diego, CA. He took part in the Tet of 1968 and RUN from December 1967 to May 1968. He received the Meritorious Unit Citation (Navy), National Defense Service, Vietnam Campaign Service, Republic of Vietnam Campaign Medal.

By discharge on May 13, 1970 he had achieved the rank of CS 3. His memorable experiences were being in Vietnam at Tet of 1968 and being with a great crew on board ship.

**DONALD TRAUSNECK** was born July 30, 1946 at New York and graduated from Syosset High School in 1965. He received his B.A. degree in Health and Physical Education at East Carolina University in 1973, and Associate in Applied Science degree in Computer Information Systems at Wytheville Community College in Virginia, 1993.

On June 27, 1965 Trausneck joined the US Navy and took basic training at Great Lakes in 1965. He served on the *USS Randolph (CVS-15), USS Benewah (APB-35), USS Mark (AKL-12), USS Rockbridge (APA-228), and USS Pocono (LCC-16)*. He was in Republic of Vietnam service and *USS Benewah (APB 35)* Navigation Department. By discharge on June 25, 1971 he had achieved the rank of QM2 (E5). His memorable experiences included NATO cruise, Caribbean cruise and Med cruise, and being a member of Scottish-American Military Society and the Naval Academy Athletic Association.

Trausneck is single and his civilian employment has included working in various newspaper and public relations positions, and is currently Public Affairs Officer for VFW Post 1115, Hillesville, VA, t he seconds largest and most active VFW post in the state.

**JOHNNY R. "BOB" TRUJILLO** was born April 30, 1945 at Pueblo, CO.

Trujillo joined the Army in March 1966 and was stationed with Germany 7th Army, 9th Division, Vietnam, 1967-1968, 62nd Transportation Vietnam, 1970-1971. He was in the Tet Offensive, Coronado operations, and at Mekong Delta. During his career he received the Army commendation and NDSM, Combat Award, VSM, VCM, and President Unit Citation. By discharge on June 12, 1971 he achieved the rank of E5.

According to Trujillo, he had many memorable experiences; some good, some bad, but felt he could not center on just one.

Trujillo and wife, Victoria, have two children, Johnny A and Robert. They have five grandchildren: Albert, Nick, Domoque, Jennifer and Theresa. Trujillo retired in September 1999 after being a carpet layer, clerk and letter carrier.

**WAYNE J. UDWARY**, GMG2, born Sept. 4, 1947, at Troy, NY. Graduated from Averill Park High School in 1965. Joined US Navy Oct. 20, 1966; attended Basic Training and Gunners Mate A School at Great Lakes, IL. Assigned to the *Dennis J. Buckley (DD808)* out of San Diego, CA from June 1967 to August 1968. On return from West Pac Tour, reassigned to River Assault Training at Mare Island, Vallejo, CA from September 1968 to November 1968. Assigned to RivRon 9 on Tango T-91-12 as Chief Gunner from December 1968 to January 1969. Boats were turned over to the Vietnamese in January, 1969. I served as Naval Advisor for February and March of 1969. Re-assigned to RivRon 595 on *A-91-2* as Gunner then Boat Captain. Wounded when *ASPB A-91-2* was in a VC ambush from both sides of the river and was hit by a B-40 rocket on June 12, 1969. Lost sight of right eye and shrapnel wounds to the right side of my body.

Medical discharge on Sept. 22, 1969. Received Purple Heart, Navy Unit Commendation with Combat V, VCM, VSM, NDSM.

Married Ruth Scouller June 28, 1970 and reside in Sand Lake, NY. I have three children, Daniel (PhD in Chemistry- Johns Hopkins University); Rebecca (BS Computer Science, Siena College-Database Administrator for Cal-Tech University) and Kevin (BS Physics, Siena College-employed at Crystal IS). I am currently retired from Watervliet Arsenal after 23 years of service and working part-time as a machinist for Canton Bio-Medical.

**GARY G. VANDELOO**, EN3, born Sept. 11, 1949, Sheboygan, WI, graduated from Sheboygan North High School, 1967. Joined the USN Dec. 15, 1967; attended basic training at Great Lakes, IL; served with RivRon 15; and RID 47. Participated in Operation Giant Sling Shot. Other military stations were USS Puget Sound (AD-38) (plankowner), on board March 1, 1968-Dec. 23, 1969; served in the internal combustion engine shop attaining the rank of EN3 (E-4); Feb. 1-April 12, 1970, River Assault craft training at Mare Island, Vallejo, CA and survival, evasion, resistance and escape training at Whidbey Island, WA; April 13, 1970-November 1970, River Assault Div. 132, RivRon 15, Monitor 7 and Monitor 6, as engineer and support gunner; boats were turned over to the Vietnamese, November 1970; November 1970-April 13, 1971, served as a naval advisor t o the Vietnamese in River Interdiction Div. 47, serving on tangos and monitors. Memorable experiences

include a firefight as an advisor on a tango boat. He was the only American on board, the rest were Vietnamese. They got hit from both banks of the river. Separated from active duty, April 19, 1971, Treasure Island, CA; and discharged Dec. 4, 1973, with the rank of EN3 (E-4). Received the NDSM, Combat Action Ribbon, VSM (2), VCM, Navy Commendation w/Combat V. Married Ellen, May 26, 1973, and has a daughter, Ruth (June 14, 1980). He is a public safety equipment technician at Lakeshore Technical College, Cleveland, WI.

**ROBERT "BOB" J. VARGAS**, Sergeant E5, born March 21, 1947, Chicago, IL; graduated from Farragut High School June 1966. He was drafted Oct. 25, 1966 into the US Army and sent to Ft. Campbell, KY. However, because of space limitations for new draftees, Bob was transferred to the new Ft. Stewart, GA, basic training facility. There he completed his B.C.T. as well as Infantry A.I.T.

January 1967 Bob had orders to serve in Korea with A Company 1st Bn. 23rd Infantry – 2nd Infantry Division. Bob found the first few weeks patrolling the DMZ weren't too bad but then things changed rather quickly. In early spring 1967, a guard type campaign called "barrier guard" commenced along the southern boundary of the DMZ, Before long, firefights along the line started to be a common occurrence. Sometimes shots were fired at moving bushes while at other times at legitimate North Korean infiltrators. During the night of May 22, 1967, things got real nasty. While Bob was in foxholes guarding the barrier, North Korean sappers penetrated his A Company compound (Camp Wally, about 3000 yd. from the DMZ) and blew up two Quonset barracks with sleeping GIs. Two GIs from the 2nd platoon were killed and 16 others wounded. That did it for Bob, he and several others decided to 1049 for Nam. Oct. 17, 1967, Bob reported in at HHC Company, 2nd Battalion 60th Infantry —9th Infantry Division, Tan Tru, South Vietnam. Now he wonders if that 1049 was a good idea.

Now a PFC, he decides he's had it with line companies so he volunteers for the battalion Recon Platoon, E Company. In less than two months he developed that tight feeling of camaraderie with the Recon guys. He earned the Bronze Star with "V" device in November 1967 for action in the Plain of Reeds. Things got tougher.

On Dec. 10, 1967, the unfortunate encounter occurred that combat grunts know they'll never forget. During an Eagle Flight operation, Bob experienced the loss of his friend, Gene. It is the first time he experienced the death of someone close to him; it's a sad day.

Recon's platoon leader was one of the best. Bob remembers how perceptive the LT was especially in recognizing when the morale was crap. "We are all afraid, including me," he said, "you've got to take that fear and make it work for you." That was always a reminder to Bob throughout his RVN tour.

On Jan. 8, 1967, an unfortunate gun shot accident sends Bob into the 35th Evacuation Hospital (Vung Tau) for three weeks. He reports back to Recon just in time for Tet. During late February, Battalion sets up a temporary base camp north of Dong Tam along Highway 4 that became known as the "Pink Palace." It is from there that Recon and other companies operated for the next 3-1/2 months. Bob remembers one particular March night when point man Dennis Lorenz noticed an unusually shaped group of rocks laying flat along the roadside. Taking no chances, Dennis and the LT. decide to check the area in front. As the platoon started going to its flanks, green tracers started flying. We caught Charley trying to spring an ambush. Later that night, Recon springs two of their own ambushes and gets credit for seven V.C. with no losses.

Bob attended the NCO school in Bearcat (Camp Martin Cox) in June 1968, and becomes a sergeant E5 in July. Many Go-Devils in E Company were brought to laughter by Bob imitating the comedic voice of one of Bill Cosby's character, "Mel."

His DEROS on the silver dust-off from Bien Hoa went to Fort Dix, NJ Oct. 13, 1968 where he was discharged as a Sergeant E5, Oct. 17, 1968. He never regrets serving in Vietnam.

Returning to college, Bob earned a 2-year Associate Degree in 1986. In April, 2001, Bob and another Recon comrade Bob Wisniewski decided to go back to the Delta and visit the village of Tan Tru. This time it was looking at the people through different eyes.

For his service with the 1st Bn. 23rd Infantry, 2nd Infantry Division on the Korean DMZ, Bob was awarded the Imjin Scout patch. For his service with the 2nd Bn. 60th Infantry, 9th Infantry division in Vietnam, his awards include the NDSM, VSM, VCM, ACM, GCM, CIB, BSw/V, and 2PH, Unit Citation and the Air Medal.

Today, he and his wife, Linda, reside in Glen Ellyn, IL. He is in his 34th year working for the Chicago-land electric utility and plans to retire early 2004.

Bob can be quoted with saying, "Not many days go by without thoughts and a silent prayer for the band of brothers I knew that did not come home with me. They are Gene Dirita, Raymond Cox, David Squires, and David Forsyth. God Bless them."

**ROBERT "BOB" LEE VICK SR.**, was born Feb. 1, 1939 at Richmond, VA. Bob graduated from high school and attended one year of community college.

In August 1955 Vick joined the Navy. He served on the *USS Ticonderoga VA14, USS Forrestal CVA 59, USS Henrico APA45, USS Proteus, USS Colleton APB36,* and *USS Borie DD704*. He was stationed with Fleet Training Group PT Loma San Diego, CA and Navy Recruiting, Baltimore, MD, serving in the Cuba crisis and in Vietnam. During his career he received the Combat Ribbon, National Defense, Armed Forces Exp. Vietnam Service, Vietnam Campaign and Good Conduct. By discharge on March 5, 1975 he had achieved the rank of PO1/E6.

Vick and wife, Mary Ann, had the following children: Deborah Ross, Lee Vick, Glen Vick, Raymond Vick, William Vick and Brandy Vick. Vick served as a Police Officer with the Baltimore County Police Department until retiring in January 1995.

**DAVID J. "VICK" VICKNAIR**, was born Sept. 26, 1949 in New Orleans, LA. He received his GED and attended Votech.

In March 1968, he joined the US Navy and

served on the *USS Washtenaw CTY (LST 1166)* and with ISOS Unit 1. He was located at Yokosuka, Japan and various locations RVN, LST home port, Antho-Crbay-Vinh Long. He was in the TF 115, Support Swift Boats and TF 117, HGLO. He earned the Met. Unit Com., Combat Action and Pres. Unit Citation. Before discharge in December 1971, he achieved the rank of GMG 3. His memorable experiences included LST 1166 1969 Assault Berry Island with ROK Marines and ISOS Unit 1 Anti-Swimmer Defense.

Vicknair and wife, Rozzie, have been happily married for over 30 years, and have two children, Tammy (age 29) and Toni (age 27) and one grandchild, Korie (age 6). Vicknair is a general contractor and owner of V and V Buildings, Inc.

**GARY A. VOELKER**, Spec. 5, born June 9, 1948, Saginaw, MI. Drafted into the US Army on March 20, 1968; attended basic training and AIT at Ft. Sam Houston, TX as a Combat Medic. Gary went to Vietnam in September 1968 and was assigned to B Company, 3/47th Infantry River Raiders, 9th Infantry Division at Tiger's Lair where he served until they left in August of 1969. He was promoted to Head Medic in March 1969. During his service Gary participated in

several combat operations and earned the Combat Medical Badge, Air Medal, Bronze Medal, Army Commendation Medal, and Purple Heart along with several unit citations.

Gary lives with his wife Liz in Essexville, MI. They have four children, Jennifer (31), Gary II (30), Rebecca (28) and Rachel (24) and four grandchildren. He owns his own printing business and is active in his church and various business organizations.

**JOE W. "HIRAM" WALKER**, was born Feb. 25, 1939 at Ravenna, TX.

Walker joined the US Navy on Feb. 13, 1958 and served with the following units and ships: VP-56, VP-30, VP-4, VAH-2, VT-25, VAW-111, DET-12, FASR BINH THY, VAW-120, VAW-123, *USS Coral Sea, USS Hornet and USS Saratoga*. He was stationed at Norfolk, VA, Jacksonville, FL, Naha Okinawa, San Diego, CA, and Binh Thuy Vietnam. By discharge on Nov. 1, 1976, he had attained the rank of AMSC.

He said he loved the Far East, except for Vietnam.

Divorced, Walker's son is Alan D. Walker and grandchildren are Peyton and Matthew. Walker is a US Postal Service Letter Carrier.

**DAVID JAMES WELCH** was born Feb. 9, 1940 at Utica, NY and attended three years of college.

Welch joined the US Navy on Aug. 29, 1957. He served on *USS Washoe Cty (LST 1165), USS Avenage MSO 421, USS Wainwright (DLG-28), USS McCard (DD 822) USS Diachenko (AOLT-50)*. He was stationed at NAS Pensacola, FL, NRD Buffalo, NY, and Fort Utica, NY. During his service he earned the Bronze Star, Purple Heart, two Navy Comms with (V), VNN Cross of Gallantry with Palm, Good Conduct, VNN Campaign with 7 Stars. He has a total of 17 medals.

He served two tours In Country VN: From June 1965 to July 1966, Costal Surveillance Station An Thoi, Phu Quoc Island and from April 1971 to July 1972, Surface Craft, NHA BE, Craftmaster (Mondeo). By time of discharge on Jan. 2, 1976, he had achieved the rank of Quartermaster Chief.

Welch and wife, Dorothy, have four children: James; Cindy; Bill and Gary. Their grandchildren are Steven, Alexis, Courtney, Gordon, Christopher and Earnest. In civilian life, he has worked for Consolidated Natural Gas Tran. Corp as Gas Measurement Spec. Sr.

**ED WERLE**, was born July 4, 1947 at Erie, PA and entered the US Navy Nov. 11, 1966. He attended basic training at Great Lakes, IL and Riverine training at Mare Island, San Diego, CA.

Ed served with River Division 92 on a Monitor (M-92-2) boat.

His memorable experiences of Vietnam include an intense firefight after a refueler was hit on April 16, 1969, and his boatmate, Tommy Wipf being hit and wounded during the fight. (Later, Tommy would give Ed the nickname: 'Vietnam Gunslinger'). Ed also remembers and was inspired by the courage displayed by Lieutenant Commander Tom Kelly, Medal of Honor recipient during his leadership of Riv Ron 9 after being severely wounded. Ed loved "shooting the 50" and loved fighting for what's right and fighting against evil. He is proud of the men he served with who "were the best."

He remembers flying back to the USA upon discharge with a plane full of men singing:

"We gotta get out of this place, if it's the last thing we ever do!"

Ed received the Navy Achievement medal for a mission on May 24, 1969 on the Cam River in Dinh Tuong Province when the column came under heavy enemy rocket and automatic weapons fires from the east bank, 50 meters away. The citation reads: .." he was nearly overcome by the intense heat and smoke generated in the mount due to the high volume of fire. For the next hour and 40" he maintained a highly accurate volume of devastating support fire, containing the enemy force." In addition, Ed received the Combat Action Ribbon, Purple Heart and 2nd Navy Achievement Medal.

Ed served on the *USS Benjamin Stoddard DDG-22,* Pearl Harbor, Hawaii; River Divisions 92 and 152, Mobile Riverine Force, Mekong Delta, Vietnam; Gig Coxswain for the Commadore of Command Landing Ship Squadron One, San Diego, CA.

Discharged May 27, 1970 - BM3. After discharge graduated in 1974 from Edinboro University receiving a BS degree in Geography.

He is currently employed as a maintenance mechanic at the Veterans Administration Hospital in Pittsburgh, PA, where his wife, Cheryl is also employed. Ed has three children; Ben, Mark and Anna.

Ed is an avid outdoorsman and especially enjoys hunting for black bear and deer. He currently resides on a farm in Export, PA.

**LESTER LEON "PADRE" WESTLING JR.** was born Oct. 19, 1930 at Oakland, CA. He received his education at University of the Pacific, B.A., 1952; Church Divinity School of the Pacific, Berkeley, CA, M. Div. 1955; San Francisco Theological Seminary, M. A., Psych, 1973; D. Min. 1974.

His military service includes: USCGR, 1950 to 1953; USNR-R, Dec. 27, 1963; and June 27, 1966 he joined the US Navy. During his service he served with USNR-R USNAS Sangley Point, Cavite, Philippines; USN Active Duty: 3d and 1st Medical Bns, 3d MarDiv (Reinf), NV; 3d Bn, 9th Regim, 3d MarDiv (Rein); National Naval Medical Center, Bethesda, MD; Naval Support Activity, Saigon as Circuit Rider; NAS, Alameda, CA; Naval Postgraduate School (under instruction); Naval Training Center, San Diego, CA; USS Proteus (AS-19) and Submarine Squadron FIFTEEN; Naval Weapons Station, Concord, CA; Service Squadron THREE (Circuit Rider); USS Carl Vinson (CVN-70) and Battle Group "C" as Command Chaplain; Naval Hospital Oakland, CA and Director of Pastoral Services.

Westling was in Vietnam from October 1966 through September 1967 and May 1969 through May 1970. He was in multiple operations with USMC and with Mobile Riverine Forces. He received several awards and medals including Personal: Bronze Star Medal with "V;" Purple Heart Medal; Navy and Marine Corps Commendation Medal with "V;" Navy Achievement Medal; Combat Action Ribbon; Sea Service Ribbon (three awards – major deployments); Combat Air Crew Wings (three stars); Submarine Deterrent Patrol Pin. Unit Awards: PUC (two awards); NUC (three awards); MUC; Battleship Efficiency Ribbon. Campaign Medals: National Defense S Service; Vietnam Service (with six Campaign Stars); and Vietnam Campaign Medal. He had achieved the rank of Captain (O-6) by his retirement on June 1, 1987.

His memorial experiences include: From May 1969 to May 1970 I was attached to the Naval Support Activity, Saigon as a Circuit Rider Chaplain for much of the Mekong-Bassac Rivers, connecting canals, and along the Cambodia Border. I served 65 combat and support Navy and Army units, completing my "rounds" about every three weeks. I was the only person "from beyond their places" that many of the sailors and Advisory Army Teams saw. I went on ambush with boat crews so that I was available to hold Communion Services, to Baptize and to counsel. I moved from ship, bases, and boats, unit to unit, either by "daisy chain" from one squadron to another, or by Seawolf Helicopter on combat patrol. I held 18 Christmas Eve/Christmas Day services and almost as many Easter services. By means of a Jewish officer volunteer on one of the LSTs, was able to provide appropriate attention to those on the canals and rivers of that Faith as well.

One dark night on "Waterborne Guardpost" something landed on the engine cover of a PBR with a metallic sound right at my feet. The 19-year-old Boat Captain screamed "grenade" and fell on it. Fortunately it was only a catfish, but he was instantly willing to give his life for me and for his crew. This was typical of the courage and calibre of the sailors and soldiers with whom I served, and for whom I was honored to be their Chaplain.

From October 1973 to June 1976 I was on the staff of the Naval Training Center, San Diego. During that period I volunteered for additional research activities with the Joint Center for Prisoner of War Studies on Point Loma. My project area was to produce a guidance book for Navy Chaplains, physicians and psychologists to aid in the reunion of returnees and their families in the long-term readjustment period. This allowed me to contribute my combat and post-combat experiences for the benefit of others. Later this became the basis for the writing and production of a fleet program designed to ease the readjustment of families following returns from long deployments.

I have recently published experiences from over a half-century in civilian, overseas missionary, and Navy chaplaincy ministries. "All That Glitters... Memoirs of a Minister" (ISBN O-9714100-2-X, Copyright 2003) is available from Global Publishing Services, Bend Oregon at toll-free telephone number 1-866-554-2665.

Westling and wife, Marjorie (Clark) Westling have three children; Karla Nancy (Westling) Bakke; Lester Leon Westling III and Karen June Westling and two grandchildren; Faith Westling and Hope Westling. Westling has had civilian pastoral assignments in California and Philippines prior to active duty; after was a Rector at All Saints' Episcopal Parish, Redding, CA. From 1988 to 2000 employed as Psychotherapist by Tehama County, CA Mental Health. His official retirement date was Jan. 1, 1996.

**MACKROY WHITE** was born Oct. 6, 1948 at Memphis, TN. He attended college and various US Navy schools.

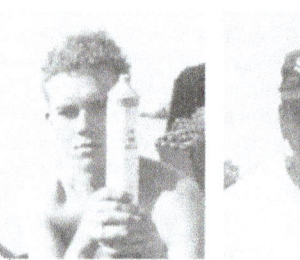

On Sept. 26, 1967, White joined the US Navy where he served with RivRon 15, ATC 151-4 and ASPB 152-4. He served at NS Rota, Spain; *USS Dale (DLG-19), USS Halsey (CG-23), USS Ramsey (FFG-2), USS Puller (FFG-23), USS Curts (FFG38),* NWS, Concord, PA. He was in various campaigns before retiring on March 31, 1988 at GM1 (E-6).

His memorable experiences included getting caught in the tail-end of a B-52 bombing and the mining of T-151-5.

**EVERETT R. "BLOND SQUID" WIEDERSBERG** was born Dec. 24, 1948 in Chicago, IL. and attended some college.

On May 16, 1967 Wiedersberg joined the US Navy. He served with Mobile Riverine Force Monitor 112-1 (Feb. 2, 1968 to Jan. 12, 1969) and *USS Orion AS-18.* He took basic training at San Diego, CA, was at Balboa Naval Hospital,  at Coronado, CA; Mare Island, CA; RVN, Norfolk, VA. He arrived RVN during "Tet '68" reported as trainer on M-112-1 and went to CuaViet River where they were mined March 28, 1968. Sent to Da Nang deep water piers for boat repair then back to DMZ and then back to Delta and finished tour. He achieved the rank of GMGSN (E-3) by discharge on March 19, 1970.

His most memorable experiences were the Bob Hope Show (Dong Tam) on Dec. 28, 1968; mining of M-112-1 and Artillery from NVN on March 28, 1968; RPG's; B-40 rockets; bullets whizzing past ears! During his career he received the National Defense Service Medal, Presidential Unit Citation, Combat Action Ribbon (Vietnam), Vietnam Campaign Medal, Vietnam Service Medal, and Navy Achievement Medal with Combat "V."

Wiedersberg has three children; Kristen, James and Timothy. He has five grandchildren: Chelsea; Rebekah; Morgan; Alisha and Bradley. His civilian employment included being a IRS tax adjuster, custodian, cab and school bus driver, warehouse laborer, painter, welder, store clerk, writer, poet, construction, fast food assistant manager, hotel/motel manager/night clerk/auditor/security, deliverer, collector, gas pumper, carpenter, car salesman and stockhandler. He medically retired in 1981 due to four back surgeries, has had diabetes for two years and neck surgery, PTSD and heart attack on May 20, 2003.

## NORM WILKINSON,

Sergeant (E-5), was born Aug. 16, 1945 at Wilmington, DE. He attended two years of college. Joined the Army Aug. 31, 1966 and was stationed at Fort Jackson, SC for basic training; Fort Lewis, WA for AIT; Fort Ord, CA; Vietnam, Fort Bragg, NC and Fort Dix, NJ as training instructor.

Assigned to Co. B 4/47th Inf., 9th Inf. Div. In Vietnam. Sgt. Wilkinson was discharged Aug. 30, 1972. His awards include the National Defense Medal, Good Conduct Medal, VCM, VSM w/Device, Expert Rifle, ARCOM w/OLC, BSM w/OLC, Purple Heart w/OLC and CIB.

He is past national vice president of US Jaycees, past president DE Jaycees, member of Delaware City Jaycees, Lions Club, American Legion and MOPH and Vietnam Veterans.

He married Pat Kelly on June 20, 1970 and they live in Delaware City. Worked in purchasing over 25 years, corporate buyer, Hercules Inc.; plant buyer, CIBA Geigy; and currently purchasing agent, Wilmington Housing Authority.

## GARY "THE KID" PAUL WILLIAMS,

Sergeant E-5, graduated from Whitesboro High School, Whitesboro, NY, in 1966, and attended John F. Kennedy College, Wahoo, NE for two semesters. He volunteered for the draft March 1967, attended basic training at Ft. Benning, GA and AIT training at Ft. Polk, LA (Tigerland) which is where he established friendship with Jack Wilson. From August 1967 to August 1968, he served in B Co., 2nd Bn., 60th Inf., 9th Inf. Div. In Vietnam. He graduated from NCO Academy at Bear Cat March 1968 and was promoted June 1968 to sergeant, E5. He completed his tour as the acting platoon leader, 4th Plt.

He received the Combat Infantry Badge, Bronze Star Medal, Air Medal, Good Conduct Medal, RVN Cross of Gallantry Unit Citation and Civil Actions Honor Medal 1st Class Unit Citation. The awards he regards the most include the Valorous Unit Citation, which was received for fighting at Ben Tre City, Tet, and the Presidential Unit Citation which was received June 1968 by B Co. as the battalion's point element in the Plain of Reeds.

Sadly, he experienced the loss of his best friend, Jack, at Ben Tre. After leaving Vietnam, his last eight months were served at Ft. Carson, CO. He was involved in the project transition program which included working with juvenile delinquents at the Zebulon Pike Detention Center. That experience renewed his interest in the social work profession. He eventually attended Syracuse University for his undergraduate and graduate program, earning his masters in social work.

He has worked for 20 years assisting veterans and continues to be employed at the Syracuse Vet Center of the Veterans Administration. He has remained active in the Reserves and holds the rank of major. He is presently assigned to Ft. Hood, TX, as a social work officer.

He married Melanie Wiltse, who was employed as a RN at the VAMC. Their daughter, Melissa graduated from the University of Delaware with a dietetics major. Their son, Gary Patrick, graduated from Baldwinsville Academy Central School. For recreation, he plays softball and ice hockey. He enjoys fishing on the St. Lawrence River and plans a retirement residence in Clayton. He is proud to have been part of one of the best infantry units in history and to have had the tremendous opportunity to meet some of the nicest people; Lt. Guy Greenfield, Sgt. Gary Mack, Sgt. Jerry Pry, Lt. Louis Heil, Capt. James Foresberg, Spec. Paul Childress, Spec. William Bell, Lt. Ken Golden, Sgt. Joseph Eckert, Lt. Col. Ret. Joe Mancuso. He says there are many more faces he remembers, and yet is unable to recall their names.

## OSCAR CLYDE "GUNNER" WILSON,

was born Aug. 29, 1947 at Clayton, GA. He graduated from Highlands High School, at Highlands, NC, in 1965.

On Nov. 17, 1965 Wilson joined the US Navy. He served on the *USS Eaton DD510* and with Rivron 15 Monitor M152-1. He was stationed at Norfolk, VA from February 1966 to May 1968, and with RivRon 15 June 1968 to September 1969. He took part in Operation Giant Sling Shot and Operation Sea Lords. He received the Purple Heart, Navy Achievement Medal with Combat V, Natural Defense Medal, Combat Ribbon, Vietnam Service Medal, VLM. He achieved the rank of GMG2 (Gunner Mate) E-5 by discharge on Sept. 1, 1969.

After a tour of duty with the *USS Eaton DD510* to Vietnam, he asked to be sent to the River of Vietnam. After training in Vallejo, CA and live 105 Howitzer firing at a Marine base, he landed in Saigon on his 21st birthday, Aug. 29, 1968.

He states: "We were sent to Cat Lo to outfit our boat and then to Dong Tam with the 9th Inf. After several small operations, we went out on Operation Sling Shot. It was to be the longest operations, 44 days. We fought long and hard. It was the early morning of Nov. 12, 1968, that was about 21 days into the operation, that some relief boats were coming down a river that told us five days to go 35 miles and were ambushed. A good friend, James Alexander Myers Jr., GMG2 was killed. I think he was the only death out of 82 of us who went over at the same time. He was with Rivron 13. All of the men on his boat were wounded. I was wounded Nov. 19, 1968, losing the vision in my right eye. James Name is on panel 39W lint 55 at the Wall. He was from New Harmony, IN. Gone but never forgotten. (I have been to the Wall three times.)

## ROBERT L. WILSON,

was born March 14, 1936 at Mexico, MO and graduated from high school.

On Sept. 23, 1955 he enlisted in the Navy. He served with N.T.C. G Lakes, IL; *USS Owen DD 536, USS Cowell DD 547, USS Mahan DLG 11, RTC San Diego, CA, USS Tausig DD746, USS Rupertus 851,* CCB-92-01 COMRIVRON 9, COMRIVRON 15 STAFF/COMPHIBPAC, Coronado, CA; COMNAVSURFPAC, Coronado, CA.

During his career he earned five Good Conduct Awards, Vietnam Service Medal with four Bronze Stars, Vietnam Campaign Medal with Device, Navy Commendation Medal with the letter V and Gold Star, Navy Achievement Medal with the letter V and Gold Star, Combat Action Ribbon, Presidential Unit Citation with Star, Navy Unit Commendation, Meritorious Unit Commendation, Good Conduct Medal with four Stars, China Service Medal, National Defense Service Medal, Armed Forces Expeditionary Medal, Vietnam Service Medal, Republic of Vietnam Campaign Medal, Navy Expert Rifleman Medal, Navy Expert Pistol Shot Medal. V = Received under combat conditions. Gold Star = Second Award. Wilson achieved the rank of GMGC – E7 by date of discharge on June 15, 1976.

His memorable experience, he says, "We were ambushed just south of the Crossroads. Being the Boat Captain on *CCB 92-1*, I was somewhat responsible for accommodations. We quite often had Senior Officers onboard; including RIVRON 9 (Commander Ferguson). With no "head" facilities, we constructed a small privy of 2x2 pine board and wrapped a poncho around it; in which we placed our bucket and rope. I asked my 2nd Class Engineman to procure a commode seat form the *USS Benewah's* "head." In this ambush we took a B-40 from Starboard Quarter which passed through 2-5 gallon cans of water; striking our privy. All that remained were splinters of wood and a small piece of the lid which I have as a souvenir today.

Robert and wife, Donna L Wilson, have two children, Alan Jean and Christina Anne and three grandchildren, Elizabeth, Michael and Catherine. Wilson retired in 1998 from maintenance in Mexico Public Schools.

**GARY ALAN "WINK" WINGER,** was born Feb. 18, 1950 in Mayville, ND and received his B. A. Buss. Admin. At Mayville State University.

On Nov. 18, 1968 Winger enlisted in the Navy. During service he received basic training at San Diego, CA and served with YFU 56 NSA Danang, *USS Sphinx,* ARL 24 Outside Repair. He also attended naval schools at Great Lakes and various locations in California. He served two years in-country, the first year up north and the second year in the Delta.

During his career received the National Defense Service Medal, Vietnam Service Medal, Vietnam Campaign Medal and Combat Action Ribbon. He had achieved the range of EN 2 E-5 by discharge on Nov. 16, 1971.

His memorable experience was the NSA Danang Fleet of YFU's and LCU's ran over 1500 sortier from Dong Ha I CTZ to Danang redeploying the 3rd Marine Division and elements of the 1st Marine Aircraft Wing in Operations Keystone Eagle and Keystone Cardinal. Our mission was to get the Marines safely down river and then on to Danang. We were constantly under the threat of hitting mines, the mine sweeps did an excellent job. We received a Unit Citation for our job well done.

Winger and wife, Jacqueline, have two children, Kami Danner and Brooke Winger, and one grandchild, Chance Danner. Gary is presently employed as City of Mayville City Auditor.

**HENRY "HANK" W. WINSTON,** was born Dec. 9, 1943 at Richmond, VA. He completed 12 years of school.

In October 1964, Hank joined the Navy and served in New London, CT; *USS Essex CUS9,* River Assault Squadron Nine, Isibella P. R., MCB-62 Gulfport, MS, Navy Recruiting Command, Richmond, VA, *USS Welch PG-92,* ACU-2, Little Ck., VA, *USS Nashville LPD-13,* Sima, Norfolk, VA, and served in Vietnam from May 1968 to May 1969, serving with the US Army 9th Infantry Division out of Dong Tam.

During his service, he received the Presidential Unit Citation, Republic of Vietnam Armed Forces Meritorious Unit Citation, Gallantry Cross with Palm and one Gold Star, National Defense Medal, Navy Commendation Medal with Combat V and two Gold Stars, Vietnam Campaign Medal, Vietnam Service Medal, Combat Action Ribbon, C/C 16 Rifle Expert Medal, Sea Service Ribbon, Navy Unit Commendation, Navy Expeditionary Medal, Humanitarian Service Medal, Fifth Good Conduct Award and Enlisted Surface Warfare Specialist Breast Insignia. He had achieved the rank of Senior Chief Boatswain Mate by date of discharge in March 1987.

Winston's memorable experiences included being Boat Captain of Assault Support Patrol Boat 92-3. Trying to help the South Vietnamese people. They were against the Viet Cong Communists and what they stood for. My rank at this time was Boatswain Mate Second Class.

Hank is single and working as Mechanic II at Chesapeake General Hospital.

**LARRY ALLEN "REBEL" WISEHEART,** was born Dec. 17, 1947 at Birmingham, AL. In 1966 he graduated from Decatur High School, Decatur, AL, attended Boston University in Boston, MA and in 1987 graduated from Northeastern University, Boston, MA with a BS in Accounting. He also received additional education at Salem State College, Salem, MA.

On March 24, 1967 Wiseheart was inducted into the US Navy. He served on *USS Coral Sea (CVA-43),* an attack aircraft carrier, with the Mobile Riverine Force ATC's (Tango boats) at Dong Tam, and COMNAVFORV at Saigon, Vietnam.

During his service, he received the Armed Forces Expeditionary Medal (Korean) Pueblo Incident, Navy Unit Commendation First and Second Awards, The Vietnam Service Medal with Bronze Stars, The Republic of Vietnam Campaign Medal, the Purple Heart (Dong Tam), Republic of Vietnam Defense Commemorative Medal, Overseas Service Commemorative Medal, Combat Service Commemorative Medal, US Navy Commemorative Medal and US Armed Forces Retired Service Commemorative Medal. He had achieved the rank of Yeoman 2nd Class (E-5) by the time of disability retirement on June 10, 1970.

He states all of his service time was memorable; from the firefights in the delta and offshore landing to living and working in Saigon as an office clerk working for Admiral Zumwalt; to the beautiful liberty ports throughout the Pacific to the homecoming in San Francisco. Then the heartbreaks of returning to an angry and nonsupporting society.

Married to Helen D. (Frost) Wiseheart since Sept. 27, 1973 with five children: Lorene Ann (Monahan), Gretchen Lee, Justin Sinclair, Timothy Michael and Larry Allen II; plus my dearest granddaughter Kaylee Ann Monohan.

Wiseheart is presently the Postmaster, Prides Crossing, MA located within Beverly, MA, birthplace of the US Navy, and has worked for the postal service for over 30 years. His retirement date was Dec. 17, 2002.

**GREG WITT, RD2,** was born on March 7, 1947 in Oak Hill, WV. Graduated from Fayetteville, WV High School and attended Marshall University.

Enlisted in the US Navy in September 1966 and attended basic training at Great Lakes, IL. During his enlistment he served aboard the *USS Whitfield County LST 1169, USS Washoe County LST 1165, USS Weis LPR 135, USS Hampshire County LST 819 and USS Gallup PG 86.* These commands were assigned to Task Force 117, River Squadron 9 of the Mobile Riverine Force. As part of these operations he spent time in-country Vietnam during 1967, 1968, 1969 and 1970. He earned the Combat Action Ribbon, Navy Unit Commendation, Meritorious Unit Commendation, National Defense Service Medal, Vietnam Service Medal with five stars, Vietnam Gallantry Cross Unit Citation and the Republic of Vietnam Campaign Medal. He was honorably discharged in July 1970.

**KENNETH J. WOOD,** was born Oct. 21, 1949 at Westerly, RI. After high school he received his B.S. in Criminology.

Wood enlisted in the Army on June 6, 1967 and served with C/3/60th from February 1968 to June 1969, MACV Command, June 1969 to June 1970, C/3/60th M.R.F., MACV – Sniper IV Corp. he took part in the Tet Offensive/ Tet Counter Offensive/ Phase IV VN Counter Offensive/ VN Counter Offensive Phase V/Vn 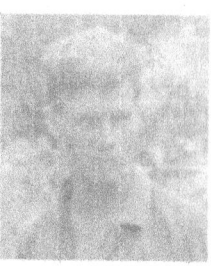 Counter Offensive VI, Tet 69 Counter Offensive, VN Summer – Fall 69/VN WIN Spring 1970/VN.

During his service, he received the NDSM/ VSM/RVNCM/VNCM/Silver Star/Bronze Star with V 2 AWD/ARCOM with 2 WD/ CT. B./ AM 3 AWD/ GEMDL , Presidential Unit Citations. Before being discharged on June 16, 1970 he had achieved the rank of SSG-E-6.

Wood is not married but worked for the Federal Government, retiring on Dec. 1, 2000.

**LORENZO A. WRIGHT,** USN, BM3, born Sept. 28, 1943, El Sobrante, CA.

Graduated from Phoenix High School 1966, joining the Navy in September as a "Kiddie Cruiser." I went from boot camp in San Diego to VT-27 NAS Corpus Christi, TX, as an Airman. I transferred to Seaman and performed duties as leading Chief Yeoman, and then to 1st Lieutenant Yeoman. September 1968 I received orders to "NIOTC" (Naval Inshore Operations Training Center) at Mare Island, Vallejo, CA. I received three months of training for River Gunboats, which included a week of gunnery school and a week of "SERE" (Survival, Evasion, Resistance, and Escape) training at Warner Springs, CA

I departed from Travis Air Force Base January 1969 to Tan Son Nhut Airport, Saigon. Flew down to Dong Tam in a C-130 aircraft and assumed duties with River Division One Eleven, on an Armored Troop Carrier "Tango 111-13" as a .50 caliber and .20 millimeter gunner. Late June of 1969 I was transferred to River Division 131.

Major campaigns included "Giant Slingshot" among a number of others.

Some memorable experiences were: firefights, night ambushes, transporting 9th Infantry into "God Forsaken Places," and cruising the rivers and canals of the Mekong. A few kilometers from the Cambodian Border, up past Tay Ninh in August 1969, our boat was protecting the canal side of an Army Fire Support Base. I participated in and experienced the many sights and sounds of a nighttime attack on the base, that was so intense, it required the assistance of Spooky," a C-135 aircraft with two .30 caliber Gatlin guns, to help ward off the NVA. Scary and awesome.

I left Vietnam January 1970 and was discharged from the Navy at Treasure Island, CA.

I was awarded the following: Navy Commendation with Combat "V," Presidential Unit Citations, Navy Meritorious Unit Commendation, Navy Unit Commendation, Combat Action Ribbon, National Defense Service Medal, Vietnam Service Medal, RVN Gallantry Cross, RVN Civil Actions Citation, Vietnam Campaign Medal, and Good Conduct Medal.

After leaving the service, I operated heavy construction equipment for 14 years, then 18 years working for the government. Was married once and have a 30-year-old son, Jason Alexander Wright. I'm now retired and reside in Central Oregon.

*Aerial view of the River Assault Flotilla One flagship, USS Benewah (APB-35). (Courtesy of S.C. Skaggs.)*

# ROSTER

*The following list includes both members of the MRFA and all known Mobile Riverine Force Personnel.*

Danny P. Abbott – USS Benewah
Richard A. Abbs – T-152-3
Tillman J. Abell, Jr. – 3rd/60 Infantry
Gordon H. Aber – ComRivRon 11
Karl Ackerman – A-132-4
John C. Adame – E-3 3rd/60th Infantry
David T. Adams – USS Benewah
Floyd R. Adams – T-91-11
Fred H. Adams – USS Askari
Joe E. Adams – B Co. 2nd/47th Infantry
Marshall G. Adams – D Co. 3rd/47th Infantry
Odis E. Adams – B Battery 3rd/34th Arty
Robert L. Adams – APL-30 and YRBM-16
Stanley Adams – RivDiv 92
Stephen A. Adams – HHC 9th Signal Bn and 3rd Bde 9th Div
John C. Adams, ENC, USNR – USS Park County
Ernest Addicott – 544 TC (MB)
David Addis – A Btry 3rd/34th Artillery
William K. Adkins – RivRon 13 M-131-1
William Adkison – USS Sphinx
Charles A. Adler, Jr. – PCF-36, PCF-98
George E. Adrian – A-1 5th/60th Infantry
Wendell G. Affield – T-112-11
William L. Agredano – C-2 3rd/47th Infantry
Marvin C. Aho – USS Tom Green County
Richard C. Aiello – T-151-6
Anthony M. Aiken – WPB-82301 Pt. Caution
Thomas F. Aiken – A-1 4th/39th Infantry
Mike Aitchison – USS Benewah
James H. Akers – CosDiv 13, PCF-36 and 98
Ronald W. Albee – C Co. 4th/47th Infantry
Roger H. Albers – M-151-2
David B. Alderman – A Co. 3rd/39th Infantry
Capt. Donald M. Alderson, USN (Ret) – CO, USS Colleton
Edward R. Aldrich – B Co. 720th MP Bn
Dennis R. Alexander – T-131-13
H. M. "Murk" Alexander – CO RivDiv 132
Jim All – YRBM-17
Charles R. Allen – T-151-2
Greg Allen – USS Nueces
Robert W. Allen – RivRon 9 Z-92-11
Roderick C. Allen – USS Askari
William K. Allen – HHC 2nd/47th Infantry
Terry L. Allen, Sr. – B-1 3rd/47th Infantry
Dan A Allers – MineRon 11, Det A
CWO Jimmie R. Allison, (Ret) – HHC 2nd/47th Infantry
Jack V. Allred – RivDiv 531
Maj Louis J. Almond, Jr., USA (Ret) – 3rd/34th Artillery
Michael T. Alogna – PCF-51
John R. Alphin – RivDiv 131
James P. Alspaugh – HHC 9th Infantry Division
David R. Altman – USS Benewah
Thomas T. Alvarado – B-4 6th/31st Infantry
George Boats Amador – USS Iolulina
Ray Ambrozy – C Co. 3rd/60th
Stephen M. Amorso – RivDiv 512
William R. Amos – 4th/47th Infantry
John P. Anamosa, LCDR, USN (Ret) – YFUs 63 and 71 NSA Danang

George Anastasion – 9th Infantry Division
Thomas J. Anathan – USS Benewah
Daniel I. Anders – B-2 3rd/60th Infantry
Martin Andersen, Jr. – 9th Signal Bn
Alan R. Anderson – AIRCOFAT, Saigon Det.
David L. Anderson – HQ 4th/47th Infantry
Donald E. Anderson – D Co. 15th Combat Engineers
Martin E. Anderson – ComRivRon 13 and 15
Michael E. Anderson – USS Tortuga (LSD-26)
Michael J. Anderson – 101st Airborne
Ronald R. Anderson – RivRon 13
Stanley F. Anderson – Z-151-3
Edward F. Andrews – B Co. 2nd/47th Infantry
Dale E. Angdahl – USS Benewah
Edward Angel – T-111-8
Allen P. Angell, CPO USN (Ret) – ComRivFlot One Staff
James B. Angermeier – A-111-5 and M-111-2
James F. Annel – C-1 4th/47 Inf.
Daniel M. Anthony – IUWG-1 Unit 2
Frank E. Anthony – D Co. 3rd/60th Infantry
Donald A. Antonovich – M-91-1
Robert J. Apostolos, Jr. – B-1 4th/39th Infantry
Jack D. Applegate – A Co. 3rd/39th Infantry
Jeffrey R. Applegate – USS Vernon County
William J. Arbogast – T-131-5 and RAID-72
Daniel D. Arden – USS Satyr ARL-23
Harold V. Arden – C Co. 2nd/47th Infantry
Charles E. Ardinger – T-151-11
LT Charlie Ardinger, Jr. – Associate
Walter A. Ardison, Jr. – A-153-48 and A-153-49
David L. Argabright – D Co. 2nd/60th Infantry
Samuel Argote – 3rd/60th Infantry
Leslie C. "Les" Arkle – T-151-6
G. Edward Arledge – USS Indra
Francis P. Armentani – 2nd/47th Inf
Dennis W. Armstrong – C-112-1
James Armstrong – A-111-8
John J. Armstrong – HHC 3rd/47th Infantry
Joe P. Armstrong, USN (Ret) – RivDiv 543
Richard B Arnold – A Co. 3rd/47th Infantry
Michael Art – A Co. 4th/39th Infantry
Patrick A. Artz – T-91-8
Stanley P. Arvin – A-2 2nd/47th Infantry
Gilbert R. Arvizu – T-151-3
Danis Ashberger – 1097th TC (MB)
Dale E. Ashley – USS Monmouth County LST-1032
Frederick Ashling – USS Satyr
William H. Ashton, Sr. – USS Monmouth County
Joseph A. Ashworth – T-112-10
Charles Asta, Jr. – USS Benewah
Dale E. Atherton – C-1 4th/47th Infantry
John Attaway – USS Windham County
Hugh M. Atwell – HHC 4th/47th Infantry
D. Jerry Aubuchon – NSA Da Nang
Derrell W. Aud – C-1 3rd/47th Infantry
Richard Augustyniak – E Co. 3rd/60th
Rodger T. Auld – T-112-9
Donald J. Austin – HHC 2nd Bde 9th Inf Div
Lloyd W. Austin – D Co. 4th/47th Infantry
Dale Avery – E Co. 2nd/60th Inf

Lyle C. Avery – HHQ Batt 3rd/34th Artillery
John Ax – C-2 2nd/47th Infantry
Carl Ayres – A-91-6
Dean W. Ayres – 709th Main Bn and 99th Combat Support Bn
Dennis J. Bacanskos – 11th Trans Bn
Warren Bacciocco – Special Boat Unit XXII
Christian Bachofer – ComRivDiv 92
Robert Bachstadt – B Co. 3rd/60th Infantry
William H. Back – 2nd/47th Infantry
Karl A. Bacon – B-3 3rd/60th Infantry
Thomas K. Bacon – 4th/47th Infantry
Dennis L. Bacon, Sr. – RivRon 15 A-151-21
Arthur "Art" Badger, Sr., USAF (Ret) – R-132-1
Terry Bafus – Navsupact An Thoi
Michael H. Bailey – RivDiv 532
Quentin L. Bailey, ENC – USS Caddo Parrish
Robert T. Bak – Z-132-2
Bobby Baker – M-131-2
Donald L. Baker – B Co. 3rd/47th Infantry
Dwain C. Baker – USS Jerome County
Dwayne Baker – B Co. 9th S&T
George J. Baker – SEAL Team 1, Det. G
Luther G. Baker – USS Tutuila ARG-4
Robert W. Baker – USS Tom Green County
Ronald L. Baker – T-91-10
Tom Baker – USS Magoffin
Wayne R. Baker – USS Page County
E. I. "Wynn" Baker, Jr. – USCGC Ingham (WHEC-35)
E. H. Baker, Ph.D. – HHC 2nd/47th Infantry
Lt. George E. Baker, USN – T-151-2
Ronald L. Bakert – APL-26
Ralph J. Bakle – A-132-8 and M-152-1
Gary L. Bales – USS Monmouth County
Terry J. Balfe – B-4 3rd/60th Infantry
Peter Bali – B Co. 3rd/60th Infantry
David J Ball – HCU-1
Franklin D. Ball, USN (Ret) – RivDiv 512, 515, and 594
John Ed Ballard – A Co. 3rd/47th Infantry
Dennis Ballentine – A-111-2
John R. Balliet, III – RivDiv 153 A-54
Robert E. Balls – C-91-1
Ronald J. Baltierra – HHC and B Co. 2nd/47th Infantry
Robert Bambury – USS Henrico
Michael J. Ban – 4th/39th Infantry
John B. Banack – USS Bradley
Floyd R. Banbury, USN (Ret – USS Colleton
Michael Bancroft – Co. B 1st Platoon 4th/39th Inf
Preston R. Banks – HHC 3rd/47th Infantry
LCDR Paul E. Banks, USN (Ret) – APL-26
Charles A. Baran – HHC 9th Infantry
Bill Barber – USS Harnett County
Franklin D. Barbour – B Co. 2nd/60th Infantry
Plumer M. (Mitch) Barden, Jr. MSG USA (Ret) – Co B 3rd/60th Infantry
Dale F. Bare – C-131-1
Dale R. Bareis – B-2 3rd/47th Infantry
Paul B. Barger – T-152-13
John E. Bargman – 2nd/47th Inf
Raymond G. Barker – NSA Saigon, YRBM-17

Roy E. Barley – E Co. 50th LRP
Steve Barnaby – B-2 4th/39th Infantry
David M. Barnas – B Co. 6th/31st Infantry
Brice H. Barnes – B Co. 2nd/47th Infantry
Don Barnes – USS Clarion River LSMR 409
James E. Barnes – Amphib Scouts and Raiders
Michael Barnes – 2nd Bde 3rd/47th Infantry
Wayland E. Barnes – USS Colleton
William M. Barnes – C-2 4th/39th Infantry
Col Paul Z. Barnes, USA (Ret) – HHC and B Co. 3rd/39th Inf.
Gary W. Barnett – B-2 3rd/47th Infantry
Edmond Barnett, III – 4th/39th Infantry, Bearcat
Gerald E. Barney – A-1 9th Signal Bn
Robert M. Barnhill – USS Mercer
Walter P. Barnick – NSA Det Dong Tam
Art Baron – ComRivFlot I
Barry Baron – D-2 4th/47th Infantry
John B. Barousse – USS Clarion River
Isaac Barraza – A Co. 3rd/34th Artillery
James M. Barrett – CosDiv 13, PCF-23
Terry G. Barrix – A Co. 6th/31st Infantry
Herbert P. Barron, Sr. – A Co. 3rd/39th Infantry
Walter G. Barrus, Jr. – USS Garrett County
Charles K. Barry – 1st Plt 15th Engineers
Edward L. Barth, Jr. – USS Krishna
Stanley A. Bartkewicz – B Btry 3rd/34th Artillery
Virgil D. Bartolomucci – B Co. 2nd/47th Infantry
Dwight J. Barton, Jr. – C-2 2nd/47th Infantry
Hershel V. Barton, USN (Ret) – COMRIVFLOT-ONE DET
Jack Barwick – R-112-1
Anthony J. Basile – Harbor Clearance Unit 1 YLLC-2
William Baskin – RID-45
Col Dennis A. Bassett – A Co 3rd/60th Infantry
Phillip R. Bateman Photography – B Co 4th/47th Infantry
William M. Batson, Jr. – HHC 4th/47th Infantry
Carmine Battista – USS Askari
Douglas Bauer – USS Windham County
David J. Bauer, Sr. – USS Benewah
John H. Bauler – C-1 4th/47 Infantry
Larry A. Bauthues – APL-30
Ronald J. Baving – T-92-9
LTC Lawrence W. Bayer, USA (Ret) – XO, 3rd/60th Infantry
Rudy Bayersdorfer – HHC 2nd Bde 9th Infantry
Ronald E. Bayes – USS Askari
Ronald R. Beach, Sr. – USS Satyr
Claude P. Beal – B-1 4th/39th Infantry
Terry Beall – USS Luzerne County
James H. Bean – USS Page County
Raymond D. Beard – LST-1009 and LSM-102
Tom Beaster – USS Westchester County
John Beaumonte – D Co. 4th/47th Infantry
Patrick D. Beaver – Coastal Squadron 1
John Beck – B Co 3rd/60th Infantry
Capt. John J. Becker, USN – CosDiv 13
Cliff C. Bedell – USS Mercer
Paul G. Bednarik – 4th/47th Infantry
Bob Beecroft – USS Tioga County and IUWG-1
Harry E. Beerman – USS Benewah
John E. Beerman – 3rd/47th Infantry
Jere Beery – USS Westchester County
William Befort – B-1 4th/47th Infantry
Gary J. Begin – A-4 3rd/60th Infantry
Walter J. Begley – A-1 4th/47th 2nd Brig
Frank R. Begovich – CO B Co. 2nd/47th Infantry
William R. Behm – TF-116

Larry L. Behrens – C Co. 9th Signal 9th Infantry
Norman A. Belanger – U.S. Navy
William Belden III – E Co. 6th/31st Infantry
James Belec – Wilhoite DER 397, Lowe DER 325
Mike Belisle – Z-151-1
Corwin A. Bell – River Assault and Interdiction Division
Dewey B. Bell, Jr. – M-92-1
Paul E. Bellmore – USS Hickman County and FMF HM3
Boedean Belt – A Co. 3rd/60th Inf
DeWayne Beltran – D Co. 3rd/60th Infantry
Angel Benavides – D and A Co. 3rd/60th Infantry
Gery Benedetti – T-112-2 and T-112-6
Jack R. Benedick – C Co. 4th/47th and 3rd/60th Infantry
LCdr. Albert H. Benge – ComRivDiv 92
Edwin Benjamin – PCF-103
William B. Benko – A Btry 3rd/34th Arty
Steve Benner – D Co. 6th/31st Infantry
Tom Bennett – RivDiv 512, PBR-8102
Clyde R. "Bob" Bennett, Jr. – HHC 2nd/47th Infantry
James Bennett, Jr. – HQ Co. Support Cmd
Thomas F. Bennis – ComRivFlot I
Daniel R. Benoit – C-3 3rd/39th Infantry
Frederick Benson – B-2 2nd/39th Infantry
Patrick H. Benson – 3rd/47th Infantry
Richard Benson – USS Brule
Clarence Bentson – C Co. 2nd/60th Infantry
Tony Benz – C-3 9th Signal BN
Bonifacio C Bercero – USS Askari
Richard V. Bergling – NSA
Ernie M. Bergman – USS Windham County
Rick G. Bergman – C-3 2nd/47th Infantry
Henry W. Bergman, II – C Co 3rd/34th and 3rd/60th Inf.
James W. Bergstrom – 6th/31st Infantry
Albert J. Berhalter – A Co. 2nd/60th and 3rd/47th Inf
Mike Berkemer – USS Benewah
Jerald G. "Jerry" Bernhardt – A Co. 3rd/39th and 3rd/60th Infantry
Capt. Pete Bernier, USNR (Ret) – RivDiv 112
Miguel O. Berry – C Co. 3rd/47th Infantry
Rodney L. Berry – T-92-5
Dale Bertsch – HHC 2nd/60th Infantry
Ernest A. Berube – B Co. 2nd/39th
Lawrence P. Besmer – USS Satyr
Bud Bessey – USS Askari
Paul D. Bessler – USS Benewah APB-35
Harold Best – USS Satyr
LCDR Dale S. Betz, USN (Ret) – USS Krishna
Bill Bevington – USS St. Francis River
Rodger W. Beyer – USS Hunterdon County
Jim Beyersdorf – U.S. Navy
Wesley A. "Wes" Bickel – A-1 2nd/47th Infantry
Bernard F. Bickford – RivDiv 153
Donald E. Bickhart – RivDiv 91
Dan Biddle – 2nd Bg 3rd/47th Infantry
Ira V. Biddle – RivDiv 92 Staff
Dennis J. Bieak – IUWG-1 Unit 2
Fred A. Bieniasz – Rivsec 512
Ralph H. Bigelow – T-131-8
James C. Biggs – USS Tioga County
Charles Bigley – B-2 2nd/47th Infantry
Larry J. Billinger – A Co. 3rd/60th Infantry
Rick Bills – APL-55
Robert C. Billstein – U.S. Coast Guard
John F. Bina – River Assault Squadron 13

Donald Bisaillon – STABRON-20, Boat 2407
Courtney "Curt" Bischoff – 9th Inf Div DISCOM Support Command
Robert Bischoff – Cdr A Co. 4th/47th Infantry
Bruce D. Bisely – A-111-7
George K. Bissett – RivDiv 571 PBRs
Larry Bissonnette – River Division 593
David J. Bittell – USS Colleton
Stephen Bivins – 3rd/60th Infantry
Charles L. Black – A Co. 3rd/39th Infantry
Danny Black – 3rd/34th Arty
James B. Black – 3rd/60th Inf
William F. Black – A-2 3rd/60th Infantry
SSG David L. Black, USA (Ret) – A Co 3rd/39th Inf 9th Inf Div
Edward L. Blackledge – A Co. 3rd/60th Infantry
Larry Blackman – USS Clarion River
LTG Paul E. Blackwell, Sr. – Cdr D Co. 3rd/60th Infantry
Lawrence W. Blair – C-2 3rd/47th Infantry
Robert B. Blair – USS Clarion River
Francis E. Blake, Jr. – Recon Plt 3rd/39th Infantry
Thomas Blakley – CosDiv 13, PCF-98
John Blakney – 2nd/47th Artillery
Robert C. Blanchard, USN (Ret) – RIV PAT FLOT 5 Staff
James R. Blanchette – USS Jennings County
John S. Blanchfield – D Co. 4th/47th Infantry
Donald J. Blankenship – A-111-3 and A-152-21
LTC Joseph R. Blatnica, USA (Ret) – B Co. 9th Med BN
Nick Blazek – HQ 2nd Bde 9th Infantry
Col. James H. Bledsoe, USA (Ret) – 3rd/60th Infantry
Ronald C. Bleemer – USS Floyd County
Wayne H. Blessing – A Co. 2nd/39th Infantry
Gary R. Blinn – PCF-97
Larry Bloemer – 2nd/47th Infantry
John M. Blondell – C-4 4/47th Infantry
Michael W. Blum – T-112-6
Lawrence P. Blumette – USS Blanco County
Ronnie Lee Boal – NSA Da Nang
Mark T. Boatwright – 9th MP Company
Roger L. Bobby – USS Haverfield
Ralph E. Boblitt – RivRon 11
GMG2 Fred L. Bock – USS Benewah
Wayne T. Bodey – USS Nueces
Roy H. Boehm – SEAL Team 2
Richard C. Boespflug – RivRon 9
Patrick Boffa – PBR
Walter Boffalow – C Co. 2nd/47th Infantry
Barry Bogart – PCF-72, 94, 36 and 5
Jerome H. "Jerry" Bogart – USS Tom Green County LST-1159
Wayne N Bogart, USN (Ret) – USS Colleton APB-36
Thomas R. Bogner – 2nd/39th Infantry
William Bohlen – T-111-10
David W. Bohmer – A Co. 3rd/60th Infantry
Raymond L. Bohn – River Division 153
Edward J. Bohrer – USS Hickman County
John H. Boldt – A-1 3rd/47th Infantry
Maj/General Lucien Bolduc, Jr. USA (Ret) – CO 3rd/47th Infantry
Lynn Bolen – MACV
Gary W. Bolin – RivRon 521
William V. "Bill" Bolin – USS Indra ARL-37
John W. Boling – IUWG-1 Unit 2
Ron Boller – Naval Advisor RAID-75

Rick Bolt – USS Sphinx
Robert Bolton – D Co. 3rd/47th Infantry
Tim Bompiani – T-131-1
Larry J. Boneck – USS Nueces
Bill Bonno – NSAD Qui Nhon
James K. Booher – A Co. 2nd/47th Infantry
John R. Booher, Jr. – A Co. 2nd/60th Infantry
Johnnie Booker – 3rd/47th Infantry
David Boone – 1097th TC (MB)
Robert R. Borchard – USS Sphinx
Dennis E. Borlek – RivDiv 112
James T. Born – Mobile Support Team Two
Dennis R. Bornhoft – USS Benewah
Jose M. Borrero – NAVSUPPACT, Da Nang
Charles W. Bort – IUWG-1
Dwight Bosselman – C-91-1
Lexie Boswell – RivDiv 111
Richard "Dick" Botelho – C Co. 5th/60th
Jacques Boulanger – M-91-1
Wayne H. Boulette – USS Colleton
James E. Bound – USS James Cowens
Louis G. Bousquet – RivDiv 542, PBR-95
Rick Boutcher – A-91-3
John K. Bowen – B-4 3rd/47th Infantry
Donald E. Bowers – C Co. 3rd/60th Infantry
Mark Bowers – RivSect 544
Byron O. Bowlou – Assault Craft Unit One
Fred M. Bowman – USS Colleton
Robert Bowman – D Co. 3rd/47th Infantry
Richard A. Boyce – C Co. 2nd/39th Infantry
Arthur E. Boyd – 5th Trans Bn, LCU-1507
Leo Boyd – NavSupAct Dong Tam
Ronald D. Boyd – B-2 3rd/60th Infantry
Roy L. Boyer – IUWG-1 Unit 3, Qui Nhon
Glen Boyette – T-112-11
Mitchell Boyette – USS White River LSMR-536
Dennis Boyle – USS Benewah
Tom Boza – 9th Inf 9th Sig MARS
Wayne "Brad" Braastad – RivRon 11 A-112-2
Tom R. Brabeck – ACU1 LCU 1485
Dennis Bracall, Sr. – RN 103
Kenneth H. Bracy – ComRivRon 9 - Det A
Edward D. Bradac, Jr. – T-91-1
Raymond H. Bradbury – USS Nueces
Bob Bradford – B-3 3rd/60th Infantry
Larry G. Bradley – YRBM-17
Robert Bradley – 3rd/34th Artillery
Van Bradley – USS White River LSMR-536
John T. Brady – NSA Danang and HCU-1
Michael M. Brady – A-111-1
Philip X. Brady – A-92-1
Thomas J. Brady – B-2 3rd/47th Infantry
John Bragg – C Co. 2nd/60th Infantry
Thomas L. Bragg – U.S. Navy
Donald Bramley – D Co. 15th Combat Eng.
Roy B. Branch – HHC, 4th/47th Infantry
Anthony H. Brand, Jr. – MSB Det. Alfa
Eric J. Brandeberry, Sr. – 1097th TC (MB)
Bruce T. Branigan – D Co. 3rd/60th Infantry
Patrick Brannon – A-112-2
David L. Branstetter, MAC, USN (Ret) – T-48
Randall D. Brassie – B-2 2nd/60th Infantry
Donald Brath – C and HQ Co 3rd/47th Infantry
Larry A. Bredahl – 3rd/60th Infantry
Thomas J. Breidel – R-92-2
Alan F. Breininger – CSO RivDiv 91
Cecil V. Breland – RivDiv 92
Jud (Joe) Breland – USS Colleton
Edward T. Brennan – E Co.(4) 3rd/60th Infantry
Larry Brennan – A-112-5

Lawrence J. Brennan – DaNang Harbor Security
William L. Brennan – USS White River
Greg Brenner – A-91-5
Edmund K. Brewer – HHC 3rd/47th Infantry
E. C. Brewer, Jr. – RivDiv 153 ASPB-13
Michael G. Brewton – 2nd/60th Infantry
Richard E. Bridgewater – C Co. 4th/47th Infantry
Sammy J. Brieden – HHQ 9th Infantry Division
Andrew M. Brigante – Co. C 2nd/39th 9th Inf Div
James W. Brinker – 199th Infantry
Lonnie E. Brinker – PCF-71 and PCF-24
Tim Brinkley – A-3 2nd/39th Infantry
Wayne F. Brinton – USS Iredell County
William "Bill" Brinton – Co. B 4th/47th Inf
Edward H. Brisbois – Amphib Attack Boats WWII
Peter Brisette – T-91-11
James H. Brittle, USN (Ret) – USS Benewah
Lewis R. Britton – NSA Det Dong Tam
Robert Brock – USS Askari
Stan Broda – T-91-13
Stephen E. Brodell – River Sect. 521
MR2 Craig J. Bronish – USS Benewah
Daryl D. Brookins – USS Benewah
Dale K. Brooks – USS Satyr ARL-23
Jerry D. Broom – USS White River and USS Tom Green County
Donald P. Brosnan – 2nd Brigade CSM
Hank Brote, Jr. – Naval Advisory Group
Robert A. Brower – PBR 458 Cat Lo SVN
BMC John E. Brown – T-92-4
Charles E. Brown – Co. A 3rd/47th Inf
Charles R. Brown – USS Benewah APB-35
David A. Brown – USS Tom Green County
David W. Brown – A-91-7 and RivRon 9 Staff
Douglas Brown – 1097th TC (MB)
Eric V. Brown – RivRon 153
Estel R. "Dick" Brown – A Co. 2nd/47th Infantry
Gary Brown – A-131-2
J. C. Brown – 15th Engineers E Co.
J. C. Brown – RivDiv 13 A-131-5
James A. Brown – T-91-7
James E. Brown – RivRon 5 Sec 512 & USS Garrett County
James J. Brown – C Co. 6th/31st Infantry
James S. Brown – C-3 3rd/60th Infantry
James T. Brown – Co. A-2 1st/15th Combat Eng
Jay S. Brown – USS Washtenaw County
Kenneth L. Brown – A Co. 3rd/60th Infantry
Leroy L. Brown – CO HHC S-4 2nd/47th Infantry
Melvin T. Brown – B-1 4th/47th Infantry
Peter A. Brown – IUWG-1 Unit 3, Qui Nhon
Rev. Daniel A. Brown – USS Madera County
Richard W. Brown – D Co.15th Eng and 3rd/47th Inf
Stephen V. Brown – YRBM-17
Terry L. Brown – USS Hampshire County LST-819
W. Ray Brown – A-112-6
William T. Brown – B Troop 3rd/5th Cav
James A. Brown, Jr. – RivRon 13, BC, T-131-2
GMGC Kenneth J. Brown, USN (Ret) – USS Askari
GMGC Warren Brown, USN (Ret) – T-152-7
Lcdr Larence H. Brown, USN (Ret) – RivDiv 513 and 552
John F. Brownell, Jr. – B-3 3rd/47th Infantry
Gary D. Bruch – RivDiv 153
Ray Bruder – USS Krishna
Coleman Brumley – USS White River
Patrick Brumm – 9th Infantry Division

Jack A. Brunet – HHQ 3rd/39th Infantry
Gary C. Bruno – USS Benewah
Oliver L. Bryan – B Co 4th/47th Inf
Jimmy R. Bryant – RivDiv 591
Kenneth V. Bryant – B-3 2nd/39th Infantry
Kermit E. Bryant, Jr. – USS Whitfield County
MGen Walter J. Bryde, Jr. – HQ 3rd/34th Artillery
Floyd H. Buch, Jr. – C Co. 3rd/60th Infantry
Terry Buchanan – RivDiv 111
Woodrow Buchanan – A-2 3rd/60th Infantry
William R. Buchannan – B-3 3rd/60th Infantry
Curtis Buck – A Co. 2nd/47th Infantry
Kenneth A. Buckley, USA (Ret) – 9th Infantry Division
Clayton L. Buettner – Z-151-1
Bill Buffie – DesRon 21
Charles J. Bugajsky – C Co. 3rd/47th Infantry
Dean B. Bugenhagen – T-111-6
Robert Bukoski – D Co. 2nd/60th Infantry
Allen Bullock – USS Vernon and USS Tom Green County
Jerry Lee Bullock – A-111-7
Roy A. Bumgarner – USS Askari
Dempsey L. Bumpass – Stab Boat Sqd-20
Robert P. Buono – A-1 2nd/47th Infantry
William J Burcroft – USS Benewah
Michael A. Burden – USS Monmouth County
William R. Burge – USS Benewah
John S. Burger – USS Washoe County
Robert A. Burgette – USS Benewah
James D. Burk – C Co. 2nd/39th Inf
James W. Burke – 1097th TC (MB)
Michael Burke – 45th IPSD - Scout Dogs
Timothy Burke – A Co. 2nd/47th Infantry
John J. Burke III – USS Nueces
Timothy M. Burket – USS Colleton
Larry E. Burkett – 1097th TC (MB)
Richard M. Burkhart – 3rd/47th Infantry
Harold L. Burlage – T-131-10
Gerald W. Burleigh – RivRon 13, T-27
Daniel W. Burmeister – C-3 3rd/60th Infantry
Claude Burnett – A Co. 9th Signal Bn
Ralph W. Burnette – A Co. 4th/47th
Carroll E. Burns – 9th Admin Co.
Lionel Burns – YRBM-16
Michael P. Burns – A-112-3
Richard H. Burns – HHC 3rd/60th Infantry
Joseph E. Burns, Jr. – HHC 4th/39th Infantry
Capt. James Burpo, USN (Ret) – CO USS Washtenaw County
Douglas M. Burrell – HHC 2nd/47th Infantry
David E. Burt – RivDiv 112
CAPT Thomas E. Burton – CSC/NAU Vung Tau
Van Burum – 2nd/39th Infantry
John A. Burvis – B Co. 3rd/60th Infantry
Louis Buscareno, Jr. – B Co. 3rd/60th Infantry
Lennie Bushek – E Co. 3rd/47th Infantry
Lauren L. Bushnell – C Co. 4th/47th Infantry
Gerald O. Busic – USS Garrett County
Luis R. Bustos – A Co. 3rd/39th Infantry
Joseph A. Butchart – HQ A Co. 15th Engineers
David A. Butcher – AGMR-2
Allen R. Butler – IUWG-1 Unit 4
Sgt Ronald W. Butler – A Co. 3rd/60th Inf
William "Nelson" Butler – B Co. 2nd/47th Infantry
William Butler, III – 2nd/60th Infantry
David K. Butler, Sr. – M-112-1
Randy Butt – USS Sphinx and USS Mark
Robert C. Byram III – CosDiv 13
James J. Byrnes – LCM-P7713

William F. Byrnes – A-1 4th/39th Infantry
Thomas G. Byrnes, III – Operation Seafloat
Larry M. Byrom – D Co. 2nd/47th Infantry
Philip A. Byrum – B-3 3rd/60th Infantry
Danny Ray Cable – USS Washtenaw County
Alfred M. Cady, III – USS Benewah
Paul W. Cagle – RivDiv 532
Terry R. Calandra – D Co. 4th/39th Infantry
Charles Allen Caldwell – Costal River Squadron 1
Robert W. Caldwell, Jr. – USS Nye County
Anthony J. Caliari – C-3 4th/47th Infantry
Gary Callender – A Co. 3rd/60th Infantry
Albert M. Calloway – 2nd/39th Infantry
Richard J. Calton – Recon Plt 2nd/47th Infantry
G. Thomas Calvin – B-3 3rd/60th Infantry
Joseph V. R. Camara – T-111-8
Dave Camarca – T-92-2
Bruce Cameron – USS Washtenaw County
Cary M. Camp – USS Bulloch County
Jerry Camp – USS Mercer
David R. Campbell – USS Satyr
Patrick D. Campbell – B Battery 3rd/34th Field Artillery
Ronnie E. Campbell – T-91-8
Terry Campbell – 9th MP Battalion
Tom Campbell – USS Mercer
Tommy J. Campbell – HHB, 9th Infantry
Victor H. Campbell, III – USS Benewah
Paul F. Campbell, Jr. – C Co. 3rd/34th Artillery
Walter Campbell, Jr. – RivDiv 512 PBRs
BM1 Charles Campbell, USN (Ret) – M-92-2
CDR Horace J. Campbell, USNR (Ret) – USS Litchfield County
Frank Campese – RivRon 13
David M. Campione – USCG Cutter Point Mast
Stephen J. Campodonico – USS Benewah
Capt. Davis S. Cangalosi, USN (Ret) – CTF-117 Staff
Doyle Cannon – T-91-3
Larry T. Canut – B-2 2nd/39th Infantry
Donato F. Capasso – M-131-1
Jonthan B. Capece – 4th/47th and 3rd/39th Infantry
Anthony J. Caravello – A Co. 2nd/47th Infantry
Hector J. Cardenas – USS Carronade
Joseph Cardone, Jr. – B-3 3rd/60th Infantry
Richard L. Cardoos – B Co. 3rd/47th Infantry
David A. Carey – 9th Signal Bn
James D. Carey – T-132-6
Robert R. Carey – M-111-2
David W. Cargill – HHC 9th Infantry Division
Frank A Carlson – NSA Saigon Cat Lo
Paul D. Carlson – Mortar Plt 4th/39th Infantry
Robert W. Carlson – Battery B 2nd/4th Artillery
Col. Gerald Carlson, USA (Ret) – 6th/31st Infantry
RADM William C. Carlson, USN (Ret) – USS White River
George Carlstrom, Jr. – A Btry 3rd/34th Arty BN
Larry E. Carlton – T-91-4
Lee R. Carmean – USS White River LSMR-536
Mark K. Carmichael – USS Clarion River
David Carmicheal – USS Sphinx ARL-24
Paul Carnes – USS Colleton
Jerry Carpenter – Vung Tau
Kenneth C. Carpenter – USS Whitfield County
Raymond Carpenter – T-111-2
Robert C. Carpenter – RivDiv 552
Alan H. Carpien – STAB Squadron 20

William C. Carr – NavSecGruDet Saigon
Dan Carrell – T-91-4, A-92-6 and A-6841
SFC John M. Carrico, USA – HHC 21st TSC
Douglas M. Carrington – USS St. Francis River LSMR-525
Angel M. Carrion – M-112-2
Edward I. Carroll – HHC 2nd Bdg Avn Section
James J. Carroll – 1097th TC (MB)
Tom A. Carroll – HHC 3rd/60th Infantry
Joe Carson – 2nd Platoon 9th MP Co.
Dennis W. Carstens – Field Plt - 9th MP Co.
Alvin L. Carter – Co Co. 4th/47th Inf
John A. Carter – B Co. 3rd/60th Infantry
Lonnie W. Carter – A Battery 3rd/34th Arty
Robert E. Carter – B Co. 2nd/47th Infantry
Thomas R. Carter – 1099th TC (MB)
William K. Carter – YRBM-16
Arthur G. Carter, USN (Ret) – YRBM-17, Dong Tam
Gregory L. Carthew – YRBM-16
Darrell Cartmill – M-131-2
Ernest Cartmill – A Co. 5th/60th Inf
James J. Caruso – A Co. 4th/47th Infantry
GMG2 Steve Carvey – USS White River
Norman J. Case – EOD Team 48
Bill Casey – 3rd/39th Infantry
Claude M. Casey – B-3 3rd/60th Infantry
William J. Casey – HQ Co. 4th/39th Infantry
Charles M. Cashmore – USS Nueces
Frank O. Cason – B-3 3rd/39th Infantry
Leal R. Cason – USS Mercer
Michael J. Cassidy – 9th Infantry Division
Edward (Sonny) Castellano, Jr. – A Co. 4th/47th Infantry
Joe Castiglia – D Co. 2nd/47th Infantry
Jesus "Jesse" Castillo – Co.C and E 3rd/47th Inf
Edward Q. Castle, USN (Ret) – COMRIVFLOT ONE
David A. Castleman – A Batt 1st/11th Artillery
Victor E. Castonguay – T-92-8 and T-47
Norman J. Catelli – C Co. 2nd/47th Infantry
Constantine J. Caterini – A-111-6
YNC A. C. Cates, Sr., USN (Ret) – USS Krishna
Robert J. Cathcart – HAL-3 Seawolves
Duane Catherman – NavDet Danang - Dong Ha
R. Lynn Catron – NSA Da Nang
William F. Catron – River Sect. 513
Max E. Catt – USS Canopus
Richard J. Caucutt – 4th/47th Infantry
John Cavano – USS White River LSMR-536
SSG Tom Center, USN (Ret) – T-91-4 and TF-115
William R. Cessna – USS Askari
Gerald Chamberlain – A Co. 3rd/47th Infantry
Gregory D. Chambers – USS Tutuila ARG-4
Craig L. Champion – D Co. 3rd/47th Infantry
Rock Champlain – USS Boston
Gerald M. Champney – T-132-3
Richard Chan – NSA Dong Tam
Melvin W. Chandler – C-1 3rd/47th Infantry
Michael G. Chandler – USS Park County
Roy Chaney – 15th Combat Engineers
Jim (JR) Channel – RivDiv T-92-12
Gerald B. Chapman – USS Colleton
Mancell Chapman – C Co. 3rd/60th Infantry
Rick J. Chapman – Z-111-7
Ronald J. Chapman – USS Satyr
Thomas Chapman – USS Satyr
Ronnie E. Charles – B-2 4th/39th Infantry
Joseph E. Chassereau, Jr. – USS Parsons

HMC Norman W. Chatman, USN (Ret) – USS Colleton
Gilbert B. Chavez – T-132-12
Howard Chemikoff – USS Reclaimer
Cleve Chick – E Co. 4th/47th Infantry
Milton P. Chick – 9th Admin Co.
Eldridge C. Childress – HHQ 2nd Brigade
Thomas A. Childress – USS Krishna
Capt T. V. Chiomento, Jr., USN (Ret) – USS Mercer and USS Askari
Bernard J. Chismar – 4th/47th Infantry
Sanford "Sandy" Chotiner – B Co. 3rd/47th Inf
Donn E. Christensen – C Co. 3rd/60th Inf
Chris Christian, USN (Ret) – USS Colleton
John P. Chrzanowski – A Co. 4th/47th Infantry
Pasquale Cicarelli – YRBM-16, NSA Ben Tre
Arthur Ciccarelli – A Co. 6th/31st Infantry
Edwin Cintron – M-91-1 and T-91-4
LeRoy Ciscon – A Co. 2nd/60th Infantry
George D. Clancy, Jr. – NSA Danang - NSF Danang
Mike Clarahan – USS White River
Joseph Clarino – HQ Co. 2nd/47th Infantry
Bob Clark – RivDiv 153 and RID-47
Greg Clark – A/D Co. 86th Combat Enginer BN
Harold Clark – USS Benewah
Michael H. Clark – A Co. 4th/39th Infantry
Robert P. "Bob" Clark – NSA Tan My
Stephen W. Clark – 3rd/47th Inf and APL 26
Vaughn T. Clark – A Co. 3rd/60th Infantry
CDR Charles W. Clark, Jr. – CO USS Monmouth County
Philip J. Clark, Jr. – T-132-1 and T-132-2
David A. Clarke – HHC 2nd/47th Infantry
Amida N. Claude – T-112-5
Robert "Bob" Clausen – C-3 3rd/60th Inf
Norman G. Clavet – A-92-2
Dennis L. Clay – A Co. 9th Avn BN
John H. Claybrook – HHC 2nd/47th Infantry
Danny G. Clayson – YRBM-20
Eugene Cleary – A-1 3rd/47th Infantry
Richard L. Cleaves – 1097th TC (MB)
Thomas W. Cleland – TF-115
Thomas M. Clemens – 4th/47th Infantry
Leroy "Clem" Clement – AIRCOFAT CRB Det TSN
Lt. Tom Clement, USN – T-152-12
Darrell Clevenger – USS Brule
Robert L. Cline – USS Caddo Parish
Frank A. Clouse – T-92-4
David C. Clutch – C-91-1
Thomas C. Coate – D-1 6th/31st Infantry
Elbon L. Cobb – T-92-2
Charles W. Cobb, Jr. – USS Krishna
SGM Patrick F. Cochrane – T-112-4
Stan W. Cockerell – C-2 4th/47th Infantry
Richard R. Cockrell – M-91-2
Daniel L. Coe – USS Krishna
James C. Coe – A Co. 2nd/47th Infantry
Gary L. Coffin – USS Windham County
GMG1 Gregory Coffman, USN (Ret) – RAS 13 T-131-5
Dan Cohen – M-111-2
Harold Cohn – USS Hunterdon & Harnett County
Ronnie Cohorst – T-131-9
David R. Colbert – YFR-889 - Nha Be
Wayne Colbree – T-92-4
James R. Coleman – PBR-512 and PBR-531
Johnnie A. Coleman – CTF-117 Staff
Roger L. Coleman – 2nd/4th Art and 3rd/39th
Ronald D. Coleman – D Co. 15th Engineers

129

George H. Coleman, III – 544th Trans Co.
Brian Collage – T-112-11
Kenneth V. Collie – USS White River
Reuben W. Collier, Jr. – ComRivFlot One Det Dong Tam
Alfred Collins – T-151-11
Brian Collins – C Co. 2nd/47th Infantry
Floyd T. Collins – T-91-6
John Collins – M-91-1, T-91-3 and Z-92-11
Michael L. Collins – YR-71
Thomas L. Collins III – C Co. 2nd/47th Infantry
CAPT John P. Collins, Jr., USN (Ret) – CO/CSO RivDiv 92
RADM Robert M. Collins, USN (Ret) – CTF-117
Herbert P. Colomb, Jr. – USS Benewah
James A. Colombo – CosDiv 14, PCF-43, PCF-44
Sgt Charles A. Colon, USA (Ret) – C Co. 2nd/60th Infantry
Ronald L. Columbus – T-132-12
Kevin Comp – LST 825 and LST 601
James A. Compton – A-111-3
Rodney E. Compton – B-1 3rd/47th Infantry
Wes Compton, USN (Ret) – USS Satyr
David Conant – USS Mercer
Robert B. Conaty – XO - RivDiv 131
Dean Conaway – T-132-16
Mike Conder – 2nd/47th Infantry
BMCM (SW)Ted W. Condiff, USN (Ret) – T-112-4
Orval W. Conine – 9th Inf 4th/47th Infantry
Andrew C. Conklin – 3rd/39th Inf
Col. John C. Conlin, USMC (Ret) – XO 2nd Bde 9th Infantry
Charles John Connell – CosDiv 11 "Seafloat"
Lee J. Connell, Jr. – C Co. 4th/39th Inf and HHC 2nd/60th Inf
Michael B. Connolly – RivRon 13 River Assault Div 132
William Conrad – USS Sphinx
Thomas Conroy – C-3 4th/47th Infantry
John J. Considine – B-1 1st/31st Infantry
Richard T. Coogan – B and A Cos. 9th Inf 15th Combat Eng
Gregory W. Cook – B-1 3rd/47th Infantry
Jack H. Cook – PCF-102
Kerry P. Cook – C-3 3rd/47th Infantry
Larry D. Cook – 3rd/47th Infantry
Randall G. Cook – USS Monmouth County LST-1032
Thomas L. Cook – PBR Mobile Base I
Martin W. Cook, Jr. – D Co. 3rd/60th Infantry
Clinton D. Cookson – A Co. 3rd/60th Infantry
Robert Allen Cooley – RAID 72 ATF 211
Robert H. Coombs – USS Washtenaw County
Patrick K. Cooney – A Co. 3rd/60th Infantry
Bennie L. Cooper – HQ Co. 3rd/47th Infantry
Clarence G. Cooper – River Section 511
Gene R. Cooper – USS White River
Joel S. Cooper – T-131-5
Jon B. Cooper – NSA Da Nang
Wayne A. Copas – T-92-10
Robert S. Copeland – E/75 Inf RGR (ABN) 3rd/9th Inf Div
Dale G. Coppins – A-1 2nd/47th Infantry
Gary E. Corbett – C Co. 6th/31st Infantry
Glen Corbett – C-3 3rd/47th Infantry
James V. Corey – 1097th TC (MB)
Barry R. Cormier – A-3 3rd/60th Infantry
LtGen John H. Corns, USA – HQ 2nd Bde
Richard L. Corrick – R-112-1
Joe B. Cortinaz – B Co. 5th/60th Infantry

Giles T. Corum – B Co. 4th/47th Inf
Chuck Cosgrove – HAL-3 Seawolves
Salvadore I. Costa – M-92-1
Clarence R. Cottrell – 4th/47th Infantry
Mike Coughlin, Sr. – USS Whitfield County LST 1169
James Coulson – LST 603 and 1073
Edward L. Courtois – A Btry 2nd/4th Artillery
Bernard L. Couturier – D-3 3rd/60th Infantry
Gary L. Covey – A-132-3 and Z-131-1
John R. Cowan – A-2 2nd/47th Infantry
Ronald G. Cowan – USS Carronade
Guy J. Coward – B Co. 2nd/47th Infantry
Thurman Coward, Jr., USN (Ret) – ComRivFlot One Staff
Ronny E. Cowart – M-112-1
Richard "Dick" Cowden – YRBM-21
Stafford Cowles – E Co. 4th/47th Infantry
Austin L. Cox – C Co. 9th Medical
Charles Cox – Commander, RivDiv 111
Fred Cox – IUWG-1
Richard Cox – Coastal Division 11
Col Laddie M. Cox, USA (Ret) – CMDR S-4 B Co. 4th/47th Inf.
Charley Crabtree – A Co. 2nd/60th Infantry
Richard J. Cragg – USS Merrick AKA 97 RivSec 532
Gail T. Crago – B Battery 3rd/34th Arty
Robert Crago – NSA DaNang
James B. Craig – HQ Co. 2nd/47th Infantry
Stephen H. Craig – B-3 3rd/47th Infantry
William Crain – A Co. 3rd/47th Infantry
William F. Crain – World War II
Irving P. Cramer – M-91-2
Mike Cramer – C Co. 4th/47th Infantry
Steve Crandall – YRBM-20
William A. Crane – NavSpecWarGru 2
Sam Crawford – USS Satyr
Steven A. Crecy – E Co. 15th Eng BN
GMGC Thomas D. Creel, USN (Ret) – RivDiv 15
Pete Crellin – USS Sphinx
Joseph F. Criscione – LCU-1499
Paul S. Crisp – B Co. 3rd/60th Infantry
Ronnie Crisp – 9th Infantry
LtGen George A. Crocker, USA (Ret) – C-3 3rd/47th Infantry
Lynn Crockett – C Co. 4th/47th Infantry
Roger K. Crofford – A-111-6
Dave Cronin – RivDiv 512
Bernard Crook, LCDR, USN (Ret) – IUWG-1 Unit 4 (Nha Trang)
Daniel P. Crossley – 5th TC (HB)
LTC Richard E. Crotty, USA (Ret) – HHC 3rd Bde, 9th Infantry
Dennis L. Crouch – IUWG-1
Charles Crouse – APL 26
Sandy Crowder – 2nd/60th Infantry
David L. Crowell – USS Jerome County
Larry J. Crowley – River Division 92
J. Kevin Crowner – USS Colleton
Harry G. Croy – HHQ 1st BDE 9th Inf. Div.
Nicky Cruz – E Co. 2nd/39th Infantry
Ben Cueva – PCFs
Walter R. Cullen – Z-152-1
BMCM (SW) Gene Culligan, USNR (Ret) – RAS 9 RivDiv 91
James D. Culverhouse – USS F. E. Evans
Gary A. Cunningham – D Co. 3rd/60th Infantry
William "Budd" Cunningham – IUWG-1, WesPacDet Unit 3

William A. Cunningham – A Co. 3rd/60th Infantry
Stephen M. Cupp – USS Iredell County
Barry E. Curbow – IUWG-1 Vung Tau
J. Scott Curran – A-112-2 and M-112-1
Hugh C. Curran, CDR USNR (Ret) – USS Askari and RivFlot 1
Francis X. Curran, III – USS Tutuila
William J. Currier – HSB 3rd/34th Arty
John Curry – T-131-11
William Curry – 4th/47th Infantry
Barry W. Curtis – USS Tom Green County
Don Curtis – SCRF DaNang
Richard W. Curtis – NSA An Thoi (APL 21) & Can Tho (APL 30)
Vern L. Curtis – HSAS Saigon and Chu Lai
Jerry H. Curtis, Sr. – ComRivRon 11 M-111-1
Alan R. Cusick – USS Tom Green County
LCDR Michael J. Cusick, USN – M-92-2
David Czech – B-3 4th/47th Infantry
Allan Czecholinski – USS White River
Howard Czoschke – USS Park County
William R. Dabel – C-1 3rd/39th
Larry E. Dahl – D-1 4th/47th Infantry
Richard Dahl – 3rd/60th Inf
Forrest W. Dahlstet – PCF-32, PCF-69
David R. Daigh – USS Askari
Joe W. Dale – USS Satyr
Orville L. Daley – USS Askari ARL-30
Robert F. Daley – 3rd/39th and 4th/47th Infantry
Stephen Dall – YR-71
Richard A. D'Aloisio – TF-211, Dong Tam
Stanley Dameron – B-3 3rd/39th Infantry
David V. Damits – B Co. 4th/47th Infantry
Peter Danchuk – USS Windham County
Tom Dandurand – USS Askari
H. E. Dan Danford – T-111-3
Jerry E. Daniel – T-131-12 and T-131-9
R. L. "Dan" Daniels, USN (Ret) – NSA Da Nang and NSA Nha Be
William E. Danner, Jr. – HQ 4th/47th Infantry
William G. Dargavel – M-91-2
EN1 Henry E. Dassler – C-91-1
Robert C. Datres – USS Colleton
Robert E. Daubenspeck – APA-37
David Davey – RivRon 15
Michael David – 6th/31st Infantry
Robert D. Davids – USS Mark AKL-12
John W. Davidson – USS Brule
Albert Davis – A-111-2
Andrew T. Davis – IUWG-1, Unit 3, Qui Nhon
Charles R. Davis – USS White River
Dale K. Davis – RivDiv 512 and 543
Donnie W. Davis – B Co. 2nd/60th Infantry
Gregory S. Davis – 2nd Bn 11th Marine Reg
James H. Davis – C-92-1 and T-92-2
Merrill Davis – USS Askari
Michael R. Davis – USS Colleton
Richard B. Davis – B Co. 15th Combat Eng.
Ricky Davis – A-1 3rd/47th Infantry
Robert E. Davis – M-112-2
Ronald L. Davis – C-151-4
Wesley G. Davis – USS Terrell County
Troy D. Davis, CSM USA (Ret) – Hq 2d Bde/9 Sig
Patrick B. Davis, Jr. – C-132-1
Rolland H Davis, Jr. – A Co. 3rd/39th Infantry
MAJ Wilbert Davis, USA (Ret) – B Co. 3rd/60th Infantry
SFC David J. Davis, USA (Ret) – HQ and C Co. 3rd/60th Infantry

Lt John D. Davis, USN (Ret) – PCF-80 and PCF-19
Frank A. Day – T-151-4
Terrence De Gelder – 5th/60th Infantry
Juan De La Garza – 2nd/60th Infantry
Frank De La Oliva – Harbor Clearance Unit One
Peter De La Pena – C-3 3rd/60th Inf and UDT-B (H) LRRP
Joaquin De Leon, Jr., USA (Ret) – E Co. 3rd/47th Inf
Louis J. De Old – B-1 3rd/60th Infantry
Edwin A. Deagle, Jr. – 2nd/60th Infantry
James Dean – USS Wexford County LST-1168
John R. Dean – B-2 3rd/60th Infantry
Ralph L. Dean – USS Nueces
Rudolph Dean – NSA Det Cat Lo
Robert DeAndrea – STABRON 20
James H. Deason – A Co. 2nd/60th Infantry
Newton B. Deavenport – HHC 2nd/39th Infantry
Carl J. Decker – USS Sproston (DD-577)
Ronald K. Decker – YRBM-9, Vinh Long
Michael T. Deckman – USS Garrett County
Donald R. Dedon – A-92-8
W. John Deegan, III – C-132-1 and Z-132-2
Michael B. Deffendoll, Jr. – USS Colleton (APB-36)
Warren H. Degen – RivRon 15 Z-151-1
Charles J. Deitz – USASupComm
Mark Del Maestro – LCU-1477
Stephen Del Rossi – USS Mercer
Patrick Del Rosso – RivRon-13 and 15
Max J. DelaCruz – C Co. 3rd/47th Infantry
Terry Delaney – USS White River
Emmett A. Delgado – RivRon 9 T-92-6
Wayne Delk – 9th Div D Co. 3rd/60th Inf
Eugene S. Delleart, Jr. – B Co. 3rd/60th Infantry
Michael Dellerson – USS Satyr
Charles R. DeLong – 2nd/47th Infantry
Buddy DeLuce – USS Sedgewick County
Anthony J. DeLuna – 1st Armored Cavalry
Eugene "Bud" Demetriou, Jr. – USS Nueces
Rodney Den Hollander – A Co. 3rd/47th Infantry
Edward E. Den Hollander, Jr. – C-1 3rd/47th Infantry
Paul J. DeNicola   3rd/60th Infantry
Gerard Denkus – E Co. 3rd/47th Infantry
Gary W. Denning – M-132-2
James W. Dennison – C-1 4th/47th Infantry
A. E. Gene Denny – USS Jennings County
Stanley A. Denson – 3rd/47th Infantry
John A. Denue – RivRon 13 T-24
William C. Derringer – Boat Captain, T-92-12
Kenneth A. Desautels – IUWG-2 Quin Nhon
John P. Descoteaux – T-92-6
Nick L. DeShullo, Jr. – A-1 3rd/60th Infantry
CDR David A. Desiderio, USCG (Ret) – USCGC Pontchartrain (WHEC-70)
Raymond N. Desilets – 15th Combat Engineers
Gary P. DeStefanis, Sr – C Co. 2nd/60th Infantry
Frank Dettmers, Sr. BMC (Ret) – A-131-6, CCB 31, and T 54
Buddy Deuell, III – T-132-3
William E. Deutcher, Jr. – 3rd/60th Inf
Carlton DeVaughn – C-4 3rd/47th Infantry
Tom D. Devier – USS Hunterdon County
David E. Devine – C-132-1
Barry K. Devliegher – T-7 and T-51
David J. DeVour – D Co. 3rd/60th Infantry
David Dewitt – NavSupAct Dong Tam
Capt Stephen T. Dexter – APL-30

Steve L. Diano – IUWG-1 and IUWG-4
Fred A. Dias – USS Benewah
Camillo J. DiBiaso, Jr. – 2nd Brig C Co. 3 Plt 3rd/60th Infantry
David L. Dice – NSA Det Binh Thuy
Russell H. Dice – 1097th TC (MB)
Francis R. Dickerson – C-3 4th/47th Infantry
James F. Dickson – CTG 116.2
John W. Dickson – RivDiv 111
Philip L. Dieteman – B Co. 3rd/60th Infantry
Jacques Dietz – CBMU-302 Dong Tam Det.
William J. Diggins – RivRon 15, T-51
Welton B. Dillard – R-112-1
Larry Dimmitt – USS Dennis Buckley and USS Hamner
Steve D. Dimond-Smith, Ph.D. – ComNavForV Staff
Howard D. Dion – D Co. 2nd/60th Infantry
Joseph "Joe" Ditchkus, Jr. – Naval Advisory Group
Philip "Archie" Ditmars – T-91-8
Gene E. Dittamo – B Co. 4th/47th Infantry
C. Dave Divelbiss – RivFlot I Staff
Dallas Divelbiss – RivRon 15
Ronald A. Dix – River Division 512
Marty Dix, USN (Ret) – USS Page County
Roger L. Dixon – USS Pitkin County
Stephen C. Dixon – RID 40
Joseph J. Dizona, Jr. – NSA Nha Be
Lon Doaty, Jr. – RivDiv 111
William A. Dobey – USS Windham County and White River
Robert D. Dockendorff – NSA Saigon Det Dong Tam
Daniel S. Dodd – Navy Combat Photographer
James D. Dodds – Z-151-1
Michael R. Doe – Boat Captain T-91-9
Lee D. Doehring – USS Askari
James E. Doescher – A Co. 3rd/39th Infantry
James R. Doherty – USS Indra
Brian D. Dolan – A-112-3
Jay A. Dolfin – C Co. 3rd/39th Infantry
James G. Dolphus – B Co. 4th/47th Infantry
Charles A. Domicello – C 1-9 (3rd MarDiv)
Nicholas Dones, Jr. – B Co. 4th/47th Infantry
William Beatty Donham II – T-111-8
Lanny R. Donnell – 3rd/60th and C Co. 2nd/47th Inf
Michael J. Donnelly – M-91-2
Tom E. Donnery – Z-151-1
Richard F. Donovan – RivDiv-513
SMSGT Charles A. Doolan, USAF (Ret) – USS Blanco County LST-344
Patrick E. Dooley – HHC 3rd/60th Infantry
MSG Jesse T. Dooley (Ret) – 1SGT HHC 2nd Bde, 9th Inf
William E. Doolittle – T-91-8
James M. Dorland – USS Colleton and USS Hunterdon County
Phillip L. Dorn – USS Satyr
Robert J. Dorrett – B Battery 1st/84th Arty
Victor J. Doster – C-1 3rd/47th Infantry
Kenneth L. Dotter – USS Askari
ETC Donald Doubleday, USN (Ret) – USS Benewah
John W. Dow – IUWG-1 Unit 2
Mickey Downing – USS Tom Green County
Phillip B. Dowsett – M-112-1
Robert C. Doyle – NILO Ben Tre (NavForV)
Normand L. Doyon – RivDiv 554, PBR-180
David Drake – NSA Danang and YRBM-21

Richard A. Dral – B Co. 3rd/60th Infantry
Michael J. Draper – HAL-3
John Edward Driessler – 1st Platoon Bravo 2nd/47th Inf
David Driggers – T-112-6 and M-112-2
Stephen P. Drop – B-3 2nd/47th Inf
Robert Drozal – A Co. 3rd/47th Infantry
Roger B. Drucker – C Co. 9th Signal BN
Ed Drumheller – U.S. Navy, Bihn Thuy
Rodney Dubbert – USS Tioga County
Leonard Dube, SGM – 159th Trans Bn
Lawrence H. Dudley – B Co. 4th/47th Infantry
Thomas J. Duff, Jr. – 15th Combat Engineers
William J. Duggan – RAS 13 M-131-2
David DuHon – USS Windham County
George Duley – HHC 3rd/39th Infantry
Steve Dumek – IUWG-1-4, Qui Nhon
Richard E. Duncan – AIRCOFAT
Larry Dunham – IUWG-1, Unit 5
Timothy E. Dunigan – C-2 3rd/47th Infantry
Bruce M. Dunlap – USS Mark
Edward K. Dunleavy – USS Washtenaw County LST-1116
Larry L. Dunn, USN (Ret) – USS Hunterdon County
Rev. Kenley W. Dunscomb – T-111-9
Kenneth J. Dunwoody – YRBM-21
Frank Durham – St. Francis River
Johnny Durham – PCF-26
Ronald Durham – Coastal Divisions 11 and 15
Keithlin D. Durkee – C Btry 1st/11th Artillery
David R. Durling – 9th Military Int Detachment
Sherman DuRousseau – T-131-3
Robert B. Durrett – T-112-7
Barry Duschanek – T-152-2
Richard P. Dust – B Co. 709th Maint. BN
Tom "Doc" Duthie – E Co. 4th/47th Inf
Bobby D. Duvall – B-3 3rd/60th Infantry
Jimmy Dye – B Co. 2nd/47th Infantry
Bill E. Dyer – C Co. 4th/47th Infantry
Dennis L. Dyer – 1097th TC (MB)
George "Tom" Dyer, Jr. – LSTs 1165, 1170, and 1180
Robert A. Dyson – B Co. 2nd/47th Infantry
Glenn A. Eakes – T-152-13
John R. Eakin – USS Jennings County
John T. Eanes – B-2 2nd/47th Inf
Patrick J. Eardley – C-1 3rd/47th Infantry
Clayton E. East – USS Krishna
Tommie C. Easter – 86th Engineers
SGM Darrell D. Easter, USA (Ret) – B Co. 4th/47th and 3rd/47th Infantry
Ronald W. Easterday – HHC 2nd/47th Inf
Paul Eastham – T-132-11
Edgar W. Eaton – B-2 3rd/60th Infantry
Sam Eaton – YRBM-21, Nha Be
Vernon K. Eaton, USN (Ret) – HAL-3 Seawolfs
Larry R. Eberlin – IUWG-1 WESTPAC Det 4 Nha Trang
William O. Ebert – C-151-1 and T-51
Peter H. Eckhardt – 6th/31st Infantry
Jim Eder – B-3 4th/47th Infantry
Douglas N. Edgar – A Co. 4th/47th Infantry
Leon P. Edmiston – B-3 3rd/60th Infantry
Allan R. Edquist – T-92-3
Chester B. Edwards – Riv Flot 1 A-111-1
Jeffrey Scott Edwards – C Co. 3rd/47th Infantry
Ken Edwards – USS Washoe County
Ronald C. Edwards – C-2 3rd/60th Infantry
William H. Edwards – 5th Trans Co. (HB)

James W. Egan – T-92-7
John T. Ege – C Co 4th/47th Infantry
Marlin Egersten – E Co. 3rd/47th Infantry
James A. Eggers – USS Colleton
Michael R. Eggleston – T-131-3 and T-131-10
Joseph B. Ehrenhardt – 335 Radio Research Co.
Richard Ehrler – LRRP E Co. 50th ABN
Dwayne Ehrmann – M-131-2
Jay C. Eichhorn – USS Indra
Henry E. Eick – USS Clarke County
Michael J. Eigo – T-132-9
Robert J. Eikleberry – E Co. 6th/31st Infantry
Robert Eisenbaugh – C-1 4th/47th Infantry
Ron Eitel – 65th Infantry Platoon
William C. Elbert – A-1 3rd/39th Infantry
MSCM David C. Elcess, USN (Ret) – USS Colleton
Lester Eldredge – USS Washtenaw County
Capt. James D. Eldridge, Jr. – CSO/CO RivDiv 91
Edward Elias – C Co. 3rd/47th Infantry
Dave A. Elledge – A Co. 2nd/39th Recondo
Alan L. Eller – 3rd/39th Infantry
James O. Eller – C-131-1
William Eller – USS Hunterdon County
Lou Ellingson – PCF-18
Thomas A. Ellingson – APL-21
Jerry W. Elliott – RivRon 15
Keith Elliott – HHC 2nd/47th Inf
Wesley Clay Elliott – 18th MP
Christian M. Ellis – B Co. 2nd/47th Infantry
Col. Bruce H. Ellis – B Btry 1st/84th Artillery
Edward R. Ellis – B-1 2nd/47th Infantry
James Ellis – B-2 2nd/47th Infantry
John C. Ellis – E Co. 3rd/60th Infantry
Michael Ellis – A-1 4th/47th Infantry
CWO4 Robert A. Ellis, USN (Ret) – YFU-55, 66, and 76
Jerry D. Elmore – USS Hampshire County LST-819
Harold L Elson – ComRivFlot One Staff
Robert L. Elston – B Co. 2nd/47th Infantry
Steven B. Elwood – USS Brule
Al Ely, III – USS Garrett County
Cecil W. Emerson – USS Nueces
Christopher Emerson – A-112-4
G. Jake Emerson – USS Indra
Carroll E. Emery – USS Benewah
Rolf A. Emilson – HHC 2nd/47th Infantry
Edward Emond – PCF-68
Thomas J. Emperor – A Co. 2nd/47th Infantry
Allan Engel – ComRivRon 15
Kip Engel – IUWG-1 Unit 2(Skimmers)
Donald English – River Section 541
SFC Dale Englund, SFC (Ret) – B Co. 3rd/47th Infantry
William S. Ennis – IUWG-1
Olaf Entwit – USS Indra
Paul F. Erasmus – USS Askari
Edward G. Erbar – D-4 6th/31st Infantry
James R. Erickson – A Co. 3rd/60th Infantry
James W. Erickson – 9th Infantry Division
John A. Erickson – A-112-1
John W. Erickson – T-92-1
Steve Ersch – USS Colleton
Ronald K. Ertel – C and D Co. 2nd/39th Infantry
Monte R. Ervin – 3rd/39th Infantry
Raymond O. Erwin – USS Washoe County
Richard Espeland – NavSuppAct Saigon
John W. Espinoza – A Co. 3rd/60th Infantry

Valray E. Estell – USS Benewah
Mike Estes – USS Benewah APB-35
Milton Estrella – A Co. 4th/47th Infantry
Raymond D. Etheridge – RivRon 15 T-26
Ted G. Etheridge – B Co. 3rd/39th Infantry
Thomas J. Etheridge – A-92-4
Larry C. Ethridge – USS Askari
Gerald T. Eubank – HHC (G3), 9th Infantry
Col Monte G. Euler – A Co. 4th/47th Inf
Alfred Evans – NavSuppAct Danang
Denn J. Evans – USS Tom Green County
Gus W. Evans – C-151-2
Kenneth D. Evans – B Battery, 1st/11th Arty, 2nd/47th Inf
Ronald Evans – D Co. 2nd/60th Infantry
Teddy Evans – A Co. 3rd/60th Infantry
Daniel E. Evans, Jr. – B-1 4th/39th Infantry
Bill Evans, YNC Ret – USS Iredell County
Robert L. Evely, Jr. – C Co 4th/47th Infantry
Frank Everitt III – 3rd/60th Infantry
Lloyd Ewald – T-152-12
Julian J. Ewell – CO, 9th Infantry Division
Frank J. Fabian – A-4 3rd/60th Infantry
Kenneth B. Fahnestock – 3rd/60th Infantry
David Terry Fairbanks – A Co and Como Plt 4th/47th Inf
Karl Faires – HHC 2nd/47th Infantry
John E. Fairley – USS Luzerne County
George R. Falco – A-4 4th/39th Infantry
Richard M. Falda – A-112-6
Bruce W. Falkum – D Co. 2nd/60th Infantry
Dennis G. Farah – D-2 5th/60th Infantry
Jesse Farias – B Co. 2nd/47th Infantry
Anthony Farina – K Co 179th Inf 45 Div
Salvadore J. Farina – RivDiv-543
Jan M. Faron – T-91-10, A-91-2, and A-91-6
James E. Farris – USS Outagamie County
Will Farris – B-1 3rd/60th Infantry
Michael Farver – 5th/60th Infantry
Michael Fasse – Co. 3rd Plt 3rd/60th Inf
Edward J. Fast – USS Colleton
Michael O. Faughn – USS Krishna
Norman Faught – 9th Signal Bn
Billy J. Faulkner, BMC (Ret) – River Section 542
Edward J. S. Faulkner, Jr. – USS Benewah
Thomas J. Favaro – B Co. 3rd/60th Infantry
Michael Febres – C and D Cos. 3rd/47th
Gary R. Feicke – B Co. 3rd/39th Infantry
Richard B. Feinstein – Ops Officer, RivRon 9
EN3 Cliff Fejfar – T-151-4
Don H. Fellabaum, Jr. – USS Brule AKL-28
Ralph L. Fellick – B Co. 2nd/39th Infantry
James R. Felton – C Co. 3rd/60th
Garold Fencl – USS Carronade IFS-1
James A. Ferguson – USS Benewah
Lawrence C. Ferguson – T-92-5
Paul Ferguson – USS Benewah
Sam Ferguson – A Co. 3rd/47th Infantry
CDR Kirk Ferguson, USN (Ret) – COMSTABRON 20
Stephen M. Ferragamo – B Co. 2nd/47th Infantry
Joseph P. Ferrara, Jr. – CO River Division 151
Anthony "Tony" Ferrarini – B-3 3rd/60th Infantry
Louis Ferraro – USS Windham County LST 1170
Steven H. Ferris – DD-806 and MRF-514
Albert P. Festag – USS Askari
Terrence Fetters – HHC 3rd/47th Infantry
Ted F. Fetting – 9th Inf B Co. 2nd/60th Inf
Ross W. Feurt – 1097th TC (MB)
Terry L. Feustel – Z-111-7 and M-111-1

Samuel Figueroa – B Btry 3rd/34th Artillery
Ronald Fillingham – B Co. 2nd/47th Infantry
Dale E. Fincannon – D-3 3rd/60th Infantry
William M. Findlay – WPB-82316 CGC Point Mast
David Finley – River Division 571
Kenneth L. Fischer – USS Mispillion
Robert F. Fischer – HHC DISCOM
Thomas L. Fischer – USS White River
BMC William L. Fischer, USN (Ret) – River Sect 532, PBR-97
Charles E. Fishe – B and E Co. 6th/31st Infantry
Jon W. Fisher – A Co. 3rd/60th Inf
William R. Fisher – APL-26
William R. Fisher – T-132-3
William H. Fissel, III – 9th S&T Bn
Dwight E. Fitch – USS Satyr
Larry E. Fitchner – T-92-7
Glenn D. Fittro – Boat Captain, A-91-3
David G. Fitzgerald – VAW-11
Dean J. Fitzgerald – Associate
Mike Fitzgerald – E Co. 3rd/39th Infantry
William C. Fitzgerald – M-91-3
Richard J. Flagler – 1SG 3rd/60th Infantry
Michael L. Flaharty – LCU-1624
Robert F. Flaige – E Co 3rd/60th 9th Inf
Bill Flamm – RivRon 15
Charles J. Fleming – B-3 3rd/60th Infantry
Clayton Fleming – T-92-4
Samuel Fleming – A-111-4
Bob Flesey – USS Askari
Charles E. Florence – PCF-31
Edward E. Flores – A Co. 3rd/47th Infantry
James "Jim" Flores – HHQ 3rd/60th Inf
Joe W. Flynn – D Co. 3rd/60th Infantry
William C. Foddrill – A-112-8
James L. Fogarty – D-3 4th/9th Infantry
Patrick M. Fogarty – 4th/47th Infantry Medic
Jack M. Fogel – T-22, T-50, & T-51, Zippo 1
Paul L. Fogle – YRBM-20
Robert E. Foley – 458th
William R. Foley – IUWG-1 Unit 5
Carl E. Foley, USN (Ret) – Co. B 3rd/60th 9th Inf Div
DK1 Thomas F. Foley, USN (Ret) – USS Benewah
Robert Folks – C-2 3rd/60th Infantry
Eugene N. Fontaine, Sr. – D-4 4th/47th Infantry
Ronnie E. Fontenot – YRBM-16
Thomas E. Fooshee – RivDiv 532
Ron Foraker – B Co. 2nd/47th Infantry
Carl Forbes – USS Whitfield County
Russell Forbes – A Co. 4th/39th Infantry
Thomas E. Forbes – E and D Co. 3rd/60th Infantry
Ken Ford – ComRivFlot I Staff
ENC Donald D. Ford, USN (Ret) – USS Colleton
Allan W. Forde – Americal
Bruce G. Fordham – RivDiv 152 T-11 Song Ong Doc
Clinton Fordice – TF-115, Dong Ha
Halford G. Fore – 3rd/60th Infantry
Thomas G. Forrest – PCF-102
LTC James H. Forsberg, (Ret) – 2nd/60th Infantry
Lloyd Foss – USS Mahnomen County
LTC Kenneth A. Foss, Jr., USA (Ret) – CO HHC and Co. E 709th Maint Bn
George W. Foster – YRBM-21
Harold Foster – USS Guide
Joseph W. Foster – USS Hunterdon County
LCDR John A. "Jack" Foster, USN (Ret) – CTF 116 Staff

William R. Fountain – A-3 3rd/47th Infantry
Jere L. Fournier – USS Benewah APB-35
Neil A. Fovel – 3rd/47th Inf
Gordon Fowlie – USS Mercer
David K. Fox – 2nd/4th Artillery
Joseph D. Foy – D-2 4th/47th Infantry
Ricky France – B Co. 2nd/47th Infantry
Bob Frank – 2nd/47th Infantry
Edward J. Frank – T-152-49
Fred A. Frank – B Co. 2nd/60th Infantry
Ron Frank – USS Askari
John Frank, Jr. – IUWG-1 Unit-2
Herbert P. Franklin – USS Benewah
James R. Franklin – B-3 4th/47th Infantry
Paul R. Franklin – C Co. 4th/47th Infantry
Hollis G. Franks – B Co. 4th/47th Infantry
Jerry L. Frankum – A-112-7
BMCS Robert Franson – A-112-6
Terry E. Frasher – USS Benewah
William H. Frede – T-112-2
Lonnie Frederick – B Co. 3rd/60th Infantry
Gene W. Frederickson – USNH Marianas Islands
Dave Fredrick – IUWG-1 Cam Rahn Bay
James R. Fredrick – 3rd/47th Infantry
Roger Fredsall – BSU-1
Frank W. Free – RivDiv 552
Richard E. Freel – T-112-10
Grub Freeland, SFM – USS Tutuila ARG-4
Ed L. Freeman – Cdr. 9th MP Company
Manuel J. Fregoso – RivRon 15
Robert A. French – C-2 4th/47th Infantry
Theron Z. French – YRBM-17
Capt Dana P. French, Jr., USN (Ret) – ComRivDiv 112
William R. Friel – D Co. 4th/47th Infantry
Ralph J. Fries – River Sect. 543 and 535
Robert L. Frisby – B Co. 9th Medical Bn
Herman L. "Reb" Fritsch – T-92-2
Courtney L. Frobenius – B-2 3rd/60th Infantry
Capt James C. Froid, USN (Ret) – ComRivRon 9
Elmer J. Fromm – RivDiv 514
Fred Frost – E Co. 2nd/60th Infantry
James H. Frost – Coastal River Squadron 1
Daniel W. Fruge – USS Sutter County
Michael "Mike" Fry – USS Jennings County
Larry Fugh – USS Inflict MSO 456
Dan T. Fuller – RivDiv 594
James E. Fuller – C Co. 3rd/47th Infantry
Stephen B. Fuller – M-92-1
John M. Fulton – HHC 3rd/47th Infantry
LTG William B. Fulton, USA (Ret) – CO 2nd Bde, 9th Inf. Div.
Cdr. Stephen H. Fulton, USN (Ret) – OIC PCF-40, 55, 89, and 101
Ray Funderburk – PIO 9th Inf Div
James F. Fungaroli – A-151-4
Charles Furr, Jr. – USS Benewah
Tom Gabig – D Co. 2nd/60th Infantry
Edwin M. Gaertner – T-112-11
Walter T. Gage – 3rd/47th and 3rd/39th Infantry
Gerald A. Gagle – USS Tom Green County
John D. Gagliardo, USN (Ret) – USS Mercer APB-39
Neville F. "Bud" Gaines – USS Satyr
Frank L. Gale – HAL-3 Det 7 - Seawolves
Jerry D. Galinski – USS Tioga County
Lawrence Gallagher – B-1 4th/39th Infantry
James Gallas – USS Luzerne County
Vincent J. Galle – Z-131-1
Frank R. Gallegos – USS White River

Peter Gallegos – E Co. 3rd/60th Infantry
William J. Gallerie – Z-151-1
Dallas A. Gallo – IUWG-1
John C. Gallo – A-3 4th/47th Infantry
John J. Gallo – D Co. 3rd/60th Infantry
Donald B. Galloway – C Co. 3rd/47th Infantry
Philip E. Galluccio – USS Vernon County
Mario L. Gambino – B-2 3rd/60th Infantry
Rick Gandenberger – MACV
Terry S. Gander – B-2 3rd/60th Infantry
Charles Ganster – T-112-9
Arpail J. Gapol – HQ 9th Infantry Division
Geraldo Gapol – A-3 3rd/39th Infantry
Kurt Garbo – RivDiv 153 T-39
Arturo Garces – A Co. 3rd/60th Infantry
Ed L. Garcia – USS Kemper County
Horacio R. Garcia – T-91-12
Jimmie Garcia – RivDiv 132 and 152
Ron Garcia – USS Windham County
Martin M. Garcia, Jr. – B-2 2nd/47th Infantry
Ronald W. Gardner – C-132-1
Tom Gardner – B Co. 3rd/60th Infantry
Adrian C. Garibay – C-3 2nd/47th Infantry
John M. Garland – USS Tutuila
Tommy L. Garland – RivDiv 153 ASPB-41
Douglas N. Garrison – USS Krishna
Lee A. Garver – USS Benewah
Anthony J. Garvey – C-2 4th/47th Infantry
Domingo M. Garza – C Co. 3rd/60th Infantry
CSM Homer M. Garza, USA (Ret) – C Battery, 3rd/34th Artillery
Gregory L. Gass – A-91-7
Harold R. Gassert – 2nd/47th Infantry
Daniel G. Gatchell – USAMMAV Cam Ranh Bay
Ernest L. Gatchell – T-132-21
Michael L. Gates – RivDiv 533
Steve Gatts – USS Askari
Kenneth C. Gaugh – USS Clarke County
Richard Gausline – USS Benewah
Capt. James B. Gautier, USN (Ret) – CO, RivDiv 111
Lee D. Gavet – A Co. 4th/47th Infantry
LCDR William J. Gavigan, USN (Ret) – CO USS Satyr
Martin P. Gavin – USS Park County
CWO-4 Vurgel I. Gay, USN (Ret) – River Assault Division 112 T-112-13
Butch Gayhart – 5th/60th Infantry
Gerald J. Gaylord – RAS 15 and RID-42
Edward Z. Gazdag, Sr. – USS Askari
Frank C. Geddings – RivDiv 591, RivDiv 554
Michael G. Geen – 9th Inf Div 4th/47th Inf
Daniel J. Gehlhausen – A Co. 2nd/47th Infantry
Kenneth L. Geil – USS Mercer
Neil F. Geis – Costal Squadron I
Paul Gellert – USS Holmes County
James P. George – A-91-1
Paul S. George – A-112-8
David R. Georgius – AIRCOFAT
William M. Geraghty – USS White River LSMR-536
Loyd W. Gerardot – A Co. 15th Combat Eng.
John W. Gerbing – 4th/47th Infantry
Thomas R. Gerhart – M-132-1
Richard L. Gerke – USS Blanco County and USS Holmes County
Dennis A. Gershman – USS Harnett County
David A. Geschwind – USS Clarion River
Danny J. Getgood – 3rd/39th Infantry
John D. Ghee – A Co. 9th Support Bn

John W. Giaconia, Jr. – C-2 2nd/60th Infantry
John K. Gibbs – RivDiv 112 and 115 M-112-1
John L. Gibbs – NSA Saigon NavDet Nha Be
Dale Gibson – D-1 3rd/60th Infantry
Henry D. Gibson – HHC 2nd/47th Infantry
Wilmer P. Gibson – B Co. 3rd/60th Infantry
Larry Gieseke – USS Caddo Parrish
Linus F. Gilbert – HQ Co. 3rd/34th Artillery
John F. Gilhooley – USS Westchester County
Charles W. Gill – C Co. 2nd/47th Infantry
James P. Gillen – 1098th TC (MB)
James Gillespie – E Co. 2nd/60th Infantry
Johnny C. Gillespie – T-112-7, T-112-9, A-112-5
SFC Dennis R. Gillespie, USA (Ret) – C-2 3rd/60th Infantry
William J. Gilley – T-112-1
Tim R. Gillibrand – T-151-1
John L. Gilmartin – RAS 15 C-151-2
Ronald Gimbert – CosDiv 14
Andrew Gira – C Co. 6th/31st Infantry
Dennis E. Girard – T-112-10
Barney Girdner – 9th Inf. Div. MP Co.
Richard Giroir – USS White River
Roy J. Giroir – Costal Division 13
David Gisch QM2 – USS White River
Tony P. Gisclair, Sr. – PCF-56
Phillip T. Givens – T-131-8
Capt. Thomas J. Glancy, Jr., USN (Ret) – TF-117 Staff
Gary M. Glanert – USS Washtenaw County
Eugene Glasco – ATSB Hatien
James D. Glenn – USS Askari
Dan Glidden – RPG 53 Ben Luc
Thomas G. Goasa – LSMR-409
Delbert Goben – LCM-38
Keith E. Godfriaux – USS Terrell County
James R. Goepel – A Co. 3rd/60th Infantry
Rickie M. Goff – B Co. 2nd/47th Infantry
Clarence E. Goforth – B Co. 2nd/47th Infantry
Timothy S. Goins – Recon E Co 3rd/60th Infantry
Terrence E. Golden – U.S. Navy
Phillip I. Gomez – RivRon 9 A-92-4
Tony Gomez – 4th/47th Inf 9th Div
Leonard Gonzales – Recon 3rd/39th Infantry
Raymond T. Gonzales – B Co. 3rd/60th Infantry
Pete Gonzalez – M-151-1
Roberto C. Gonzalez, Jr. – D-1 6th/31st Infantry
George Good – USS Tom Green County
Dr. Larry R. Good, DDS – NSA An Thoi
Carol G. Goodman – USS Askari
Edward F. Gorczyk, Jr. – A-91-3
Edward F. Gorman – B Co 2nd Plt 3rd/60th Inf
Ron Gorman – RivDiv 91 T-91-10
Walter W. Gorr – USCGC Point Jefferson
Roger D. Gorzney – C Co. 2nd/39th Infantry
Frederick E. Gottwald – C Co. 3rd/60th Infantry
Theodore C. Graban – A-112-7
David D. Graczyk – C Co. 9th Signal BN
Robert L. Graeter – USS Harnett County
Bruce M. Graff – USS Passumpsic
Edward J. Graff – A Co. 2nd/47th Infantry
Dennis Graham – 15th Combat Engineers
George T. Graham – HHC 3rd/47th Infantry
Howard T. Graham – USS Windham County
Timothy H. Graham – T-111-10
Gary R. Grahn, USN (Ret) – A-111-7
Richard E. Grambo – A Co. 4th/47th Infantry
Ralph E. Grampp – D Co. 3rd/60th Infantry
James W. Grant – CosRivRon 2 - SBU-24
Robert C. Grant – A-1 6th/31st Infantry

133

Roy E. Grassinger, Jr. – C-2 4th/47th Infantry
Daniel H. Graves – A-111-1
Dave Graves – B Co. 3rd/60th Infantry
Francis Graves – USS Tigonderoga CVA-14
David E. Gray – B Co. 6th/31st Infantry
Donald L. Gray – Z-132-2
Edward W. Gray – A-91-8, A-92-4
Eugene W. Gray – USCGC Point League
Peter A. Gray – USS Indra
Richard L. Gray – C Co. 3rd/60th Infantry
Robert L. Gray – River Section 523
Victoria S. Gray – Coastal Group 36
Steven A. Grchan – B-1 4th/47th Infantry
Gilbert Greber – USS Benewah
John Greco – NSAD Cua Viet, YFU-63
David G. Green, Sr. – A Btry 2nd/4th Artillery
Ronald Greene – IUWG-1
Toni S. Greene – B Co. 4th/39th Infantry
LTC Mervin Greene, Sr., USA (Ret) – B Co. 3rd/60th Infantry
Milton L. Greenfield, Jr., USN (Ret) – USS Sutter County
Lawrence A. Greenhaw – USS Satyr ARL-23
Donald Greenough – A-92-2
Gilbert Greenwald – USS Askari
Kenneth Greenwell – USS Holmes County and LST 344
Jerry Greenwood – B Co. 5th/60th Infantry
Curtis Greer – C-2 3rd/60th Infantry
Joseph W. Greer – YRBM-20
Larry E. Greer – USS White River
Michael L. Gregory – YRBM-16 and YRBM-20
Ruhlin L. Gregory – B Co. 3rd/60th Infantry
Henry H. Gregory, Jr. – C-2 4th/47th Infantry
Barry E. Greiner – B Btry 3rd/34th Artillery
Paul D. Grew – T-132-2
Raymond C. Grewe – USS White River
Gerhard Grieb – A Co. 3rd/39th Infantry
Dwight A. Griffin – LST-902
Kenneth A. Griffin – USS Henrico
Robert E. Griffin – RivRon-13
Thomas R. Griffin – HQ Btry 2nd/4th Artillery
Thomas S. Griffiths – USS Satyr
Roy Grigsby – Point Defiance LSD-31
H. Glenn Grimes, Sr. – T-111-2, A-111-5, and A-111-7
Donley Grindstaff – 6th/31st Inf
William Griswold – C-91-1
Maurice E. Gritton – B Co. 3rd/39th Infantry
Lee D. Groat, Jr. – RivRon 15 T-151-1
Donald B. Groce – T-92-5 and ZIPPO 5
Richard Grodecki – USS Guide
William D. Groesbeck – RivRon 9
Ralph E. Groschen (..shen) – D Co. 2nd/60th Infantry
Richard E. Grossa – B Co. 3rd/39th Infantry
Ronald C. Grossarth – 3rd/47th Inf
Randall M. Grottke – T-91-11
Donald E. Grout – USS Benewah
Robert L. Grout – T-131-2
Marvin D. Grover – C-1 4th/47th Infantry
Ray K. Grover – C Co. 2nd/47th Infantry
Robert K. Grover – USS Tom Green County
Max F. Gruenberg, Jr. – USS Whitfield County
Thomas Ray Grune – D Co. 2nd/60th Infantry
John J. Guarnieri – River Div 151 T-34
Frank J. Gubala – A 3rd/47th Infantry
James D. Guest – T-132-2
Gerald P. Guillot – B Co. 3rd/60th Infantry
Thomas Guise – USS Sphinx

Edward Gulliksen – NSA Saigon, APL-26
BRIG. GEN. Frank L. Gunn, (Ret) – 9th Infantry Division
John Gunsch – 3rd/34th Artillery
Skip Gunther – PCF-21
Charles J. Gurey – USS White River
Karl E. Gustafson – T-131-4
Steven E. Gustuson – A-152-1
David A. Gutierrez – T-111-8 and T-151-38
Daniel E. Guy – IUWG-1 Unit 2
Louis D. (Dave) Guzdzial – RivRon-15 (Staff SK)
Nick C. Haas – USS Clarion River LSMR-409
Jerry L. Hackney – USS Benewah
Mark W. Haddow, Sr. – T-132-4
Michael C. Hadley – B Co. 2nd/47th Infantry
Steve Hadley – E Co. (Recon) 3rd/47th Inf.
William M. Hadly – BN S-3, 4th/47th Infantry
John C. Hadvance – USS Jennings County
Mike Haecker – NSA Saigon Det Nha Be
Durwood Hafenrichter – B Co. 4th/47th Infantry
Thomas Hagel – B Co. 2nd/47th Infantry
Roger D. Hager – B Co. 2nd/47th Infantry
Pat Haggerty – USS Westchester County
Gerald G. Hahn – 3rd/60th Infantry
Harry Hahn – M-131-1
Lynn Hahn – RivRon 9 A-91-6
Michael A. Hahn – USS Benewah
John T. Haidul – 15th Combat Engineers
Thomas J. Hain – B Co. and HHC 4th/47th Infantry
James E. Haines – B Co. 4th/39th Infantry
Gary P. Hale – C Co. 3rd/39th Infantry
Kenneth Hale – U.S. Navy
Jimmie Don Haley – T-131-8
LTC Noah Halfacre, USA – E Co. 6th/31st Infantry
Billy D. Hall – C Co. 3rd/47th Infantry
Herman M. Hall – RivDiv 111
Jeffrey L. Hall – B Co. 4th/47th Infantry
Keith R. Hall – 2nd and 3rd Bde, 9th Inf
Paul C. Hall – 3rd/39th Infantry
Steve Hall – 4th/39th Infantry
Thomas R. Hall – USS Satyr and Uss Krishna
CDR Daniel B. Hall, Jr., USNR (Ret) – RivFlot One
1st SGT Paul T. Hall, USA (Ret) – USS Kemper County
BG Ed Y. Hall, USA (Ret) – MACV Team 100 Rung Sat
Oliver G. Halle – CosDiv 11, PCF-70
Tom Hallinan – USS Benewah APB-35
Robert E. Halloran – USS Harnett County
Capt. William R. Halloran, USN (Ret) – CTF-117 (N2)
Douglas T. Halsted – YRBM-17
Joe Halterman – B Co. 2nd/60th Infantry
Barry W. Haltom – USS Hunterdon County
Michael A. Halvorsen, USNR (Ret) – IUWG-1 WesPacDet Unit 1
Willian F. Hamann – USS Benewah
Hubert Hamilton – USS Askari
Robert J. Hamilton, Jr. – HQ Co. 2nd/47th Infantry
Roger N. Hamilton, Jr. – USS Mark
Steve Hammell – A-152-3
David A. Hammond – C-2 4th/47th Infantry
William "Bill" K. Hammond – Naval Support Da Nang and USS Guide
Robert M. Hammond, Jr. – 3rd/34th Artillery
Robert B. Handel – HHQ 2nd/47th Infantry

Jeffie L. Hanks – USS Benewah
Richard G. Hanks – USS White River
John J. Hanley – USS Nueces
SFC Michael D. Hanmer – RivRon 13 and RivRon 153
David C. Hanna – A Co. 3rd/60th Infantry
Wilbert Hannah – USS White River
Stephen F. Hanold – B Co. 3rd/47th Infantry
David D. Hansen – Swift boats
Larry B. Hansen – A-132-2
Rev. Henry W. Hansen, Jr. – USS Washtenaw County
Fred J. Hanseroth – USS Hunterdon County
Bond R. Hanson – FMS-811 and FMS-789
Jeffery C. Hanson – T-92-12
Michael V. Hanson – A Co. 2nd/47th Infantry
John S. Hanttula – M-112-2
Wayne M. Hapgood – RivRon 15
Radie L. Harbour – RivDiv 531
Clyde M. Hardman – D-3 6th/31st Infantry
Alan E. Hardtarfer – ComRivRon 11
Ben N. Hardy – ComNavSupAct Saigon ATSB
Larry V. Hare – T-91-5, T-92-7, and T-92-9
William F. Hare – USS White River
John D. Harman – USS Oak Hue (LCD-7) and APL-26
William A. Harman – T-132-2
Bernard N. Harmon – NSA Saigon APL-55
BM3 Joseph E. Harper – USS White River
Martin Harr – B Co. 3rd/60th Infantry
Fred Harrell – C Co. 4th/47th Inf
James R. Harrell – B Co. 3rd/39th Infantry
James Harrier – C Co. 5th/60th Infantry
Robert E. Harrill – USS Jennings County
David A. Harrington – A-2 3rd/47th Infantry
George Harrington – B-3 3rd/47th Infantry
Dallas L. Harris – HHC 2nd/60th Infantry
James P. Harris – USS Satyr
Jimmy D. Harris – RivFlot I, APL-30
Mark E. Harris – 1097th TC (MB)
Michael A. Harris – T-152-1
Michael J. Harris – IUWG-1, Unit 3
Phillip Harris – HHC 4th/47th Infantry
Rod Harris – USS Clarion River
W. J. Harris – 3rd/34th Artillery
William M. Harris – A-132-10
Alfred D. Harris, Sr. – 3rd/60th Infantry
Robert L. Harris, Sr. – RivDiv 131
David L. Harrison – D Co. 9th Medical Bn
J. Albert Harrison – C-2 3rd/47th Infantry
Frank A. Hart – HQ 4th/39th Infantry
George R. Hart – 3rd/39th Infantry
Thomas R. Hart – Associate
Charles E. Hartle III – USS Tutuila ARG-4
Pat Hartley – USS Mercer
Ernest J. Hartman – C-1 4th/47th Infantry
Robert C. Hartman – C-3 3rd/39th Infantry
Bruce H. Hartshorn – C Co. 4th/39th Infantry
Elmer S. Harvey – USS Harnett County
Ray W. Harvey, Jr. – USS Clarion River LSMR-409
Charles Harvey, USN (Ret.) – ASPB-112-2 and CCB-112-1
James A. Hasselmann – C Btry 3rd/47th Infantry
Charles Hasson – T-112-10 and T-152-50
Michael E. Hasson – USS Kemper County
Wade Hasty – USS Benewah
Norman D. Hatch – USS Krishna
Robert P. Hatch – A Co. 3rd/39th Infantry
CAPT James A. Haug – C-3 5th/60th Infantry

Richard Hauner – D-3 15th Combat Eng.
Leonard L. Haverkamp – C Batt 1st/11th Artillery
Bob Hawkins – RAG-24
David M. Hawkins – T-112-8, A-112-2
Drennon D. Hawkins – Det. Cat Lo, Run
J. Bruce Hawkins – RivDiv 92
Kent W. Hawley – YRBM-20
Keith L. Hawn – C Co. 3rd/60th Infantry
Arthur Hayday, Sr. – D and A Co. 2nd/47th Infantry
Dan J. Hayden – T-91-5
Joseph L. Hayden – C Co. 3rd/47th Infantry
LTC Thomas Hayden, USA (Ret) – A-1 3rd/60th Infantry
Junious I. Hayes – HHC 2nd/47th Infantry
Thomas F. Hayes – 1097th TC (MB)
LTC Daniel P. Hayes, USA (Ret) – HQ 3rd/34th Artillery
Robert F. Haygood – 329th Heavy Boat Co.
Jerry A. Haynes – C-3 3rd/60th Infantry
EN2 Leo H. Haynes, USN (Ret) – RivDiv 594, PBR-8120
Richard W. Haywood – 3rd/60th Inf and 6th/31st Inf
David A. Hazelett – RivRon 15
Ernest R. Hazelwood – USS Krishna
Harold P. Hazen – B Co. 3rd/47th Infantry
Dave Head – B Co. 15th Engineers
Joseph R. Headrick – USS Benewah
Francis J. Headworth – RivDiv 511, PBR-111
Wilfred A. Hearn, Jr. – USS Benewah
Dutch R. Hearne – Btry A 6 MSL Bn 61 Arty
James A. Heath, Jr. – 1097th TC (MB)
Capt. Robin Heath, USA (Ret) – B Co. 3rd/47th Infantry
Everette Hebert – River Division 533
Leonard R. Heck – R-92-1
John Hecker – CosDiv 11 and 15
Leonard M. Hecker – USS Terrell County
Harold F. Hector, Jr. – B Co. 3rd/60th Infantry
John O. Hefner – A-112-1
Eugene F. Heid – C Co. 3rd/47th Infantry
Roger F. Heilpern – MRF-IO
Charles Heindel – C-91-1
Richard Heindel – RivRon 9
Dallas H. Heine – USS Tutuila
Robert C. "Bob" Heiney, MSW – APL-30 and NSA Nhu Be
Norman W. Heino – T-111-1
Henry Heintz – USS Nueces
John D. Helf – B Co. 2nd/47th Infantry
Henry J. Helgeson – USS Satyr
Lee Helle – 458th Trans. Co.
Gerald P. Heller – IUWG-1
Frank P. Hellige – C Co. 5th/60th Infantry
Eric P. Hellman – USS White River
Richard Helmick – USS Colleton
Robert J. Helms – 4th/47th Inf
Howard Helterbrand – T-132-9
Stephen L. Hemmer – USS Benewah
Dennis L. Hemphill – C Co. 3rd/47th Infantry
Donald D. Hemsworth, Jr. – T-132-25
Danny F. Henderson – Boat Captain, T-111-5
Earl T. Henderson – D Co. 2nd/60th Infantry
Dan Hendricks – B-4 3rd/60th Infantry
George Hendricks – 9th Signal Bn
James E. Henke – A Co.4th/47th Infantry
Dr. Stephen Henley – USS Benewah
Michael J. Hennessey – T-151-6
Bill Henning – 15th Engineers

Gerard L. Henningsen – AIRCOFAT
James V. Henriksen – USS Cabildo
Edward L. Henry – T-92-10
James Henry – 3rd/47th Inf
Jerry Wayne Henry – USS Sphinx
John R. Henry – NSA Binh Thay
Lt. Randy L. Henry, USN (Ret) – T-92-9
William C. Hentz III – USS Sphinx
Herbert H. Hepworth – T-91-13
Bruce D. Herbert – USS Brule
Sgt. Fredrick L. Herbert, USA (Ret) – B Co. 3rd/60th Infantry
Larry A. Hereford – A and C Co. 3rd/60th 15th Combat Eng
John Herkle – RivDiv 531, 521, and 532
Michael Hermann – T-111-10
James A. Herndon, Jr. – USS Tutuila
Phil Herr – Junk Base 36 Advisor
Thomas M. Herritage – PCF-94
Mark J. Herrmann – RivDivs 593 and 515
Nicholas J. Hesse – RivRon 11
George H. Hessenius – HQ 65th Infantry
Joseph L. Hetherington – B-2 3rd/60th Infantry
William "Bill" Hewitt – T-91-5
Bruce Hiatt – USS Benewah
Bobby Hickerson – C Co. 3rd/47th Infantry
Les L. Hickman – T-151-1
Willis M. Hickman – R-92-1
David Hicks – USS Tioga County
Thomas A. Hicks – USS Washoe County
Rudy Hicks, Sr. – A Co. 2nd/39th Infantry
Larry W. Hidbrader – USS Benewah
Bruce R. Hierstein – B-3 4th/47th Infantry
Wayne T. Higdon – USS Satyr
Gordon Higgins – RivDiv 153
Danny L. Higgins, USN (Ret) – T-91-8
Mark Higgs – USS Benewah
Henry Hild – A Co. 3rd/47th Infantry
Ronald O. Hildreth – C Battery 3rd/34th Arty
Jim Hildwine – 2nd/47th Infantry
Fred L. Hile – 2nd/47th Infantry
Richard S. Hile – ComNavForV Staff
Richard J. Hilko – B-1 2nd/60th Infantry
Carl L. Hill – T-152-1
David F Hill – HHB 9th Div Arty
Greg M. Hill – M-91-3
Jerry W. Hill – A Co. 4th/47th Inf 9th Inf Div
John H. Hill – Coastal Div 12 Swift Boats
Gordon K. Hillesland – NSA Dong Tam
Terry Hillestad – IUWG-1
Joe A. Hilliard – Boat Captain T-44
Charles Hilligoss – T-151-1
James "Jim" Hilsheimer – USS Mercer
Charles A. Hilton – A Co. 2nd/47th Infantry
Clyde A. Himes, Jr. – 2nd/47th Infantry
Randal G. Hingson – ISB Long Phu
John H. Hinkle – 2nd/47th Infantry
Lucien Hinkle – HQC 3rd/60th Inf 9th Inf Div
Denver L Hipp – RivRon 15 Staff
Gary Hite – Division 104, PCF-53
Donald W. Hobbs – B Co. 3rd/39th 9th Inf Div
Jerry R. Hobbs – 9th Aviation BN
William T. Hobdy – Co. B 3rd/60th Infantry
Alvin L. Hobgood – C-3 4th/47th Infantry
Russell K. Hocker – B Co. 3rd/47th Infantry
Bill Hodges – T-131-9
Kenneth L. Hodgkins – RivRon 13 and 15
Alan Joseph Hodgkinson – HQ Co. 3rd/60th Infantry
Robert T. Hoelle, Jr. – B-1 4th/47th Infantry

Anthony J. Hoene – IUWG-1, Cam Rahn Bay
Zehner A. Hoffman – USS Brule
John A. Hoffmann – RivRon 13 T-132-12 and 132-8
Curtis J. Hofstetter – E Co. 3rd/60th Inf
J. Thomas Hogle – C Co. 4th/47th Infantry
Michael H. Hoks – T-112-3
Kenneth L. Holcomb – E Co. 2nd/39th Infantry
Michael R. Holcomb – T-91-5
Alvah Max Holcomb, SGM Ret – D Co. 4th/47th Infantry
Ed Holcombe – USS Colleton
Henry K. Holcombe – USS Sphinx
Steven C. Holden – USS Pitkin County
Shields R. Holder – C-91-1
Bruce J. Holdsworth – USS Benewah
Donald G. Holland – USS Whitfield County
John R. Holland – 4th/39th Infantry
Tim Hollar – C Co. 3rd/60th Infantry
Norval Holley – USS Nueces
Byron E. Holley, M.D. – HHC Med 4th/39th Infantry
Robert Hollingworth, Jr. – 1097th TC (MB)
Rodney Hollowbush – C-1 5th/60th Infantry
Robert J. Holman – D Co. 2nd/60th Infantry
Bill Holmes – USS FD Roosevelt (CVA-42)
Don Holmes – Coastal Surveillance
Donald A. Holmes – 4th/47th Infantry
Leonard L. Holmes – B-2 3rd/60th Infantry
Ron Holmes – C Co. 3rd/60th Infantry
Ronald E. Holmes – B Co. 2nd/47th Infantry
Wesley Holmes – T-111-6
Edward J. Holst – HQ Co. 3rd/39th Inf
Norman R. Holst, Jr. – E Co. 2nd/39th Infantry
Tim E. Holt – B-1 2nd/47th Infantry
William E. Holt – T-132-9
RMCS James C. Holt, USN (Ret) – ComRivFlot I
Alfred L. Holtan – B-2 4th/47th Infantry
Quinton Holton, II – Cmdr Btry A, 3rd/34th FA BN
William H. Holtz – YRBM-16 PBRs 115 and 116
James (Buddy) Hood – USS White River
Joseph M. Hood – Cos. D and E 3rd/39th Inf
Harry J. Hooks – A-2 3rd/60th Infantry
John E. Hooper – RivRon 15 T-43
Galen H. Hoover – River Inter. Div 40 and 45
Madison F. "Max" Hoover – USS Askari ARL-30
Robert Hoover – T-112-13
Joseph Hope – C-131-1
Rodney H. Hope – ACV 903 3rd/39th Cavalry
Allen B. Hopkinson – HHQ 5th/60th Infantry
Steven R. Hopper – C Co. 4th/47th Infantry
George Horgan – USS Whitfield County
Jack Horn – C Co. 2nd/47th Infantry
Jim R. Horne – ComRivFlot I Staff
RADM Chuck Horne III, USN (Ret) – CosRon 1
Al "Lil Jack" Horner – C-112-1
George L. Horning – USS Hissen
Gary Horton – T-91-11
George A. Horton – T-112-9
Timothy J. Horton – B Btry 3rd/34th Arty
Lewis H. Hosler – B Co. 2nd/47th Infantry
Robert W. Hotz, Jr. – IUWG-1 Unit 4
HTC Joseph W. Houghton, USN (Ret) – USS Sphinx
Robert R. Houle – USS White River
Thomas M. Hounsell – RivDiv 574 and RivDiv 554
Billy B. Howard – A Co. 9th Signal Bn
Jerry O. Howard – USS Askari
John S. Howard – Mine Squadron 11, MSB-49
Nathaniel "Doc" Howard – USS Mercer APB-39

Tim Howard – E Co. (Recon) 3rd/47th Inf
Wesley Howard – USS White River
Wayne E. Howard, HMCS USN (Ret) – USS Luzerne County LST-902
Michael R. Howard, Jr. – B Btry 3rd/34th Arty
CW3 John F. Howard, Jr. USA (Ret) – A Co. 709th Maint. BN
Charles E. Howe – B-1 3rd/60th Infantry
Gerald L. Howe – USS Nueces
Jerry Howe – USS Sumner County
John Howell – CosDiv 13 PCF-32
Roy Howell – RivDiv 513
Bernard G. Howlett – USS Carronade IFS-1
James "Jim" Hoyer – 1097th TC (MB)
Theodore "Ted" Hoyt – 9th Inf Div 9th Signal Corps
Ronald F. Hubert – C Co. 2nd/47th Infantry
Tom Hubik – USS Askari
Kenneth D. Hudson – B Co. 2nd/47th Infantry
Paul Hudson – RivDiv 515 and 571
Thomas J. Huebner – TF-116
Dana R. Huff – IUWG-1, Unit 3
Morris F. Huggins – 65th Infantry Plt
Don A. Hughes – D Co. 15th Engineers
Freddie L. Hughes – USS Colleton
John L. Hughes – E Co. 3rd/60th Infantry
Michael Hughes – USS Pitkin County
Richard R. Hughes – USS Page County
Ross P. Hughes – E Co. 4th/47th Infantry
Herschel Hughes, Jr. – USS Colleton
LTG Patrick M. Hughes, USA (Ret) – Plt Ldr D Co. 4th/39th Inf.
Thomas M. Hughey – 4th Riv Adv Tsam 108
Cornelius J. Huhn – E Co. 3rd/60th Infantry
John Huhn – A-1 4th/47th Infantry
John A. Hulbert – 18th CAC, 1st Avn Bde
William W. Hulse – USS Pickaway (APA-222) and Mike 8
Jim Hulsey, Jr. – 4th/47th Infantry
Wray Humbyrd – PCF-71 and PCF-24
George Frank Humphreys II – E Co. 3rd/39th Infantry
Nelson G. Hundley, Jr. – USS Benewah
William Hunsinger – RivDiv 153
Lester L. Hunsucker – USS Colleton
Dale Hunt – U.S. Navy
David R. Hunt – PBR-458
Herbert Hunt – B Co. 3rd/47th Infantry
John D. Hunt – HHC 2nd BDE 9th Infantry
Marshall "Harley" Hunt – RivDiv 535
Roy Hunt – 3rd/47th Infantry
MG Ira A. Hunt, Jr. – HHQ 9th Infantry Div.
Robert B. Hunt, QMC, USN (Ret) – RivSec 533, PBR-153
Alfred A. Hunter – LST-996
Larry L. Hunter – USS White River
Gary E. Hurst – YRBM-17 Dong Tam
L. F. Hurst, Jr. – T-132-6
Jerry Hurt – T-151-11
John D. Hurt – River Section 533/534
Angus R. Huskey – RivFlot I, APL-26
Richard Hutchinson – D-2 15th Engineers
William Hutchson – Brown Water Navy
Henry R. Huthmacher – USS White River
Ron Hutson – M-91-3 and T-91-8
Don Hutton – Associate
Glenn Hyatt – 3rd/39th Infantry
Alan G. Hyde – 9th Signal BN
Jerry Hyde – USS Askari
William A. Hyer – C-3 4th/47th Infantry
Frank Hynan – 15th Engineers

John N. Iannucci – B Co. 3rd/60th Infantry
Ralph Iannucelli – 28th Eng Detachment 3rd/39th
Ralph Iannucelli – 3rd/39th Inf
Lt. Jerry O. Imgarten – B-2 3rd/47th Infantry
John Ippolito – A-131-3
Glen W. Irish – B Co. 2nd/47th Infantry
Richard L. Irvin – RivRon 15
Richard W. Irvin – A Co. 3rd/60th Infantry
Loren Irving – 9th Inf. 709th Maint. Bn.
Truman E. Irving – USS Mark
William J. Irwin – B-3 2nd/39th Infantry
Billy M. Isabell – 3rd/60th Infantry
Gary V. Isbell – T-131-32
William N. Isetts – USS Askari
Larry D. Iverson – A-3 2nd/39th Infantry
Walter W. Ivie – A Co. 3rd/47th Infantry
Bobby R. Ivory – C Co. 86th Combat Eng
James A Ivy – A-92-4
Alexander Jackson – A Co. 3rd/47th Infantry
Daniel Jackson – T-111-1
Harry R. Jackson – C Battery 1st/84th Artillery
Jerry Jackson – HCU 1
Larry Jackson – T-111-1
Don P. Jackson, USN (Ret) – IUWG-1, Vung Tau
Paul C. Jacobsen – USS Tutuila
Jeff Jacobson – T-151-31
Archie Jakab – E Co. 3rd/60th Infantry
David W. Jakeman – A-1 4th/39th Infantry
David G. James – D-2 2nd/60th Infantry
Donald R. Jameson – B Co 3rd/60th 9th Inf Div
Andrew G. Jancosek – USS Benewah
Alexander F. Janisieski – USS Krishna ARL-38
Lannis W. Janssen – C-2 4th/47th Infantry
David V. Jarczewski – C Co. 4th/47th Inf 9th Div
Bruce E. Jarose – E Co. 2nd/39th Infantry
Russell E. Jarousek – A-2 4th/47th Infantry
Joseph H. Jarreau – USS Tom Green County LST-1159
Garry M. Jarrett – B-2 3rd/60th Infantry
Lanny G. Jarvis – AIRCOFAT
Frank Jaskot – USS Sphinx
Michael A. Jasper – T-111-12
John A. Jasperson – C-1 4th/47th Infantry
David G. Jauhola – NSA Dong Tam
Jerry Jaworski – A Co. 2nd/47th Inf
Isaac Lynn Jeane – 2nd/47th Inf and 9th Med BN
Bobby D. Jefcoat – B-3 4th/47th Infantry
Richard W. Jefferies – USS Carronade
William H. Jeffers – USS White River
Paul H. Jefferson – T-132-26
Earl W. Jeffries – E-3 3rd/60th Infantry
Bradley E. Jenkins – HHSB 3rd/34th Arty and 2nd/47th M
Don J. Jenkins – A-2 2nd/39th Infantry
Irving Jenkins – B Co. 3rd/47th Infantry
Richard Jenkins – B Co. 2nd/60th Infantry
Roland D. Jenkins – A-3 2nd/39th Infantry
Gary Jenks – USS White River LSMR-536
Richard P. Jennings – S3, 3rd/60th Infantry
Bruce A. Jensen – T-111-3
Gregory R. Jensen – USS Satyr
Ralph L. Jensen – A Co. 3rd/47th Infantry
Wayne W. Jensen – PCF-5
Frederick L. Jensen, Jr. – B Co. 2nd/39th Inf
Roger Jerram – 2nd/60th Infantry
Arthur J. Jervis – RivRon 15 River Div 153
Michael H. Jeter – C-3 4th/47th Infantry
Ben Jetton – USS Benewah
Homer Jewell – USS Washtenaw County
Fred Jewett – A Co. 9th Signal BN

Henry L. S. Jezek – 2nd/47th Infantry
Frank D. Jimenez – 3rd/47th Infantry
Carroll Joachimi – USS St. Clair County LST-1096
M/Sgt Roger Jodoin, USA (Ret) – ComNavForV
Brian A. Johansen – USS Tutuila
Charles M. Johns – B-2 2nd/47th Infantry
Arvel L. Johnson – HHQ 4th/47th Infantry
Bruce L. Johnson – C-2 4th/47th Infantry
Cecil Johnson – T-92-7
Cecil A. Johnson – USS Benewah
Debra Johnson – D-4 3rd/60th Infantry
Donald A. Johnson – T-132-10
Doug Johnson – B Co. 9th Medical Bn
Duane B. Johnson – 15th Combat Engineers
Ed Johnson – B Co. 2nd/47th Infantry
Eric Johnson – USS Benewah APB-35
Franklin Johnson – T-111-8
George Johnson –
Herchel D. Johnson – A Co. 3rd/39th Infantry
J. R. Johnson – E Co. 3rd/47th Infantry
James B. Johnson – A-1 4th/47th Infantry
Kelly Johnson – B Co. 2nd/39th Infantry
Les Johnson – Zippo-4
Lionel Johnson – USS Washtenaw County
Maurice R. Johnson – D Co. 2nd/39th Infantry
Michael Johnson – USS Tom Green County
Ralph G. Johnson – COSRON 1PCF 9/10
Ray E. Johnson – USS Washtenaw County LST 1166
Raymond "Padre" Johnson – RivFlot I
Richard G. Johnson – T-152-6
Robert E. "Bob" Johnson – USS Terrell County
Roger A. Johnson – USS Whitfield County
Sam Johnson – A Co. 4th/47th Inf
Stan E. Johnson – USS Whitfield County
Steve Johnson – A-111-7
Willard G. Johnson III – A Co. 2nd/47th Infantry
Jimmy M. Johnson, Sr. – E Co. 4th/47th Infantry
Col. James D. Johnson, USA (Ret) – HQ 3rd/60th Infantry
George K. Johnston – A-1 3rd/47th Infantry
Gerald Johnston – USS Nye County
Jace Johnston, Jr. – C Co. 2nd Br 4th/47th Infantry
Dale S. "Doc" Jones – B Co. 4th/47th Infantry
David D. Jones – USS Currituck VP-50
David R. Jones – Z-111-7
David W. Jones – USS Washtenaw County
Eugene P. Jones – USS Washtenaw County
Everett R. Jones – RivRon 15
Frank Jones – RivRon 15, T-48
Guinn H. Jones – A-4 2nd/47th Infantry
Howard M. Jones – E-1 2nd/39th Infantry
John L. Jones – 1st Plt, A Batt 84th Arty
Johnnie B. Jones – B-1 3rd/47th Infantry
Johnny R. Jones – R-92-1
Lones Jones – D Co. 4th/39th Infantry
Richard L. Jones – USS Tutuila ARG-4
Robert S. Jones – Mineron Eleven Det Alpha
Roy Lee Jones – USS Askari
Stephen "Steve" Jones – USS White River (LSMR-536)
Wylie B. Jones – 78 Ord Att (1965-66) and Navy
Stanley Jones, III – RivDiv 15 T-17
John D. Jones, Jr. – T-91-9
Durward L. Jones, RDC, USN (Ret) – USS Colleton
Paul A. Jorczak – T-92-5
Guy F. Jordan, Jr. – MineRon-11 Divs 111-113
Jim Jorgensen – C Co. 4th/47th Infantry

David B. Joslin – ATF-211
Henry L. Joyce, III – C Co. 2nd/47th Infantry
Mackey D. Joyner – USS Krishna
Louis R. Judson – A Co. 3rd/39th Infantry
Ron Julin – HHC 3rd/47th Infantry
John R. Justice – A Co. 15th Engineers
LT David P. Justin – A Co. 3rd/60th Infantry
Maynard G. Kaderlik – USS Nueces
Vern Kahler – APL-26
Michael Kahlhamer – 9th Division 4th/47th Inf
Harry A. Kahn – RivDiv 132
William M. Kahn – RivDiv-131
Myron T. Kaiser – C Co. 2nd/39th Infantry
Rudy Kaldi, Jr. – C and D Co. 2nd/47th Infantry
Terry R. Kalinowski – USS Benewah
Kenneth K. Kalish – River Patrol Section 523
Fredrick L. Kalles – RivRon 15 T-152-12
Richard T. Kane – B-1 4th/47th and D Co. 5th/60th Inf
Joseph H. Kanick – B-3 3rd/47th Inf and HHC 2nd/47th Mech
David A. Karaus – A Co. 3rd/39th Infantry
Michael L. Karl – Rivron 13 and 15
BT3 Tim Karwoski – USS Terrell County
Edward S. Kasik, II – C-2 3rd/47th Infantry
Paul R. Kasper – 15th Engineers - Zippo
Ronald J. Kasperek – USS Garrett County
Harold Kau-Aki – D-1 3rd/60th Infantry
Alexander C. Kaufbusch – A Co. 3rd/60th Infantry
James Kaufman – A-132-2
John J. Kauneckas – USS Harnett County
Jack Kavanaugh – ACV 3rd/39th
Allen T. Kawabata – T-111-10
Gerald J. Kawecki – 3rd/47th Infantry
Jerry Keane – C Co. 3rd/47th Infantry
Eugene F. Keany – 1099th TC (MB)
Thomas W. Kearbey – USS Tom Green County
Kent Keasler – USS Krishna
William J. "Bill" Keating – A-1 3rd/47th Inf
Thomas Keefe – T-111-10
CPT Milton C. Keene, USA (Ret) – A Co. 3rd/60th Infantry
Francis M. Keim – RivFlot I
Jeff Kelleher – River Division 535
Dane K. Keller – RivDiv 532 PBR-121
Jimmie E. Keller – D Co. 2nd/47th Infantry
Jay Morgan Kellers II – T-111-4
Daniel L. Kelley – C-3 6th/31st Infantry
James V. Kelley – A Co. 4th/47th Infantry
Ken Kelley – River Section 553
SKI Michael Joseph Kelley – USS Nueces APB 40
Capt. Thomas G. Kelley, USN (Ret) – RivDiv 152
John A. Kellner – 2nd/60th Infantry
Dale Kelly – T-111-4
Floyd L. Kelly – MinDiv 112
Patrick M. Kelly – C-151-1
Timothy J. Kelly – C-3 2nd/47th (Mech) Infantry
Francis Y. Kelson – A Troop 3rd/5th Cavalry
Ronald C. Kemp – A-1 3rd/39th Infantry
Ronald T. Kemp – T-132-5
Robert D. Kenady – A-92-6
Jerry B. Kendall – YOGS 56 and 76
John Y. Kennedy – 3rd/34th Infantry
Larry J. Kennedy – T-131-11 and M-131-1
Steve W. Kennedy – USS Sphinx
Steven D. Kennedy – M-111-2 and T-131-8
James F. Kennedy, LT USN (Ret) – USS Washtenaw County
Joseph A. Kenny – 458th PBR Co.
Michael T. Kenny – YRBM-16
CAPT Robert J. Kermen, USNR – RAS 11 RAD 112 T-112-7
John R. Kern – 1097th TC (MB)
Robert D. Kernechel – M-111-3
Paul Kershner – T-112-12 and T-152-50
Ralph L. Kettmann – YRBM-16
Steven K. Kidd – T-131-3
Herbert Kidwell, Jr. – USS Indra
Patrick A. Kiernan – Dong Tam
BMCS Leslie M. Kildow, USN (Ret) – RivDiv 514
Sam J. Kilsby – T-111-10
Robert Kimball – HHC 4th/47th Infantry
Chuck L. Kimble – A-132-12, T-132-21
Kenneth Kincaid – C Co. 5th/60th Infantry
Larry Kincheloe – CDR B Co. 3rd/60th Infantry
Paul E. Kinchen – U.S. Navy
August F. Kindla – T-151-4
Bruce P. King – NSA Saigon Nha Be Det
David Lloyd King – USS Polk County
Pete Kinne – A Co. 3rd/60th Infantry
Lloyd B. Kinnicutt – 25th Infantry
Larry G. Kinser – B Co. 4th/47th Infantry
Jon Kio – E Co. 3rd/60th Inf
Michael J. Kirby – A Co. 6th/31st Infantry
Thomas R. Kirby – USS Benewah
Jim Kirk – C Co. 4th/39th Infantry
Howard C. Kirk III – E Co. (Recon) 3rd/47th Inf.
Kenneth D. Kirkland – USS Askari
Ron Kirkwood – Z-152-5
George A. Kitchen – CO RivDiv 92
John R. Kitchura – A-152-3
Marvin F. "Buddy" Kittrell – IUWG-1 Vung Tau
James E. Klapec – B-2 3rd/60th Infantry
Robert Klapp, Jr. – USS Whitfield County
Terry Alan Klasek – USS Summit County and NSA DaNang
John M. Kleba – IUWG-1
Roger J. Klegin – E-4 4th/47th Infantry
Robert J. Kleiman – RivDiv 533, 573, and 535
James R. Klein – B Co. 3rd/60th Infantry
Michael L. Klein, MD – 3rd/60th Infantry
Thomas H. Klemash – Coastal Squadron 1/Coastal Division 12
William J. Klenk – HHC 2nd/47th Infantry
Donald R. Kline, Jr. – C Co. 4th/47th Infantry
SFC Eric L. Klinedinst, USA – A Co. 4th/47th Infantry
John W. Klink – 170th Ordinance Det
Lawrence M. Klisura – 2nd/39th and 5th/60th Infantry
Stephen H. Klosterman – USS Askari ARL-30
BMCM James W. Klug, USCG (Ret) – USGS Point Marone
Ronald N. Klump – A Co. 3rd/39th Infantry
Chris R. Knabe – M-92-1
Theodore M. Knapp – T-152-2
Capt. William D. Kneisler – MIUW-213
Rev. David E. Knight – Chaplain, 4th/47th Infantry
John W. Knopf – 3rd/47th Inf
David A. Knotts – D Co. 3rd/47th Inf and HHC 3rd/60th
Gordon C. Knowles – ComRivFlot I
David Knowlton – 3rd/39th Infantry
Gen William A. Knowlton – ADC 9th Infantry
Michael A. Knowlton – YRBM-18
Gary L. Knox – RivRon 9 A-91-8
John A. Koch – D Co. 4th/47th Infantry
Maurice P. Koch – RivDiv 531, PBR-101
John R. Koeppen – A-4 6th/31st Infantry
David G. Koffler – CosDiv 13
Edward "Rusty" Kohler – 9th MP Co.
Francis X. Kohut – USS White River
Walter R. Kolling – USS Benewah
Lucian Kolodziejczak – B Co. 3rd/47th 9th Inf
Joseph Kolodziejski – B Co. 15th Combat Eng.
Lee Kolstad – D Co. 15th Engineer Bn
Larry J. Koltz – T-91-10
Fred Kopatch – B-2 3rd/60th Infantry
Thomas Kopp – USS Holmes County
Robert D. "Bob" Koppes – USS Tom Green County
Richard Koral – 3rd/34th Artillery
John E. Kordinak – B Co. 3rd/47th Infantry
Robert P. Kortekaas – B Co. 2nd/47th Infantry
Neil W. Koski – M-111-3
Allan R. Koster – A Co. 2nd/47th Infantry
Edward T. Kostiha – RADs 111 and 151 and NAG RAID 72
Dennis Kotila – T-131-2
William F. Koupeny – M-92-1 and C-92-1
Rev. Charles M. Kovich – C and D Cos. 3rd/60th Infantry
Bruce R. Kowal – HQ 3rd/60th Infantry
Bradford T. Kowhan – 212 Dong Tam
Frederick W. Kraft – RivFlot I
Bernhard J. Krajewski – A-92-4
John F. Kralemann – IUWG-1, Unit 4
Howard W. Kramer – D Co. 3rd/60th Infantry
Lloyd J. Kramer – RivDiv 591, PBR-72
Donald Kraniak – USS Mercer
Robert D. Kraus – TF-115
Stanley Krawiec – B Co. 2nd/47th Infantry
Capt. Richard Krebs, USNR (Ret) – USS Washoe County
Capt Donald E. Krehely, USN (Ret) – USS Colleton
Joseph L. Kreis – Sea Float/Operation Slingshot
Ron Kresel – B Co. 3rd/60th Infantry
Bruce K. Kress – D-4 4th/47th Infantry
Gerald D. Kreul – USS Sphinx ARL-24
David E. Kroenke – Task Force 116 Saigon
Edward M. Krstulovic, Jr. – MACV Naval Advisory Group
LCDR Edward M. Kruk, USN (Ret) – Com Riv Flot One A-92-1
Walter Leon Krustchinsky – USS Benewah APB-35
Ted Krystia – RVN
Stan Krzesinski – T-112-7
Sam J. Kubala – A-91-1
Keith R. Kucera – M-131-3
Gary Kuehne – 2nd/39th and 5th/60th Infantry
Paul Kuhn – T-112-6
Phillip L. Kuhn – USS Mark
Richard P. Kulpa – B-3 3rd/60th Infantry
Dale A. Kumher – NavAdvGrp Da Nang
Daniel H. Kunkel – E-2 4th/47th Infantry
Lee A. Kunkle – B-2 4th/39th Infantry
John E. Kurian – USCG-82303
Larry R. Kurth – A-4 2nd/47th Infantry
Donald L. Kvislen – T-112-7
Roman C. Kwarta – A-3 4th/47th Infantry
Ray Labaha – USS Tutuila (ARG-4) and IUWG-1, Unit 2
Joseph A. Lacapruccia – M-92-2
Albert R. Lacewell, Jr. – HQ 3rd Bde, 9th Infantry
Bob Lacey – A Co. 4th/39th Infantry

Richard LaChance – A-112-4
Travis T. Lackey, Jr. – USGS Pontchartrain
Raymond E. Lacks, Jr. – D Btry 2nd/4th and 3rd/9th
Thomas S. Ladd – M-92-2 and T-151-9
John L. Laemmar – T-131-11
Thomas R. Laflam, Jr. – RivDiv 531/592
John M. Lahare – T-92-8
Richard Lahart – USS Clarion River
LTC Nicholas M. Laiacona, USA (Ret) – C-1 3rd/60th Infantry
Larry A. Lail – USS Acme
Henry Lain – RivRon 13 and 15
Robert W. Laing, Jr. – 3rd/39th Cavalry (ACV)
Larry C. Lamb – C-3 3rd/47th Infantry
Elmer E. Lambert – USS Askari
F. Richard Lambert – TF-117 Staff
Gene Lambert – HHQ 2nd/47th Infantry
Stanley H. Lambert – USS Mark AKL-12
Wayne T. Lamond – USS Montrose
Robert A. Lamoureux – C Co. 3rd/47th Infantry
Norman A. Lampert – M-112-1 and M-152-2
Tom Lanagan – 3rd Boat Group
Kenneth G. Lancaster – B-3 3rd/60th Infantry
Bill Lance – A-111-1 and T-111-13
Robert C. Land – C-111-1 and C-131-1
Dennis Lander – T-50
Hurlust Landers – A-111-4
Elton Landrum – PBR 543
Kenneth R. Lands – RivDiv 512
Billy D. Lane – USS Benewah APB-35
James L. Lane – NavComSta CRB
John J. Lane – T-92-8
Donald J. Lane, Jr. – A Co. 5th/60th Infantry
Douglas Laney – T-112-12
James Langford – IUWG-1 Unit 2
Ken R. Langham – C Co 1st Platoon 2nd/47th 9th Div
BMC William T. Langham, USN (Ret) – TF 115
Joseph Lango – WHEC-39
Phillip W Langston – CSO RivDiv 152
Welsey K. Lanham – USS White River LSMR-536
Charles C. Lanier – A Co. 3rd/47th Infantry
James R. Lanier – 2nd/47th Infantry
Richard B. Lanphear – RivRon 9
John "Doc" Lantz – USS Page County
A. Taylor Lapham, Jr. – CGC Point Grey Div 13
Danny Lara – 3rd/60th Infantry
GMG2 Ron Laratta – RivSec 532
Gerald H. Lariviere – D-3 3rd/60th Infantry
David W. Larkin – T-111-1
Charles R. Larntz – A-111-5
Kendall A. Larsen – LST Support - RivFlot I
Robert D. Larsen – USS Tioga County
Dennis Larson – USS White River
Stanley W. Larson – USS Askari
Arthur LaRue – Z-151-3
Tom Laskowski – USS Washoe County
Peter J. Lassen – T-112-9
Paul F. Latata – USS Askari
Earl W. Latta, Jr., LTC Aus (Ret) – HQ (G-4) 9th Infantry
Robert Laudermilk – 5th Trans Co. (HB)
Thomas A. Lavender – M-132-1
Robert C. "Tink" Lawing, Jr. – USS Montrose
Michael J. Lawler – T-91-8
Daniel W. Lawless – HHQ 2nd/47th Infantry
Larry Lawniczak – PCF-60
Standlee G. Lawrence – T-92-12

Cam Lawson – RivRon 13
James H. Lawson, Jr. – C-2 3rd/47th Infantry
Thomas E. Lawson, Sr. – E Co. 2nd/60th Infantry
William S. Lawton – USS Pitkin County
Steven H. Lawyer – A Co. 3rd/47th Infantry
Robert A. "Bob" Lazzell, USA (Ret) – HQ Co. 15th Combat Eng
Don B. Leach, Jr. – 3rd/60th Infantry
M. John Lebens – CBMU-302, Dong Tam Det.
John LeBorgne – 3rd/39th Inf
William J. Leckey – PCF-6
Tere J. Ledinsky – PCF-50
Jerry R. Lee – USS Sphinx ARL-24
Robin E. Lee – RivDiv 152
Harold S. Lee, USN (Ret) – USS Krishna
Jerry R. Leeds – TF-115
James H. Lehne – C Co. 2nd/60th Infantry
Edward Leib, Jr. – HQ Co. 1st/11th Infantry
Stephen Leiker – B-1 4th/47th Infantry
Phillip B. Leith – B Co 2nd/47th Infantry
Billy LeJeune – U.S. Army
Russell Lembke – USS Satyr
Bob Lennon – USS White River
F. Richard Lennon – 1st AmTrac Bn
Phillip G. Lent – C-3 3rd/60th Infantry
Gregory L. Lentz – Operation Market Time
Lt Col William A. Lenz, USA (Ret) – Cdr C Co. 3rd/47th Infantry
Dennis P. Leonard – B Co. 3rd/47th Infantry
Robert D. Leonard – B Co. 4th/47th Infantry
Robert J. Leonard – USS Hampshire County
Kenneth D. Leone – A Co. 3rd/60th Infantry
Wayne R. Lepore – T-131-4
Gregory S. Lermond – B Battery 2nd/4th Artillery and 2nd/47th
Paul R. Lesneski – Com RivRon 9 CCB-92-1
Tsgt Earl M. Leuelling, Jr. – USS Benewah
James T. Levandowski – A Co. HQ 3rd/47th Infantry
William H. Leverock – C Co. 2nd/47th Infantry
David G. "Jerry" Levesque, Jr. – USS Guide MSO-447
Kenneth Lew – USS Tutulia
William J. Lewandowski, USN (Ret) – USS Harnett County
Bill Lewellen, Jr. – HHC 2nd/47th Infantry
Harvey C. Lewis – USS Garrett County LST-786
Lawrence G. Lewis – A-1 3rd/47th Infantry
Miles C. Lewis – USS Whitfield County
Robert H. Lewis – B Co. 4th/47th Infantry
Roger M. Lewis – IUWG-1 Unit 2
Samuel H. Lewis – Nha Be
Robert E. Lightwine – T-112-11
Bradley G. Lillmars – T-92-4
Sam Liming – A Co. 3rd/47th Infantry
Richard J. Limpert – B Co. 4th/47th Infantry
CDR Ernest T. Lindberg – RivRon 11
Randall E. Lindberg – HA(L)-3 Det 2 Seawolves
Rod Lindberg – USS Vernon County
William K. Lindloff – R-112-1
Marvin L. Lindmark, Jr. – A Co. 9th Avn Bn
Jim Lindsay – B Co. 3rd/47th Infantry
Michael Lindsay – USS White River
Douglas R. Lindsey – YRBM-17, Dong Tam
Robert C. Lindsey – USS Clarion River
Walter F. Lineberger, III – XO RivDiv 91
William Linenberger – USS Vernon County
Larry G. Linkous – PCF-78 and PCF-101
James T. Lipham – USS Engage MSO-443
David C. Lipko – HHQ 9th MP Co.

Jerry L. Lippincott – IUWG-1, LCM-877
Robert C. Lisko – E-1 3rd/60th Infantry
Alan L. Lithwin – 1097th TC (MB)
Arthur J. Little – B-1 4th/47th Infantry
Bobby G. Little – D Co. 3rd/60th Infantry
Dennis R. Little – T-112-12
Don H. Little – USS Windham County
Brett Littrell – USS Boston
Stephen K. Livelsberger – D Co. 3rd/47th Infantry
Tom Lively – C Battery 3rd/34th Inf
John M. Livingston – 9th Infantry, 483 MP Plt
Willie B. Lloyd – USS Tom Green County/USS Hampshire County
Thomas J. Lloyd, Sr. – USS White River
Jake Lo Cascio – Naval Advisory Unit
Douglas A. Lockard, Sr. – USS Askari ARL-30
Ken Locke, Sr. – USS White River
Robert K. Locker – USS Whitfield County
Joe Lodyga – D Co. 4th/39th Infantry
John Loeb – A-132-2
Cdr Nathan O. Loesch, USNR (Ret) – RivFlot One
George U. Loffert, Jr., USA (Ret) – HHC 2nd/47th Infantry
Thomas M. Logan – USS Satyr
Joseph Loglisci – A Co. 2nd/60th Infantry
Edward E. Lohf – C Co. 4th/47th Infantry
Cecilo Lois – T-91-5
Dominic A. Lombardi – MACV
Roy E. London – B-4 3rd/60th Infantry
Daniel E. Long – USS Jennings County
Jerry R. Long – NavDet Dong Tam
Larry D. Long – B Co. 3rd/60th Infantry
Robert E. Long – A-91-1
John P. Long, Jr. – USS Benewah APB-35
James L. Long, Sr. – ComRivFlot One Staff
Robert K. Long, Sr. – 3rd/34th Artillery
Steven Loomis – Naval Advisory Group (VANNSY)
Frank J. Lopez – B Co. 4th/47th Infantry
Adm. Thomas J. Lopez, USN – RivDiv 153
Richard E. Lorman – T-152-6
Kelly Loudon – Naval Advisory Group ISB Rach Soi
William J. Lounsbery – MCS-7
Robert A. Love – T-131-7
Clyde W. Lovell – River Squadron 15
Loyd V. Lovell – USS Tom Green County LST-1159
Steve Lovely – M-132-1
Col. Karl Lowe – 6th/31st Infantry
James A. Lowe – APL-26
Russell Wm Lowenstein – 3rd/34th Artillery
James R. Lown – B Co. 2nd/47th Infantry
Jess Loya – B-2 3rd/47th Infantry
Leonard T. Luba – SCRF - Danang
Antoni Luca – 4th/39th and 2nd/39th Infantry
John M. Lucas – HHQ Co. 2nd/47th Infantry
John S. Lucas – USS Washtenaw County
Lilyard N. Lucas – Z-132-2
Randy Lucht – USS Terrell County
John A. Lucidi – C Co. 3rd/47th Inf
Allan Ludi – TF-194
William M. Lueck – A-151-1
Stephen Luft – B Co. 4th/47th Inf
Jim Lukaszewski – APL-30
Steven W. Luke, Sr. – USS Page and USS Bulloch County
David E. Lull – B-2 2nd/47th Infantry
Peder C. Lund – B Co. 3rd/60th Infantry

Jim Lundgard, II – B Co. 3rd/47th Infantry
Erick C. "Doc" Luoma – IUWG-1
Richard Lussier, USN (Ret) – USS Nueces
Louis Luth – B Co. 3rd/47th Infantry
Stephen E. Luth – RivRon 15 M-151-2
Corrado R. Lutz – PCF-23
Michael J. Lux – T-132-5
George B. Luzaich – USS White River
James P. Lyde – USS Benewah
William E. Lyden, Jr. – USS Sphinx
Leroy Lynch – C Co. 3rd/39th Infantry
LCDR Charles W. Lynch, USN (Ret) – OIC, APL-26
Allen F. Lynd – HHC 3rd/47th Infantry
David R. Lynn – IUWG-1, 3, and 4
Richard G. Lynn, Jr. – A-151-3
Rev. Larry J. Lyons – C-112-1
Barry R. Mabus – A Co. 3rd/39th and C Co. 5th/60th Mech
Richard E. MacCullagh – CTG-117.2
Frank T. MacDonald – USS Harnett County
Gary A. MacDonald – A Co. 9th Signal Bn
James A. MacDonald – TF-116, PBR-732
James H. MacDonald – B Co 3rd/60th Inf
LCDR Scott A. MacDonald, USN – USS Askari
Richard H. Machesky – A-92-1
George W. Machin – T-112-6
Manuel M. Macias – IUWG-1
Larry MacIntire – USS Tutuila ARG
David J. Mack – A-1 4th/47th Infantry
William B. Mack – LSB Dong Tam
Charles L. Mackay – River Section 511
Mac MacKechnie – A Co. 5th/60th Infantry
Kenneth M. MacKellar – C Btry, 3rd/34th Artillery
Mike Mackenzie – RivRon 9
Clarence R. Mackey – USS Nueces
John Madison – Co. B 4th/47th Inf
Richard C. Madison – 9th MP Co.
Hildebrando Madrigal – A Co. and Recon 3rd/39th Infantry
Robert W. Maginnis – A Trp, 3rd/5th Cavalry
David L. Magnuson – 9th Infantry Division
John Magriplis – 3rd/34th Arty
John J. Maguire, Jr. – B-2 3rd/60th Infantry
Rudy Mahanes – T-131-12
Brian J. Mahin – T-132-9
Dennis M. Mahon – A Battery 3rd/34th Arty
Brian J. Mahoney – USS Sphinx ARL-24
Gary W. Maibach – C-1 4th/47th Infantry
David L. Maier – USS Westchester County
Gash E. Mains – A-92-1 and A-92-8
William V. Mains, Jr. – NavDet Can Tho
Stephen "Ken" Mairs – B Co. 2nd/47th Infantry
Frank S. Maj, Jr. – A Co. 2nd/47th Infantry
Jimmie Majerus – A-117-7
Nelson Makinson – 4th/47th Inf
James A. Malarik – B Co. 2nd/47th Infantry
Cdr. Charles Malmgren – USS Kemper County
Robert W. Malone – RivDiv 112
John Maloney – USS Iredell County
Larry Maloney – 9th Infantry Div.
LTC Joe Mancuso – 2nd/60th Infantry
Charles R. Mandelbaum – E Co. 15th Engineers
Chuck Maness – USS Benewah
Arthur L. Mann – A-91-3
Earl K. Mann – M-111-1
Steven Manners – E Co. 2nd/60th Infantry
David F. Manning – 9th Avation BN
Gary Manninger – A-92-5
Raymond L. Mans – B-2 4th/47th Infantry

Martin J. Mansfield, Jr. – HQ Det. 11th Trans BN
William H. Manville – USS Benewah
Cpt Steve Maquire – 6th/31st Infantry
Lee Marble – USS Satyr
Robert H. Marburger – C Co. 2nd/60th Infantry
Earl D. March – 9th Div Arty
Raphael Marchese – HHQ Co 3rd/47th Infantry
John A. Marciniak – Battery A 1st/84th Artillery
Sheldon H. Marcus – A Co. 709th Maintenance
Ronald K. Marhenke – T-91-5
David P. Marion – US Army, MACV Advisor Team 88 & TF-115
Samuel Marks – USS Tioga County
Ronnie J. Markum, Sr. – USS Hunterdon County
Dennis L. Marlen – B Co. 2nd/47th Infantry
Lansing Marlow – C-2 2nd/60th Infantry
William C. Marlow – C-3 4th/47th Infantry
Roger A. Marnell, USA (Ret) – 65th Infantry Platoon
Dennis J. Marnick – E-2 3rd/47th Infantry
Wes Maroney – HHC 1st Bde, 9th Infantry
Edward Marquart – 5th/60th Infantry
Michael Marquez – A-3 3rd/60th Infantry
Kenneth Marr – 1097th TC (MB)
Robert G. Marreel – A Co. 2nd/47th Infantry
Joseph M. Marron – D Co. 9th Med Bn
Dallas L. Marshall – A-2 4th/47th Infantry
Patrick N. Marshall – USS Jerome County
John P. Marshall, Jr. – MSM-1, Nha Be
Robert L. Marshall, Jr. – CosDiv 11, PCF-619
Chief Larry R. Marshall, USN (Ret) – MACV
William L. Martel – RivRon 13
George J. Marthenze – T-91-10
Anthony L. Martin – USS Chesterfield County
Bill Martin – USS Wexford County
Cecil H. Martin – River Sect 531
Elbert Martin – B Co. 4th/47th Infantry
Frederick H. Martin – USS Brule
James A. Martin – USS Hunterdon County
James J. Martin – C Co. 2nd/47th Infantry
John E. Martin – HHB 3rd/34th Arty
Randall L. Martin – USS Colleton
Richard W. Martin – HQ (FO) 3rd/34th Artillery
Ronan R. Martin – M-92-2
Andrew S. Martin, Jr. – HQ 2nd/47th Infantry
BMC Robert C. Martin, USN (Ret) – USS Benewah
Wayne Martin, USN (Ret) – M-131-1
Jean-Guy Martineau – USS Tutuila
Antonio Y. Martinez – A Co. 2nd/47th Infantry
Julian A. Martinez – B-2 4th/47th Infantry
Lyonso "Marty" Martinez – B Co. 4th/39th Infantry
Socorro R. Martinez – B-2 4th/39th Infantry
GMG1 Jaime L. Martinez (Ret) – RivRon Div 111 A-111-4 and M-111-1
Frank O. Martinolich – A Co. 3rd/60th Infantry
Rudolph A. Martiny – 2nd/60th Infantry
William L. Masasso – IUWG-35, Cat Lo
Al Masella – 3rd/34th Artillery
Albert A. Maslankowski – B Co. 3rd/60th Infantry
Thomas A. Mason – Ops Officer, RAS 9 and 13
C. Steven Massey – USS Satyr
John Massie – B Co. 4th/47th Infantry
PCCM James H. Masters, USN (Ret) – USS Askari
John F. Masterson, Jr. – C Co. 2nd/47th Infantry
David A. Mastracchio – 3rd/60th Infantry
Gerald B. Matheis – B-2 4th/47th Infantry
Lee H. Mathers – M-112-1

William Dennis Matheson – T-151-10
Robert L. Mathias – B-3 3rd/60th Infantry
Clarence R. Mathis – LRRP
Oscar T. Mathison – A-2 4th/47th Infantry
Steve Mathovich – A-112-5
David J. Matthias – A Co. 2nd/47th Infantry
Joseph T. Mattie – M-112-2
MG William Matz, Jr., USA (Ret) – CO C Co. 3rd/47th Infantry
Joseph B. Mawn – IUWG-1
Richard J. Maxwell – YRBM-16
Keith D. May – B Co. 3rd/60th Infantry
Dennis May, Jr. – C Co. 15th Eng. BN
BMCS Bob May, USN (Ret) – YTB-178
Jerry L. Maygarden – USS Luzerne County
Donald W. Maynard – C-2 4th/47th Infantry
Paul A. Mayne – YRBM-16
Roderick N. "Rod" Mays – C Co. 3rd/47th Infantry
Ronald J. Mayville – C Co. 5th/60th Inf
Charles E. Mc Clung – HHC 2nd BDE, 9th Inf.
Willie Mc Tear – 9th Inf Div 4th/47th Infantry
Ronald L. McAbee – M-92-1
Michael G. McAdory – Mobile Support 5, DaNang
Floyd H. McAfee – XO 3rd/47th Infantry
James McAllister – T-92-4
William "Bill" McAndrew – USS Schenectady (LST-1185)
Steven S. McAvoy – USS Askari and USS Satyr
Jack McBride – HHC 5th/60th Infantry
Terry A. McBride – C-3 4th/47th Infantry
Gary E. McCabe – A-3 3rd/47th Infantry
Howard McCafferty – T-111-9
Bill McCall – RivFlot I
Ted S. McCall – Naval Support Activity
Larry D. McCallister – C-2 4th/47th Infantry
David G. McCann – RivRon 15
Geoffrey McCarron – A Co. 5th/60th Infantry
1 LT Joseph A. McCarthy – A Battery 3rd/34th Artillery
Lawrence T. McCarthy – USS Askari ARL-30
Robert M. McCarthy – E Co. 2nd/60th and 3rd/47th Inf
A. J. McCaskey – A Co. 4th/47th Infantry
Bill McCaskill   2nd/47th Infantry
James D. McCaughan – R-92-3 and A-92-5
Ron C. McClain – 3rd/60th Infantry
William H. McClain – E-2 4th/47th Infantry
Henry E. McClamrock – RID-48
Kenneth McClelland – YRBM-21
Joseph W. McClister, Jr. – Sea Float LCM 920
Ronald McClurg – Co B 4th Plt 2nd/69th Inf 9th Div
Lance E. McClymond – Z-92-11
Robert L. McCollom – B Co. 9th Sig BN
Ross R. McCollum – B-1 3rd/60th Infantry
William McCollum – T-111-2
Randall McComas – Co E 15th Eng
Dennis McCormick – A-1 2nd/39th Infantry
Michael A. McCormick – USS Mark
Michael J. McCormick – Beachmaster Unit 1
Thomas McCormick – 5th/60th Inf
Ken McCorry – RivDiv 515, STAB Sqdrn 20
Joseph F. McCoy – USS Pitkin County
Terry M. McCoy – A Co. 3rd/60th
L. H. McCrary – C-112-1
Donald "Doc" McCue, USN (Ret) – USS Nueces
John C. McCurdy – T-152-5
Robert McDevitt – RivDiv 595/153 and NAVFORV
Ricky G McDivitt – RivRon 15 T-51

Thomas J. McDonagh – USS Indra
Bruce T. McDonald – D-3 4th/47th Infantry
Joseph W. McDonald – CBMU-302 Dong Tam Det.
Russell H. McDonald, Sr. – APA-212
Dennis D. McDougall – A-3 3rd/60th Infantry
Ronald B. McEckron – B-1 3rd/60th Infantry
Bernard McFadden – HHQ 2nd/47th Infantry
LCDR Donald R. McGarrigle, USN (Ret) – AIRCOFAT, Saigon Det.
Charles E. McGaugh, Jr. – USS Colleton
George S. McGee – A-111-7
Hugh P. McGee, Jr. – USS Conquest, MSO-488
Charles McGillicuddy – 44th Medical Brigade
Charles "Frank" McGinnis – RivDiv 91, 92, and 595
Dean McGinnis – A-92-3
Donald D. McGriff, BMC (Ret) – T-131-6
Don McGrogan, BMCS (Ret) – IUWG-1
Michael E. McGuire – E Co. 3rd/47th Infantry
Ken McGwin – USS Westchester County LST 1167
Lcdr John J. McHale, USNR – CTU 73.1.2
Edward McHenry – B Co. 2nd/47th Infantry
Morgan P. McHenry – RivDiv 553 RAD 595-153
Richard H. McIntosh – USS Nueces
H. Bruce McIver – T-131-7, RAID-72
Philip S. McKay – RivDiv 573
Charles E. McKay, Jr. – USS Benewah and YRBM-18
Lee "Tex" McKean – USS White River
David R. McKee – C-3 3rd/60th Inf
Terry L. McKenty – IUWG1 Unit 2, Boat 39
Richard P. McKenzie – 1098th TC (MB)
Lawrence R. "Mac" McKeough, Lt USN (Ret.) – USS Tutuila
Oscar L. McKnight – 3rd/39th Infantry
Ronnie K. McLain – RivRon 9
John R. McLaughlin – M-92-2 and T-131-4
Phil F. McLaughlin – Landing Ship Squadron 3
Walter McLaughlin – PCF-79 and PCF-81
Thomas L. "Mac" McLemore – T-112-7
James J. McMahon, Jr. – Mine Division 112
Cary A. McMasters – B Trp 3rd/5th Cavalry
Patric McMenamin – 9th Med
Robert W. McMillan – 4th/47th Infantry
Wade H. McMillin, Jr. – USS White River
Bill McMullen – C Co. 6th/31st Infantry
Richard A. McMurry – TF-116, PBR-105
Kyle S. McMurtery – C Co. 2nd/60th Infantry
Tom McNallan – Z-132-2
Dennis McNally – E Co. 2nd/50th Infantry
BMCM Jimmie F. McNamee – Boat Captain, M-91-1
Hugh N. McNeal – T-151-4
William E. McNeese – C-112-1
Bernard McNeil – 1st Transportation Co.
Uriah L. McNiel – IUWG-1 Unit 2
Donald McNurlin – HHC 3rd/60th Infantry
Melvin McNutt – AC Div 12
Myron J. McNutt – T-91-5
Kevin R. McPartland – USS Luzerne County LST 902
Richard "Dick" McQueston, Jr. – YTB-784
Cyril "Bud" McQuillan, Jr. – E Co. 2nd/39th and HHC 2nd/47th
David B. Mead – USS Caddo Parish
Richard E. Meade – NSA Danang, YOG-76
W. David Meador – C-131-1
Alfred A. Meadows – HHC 3rd/60th Infantry

Russell F. Meadows – HHC 2nd/60th Infantry
Dennis Medders – USS Colleton
Juan Medina – C-2 4th/47th Infantry
Juan Medina – A-112-1
Wendell D. Medlin – T-112-5
Eugene P. Meechan – USS Montrose
James E. Meehan, Jr. – IUWG-1 Unit 4 Nha Trang
Wayne R. Meeks – RivRon 15
RMC Jack R. Meeks, USNR (Ret) – RivRon 13 T-131-2
Jim "Dutch" Meeuwenberg – IUWG-1
Gerald J. Meier – D-2 3rd/60th Infantry
George Meining – USS White River LSMR-536
Mark V. Melanson – C-152-1
Calvin F. Mellinger – USS Benewah
Richard Mellinger – USS Benewah APB-35
Robert Melnikof – A Btry 3rd/34th Artillery
Stan Melton – T-91-5
Dan Mendini – 9th Inf on loan to 3rd Vietnamese Armor
James A. Mendonsa – A Battery 2nd/4th Artillery
Ronald R. Menner – CO C Co. 3rd/47th Infantry
Alejo B. Meno – A Co. 3rd/39th Infantry
Angel L. Mercado – C-151-2
Douglas J. Mercer, Jr. – HHC 4th/47th Infantry
Phillip H. Mercurio – USS Colleton
Ronald S. Mercurio – 4th/39th Infantry
Stephen A. Meroshnekoff – IUWG-1, Unit 2
William M. Merritt III – 3rd/49th Inf and 2nd/60th Inf
Larry Messmer – IUWG-1 Unit 2, LCPL-45
William L. Messmer – CO RivDiv 152
Donald E. Messner – 1097th TC (MB)
David Mete – A Co. 3rd/60th Infantry
Glenn L. 'Skip' Metheny – 40th MP BN, MACTHAI
Adam C. Metts – T-111-2
Capt Roger C. Metz, Jr., USNR (Ret) – USS Askari
Terry Metzen – C-4 3rd/60th Infantry
Allen H. Metzger – NSA Danang
William P. Metzler – B Co. 5th/60th Infantry
Dennis R. Meyer – R-92-1
Maj. Charles C. Meyer – HHB 9th Division Arty
Walter G. Meyer – USS Benewah
Donald C. "Cal" Meyer, Jr. – C Co. 2nd/39th Infantry
Christopher Meyers – 456 Strat. Aerospace Wing
Robert X. Meyers – 1097th TC (MB)
Willy G Meyers – HCU-1, LLC-2
Pierce B. Michael, Jr. – HHC 15th Combat Engineers
Keith Michaels – USS Satyr
George Michelbrink – CCB-151-2
John E. Mickelson – ComRivPatFlot 5
Daniel J. Middendorf – B Co. 3rd/60th Infantry
Jack Middleton – A Co. 9th Signal Bn
Jimmie D. Middleton – C-3 3rd/34th Arty
Walter C. "Ski" Migalski – RivRon 15 T-151-10
W. Michael Mikulak – B Co 3rd/47th Inf 9th Inf Div
Jacob Miler – D Co. 4th/39th Infantry
Alexander C. Miller – T-112-4
Andrew G. Miller – PCF Div 101 and 105
Charles H. Miller – USS Washoe County
Dale G. Miller – A-4 2nd/47th Infantry
Dennis C. Miller – USS Mattaponi
Dennis R. Miller – USS Askari
Deono Miller – B Co. 4th/47th Infantry
J. Gerald Miller – USS Vernon County
John C. Miller – Coastal Squadron 1
John L. Miller – RivRon 11 A-111-5

John P. Miller – C Co. 3rd/47th and 3rd/60th Infantry
Michael T. "Mickey" Miller – RivRon 9, 13, and 15
Minter M. Miller – USS Colleton and USS Garrett County
Nicholas P. Miller – Chief Staff Officer Riv Assault Div 152
Rick Miller – B-2 4th/39th Infantry
Rodger L. Miller – D Co. 3rd/60th Infantry
Ronald R. Miller – USS White River
Terrence L. Miller – USS Floyd County
Thomas G. Miller – APL-26
Thomas H. Miller – USS Tioga County
William A. Miller – Costal Div 11, PCF-23
Claude Miller, Jr. – HHC 3rd Brigade
Frederick H. Miller, Jr. – T-92-2
ENC (DV) John W. Miller, USN (Ret) – T-91-11
William M. Miller, USN (Ret) – M-92-1
Robert S. Millican – RivRon 9 A-92-4
Andrew Milligan, Jr. – 2nd A/D 1953 AACS/AFCS
Robert J. Mills – T-151-13
Michael "Phoenix" Milne – HQ 9th Infantry
Raymond P. Mimm – 3rd/60th Infantry
Edward S. Mindlin – USS Satyr
Joseph D. Mingledorff – USS Nye County LST 1067
Michael Mink – Recon 2nd/47th Infantry
William S. Minton – B-2 3rd/47th Infantry
Juan D. Mireles – 2nd/47th Infantry
Ron Miriello – T-91-13 and A-92-4
Thomas Miserendino – USS Sphinx
Edgar R. Mitchell – T-112-7
George F. Mitchell – RivRon 11
J. Pat Mitchell – USS White River
John S. Mitchell – USS Jennings County
Michael K. Mitchell – 1099th TC (MB)
Robert K. Mitchell – C-1 3rd/60th Infantry
Ronald Mitchell – T-152-3
Nick Mitschkowetz – APL-30
Daniel H. Mock – B-3-7 199th Infantry
Ted R. Moen – A Co. 5th/60th Infantry
Allan D. Moffatt – T-91-12
Donald W. Moffatt – NSA Det Cat-Lo
Phillip S. Mohler – USS Sphinx
Michael J. Mokler – 2nd/47th Infantry
Terrance Molloy – E Co. 3rd/47th Infantry
Gary F. Monell – 1099th TC (MB)
James D. Money – E Co. (RECON) 3rd/47th Inf
James L. Mongan – USS Benewah
Bruce K. Monks – USS Page County
Clayburn A. Monks – 3rd/34th Artillery
Mike Monroe – T-91-10
Leo Mons – C Co. 2nd/60th Infantry
John A. Montagne – USS Washtenaw County
Tony Montana – NSA Saigon
Lewis W. Montgomery – LT-529, 389th Trans Co.
Albert R. Montillo, Jr. – B Co. 3rd/60th Infantry
Antonio Monzon – 2nd/60th Infantry
Darwin L. Moody – T-112-10
Richard Moody – USS Brule (AKL-28)
Paul L. Moody, Jr. – USS Pivot (MSO-463)
Joseph R Moon – Z-151-2
David J. Mooney – A Btry 3rd/34th Artillery
Albert R. Moore – USS Benewah and IUWG-1
Allen R. Moore – A-153-3
Craig A. Moore – C Co. 4th/47th Infantry
Dennis P. Moore – A-132-10
Guy P. Moore – B Co. 2nd Brigade 3rd/60
J. Russell Moore – A-91-5
James "Jim" Moore – RivRon 15 T-31

Joe M. Moore – 3rd/60th Infantry
Larry J. Moore – 2nd/47th Inf
Patrick A. Moore – M-152-1
Reynold E. Moore – S-2 HQ 2nd Bde
Robert D. Moore – A-92-3
Robert E. Moore – A-2 3rd/39th Infantry
William R. Moore – M-132-1
John B. Moore, Jr. – C Co. 3rd/60th Infantry
Joseph L. Moore, Jr. – USS Colleton
Kenneth George Moore, USN (Ret) – USS Terrell County LST-1157
Lee E. Mooreman – E Co. 2nd/60th Infantry
Charles "Chuck" Moran – RivDiv 91 T-91-5
Frank H. Moran – B-3 4th/47th Infantry
Michael E. Morehead – River Squadron 15 M-151-6
Donald C. Morency – CTF 117 Staff
Albie T. Morford – USS Jennings County
Carl W. Morgan – A-4 2nd/39th Infantry
Dan Morgan – NSA Dong Tam
Rodney Morgan – RivSec 532, PBR-144
Ronald D. Morgan – T-111-9
David H. Morris – HHQ 3rd/47th Infantry
Donald Morris – HHQ Co. 4th/47th Infantry
Frank M. Morris – T-92-7
Robert W. Morris – 4th/47th Infantry
Tom Morris – TF-117
William J. Morris, Sr. – T-112-12
Col. Rodney W. K. Morris, USA (Ret) – A Co. 3rd/60th Infantry
John J. Morrison – IUWG-1, Vung Tau
John W. Morrison – B-4 2nd/47th Infantry
Lynn N. Morrison – B Co. 4th/47th
Thomas M. Morrissey – T-151-5
Ted L. Morrow – T-91-13
Gary T. Morse – USS Colleton
James A. Morse – CTF-116/117
Robert E. Morse – USS Benewah
William C. Morstad – USS Washtenaw County
G. Thomas "Morto" Mortensen – A-92-8
Gary N. Morton – USS Askari
Pat K. Morton – C-2 2nd/47th Infantry
Roy D. Moseman – C-2 4th/47th Infantry
Terry Moser, USN (Ret) – USS Krishna
Dennis E. Moshopoulos – T-132-21
Nicholas Motto – USS Clarion River and USS Washtenaw County
John C. Moxness – A-4 4th/47th Infantry
Dennis H. Moyer – USS Washtenaw County
Thomas P. Mozingo – RivFlot-1 T-112-5
Donald Mraz – NavSupFac Cam Rahn Bay
Dennis Mrosewske, Sr. – A Co. 3rd/60th Infantry
Brian J. Muegge – LCU-59 and YFU-89
Dennis J. Muehlstedt, Sr. – 2nd/47th Infantry
Clifford H. Mulder – RivDiv 543, NSAD Cua Viet
Patrick J. Mullen – PBR-533
Jack F. Mulligan – A Co. 3rd/47th Inf
Jesse R. Mullins – A Co. 5th/60th 9th Inf Div
Roddy Muniz – B Co. 2nd/60th Inf
Karl L. Munn, Jr. – T-92-7
William Muns – 9th Admin
David B. Murphy – Naval Aviator-Memphis NAS
Herman Murphy – USS Benewah
James R. Murphy – C-1 5th/60th (Mech) Inf.
Kenneth Murphy – USS Whitfield County
Robert W. Murphy – 1st AVN BDE
RMC Michael J. Murphy, USN (Ret) – USS Krishna
Alan Murray – LST-980 and LST-1165
David T. Murray – RivDiv 153, ASPB-6848

Patrick L. Murray – T-92-5
Carlton W. Musgrove – 2nd/4th Field Artillery
Rick D. Musil – USS Hampshire County
William Myatt – USS Benewah
Capt. Benjamin F. Myatt, Jr. – Cdr B Co. 3rd/47th Infantry
Hervy L. Myers – B Co. and HHC 4th/39th Infantry
Ira Myerson – M-131-1
Ronald F. Naegelin – C Co. 2nd/60th Infantry
Clarence W. Nairmore – PCF-35
James R. Nalbone – USS White River
James O. Nall – C-1 4th/47th Infantry
Marvin C. Napier – A Co. 2nd/60th Infantry
Stephen R. Napieralski – A Co. 2nd/47th Infantry
Thomas S. "Doc" Naples – NSAD Tan My/Hue
W. T. Naramore, Jr. – A Co. 3rd/39th Infantry
Clem Narcisse – A Co. 2nd/60th Infantry
Ronald Nardini – NSA Det Dong Tam
Michael S. Nash – HAL-3
CW3 James T. Natividad, USA (Ret) – HQ Co 3rd/60th Infantry
Saul Nava – A Co. 4th/47th Infantry
Timothy J. Neary – USS Jamestown AGTR-3
Mel Neef, Jr. – NSA Saigon Det Cat Lo
Roger H. Neeland – B Co. 3rd/60th Infantry
Jon A. Neely – C-2 2nd/47th Infantry
Marvin L. Neer, Jr. – C Co. 2nd/47th Infantry
Michael T. Nehring – T-152-8
David R. Nehrlich – B-1 5th/60th Infantry
Cdr. James R. Nelson – ComRivDiv 112
Charlie Nelson – C-1 4th/47th Infantry
David R. Nelson – A-1 4th/47th Infantry
Gary L. Nelson – Z-92-11
Johnny L. Nelson – APL-26
Lawrence H. Nelson – MineDiv 113
Mel F. Nelson – C Co. 4th/47th Infantry
Phil Nelson – E Co. 2nd/39th Infantry
Thomas H. Nelson – C-1 2nd/60th Infantry
CAPT Carl A. Nelson, USN (Ret) – RSSZ
Richard E. "Doc" Nelson, USN (Ret) – RivRon 15 Staff
Paul J. Nemitz – USS Benewah
Dennis L. Nester – D-3 6th/31st Infantry
Lawrence J. Neuen – US Army - Saigon
Norman Neuleib – USS Askari ARL-30
Burton C. Newby – USS Krishna
Bennie R. Newcomb – 3rd/60th 9th Infantry
Edwin C. Newland – A-111-7
Aaron G. Newman – C-112-1
Cecil Newman – USS Sphinx
Howard E. Newman, Jr. – B Co. 3rd/47th Infantry
Thomas D. Newsham – HHC and B Co. 15th Combat Engineer Bn
James B. Newsome – T-132-3
Wesley H. Newsome – T-92-9
Jerry Newton – 2nd/47th and 4th/39th Infantry
Donald E. Nichols – 2nd/60th and 5th/60th Infantry
Philip J. Nichols – A-1 4th/39th Infantry
Robert C. Nichols – B-3 3rd/60th Infantry
Roy E. Nichols – C-92-1
Wally Nichols – USS Nueces
Maj. Joseph D. Nichols, III – Cdr C Co. 3rd/60th Infantry
John Nielsen – B Co. 2nd/39th Infantry
Tom Nielsen – T-132-6
Donald E. Nieman – 2nd/60th Infantry
Joe Niemojewski – RivDiv 151
Ed Nieuwsma – NAG Rach Gia

Donald Nimsger – USS White River
Dan Ninedorf – USS Mark
David J. Nishioka – FDC Batt B 3rd/34th Arty
Robert D. Nist – STABRON 20
Dennis R. Nitz – USS Terrell County
Paul B. Nitzel – B-1 4th/47th Infantry
Bill Nixon – C Co. 6th/31st and 1st/11th Arty
Donald L. Noble – M-91-2
Lynden R. Noe – USS Benewah
Roger Noel – A Co. 9th Signal BN
Ronald S. Nolan – A-132-9
Richard M. Nolden – T-91-6 and T-92-10
James P. Nolles – Co. D 5th/60th
Jasper Northcutt – B Co. 2nd/47th Infantry
William Northcutt – 9th Signal Co. C 52nd Sig BN
Darrel R. Northington – T-132-5
Jeffrey E. Northridge – B Co. 2nd/47th Infantry
Kenneth W. Novack, Sr. – Co C 3rd/47th Inf
Roy C. Novello – C-2 3rd/60th Infantry
Ivars Noviks – A Co. 99th Spt. BN
David Nowacki – T-111-5
John P. Nowak – NavSuppAct Saigon
Dennis L. Noward – USS Colleton
Ronald N. Nowell – C-91-1
Roscoe C. Nowlin – C Co. 4th/47th Infantry
James L. Noyes – C Btry 3rd/34th Arty
David D. Nulf – USS Krishna and USS Satyr
Kenneth A. Nunez – USS Sedgewick County
Matthew J. Nutt – RivDiv 111 T-111-3
Richard G. Nutt – USS Benewah
Thomas Nyman – USS Sutter County
Pete Oakander – RAS 13 C-131-1
James C. Oakes – A-92-5 and T-92-10
Donnie H. Oaks – D Co. 3rd/60th Infantry
John Oakwood – USS White River
Calvin S. Obergfell – T-132-2
Max Oberkiser – USS Krishna
Robert J. Oblinger – HHC 2nd/47th Infantry
Gary O'Brien – USS Mercer APB-39
Michael D. O'Brien – T-131-1
Michael Obsitnik – NavAdGroup Rach Gia
James Ochs – 39th Combat Engineers
George R. O'Connell – USS Terrell County LST-1157
Vincent J. O'Connor – YRBM-20, NSA Saigon
John M. Odom – E Co. 3rd/60th Infantry
Lawrence J. O'Donnell – USS Tortuga LSD 26
Ross Francis O'Dowd – T-92-7 and T-131-4
Dale C. Ogdahl – C Co. 4th/47th Infantry
Clayton Ogden – RAS-15, T-53 and USS Satyr
David J. Ogle – NavSuppAct Cat Lo
David P. Ogle – D Btry 2nd/4th Artillery
Gerald B. O'Grady, III – Coastal Division 15
Donald E. Ohmes – Co. A 3rd/47th Infantry
Bill O'Kelley – B Btry 3rd/34th Arty
Dennis Oliver – USS Luzerne County LST-902
Roger D. Olmanson – 303 RR Bn 509 RRGP (9th Inf)
Kenneth Olmsted – USS White River
Ronald K. Olney – RivRon 13 T-132-1
Stanley J. O'Loughlin – 3rd/60th Infantry
Donald Olschafskie – IUWGI Unit 5
Billy W. Olsen – Co C 4th/47th Infantry
Harry L. Olsen – USS Tutuila
Dale E. Olson – T-112-8
Daniel D. Olson – USS White River LSMR-536
George L. Olson – PBR 458
Keith T. Olson – 458th Trans. Co.
Patrick S. Olson – C Co 1st Plt 2nd/60th 9th Div
Robert M. Olson – CSC Vung Tau

141

Steven Ray Olson – USS Mark AKL-12
George H. Oltman, Jr. – C Batt. 1st/11th Artillery
Richard K. Omara – PCF-102
Andrew F. O'Mara – 2nd Plt, 9th MP Co.
Stephen J. Ondrovic – B Co. 2nd/47th Infantry
Dow D. O'Neal – T-131-1
Mike O'Neal – USS Satyr
Danny O'Neel – RivDiv-112
MKC John J. O'Neil, Jr., USCGR (Ret) – U.S. Coast Guard
Joseph G. Opatovsky – PCF-103
Ronald O'Reilly – USS White River
Robert L. Ormond – USS Askari
Barry J. Orner – B-2 3rd/47th Infantry
Larry Orr – HHC and B Co. 2nd/47th Inf
John J. Ortega – T-112-2
Gregg R. Orth – 3rd/60th Infantry
Wayne S. Ortiz – B-2 3rd/60th Infantry
Melvin R. Osborn – B Co. 3rd/60th Infantry
David J. Osinski – USS Askari
Joseph K. Osman – RivDiv 554
Charles Ostrov – HHC 2nd/47th Infantry
Dennis N. O'Toole – IUWG-1
Larry Ott – C-2 3rd/47th Infantry
LtCol Luther D. Ott – 9th Signal Bn
Ronald D. Ottens – C Btry 3rd/34th Artillery
Bill Otterlei – A Co. 3rd/39th Infantry
Edward L. Ottney – 120th Aviation Co.
David Oulette – D Co. 3rd/60th Inf
Joseph R. Overbeek – 4th/47th Infantry
John J. Overleese – USS Henrico
Don Overstreet – C Co. 3rd/39th Inf
Bob Owen – USS Benewah
Robert S. Owen – IUWG-1
John Owenby – A Co. 3rd/47th Infantry
Maclyn "Mac" Owens – NSA Danag and Cua Viet
Capt. William L. Owens, USN (Ret) – RivDiv 571
Alfred Tom Owenson – USS Mercer
William M. Owings – USCGC Bering Strait W382
John C. Oxley – E Co. 3rd/47th Infantry
Ed Paananen – HQ 3rd/47th Infantry
Don Pacheco – PBRs and LST-1161
Michael Pacholka – MDMAF C-112-1
Dennis J. Pack – B Co. 3rd/47th Infantry
Jerry Pack – 1st Trans Bn
Chuck Packer – USS Rowan
Bruce Packman – USS Hunley
Joseph Paczkowski, Jr. – USS Schenectady LST 1185
Nicholas J. Padrevita, Jr. – USS Tutuila
Donald S. Pady – 3rd/34th Artillery B Battery
Charles Page – USS White River LSMR-536
Jimmy E. Page – A-112-2
Larry Pagnoni – A-3 3rd/47th Infantry
Lt. Gen William Pagonis, USA – CO 1097th TC (MB)
Cecilio H. Palacias – HQ Co. 3rd/34th Artillery
CWO4 Tony Z. Palag – USS Hunterdon County
Charlie Palek – B Co. 3rd/47th Infantry
Steven Palladino – YRBM-16
Larry H. Palletti – HHC, 9th S&T Battalion
Charles Palmer – T-132-10
Dale F. Palmer – E-3 2nd/39th Infantry
Michael R. Panfil – HHC 3rd/47th Infantry
Anthony Panichelli – B 2 2nd/47th Infantry
Michael A. Paoletto, Jr. – IUWG-1
Rev Frank D. Papandrea – A-2 2nd/47th Infantry
Jerry L. Pape – ComRivFlot I
J. Dennis Papp – 9th Admin Co.
James W. Paquette – PCF-24

Thomas A. Paquette – T-111-8
Lyle W. Parin – USS Floyd County
James E. Paris – C Co. 4th/47th Inf
Robert G. Parish – T-92-2
Morris W. Parish, Sr. – C-3 3rd/47th Infantry
James T. Parker – B-3 3rd/60th Infantry
Ronald B. Parkey – D-1 2nd/60th Infantry
Doug Parkhurst – C Co. 3rd/60th
Robert J. Parkhurst – USS Windham County
Daryl Parks – 2nd/47th Infantry
George M. Parks – Co. B 4th/39th Infantry
Michael E. Parks – B Co. 2nd/47th Infantry
Jerry Parmley – River Division 532 PBR
Cecil Wayne Parrish – Co. C 5th/60th Bandido Charlie
John Wayne Parrish, Jr. – Co. A 4th/47th Inf
Vincent Parry, Jr. – PBR Mobile Base #2
Jim E. Pasternak, USA (Ret) – C-2 4th/47th Infantry
James L Patin, Jr. – CCB-152-1
James E. Patrick – YRBM-17
Gerald L. Patrie – IUWG-1
Lyle L. Patrie – USS Whitfield County
Robert Patterson – HHC 4th/47th 9th MI
Capt. William Patterson, Jr., USNR – M-131-2
Lt Col. Robert J. Patterson, USA (Ret) – 9th Infantry Division
John Patton – IUWG-1 Unit 1
Kurt Patton – Mike 5 and T-37
John D. Patty – USS Monmouth County
Larry Paul – 2nd/60th Infantry
Steven Paul – RivDiv 112 A-112-4
BMC David L. Paust, USN (Ret) – M-131-1
MAJ Steve G. Pavlou (Ret) – A Co. 2nd/47th Infantry
Robert D. Pawlicki – T-111-11
Harold L. Payne – APL-30
Kyle Payne – D-1 4th/47th Infantry
Leland E. Payne – C-1 4th/47th Infantry
Earnest R. Peacher, USA (Ret) – A Co. 2nd/47th Infantry
Jack T. Peachey – M-111-1
David B. Pearson – A Co. 2nd/47th Infantry
Richard P. Pearson – USS Indra
Robert Pearson – IUWG-1 Unit 2 Boat 72
Ronald D. Pease – E Co. 4th/47th Infantry
Randall Peat – T-132-12
Dan E. Peckham – C-91-1, A-91-8
Rodney C. Peeler – 2nd/60th Infantry
Courtney B. Peeples – A-112-4
Roger E. Peiffer – USS Washtenaw County
James A. Pelfrey – C Co. 3rd/47th Infantry
John M. Pellenz, Jr. – C Co. 4th/39th Infantry
Rene J. Pelletier – HHC 4th/47th Infantry
Thomas E. Pelletier – 458 Trans Co. 18th MP Bde
Manuel J. Pena – USS Vernon County
Ron Pendergraph – HHQ 3rd/47th Infantry
David L. Pendergrass – CosDiv 12
William A. Pendergrass – RivRon 13
Glenn M. Pendley – HHC 3rd/39th Infantry
Richard R. Penney – YFU-64
Gaylord E. Penton – USS Garrett County
Luis F. Peraza Casanova – D Co. 3rd/60th Infantry
Ernest "Mitchell" Perdue – B Co. 3rd/60th Inf
Anthony L. Perez – USS Iredell County
Esiquio G. Perez – Co. D 3rd/60th Inf
Kenneth W. Perkins – A Co. 2nd/60th Infantry
Thomas W. Perkins – HHC 2nd/47th Mech. Infantry

William A. Perkins – T-111-2
William M. Perkins – Cmdr, B Co. 3rd/60th Inf.
Dominick J. Perotti – T-92-10
George J. Perrault, USN (Ret) – USS Tioga County
Bill Perricotti – D Co. 2nd/47th Infantry
Edward Perry – A-112-6
John "Ron" Perry – T-132-11
Virgil H. Perry – A-131-4 and A-131-1
Anthony H. Perry, III – MMA Det. 2
David L. Persson – B Co. 4th/47th Infantry
Thomas W. Pesce – USS Mercer
Roger Pete – T-112-2
Terry R. Peters – USS White River
Clinton L. Peters, Sr. – T-151-3
Dr. Peter Petersen – CO 3rd/60th Infantry
Clyde W. Peterson – T-152-4, Z-152-2
Ronald A. Peterson – PCF-18
Harold A. Peterson, Sr. – 2nd/47th Infantry
Joseph A. Petrilli, Jr. – B Co. 2nd/60th Infantry
Louis Petronelis – Army
Robert A. Pettit – USS Askari
Carl T. Petty – 3rd/60th Inf
Peter E. Pfaff III – RivDiv 92
Floyd Pfannenstiel – USS Holmes County
Sam L. Pfiester – Coastal Group 43
Chung C. Pham – SVNN, MRTF 75th
Bob Phelan – HHC 3rd/60th Inf
James L. Phelan – B Co. 3rd/60th Infantry
Thomas H. Phelps – A-16, T-37, and T-49
Robert K. Phelps, Jr. – USS White River
Harry N. Phillips – C Btry 3rd/34th Arty
Keith Phillips – A-132-1
Patrick T. Phillips – A-112-3
Timothy A. Phillips – 3rd/60th and 5th/60th Infantry
John M. Philp – A Co. 2nd/47th Infantry
DeVant L. Phoenix – A-131-6
William Piatti – C Co. 4th/47th Infantry
Tony Piazza, Jr. – USS Brule AKL-28
Darrell E. Pickett – HHC and B Co 2nd/47th Mech 9th Inf Div
LT Freddie Picou, USN (Ret) – T-112-4
Robert Pierce – HHC 3rd/47th Infantry
Ronald Pierce – T-112-7 and T-112-2
Walter Pierce – 4th/39th Inf
Ed Pietzuch – HAL-3
Robert W. Pilcher – E-4 Co. 4th/47th
Henry M. Pillsbury – D Co. 2nd/47th Infantry
Raymond G. Pineau – D and E Co. 4th/47th Infantry
Frank Pinegar – NSAD Binh Thuy
Norman W. Pinkleton – Inshore FSU 1
Paul J. Piper – USS White River
James W. Pippin, Jr. – RivRon 13 and RID 45
Rip Pisacreta – USS White River
Augustus Pisano – B-4 2nd/47th Infantry
Roger D. Pitts – T-112-5
Joe Frank Pitzer – Z-151-1
Jack F. Platter – E Co. 3rd/47th Infantry
LT COL Nathan Plotkin, USA (Ret) – HQ 2nd Bde, 9th Inf. Div.
Kit Carson Plotner – C-3, 3rd/47th Infantry
Darrell L. Plough – A Co. 3rd/60th Infantry
Gordon R. Plowman – A-3 3rd/47th Infantry
Joe Pocs – USS Guide MSO-447
L. Blaine Poe – IUWG-1 and IUWG-4
Leonard G. Pohlod – HHC 4th/47th Infantry
David D. Poindexter – T-92-10
Russell A. Pollard – Cdr B Co. 4th/39th Infantry

Dewey I. Pollock – T-131-3
Tony Pope – A-HQ  4th/47th Infantry
Ronald J. Popke – RivDiv 523, PBR-52
Del W. Poppelreiter – B Co. 4th/47th Infantry
Charles R. Porter – C-3 3rd/39th Infantry
William M. Porter – USS Windham County
Ray Porterfield – B Co. 3rd/47th Infantry
William R. Posey, USN (Ret) – YTB-785
William A. Posson – USS Hampshire County
YNC John Post, USN (Ret) – USS Indra
David L. Potter – U.S. Navy
Joe A. Potter – C-3 3rd/39th Infantry
William F. Pottichen – A-1 3rd/39th Infantry
Francis M. Powell – USS Benewah
Frank L. Powell – USS Nueces
Paul F. Powell – B-3 15th Combat Engineers
Mark E. Powers – C Co. 4th/47th Infantry
David Poynter – RivRon 13
David Prado – USS Tanner AGS-15
Hilton M. Preau II – Co. B 2nd/60th Infantry
Doug Prescott – B Co. 4th/47th Infantry
Mike Prescott – C-2 3rd/47th Infantry
Dave Preston – IUWG-1 Unit 4 Nha Trang
LCDR Leonard R. Previto, USN (Ret) – CTF-117
LTC Richard C. Prewett, USA (Ret) – A Co. 4th/39th Infantry
John H. Pribnow – D Co. 3rd/60th Infantry
Gary Price – USS Colleton
Patrick W. Price – RivDiv 591
Robert J. Price – ATCU-100A, Can Tho
Bob "Doc" Pries – B Co. 2nd/47th Infantry
Rudolph Pries, Jr. – M-111-1
Robert N. Primm – RivRon 13
Alan D. Pritts – A-111-6
Michael Prochko, Jr. – D Co. 2nd/60th Infantry
Cecil A. Proffitt – M-111-1
Robert E. Proper – B Co. 4th/47th Infantry
James R. Propst – A-3 3rd/47th Infantry
Chris Proscia – C Co. 3rd/60th Infantry
John W. Protosow, Jr. – HHC 3rd/60th Infantry
Donald L. Pryber – Coastal Surveillance Group
James E. Przytarski – B Co. 2nd/60th Infantry
Richard Puff – 9th Admin Co.
Gerard "Jerry" Pujat – C-3 3rd/47th Infantry
Joseph L. Pulice – B-2 3rd/60th Infantry
Sam Pulis – USS White River
Jack M. Pulliam, Jr. – NSA Da Nang
Duane K. Pullian – River Sect. 533, PBR-153
BMC Norman E. Pully, USN (Ret) – USS Benewah
Joe Pursel, Ph.D – Naval Advisory Group
John C. Puskar – HHQ C Btry 3rd/34th Arty
Lewis Putnam – M-91-2
Thomas W Quade – NavSupAct Det Sa Dec
Capt. Carl R. Quanstrom, USN (Ret) – CDR Oper. Market Time
John Quaty – B Co. 3rd/60th Infantry
Roger D. Queen – C Co. 2nd/60th Infantry
BMCM (SW) George Queen, USN (Ret) – USS Benewah
CDR Jay E. Quick, USN (Ret) – Commander TF 117 Senior Advisor VNN ATF
David M. Quickel, III – 478th Avn BN
David M. Quickel, Jr. – USS Benewah
Michael Quigley – YRBM-16, Binh Thuy
Christopher Quijada – USS White River
Ken Quinlan – River Section 535
Thomas F. Quinlan – E-3 3rd/47th Infantry
Lloyd V. Quinn – M-92-1
William F. Quinn – VAL-4

John Quinzio – DesRon-9
Kenneth L. Rachels – C and HQ Co. 3rd/34th Arty
Leland Raddatz – A Co. 709th Maint. Bn
Robin Rader – NSA Da Nang
James J. Radetzky – HHQ 2nd/47th Infantry
Fred B. Radtke, Jr. – YRBM-17
Lt. Col. William P. Radtke, USA (Ret) – 3rd/60th Infantry
Edward J. Rafferty – A Co. 2nd/47th Infantry
Marvin Raffler – B Co. 3rd/60th Infantry
Lee Finley Ragland – A-4 2nd/47th (Mech) Infantry
Michael J. Rahill – T-91-2
Donnie J. Rains – T-151-2
Loy K. Rainwater – USS Guide
Walter A. Rakaczewski – B-2 2nd/47th Infantry
Richard E. Raleigh – Naval Adv Group RAID 74
Jerry Raley – T-112-13
George "Joe" Ralph – 135th Helicopter Co
Jim Ralston – USS Whitfield County
Joe Rambo – E Co. 2nd/39th Infantry
Jurgen K. Ramil – Security Plt
Armando Ramirez – Naval Support Activity "My Tho"
Rene R. Ramirez – M-112-1
Manuel C. Ramos – B-2 3rd/60th Infantry
Ronald W. Ramsey – USS White River
Andrew M. Ramsey, Sr. – A-1 3rd/47th Infantry
Jonathan H. Randall – C-112-1
GMG1 Eugene Randall, USN (Ret) – USS Benewah
Michael R. Rankin – CBMU302
Peter B. Rankin – RivDiv 111
Jerrold W. "Jerry" Ranson – T-131-1
Ernest W. Rapp – USS Colleton
Anthony S. Rascano – HQ Co. 3rd/39th Infantry
Lynden E. Rasch – T-91-3
T. David Rasco – D and E Co. 3rd/39th 9th Inf.
Gilbert Rascon, Jr. – NASD Tan My
Kim H. Raseman – 335th Radio Research Co.
Rasmus W. Rasmussen – RivRon 9 T-91-6
Lucius R. Rast – D Co. 2nd/60th Infantry
Tom Rastall – 1st/84th Artillery
John Scott Rath – B-2 3rd/60th Infantry
Ray Rathburn – RivDiv 515
Grey "Doc" Rather – RivDiv 11 and 13
Jimmie Ratliff – USS Tioga County
Richard J. Rau – RivRon 13
Jack C. Rauscher – T-132-1
Owen M. Raven – A Co. 9th Signal BN
Hendrix F. Rawl – MineRon 11, Det AMSB-18
Paul Ray – 5th Heavy Boat Co.
Paul A. Ray – M-151-5
Ronnie D. Ray – B Co. 2nd/47th Infantry
William P. Ray – C Co. 2nd/47th Infantry
GMCM Kenneth S. Ray, USN (Ret) – USS Vernon County
David W. Raybell  M-111-3
Michael "Terry" Rayburn – USS Mercer
Roger K. Rayl – 9th Infantry Division
Charles E. Raynor – USS Benewah
Dale M. Ream – B Co. 3rd/47th Infantry
Russell Reamer – A-3 3rd/47th Infantry
Robert D. Reardon – NSA Da Nang
Jeffrey T. Reaves, Jr. – C-2 3rd/47th Inf
William Reddan – YRBM-17, Dong Tam
Michael J. Redding – USS Washtenaw County
Ted Reddinger – RivRon 9 T-91-11
William B. Redington – M-91-3
Col. Henly "Ed" Reed – HHC 2nd/60th Infantry

Larry T. Reed – B-2 3rd/60th Infantry
Lon Donald Reed – IUWG-1 Vung Tau
Robert A. Reed – T-111-3
Samuel W. Reed – US Navy DD-778
Edgar W. Reed, Jr. – T-92-9
Donald W. Reeder – USS Sphinx
Robert L. Reedy, Jr. – A Co. 3rd/47th Infantry
Raymond J. Reiblein – D Troop 3rd/5th Cavalry
Bill Reichert – USS Newman K. Perry
Gerald B. Reid – Z-152-1 and T-152-5
Robert K. Reidel – C-4 3rd/60 Infantry
Ed Reilly – B Co. 69th Engineers
Edward J. Reilly – 39th Cav. Platoon
Gary Reis – HHQ Co. 2nd/60th Infantry
Michael A. Reistetter – A-2 2nd/60th Infantry
David P. Reistetter, PE – NavPhibBase Coronado
Gary Reite – 9th Infantry Division
Richard D. Rekart – T-92-2
George C. Rekow – PCF-5, PCF-59, PCF-60
Ed Remmers – River Squadron 9
David J. "Dave" Remore – E Co. 3rd/60th Infantry
Dale A. Renbjor – NSA Saigon
Steven A. Renfro – CosDiv 15, 14, and 11
James R. Renick, Jr. – RivDiv 535
Lannie Mack Reninger – USS Windham County
Frank A. Renn – T-131-2
Clint "Ace" Reno – USS Askari
CAPT William J. Renton, USNR (Ret) – USS Askari
Richard "Rick" Ressegger – C Co. 2nd/47th Infantry
Federico Rey – D Co. 15th Combat Eng
Allan A. Reynaud – IUWG-1
Daniel A. Reynolds – TF-115
Leonard M. Reynolds – B-3 4th/47th Infantry
Paul G. Reynolds – HHQ 3rd/60th Infantry
Ronnie F. Reynolds – C Co 2nd Plt 4th/47th Infantry
William L. Reynolds – C Co 4th/47th Infantry
David A. Rhew – 3rd/60th Infantry
Wayne W. Rhinehart – D Co. 3rd/60th Infantry
Michael R. Rhode – A Co. 2nd/60th Infantry
Eudon A. Rhymer – USS Colleton APB-36
Billy G. Rice – RivRon 9
Danny G. Rice – C Co. 15th Engineers
Gregory M. Rice – RivRon 13 RAD 131
Ronald L. Rich – T-111-9
Tim L. Richard – C-92-1
Franklyn D. Richards – Z-131-1
Ronald G. Richards – A Co. 2nd/47th Infantry
Gene Richardson – 2nd/60th Infantry
John H. Richardson – A Co. 3rd/47th Infantry
CDR David Richardson, USN (Ret) – USS Hampshire County
LCDR B. J. Richardson, USN (Ret) – T-112-9
Pete Richenburg – USS Colleton
Daniel L. Richey – B Batt 1st/11th Artillery
Michael D. Richey – C-3 3rd/47th Infantry
David J. Richter – USS Washtenaw County
James R. Richter – USS Park County
SKC Gerold G. Ricks, USN (Ret) – USS Vernon County LST-1161
Edward E. Riddle – T-91-9
BMC Bobby G. Rider, USN (Ret) – M-111-3
David L. Ridgell – 3rd/34th Artillery
Guy C. Ridgely – Uss Washoe County
Capt Walter J. Riedemann, USN (Ret) – CO USS Tom Green County
John C. Rieger – USS Sphinx

Lt Ray E. Riesgo, USN (Ret) – CDR RivDiv 111
Nolan L. Riggs – USS Krishna
SSG Willie Rigney, Jr. – A-1 3rd/60th Infantry
Dave Riley – Coastal Division 12 and 13
William R. Riley – C Co. 4th/47 Infantry
Capt Douglas B. Rill, USN (Ret) – T-91-10
Johnnie P. Rindy – River Division 534
Wayne Ringate – USS White River
Sammie J. Ringer – R-112-1
Phillip Ringhand – USS Sedgewick County
Donald L. Riske – T-91-4
Herbert G. Risse – USS Mercer
Angel L. Rivera – C Co. 2nd/47th Infantry
Antonio Rivero, USN (Ret) – IUWG-1
James A. Roach – C-4 3rd/47th Infantry
Donald R. Robbins – USS Benewah
James O. Robbins – ComRivFlot I
Carl W. Robert – T-151-5, Z-151-1
Christopher P. Robert – HHC 9th Inf Div
Albert D. Roberts – USS Askari
David A. Roberts – RivDiv 132 and 153
Edward B. Roberts – River Section 511 and 512
Gary D. Roberts – B Co. 2nd/47th Infantry
John Roberts – YFU-24
Randall J. Roberts – B Co. 9th Signal BN
James D. Robertson – HHC and C Co. 4th/39th Inf.
Jeffrey C. Robertson – T-111-9
Terry L. Robertson – T-131-9
Daniel K. Robin – T-112-5
David E. Robinson – USS Washoe County
Gerald Robinson – USS Hampshire County LST-819
John H. Robinson – 9th MP Company, Dong Tam
William B. Robinson, Jr. – USS Mark AKL-12
Randall D. Robison – NavSuppAct Saigon
Russell G. Robison – NSA Dong Tam
William "Doc Rock" Rockwell, USA (Ret) – B Co 4th/47th and E Co 3rd/39th Inf
Allen Rodenberg – Army
Larry D. Rodgers – T-92-8 and A-92-4
Patrick J. Rodgers – USS Sumner County
Stephen J. Rodgers – VAL-4
William E. Rodman – USS Askari
Thomas G. Rodriguez – 6th/31st Infantry
Louis Rodriquez – RivRon 15 T-50
William Rodriquez – A-91-1
Timothy Rogan – C-3 3rd/60th Infantry
Haywood C. Rogers – 112 Mine Div MSB-18
James H. Rogers – A Co. 3rd/60th Infantry
Jon V. Rogers – C-2 3rd/47th Infantry
Charles E. Rogers, Sr. – B Co. 2nd/47th Infantry
Kent H. Roiecki – B-1 3rd/60th Infantry
Henry E. Rolen – E Co. 3rd/60th Infantry
Charles D. Rollins – USS Carronade IFS-1
Dominic C. Romano – C-3 3rd/47th Infantry
James W. Romerdahl – T-92-13
Anthony D. Romero – D-3 3rd/60th Infantry
Frank Romero – T-151-5
Mark L. Romey – Costal Division 13
CDR Lawrence E. Ronan, USN (Ret) – EOD Group I
Richard N. Rongstad – CHNAVADGRP NSA Saigon
Patrick M. Rooney – T-152-7
Curtis Roquemore – E Co. 4th/47th and 3rd/47th Infantry
Raymundo Rosales – B Co. 3rd/47th Infantry
Lance H. Rose – USS Benewah
Lawrence Rose – CRIP 9th Div Inf

Reed Rose – B Co. 2nd/47th Infantry
William A. Rose, USN (Ret) – USS St. Clair County
Jay Rosenberger – NAS Tan My and My Toa
Joseph K. Rosner – RivRon 15, M-6
Edward W. Ross – 3/34th Artillery
George F. Ross – C Co. 4th/47th Infantry
Jerry D. Ross – M-91-3
Charles C. Ross, Jr. – RivRon 131 and 132
Larry Rossebo – A Co. 2nd/60th Infantry
James D. Rosselli – C Co. 3rd/60th Infantry
G. Philip Rossman, II – B Co. 4th/47th Infantry
Glen W. Roth – RivDiv 552
J. Robert Roth – USS Benewah
John M. Roth – USS Askari ARL-30
Morton F. Roth – 15th Combat Engineers
E. J. Roulett – HHQ 3rd/47th Artillery
Grayson D. Roulston, Major, USA (Ret) – B-2 Co. 3rd/60th Infantry
Steven T. Rouse – Naval Advisory Group, T-53
Charles R. Rousey – C-2 4th/47th Infantry
Reuben P. Routh – 446th Trans Co.
Matthew F. Rovner – USS Colleton
Larry Rowan – USS Sutter County
Guy C. Rowland, Jr. – LPH-3
Ron Roy – B-1 2nd/60th Infantry
Robert G. Royer – USS Indra
James L. Rozema – A-91-3
Michael Rozier – B Co. 5th/60th Infantry
John Rubin – YRBM-16
Col. George R. Rubin, USA (Ret) – HQ 2nd and 3rd Bde, 9th Inf
RADM Merrill W. Ruck – PCF Div. 103, Cat Lo
James B. Rudd – USS Clarion River
Roy D. Rudolf – M-92-1
Jay H. Ruff – RivRon 13
Charles A. Ruggles – B-3 3rd/60th Infantry
Pieter A. Ruig – 3rd/47th Inf 9th Inf Div
Ronald B. Rulon – D Co. 15th Eng. Bn
Donald K. Ruplinger – A-2 2nd/39th Infantry
David J. Russell – T-111-11
Carleton T. Russell, Jr. – HCU-1, YLLC-4
Vito J. Russo – B Co. 2nd/60th Infantry
William R. Rusth – M-111-2
Sandy Ruta – D Co. 4th/47th Infantry
Larry L. Ruthrauff – T-111-12
Steven L. Ruud – 1099th TC (MB)
Al Ryan – USS Benewah
Daniel E. Ryan – B Btry 3rd/34th Arty
John W. Ryan – 3rd/60th Infantry Medic
Delos "Dee" R. Ryant, Jr. – USS Pulaski County LST-1088
Eugene J. Sabaitis – Coastal Surveillance Ctr.
James O. Saboe – C Co. 3rd/47th Infantry
Donald Sack – C Co. 3rd/60th Infantry
William Saffell – 335th Radio Research Co.
Leonard V. Saffen – M-91-2
James Saffo, Jr. – 4th/47th Infantry
Robert C. Sage – A Co. 15th Combat Eng.
William K. Sailing – USS Benewah
Michael Salaba – RivRon 11 A-112-4
Charles Salem – A Co. 2nd/47th Infantry
Burke A. Salsi – PCF-12 and CosDivs 12 and 11
Ken Saltz – B Co. 3rd/60th Infantry
Robert N. Salvador – USS Washtenaw County
Tom S. Salvaggio – A Co.4th/47th Inf
Ronnie Salyer – M-131-1
Loren Salzman – 4th/47th Infantry
Rev. Donald Sampley – Z-152-1
Eric Samson – USS Nueces

Harlan Samuels – E-3 Co. 4th/47th Infantry
David C. Samuelson – Naval Support Saigon (Det 552)
Tom Sanborn – A Co 4th/47th Infantry
Eduardo R. Sanchez, Jr. – USS Sphinx
Roger Sandeen – D Co. 3rd/47th Infantry
Billie J. Sanders – C-112-1
John Sanders – USS Askari
Joseph L. Sanders – USS Satyr
Robert L. Sanders – USS Benewah
Wade R. Sanders – CosDiv 13, PCF-98
Thomas H. Sandin, III – Z-131-1, T-132-23
Raymond Sandoval – C Co. 4th/47th Infantry
David Sandquist – USS Nueces
Rod J. Sangster – Strike Boat Sqd-20
Edward Sanicki – D Co. 2nd/60th Infantry
HMC Thomas J. Sanko, USN (Ret) – USS Benewah
Ron Santoro – RivRon-15
Jerry W. Sapp – River Section 533
Robert E. Sarka – USS Colleton
Sylvester J. Sasnett, Jr. – STAB Squadron 20
Reno A. Sassatelli – BSU-1 Det 1-A
John Sassian – D Co. 2nd/60th Infantry
Terry M. Sater – T-131-6 and T-131-9
Jorge Sauceda – NSA Dong Tam
Jose L. Sauceda – C Co.4th/47th Infantry
LCDR Gerald Saucier, USN (Ret) – CO USS Benewah
Norman J. Saunders – B Co. 3rd/39th Infantry
David J. Savage – USS Satyr
Gerald P. Savarese – C-3 3rd/47th Infantry
Clifford E. Savell – RivDiv 15 Zippo 4 T54
Jerome J. Sawick – B Co. 2nd/60th Infantry
BMCS (DV) Elbert W. Sawley, Jr. – USS Mauna Loa AE-8
Dennis Sawlsville – A-112-5
Tim Sayeressig – 3rd/47th Infantry
William H. Sayers – A Co. 3rd/60th Infantry
Donald L. Saylor – M-92-1
Raynard E. Saylor – A Co. 2nd/47th Infantry
RADM William L. Schachte, USN (Ret) – PCF-45
Robert Schade – A Co. 3rd/39th Infantry
SFC Martin Schadeberg, USA (Ret) – 1097th TC (MB)
Kerry N. Schaefer – RivDiv 514
Robert Schaffer – D-1 3rd/60th Infantry
Carl W. Schaldecker, Jr. – C-1 3rd/39th Infantry
Michael E. Schaming – B-2 3rd/60th Infantry
John Schank – HHC 5th/7th 1st Air Cav
Robert J. Schelb – T-91-8
Dennis J. Schelinski – D Co. 15th Combat Eng.
Richard C. Schelke – C-4 3rd/47th Infantry
Dave J. Schell – RivRon 15, T-41 and T-49
Charles D. Schellenger – B Co. 3rd/60th Infantry
Jonathan N. Schenz – Army
David E. Scherf – USS Tioga County LST-1158
Paul J. Schettine – USS Colleton
Robert L. Schifferns – USS Tutuila
BMCM Duane J. Schinn, USN (Ret) – RivRon 11 M-111-2
Joe Schladweiler – HHC 2nd/47th Infantry
Charles R. Schlaffer – T-92-9
John M. Schleicher – IUWG-1
Armin P. Schmalz – 1097th TC (MB)
James E. Schmelz, Jr. – USS Satyr
Conrad J. Schmer – USS Holmes County
Aloys L. Schmidt – USS Madera County
Gary D. Schmidt – D Co. 2nd/60th Infantry
Larry G. Schmidt – 1097th TC (MB)

Walter C. Schmidt – NSA Vinh Long/RS-57
Garry A. Schmieder – 5th/60th and 2nd/47th Infantry
William P. Schmitt – 3rd/60 Infantry
Richard L. Schmutte – M-91-2
George W. Schneider – USS Benewah
Lester J. Schneider – T-112-13
Ronald L. Schneider – IUWG-1 Unit 3
Thomas F. Schneider – A Btry 1st/11th Art & B Co 2nd/39th Inf
Robert J. Schnell – 2nd/60th Infantry
Thomas Schnorbus – 3rd/47th Inf
Robert H. Schnurbusch – Mine Squadron 11, Det A
Mark F. Schoenberger – B Co. 3rd/39th Infantry
Harold A. Schoenfeld – USS Tom Green County
Harry D. Schoenian – C Co. 4th/47th Infantry
Martin J. Scholnick – E Co. 3rd/47th Infantry 9th Div
Cdr. Richard L. Schreadley – ComNavForV
Charles A. Schroeder – USS Askari
Martin "Marty" Schroeder – B Co. 3rd/39th
Philip K. Schroeder – USS Washoe County
Jerry Schuebel – B-2 3rd/60th Infantry
Allan G. Schuerlein – A Co. 3rd/39th Infantry
Terry R. Schulte – B Co. 3rd/60th Infantry
Thomas A. Schultz – HQ Co. 3rd/60th Infantry
Bruce Schulze – USS Satyr
F. George Schuster – USS Indra
COL Sam L. Schutte, USA (Ret) – Co. B 4th/47th Infantry
Clyde A. Schwalen – D-3 4th/47th Infantry
RADM Sayre A. Schwarztrauber, USN (Ret) – Task Force Clearwater
Jon F. Scofield – USS Tioga County
Billy Scott – D Co. 4th/39th Infantry
Calvin J. Scott – A-1 3rd/39th Infantry
Donald E. Scott – B Co. 15th Engineers
Michael J. Scott – USS Satyr
Ronnie Scott – 2nd/39th Infantry
Thomas D. Scott – USS Colleton APB-36
William A. "Doc" Scott – B-2 4th/47th Infantry
GMGC Richard H. Scott, USN (Ret) – USS Benewah
Larry R. Scruggs – B Batt. 3rd/34th Arty
Dennis J. Scully – River Division 534
Joseph Sczyrek – USS Holmes County
Eugene F. Seacor – D Co. 2nd/47th (Mech) Infantry
Edward A. Seafeldt – USS Satyr
Pat Seals – 1097th TC (MB)
Al Sears – Riv Divs 591 and 593
John R. Secor – C Co. 4th/47th Infantry
Laurance See – Americal Division
Steven G. Seeberger – USS Tom Green County
James R. Seeley – USS Benewah
LaRue M. Seeley, USA (Ret) – IUWG-1, Nha Trang
Frank G. Seely – Co. C 15th Engineer BN
Daniel Seitz – HHQ 4th/47th Infantry
James W. Selby – CosDiv 13
Terry Sellers – C-4 3rd/47th Infantry
Jeffry L. Semprini – Harbor Security, Da Nang
LeRoy Senik – Michigan National Guard
Frank R. Serpas, Jr. – B-3 2nd/47th Infantry
Ernest E. Serrano – HHC 2nd/47th Infantry
William Settlemir – Com Mine Ron (11) Detachment Alpha
Charles R. Sewell – B Co. 5th/60th Infantry (Mech)
Walter S. Sexton – USS Whitfield County

Mark Seymour – YW-118 NSA Danang
James A. Shaffran – PCF-62
William J. Shall – A-151-4
Lawrence J. Shallue – HHC 2nd/47th Infantry
Robert H. Shank, Jr. – RivDiv-111 R-112-1
Larry P. Shankland – D Co. 4th/47th
E. Michael Shanklin – C Co. 3rd/39th Infantry
Michael D. Sharp – RivDiv 512
Thomas C. Sharp – T-152-11
Dean C. Shatley – USS Chesterfield County
Robert Shaw – C-132-1
Robert N. Shaw – T-91-3
Peter Shay – Seawolf HA (L) 3
SKC Eugene C. Shea, USN (Ret) – USS Colleton
Jerry L. Shearer – C Co. 3rd/60th Infantry
Joseph W. Shedlock – A-152-4
Patt L. Shelley – NSA Nha Be
LtCol Jim Shellington – A-1 3rd/60th Infantry
Gary L. Shellum – VAL-4
Donald J. Shelton – USS White River
Larry Shelton – B-1 3rd/39th Infantry
Samuel A. Shepherd – C Co. 3rd/47th Infantry
Rev. Patrick L. Sheridan – A Co. 3rd/60th Infantry
Richard A. Sherley – RivRon 13
J. Michael Sherlock – E Co. 3rd/60th Infantry
BMC Richard G. Shick, USN (Ret) – River Sect. 533
Glenn Shindler -- YRBM-16
Nelson E. Shineberger – B Co. 39th Infantry Reg
Robert A. Shinn – USS Whitfield County
James J. Shippey – R-E 4th/47th Infantry
Wayne Shippy – Alpha 8
Harry Shires – B-HQ Co. 3rd/60th Infantry
Clarence Shires, Jr. – C-1 4th/47th Infantry
Barney R. Shirey – USS Harnett County LST-821
George W. Shirey – M-92-2
Philip E. Shober – C-1 2nd/60th
Jerry Shockley – HHC 3rd/60th Infantry
Raymond H. Shockley – E Co. 4th/47 Infantry
Edward C. Shoemaker – USS Nueces
Frederic A. Short – PCF-66, PCF-72
Thomas L. Shorter – C Co. 3rd/60th Infantry
William Shreffler – B Btry 7th/9th Arty II Field Force
John Shroades – USS Mark AKL-12
Freddy Shugart – C-3 3rd/47th Infantry
Jerry A. Shullick – B Co. 4th/47th Infantry
Mike Siakooles – 286th Combat Engineers
Alejo V. Sibuma – RivDiv ASPB-6857
Edward J. Sicilia – 9th MP Co.
George Sickling – B Co. 3rd/39th Infantry
Peter G. Siebern – T-132-4
Richard Siebert, Sr. – IUWG-1 Unit 3, Qui Nhon
Leroy Siefer – 2nd/47th Infantry
Gary Sieg – D Co. 15th Engineers
E. H. "Skip" Sietmann – 101st Airborne
Rollin W. Sieveke – USS Hickman County
Mark Sigler – RivDiv 535
George H. Sikes – C Co. 4th/47th Infantry
Richard B. Silbert – USS Krishna
Arthur D. Silva – MineDiv 11 and RivDiv 534
Jim Silva – D-3 4th/39th Infantry
Jack L. Simmet – HHC 2nd Bde 9th Infantry
Franklin L. Simmons – C-2 4th/47th Infantry
John L. Simmons – A-1 3rd/47th Infantry
Raymond I. Simmons – USS Askari
CDR Douglas W. Simmons, USN (Ret) – RivDiv 515
Lesley E. Simons – T-131-4
Dennis L. Simpson – CTF-116 Staff
Frederick L. Simpson – C-4 4th/47th Infantry

Richard M. Simpson – C-1 3rd/47th Infantry
Robert E. Simpson – USS Washtenaw County
Ellis J. Sims – B Btry 1st/84th Arty
William E. Sinclair – USS White River LSMR-536
Morgan "Butch" Sincock – Mobile Advisory Team III-84
Bill E. Singleton – C-2 6th/31st Infantry
Charles R. Singleton – A-112-7
G. Dennis Singleton – T-151-11 and Z-152-2
Gary Sinkule – IUWG-1, Unit 3 Qui Nhon
Dominic C. Sirianni – T-91-1
Mark D. Sisco – C-3 4th/47th Infantry
Dennis W. Sisk – M-111-1
Gerald D. Sisk – B Co. 2nd/60th Infantry
James Edward "ED" Sitton – IUWG-1 Unit 3
A. Wayne Sizemore – C-3 3rd/60th Infantry
Gary C. Skaggs – Cdr B Co. 4th/47th Infantry
William B. Skidmore – B Battery FDC 1st/84th Arty
William H. Skidmore – USS Colleton
David D. Skinner – T-112-8
Charles W. Skoog – USS Windham County
Athan G. Skroumbelos – USS Krishna
George L. Skypeck – MACV
James D. Slade – A Co. 3rd/47th Infantry
Larry W. Slagle – 9th MP CID
Kerry R. Slahta – C Co. 9th Medical Bn
David E. Slasor – B Batt 3rd/34th Arty
Terry Lee Slater – B-2 2nd/60th Infantry
Thomas Slater – USS Hampshire County
Frank J. Sledz – A-2 3rd/39th Infantry
Norman H. Slimmer, Jr. – RivDiv 592
Donald Slinkard – RivDiv 131
Terry E. Sloat – River Assault Squadron 11
Marvin W. Slocum – C-2 3rd/60th Infantry
Walter M. Slone – HHC 9th Infantry Division
William A. Slover – XO USS Colleton
DeWayne Sloviak – HQ 3rd/47th Infantry
LCOL Richard A. Slowik – 22nd TASS
James W. Smalkowski – 32nd/47th Infantry
Bobby D. Smiddy – A-3 2nd/60th Infantry
Lawrence L. Smigielski – HHC 2nd Bde
Charles "Ron" Smith – USS Benewah APB-35
David M. Smith – C Co. 2nd/60th Infantry
Denny K. Smith – USS Satyr
Donald W. Smith – HQ Co. 2nd Brigade
Douglas M. Smith – B Trp 3rd/5th Cav, 9th Inf.
Douglas S. Smith – 2nd/47th Infantry
Emmitt Smith – HHQ 2nd/47th Infantry
Frederick E. Smith – T-91-13
Gary G. Smith – AO-63
Gary H. Smith – D-2 3rd/60th Infantry
Gary L. Smith – T-92-6 and A-92-3
Glenn I. Smith – B-3 4th/39th Infantry
Harold J. Smith – USS Benewah
J. E. Smith – C-2 4th/47th Infantry
James Wayne Smith – R-92-1
John A. Smith – B Co. 3rd/60th Infantry
John G. Smith – B-2 2nd/47th Infantry
John W. Smith – A-112-5
Larry R. Smith – USS Washoe County
Ralph R. Smith – HQ 3rd/47th Infantry
Randy D. Smith – B Co. 2nd/60th Infantry
Richard Smith – USS White River LSMR-536
Robert F. Smith – HQ 2nd/47th Infantry
Robert J. Smith – USS Krishna
Ronald C. Smith – USS Benewah
Ronald E. Smith – 2nd/60th Infantry
Ronald G. Smith – PCF-88 and PCF-102
Ronald J. Smith – T-131-7

Samuel T. Smith – IUWG-1 Unit 3
Thomas E. Smith – 9th S and T Battalion
Robert O. Smith III – A-91-1
Austin J. Smith, Jr. – YFU-80
Gary D. Smith, Sr. – YRBM-18 and YRBM-21
BMC John L. Smith, USN (Ret) – T-131-10
Dennis D. Smock – USS Mercer APB-39
Michael T. Smoley – USS Satyr
Joseph Snable – 1097th TC (MB)
D. David Sniff – USS Tutuila
Robert W. Snitgen, Jr., USN (Ret) – A-131-2
Henry L. Snook – USS Benewah
Jack L. Snow – USS Krishna
Walter H. Snow – C-151-1
John Snowden – B Co. 4th/47th Infantry
Howard W. Snyder – HQ Co. 4th/47th Infantry
Lanny R. Snyder – RivDiv 92
Gerald J. Snyders – 6th/31st Infantry
Richard Sobel – B Co. 3rd/60th Infantry
Jon B. Soder, USNR (Ret) – USS Hunterdon County
Andy Solomon – USS Mercer
David J. Soltis – A-92-4
Robert A. Somerville – A-131-4
Quentin Sommer, Jr. – B Co. 2nd/47th Infantry
Raymond Somogy, Sr. – 9th Infantry MP
Barry D. Sones – USS Sphinx
Gary Sonsteng – RivDiv 153 ASPB 57
Ryland "Lynn" Sorensen – River Assault Flotilla One
Capt. Curtis A. Sorenson, USN (Ret) – ComRivRon 11
Bill Sorrentino – USS Caroline County (LST-525)
Rosario F. Sortino – B-2 3rd/47th Infantry
Wallace C. Southerland – Z-131-1
Richard P. Sowa – T-131-3
Howard G. Spallinger – B Co. 9th Aviation Bn
David E. Sparks – C-2 3rd/47th Infantry
John E. Sparks – USS Holmes County LST-836
John E. Sparks – USCGC Sherman (WHEC-720)
Robert Sparks – 1st Armored Cavalry
Dwight K. Spear – D Co. 15th Combat Eng
G. Dwain Spears – USS Colleton
Gregory A. Spears – 571st Engr Co. (Combat)
Gary J. Speckman – T-91-5 and M-91-2
Terry L. Speelman – B Co. 2nd/47th Infantry
William Speenburgh – T-132-12 and T-32
Stephen A. Spence – A Co. 4th/47th Inf
Bradford R. Spencer – B Battery 2nd/4th Artillery
Thomas F. Spencer – RID-43
John J. Sperry – B-3 3rd/60th Infantry
Michael G. Spight – RivDiv 153 and 152
Marc Spilberg – 4th/47th Infantry
Ronald F. Spivak – C Co. 3rd/39th Infantry
Roy D. Spivey – Co. C 3rd/47th Infantry
John "Fats" Spizzirri – B-2 2nd/47th Infantry
Fred Spradley, Jr. – IUWG-1, Cat Lo
Tony Spradling – A-1 4th/47th Infantry
William Sprague – USS Benewah
J. Christopher Sprehe – RivDiv 153
Frank Springer – T-131-9
Glenn H. Springmeyer – 2nd/47th Infantry
Russell C. Sprinkle – 9th Adm 2nd/39th Inf
Aaron E. Spurway – USS Vernon County
Spyros Spyropoulos – 9th/60th Infantry
Ed St. Germain – NSA Nha Be and IUWG-1
James M. Stack – USS Askari
Frank R. Stafford – C-132-1
Lloyd Ron Stafford – Co. C 2nd/39th Inf
Larry D. Stalder – T-112-13

Richard Staley – RivRon 15
Willie A. Stallings – HHC and E Co. 2nd/60th Inf
Tony W. Stalnaker – USS Glennon
Jim Stanford – T-151-32
Henry A Stanley – USS Askari (ARL-30)
Chester C. Stanley, Jr. – C-111-1
Dwight O. Stapleton – River Assault Flotilla One
John R. Stark – 4th/47th Infantry
Michael Starr – 15th Combat Eng Air Boats
Ronald J. Stauffer – D Co. 3rd/60th Infantry
Douglas A. Stearns – D Co. 4th/47th Infantry
Pete Steberger – USS Askari
Steven K. Stedry – C-1 3rd/47th Infantry
Jimmy L. Steeley – USS Askari
Glen K. Steers – USS Benewah
Carroll G. Steeve – A Co. 2nd/47th Infantry
Paul C. Steffy – B Co. 2nd/47th Infantry
Barney J. Stefl, Jr. – B-2 3rd/47th Infantry
Joseph A. Stein – HHC 4th/47th Infantry
A. Eugene Steinkirchner, Jr. – B-3 3rd/39th Infantry
Jackie W. Steinman – 2nd/60th Infantry
Larry L. Steinmetz – RivRon 13
David E. Stenerson – RivDiv 153
Richard M. Stenzel – USS Benewah
Bennie Stephens – M-92-2
Harold Lynn Stephens – A Co 9th Aviation Bn
James L. Stephens – 4th/47th Inf
Randall L. Stephens – B-2 3rd/60th Infantry
Jeff Stephenson – USS Nueces
Mike Stephenson – A-3 3rd/47th Infantry
Howard W. Stepler – USS Askari
Charles R. Sterling – T-131-13
Robert F. Stern – E Co. 3rd/60th Infantry
Howard S. Stevens – RivDiv 534, PBR-17
Jim Stevens – B Co. 2nd/47th Infantry
John E. Stevens – USS Benewah
John J. Stevens – COS Divs 11 and 12, PCFs 58 and 40
Woodrow W. Stevens – C Co. 2nd/60th Infantry
David B. Stewart – USS Colleton
Mike Stewart – C Co. 3rd/60th Infantry
William G. Stewart – A Co. 4th/47th Infantry
Robert G. Stidham – USS Kitty Hawk
William E. Stieler – T-91-12
Kenneth Stiltner – USS Whitfield County
Jean L. Stimmell – USS Westchester County
Donald R. Stivers – A Co. 3rd/39th Infantry
Arthur W. Stock – B-3 3rd/60th Infantry
Theodore J. Stockland – USS Merrick
C. G. "Bill" Stockton – CO USS Kemper County
Don Stockwell – 9th MP Company
William F. Stoehs – River Assault Div 153
Curtis W. Stone – USS Francis Marion
Howard E. Stone – 574th Sup and Svc Co.
James A. Stone – E Co. 2nd/39th Infantry
Robert Stone – A Co. 2nd/47th Infantry
Norman E. Stone, Jr. – HQ 4th/47th Infantry
John F. Stone, USN (Ret) – USS Harnett County
Robert H. Stoner – USS Nueces
Darrell W. Storck – T-91-7
Willard Storms – D Co. 3rd/60th Infantry
Ross P. Stornello – 2nd/47th Infantry
Michael N. Stone – USS Benewah
Ronald G. Stout – RivRon 15 T-32 and IUWG-1
Dennis K. Stout, RMCM, USN (Ret) – RivDiv 152
Dan E. Stover – A-1 4th/47th Infantry
YN1 James A. Stover – NavSupDet Binh Thuy
Capt Marshall A. Stowell, USN (Ret) – CO, USS Benewah

Art Streeper – T-91-2
Russell J. Streiber – HHC 2nd/35th Infantry
Philip Streuding – B Co. 2nd/47th Infantry
CDR Joseph W. Streuli, USN (Ret) – ComCosDiv 13 CTG 115.3.7
Alan D. Strickland – A Co. 2nd/47th Infantry
Eugene F. Strickland – YRBM-17
Jerry W. Strickland – T-131-7
John T. "Jack" Strickland – D-3 3rd/60th Infantry
Kenneth L. Strickland – USS Satyr
Steve Strickland – IUWG-1
William H. Strobel, Jr. – RivDiv-153 and RID-47
Arthur R. Strong – B Co. 3rd/47th Infantry
Terry W. Strong – C-1 3rd/47th Inf
Kenneth Strong, USAR (Ret) – 1st/11th Field Artillery
R. Michael Strubel – T-91-4
Thomas R. Stuart – USS Benewah
William B. Stuart – 1097th TC (MB)
Ronald A. Stubbington – C Co. 2nd/39th Infantry
BMCM Robert Stucka, USN (Ret) – M-91-2 and A-91-5
Gary D. Studley – C-3 4th/47th Infantry
Karl K. Stueve – D Co. 3rd/60th Infantry
Terry G. Stull – A-1 3rd/47th Infantry
Neil E. Stummer – ISB/Solid Anchor
Robert J. Stumpf – 3rd/60th Infantry
John P. Sturgill – USS Colleton
John W. Sturgill – USS Satyr
John A. Sturtz – T-151-9
Bill Stute – USS Clarke County
Orlando Suarez-Lugo – RivRon 9
Dallas J. Suding – Co. C-2 3rd/60th
Jerry Sullivan – CosDiv 11, 12, and 16
LT Pete Sullivan – NGLO 12th Marines
Michael V. Sullivan – FASU Binh Thuy
Robert A. Sullivan – U.S. Navy
Edward R. Summers – M-111-2 and Z-111-7
Michael S. Sumner – C Co. 2nd/47th Infantry
Ira Sunday – USS Satyr
Ken Sundberg – HHC 5th/60th Mech. Infantry
LeRoy H. Sutlief – HHC 2nd/39th Infantry
Calvin H. Sutton – 3rd/47th and 2nd/47th Infantry
Lawrence Flint Sutton – C Co. 2nd/47th Infantry
Robert J. Sutton – RivRon 9 M-92-2, Z-92-1, and R-92-1
Virgil E. Sutton – HHC 3rd/47th Infantry
John F. Svandrlik – IUWG-1
Alan J. Svendgard – C-4 4th/39th Infantry
Mike Swank – USS Satyr
Charles R. Swank, III – HHC 2nd/47th Infantry
Brian M. Swann – HHC 6th/31st Infantry
Earl W. Swanner – RivDiv 554
Alfred E. Swanson – USS Harnett County
Jerry Swanson – USS Benewah
Jack A. Swardz – RivFlot I Staff
John E. Swart – T-132-1
Gary R. Swartz – C Co. 3rd/60th Infantry
Richard Swayne – USS Satyr
Woodrow J. Sweeney – USS White River
Michael G. Swenson – B-1 2nd/47th Infantry
Len Swiatly – USS Jennings County
Bryan Swisher – B Co. 3rd/47th Infantry
William P. Swistok, Sr. – RivRon 9 and RivRon 15
Weymouth D. Symmes – PCF-56
John W. Symons – IUWG-1 Unit 4
Stephen J. Szabo – C Co. 2nd/39th Infantry
Thomas X. Szewczyk – A Co. 3rd/60th Infantry
Rick Szpyrka – USS Conflict MSO-426

Ronald B. Szymberski – E Co. 4th/47th
Jim Taber – USS Whitfield County
James Dean Tabor – USS Windham County
Silvio Tagliamonte – 4th/47th and 2nd/60th Infantry
Michael J. Taheny – A Co. 3rd/47th Infantry
Brian T. Takeshita – C Co. 2nd/47th Infantry
William M. "Bill" Tallas – RivDiv 152
James R. Talley – RivDiv 551
Eric J. Tallstrom – STAB Squadron 20
William E. Tamboer – T-151-9
Anthony Tamuzza – USS Colleton
Richard E. Tangel – B Co. 3rd/47th Inf
John A. Tapocik – Cat Lo, Vietnam
Robert D. Tarbutton, Jr. – USS Mercer APB 39
Michael A. Tardo – NSA Da Nang
Joe C. Tarleton, Jr. – RivRon 15
Wyatt B. Tarrant – USS Benewah
Oscar Tate – A Co. 3rd/47th Infantry
Col. Clyde J. Tate, USA (Ret) – HQ 2nd Bde S-3
John Tatich, Jr. – A Co. 2nd/47th Infantry
Dennis M. Taulbee – IUWG-1 and IUWG-4
Richard L. Taunt – T-91-8, M-91-2
Bill Taylor – RAID-75
Charlie E. Taylor – C-3 5th/60th Infantry
Don Taylor – HQ 5th/60th Infantry
John E. Taylor – T-91-6
Michael W. Taylor – ComNavForV, YRBM-20
Paul R. Taylor – USS Askari
Robert L. Taylor – USS Washoe County LST 1165
Sherry Taylor – American Red Cross
Stephen P. Taylor – PCF-82, PCF-12, PCF-25
William T. Teare – USS Benewah
Richard S. Telega – T-152-12 and T-35
Edward E. Teletzke – C-91-1 and T-92-4
David L. Tennant – RivDiv 132, T-27
Glen L. Tennill – T-91-6
Eddie W. Tenpenny – USS Ticonderoga
Greg Terry – YRBM-16, YFU-59
John T. Terry – USS Nueces
Jack (Doc) Terry, Jr. – USS Colleton
Kenneth C. Terryberry, USN (Ret) – River Division 534
Joseph A. Terzi – B-1 3rd/47th Infantry
Bob Tesone – USS White River LSMR-536
Robert E. Teter – RivDiv 153
Capt. William H. Tewelow, USN (Ret) – USS Colleton
Robert G. Thacker – D Co. 15th Combat Eng.
William L. Thackrah – USS Tioga County
SGM John E. Thibado, USA (Ret) – T-112-3
Maurice J. Thibaudeau – T-132-3 and T-17
Thomas M. Thielmann – Co. C 15th Eng Bn
Daniel E. Thomas – 709th Maint Bn
Harry M. Thomas – PCF-46, PCF-52
Melvin E. Thomas – RivDiv 595
Robert A. Thomas – USS Tom Green County
William H. Thomas – A-91-7
William J. Thomas – RivDiv 153
Major James P. Thomas, USAF (Ret) – CosDiv 11 and 14
Clint D. Thomason, Jr. – USS Nueces APB-40
Jim Thome – RivRon 9
Dennis E. Thompson – USS Colleton
James L. Thompson – USS Colleton
Jawan L. Thompson – A Co. 2nd/47th Infantry
Richard Thompson – A-3 3rd/60th Infantry
Roger D. Thompson – T-131-4
Sam Thompson – 2nd/47th Infantry
Terry Thompson – USS White River

Terry G. Thompson – 1st/11th Arty and 2nd/4th Arty
Terry L. Thompson – C Co. 4th/47th Infantry
Thomas A. Thompson – B Co. 4th/47th Inf
Wayne W. Thompson – B Co. 9th Avn Bn
Clarence Thompson, CBM – C-92-1
James L. Thompson, III – T-92-2
Cpt. B. D. Thompson, USA (Ret) – 329th Trans Co, LCU-1567
Stephen E. Thoms – USS Benewah
M. Lee Thomson – C-111-1 and 151 and 152
Warren J. Thomson – B-3 3rd/60th Infantry
Leroy E. Thoreson – USS Askari
Roger J. Thornill – B Co. 3rd/47th Inf
Edmund E. Thornton – 9th Medical Battalion
Kenneth R. Thorpe – R-112-1
Dale P. Thurston – C Co. 3rd/47th Inf
Bruce B. Tidball – USS Indra
VADM Emmett H. Tidd, USN (Ret) – ComNavForV Chief of Staff
Timothy J. Tighe – USS Madera County and USS Benewah
Robert P. Tillander – USS Sphinx
Michael Tiller – RivRon 15
Steven Timchula – 15th Combat Engineers
Barry F. Timm – 2nd/60th Infantry
Harley G. Timmerman – T-132-10
John G. Tissler – FO 3rd/34th Artillery
Michael Tkalcevic – D Co. 2nd/60th Infantry
Donald M. Tobolski – CDR RivDiv 152
Frank Todaro – STABRON 20
Danny Todd – USS Satyr
Robert Tomasso – D Co. 4th/47th Infantry
Col. Dennis Tomcik – B Co. 3rd/47th Infantry
Jerry D. Toney – USS Satyr
Jimmy Toney – 3rd/60th Infantry
Harold W. Tooley – D-4 3rd/60th Infantry
Bill Toomey – C Co. 2nd/47th Infantry
Sgt. Okey Toothman, USA (Ret) – C-2 3rd/47th Infantry
Robert Torralva – Boat Captain T-152-44
Henry J. Torres – Associate
Randolph Torres – E Co. 4th/47th Infantry
Edward J. Toth – USS Askari
Richard P. Toth – B-2 3rd/60th Infantry
Fred E. Tow – USS White River
James M. Towey – B Co. 2nd/60th Infantry
Arthur Traendley – USS Wexford County
Michael Tramo – B Co. 6th/31st Infantry
Cam Tran – South Vietnames Navy
Donald Trausneck – USS Benewah
Don Trautman – 3rd/39th Infantry
William J. Trautman – C-3 3rd/47th Infantry
Phillip D. Treadway – B Co. 4th/47th Infantry
Gary L. Trebesch – B Co. 3rd/60th Infantry
Ralph Tresser – USS Benewah
Neil L. Trew – M-91-1
Harry S. Triebe, Sr. – 1099th TC (MB)
Edgar L. Tripp – RivDiv 152
David L. Trostle, Jr., USN (Ret) – RivDiv 554 and 594
Autry W. Trotter – B-3 3rd/60th Infantry
Larry Trubinski – C Co. 4th/47th Infantry
John L. Trudeau – A Co. 3rd/60th Infantry
Roland Truex – USS Jennings County
Johnny R. Trujillio – 3rd/34th Artillery
Kenneth I. Tryon – PCF Div 102 and 105
Timothy Tschida – A Btry 3rd/34th Arty
Allan W. Tucker – RivDiv 153
David J. Tucker – A-151-18

Gary Tuell – 3rd/47th Infantry
Lawrence Tully – B-2 3rd/60th Infantry
Jim Tunney – B Co. 3rd/39th Infantry
Philip E. Turnell – A Co. 3rd/39th
David Turner – USS Satyr
Dean E. (Fritz) Turner – USS Brule AKL-28
Howard D. Turner – 2nd/47th Infantry
Royal T. Turner – A Co. 2nd/60th Infantry
Willie B. Turner – USS Benewah
Robert K. Turner, Jr. – B Co. 9th Signal Bn
BM1 Richard P. Turner, USN (Ret) – RivDiv 152
LCDR Lewis D. Turner, USN (Ret) – USS Nueces CO
Darwin R. Turpin – A-1 4th/47th Infantry
Joseph M. Turton – T-49 and T-42
Col. Guy I. Tutwiler, USA (Ret) – CO 4th/47th Infantry
Erol S. Tuzcu – A Co. 3rd/60th Infantry
Lyle D. Twedt – E Co. 4th/47th Infantry
Richard E. Twigg – T-131-1
Christopher T. Tyas – 9th Division 4th/47th
Dennis L. Tye – R-92-1 and USS Krishna
David Tyler – RivDiv 132 M-3-6 T-24
David Tyma – USS Benewah
Leon A. Tyner, Jr. – D Co. 2nd/60th Infantry
Richard W. Typpo – USS Garrett County
Leahmond Tyre – B Co. 2nd/47th Infantry
David Tyson – M-91-2
Wayne J. Udwary – T-91-12 and A-91-2
Richard P. Uhlich – HHC B Co 2nd/47th Inf
Gary Ulrich – A Co. 2nd/60th Infantry
Steven Umbaugh – TF-116
Victor E. Unruh – T-151-1
Rickey Updegraff – 3rd/34th Artillery
Charles W. Upton – 329th Heavy Boat Co
Michael H. Urbom – USS Satyr
Benjamen D. Utley – C-3 3rd/60th Infantry
Dennis G. Valy – HQ Co. 3rd/47th Infantry
Stefan L. Van Camp – 2nd/39th and 4th/47th Infantry
Peter W. Van der Naillen – USS Clarion River
Ronald D. Van Dyck – 2nd/4th Artillery
Larry E. Van Trump – RivDiv 54
Charles E. Vance – USS Westchester County
Jim Vance – Z-152-1
Ron Vance – M-92-2
Gary G. VanDeLoo – RivRon 15, M-151-6 and M-151-7
S. Mark Vandling – M-132-3
Robert E. VanDruff – T-91-5 and T-92-4
Cdr. A. VanHorne, USN (Ret) – CO USS Jennings County
Robert Varain – B Co. 2nd/47th Infantry
Don Varenhorst – E Co. 6th/31st Inf
Mario Vargas – C-3 3rd/47th Infantry
Robert J. Vargas – 2nd/60th Infantry
Jaan R. Vari – IUWG-1 Unit 3
Steve Vasco – HHQ 5th/60th Mech Infantry
Richard M. Vasquez – Z-132-1
Calvin J. Vaught – NSA Cat-Lo
Captain Tom Vaught, USN (Ret) – Riverine Assault Division 131
Andres Vega – RivRon 15 C-151-2
Leroy Vegotsky – A Btry 3rd/34th Arty
Luis Velasco, Jr. – T-151-11
Larry D. Venenga – A Co. 4th/47th Infantry
Mike Venezia – U.S. Navy - Vietnam
John R. Venters – A Battery 1st/11th Arty
Willis R. Venus – RivRon 9
Donald N. Verwoerd, Sr. – USS Garrett County

Russell E. Vibberts, Jr. – HHC 2nd/47th Infantry
GMG1 Ricky M. Vice, USN (Ret) – RivRon 13 T-131-7
Robert L. Vick, Sr. – USS Colleton
G. "Jim" Vickers, Jr. – River Squadron 523
David J. Vicknair – USS Washtenaw County
Thomas Viet – E Co. 2nd/60th Infantry
Ken M. Vigil – T-152-7
Frank Vignola – RivDiv 92
Albert Villa – 3rd/47th Infantry
LCDR James M. Vincent, USN (Ret) – 3rd Coastal District
Stephen C. Vine – B Co. 2nd/47th Infantry
Melvin C. Vineyard – USS Washtenaw County
Ralph W. Vinson – IUWG-1 Unit 4
H. Allan Virginia – USS Jennings County LST-846
Gene Vise – USS Tom Green County
Steven J. Vitale – T-92-8
Gary A. Voelker – B Co. 3rd/47th Infantry
Ronald E. Voldseth – RivDiv 153 A-51
Frank J. Voll, Jr. – 2nd/47th Inf and 5th/60th Inf
Terry L. Volz – USS Luzerne County
Donald Von Eller – C Co 9th Signal Battalion
Stan Vonfeldt – A Co. 5th/60th Infantry
John T. Vorndran – A Co. 4th/47th Infantry
Leslie A. Vorphal – CosDiv-11, PCF-3
Melvin L. Voth – RivDiv 533
Brett T. Votra – HDQ and A Co. 99th Combat Support Bn
Larry W. Vowels – USS Tutuila
Robert N. Voytko – A Co. 9th Aviation Bn
Gerald A. Vroman – B-1 3rd/60th Infantry
David T. Vrooman – T-111-13
John L. Wabel – C and E Co. 3rd/39th Infantry
Joe Wadlow – TF-116
Jerry Wagner – A-3 3rd/47th Infantry
Mike Wagner – D-4 3rd/60th Infantry
Thomas E. Wagner – PCF Div. 105, PCF-60
Franklin D. Wagner, USA (Ret) – HHQ 9th Infantry Division
Jerry Wagstaff – RivRon 11 and 15
Gene Wahlstrom – NAVSUPACT Dong Tam
Michael S. Wakefield – T-112-4
Carl Waldron, Jr. – B Co. 3rd/60th Infantry
Joseph F. Walk – USS Benewah
James T. Walker – E Co. 3rd/60th Infantry
Mickey W. Walker – PCF-9
Rodney S. Walker – CCB-132-1 and T-132-15
Ronald A. Walker – T-111-9
Robert R. Wallace – River Patrol Force
Ronald R. Wallace – B-3 3rd/47th Infantry
William J. Waller – A-131-6
Michael Jon Walsh – USS Holmes County
Gilbert L. Walters – T-92-11
William Lamar Walters – C-132-2
Lonnie Walters, USN (Ret) – IUWG-1, Vung Tau
Charles Q. Walton – C Co. 2nd/47th Infantry
EM1 Johnny L. Walton – T-91-2
Robert J. Walz – M-131-1
Andrew E. Wampler – T-92-6
Donold J. Wampler – PCF Advisory Team #159
Billy L. Ward – M-112-1 and T-112-2
John F. Ward – B-3 3rd/60th Infantry
Stanford C. Ward – PBR-114, Cua Viet
Steven M. Ward – ComRivFlot I Staff
Alan W. Wargel – T-91-1
Terry Wargo – NavSupAct, APL-30
Joseph Waring – USS Tutuila ARG-4
Michael D. Warlick, Sr. – USS Brule AKL-28

David Warner – C Co. 3rd/47th Infantry
Rexford E. Warner, Jr. – A Co. 2nd/47th Infantry
Donald D. Warren – T-91-2
Ronald Patrick Warren – EOD Team 39
John R. Warren, Jr. – M-92-2
ENC Ernest W. Warren, USN (Ret) – USS Hickman County
CWO3 Donald G. Washburn, USA (Ret) – 1097th TC (MB)
CDR Lawrence Wasikowski – CosDiv 12, PCF-58
James R. Wasser – PCF-23, 103, 40, and 44
John B. Watkins – B-3 3rd/60th Infantry
Ray Watley – USS Mercer
John W. Watry – M-92-2
Calvin D. Watson – A Co. 3rd/47th Infantry
Jack Watson – C Co. 3rd/60th Infantry
John Watson – RivRon 15 (A-19, M-7)
Malcolm G. Watson – USS Askari
Marty Watson – USS Colleton
Terry Watson – 2nd/47th Infantry
Clifton Watts – USS White River
William H. Waugh, III – C Co. 3rd/47th Infantry
William W. Weathersby, Jr. – 2nd/47th and 3rd/47th Infantry
Jack D. Weaver – River Squadron 5 RivSec 511
Charles F. Webb – USS Sphinx
Clyde A. Webb – RivRon 9 A-92-7
Jerry E. Webb – YRBM-20
Perry Webb – C Co. 3rd/47th Inf
William M. Webb – A-4 3rd/47th Infantry
Fred R. Webber – NSA Dong Tam
Larry L. Webber – T-92-9
Peter F. Weber – B-2 3rd/47th Infantry
Scott Weber – B Co. 2nd/47th Infantry
Harold H. Weber, Jr. – T-132-1
Thomas A. Weber, Jr. – USS Caroline County
A. J. "Jim" Webster – IUWG-1 Unit 2
David A. Webster – USS Whitfield County
Rev. Robert J. Weckle – C-1 2nd/60th Infantry
Larry Wedemeier – B Co. 3rd/47th Infantry
James O. Weed – B-1 2nd/47th Infantry
Jessie B. Weeks – RivDiv 511
John R. Weersma – B-3 3rd/47th Infantry
Ralph Weicht – B-2 3rd/47th Infantry
William E. Weidman – T-111-12
Randall Weir – TF117
David Weis – USS White River
Sanford Weisman – USS Washtenaw County
Gerald J. Weiss – USS Benewah
John W. Weiss – C-3 2nd/60th Infantry
Gary T. Weisz – A-91-4
David J. Welch – NavSupAct Saigon
Gordon J. Welch – USS Satyr
Joe Welch – 4th/47th Infantry
Dolph W. Wellborn, Jr. – T-131-13
Henry Wells – C Co 5th/60th 9th Inf Div
Norman L. Wells – ComRivDiv 112
Robert T. Wells – River Division 92
Capt. Wade C. Wells, USN (Ret) – ComRivFlot I
Lawrence W. Wenban – Harbor Clearance Unit 1
Frank D. Wengler – HHC 2nd/60th Infantry
Stephen Wentworth – 3rd Cavalry
Ed Werle – M-92-8
Joseph F. Werner – T-132-10
Patrick F. Werner – 2nd/60th Inf
Terry Lee Werstlein – USS Benewah
Bill West – USS Colleton
Kerry West – RivRon 11 T-112-13
Robert J. West – USS Krishna

William C. West – T-131-1
Charles Westcott – RivDiv 111, 112, and 131
Terrell M. Westcott – USS Hunterdon County
James A. Westgate – USS Satyr
Lester L. Westling, Jr., USN (Ret) – NSA Saigon in IV Corps
Gen. William C. Westmoreland, USA (Ret) – ComMACV
Gerald G. Weston – C-91-1 and A-91-7
Francis Westrick – HHC 3rd/47th Infantry
Roy Wetzel – 1099th TC (MB)
William B. Wharton, USA (Ret) – Co. A 15th Combat Eng Battalion
James Fred Whatley – A Co. 4th/47th Infantry
Lewis F. Wheatley – C-2 3rd/60th Infantry
Edward Wheeler – C Co. 2nd/47th Infantry
Michael E. Wheeler – RIVPAT FLOT 5 (Staff)
George L. Whicker – A-111-8
Arlyn Whitchurch – HHC 15th Combat Engineers
Bobby C. White – B Co. 2nd/47th Infantry
Charles T. White – 3rd/47th and 5th/60th Infantry
Christopher White – T-92-8
David Allen White – RivDiv 593
David H. White – USS Satyr
Dr. Charles J. White – RivDiv 533/595
Harless White – M-91-3
Jim H. White – 15 Engr BN 9th Inf Div
Kerry A. White – C Co. 3rd/47th Inf
Richard D. White – B Co. 3rd/39th Infantry
Ronald D. White – USS Benewah
Tom R. White – C Co. 4th/47th Infantry
Trentwell "Trent" White – USS Guide
William J. White – A Co. 2nd/39th Infantry
Willie B. White – A-92-4
Frank A. White, Jr. – B Co. 2nd/47th Infantry
James White, USN (Ret) – USS Nueces APB-40
Mackroy White, USN (Ret) – RivRon 15
Phillip L. Whiteside – E-2 HHQ 3rd/60th Infantry
Terence G. Whiteside – NSA Da Nang
Edward C. Whitmarsh – 9th Inf Div A-3 2nd/60th Inf
Richard K. Whitmore – HHC 2nd/60th Infantry
Lloyd C. Whittaker – USS Clarke County
Robert E. Whittaker, Sr. – 9th MP Co. 9th Inf. Div
William "Whit" Whitworth, Sr. – D Troop 3rd/5th Cav
Terry Wibstad – USS Luzerne County
Charles D. Wie Sel – NavAdvGrp, TF-115.4
Everett R. Wiedersberg – M-112-1
Grant D. Wieler – HHC 3rd/60th Infantry
Bruce A. Wiener – Co. C 3rd/47th Infantry
James P. Wiener – PBR Mobile Base 1
Jack Wiesner – 2nd/47th and 2nd/60th Infantry
Stephen G. Wieting – USS Benewah
John H. Wigand – A Co. 9th Avn BN
BMCM Donald J. Wiita, USN (Ret) – T-111-13
Charles L. Wilber – C Co. 3rd/47th Infantry
Edward E. Wilds, Jr. – C-2 4th/47th Infantry
Roger C. Wiles – LC PL 23 and IUWG-1 Unit 2
Larry W. Wiley – USS Benewah
Michael A. Wiley – RivDiv 543
George A. Wilfong – A-2 4th/39th Infantry
William R. Wilhelm – T-152-6
Terry J. Wilkins – C-4 3rd/47th Infantry
David G. Wilkinson – PBR-109
Norman C. Wilkinson, Jr. – B Co. 4th/47th Infantry
John J. Wilks – RivRon 9 A-92-7
James M. Will – PCF-28, PCF-98, PCF-102
David Willard – USS Vernon County

Roger A. Willcutt – T-151-11
Robert J. Willegal – T-112-6
Dennis D. Willess – CosDiv 13, PCF-71, PCF-60
Bruce F. Williams – HQ 3rd/47th Inf 9th Inf Div
Darrell D. Williams – USS Askari
David S. Williams – USS Iredell County LST-839
Donald E. Williams – T-132-8
Gary L. Williams – C-2 3rd/60th Infantry
Jack N. Williams – RivDiv 92 and 13
Larry W. Williams – B Co. 3rd/39th Infantry
Reginald N. Williams – B-1 3rd/47th Infantry
Robert P. Williams – 1097th TC (MB)
Robert W. Williams – C Co. 6th/31st Inf
Walter Williams – RivDiv 552
Clyde L. Williams, III – A Co. 2nd/47th Infantry
Keston K. Williams, Jr. – 9th Infantry Division E Co.
Gary Williams, LTC, USAR – B Co. 2nd/60th Infantry
CDR Jim Williams, USN (Ret) – CTF-117
Ed F. Williamson – Operation Sealords
Stanley L. Willingham – USS Colleton
Larry G. Willis – A Btry 3rd/34th Artillery
Randolph L. Willis – A-4 3rd/60th Infantry
Donald E. Wills – E Co. 15th Engineers
Lester Wilmes – C Co. 2nd/39th
Buddy Wilson – YTB-784 and YFU-4
David C. Wilson – U.S. Navy
Donald E Wilson – M-112-1
Donald W. Wilson – T-111-5
Douglas B. Wilson – C-1 4th/47th Infantry
Frederick J. Wilson – RivDiv 153, A-56
Oscar C. Wilson – M-152-1
Richard L. Wilson – NSA Cam Rahn Bay
Robert L. Wilson – C-92-1, M-92-5
Ronald E. Wilson – B Co. 4th/47th Infantry
Ronald I. Wilson – D Co. 15th Combat Eng
Curtis M. Wilson, Jr. – C Co. 2nd/47th Infantry
John K. Wilt, Jr. – USS Ranger (CVA-61)
Jack J. Winch, Jr. – HHC 4th/47th Infantry
Ronald Winchell – C Co. 3rd/60th Infantry
Jeffrey W. Winegardner – C Co. 4th/47th Inf
Russell A. Winemiller – USS Tutuila (ARG-4)
Gary A. Winger – USS Sphinx
Dale R. Winkel – C Co. 3rd/60th Infantry
Steve Winkler – D Co. 2nd/60th Infantry
BMCS Henry W. Winston, USN (Ret) – Boat Captain of A-92-3
Tom Wischman – USS Indra ARL-37
Rhett S. Wise – A-2 3rd/47th Infantry
CWO4 Orville G. Wise, Jr., USN (Ret) – T-131-5
Larry A. Wiseheart – ComRivRon 13
Robert J. Wisniewski – E Co 2nd/60th Inf
Jeffrey L. Withers – RivRon 9 and 11
Warren R. Withers – A-111-2
Robert E. Witmer – USS Krishna
Greg Witt – USS Whitfield County
Thomas F. Witt – YRBM-21, Dong Tam

Larry E. Wodack – Co. C 3rd/47th Inf
John T. Wofford – T-132-6
Frank Wojciechowski – USS Caroline County
Kerry J. Wojcik – USS Westchester County
Jim Wolak – USS Washtenaw County
Albert F. Wolfe – USS Askari
Charles Wolfenberger – A Battery 3rd/34th Artillery (Barges)
Lary Wolff – RivDiv 574 and 514
William F. Wolffer, Jr. – B-2 3rd/60th Infantry
Bruce "Doc" Wolfson – 3rd/39th and CRIP 3rd Bde HQ
James P. Wollner – 15th Eng. Bn 2nd Airboat Platoon
Henry A. Woloszyn – A Co. 2nd/39th Infantry
William R. Wolverton – T-111-5
Gary Wood – USS Westchester County
Kenneth J. Wood – C Co. 3rd/60th Inf
Joseph T. Woodall – CosDivs 11, 13, and 15
Andrew J. Woodgeard – C Co. 4th/39th Infantry
Richard Woods – A-91-2
Roy E. Woods – A-111-3
Tim Woolums – USS White River
James A. Wooten – M-152-1
Theodore E. Worcester – B Batt 3rd/34th Artillery
John W. Woronicak – USS Benewah
George C. Worthington – RivDiv 152
Herbert Worthington – C Co. 3rd Brigade 2nd/60th Infantry
John L. Wotring – B-3 3rd/47th Infantry
Charles T. Wright – 1097th TC (MB)
Dennis A. Wright – USS Krishna
Jerry H. Wright – M-92-1
John T. Wright – IUWG-1 Unit 2 and Unit 4
Larry L. Wright – HQ C Co. 4th/47th Infantry
Lorenzo A. Wright – RivDiv 111-13 and 131
Melvin G. Wright – USS Askari
Michael A. Wright – B Co. 4th/47th Infantry
Robert L. Wright – 1099th TC (MB)
Thomas A. Wright – 2nd/47th Infantry
L. T. "Tom" Wright, Jr. – D Co. 3rd/60th Infantry
William H. Wulff – B Co. 3rd/47th Infantry
BMC (SW) Edward L. Wyman – USS Washoe County
Harry M. Wymore – PBR-110
Albert G. Yaek – A-111-7
Richard K. Yager – A Co. 4th/47th Infantry
Francis R. Yanovitch – PCF-39
Joseph T. Yarashus – T-111-6
Robert M. Yarnall, Jr. – 9th Signal Bn
Steve Yawn – RivRon 11
1SG Fred "Yab" Ybanez, USA (Ret) – C-1 3rd/60th Infantry
Dennis L. Yeakel – USS White River
James P. Yeiser – A Co. 3rd/39th Infantry
Doug Yelmen – ACU-1, Dong Ha
Thomas H. Yelverton – HHC 3rd/47th Infantry

LCDR Walter F. Yielding, USN (Ret) – CO USS Mark AKL-12
Lawrence Yoder – Uss Westchester County LST-1167
Robert T. Yoka – 3rd/47th Infantry
Maj. Charles N. Yongue, USA (Ret) – A-1 145 AB
Terry York – A-112-7
Jerry Young – USS Colleton APB-36
John W. Young – C Co. 4th/47th Infantry
Kennard A. Young – B-2 2nd/60th Infantry
Mark R. Young – B-2 3rd/60th Infantry
Rex A. Young – 3rd/39th Inf
Rick Young – USS Colleton
Tom Young – USS Brule
William J. Young – USS Tom Green County
Henry L. Young III – H Btry 29th Artillery
Spurgeon Young, Jr. – A Co. 4th/39 Inf
Larry A. Youngblood – USS Jennings County
James O. Younts II – C Co. 2nd/47th Infantry
George P. Yung – CTF-115
Mark R. Zabkowicz – C Btry 2nd/4th Artillery
William Zachmann – RivDiv 92 M-91-1
Joseph Zagar – RivDiv 535
John E. Zahurak – T-92-1
Frank P. Zamski – D-4 4th/47th Infantry
George R. Zane – USS Wexford County
Albert C. Zapanta – E Co. 75th Rangers
Tom Zaputil – 5th/60th Infantry
Tony Zatkovic – USS Coral Sea
Nickolas J. Zeveski – RivRon 13
John Zia – USS Colleton
Patrick T. Ziegler – USS Krishna ARL-38
Philip E. Ziegler – NILO My Tho
Edward J. Ziek – B Co. 3rd/60th Infantry
Richard J. Ziemba – USS Whitfield County
James E. Zieminski – RivDiv 153, ASPB-6854
Joseph W. Zieris – USS Ranger (VA-165)
Keith N. Zierk – B-2 5th/60th Infantry
John Ziesing – T-151 and T-152
Thomas Zigoris – 9th MI Det - Dong Tam
Vincent Zike – A-1 3rd/47th Infantry
Carl E. Zilch – D Co. 2nd/60th Infantry
Charley C. Zilhaver – D Co. 3rd/60th Infantry
LT Robert J. Zimmer, USN – XO USS Mercer APB-39
Randall V. Zimmerman – C Co. 3rd/39th Infantry
Richard M. Zimmerman – B Co. 3rd/39th Infantry
Ronald L. Zimmerman – PCF-74
William E. Zimmerman – IUWG Unit 2 Cam Rahn Bay
Larry E. Zinneman – C-2 2nd/60th Infantry
Joseph E. Ziss – HHQ 3rd/39th Infantry
John R. Zivic – USS Vernon County
Randy Zobel – B Co. 2nd/47th Infantry
Joseph Zuppardo – 231 Trans. Co.
Edward Zwaduk, Jr. – C-3 3rd/39th Infantry
Theodore Zwislewski – M-132-1

# INDEX

## A

Abrams, General Creighton 48
Adams, Eddie M. 52
An Giang 53
An Long 36
An, LTJG 20
An Thoi 18, 22
An Xuyen 16, 26, 53
An Xuyen Province 10, 16, 51
Ap Bac 25, 29, 30
Ap Thanh My 12
Arbogast, Bill 68
Arens, Frederick V. Jr. 52
Athanasiou, Ronald S. 53
Aurin, LT R.J. 21

## B

Ba Ngoi Vilage 16
Ba The Canal 25
Ba Xoai 20
Bac Lien 53
Bakle, Ralph 22, 70, 71, 72, 73
Ballard, LCDR R. 19
Bannister, Howard W. 52
Barber, Barry M. 53
Barbour, LCDR Richard E. 33
Baria 14
Barnes, LCDR H.L. 19
Barr, Edward N. 53
BARRIER REEF 20, 21, 24, 25, 29, 31, 33, 36, 39, 44, 48
Basco, Harvey Lee 53
Bassac River 29, 46
Baumer, James C. 53
Bay Hap River 41
Bechwith, CAPT R. 19
Bell, Dave 68
Bell, LT C.A. "Al" 68
Bell, Navy Lieutenant Al 67
Ben Heo 21
Ben Keo 23, 29, 36
Ben Keo (Tay Ninh) 8
Ben Luc 8, 9, 13, 19, 21, 23, 28, 29, 36
Ben Tre 46, 67
Benak, Joseph F. 53
Benson, ADR1 C.R. 45
Bernstein, Leonard 62
Berry, LT N.W. 20
Bien Hoa 52, 53, 69
Bien Hoa Province 35
Binh Duong Province 29
Binh Thuy 13, 14, 19, 36, 41, 45, 51
Bishop, LT J.B. 20, 22
Blackwell, BMC 24
Blair, CAPT C.H. 21
BLUE SHARK 46
Bobb, John F. 52
Boink, LT 33, 34, 37
Bonachi, Pete 64
Border Interdiction 22, 26
Boron, David J. 52
Borquist, LCDR B.W. 21
Bortell, LTJG C. 19
Boschen, CDR H.C. 17, 18, 22
Bouchet, Signalman Second Robert Louis 59
Boyce, Samuel M. 52
Boyd, LCDR J.P. 22
Boyer, Bill 71
Boyer, BTSN 71
Brannen 76
Breckenridge, LCDR D.R. 17
BREEZY COVE 20, 22, 26, 30, 31, 32, 34, 36, 37, 39, 41, 44, 45, 48, 50, 51, 63
Brisbois, Commander M.B. 40
Brown, Dr. Noel 62
Brown, Radarman Second Anthony Barton 59
Bruckart, Donald L. 52
Brunton, Stephen C. 52
Bryson, LTJG A.Y. 19
Buck, Frank H. 52
Burnes, Quartermaster Second Howard Frank 59
Butterfield, LCDR J. 19
Buzzell, LTJG R.H. 51
Byassee, Norman K. 53

## C

Ca Mau 8, 10, 30, 33, 34, 36, 37, 38, 41, 45, 50, 51
Ca Mau City 33
Ca Mau Peninsula 43, 45, 51
Cai Lon River 12, 38
Cai Nuoc 50
Cai Tu River 12
Cain, BM1 28
Cain, Captain Donald M. 28
Cam Ranh Bay 19, 57, 58
Cambodia 25, 31, 32, 36, 41
Camp Nguyen Van Nha 14
Camp Nguyen Van Nho 9
Camp Tien Sha 11
Campos, Jose B. 53
Can Gao Canal 8
Can Giouc 21
Can Giouc City 27
Can Giuoc 42
Can Tho 14, 19, 22, 25, 36
Carroll, Kenneth A. 52
Carson, Sgt.J.M. "Joe" 56
Carter, Jackie C. 53
Cartwright, Richard C. 53
Cat Lai 36
Cat Lo 44
Catlett, LTJG G.L. 17
Catone, Lieutenant 23
Causso, Sgt. Dennis 68
Cawley, Robert W. 52
Cerreta, Major Mike 68
Chambless, SMC 24
Champion, LT R.H. 19
Chapman, Rick 76
Chapman, Ronald 52
Chau Doc 24, 25, 29, 30, 36, 51
Chau Van Theatre 25
Chavous, Samuel C. Jr. 52
Cheek, Richard A. 52
Chon, RADM Tran Van 44, 51
Christensen, CDR C.R. 41
Christensen, Commander 51
Chuong Duong 16
Chuong Thien 53
Chuong Thien Province 12, 13, 67
Clark, CDR B. 22
Clark, CDR R.A. 22
Colby, Ambassador William E. 16
Comer, William M. Jr. 52
Connolly, LT Commander 70
Connolly, LT M.B. 20, 21
Cook, Larry 65, 66
Couch, LT 44
Cox, Roy A. 52
Crago, Robert 66
Crane, LT M.F. 18
Cross, Sammy J. 52
Cua Dai 20
Cua Dai River 17
Cua Dai River Basin 11
Cua Viet 22
Cua Viet River 39
Cunningham, Budd 57
Cutler, Thomas J. 61

## D

Dale, Chester D. 53
Dameron, Larry R. 53
Danang 11, 17, 22, 48
Dannheim, Lieutenant Commander W.D. 51
Darville, Edward R. III 52
Davidson, PR1 25
Davis, Boatswainmate Third Terry Lee 59
Dead Man's Trail 65
Dellinger, Charles H. 52
Demski, EN 3 N.H. 50
Dennis, BMC 27
Diamond, Bill 64
Diamond, William T. Jr. 52
Dinapoli, Seaman Michael Joseph 59
Dinh Tuong 52, 53
Doan Thi Diem Street 48
Dodd, Dan 3, 7, 10, 13, 14, 15, 16, 35, 37, 40, 42, 45, 49, 55
Dodson, J.D. 75
Dong Ha River 22
Dong Hung 8, 9, 10, 14, 67
Dong Tam 9, 12, 20, 31, 56, 59, 60, 71
Dosell 61
Drew, JO3/JOSN Robert S. 39, 43, 48
Ducharme, CDR G.W. 22
Duffy, Keith W. 53
Duggan, LTJG 24
Dunning, Timothy C. 53
Durbi, Ronald W. 52
Dyer, LCDR W.G. 19
Dyer, LT 40

## E

Edmundson, CAPT J.E. 22
Eischen, LT G.N. 20
Ellis, LT G.J. 20
Engstrom, LTJG J.G. 18
Eo Lon Canal 46
Ethridge, LT S.V. 49
Evenson, Michael A. 52

## F

Fallow, EM1 John S. 45
Farley, GMG2 28
Faulk, CAPT J.E. 19
Faulk, CAPT J.R. 19
Fell, David G. 53
Ferguson, Michael L. 53
Finke, CAPT E.I. 22, 44, 48
Fire Support Base Barbara 9, 13
Flanagan, RADM W.R. 19
Foddrill 68
Ford, LTJG William L. 41
Fourth Riverine Area 16
Frantz, LTJG Stephen W. 39, 43, 48
Fulton, General 4
Funke, Thomas G. 53

## G

Gage, RMC 28
Gaines, GMG3 Stanley H. 28
Ganh Hao River 36
Garcis, GMG1 8
Gardner, LT W. 19
Garza, Richard Jr. 53
Gaspar, Jose 59
Gatto, LCDR D.P. 18
Gaudet, Thomas W. 53
Gia Dinh 52, 53
Gia Dinh Province 16
GIANT SLINGSHOT 8, 9, 20, 22, 23, 26, 27, 28, 29, 36, 39, 44, 48, 67
Giao Hoa Canal 67
Girard, EN1 28
Go Cong 52, 53
Go Dau Ha 21, 23, 24, 29
Go Dau Ha City 27
Going, Wallace 52
Goodwin, GMG2 25
Gottemueller, LTJG G. 19
Graham, LT W.H. 20
Grand Canal 29, 30, 33
Griffin, Patrick J. 52
Groce, BM1 27
Grosz, GMG2 28
Guam 34
Gulf of Thailand 10, 18, 25, 46

## H

Ha Tien 20, 36, 51
Hagl, Edward J. 52
Hai Yen 51
Hall, Herman Michael "Mike" 63
Ham Rong 44
Ham Rong Village 49
Hamm, CDR R.G. 22
Hamm, Gerald E.B. 53

Hamman, Commander 23
Hanna, William A. 53
Harrington, Iris H. 53
Harris, BM2 70, 71
Harrison, Theodore Jr. 52
Harvey, LTJG Walter R. 23
Hau Giang River 46
Hau Nghia Province 27, 28
Haynes, EN2 Leo H. 28
Hazard, LTJG S.B. 19
Hererra, EM1 23
Hoang, CPO Lee Anh 26
Hockaday 76
Hogan, LTJG J.M. 20
Hoi An 36
Hollis, John E. 53
Hollister, GMG3 27
Hope, Bob 74
Houghtaling, Floyd W. III 53
Howe, BMC J.D. 50
Howell, Adrian E. 52
Hua Nghai 53
Hua Nghia 52
Hue River 22
Hughes, Herschel, Jr. 59
Hunford 76
Hung, PO2 Vu Ba 26
Hunt, Bruce C. 53
Hunt, EN3 Bruce C. 45
Hunt, James R. 53

**I**

Ibanez, Aristotoles D.R. 53
Isble, Don 75

**J**

James, Marc S. 52
Jefferis, CDR L.R. 18
Johnson 76
Johnson, Frankie R. 52
Johnson, GMG1 25
Johnson, Chaplain Raymond W. "Padre" 60, 61, 62
Jones, LT S.H. 22

**K**

Kahn, LT W.M. 22
Kam Can City 16
Keller, Richard L. 53
Kellerher, Commander T.A. 40
Kelley, James 50
Kennedy, John F. 62
Kenney, Harry J. 52
Kiem, CDR 18
Kien An 25, 51
Kien Giang 53
Kien Giang Province 8, 10, 12, 67
Kien Hoa 52, 53
Kien Hoa Province 67
Kien Luong Province 38
Kien Phong 53
Kien Tuong 52
Kien Tuong Province 28
Kim, Dang Van 26
Kin Moi Hai 34
King, VADM J.H. Jr 44
King, Vice Admiral 51
Kinh Bo Bo 23

Kinh Cai Nhap 49
Kinh Gay 23, 27
Kinh Lagrange 23, 27
Kinh Ngang Canal 44
Kinh Tu Canal 41
Kissinger, Henry 62
Klomstad, Ronnie G. 53
Kneece, Charles L. 52
Knott, BM2 27
Knowles, David Du Wayne 52
Kovi, BM1 25
Krebs, LT R.F. 20
Krekelberg, Raymond J. 53
Kucera, CDR R.C. 17, 22

**L**

Land, David A. 53
Lane, Zeph 67
Lapping, Colonel S.F. 40
Leach, LTJG 25
LeClerc, JO1 Joe 39, 43
Leonard, Jerry S. 53
Lepak, LT R.R. 20
Lewis, BMC 24
Lien, James L. 52
Little, William H. 52
Lo, LT 20
Long An 42, 52, 53
Long An Province 27, 28, 29, 35, 62, 68
Long Binh 47
Long Phu 44
Long Tau Shipping Channel 38, 42, 47
Long Xuyen 8, 12
Lorman, Richard 74, 77
Lucas, Lilyard N. 73
Luksich, LT J.W. 20
Lundberg, WO-2 J.R. 19
Lynn, LTJG George G. 39, 43, 48

**M**

Mangan 76
MARKET TIME 18, 39, 44, 46, 48, 57, 58
Marquez, Michael 76
Marriner, BMC 24
Marsh, LCDR L.S. 57
Martin, Lt. J.A. 16
Martinez, Richard E. 53
Mason, LT T.A. 19
Mason, Terry D. 53
Matthews, RADM H.S. 32, 38
Matzner, CDR R. 22
Mayo, Dudley W. 53
McCall, Victor G. 53
McDaniel, W.O. 39
McDowel, Signalman Second Donald Francis 59
McGinley, LT T.P 19
McIver, H. Bruce "Mac" 67
McKen, Electronics Repairman Second Norman Laforest 59
Meenan, Radioman Second Thomas James 59
Mekong Delta 16, 51, 60, 62, 63, 68, 77
Mekong River 16, 30, 32
Messemer, LT W.L. 21
Mihalic, LTJG 26

Miller, Gunnersmate Third Herman A. II 59
Miller, Joseph A. Jr. 53
Miller, LCDR C.L. 18
Mitchell, James C. Jr. 53
Mitchell, Seaman Ron 62, 63
Moc Hoa 8, 21, 23, 24, 28, 29, 34
Montgomery, LCDR R.G. 19
Moore, Albert B. 4
Moore, Richard S. 43, 47
Moore, Seaman Daniel Eugene Jr. 59
Moran, LT 45, 51
Moras, Robert J. 52
Morgan, Jackie R. 52
Morris, Lieutenant (junior grade) William T. III 59
Morto, Douglas G. 52
Moseman, Roy 5
Murphy, LCDR W.G. 19
Murphy, RM 3 M.J. 50
My Tho 36
Myers, James A. Jr. 53

**N**

Nam Can 43, 44, 50
Nam Can District 44
NcNeely, LT E.E. 20
Neak Luong 31
Neese, LCDR J.F. 20
Nelson, Eugene 52
New Song Ong Doc 31
Newan, CPL 56
Nha Be 16, 19, 21, 22, 36, 46, 47, 48
Nha Be Navy Base 35, 38, 42, 46, 47
Nha Be River 53
Nha Trang 17, 18, 19, 22, 57, 58
Nhan, Lieutenant Commander 51
Nhon Trach 46
Nhon Trach District 35
Nhuong Nghia 11
Nickerson, LTJG 26
Niemi, EN3 27
Ninh Moa 16
Ninh River Thuan Province 16
Nixon, President 58, 67, 68
Nui Gia Mountain 25

**O**

O'Connor, LT T.F. 20
Old Song Ong Doc 31, 50
Ortiz, LTJG A.O. 51
Oulette 76
Overstreet, CDR G.H. 19

**P**

Parker, Lonnie R. 53
Parshal, EN3 27
Parson, Doyle H. 53
Parsons, LCOL T.D. 22
Patrick, CDR J.C. 1
Pawlicki, Robert Daniel "Polak" 63
Pearson, David A. 52
Pedersen, LTJG William A. 41
Perex, ENEN Michael C. 28
Perkins, CAPT D.E. 18

Perry, Charles L. 52
Perysian, Joseph S. 52
Peters, Rodney W. 53
Pham Van Tran 26
Phnom Penh 32
Phong Dinh 52
Phu Cuong 21, 29, 36
Phuoc Tuy 53
Phuoc Xuyen 33
Pierce, SM1 27
Pinegar, LTJG 23
Pino, Lt. Anthony 65, 66
Plain of Reeds 68
Plona, AMS3 James P. 41
Poe, LT J.R. 21
Poole, Lieutenant Commander William W. Jr. 59
Porter, Captain R. 9
Pribnow 76
Prouty, LTJG C.S. 18
Pyle, Nicholas I. 52

**Q**

Quan Lo River 33
Quang Nam 53
Quang Ngai Province 16
Quang Tri 52, 53
Quang Xuyen 42, 46
Quang Xuyen District 35
Qui Nhon 57
Qui, LCDR Duong Van 17
Qui Nhon 17, 19, 20, 48, 58
Qui Nhon Province 16
Quyet Thang 16

**R**

Rach Ba Rai River 63
Rach Cai Nhap 50
Rach Gia 25, 26, 38, 41, 42
Rach Gia Ha Tien Canal 25
Rach Gia River 60
Rach Nga Ba Cai Tau 14
Rach Nuoc Trong 12
Rach Ong Dinh 49
Rach Soi 25, 36, 38, 42
Ramirez, Nelson 52
Ramos, ADJ3 Jose Pablo 41
Rand, WO-1 Benjamin W. 49
Ratliff, AEC J. 51
Rauch, CAPT C.F. Jr. 22
Ray, GMG3 27
READY DECK 22, 36, 39, 44, 48
Rees, LTJG 27
Republic of Korea 58
Rhea, LCDR K.J. 41
Rhodes, Dusty 68
Riesco, Commanding Officer Ray 61
Rivers, Sandy M. 53
Rochez, EN 2 E.V. 51
Roller, LCDR D.G. 39
Roper, LT J.E. 20, 21
Ross, GMG3 Charlie 70, 71, 72
Rost, James F. Jr. 53
Roy, Billy D. 52
Roy, Charles S. 52
Rundle, Cary F. 53
Rung Sat 15, 19, 35, 38, 42, 46, 47

Ruoho, John R. 53

## S

Saigon 9, 11, 13, 14, 16, 20, 21, 22, 23, 48, 49, 65, 68
Saigon Harbor 48
Saigon River 16, 21, 29
Sampsell, BM 1 H.E. 49
Sanders, BM2 27
Santiago, Oscar 4
Santiam 42
Schisler, LTJG Richard C. 39, 43
Schnurrer, Reinhard J. Jr. 53
Schuman, CDR M.S. 19
Scott, Eddie 70
SEA TIGER 39, 44, 48
Sea Tiger 17, 36
SEARCH TURN 20, 22, 25, 26, 36, 38, 39, 41, 44, 48
Serig, CDR W.E. 19
Shanahan, CAPT J.J. 17, 18, 20, 21
Sharp, Ray L. 53
Sharp, Stephen C. 53
Sheppard, Thomas E. 53
Siedentopf, Mark 53
Sienicki, LCDR E.F. 39
Sienicki, LCDR Edward E. 43, 48
Sigmond, CDR A.C. 21
Singler, Quartermaster Third Delbert Leo Jr. 59
Skaggs, G.C. 75, 77
Skaggs, S.C. 76, 125
Skipjack 50
Smelley, LT A.R. 20
Smith, Maynard L. 52
Smith, Michael J. 52
Smith, Thomas H. 53
Smith, Wiselee 52
SOLID ANCHOR 23, 37, 39, 40, 41, 44, 45, 48, 49, 50, 51
Son Tay 44
Song Bo De 50
Song Cau District 16
Song Cua Lon 50
Song Dong Dung 32
Song Ong Doc 8, 19, 20, 26, 31, 32, 34, 36, 37, 41, 45, 46, 51, 62, 63, 70, 71, 73
Song Ong Doc District 10
Song Ong Doc River 34, 35, 46, 50
Song Trem Trem 36
South China Sea 53
Souval, LCDR Paul T. 33
Spaugy, LT D.A. 20
Spruit, Captain R.E. 51
SS President Coolidge 47
SS Raphael Semmes 38
STABLE DOOR 57, 58
Stanford 50

Stauber, BM1 8
Steffy, P.C. 69, 74
Stephenson, JO2 Don H. 39, 43, 48
Streuli, LCDR J.W. 18
Strey, LCDR D.W. 20
Stubblefield, LTJG 38
Studds, BM1 28
Stumpf, R.J. 76
Sturvist, LT G.H. 21, 22
Sullivan, LT D.J. 18
Sullivan, R.D. 52
Swain, LCDR J.R. 19
Swift, Eugene E. 52

## T

Ta Keo Creek 42
Tam, Fireman Nguyen Viet 38
Tan An 8, 21, 36
Tan Bang 8, 9, 10
Tan Chau 51
Tan My 36
Tan Son Nhut 13
Tan-Tru 75
Tapper, Sonar Technician First Freddie Leslie 59
Tapscott, LTJG J.W. 34
Tapscott, LTJG K.W. 36
Tay Ninh 21, 23, 52, 53, 67
Tay Ninh City 23, 28
Tay Ninh Province 28, 29
Tay Tinh City 27
Tay Tinh Province 27
Taylor, LTJG Michael W. 39, 43, 48
Taylor, William R. 53
Thailand 67
Thames, LCDR L.H. 20, 31
Thanh Duc 35
Thanh Phu 46
Thi Tran 44
Thi Vai River 14
Thibadeau, BM1 John 67
Thieu, CAPT Vuong Huu 44
Thieu, President 48
Thinh, LT 20
Thoi Binh 8, 36
Thomas, Budda 4
Thomas, LCDR 24
Thompson, Terry N. 53
Thu Duc 9, 11, 13, 14
Thua Thien 53
Thuyen Nhon 20
Tidd, Capt. Emmett H. 16
Tief, Colonel F.W. 48
Tiger's Lair 65
Todd, LTJG J. 19
Tomcik, Lt. Dennis 65
Torcivia, Anthony R. 53
Touhey, LCDR R.J. 21
Tra Cu 8, 21, 23, 27
Tra Cu City 28

Trai Cheo Canal 50
TRAN HUNG DAO 20, 24, 29, 31, 45, 48, 51
TRAN HUNG DAO I-X 39
TRAN HUNG DAO I-XVII 44, 48
Tran Van Chon, Commodore 16
Trung Hung Dao 21
Tuyen Nhon 21, 23, 27, 28, 36
Twin Rivers area 12, 13, 14

## U

U-Minh Forest 8, 9, 10, 11, 12, 13, 14, 35, 36, 41, 48, 51
USCGC Dallas (WHEC 716) 26
USCGC Ponchartrain (WHEC 70) 38
USCGC Yakutat 46
USNS Herkimer 38
USS Askari (ARL 30) 8, 31, 53
USS Benewah (APB 35) 3, 31, 53, 59, 76
USS Colleton (APB 36) 53
USS Garrett County (AGP 786) 20, 44, 46, 50, 51
USS Garrett County (LST 786) 26
USS Garrett County (LST 821) 34
USS Harnett County (LST 821) 20, 25
USS Hunterdon County (LST 838) 25, 31, 45, 46
USS Hunterdon County (LST 823) 31, 45, 46
USS Jennings County (LST 846) 34
USS Krishna (ARL 38) 32, 51, 53
USS Mercer (APB 39) 53
USS Nye County (LST 1067) 53
USS Outagamie County (LST 1073) 53
USS Reclaimer (ARS 42) 51
USS Satyr 30, 31
USS Southerland (DD 743 37
USS Tom Green County (LST 1159) 53
USS Westchester County (LST 1167) 53, 53, 76

## V

VADM Jerome H. King 48
Vam Co Cong River 27
Vam Co Dang River 23
Vam Co Dong River 8, 9, 22, 23, 24, 27
Vam Co Tay River 8, 22, 23, 24, 27
Vam Song Ong Doc 26, 31, 34
Van, Chinh Vo 34

Van Kiep 14
Van Kiep National Training Center 9
Vanzuyen, COL W.M. 22
VC Canal 37
VC Lake 37, 41
Vin Ghiu 70
Vinh Chau District 46
Vinh Gia 24, 25
Vinh Gia Special Forces Camp 24
Vinh Long 16, 52, 53
Vinh Phong 12
Vinh Phouc 12
Vinh Te 20
Vinh Te Canal 24, 25, 72, 73
Voelker, "Doc" 66
Voelker, Gary A. "Doc" 65
Volkle, LCDR T.C. 17
Vriesenga, Tom 68
Vung Ro 58
Vung Tau 14, 18, 19, 22, 57

## W

Wages, CDR C.J. Jr. 19, 22
Walter, CDR D.J. 20
Warnick, EN3 27, 34
Warren, Jeider J. 52
Watts, LTJG 24, 25
Webb, Frederic P. 52
Welles, Orson 62
Wemette, Scott F. 53
Westlie, Daniel L. 52
Wetherill, Major General
Whitesell, SM1 John R. 28
Wicklund, BMC 28
Wiglesworth, Ernest W. Jr. 52
Willeford, James R. 53
Williams, Jerry L. 52
Williams, SN Dale R. 28
Woodard, John D. 52
Woolard, LTJG R. 20
Worth, ADJ 2 R.E. 51
Wurtzburger, EN3 27
Wyrick, David H. 52

## X

Xucuhko, LTJG 41

## Y

Yaeger, LCDR E.F. 21
Yost, CDR P.A. 18, 22
Young, James E. 53
Young, LT J.C. 20
Yu Quoc Thuc, Minister 16

## Z

Zumwalt, Admiral 70

www.ingramcontent.com/pod-product-compliance
Lightning Source LLC
Chambersburg PA
CBHW060233240426
43671CB00016B/2932